ENCYCLOPEDIA OF
EUROPEAN SOCIAL HISTORY

EDITORIAL BOARD

ENCYCLOPEDIA OF
EUROPEAN SOCIAL HISTORY

FROM 1350 TO 2000

VOLUME 2

Peter N. Stearns

Editor in Chief

Charles Scribner's Sons

an imprint of the Gale Group

Detroit • New York • San Francisco • London • Boston • Woodbridge, CT

1 3 5 7 9 11 13 15 17 19   20 18 16 14 12 10 8 6 4 2

Printed in United States of America

Library of Congress Cataloging-in-Publication Data
Encyclopedia of European social history from 1350 to 2000 / Peter N. Stearns, editor-in-chief.
    p.   cm.
    Includes bibliographical references and index.
    ISBN 0-684-80582-0 (set : alk. paper) — ISBN 0-684-80577-4 (vol. 1)—ISBN
0-684-80578-2 (vol. 2) — ISBN 0-684-80579-0 (vol. 3) — ISBN 0-684-80580-4 (vol. 4)
— ISBN 0-684-80581-2 (vol. 5) — ISBN 0-684-80645-2 (vol. 6)
    1. Europe—Social conditions—Encyclopedias. 2. Europe—Social life and
customs—Encyclopedias. 3. Social history—Encyclopedias. I. Stearns, Peter N.
HN373 .E63 2000
306′.094′03—dc21

                                        00-046376

CONTENTS OF THIS VOLUME

CONTENTS OF OTHER VOLUMES

ALPHABETICAL TABLE OF CONTENTS

xiii

COMMON ABBREVIATIONS USED IN THIS WORK

A.D.	*Anno Domini,* in the year of the Lord
AESC	*Annales: Économies, Sociétés, Civilisations*
ASSR	Autonomous Soviet Socialist Republic
b.	born
B.C.	before Christ
B.C.E.	before the common era (= B.C.)
c.	*circa,* about, approximately
C.E.	common era (= A.D.)
cf.	*confer,* compare
chap.	chapter
CP	Communist Party
d.	died
diss.	dissertation
ed.	editor (pl., eds.), edition
e.g.	*exempli gratia,* for example
et al.	*et alii,* and others
etc.	*et cetera,* and so forth
EU	European Union
f.	and following (pl., ff.)
fl.	*floruit,* flourished
GDP	gross domestic product
GDR	German Democratic Republic (East Germany)
GNP	gross national product
HRE	Holy Roman Empire, Holy Roman Emperor
ibid.	*ibididem,* in the same place (as the one immediately preceding)

i.e.	*id est,* that is
IMF	International Monetary Fund
MS.	manuscript (pl. MSS.)
n.	note
n.d.	no date
no.	number (pl., nos.)
n.p.	no place
n.s.	new series
N.S.	new style, according to the Gregorian calendar
OECD	Organization for Economic Cooperation and Development
O.S.	old style, according to the Julian calendar
p.	page (pl., pp.)
pt.	part
rev.	revised
S.	*san, sanctus, santo,* male saint
ser.	series
SP	Socialist Party
SS.	saints
SSR	Soviet Socialist Republic
Sta.	*sancta, santa,* female saint
supp.	supplement
USSR	Union of Soviet Socialist Republics
vol.	volume
WTO	World Trade Organization
?	uncertain, possibly, perhaps

ENCYCLOPEDIA OF
EUROPEAN SOCIAL HISTORY

Section 5

PROCESSES OF SOCIAL CHANGE

MODERNIZATION

Peter N. Stearns

The concept of modernization was developed primarily by historical sociologists, and primarily in the United States, during the 1950s. The theory derived in part from earlier work by seminal social scientists, such as Max Weber, dealing with cumulative historical developments such as bureaucratization and organizational rationalization. In addition to these credentials, modernization took from Marxism the idea of progressive historical change while denying the need for revolution as its motor. Modernization provided a more optimistic, less violent view of major change. The theory's sweep and implicit optimism were seen as an alternative to Marxist formulations and took root in the context of the cold war. It also put economic change, including industrialization, in a wide political and social context. Major scholars who outlined the theory and organized empirical studies on its base included Daniel Lerner, Alex Inkeles, and Myron Weiner. Cyril Black and Gilbert Rozman took the lead in historical applications and comparisons.

Modernization theorists contended that there were fundamental differences between modern and traditional societies involving changes in outlook and in political, economic, and social structure. Western Europe (and perhaps the United States) first developed these modern characteristics, which would, however, become standard in other societies over the course of time. Finally, in many formulations the key features of modern society were not only different from but preferable to those of traditional units: they involved more wealth and better health, more political freedoms and rights, more knowledge and control over superstition, and even more enlightened treatment of children.

Modernization theory was widely utilized for two decades, by social historians as well as social scientists. Social historians in the 1970s could easily refer to such developments as the modernization of the European family. Modernization of child rearing, for example, included new levels of affection for children and a reduction in harsh discipline, and historians found evidence of this process in the eighteenth and

nineteenth centuries. A cluster of scholars worked on patterns of modernization in social protest, from rioting in defense of older, threatened standards to articulate political movements on behalf of newly claimed rights. These imaginative extensions of the theory added to the more obvious uses of modernization such as the expansion of education or greater geographic and social mobility.

Modernization theory also required definitions of traditional society, now sometimes called premodern. Shared characteristics of premodern societies ranged from lack of widespread literacy to an inability to conceive of political issues in abstract terms; premodern people, so the argument went, could only attach politics to the persons of particular monarchs or representatives. "Traditional" personalities looked to the past for guidance and, oriented to groups, lacked a commitment to individual identity. Sweeping generalizations about traditional societies, not always supported by careful research, proved to be one of modernization theory's greatest vulnerabilities.

Attacks on modernization emerged by the mid-1970s, led by critics like Dean Tipps, who argued against the use of purely Western models to measure modern world history. The concept fell into increasing disfavor; but it continues to have partisans and, more broadly, it often slips into untheoretical historical discourse. No longer widely debated or formally utilized by European social historians, modernization nevertheless deserves attention not simply as a relic but as an attempt to link various processes of change during the past several centuries.

MEANINGS AND USES OF THE CONCEPT

As a term "modernization" can be used with many meanings. It can refer simply to technological change: during the nineteenth and twentieth centuries military modernization, in this sense, can mean little more than updating weaponry. Economic modernization, though a bit broader in implication, can be little more than a synonym for industrialization. Thus one could say that the French economy began to modernize in the 1820s, or the pace of modernization accelerated under Napoleon III in the 1850s.

However, the core meanings of the modernization concept, beyond surface descriptions, are twofold, with both aspects closely related. First, modernization often is used to describe patterns outside western Europe that are replicating patterns previously manifested within western Europe, or patterns that will or should develop in future. Thus Kemal Atatürk (first president of Turkey) attempted to modernize Turkey from the 1920s onward, mainly by attempting to introduce social forms that were already part of western European social history, broadly construed, a more secular society, wider education, industrial development, family planning, changes in the roles of women, and so on. This use of modernization treats modern European social history as a template for measuring or predicting developments outside of western Europe. Global modernization, particularly in optimistic 1960s formulations, assumed that all societies could ultimately modernize—that the social history of all civilizations would ultimately draw them closer to the trajectories of western Europe. But the formulations could also be used to identify lags: Why did Turkey modernize more slowly than the Soviet Union? Would India be able to modernize? In addition, the model could be used as a framework for comparisons of different modernization patterns, such as Soviet versus Western.

This first use of modernization theory, to summarize western European patterns as a predictive or at least descriptive model, assumed that such patterns could be agreed upon. Familiar components included industrialization, urbanization, the demographic transition (dramatically lower birth rates but also lower infant death rates), the rise of science, mass education and literacy, the growth of government and business bureaucracies, and changes in political structure, including wider suffrage. But there were areas of debate: Did modernization involve growing secularization or could/should it include new kinds of religious interests? Did it necessarily expand political participation and freedom? And there were areas of extension that went beyond some of the staples of modern European history: some modernization theorists thus posited the emergence of a modern personality type, contrasting with more traditional personalities in being more individualistic, more committed to a belief in progress, and less fatalistic.

The second meaning of modernization applied more directly to western European social history, though it undergirded the global application as well:

modernization theory suggested an intertwining of otherwise discrete processes, so that somehow (it was not always clear how, save in rough chronological lockstep) the processes supported each other and conjoined. Thus economic modernization—in the sense of industrialization, technological change in agriculture, and the growth of business units—occurred in relationship to several other major, parallel changes: the spread of education; the diffusion of more scientific outlooks; changes in the state, such as new levels of political participation, shifts in governmental function (more promotion of economic growth, less promotion of particular churches), and bureaucratization; changes in family structure, such as new levels of birth control and growing emphasis on the nuclear as opposed to the extended family; and a decline of privileges of birth and a rise of legal equality and opportunities for social mobility. The range of interconnections could be awesome, particularly when modernization involved not only structural changes—like the spread of factories or urbanization—but also shifts in outlook, including new attitudes toward children or, at its most ambitious, the new personality types. In both its meanings, modernization theory obviously assumed major and mutually related changes between traditional and modern societies.

The theory had a number of potential advantages. It could provide a shorthand: rather than running through all the discrete developments that made a modern society different from a traditional one, modernization theory would sum them up. It suggested attention to process: modernization took place over decades or possibly centuries in cases, such as western Europe, where there was no established model to imitate. The emphasis on interrelationships was attractive not only to social scientists interested less in history in detail than in history as a source of large, intelligible trends, but also to social historians concerned about linking their special topics—like family history—to more general developments, including some of the staples of modern political and intellectual history. Modernization theory made it possible to integrate more easily. Changes affecting ordinary people—the social historian's preferred focus—related to more familiar shifts in elite policy and behavior, if the whole society ultimately was heading in a common, modernizing direction. Changes in one facet of behavior, such as sexuality, could be linked not only to shifts in other clearly sociohistorical facets, such as attitudes to the body or health, but also to trends in political or intellectual life.

Finally, many historians of Europe who dealt with areas outside the western European core and with periods before the nineteenth century found modernization theory useful. Russian experts, for example, were able to link some of the major trends in Russian history to apparently common, if earlier, modern patterns in Britain or France. Students of early modern European history, dealing with what might otherwise seem a rather remote seventeenth century, for example, gained new salience by suggesting that in order to understand the European modernization process, one had to go back to its prior stages, to patterns first shaped three or four centuries ago. The emphasis on process and interrelationship in modernization theory encouraged broad thinking yet at the same time could generate new claims for the significance of specialized areas of study.

Discussing modernization theory in the context of European social history involves three stages: first, defining what the theory implies in greater detail; second, noting some of the questions the theory inherently raises, to which social historians have supplied varying answers; and third, probing the various objections to the theory that have so dramatically reduced its acceptance among social historians (without, however, fully eliminating its use).

STRUCTURAL AND BEHAVIORAL MODERNIZATION

Western and eastern Europe obviously underwent a series of transformations in the framework for social and personal life, mostly beginning in western Europe in the eighteenth century. These changes include industrialization—with its conjoined features of expanded manufacturing, rapid technological shifts, and alterations of the organization of work, particularly through factories—and ultimately the increase in available wealth, however inequitably distributed. They also include the growth of urban influence and then the rapid growth of cities themselves. Change in basic social structures also involved the expansion of governments, including larger and more specialized bureaucracies, and, by the nineteenth century at least, the redefinition of government functions. The state's gradual assumption of responsibility for the education of all children, public health activities, mass military conscription, and some preliminary regulatory and welfare functions fall in the category of structural modernization, in altering the relationship between state and society.

The modernization of social frameworks could include at least three other facets. First, with industrialization and also the legal changes encouraged by the French Revolution (including equality before the law and the abolition of guilds), social class, based on property, earnings, and to a lesser extent education, began to replace social order or estate, based on legal privilege as well as property, as the structure for social relationships. With this shift also came new popular definitions of, and interest in, social mobility; it seemed possible and desirable for more people to acquire schooling and money and so move up in status. Earnings replaced inherited legal status as the building block for social hierarchy.

Second, many modernization theorists were also comfortable with the idea of cultural modernization, whereby Europeans increasingly embraced a belief in progress and science and a growing interest in individual identities. These changes were associated with the scientific revolution and the Enlightenment, particularly as now understood by cultural-social historians eager to probe popular beliefs as well as more formal intellectual activities. The decline of credence in magic, or at least public approval of beliefs rooted in magic, and their replacement by more rational calculations such as insurable risk would be part of a cultural modernization that redefined the structures of life as much as the fundamental alterations in government functions did. In a similar vein, though less strictly tied to the Enlightenment, the rise of national identities, replacing or modifying more traditional local and religious loyalties, were taken by some historians as signs of a modernizing mentality in western Europe. This development, beginning around the time of the French Revolution, was actively encouraged by expanding networks of newspapers and state-sponsored schools in the nineteenth century.

Finally, the idea of a modernization of health continues to appeal to some scholars. At first gradually and unevenly, then by the later nineteenth century quite rapidly, health conditions improved in western Europe. Measures such as vaccination, gains in food supply and the reliability of food transportation, the ultimate impact of public health programs such as sewage systems, and in the long run the results of more sanitary and effective medical procedures did improve longevity—while at the same time tolerance for traditional high levels of mortality decreased.

With structural modernization defined, some modernization theorists turned to related (perhaps resultant, perhaps merely concomitant) changes in people's behaviors, particularly in private areas over which they have greatest control, and in the values they apply to their behaviors and their environment. Here is where the modernization of the family entered. The concept of family modernization included growing emphasis on the nuclear unit as opposed to more extended family relationships. It also included, ultimately, a commitment to unprecedented levels of birth control, designed both to protect the family's economic standing and to permit greater attention to, and expenditure on, individual children. It could include reevaluation of traditional child discipline. In some formulations, family modernization also meant the transition of the family from a unit largely intended as the basis for economic production, and formed with this goal in mind through arranged marriages and dowries, to a unit more focused on emotional and recreational satisfactions, with production increasingly moving out of the domestic setting.

Some social historians applied the idea of behavioral modernization, within the framework established by cultural modernization, to other developments they identified in eighteenth- and nineteenth-century Europe, especially in the west. Naming was one example. We know that by the late eighteenth century western Europeans had changed practices of naming infants in at least three respects, on average. First, they named infants relatively early, rather than waiting, as some Irish peasants once did, as much as two years to make sure the infant survived. Second, they no longer reused a name after a child died: new names were attached to each child born. Third, they gradually began to favor names based on criteria other than family tradition or religious figures, a shift that began to generate a certain faddism in name popularities that has continued to the present day. This set of changes can be taken as a sign of secularization in outlook and also of individuation, as parents came to see children as individual figures and to seek names that would encourage each child to do the same.

Similarly, historians of crime and historically minded criminologists explored the application of modernization theory to their area of interest. They examined how modernization brought a reduction in the ratio of crimes of violence to those of property, along with changes in policing and crime techniques. Some scholars, noting the unquestionable decline in murders per capita in western Europe from the Middle Ages at least until the late twentieth century, also discussed more effective social control and personal restraint and the link between these social and behavioral changes and broader processes of political and economic modernization.

The modernization of protest, particularly when it involved new beliefs about the relevance of political rights and a new capacity to raise novel demands, even more clearly linked behavioral changes to the larger patterns of structural modernization, including the redefinitions of the state. New state functions increased popular belief that the state should be a target of protest and that overtly political means could be used to obtain new rights.

On another, personal front, heightened consumer interests, now traced clearly to the eighteenth century in western Europe, seemed to signal a new commitment to materialism and material progress and also a new capacity to express personal meaning and identity in the acquisition of objects such as clothing—another possible sign of personal modernization. Few social historians have shared the sociological theorists' enthusiasm for a sweeping modernization statement that would attribute crime, education, protest, and consumerism to a modernized, as opposed to traditional, personality, but obviously social history findings have established ingredients that seem to reflect significant shifts in this direction.

QUESTIONS ABOUT MODERNIZATION

The above presentation of the main lines of structural and associated behavioral modernization suggests a tidy package—which is what advocates of the theory seek. Modernization, according to its advocates, should link a variety of major changes that distinguish a traditional from a fully modern society, and its clarity in summing up changes in western Europe should permit application of an empirically derived modernization model to other areas.

Yet, even in its most successful formulations, modernization theory has some obvious weaknesses and raises several crucial questions—some would add, like any very ambitious social-historical theory. Most obviously, causation was unclear. Modernization theory was primarily descriptive, talking about linkages whose concomitant occurrence could be traced. Unlike Marxism, it does not really seek to assess what would cause the whole process to start. Yet the interconnections among trends that modernization theory insists upon imply causation. The problem is that the theory itself does not clearly stipulate priorities; it does not clearly indicate what factors came first in launching the whole process. To the extent that most social historians, confronted with some of the big changes in modern history, also seek to explore the factors that prompted them, modernization tantalizes more than it satisfies.

What, for example, was the role of education in the European modernization process? Many non-European observers, looking in the nineteenth century at Europe's industrialization, felt that education was a key factor in causing economic change. Thus Muhammed Ali, the reform leader who seized power in Egypt in the 1820s and 1830s, sent students to European technical schools. Japanese reformers in the 1860s, like Yukichi Fukuzawa, saw educational reform as the key means of introducing Western-like commitments to science and innovation into Japanese culture. But actual educational change occurred very slowly in European social history. Literacy had advanced by the later eighteenth century, though often to rudimentary levels, but exposure to formal schooling was in most places haphazard and incomplete until after the 1860s. Further, several social historians have shown that until the late nineteenth century the connection between educational achievement and industrial development was loose at best—as witnessed by the individual success of relatively uneducated workers or, at a more macro level, the industrial achievements but educational lag of Great Britain. So the question of where education fits in the causation stream of European modernization goes unanswered.

The issue of technology change is another example. Modernization theory obviously assumes major changes in industrial and military technology, and technology levels form one of the most obvious contrasts between traditional and modern societies. But modernization theory does not indicate causal priorities, whether new technology causes or results from basic initial modernization. Once again, the theory invites causal analysis—from what stage of structural or behavioral modernization did a key invention like the steam engine flow, for example—but offers no clear resolution.

Linked to the problem of causation is modernization theory's chronological imprecision, particularly when applied to European social history. When, in time, does modernization definitively begin? Unlike Japan after 1868, western Europe made no explicit decision to reform in modernizing directions. The above discussion suggests the eighteenth century as seedbed, but many historians would place key changes earlier. Was the Renaissance, with its more secular outlook and commercial emphasis, part of the modernization process? Some medievalists, eager to claim their period's role in ongoing trends, have argued that the inception of the modern European state goes back to the twelfth century, when greater centralization, expansion of governmental function, and the beginnings of bureaucratic specialization can clearly be traced. How can this claim, empirically accurate, be assessed in terms of modernization theory? Because the criteria for the inception of modernization are vague, answering chronological questions of this sort is difficult. Yet, without the capacity to deal with these issues, can the theory be of use in European social history?

Problems of chronological origins are not necessarily irresolvable. Because modernization theory insists on the cooccurrence of major changes, it is pos-

sible to argue that a single strand of development, such as the expansion of the central monarchies in the high Middle Ages, does not constitute the process, however much such changes may unintentionally prepare the way. But the theory remains vague, and this kind of sorting out has not occurred.

The same problems of definition, causation, and chronological precision apply when the theory is extended to other parts of Europe. Russia provides a classic example. Peter the Great's selective Westernization program, initiated around 1700, brought major change to Russia. Military technology and organization, aspects of economic production (particularly in metallurgy and arms), and elite culture and education all shifted significantly. Virtually all surveys of Russian history refer to Peter's major role in Russian modernization. But is this when modernization began in Russia? Did Peter's forceful changes merely accelerate earlier developments, or were his initiatives too lopsided and forced to initiate a broad modernization? Again, the answer to when modernization begins may be sought in the coherence of change, particularly in terms of social history. A historical setting like eighteenth-century Russia, in which commerce and merchant groups did not significantly advance, mass culture was unaltered, and conditions of serfdom became more rigorous, is not a setting that clearly suggests modernization. Dissociation of Peter's reforms from modernization would not downgrade the reforms' significance, but it would remind us that not all major change, even within the last three centuries, can be lumped under a single heading. Yet modernization theory is not in fact historically precise enough to permit a definitive response to this aspect of the Russian case: the issue of when modernization begins opens more questions than answers.

The same issue of definition applies to the end of the modernization process. At what point, and by what criteria, can one say that a society is modernized, such that further major change no longer attaches to a modernization process? When a society is urban, industrial, bureaucratized, individualistic—is it modernized? Current theoretical formulations that refer to postmodern societies, as in western Europe after World War II, suggest an end to the modernization process and its replacement with another set of basic trends. But the postmodern concept, outside of specific realms such as art and architecture, is itself rather vague. Some basic modernizing features seem to persist, in western Europe and elsewhere, for example, in the changes in peasant habits that see peasants become avid consumers, eager for complex technology, with reduced interest in the land. The result is another incompletely resolved problem for analysis: Is the concept of modernization useful in dealing with advanced industrial societies in the twenty-first century and, if not, when and by what criteria did its utility cease?

Issues of causation and chronology are joined by those of geography. Here, to be sure, modernization theory is quite clear: basically similar processes should occur when a society modernizes, regardless of where it is located. Yet most European social historians remain attached to older historical habits that insist, to some degree at least, on peculiarities of place. They are thus inclined to point to significant distinctions between the modern history of, say, France and that of England—even though in modernization theory the two nations should be readily coupled. French industrialization emphasized craft products more than British industrialization did, it relied on a larger female labor force, and it generated a more politically radical working class. Modernization would insist on the common elements in the industrialization process, and perhaps rightly so; but many social historians would be uncomfortable with dismissing these important regional differences. And if this problem applies to two close Western neighbors, the comparative issues loom even larger if eastern and western Europe are to be seen sharing a historical dynamic (if at slightly different times), or if the United States (a clearly modernizing society) is amalgamated with western European history. Modernization theory can make allowance for differences in specific context in terms of when the basic process of change begins, but it does not so readily accommodate other distinctions.

This problem of geography relates, in turn, to a final general set of questions, this one about the traditional society from which modernization departs. At an extreme, modernization theorists, in their enthusiasm for common processes of change, might imply an undifferentiated traditional society, which change will itself gradually erase. Comparative scholars more commonly noted the importance of different traditional contexts, caused, for example, by religious distinctions: thus Russia's Christianity contrasted with Japan's cultural heritage, leading to sensitive discussions of different paths to modernization. Even with these allowances, however, the emphasis on common processes remained strong.

Yet most social historians, looking at parts of Europe before the eighteenth century, remain far more interested in regional patterns. Guild structures, for example, loomed far larger in eighteenth-century Germany than in England. Would this difference be wiped away by a common modernization, or would it produce deep differences in the process of change in both countries? Family systems, too, varied considerably. In many parts of Europe, social historians have discov-

ered that the nuclear family was the predominant unit by the later Middle Ages. Thus the assumption by some modernization theorists that a common traditional extended family pattern everywhere inevitably yielded to nuclear family organization loses accuracy in the case of western Europe and much of North America. In other words, empirically "traditional" societies varied greatly, and to the extent these variations continued to affect aspects of modern social history, the resulting diversity seriously compromises modernization's accuracy and claim to universality.

OBJECTIONS TO MODERNIZATION THEORY

Modernization theory not only raises huge historical issues, it also has provoked ringing dissent and attack. Social historians were reacting vigorously against the theory by the early 1980s: while one held out for "better than no model at all," other comments included "too big and slippery for deft manipulation," "historically crude," "elusive," and "inadequate . . . for comprehending the diversity of the human experience during several centuries of social transformation."

By this point, modernization theory ceased to be applied to many aspects of historical change. Historians who had used modernization to describe changes in protest or family patterns, for example, dropped the reference. Models of changes in protest forms and goals persisted or, as in the case of the family, the links between traditional and more recent patterns might be reevaluated and made more complicated; but either way, modernization no longer seemed to help. Modernization theory seemed irrelevant to major new discoveries, such as the existence of an active consumer culture in western Europe in the eighteenth century. Even when this early culture was directly linked to more recent consumer patterns, analysts no longer made modernization references at all; the links were evaluated and explained more discretely. New findings in the history of crime—for example, that violence shifted in the late nineteenth century from attacks against relative strangers to attacks against family members—similarly implied no new facet of modernization.

Three basic objections emerged by the mid-1970s. First, and most vigorously, scholars from various disciplines objected to modernization's ethnocentric qualities: that all societies should be measured and all predictions should be founded on western Europe as a standard model. This critique was an extension of the geographical homogenization questions about modernization, and it has proved very powerful. Modernization references still are applied to "non-Western" societies such as Latin America and China on the basis of presumed previous Western trends, but all-out partisans are now few in number.

Second, modernization's characteristic optimism drew criticism, even when applied to western Europe. The blanket notion that modern people are in all ways better off than premodern people is not now widely accepted. Here social historians like E. P. Thompson have contributed powerfully, though earlier theories such as Marxism already constrained optimism. Studies of the relationship between modern work and premodern work, in terms of stress and satisfaction alike, call linear progressive models into question; many features of work have arguably deteriorated with greater time pressures, de-skilling, and removal from community life. The same applies to aspects of leisure, or community cohesion, or even child rearing (which once was seen as a dramatic area of modern advance). Ironically, these evaluative objections do not destroy other features of the theory: a society might modernize and get worse, or at least generate mixed results. But in practice, greater skepticism about the benefits of modern life has contributed to modernization's fall from grace.

Finally, and most important in terms of European social history, modernization's implications of ultimate, basic uniformity in the direction of change have drawn attack. Precisely because social historians see societies composed of radically different groups, they have trouble accepting common ultimate dynamics. What does modernization mean, for example, when the experiences and values of workers and the middle class vary so? Where modernization theory once assumed that, ultimately, peasants would modernize (technologically, politically, and culturally) and so merge with urban groups, social historians are now more prone to note persistent distinctions, based on differences in power and prior class culture.

The new levels of attention historians paid to gender called forth similar objections, along with an obvious empirical problem. Modernization theory had focused very little on the issue of gender. Historians now asked, did men and women "modernize" in the same ways? If modernization meant individuation, for example, how can this apply to the special domestic, subservient ideology created for women in the most "modern," middle-class families in western Europe during the century of industrialization? More fundamentally, does modernization mean more or less formal participation for women in the workforce? The answer is clearly less (except for key cases like Russia, where industrialization proved compatible with continuing high levels of women's work). But if the mod-

ernization process persists into the mid-twentieth century, then it embraces a massive reinsertion of women into the labor force. Applying the modernization formula is immensely complicated, precisely because of the diverse experiences of different social classes and of men and women.

The combined force of these objections accounts for the waning commitment to modernization theory; its moment of glory in social history has thus far proved brief. In the international arena, world economy theory, arguing for the durable importance of economic relationships first set up in the fifteenth century, is now far more widely used than modernization; it stresses diversity between dominant and subordinate international trading areas and is often pessimistic about outcomes, in marked contrast to the modernization model.

For European social history itself, no model with modernization's sweep has arrived to reclaim the power of synthesis: no overarching framework unites various facets of social change. Important theoretical statements have been devised or revived: considerable work on personal habits and family relationships, for example, utilizes Norbert Elias's theory of the "civilizing process," in which, beginning with the European upper classes, people gained and expected greater restraint over the body and over emotions. But this theory's range of application is more limited than modernization's.

Yet modernization theory has not perished. A group of staunch partisans, mainly survivors of the ambitious cluster of sociologists who first delineated the theory in the 1950s, continues productive work, in general statements and also in using the theory to frame the modern social and political history of places like Russia or China. Gilbert Rozman's syntheses are a case in point. A second locus of the theory involves the casual references to a city "becoming modern" or peasants "responding to modernization" in social history studies that shy away from larger theoretical pronouncements. This second use suggests the ongoing momentum of the theory in summing up related changes in societal structure, and perhaps some ongoing utility as well.

Finally, though hesitantly, a few social historians have tried to refine the theory by noting the key difficulties attached and urging a more selective application. Here, the basic approach is twofold. First, addressing both western European and world history, these cautious advocates urge a clearer agreement on what did, in fact, change very widely—the commitment to mass education is a case in point—where modernization really can describe seemingly universal social impulses. At the same time, areas of greater di-

9

versity or complexity must simply be dropped, in an admission that modernization cannot accurately cover all facets of social change and continuity. Thus it is silly to talk of the "modernization of women" without immediate restrictions and complications—even in western European society alone. The second component of the refinement of modernization theory involves urging social historian critics to see the forest as well as the trees, to look at longer-run patterns as well as short-term complexities. For example, critics argue that talking about a shared modernization process makes little sense for middle-class owners and factory workers in the 1870s, despite some common involvements in new levels of schooling, work organizations, and the like. But others would respond that looking at a broader picture, as class differentiations ultimately moderated somewhat, may provide greater

support for the idea of participation in common processes—processes that would not produce identical cultures or behaviors, but that would bring some genuine convergence.

Since 1980 modernization theory has inspired relatively little new work in social history. References are infrequent, sometimes dismissive, casual at best, beyond the core of true believers. Yet the need and, perhaps, the possibility for some overarching linkages among major facets of social change over the past three centuries is hard to deny. This, surely, is why modernization continues to crop up as a subliminal scholarly shorthand, in dealing with huge processes such as technology and culture—both in western European history and in the history of places like Russia and Spain, whose relationship to Western history forms part of the essential analytical framework.

See also **Generations of Social History** *(volume 1), the section* **The Periods of Social History** *(volume 1), and the other articles in this section.*

BIBLIOGRAPHY

Black, Cyril E., et al. *The Modernization of Japan and Russia.* New York, 1975. An important historical application and comparative work.

Black, Cyril E., and L. Carl Brown, eds. *Modernization in the Middle East.* Princeton, N.J., 1992. One of the most recent full uses of the theory.

Brown, Richard D. *Modernization: The Transformation of American Life, 1600–1865.* 1976. Reprint, Prospect Heights, Ill., 1988. Applies the theory to social history.

Eisenstadt, S. N. *Tradition, Change, and Modernity.* 1973. Reprint, Melbourne, Fla., 1983. A classic statement of the theory.

Inkeles, Alex. *One World Emerging?: Convergence and Divergence in Industrial Societies.* Boulder, Colo., 1998. A full statement by a slightly chastened true believer.

Inkeles, Alex, and David Smith. *Becoming Modern: Individual Changes in Six Developing Countries.* Cambridge, Mass., 1976.

Lee, Joseph. *Modernization of Irish Society, 1848–1919.* Dublin, 1989.

Lerner, Daniel. *The Passing of Traditional Society.* Glencoe, Ill., 1958. Offers an early statement.

Levy, Marion J., Jr. *Modernization and the Structure of Societies.* 1966. Reprint, New Brunswick, N.J., 1996.

Rozman, Gilbert, ed. *The Modernization of China.* New York, 1981. A very challenging application.

Stearns, Peter N. *European Society in Upheaval.* 2d ed. New York, 1975. Applies modernization as a framework for modern social history; the approach was dropped in the third edition.

Tipps, Dean C. "Modernization and the Comparative Study of Societies: A Critical Perspective." *Comparative Studies in Society and History* 15 (1973): 199–226.

Weiker, Walter. *Modernization of Turkey: From Ataturk to the Present.* New York, 1981.

Weiner, Myron, ed. *Modernization: The Dynamics of Growth.* New York, 1966. Includes some of the strongest statements about personality modernization.

TECHNOLOGY

Kristine Bruland

The relationship between technology and social history raises two kinds of considerations. The initial section of this essay takes a conceptual approach, examining the nature of technology itself. Is technology a separate force, as is often assumed by historians of technology, or does it interact with society in more complex ways, such that social forces may help explain technological developments and vice versa? The second category of considerations involves the actual development of technology as part of European social history, which is taken up in the second section of this essay. In terms of chronology, the conventional division between technology before and after the industrial revolution forms the main organizing principle.

CONCEPTUAL ISSUES

What are the relationships between processes of technological change and the social context? Until very recently technological change has usually been viewed primarily in terms of hardware: impressive, ingenious and increasingly sophisticated engineering solutions to the problems posed by production tasks. For a long time these solutions tended to be seen as rather autonomous in character, so that they could be understood without much in the way of social context. For example, the five-volume *History of Technology* edited by Charles Singer and collaborators and published between 1954 and 1958 follows technology from the earliest stages of human evolution to the twentieth century. Its 4000 pages cover technical developments (in terms of hardware and specific operative practices) in metalworking, textiles, pottery, and other areas in considerable detail but contain only one brief article by Gordon Childe on technology in terms of social practice.

The role of social factors in the history of technological change gives rise to a range of explanatory problems at different levels. There is, for example, a quite abstract level at which the general propensity of an economic system for such change is explored; this

is the level that David Landes (1998) has explored. Then there are questions about why particular sectors of the economy exhibit a propensity for technical change; here one would have to consider questions of how technological opportunity emerges as well as questions of industrial structure; the development of markets, patterns, and levels of demand; the structure and capacity of producer goods industries; state economic policy; and so on. Finally there are questions about why specific technologies develop and what factors shape their diffusion. All of these levels have been researched, in one way or another, from a social perspective. But it is probably this last which has formed the most important focus of recent research. Social factors have been to the forefront in the analysis of how technologies originate and diffuse. As a recent study covering aircraft, fluorescent lights, steel, atomic energy, and electricity production and distribution claimed:

> Technologies do not, we suggest, evolve under the impetus of some necessary inner technological or scientific logic. They are not possessed of an inherent momentum. If they evolve or change, it is because they have been pressed into that shape. . . . Technology does not spring, ab initio, from some distinterested fount of innovation. Rather it is born of the social, the economic, and the technical relations that are already in place. A product of the existing structure of opportunities and constraints, it extends, shapes or reproduces that structure in ways that are more or less unpredictable. (Bijker and Law, 1992, pp. 5, 11)

The more traditional and still to some extent dominant view is that technology is something that might have profound social effects but which has developed and spread on the basis of rather autonomous processes of artisan development or, in the modern era, scientific and engineering advance. This kind of determinism has in recent years been supplanted by approaches that seek to set technical or engineering processes against the background of the social environments in which they are generated and put to work. From this perspective, technology immediately begins to look more complicated, and we can begin to see ways in which the social environment shapes technological evolution, as much as it is shaped by it.

Modern perspectives begin by conceptualising technology in ways that move beyond the level of material technique. Of course technology does involve hardware (machines, tools, infrastructure) and technique (in the sense of routines of technical practice), but it also involves at least two other primary dimensions, namely knowledge and organisation, both of which are social phenomena. Technology involves, for example, the production and maintenance of knowledge, both in terms of formal scientific and technical disciplines and also as an equally important array of tacit knowledge. These human skills—sometimes codified, but equally often developed gradually by individuals and taking the form of acquired skills—are an integral part of all processes of production and work. Then there are the crucially important processes of organisation and management through which hardware and technique are set to work. On the one hand these organisation and managerial issues involve decisions about how production processes are to be subdivided, operated, integrated, and supervised; this element of technological practice has a complex history of its own. The publication in 1974 of Harry Braverman's *Labor and Monopoly Capital* was a key event in this area. Braverman argued that the history of modern capitalist production is characterised by a consistent attempt to separate conceptual aspects of production (in terms of human skill and control) from the actual process of work; technological change in the modern era thus involves a persistent "degradation of work," and modern management is essentially a method for organising this. There is now a wide literature on the history of work organisation and its links to technological change and society. However, there are also equally important managerial issues involved in integrating technological aspects of production with the wider processes of commercial calculation, marketing, financial organisation, and so on, which firms must undertake. Finally, these elements of knowledge, hardware, and organisation at the firm level occur within a much broader and extremely complex social framework of economic, political, and cultural relationships. This social environment both facilitates and constrains the development, use, and spread of technologies in many ways: for example, through cultural attitudes that affect levels and types of education or that place different valuations on technical or economic achievement.

Central to modern conceptual approaches, therefore, is the idea that the histories of technologies should be seen in their economic and social context and that the focus should extend wider than to embrace just technical artefacts. The point here is that the evolution of technologies involves complex social processes of conflict, negotiation, compromise, and adaptation, and technological change cannot be understood in isolation from these social dimensions. In these approaches, society is not seen as adapting to a deterministic process of technological change, but rather it is social values and decisions that shape the path of technological development. It is a short step from this to the idea that differences in technological performance between societies have at least some of their roots in social structure and social forms, although how these differences operate is as yet far from clear. Nonetheless, technological developments have important impacts on the social world, on the environment, the way we work, and on our general social interrelations. So understanding the evolution of technology in the long run is in part a process of understanding the history of the wider society in which technology is embedded. Socio-technical interplay has only recently emerged as a systematic theme in historical studies. While study of technical and social interaction has frequently been found in historical work, there has also often been a strain of technological determinism, which has raised considerable problems in understanding technological dynamics and their relation to the social context.

Society and technology in the very long run.

The link between human society and technology goes back a long way. The evolution of human societies and even the dominance of *homo sapiens* as a species are intimately joined with the evolution of technology. Early hominid fossil records, for example, are usually found in close proximity to remains of stone implements, and the extension of human society over the earth's surface seems to be founded on mastery of a number of apparently simple (but arguably rather complex) technologies: stone weapons, the management of fire, and the construction of shelter, for example. These technologies emerged in the distant past and characterised the paleolithic and neolithic periods, in which humans evolved complex understandings of animal behaviour, pyrotechnology, weapons manufacture, medical practice, materials, and so on. It has been argued that even these distant technologies can be analysed in terms of evolutionary sequences; the archeological record of such tools exhibits considerable variation, which led George Basalla to argue that

> The modern technological world in all its complexity is merely the latest manifestation of a continuum that extends back to the dawn of humankind, and to the

14

first shaped artefacts. Stone implements may not offer a crucial test for the evolutionary thesis, but they provide the best illustration of continuity operating over an extended period of time. (Basalla, 1988, pp. 30–31)

From the neolithic period (from ca. 5000 B.C.) this very slow evolution developed into a number of very profound technological revolutions, of which probably five are especially significant, apart from those mentioned above: the domestication of animals, cultivation of food and "industrial" plants (such as plants used for vessels, construction materials, fibres, and so on), the development of pottery, the development of textiles, and the evolution of metallurgy.

The evidence for the emergence and use of these technologies is primarily archeological, but over this period we have the first sustained phase of what can reasonably be called "radical" change. H. S. Harrison remarks that

> The centuries following the development of the initial features of Neolithic culture, during which the hunter and gatherer first became a farmer and stock breeder, were the most significant in the history of human progress. Steps were taken then that were essential to the building of civilizations upon which later cultural revolutions depended. . . . the evidence indicates that the ferment leading to the development of the new culture was in progress before 5000 B.C. Centuries, and not years only, were consumed in the processes which led to the cultivation of cereals and the domestication of hoofed animals. New opportunities and stimuli emerged that led into other fields of discovery and invention. (Harrison, 1958, p. 79)

Harrison points to three further key features of these technological revolutions, which are found persistently in the historical literature and are relevant also in understanding modern large-scale technological change. First, the time periods involved in these shifts are long—the development of radically new technologies is slow, and therefore for long periods new techniques (such as metal implements) co-exist with the old (such as implements of wood and stone). Second, technical advance has an evolutionary character with new developments opening up further opportunities and thus gradually speeding up the overall process of change. Third, there is a close relationship between large-scale technological change and the social context. The emergence of new technological regimes interacted in significant ways with technical divisions of labour, productivity, and patterns of exchange. In particular, historians have emphasized the fact that increasing productivity raises the question of the distribution of the gains from growth; this is central to questions of the emergence of hierarchy, order, and power in human society. In the very long run, shifts in technological regime cannot therefore be separated from the evolution of social forms as such.

Early social conflict and technological change: the case of the water mill. With respect to modern and premodern eras, it has long been recognised by historians that the diffusion of major technologies is often closely linked to social factors such as patterns of ownership, economic organisation, and income distribution. A classic analysis of such factors was developed by Marc Bloch in his study of the diffusion of water-powered mills in England. The grinding of corn in England, as in all medieval societies, was an activity of key economic significance; the technological alternatives were handmills, which operated on a very small scale with human muscle power, and water mills, which operated with considerably greater speed and efficiency. Yet water mills diffused very slowly as a technique for corn grinding in the period after the eleventh century. The reason for this lies not in the technique itself but in the way the technique was integrated with particular patterns of ownership and social control. After the Norman Conquest of England control of rivers and streams became part of an attempt to impose a new social system based on manorial rights through which landowners claimed income and services from other social classes:

> Manorial rights were not an institution native to England. The Norman conquerors had imported them from the continent as one of the principal elements in the manorial system which after the almost total dispossession of the Saxon aristocracy they methodically established. (Bloch, 1985, p. 75)

The watermill was in effect monopolised by the seigneurial class and used as a method of revenue extraction. As part of this process, handmills were proscribed, with a wide variety of attempts to eliminate their existence and use, often by force. This attempt to facilitate use of the water technology by direct suppression of the competing technology failed in the long run, and the consequence was a very slow spread of the apparently superior technology. Bloch's key point in analyzing this process was the deep interconnection between social power, embedded interests, and the processes of use and diffusion of a technology. The fates of the competing technologies were therefore shaped by the fact that different social classes championed them for different economic ends, and the diffusion of the technologies depended on the outcome of sustained social struggle.

Comparative technological development across societies. Social factors have also been deployed around the major historical problem of differences in the rates and direction of technological change across societies. There can be no doubt that many societies are capable of sustained and ingenious invention. Joseph Needham's magisterial *Science and Civilisation in China* showed beyond any doubt that China pioneered a wide range of technical advances; similar points can be made with respect to the Arab world in such key areas as written texts, mathematics, and so on. Yet, as Joel Mokyr has remarked, "The greatest enigma in the history of technology is the failure of China to sustain its technological superiority." Mokyr surveys a plethora of explanations for this but ultimately supports the view that a constraining social order was the core of the problem:

> The difference between China and Europe was that in Europe the power of any social group to sabotage an innovation it deemed detrimental to its interests was far smaller. First, in Europe technological change was essentially a matter of private initiative; the role of the rulers was secondary and passive. Few significant contributions to non-military technology were initiated by the state in Europe before (or during) the Industrial Revolution. There was a market for ideas, and the government entered these markets as just another customer or, more rarely, a supplier. Second, whenever a European government chose to take an actively hostile attitude towards innovation and the nonconformism that bred it, it had to face the consequences. . . . the possibilities of migration in Europe allowed creative and original thinkers to find a haven if their place of birth was insufficiently tolerant, so that in the long run, reactionary societies lost out in the competition for wealth and power. (Mokyr, 1990, p. 233)

Although serious histories of technology have been written around the centrality of social forces in technological evolution for many years now, it would be a mistake to think that technological determinism is dead. It is common for writers and analysts (with the notable exception of James R. Beniger) to speak as though the revolution in information and communications technologies is autonomous and is reshaping society, but it is hard to doubt that this area too will come to be seen in the kind of context outlined above.

MAJOR DEVELOPMENTS IN TECHNOLOGY

Medieval and Renaissance technology. Most approaches to the development of technology in European culture stress the inventiveness of medieval and renaissance Europe, combined with relatively slow or limited diffusion and use of new technologies. Historians such as Bloch, Lynn White, and Bertrand Gille have shown the medieval development or adoption of a wide range of technologies, such as new forms of plow and harness in agriculture, the open field system, moveable type, and powered machinery. In an recent overview, Frances and Joseph Gies showed the importance of complex infrastructural developments, such as bridges, cathedrals, and fortifications on the one hand and on the other hand, of commercial innovation such as milling, textiles, glass, double-entry bookkeeping, and general accounting techniques. But it really cannot be claimed that these technologies came into widespread use. Mokyr makes a similar point with respect to Renaissance technologies. Clearly we should be cautious about using catchall terms such as the "Renaissance" to describe such a wide and differentiated period, but however we label it the period 1500–1750 generated a wide range of new technical developments in agriculture, mining pumps, precision instruments, tools, and other technologies. But the period is at least as interesting in terms of what did not happen, namely the widespread application of these technologies in a context of technical and productivity advancement. This is primarily a matter of the social and institutional context. Europe was only in the early stages of evolving the social framework which would sharply stimulate not only the development of technologies but their widespread application.

Still, the early modern period did see steady technological evolution in major branches of the European economy. It was in this period that western Europe gradually shifted from being a borrower of Asian technologies such as explosive powder, the compass, and printing, to being a technological leader. Gradual changes in mining and metallurgy boosted European technology by 1600. Adaptations in the printing press, with the use of movable type, propelled Europe to a clear advantage in printing even earlier. By 1700 new technologies in many branches of textiles made Europe a world leader in that area.

The decades from the late seventeenth century to the advent of James Watt's steam engine (1765) saw an accelerating pace of technological change spurred not only by Europe's lead in world trade, but also by growing artisanal freedom from guild restrictions in England and Scotland and by some spillover from the scientific revolution. Social and cultural causes, in other words, explain technological change along with world economic position, while the technological changes in turn fed further social shifts. For the first time since the Middle Ages agricultural technology received attention (at the same time that Europeans were introduced to New World crops like the potato). New methods of drainage expanded available land in places like Holland, while the seed drill and even wider use of the scythe instead of the sickle for

The Crystal Palace. The Crystal Palace was built of iron and glass for the Great Exhibition of 1851. ©HULTON GETTY/ LIAISON AGENCY

harvesting led to modest increases in productivity. The other main sector in which there was significant technological advance was domestic manufacturing, where new techniques such as the flying shuttle for weaving (1733), while still relying on manual or foot power, partially automated processes and so increased productivity. These developments soon proved compatible with water or steam power, combining to generate the technological basis for the industrial revolution proper. In the interim, new technologies fed the rapid commercial and manufacturing expansion of rural and urban areas in western Europe and fostered other changes such as the growth of consumerism.

Industrialization and the new technological era.

Many of the issues involved in the interaction between society and technology become critical in the modern period, characterized as it is by incessant technological change and continuous productivity growth. What is often referred to as the industrial revolution began in England in the late eighteenth century and is usually and rightly regarded as a technological watershed, yet its interpretation gives rise to major problems of technological determinism.

Influential explanatory accounts ascribe the industrial revolution to the effects of the deployment of new techniques as the primary agent of economic advance. The strongest version of this argument is written around the steam engine:

> If we were to try to single out the crucial inventions which made the industrial revolution possible and ensured a continuous process of industrialization and technical change, and hence sustained economic growth, it seems that the choice would fall on the steam engine on one hand, and on the other Cort's puddling process which made a cheap and acceptable British malleable iron. (Deane, 1965, p. 130)

In effect, the rise of the Watt steam engine has long been treated in British historiography as a decisive event in industrialization. The heroic approach began with the first systematic work on the industrial revolution, *Lectures on the Industrial Revolution of the Eighteenth Century,* by Arnold Toynbee (1852–1883), which focused on the Watt steam engine and the "four great inventions" which revolutionized the cotton textile industry—the spinning jenny (1770), the water-frame (1769), Crompton's spinning mule (1779) and the automatic mule (1825) of Richard Roberts. Toynbee took an essentially determinist view of technology; for example, in seeking to explain the rise of urban industrialization and the decline of the outwork system, he suggested that the emergence of the factory was "the consequence of the mechanical discoveries of the time," and indeed that the steam engine was the basic permissive factor in economic liberalisation. Toynbee had a major impact on subsequent economic history. His technological emphases were repeated in Paul Mantoux's classic *Industrial Revolution in the Eighteenth Century* and in a wide range of later works up to and including Landes's *Unbound Prometheus*, which remains the major work on technological development in Western Europe. Mantoux focused the second part of his work, titled "Inventions and Factories," on exactly the same sequence of textile inventions to which Toynbee drew attention, plus Henry Cort's iron process (1783–1784) and the Watt engine. Landes did likewise, adding a discussion of power tools and chemicals. It is only in recent years that a counteremphasis has emerged in which small scale innovation has been placed in the forefront of analysis. Donald McCloskey, for example, emphasized that by 1860 only about 30 percent of British employment was in "activities that had been radically transformed in technique since 1780" and that innovations "came more like a gentle (though unprecedented) rain, gathering here and there in puddles. By 1860 the ground was wet, but by no means soaked, even at the wetter spots. Looms run by hand and factories run by water survived in the cotton textile industry in 1860." G. N. von Tunzelmann (1981) argued that "the usual stress on a handful of dramatic breakthroughs is seriously open to question," and that what mattered was the variety and pervasiveness of innovation.

This general account has not gone without challenge, however. For a start it runs into serious problems of chronology: in the words of G. N. von Tunzelman, "if the Industrial Revolution was to be dated from around 1760, as Toynbee believed, then the Watt engine can hardly have triggered off industrialization, since it was not being marketed commercially until the mid-1770s." Even where there is a clear temporal correlation between expanded output and technical change, as in cotton and in the period 1760–1800, the causal relations are not at all obvious. Others have pointed out that the large factory was uncharacteristic in the eighteenth century; that historians of industrialization have seriously neglected agriculture, "the dominant sphere of the economy at this time, and also the most intensively capitalist of any sector," as Keith Tribe has called it; that hand techniques persisted in sector after sector until well into the nineteenth century, and that it is therefore, according to Raphael Samuel, "not possible to equate the new mode of production with the factory system." All of these considerations suggest a need for a closer look at the social aspects of technological change during the industrial revolution.

Social determinants of innovation in the industrial revolution. Although economic historians have, on the whole, a much more complex understanding of the industrialization process than economists, they have nonetheless followed economists in focusing on aspects of the economic environment (entry conditions, for example, or the structure of factor prices), or the impact of technological change on, for example, productivity growth, rather than on the sources and character of technological change as such. The approach taken by much of the literature on the social dimensions of industrialization has been similar in that it focused on the impacts of technology but not on the dynamics of innovation itself. This was probably because of the long lasting influence of the first systematic examinations of industrialization, the Parliamentary Select Committee hearings that began in the early nineteenth century, and the substantial literature on industrialization to which they gave rise. Within this literature the emphasis was on working conditions, health effects, mortality, and other impacts on the new working class. This type of approach was followed through in the classic sociological study of industrialization, Neil J. Smelser's *Social Change in the Industrial Revolution* (1959), and then in modern social history.

The approaches of social and economic historians have said little about the technologies themselves. So although technological change is treated as a major factor in early industrialization, it is rarely itself explained in any systematic way. In some cases this occurs because of an explicit or implicit technological determinism, as noted above, which sees technology as an autonomous explanatory force. It is quite common in the literature to find arguments to the effect that the transition to the factory, the rise of new forms of enterprise, or the development of cost accounting, for example, are responses to technological change. It is rare, on the other hand, to find detailed or systematic treatments of the evolution of specific technologies.

Indeed, with the exception of the literature on steam power, we have no systematic histories of the core technologies of early industrialization. Instead

18

what we have had until very recently is *Hamlet* without the Prince: an economic historiography written largely around the impact of new technologies, but with little analysis of the processes that produce specific areas of technological development, or that determine why some technologies succeed and some fail.

Where we have had attempts to explain the development of technological change in the industrial revolution, the explanations have emphasized the new social context of commercial calculation. Landes, for example, in *Unbound Prometheus,* writes of technical change in European industrialization as an effect of a conjunction of Western "rationality" (by which is meant means-end calculation) and a "Faustian spirit of mastery." Samuel Lilley, on the other hand, emphasised the causal effectivity of the control, decision-making capacity, and incentives to innovate that characterize the capitalist entrepreneur:

> The capitalist entrepreneur is aware—to a degree that no previous exploiter is aware—of how much he stands to gain from this or that technical change. He probably also has enough technological knowledge to judge the practicability of an invention, perhaps even to invent for himself. And the cold steel of competition reinforces this awareness and eliminates those who do not possess it. Hence derives the extreme sensitivity of response to technological opportunity that eighteenth century entrepreneurs repeatedly exhibited. (Lilley, 1978, pp. 219–220)

It should be emphasized that these aspects of the new technological environment are essentially social: they rest on new powers of ownership and control in production. However, we can go beyond these general factors into accounts of the determinants of specific lines of technical change. Modern analysis suggests that the technological change process is not general but focused, and that this is one of the primary explanatory problems which technological advance presents. Against this background the history of technological change is in fact one of advance in quite specific directions, often concentrated not just on particular sectors of the economy but on particular processes within sectors subject to change. In a word, there appear to be priorities. The theoretical problem here has been most succinctly outlined by Nathan Rosenberg:

> In the realm of pure theory, a decision maker bent on maximising profits under competitive conditions will pursue any possibility for reducing costs. . . . What forces, then, determine the directions in which a firm actually goes in exploring for new techniques? Since it cannot explore all directions, what are the factors which induce it to strike out in a particular direction? Better yet, are there any factors at work which compel it to look in some directions rather than others? (Rosenberg, 1977, pp. 110–111)

If the explanation of technological change should be understood in terms of explaining the direction of technological change, then we should seek to explain why technological advance has specific trajectories. This is in large part a matter looking at the social and technical problems which the innovator seeks to solve. Rosenberg has proposed three such "problem areas": technological complementarities, in which imbalances between technical processes induce correcting innovations; supply disruptions of various kinds, leading to innovations to provide substitute products and processes; and labour conflict, in which strikes or plant-level struggles generate "a search for labour-saving machines."

The latter issue was particularly important during the industrial revolution; it gave rise to Marx's famous remark that "it would be possible to write a whole history of the inventions made since 1830 for the sole purpose of providing capital with weapons against working class revolt." This claim has in fact been researched in terms of the sources of innovation during industrialization, and a number of confirming instances have been found. Kristine Bruland (1982) described three important technologies deriving from an attempt to "innovate around" labor conflicts, showing that a number of key innovations in textiles (including the first fully automatic machine in history) could be ascribed to the desire of entrepreneurs and engineers to automate their way around persistent conflicts with powerful shop-floor operatives. Conventional interpretations of industrial technology, in other words, do not deal adequately with the pace and extent of adoption of new technologies or the nature of social and cultural, rather than "great inventor," causation. More recent interpretations have revealed the role of social forces in the construction of "heroic inventors," as in Christine MacLeod's study of Watt and the steam engine.

By the mid-nineteenth century the pace and extent of new technologies unquestionably accelerated. Railroads and steamships transformed transportation from the 1820s onward, and the telegraph began to do the same for communication. Metallurgy was revolutionized by the substitution of coal for charcoal and the invention of the Bessemer process (1850s) for making steel. Printing was automated and larger printing presses were introduced. By the 1870s, use of electrical and gasoline motors anchored the set of new technologies sometimes referred to as the second industrial revolution.

The basis for invention increasingly shifted from individual tinkerers, usually of artisanal background, to organized, collective research in large companies, government agencies, and universities.

German firms pioneered the formal research and development approach. The United States became a significant innovator where previously it had borrowed; its contributions included the introduction of interchangeable parts, which speeded the manufacture of weaponry and machinery, and the expansion of looms and other equipment later in the nineteenth century. The second industrial revolution also involved the application of new technology outside the factory, to agriculture (harvesters and other implements), crafts (loading equipment, mechanical saws, and the like), and office work (typewriters and cash registers). Even the home became the site of technological change with sewing machines and vacuum cleaners, among other conveniences.

The modern industrial era. The emphasis on social forms as a central explanatory element of technological change does not stop with the industrial revolution. Many researchers have pushed it into the modern technological epoch, a field of study which developed rapidly in the 1990s, especially focusing on analyses of technology which conceptualise technologies not as artefacts but as integrated systems, with supporting managerial or social arrangements. A particularly influential body of work has been that of Thomas P. Hughes, whose history of electrical power generation and distribution emphasizes that the development of this core technology of the "second industrial revolution" must be understood in terms of

"systems, built by systems builders." His work encompasses the electrification of the United States, Britain, and Germany between the 1880s and 1930s. As Hughes shows, the evolution of electric power systems was different in each country, despite the common pool of knowledge to draw on. Reasons for these differences are found in the geographical, cultural, managerial, engineering, and entrepreneurial character of the regions involved. The "networks" which he studies refer not only to the technology but also to the institutions and actors involved. Such an approach, treating technologies as complex integrated systems of artefacts and social organization, has been carried out with regard to a wide range of technologies such as radio, jet engines, and railways.

Interest in the process of technological change crested again with the final decades of the twentieth century. New procedures of genetic engineering, computation, and robotics transformed the technological landscape in what some observers termed a third industrial—or postindustrial—technological revolution. Europe now participated in a literally international process of technological innovation, lagging in some areas (in computerization, behind the United States) but advancing rapidly in others, such as robotics. The full effects of this latest round of technological upheaval have yet to emerge, but the complex relationship between technological and social dynamics will surely remain a major topic for European social history in the future.

See also other articles in this section.

BIBLIOGRAPHY

Basalla, George. *The Evolution of Technology.* Cambridge, 1988.

Beniger, James R. *The Control Revolution: Technological and Economic Origins of the Information Society.* Cambridge, Mass., 1986.

Bijker, Wiebe E. and John Law, eds. *Shaping Technology/Building Society: Studies in Sociotechnical Change.* Cambridge, Mass., 1992.

Bijker, Wiebe E., Thomas P. Hughes, and Trevor J. Pinch. *The Social Construction of Technological Systems: New Directions in the Sociology and History of Technology.* Cambridge, Mass., 1987.

Bloch, Marc. *Land and Work in Medieval Europe: Selected Papers.* Translated by J. E. Anderson. Berkeley, Calif., 1967.

Bloch, Marc. "The Watermill and Feudal Authority." In *The Social Shaping of Technology: How the Refrigerator Got Its Hum.* Edited by Donald Mackenzie and Judy Wajcman. Philadelphia, 1985. Pages 75–78.

Braverman, Harry. *Labor and Monopoly Capital: The Degradation of Work in the Twentieth Century.* New York, 1974.

Bruland, Kristine. "Industrial Conflict as a Source of Technical Innovation: The Development of the Automatic Spinning Mule." In *The Social Shaping of Technology: How the Refrigerator Got Its Hum.* Edited by Donald Mackenzie and Judy Wajcman. Philadelphia, 1985. Pages 84–92.

Bruland, Kristine. "Industrial Conflict as a Source of Technical Innovation: Three Cases." *Economy and Society* 11:2 (1982). 91–121.

Childe, V. Gordon "Early Forms of Society." In *A History of Technology.* Vol. I. *From Early Times to the Fall of Ancient Empires.* Edited by Charles Singer et. al Oxford, 1958. Pages 38–57.

Deane, Phyllis. *The First Industrial Revolution.* Cambridge, U.K., 1965.

Gies, Frances and Joseph Gies. *Cathedral, Forge, and Waterwheel: Technology and Invention in the Middle Ages.* New York, 1994.

Gille, Bertrand. "The Medieval Age of the West, Fifth Century to 1350." In *A History of Technology and Invention: Progress Through the Ages.* Vol. 1. *The Origins of Civilization.* Edited by Maurice Daumas. New York, 1969. Pages 422–572.

Gille, Bertrand. "The Fifteenth and Sixteenth Centuries in the Western World." In *A History of Technology and Invention: Progress Through the Ages.* Vol. 2. *The First Stage of Mechanization, 1450–1725.* Edited by Maurice Daumas. New York, 1969. Pages 16–148.

Harrison, H. S. "Discovery, invention and diffusion." In *A History of Technology.* Vol. I. *From Early Times to the Fall of Ancient Empires.* Edited by Charles Singer et. al Oxford, 1958. Pages 58–84.

Hughes, Thomas P. *Networks of Power: Electrification in Western Society, 1880–1930.* Baltimore, 1993.

Landes, David S. *The Unbound Prometheus: Technological Change and Industrial Development in Western Europe from 1750 to the Present.* London, 1974.

Landes, David S. *The Wealth and Poverty of Nations: Why Some Are So Rich and Some So Poor.* New York, 1999.

Lilley, Samuel. "Technological Progress and the Industrial Revolution, 1700–1914." In *The Fontana Economic History of Europe.* Vol 3. Edited by Carlo M. Cipolla. London, 1978. Pages 187–254.

Mackenzie, Donald, and Judy Wajcman. *The Social Shaping of Technology: How the Refrigerator Got Its Hum.* Philadelphia, 1985.

MacLeod, Christine. "James Watt, Heroic Invention, and the Idea of the Industrial Revolution." In *Technological Revolutions in Europe: Historical Perspectives.* Edited by Maxine Berg and Kristine Bruland. Chelten, U.K., and Northampton, Mass., 1998. Pages 96–116.

Mantoux, Paul. *The Industrial Revolution in the Eighteenth Century: An Outline of the Beginnings of the Modern Factory System in England.* London, 1961.

McCloskey, Donald. "The Industrial Revolution, 1780–1860: A Survey." In *The Economic History of Britain Since 1700.* Vol 1. *1700–1860.* Edited by Roderick Floud and Donald McCloskey. Cambridge, U.K., 1981. Pages 242–270.

Mokyr, Joel. *The Lever of Riches: Technological Creativity and Economic Progress.* New York, 1990.

Needham, Joseph. *Science and Civilisation in China.* Cambridge, U.K., 1954.

O'Brien, Patrick K. "Introduction: Modern Conceptions of the Industrial Revolution." In *The Industrial Revolution and British Society.* Edited by Patrick K.

O'Brien and Roland Quinault. Cambridge, U.K., and New York, 1993. Pages 1–31.

Pahl, R. E., ed. *On Work: Historical, Comparative, and Theoretical Approaches.* Oxford, 1988.

Rosenberg, Nathan. *Perspectives on Technology.* Cambridge, U.K., 1976.

Rudgeley Richard. *Lost Civilisations of the Stone Age.* London, 1998.

Samuel, Raphael. "Workshop of the World: Steam Power and Hand Technology in Mid-Victorian Britain" *History Workshop Journal* 3 (1977): 6–72.

Tann, Jennifer. *The Development of the Factory.* London, 1970.

Toynbee, Arnold. *Lectures on the Industrial Revolution of the Eighteenth Century, Popular Addresses, Notes, and Other Fragments.* London and New York, 1908.

Tribe, Keith. *Land, Labour, and Economic Discourse.* London, 1978.

Tunzelmann, G. N. von. "Technical Progress During the Industrial Revolution." In *The Economic History of Britain Since 1700.* Vol 1. *1700–1860.* Edited by Roderick Floud and Donald McCloskey. Cambridge, U.K., 1981. Pages 143–163.

Tunzelmann, G. N. von. *Steam Power and British Industrialization to 1860.* Oxford, 1978.

White, Lynn. *Medieval Technology and Social Change.* Oxford, 1962.

CAPITALISM AND COMMERCIALIZATION

Robert S. DuPlessis

The rise of capitalism, one of the formative influences on modern Europe, is the subject of an enormous and contentious scholarship. The new economic and social order formed over many centuries, but historians have long devoted much attention to the two and half centuries from the Black Death to the onset of the seventeenth-century crisis. In this period, from about 1350 to about 1620, two of capitalism's central attributes became firmly and widely entrenched: the market as the fundamental economic institution, or "commercialization," and a polarized class structure. Analysis of these traits began with the founders of modern economics and sociology. Adam Smith held that market development promoted division of labor, specialization, and productivity-enhancing innovation that engendered continuous economic growth. For Karl Marx the origins of capitalism lay in "original" or "primary" accumulation. This process transformed existing land, labor, tools, and money into capital by dispossessing peasants and artisans, simultaneously turning them into proletarianized wage laborers and the landlords and merchants who accumulated this productive property into capitalist entrepreneurs. Max Weber argued that a novel mentality to motivate both capitalist classes stemmed from the theology of the sixteenth-century Reformation.

Over the many decades, these interpretations have been fiercely debated, elaborated, and modified, and important new explanatory factors introduced. No scholarly consensus exists on how to account for the rise of capitalism. Nevertheless, the critical nature of this period is widely accepted. This discussion first examines the appearance of the marketized economy and then turns to the social relations of commercial capitalism.

ECONOMIC CHANGE AND COMMERCIALIZATION

After about 1000, European population and economy underwent brisk growth. Colonists settled and im-

proved large territories; new towns were founded and existing ones greatly expanded; crafts flourished; and local, interregional, and long-distance trade burgeoned, most of all on overland routes that spread across the Continent. Time-honored interpretations postulate that the traumatic Black Death (1347–1351), which killed up to half of Europe's population, put an abrupt end to the expansion of the High Middle Ages, but research in commercial, demographic, political, and price history has forced considerable interpretive revision. Instead of a unique catastrophe, most scholars have come to postulate a broader, protracted "late medieval crisis" extending from the early fourteenth to the mid-fifteenth century. Heralded by poor harvests, extensive famines, and destructive warfare around 1300, the troubles touched their nadir with the catastrophic great plague. Worse, they were perpetuated by several decades of recurrent epidemics; interstate conflicts, most famously the Hundred Years' War (1337–1453); and social strife, notably the French Jacquerie (a peasant insurrection) of 1358, the Florentine *Ciompi* (wool workers) revolt of 1378–1382, and the English Peasants' Revolt of 1381, all of which cut short population recovery, stoked inflation, depressed farm and craft output, and disrupted trade. From about 1400, the worst problems eased, but the next half century was a time of slow revival marked by demographic stagnation, the constant threat or, all too often, reality of war, and steep deflation.

It also turned out to be a period of gestation. During the "long sixteenth century"—beginning in 1450–1470 and continuing to about 1620—earlier economic and social trends were renewed, extended, and consolidated. Until at least 1570 nearly all of Europe experienced vigorous demographic recovery, reoccupation of vacant holdings along with notable urbanization, intensified agricultural and industrial output, and the extension of trading relations across much of the globe. But thereafter the long expansion petered out. Population growth slowed, agricultural productivity stagnated, industrial output stalled or dropped, and both overseas and intra-European trade

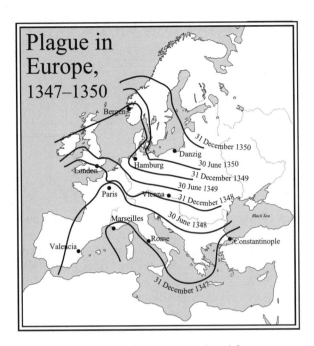

The Plague in Europe, 1347–1350. Adapted from Wilhelm Abel, *Agricultural Fluctuations in Europe,* 3d ed. (London: Methuen, 1980), p. 42.

languished. Bitter and prolonged strife in France and the Low Countries was followed by wars elsewhere on the Continent, marking the return of disruption and high taxes, which sucked money out of the economy. After about 1620 most of Europe entered the "crisis of the seventeenth century." Yet the dominance of the market economy had been established, so whereas before the late fourteenth century most peasant output was directly consumed by its producers or taken by lords as tribute, by the end of the long sixteenth century the majority went to the market.

The late medieval crisis. Market exchange played a larger role in medieval Europe than traditionally assumed. Although overwhelmingly agrarian, Europe was not a nonmonetized, autarkic "natural economy." Commerce developed after the dawn of the new millennium and centered initially in northern and central Italy. Together with the early decline of serfdom, the precocious revival of towns fostered market production by urban artisans and by peasants encouraged or compelled to supply food, raw materials, and funds to city-states. The peninsula's middleman position between the flourishing Middle East and transalpine Europe, stimulus provided by the Crusades and consequent establishment of trading colonies in the Levant and around the Black Sea, and expansion of the papacy's fiscal apparatus prompted Italians to organize commercial, financial, and transport networks throughout the Mediterranean and adjacent areas and on into northern and eastern Europe. Italian commercial dominance was firmly grounded in stable currencies and in innovations such as permanent partnerships, bills of exchange, insurance, and double-entry bookkeeping that reduced transaction costs and enhanced efficiency. During the twelfth and thirteenth centuries, demographic recovery, urbanization, conversion of labor services and other feudal obligations into cash payments, and textiles and other crafts spread across Europe. As a result markets became particularly active along Europe's "dorsal spine," extending from Florence to southeastern England, and on related networks like the Hanseatic League, organized by merchants of Baltic and North Sea towns.

The late medieval crisis complicated commercialization but did not provoke a general retreat from markets. Warfare's attendant lawlessness, destruction, inflation, taxation, and coinage debasements disorganized commerce, especially long-distance trade in cheaper items whose transport and security costs exceeded potential profits. As John Munro showed, a once-flourishing transcontinental trade in inexpensive Flemish woolens ceased. Demographic collapse reduced both the supply of and the demand for industrial goods and provoked the abandonment of land or, in some areas, entire settlements. In Germany, perhaps the most severely affected, about one-quarter of the villages in existence before the crisis were deserted by its end.

These problems proved surmountable. Once the hyperinflation of cereal prices subsided in the 1380s, not only workers enjoying high real wages due to a tight labor market but most other Europeans had more income to spend on nongrain foodstuffs and manufactures. Richard Goldthwaite argued that Italian towns prospered on the basis of demand for luxury goods, notably works of art, which expanded because wealth concentrated in the hands of those who survived the ravages of the era. What from one perspective was the late medieval crisis from another was the celebrated Renaissance. Many Flemish towns that could no longer profitably export cheap textiles turned successfully to fine woolens—whose high selling price absorbed stiff transportation and insurance rates on unsafe routes—and then revived inexpensive lines when demographic, social, and political circumstances stabilized after 1400.

The evolution of agrarian specialization suggests that many peasants took their cues from the market. For much of the fourteenth century, the price of grain remained high, so it enjoyed pride of place in European fields. But when relative prices changed, farmers quickly switched to dairying, livestock raising, and the cultivation of wine, fruits and vegetables, flax, and

24

other foodstuffs and industrial crops. Landlords, too, contributed to commercialization both inadvertently and intentionally. To be sure, some initially sought to exploit disarray and reintroduce labor services, even serfdom. But their offensive met intense resistance and succeeded only in limited regions, so trends toward commutation of feudal obligations into monetary payments and rents in cash and kind redoubled. Along with rising levies imposed by churches and states, these changes forced more farmers to sell a larger part of their produce. Many poorer peasants and full-time agricultural laborers also found jobs on large market-oriented estates established by landlords—noble, ecclesiastical, and bourgeois—who dispensed with tenants altogether, or on the farms of more substantial peasants.

High mortality, low birthrates, and rents and land values that fell by one-third to one-half, central features of the crisis era, combined to provoke an active land market for proprietors and tenants alike. These factors also spawned both subdivision and amalgamation of properties from individual holdings to entire estates. In this environment a novel attitude toward land arose. Rather than a patrimony to be carefully husbanded for transfer over generations, landed property became an exchangeable commodity valued by and in the market. The new mentality was still strongly attached to land but no longer identified a specific plot or manor with an individual family. Any piece of land was a capital asset to be put to the most lucrative use for a contractually stated period of time and disposed of if economic conditions warranted.

By the mid-fifteenth century the European economy was smaller than a century before. Some areas, notably uplands and regions of low fertility; producers distant from urban markets or trade routes; and artisans in crafts that failed to adapt to new market conditions continued to suffer. Guilds, village communities, landlords, laws, and customs often hampered experimentation with new procedures, crops, and tools. Many Europeans were too poor and the output of their farms or shops was too meager to enter the market regularly as either producers or consumers. But all economic sectors were much more vigorous than in the early fourteenth century, and per capita productivity and income were higher thanks mainly to agricultural and industrial specialization in response to relative market prices. Despite manifold signs of decline in the period, economic historians view the late medieval crisis as an era of adjustment and enhanced commercialization.

The long sixteenth century. The forces undergirding the robust growth that began about 1450 and became general before 1500 powerfully spurred commercialization. As epidemics waned and destructive warfare receded, lower death rates interacted with rising natality, initially reflecting higher incomes and the greater availability of land at affordable rents, to lift Europe's population from no more than 50 million in 1450 to nearly 80 million in 1600, boosting aggregate demand and enlarging the labor supply. Pronounced urbanization raised the proportion of Europeans living in towns of more than 10,000 people from about 5.5 percent in 1500 to 7.5 percent a century later, magnifying the numbers of people whose livelihoods depended on market involvement. The growth of cities also promoted economies of scale that by cutting prices helped widen the market. As commercial opportunities multiplied, merchants throughout Europe adopted commercial and financial innovations pioneered in Italy that decreased transaction costs and thus final prices to consumers, further quickening markets.

The declining incidence and destructiveness of intrastate and interstate conflicts lowered the cost of goods and eased tax burdens, giving consumers more disposable income. Additional market stimulus came from a budding new commercial network, even if it did not yet, in the opinions of most historians, constitute "the modern world-system" proposed by Immanuel Wallerstein. Overseas exploration, settlement, and trade grew exponentially. Seville, the staple port for Spain's New World possessions, shipped seventeen times as much by volume in the years 1606–1610 as it had in 1511–1515. Imports from Asia as well as America likewise developed smartly. One of the leading commodities, New World bullion, provided much of the enlarged money supply needed to keep the wheels of commerce turning. Production for the market motivated the establishment, in Europe's American colonies, of plantations staffed by indigenous peoples or, increasingly, enslaved Africans in what Wallerstein has aptly termed "coerced cash-crop" agriculture.

Expanding market production resuscitated old centers and launched new ones all across Europe. Long-neglected fields were plowed up, and forests were felled. By the 1530s the forest of Orléans, France, had contracted to a third of its former size. In many areas, particularly along the North Sea coast, new land was created. In a half-century more than 100,000 acres were drained and diked in the northern Netherlands alone. All this activity was made possible by massive capital investment, much by townspeople who sold the reclaimed land once it was ready for cultivation. The new owners, specialized commercial farmers who shed all auxiliary tasks to improve efficiency, purchased inputs from livestock to implements to additional labor. Under such conditions, peasants had to be closely attuned to market conditions. Thus as relative cereal prices again consistently exceeded those for other produce, farmers reversed course from their medieval forebears and increased grain growing. Landlords behaved similarly. Many English manors enclosed for sheep grazing in earlier years were plowed up and sown with wheat or rye. The proportion of western European landowners' income provided by feudal sources, such as seigneurial privileges, dues, and commuted labor services, tumbled, while income from capitalist activities, such as the sale of produce and market-determined rents, mounted. Witnesses—and handmaidens—to the ever-spreading commercialization were legions of market towns, amounting to four thousand just in Germany, so most farms were only a few miles from at least one of them. Agricultural advance also sustained the lively land market, for rising demand translated into mounting rents and related charges, making pasture and arable land excellent investments.

Industrial development had a broader impact. The city of Lille and its nearby countryside in Flanders illustrate the processes at work. Its once-thriving woolens industry devastated by the late medieval crisis, sixteenth-century Lille took up various forms of light textiles, which experienced a remarkable boom thanks to sales in much of Europe and in Spanish America. Eventually entrepreneurs, many of them Lillois, hired workers in neighboring villages, some of which became formidable competitors of the metropolis. Feeding the swelling industrial population and supplying it with raw materials greatly enlarged and enriched Lille's merchant class, developed a vigorous carting trade, and employed farmers in the immediate outskirts of town, in grain-growing districts in adjacent Flanders and northern France, in vineyards in Burgundy and the Bordelais, in grazing regions from Germany to Spain, and even on Polish serf estates.

The achievements of commercialization should not be exaggerated, however. Although wider and deeper market participation and specialization had occurred, relatively little capital had been invested in technical development that would have allowed productivity to outpace population. Why this was so is a matter of considerable dispute. To some historians, capitalists' preference for commerce, land acquisition, moneylending, and various types of conspicuous expenditure is evidence of a "traditional" mentality that valued consumption above production and placed social and political objectives above economic ones. But other scholars contend that such behavior was economically rational given the prevailing conditions of constantly expanding commercial opportunities, high rents and interest rates, lower industrial prices than agricultural prices and fluctuating markets for manufactures, cheap unskilled labor, and costly innovations with low rates of return.

Still, the results stopped economic advance. Inflation became sufficiently severe that many scholars speak of a sixteenth-century "price revolution." Because grains were central to diets and thus to budgets in nearly all of Europe, demand shifted away from other foodstuffs and especially away from industrial goods, heightening the damage to workers, who saw their real wages fall in tandem with work opportunities, and to specialized agriculturists. Florentine woolen output, for example, which had mounted from 10,000 to 12,000 pieces a year in the 1430s to 30,000 in the 1560s, dropped to 14,000 in the 1590s and just 6,000 by the 1630s. Across the last period sales of raw wool from Castile's vast herds were cut in half.

The effects of commercialization were unevenly distributed across Europe. Three distinct but interrelated zones are discernible. In the Mediterranean basin, agriculture and industry initially conquered foreign markets but were harmed by low levels of investment. Despite a few notable exceptions, like Catalonia and Lombardy, the Mediterranean region underwent a process of relative decline marked by a partial retreat from commercialization and specialization. Eastern Europe experienced the wide imposition of "second serfdom," which had dual origins in the late medieval crisis and in sixteenth-century commercialization. Despite resembling medieval serfdom by virtue of heavy obligations and restrictions placed on the peasantry, neoserfdom was market-oriented. Perhaps three-fourths of all the grain, cattle, wine, and other items produced by peasants performing compulsory, unpaid labor services on the lords' demesnes or appropriated from the surplus gathered on their individual plots was marketed in western Europe and locally. But commercialized serfdom obstructed development. Lords saw little reason to innovate, whereas peasants lacked the time and capital to improve their own holdings and had no inclination to improve their lords'. Industries making cheap goods emerged, but the narrow, impoverished market discouraged new methods.

Western Europe, particularly the quadrant comprising southeastern England, the Low Countries (Belgium and the Netherlands), northern France, and the German Rhineland and North Sea coast, reaped the most benefits. There Europe's highest rate of demographic expansion, rapidly growing town populations atop already elevated levels of urbanization, and a thick nexus of dynamic, increasingly efficient markets provided many incentives to innovate and the institutions and capital to do so. By the early seventeenth century, an area that had traditionally been on the periphery of the European economy was poised to become the core of a capitalism that was taking its first steps toward creating a global economy.

SOCIAL POLARIZATION

While few historians think that Emmanuel Le Roy Ladurie's notion of "motionless history" accurately represents the preindustrial world, many emphasize the continuities that marked it. From the Black Death to the seventeenth-century crisis—not to mention before and after the period—the basic farming unit over nearly all Europe remained the holding worked by an individual household or, notably in some sharecropping and upland areas, by several usually related and coresident households. Analogously, the small artisan workshop operated by a household produced most manufactures. Both farms and shops were integrated into larger institutions. Village communities supervised many aspects of cultivation, crop rotation, grazing, and access to common resources, such as woodlands, waterways, and waste. Corporations (guilds) regulated artisanal production and organized collective social and religious observances. All these structures retained broad ideological sanctions as the desirable means of ensuring not only acceptable livelihoods but also, through inheritance, provision for the next generation. In addition they fit snugly into the hierarchic image that ordered social perceptions and obligations.

Yet across the period these structures were undermined, and the ideal and reality diverged notably as the sixteenth century proceeded. Larger units emerged. In agriculture landlords and peasants enlarged and consolidated their properties. In manufacturing capitalists assembled urban and rural "putting-out," or domestic, networks by employing artisans, peasants seeking additional income, and women and children to process raw materials supplied on credit by the entrepreneur. Smaller units proliferated as well, especially in regions where peasant families subdivided their holdings to bequeath to all their children. All these changes reflected the weakening of village and corporate institutions as capitalists—commercializing landlords and rich peasants, putting-out organizers, and merchants—became more influential. Domestic systems, for instance, often existed in defiance of corporate privileges. As the period went on, advocates touting the benefits of the new arrangements to the economy and society claimed and sometimes acquired a degree of legitimacy for them.

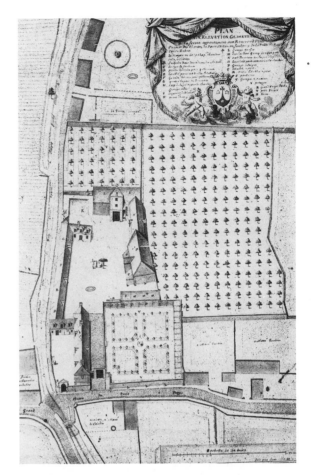

Consolidated Farm. A commercial farm outside Paris belonging to the Carmelites. Seventeenth-century print. ARCHIVES NATIONALES, PARIS/PHOTO: JEAN-LOUP CHARMET

These developments did not occur uniformly or steadily, and they were often interrupted, particularly during the late medieval crisis, when stabilization succeeded initial upheaval. But the transformation proved broad and persistent, as evidenced by the social polarization—most of all the extensive proletarianization—that accompanied sixteenth-century commercialization.

The late medieval crisis: Social upheaval to social stabilization. Echoing contemporaries, historians long believed that the Black Death severely and permanently disrupted European social institutions and behavior. Ever since Wilhelm Abel charted a close concordance between agricultural and population movements, however, scholarship has played down the singular importance of the plague, pointing instead to a host of problems that accumulated after the late thirteenth century. Chief among them was the demo-

Gender Division of Labor. A painting by Jehan Bourdichon (c. 1457–1521) shows an idealized fifteenth-century carpenter's shop that nevertheless accurately depicts the tools. It also portrays the wife spinning; spinning was probably the most widespread female occupation. BIBLIOTHÈQUE DE L'ÉCOLE DES BEAUX-ARTS, PARIS/GIRAUDON/ART RESOURCE, NY

sible for the duration and magnitude of the troubles and for their most significant outcomes.

On the basis of this rich but contentious historiography, the outlines of another synthesis can be proposed that distinguishes two phases in the social history of the late medieval crisis. The first, which comprised the three decades or so after the Black Death, deeply shook European society, whereas the second, which roughly coincides with the end of the fourteenth century and the first half of the fifteenth century, was characterized by stabilization.

In the immediate aftermath of the plague, drastic inflation engendered by the wide abandonment of fields and the disruption of trading networks created golden opportunities for astute and unscrupulous merchants, landlords, and peasants. Further, the vagaries of survival and inheritance contributed to unprecedented individual social mobility, for many agricultural holdings and artisanal shops suddenly became available to rent or purchase on favorable terms. The same processes also encouraged geographical mobility, most notably among rural residents attracted by the new occupational positions that opened up in towns. The easing of access to mastership in craft guilds symbolized the new opportunities. Florence's silk guild, for instance, admitted just 16 new members in 1346 and 18 in 1347, the last preplague years, whereas in 1348, 1349, and 1350, 35, 69, and 67 matriculants, respectively, were accepted. Moreover in stable periods half or more of the neophytes had close relatives in the silk guild, but in the quarter century after the Black Death, the proportion was a third or fewer.

If this was a period when fortune smiled on "new men," women formed the group that probably saw the most improved conditions. The particularly lucky among them became substantial propertyholders upon inheriting assets that previously would have gone to their brothers. Because of labor shortages, gender divisions of labor were widely relaxed, and women were allowed entry to numerous jobs and guilds that formerly had barred them. For the same reason women who had been employed but suffered from discrimination saw their wages rise dramatically, particularly in relation to men's. Female grape pickers in Languedoc, for instance, paid just half the rate of their male coworkers before the Black Death, received 80 to 90 percent as much immediately after. Both men and women, however, experienced a big jump in nominal wages.

Not everyone benefited from the upheaval. Many men, of course, lost relatively, a sore point at a time when patriarchal power was widely taken as natural and inevitable. Those who bought grain in the

graphic growth that exhausted much land, thereby reducing productivity, pushing up prices, engendering famine and disease, and allowing landlords to increase rents while also encouraging them to commute feudal bonds and obligations into more easily adjusted and thus more lucrative payments in cash and kind. But population pressure had such strongly negative effects, historians now contend, only because of three additional factors: frequent and destructive wars and civil conflicts, excessive state and lordly levies that further burdened the populace while taking from it the resources needed to satisfy them, and rigid tenurial structures that discouraged innovation. In the 1990s David Herlihy and other scholars attempted to rehabilitate a version of the earlier catastrophic view. Agreeing that Europe suffered from a late medieval crisis, they regarded the Black Death and the recurrent epidemics of the next few decades as chiefly respon-

market were harmed as wars and epidemics that repeatedly interfered with farming and distribution kept cereal prices high for at least a generation after the great plague. These same occurrences also interrupted manufacture and trade, so workers were unable to profit fully from their higher wages. Worse, improved nominal rates may disguise declining real wages consequent upon elevated grain prices and the practice, adopted by many employers, of paying with depreciating copper coins. One of the grievances of the rebellious *Ciompi* (wool workers) in Florence in 1378 was precisely that they received wages in debased pennies.

As the postplague troubles played out by 1400, a new equilibrium took shape. Attention to the effects of gender ideologies and relations reveals that for women the new order entailed a clear decline in opportunities and material conditions. As population and production stabilized, albeit at below preplague levels, labor shortages eased or rather were redefined to restore male preference. The female presence on lists of property owners diminished considerably. Many corporations statutorily prohibited female membership. Forced into gender-restricted labor pools, women experienced at least a relative drop in the market value of their labor. Thus Languedoc grape pickers' wage hierarchy returned to early-fourteenth-century levels. Landlords with fixed rents and long leases or those who employed sizable numbers of farm laborers also faced the prospect of hard times. But unlike women, they had socially approved and economically lucrative ways to cope. Many switched to in-kind or sharecropping rents that yielded consumable as well as marketable produce. Titled landowners requently found salvation in marriage to members of wealthy, upwardly mobile commoner families. The most powerful acquired offices, monetary grants, or other forms of state assistance.

For most males, at least, and perhaps for families as a whole, the first half of the fifteenth century was a golden age. What is often termed the "wage-price scissors" favored the majority of the population. Food prices finally fell, grain most of all (see table 1). Yet average farm size had grown. On Redgrave Manor in England, for example, the mean holding had twelve acres in 1300, twenty in 1400, and more than thirty in 1450. Consequently marginally productive land had been abandoned. Because peasants shifted from grain to higher-priced foods, their earnings were healthy. With land cheap and plentiful but tenants scarce, farmers and their communities enjoyed enhanced bargaining power. To attract them, landlords offered lower rents. In a sample of thirty-one Brandenburg villages, for instance, rents fell at least a third

from the fourteenth century to the mid-fifteenth century. Landlords also offered longer leases, better tools and seed, and even expensive teams of oxen. Many of these improvements further enhanced productivity and encouraged greater commercialization, again augmenting farm income. Ongoing labor shortages in crafts and on the land, where vineyards, vegetable gardening, hop raising, and many other types of specialized agriculture were labor-intensive, kept employment and wages up.

Lower food prices and higher real wages, not to mention the return of more peaceful conditions that allowed the reopening of transcontinental trade routes, quickened and smoothed out both the supply of and the demand for industrial goods. Thus for the first time in over a century, many Europeans experienced rising incomes, which they used to rent or buy more land and new equipment and for training for better jobs—that is, they invested in capital that would sustain their incomes. They also improved their standard of living. Although they stuck mainly to moderately priced items, they purchased some luxury consumer goods, undaunted by aristocratic disdain and sumptuary laws, and once again traded widely across Europe.

Herlihy proposed that this material progress and the realistic expectation of its continuation had fundamental effects on demographic behavior. Previously, forces like disease or famine beyond an individual's control had been the chief determinants of population trends. Now, however, Europeans embraced new inheritance conventions that concentrated property into fewer hands, married later and increasingly did not marry at all, and perhaps practiced birth control. Taken together, these steps limited the birthrate, allowing families and individuals to achieve or maintain greater degrees of prosperity. Concomitantly, the new

TABLE 1
THE WHEAT EQUIVALENTS OF WAGES IN SOUTHERN ENGLAND

Period	Artisan	Laborer
1300–09	100	100
1440–59	241	236

Source: Abel, p. 54.

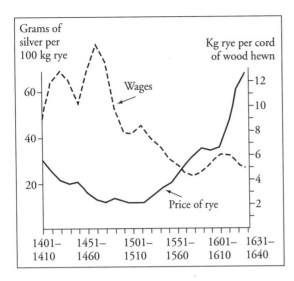

Figure 1. Wages and the price of rye in Göttingen, Germany, 1401–1640 (trinomial 10-year moving averages). From Wilhelm Abel, *Agricultural Fluctuations in Europe,* 3d ed. (London: Methuen, 1980), p. 57.

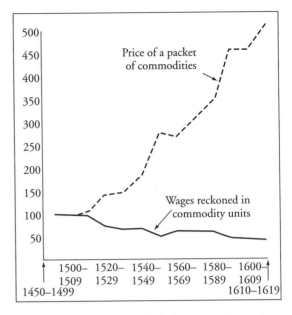

Figure 2. Purchasing power of a builder's wage in southern England, 1450–1619 (1450–1499 = 100). From Wilhelm Abel, *Agricultural Fluctuations in Europe,* 3d ed. (London: Methuen, 1980), p. 135.

low-fertility pattern delayed population recovery, which ironically helped sustain better material conditions.

In sum, despite all its tribulations, the late medieval crisis was a time when social divisions diminished. As the power and in many cases the wealth of landlords and employers of labor decreased, at least in a relative sense, material and tenurial conditions improved for the mass of the populace. In Languedoc, for instance, where rents, taxes, and tithes took about one-fourth of peasants' gross yield, down from a third or more in the High Middle Ages, a comfortable middling group constituted the majority of villagers. Rich peasants and the landless formed distinct minorities. As seigneurial levies and obligations were commuted into payments, peasant-controlled village communities took over most collective tasks from landlords. States bolstered them as useful counterweights to aristocrats and as tax-collecting entities. In a particularly dramatic manifestation of the power of village communities and the peasant solidarity they embodied, numerous rebellions shook rural Germany in the late fifteenth century, culminating in the Peasants' War of 1524–1525. In towns organized artisans supported by municipalities guided by ideological commitments and concerns about public order and tax revenues firmed up their dominance over craft production. But brisk demand for goods and services in a time of labor shortages also benefited workers outside guilds through higher wages and steadier employment.

The long sixteenth century: Polarization and proletarianization.
Strong growth, in contrast, gen-

erated social polarization. Historians influenced by Abel and the so-called *Annales* school favor a neo-Malthusian explanation, that is, swelling population in a context of technological immobility leads to opulence for the few but misery for the many. As numbers increased, the land-labor ratio tilted in favor of property owners, permitting them to raise rents and associated levies. Commercial farmers benefited from strong demand and rising prices. Both urban and rural employers of labor found the labor supply growing, allowing them to stabilize wages. The same processes disadvantaged the many people who were at once suppliers of labor and purchasers of food, for competition among them drove pay down and prices up. In England agricultural laborers saw their real wages cut in half between 1500 and 1650. But that was not the worst situation: in 1570 the wages of reapers near Paris had just a third of the purchasing power of a century before.

Other historians consider commercialization largely responsible for the increasing poverty. Growing market activity favored merchants, financiers, landed proprietors, big farmers, industrial entrepreneurs, and certain artisans who possessed capital and skills. But by drawing more of the population into labor and commodity markets, this activity put them increasingly at the markets' mercy. Thus the sixfold or sevenfold rise in grain prices that prevailed across Europe during the long sixteenth century had a disastrous im-

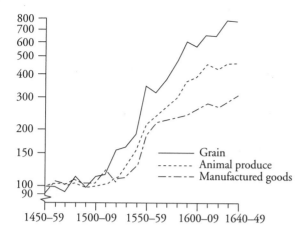

Figure 3. Index of nominal prices in ten-year averages for England, 1450–1649 (1450–1459 = 100). From Peter Kriedte, *Peasants, Landlords, and Merchant Capitalists: Europe and the World Economy, 1500–1800* (Leamington Spa, U.K.: Berg, 1983), p. 49.

pact on wage laborers. As their pay went up only three or four times, the wage-price scissors cut against them. They suffered additionally from unsteady employment as the populace was forced to spend more of its income on grain and less on other produce and manufactures. The same circumstances also damaged much of the middling peasantry. Its members had formerly achieved an adequate standard of living by combining agricultural and industrial wage labor with work on their holdings, which typically comprised a few acres that they owned and rather more that they leased. But as the sixteenth century proceeded, their additional sources of income yielded less while their costs climbed. Obliged to borrow to make ends meet, many finished in bankruptcy and dispossession. The same fate awaited numerous artisans. Modest output and minimal productivity gains kept costs high, while relative industrial prices lagged behind agricultural prices and market swings intensified. Many artisans came to depend on credit and on work provided by merchant capitalists or rich artisans.

As Robert Brenner pointed out in articles that reignited the transition debate in the 1970s, neither demography nor commercialization accounts sufficiently for early modern socioeconomic developments, most of all in the countryside. Underlining disparate outcomes across Europe, Brenner argued that social relations and social conflicts determined how demographic and commercial forces played out. Vigorous village institutions, secure tenures, and various types of collective action from negotiation to rebellion best enabled peasants to hold on to their land and to enjoy continued access to common woodlands and pastures that were vital to the survival of middling and small farms. Conversely, short tenures, weak occupancy rights, and communities that had lost common resources and solidarity proved vulnerable to landlord initiatives that hiked rents and related charges frequently or even evicted tenants.

Subsequent studies moderated some of the sharp contrasts, notably between English and French agriculture, that Brenner drew and broadened the analysis to include political and military developments along with the industrial sector. Many princes, particularly in France and Germany, sought to defend peasants and their communities from excessive lordly levies and the loss of collective property so they could serve as counterweights to aristocratic power and shore up the fiscal foundation of expanding state bureaucracies and militaries. Yet because government finances relied mainly on taxing the countryside, village communities became fatally indebted and were forced to mortgage or sell common property to landlords or well-to-do peasants. Privatization of resources meant the exclusion of villagers, who had relied on common property to provide a margin of survival. Some authorities, prodded by guilds, supported petty artisan producers, but most permitted entrepreneurial initiatives. Women, almost entirely excluded from any sort of institutional protection and herded into overcrowded labor pools, saw their already unenviable position sink further. In Languedoc their wages fell to less than 40 percent of men's. Warfare returned with a religiously inspired vengeance in the sixteenth century, ruined many villages and towns, and dealt a crippling blow to many peasants and workers already on the edge.

In consequence the social order of commercial capitalism became ever more sharply divided. A small minority of the populace accumulated wealth and capital assets. In the textile center of Nördlingen, Germany, in 1579, the top 2 percent of the citizens controlled at least a quarter of the assets. In Lyon, the French silk and commercial metropole, more than half of all wealth belonged to 10 percent of the taxpayers, and just ten individuals, all merchants, owed 7 percent of the urban tax bill in the mid-sixteenth century. At a time when the average artisan had a loom or two, 220 looms were controlled by two merchants. A few decades later two others employed nearly one thousand people between them. Infrequently attempted, big centralized workplaces almost invariably failed because no technologically generated savings offset their high cost and financial vulnerability in the always fluctuating markets. The picture was much the same in the countryside. In Poland serfs worked a quarter of the cultivated area, and lords received, at no cost, up to half of the gross output of

RESPONSES TO CAPITALISM

The effect of the plague.   All this year [1348] and the next, the mortality of men and women, of the young even more than the old, in Paris and in the kingdom of France, and also, it is said, in other parts of the world, was so great that it was almost impossible to bury the dead. . . . Many country villages and many houses in good towns remained empty and deserted. Many houses, including some splendid dwellings, very soon fell into ruins.

Source: Jean de Venette, *The Chronicle of Jean de Venette.* Edited by Richard A. Newhall. Translated by Jean Birdsall. New York, 1953, p. 49. Venette, a Carmelite friar, was a theology professor at the University of Paris.

The poor of Norwich.   Theis be the names of the poore within the saide Citie [Norwich, England] as they ware vewed in the year of our Lord god 1570. . . .

The Parishe of St. Stevenes

Robert Rowe of the age of 46 yeres, glasier, in no worke, and Elizabeth his wyfe that spinne white warpe and have five children, 2 sonnes the eldist of the age of 16 yeres that kepe children, and the other, daughters that spinne, and have dwelt here ever. . . .

John Hubburd, of the age of 38 yeres, butcher, that occupie slaughterie, and Margarit his wyfe of the age of 30 yeres that sell souce, and 2 young children, and have dwelt here ever. . . .

An Bucke of the age of 46 yeres, wydowe, souster and teatcheth children, and hath two children, the one of the age of 9 yeres and the other of 5 yeres that worke lace, and have dwelt here ever. . . .

Thomas Pele of the age of 50 yeres, a cobler in worke, and Margarit his wyfe of the same age that spinne white warpe, and have 3 children, the elldist of the age of 16 yeres that spinne, and the other of the age of 12 and of 6 yeres that go to scoole, and have dwelt here 9 yeres and came from Yorkeshere.

Source: R. H. Tawney and Eileen Power, eds. *Tudor Economic Documents.* Vol. 2. London, 1924, pp. 313–314. The census, which includes nineteen more entries, reveals the poverty of the working poor in the late sixteenth century despite the labor of most family members.

Enclosure.
A Consideration of the Cause in Question
before the Lords Touching Depopulation
5 July 1607
[Enclosures result in]
I.2. Increase of wealth and people, proved (i) *a contrario:* the nurseries of beggars are commons as appeareth by fens and forests, of wealth people the enclosed countries as Essex, Somerset, Devon, etc.; fuel, which they want in the champion, is supplied by enclosures. And labourers increased as are their employments by hedging and ditching; (ii) *a comparatis:* as Northamptonshire and Somerset, the one most champion, more ground, little waste, the other all enclosed but inferior in quantity and quality, yet by . . . choice of employment exceeding far.

Source: W. Cunningham, *The Growth of English Industry and Commerce in Modern Times.* Part 2. Cambridge, U.K., 1903, p. 898.
The speaker in this parliamentary debate sought to show the superiority of enclosed farms over open fields.

Defending the commons.
The Twelve Articles of the Upper Swabian Peasants
27 February–1 March 1525
Article Ten
Tenth, we are aggrieved that some have appropriated meadowland as well as fields which belong to the community (as above, Luke 6). We will take these properties into our hands again, unless they have in fact been legally bought. But if someone has bought them unfairly, the parties involved should reach a benevolent and brotherly agreement, according to the facts of the case.

Source: Michael G. Baylor, ed. and trans. *The Radical Reformation.* Cambridge, U.K., 1991, p. 237.
This complaint, from a widely circulated manifesto of the German Peasants' War, indicates the wide resentment caused by landlord and rich peasant appropriation of common lands.

peasant plots. By 1600 city people owned half of the best land around Pisa, Italy, and Castilian nobles held even more, some two-thirds when holdings of aristocratic-dominated ecclesiastical institutions are included. Some of the property on expanding estates had traditionally formed part of the lords' demesnes or was usurped from village communities. However, the greater part was bought from churches, in Catholic as well as Protestant lands, or, more often, from indebted peasants.

While artisans and peasants in general were losing control of productive property, a minority accumulated assets in ways similar to and often linked with those followed by merchant and landlord elites. Before the mid-sixteenth century a few Antwerp ribbon makers had shops with several dozen looms. In 1584 nine cartels, the biggest run by merchants and financiers, comprising just twenty-four master builders performed 80 percent of the work on Antwerp's massive citadel. An affluent top tenth at most likewise formed in the peasantry. In a village near Toledo in Castile, 9 percent of the residents held 54 percent of the peasant land in 1583. In a Norman community the upper 5 percent occupied a sixth of the arable peasant holdings in the early fifteenth century but three-fifths in the 1630s. Often starting with substantial amounts of inherited property, these yeomen (the English term is widely applied elsewhere) bought more land, usually from their poorer counterparts, to whom they also extended credit, or served as tenants on big consolidated farms that the landlords assembled across Europe. Such substantial commercial-minded farmers could count on significant landlord investment in tools, buildings, and drainage systems, and many earned additional income as lords' agents.

Although these elites separated from the mass of their fellows, a degree of mobility into and among them existed. Rich peasants and artisans joined the ranks of merchants and entrepreneurs, and these latter groups purchased land and titles. The entry of a new family was often sealed by marriage. Yet each elite also developed into a kind of caste, rooted in intermarriage that helped build up patrimonies preserved by impartible inheritance, practiced even in the face of local custom. Caste members enjoyed enhanced power in critical institutions that advanced their interests. Landowners and some merchants found places in rising princely governments, and merchants solidified control of many municipalities, usually at the expense of all but the wealthiest artisans. For their part, the top craftsmen dominated guilds, and yeomen dominated the village communities.

Consumption also helped these groups define and distinguish themselves. In the European countryside a massive rebuilding of lordly houses incorporated modern conveniences, from separate rooms to glass windows. Leading farmers, too, upgraded their dwellings and added capacious new barns. Probate inventories reveal that rural and urban elites accumulated silver, glassware, additional servants, and other markers of affluence and difference. Finally, elites developed a certain ethic. Cutting across creedal boundaries, their emphasis on hard work, orderliness, and propriety demarcated them from both lavish-spending grandees and what they saw as the shiftless, drunken, and rowdy poor.

The mass of the population faced worsening conditions that increasingly distanced them from both the elite and the better times of the fifteenth century. Despite possibilities of upward mobility for a few, the predominant movement was down. As rich craftsmen used their guild authority and wealth to reserve positions for their sons, the status of journeyman was converted from the penultimate rung on the ladder to coveted mastership to a synonym for permanent, albeit skilled, wage laborer. Once-autonomous small and middling artisans were hard-pressed by putting-out entrepreneurs with access to markets and the resources to weather hard times. Most domestic workers owned their tools, toiled in their homes or shops, and retained some ability to change employers or at times to produce and sell wares in the market on their own account. Nevertheless, they were well on the way to becoming proletarians who had only their labor to offer. Long a feature of certain centers, putting-out spread both geographically and among more industries in the sixteenth century, enabling a growing throng to earn little more than a bare subsistence, even when a whole family was employed. Already by the 1520s more than 85 percent of the population in a Suffolk, England, district noted for its high degree of rural industry was classed as poor. Deteriorating conditions were not restricted to domestic workers. Whereas mason's assistants in Lyon earned a living wage in all but three years between 1525 and 1549, between 1575 and 1599 their income fell short seventeen times.

Farm populations experienced similar polarization. Sometimes well-to-do farmers were pushed to the wall when landlords, eager to recoup their investments, raised rents excessively or when a meager harvest, accident, or ill health struck. But middling peasants were most affected. During the sixteenth century in Languedoc, the proportion of arable land located on farms of less than about 12 acres doubled, but that on holdings of 12 to 25 acres dropped by a third. Similar results were recorded across Europe. As the ranks of small peasants swelled, the ongoing subdivi-

Proletarianized Peasants. *The Peasants' Meal,* painting (1642) by Louis Le Nain
(1593–1648). MUSÉE DU LOUVRE, PARIS/ALINARI/ART RESOURCE, NY

sion of holdings, privatization of commons, and high rents due to skyrocketing demand for modest-sized farms impoverished and all too often dispossessed them.

Some downwardly mobile peasants recovered farms—but as sharecroppers. A larger group became cottagers, forced to eke out livings from gardens attached to their dwellings in tandem with agricultural and industrial work. Cottages with gardens multiplied from 11 percent of English holdings in about 1560 to 40 percent around 1620. Many other farmers lost any holdings and became full-fledged wage earners. In Spain, across Castile perhaps half the rural population owned no land in 1570; in Andalusia the proportion approached three-quarters. Many of the landless stayed in the countryside, grouped into large impoverished villages or squatting on wastelands, otherwise left to pigs for foraging, where they erected flimsy shacks. But farm labor scarcely provided a tolerable living. English data, which seem representative, indicate that agricultural workers' real wages were sliced in half between about 1500 and 1650. Many villagers headed for towns, where they swelled the ranks of the urban poor and beggars, or became the wandering vagrants who preoccupied authorities.

Like the elites, proletarianizing Europeans developed distinctive attributes. By the late sixteenth century, they had to devote 70 to 80 percent of their meager incomes to food in a normal year, half just to rye bread. (Wheat was considered more desirable but was usually too expensive.) No wonder that meat consumption in Sicily fell to less than half of earlier levels. What with rent, heat, and light, little money remained for consumer goods apart from cheap textiles and metalwares, and inventories indicate the sparseness of the material environment in which the majority lived.

Unlike elites, impoverished Europeans had few institutional means to promote their interests, although journeymen in a few towns formed collective associations. For the most part, however, corporations or municipalities, in whose decisions workers did not participate, dictated their wages, mobility, and labor conditions. Similarly, richer villagers manipulated communal assemblies to shift the tax burden onto the shoulders of their less affluent neighbors or to monopolize communal pastures for their own large herds. In fact, new institutions like centralized municipal welfare offices and workhouses were established to provide for but also to manage the poor.

CONCLUSION

Social divisions widened least in poorer agricultural regions that offered few opportunities to landlords and affluent peasants, in areas where resilient villages maintained communal resources, in districts where unspecialized agriculture rode out hard times, and in towns where corporate and municipal leaders defended traditional production. Great variety in exposure to commercialization, even in closely neighboring regions, continued through the eighteenth century. Holland and adjacent provinces evolved a unique, commercialized agrarian order that likewise minimized social differentiation. It was characterized by family farms, weak landlords and village communities, and employment of the landless in crafts and services oriented to the specialized holdings. But the dominant trend was toward polarization and proletarianization, whether on productive enclosed English farms or lagging Mediterranean latifundia and eastern European serf estates, and whether in urban crafts or in rural industrial districts. The late medieval economic crisis brought good times to the majority of Europeans. The concomitant of economic growth and commercialization during the long sixteenth century was material and social advancement for the few, impoverishment and wage laborer status for the many.

See also **The *Annales* Paradigm; The World Economy and Colonial Expansion (volume 1); The Population of Europe: Early Modern Demographic Patterns; The City: The Early Modern Period** *(in this volume).*

BIBLIOGRAPHY

Surveys

Abel, Wilhelm. *Agricultural Fluctuations in Europe: From the Thirteenth to the Twentieth Centuries.* 3d ed. Translated by Olive Ordish. London, 1986. Parts 1 and 2 are particularly germane to this article.

Aston, T. H., and C. H. E. Philpin, eds. *The Brenner Debate: Agrarian Class Structure and Economic Development in Pre-Industrial Europe.* Cambridge, U.K., 1985.

Dewald, Jonathan. *Pont-St-Pierre, 1398–1789: Lordship, Community, and Capitalism in Early Modern France.* Berkeley, 1987.

DuPlessis, Robert S. *Transitions to Capitalism in Early Modern Europe.* Cambridge, U.K., 1997. See especially parts 1 and 2 and chapter 7.

Goldthwaite, Richard A. *Wealth and the Demand for Art in Italy, 1300–1600.* Baltimore, 1993.

Lis, Catharina, and Hugo Soly. *Poverty and Capitalism in Pre-Industrial Europe.* Atlantic Highlands, N.J., 1979. Chapters 2 and 3 are thought provoking.

Marx, Karl. *Capital.* Vol. 1. New York, 1977. Part 8 concerns primary accumulation.

Scott, Tom, ed. *The Peasantries of Europe: From the Fourteenth to the Eighteenth Centuries.* London and New York, 1998.

Smith, Adam. *An Inquiry into the Nature and Causes of the Wealth of Nations.* Chicago, 1976.

Weber, Max. *The Protestant Ethic and the Spirit of Capitalism.* Translated by Talcott Parsons. London, 1930.

The Late Medieval Crisis

Bois, Guy. *The Crisis of Feudalism: Economy and Society in Eastern Normandy c. 1300–1550.* Cambridge, U.K., 1984. A rare examination of both economy and society.

Britnell, R. H. *The Commercialisation of English Society, 1000–1500.* Cambridge, U.K., 1993. The insights of this fine study can be applied across Europe.

Dyer, Christopher. *Standards of Living in the Later Middle Ages: Social Change in England, c. 1200–1500.* Cambridge, U.K., 1989.

Epstein, Stephan R. "Cities, Regions, and the Late Medieval Crisis." *Past and Present* 130 (1991): 3–50.

Epstein, Stephan. *An Island for Itself: Economic Development and Social Change in Late Medieval Sicily.* Cambridge, U.K., 1991.

Finberg, H. P. R., ed. *The Agrarian History of England and Wales.* Vol. 3: *1348–1500.* Edited by Edward Miller. London, 1967–1991.

Genicot, Léopold. "Crisis: From the Middle Ages to Modern Times." In *The Cambridge Economic History of Europe.* Vol. 1: *The Agrarian Life of the Middle Ages.* Edited by M. M. Postan. 2d ed. Cambridge, U.K., 1966. Pages 660–741.

Goldberg, P. J. P. *Women, Work, and Life Cycle in a Medieval Economy: Women in York and Yorkshire c. 1300–1520.* Oxford, 1992.

Herlihy, David. *The Black Death and the Transformation of the West.* Cambridge, Mass., 1997.

Hoffmann, Richard C. *Land, Liberties, and Lordship in a Late Medieval Countryside: Agrarian Structures and Change in the Duchy of Wroclaw.* Philadelphia, 1989. An exhaustive study of an underexplored area.

Munro, John H. *Textiles, Towns, and Trade: Essays in the Economic History of Late-Medieval England and the Low Countries.* Aldershot, U.K., 1994.

Poos, L. R. *A Rural Society after the Black Death: Essex, 1350–1525.* Cambridge, U.K., 1991.

Ruiz, Teofilo F. *Crisis and Continuity: Land and Town in Late Medieval Castile.* Philadelphia, 1994.

The Long Sixteenth Century

Clark, Peter, ed. *The European Crisis of the 1590s.* London, 1985.

Davis, Natalie Zemon. "A Trade Union in Sixteenth-Century France." *Economic History Review,* 2d series, 19 (1966):48–69.

Davis, Natalie Zemon. "Women in the Crafts in Sixteenth-Century Lyon." *Feminist Studies* 8 (1982): 47–80.

Davis, Robert C. *Shipbuilders of the Venetian Arsenal: Workers and Workplace in the Preindustrial City.* Baltimore, 1991.

De Vries, Jan. *The Dutch Rural Economy in the Golden Age, 1500–1700.* New Haven, Conn., 1974.

Finberg, H. P. R., ed. *The Agrarian History of England and Wales.* Vol. 4: *1500–1640.* Edited by Joan Thirsk. Cambridge, U.K., 1967–1991. The most complete overview for any country.

Hagen, William. "How Mighty the Junkers? Peasant Rents and Seigneurial Profits in Sixteenth-Century Brandenburg." *Past and Present* 108 (1985): 80–116. An important revision of East Elbian agriculture in the era of second serfdom.

Le Roy Ladurie, Emmanuel. *The French Peasantry, 1450–1660.* Translated by Alan Sheridan. Berkeley, Calif., 1987.

Sacks, David Harris. *The Widening Gate: Bristol and the Atlantic Economy, 1450–1700.* Berkeley, Calif., 1991.

Scott, Tom. *Regional Identity and Economic Change: The Upper Rhine, 1450–1600.* Oxford, 1997.

Scribner, Bob, ed. *Germany: A New Social and Economic History.* Vol. 1: *1450–1630.* London and New York, 1996–.

Vassberg, David E. *The Village and the Outside World in Golden Age Castile: Mobility and Migration in Everyday Rural Life.* Cambridge, U.K., 1996.

Wallerstein, Immanuel. *The Modern World-System.* Vol. 1: *Capitalist Agriculture and the Origins of the European World-Economy in the Sixteenth Century.* New York, 1974.

Wiesner, Merry E. *Working Women in Renaissance Germany.* New Brunswick, N.J., 1986.

Zell, Michael. *Industry in the Countryside: Wealden Society in the Sixteenth Century.* Cambridge, U.K., 1994.

PROTOINDUSTRIALIZATION

Gay L. Gullickson

In 1971 the historians Charles Tilly and Richard Tilly questioned the prevailing portrait of the industrial revolution. They did not doubt that the changes associated with industrialization had been important and dramatic: work had moved out of the home; peasants had moved off the land and into the cities; families had ceased to be production units; daily life and work had been altered by technological developments; and new classes had come into existence. What they doubted was that these changes had happened abruptly and swiftly. They were led to these doubts by the research of historians on early modern rural Britain and Europe. Most important of all for the Tillys was the work of a young historian named Franklin Mendels. Based largely on his findings of economic and demographic change in Flanders, they called for historians to study "protoindustrialization, demographic change, and industrialization as life experience" (Tilly and Tilly, 1971, p. 186). They defined protoindustrialization as "industrialization before the factory system" (p. 186), and they freely acknowledged having "lifted" the term from Mendels (p. 187).

Mendels immediately found himself in an unusual position for a young historian. In 1969 he had used the term "proto-industrialization" in his doctoral dissertation; in 1970 he had delivered a paper based on his dissertation; and now, one year later, the Tillys were calling for historians to devote themselves to the study of protoindustrialization. Worried that the term needed precise definition, Mendels hurriedly wrote and published a summary of his dissertation research. In this 1972 article he defined protoindustrialization as "the rapid growth of traditionally organized but market-oriented, principally rural industry" (p. 241). The process, he said, was "accompanied by changes in the spatial organization of the rural economy" (p. 241), and it "facilitated" industrialization proper by creating a class with entrepreneurial experience, market connections, and investment capital (p. 245). Most controversially, he suggested that protoindustrialization and industrialization were two phases of the same process.

Historians connected to the Cambridge Group for the History of Population and Social Structure in England and to the Max-Planck-Institut für Geschichte in Germany and individual American, English, French, Dutch, Swiss, Irish, and other social historians began to consider the questions posed by Mendels and the Tillys. As historians worked, they found they could agree on several things but not everything. The definition of a region remained fuzzy, but they agreed that protoindustrialization was a regional rather than a national phenomenon and needed to be studied region by region. They agreed that cottage manufacturing expanded in the eighteenth century and employed a majority of the population in various areas. They agreed that it was important to understand why and how this expansion occurred and how it affected rural behavior and values. And they generally agreed on the distinguishing characteristics of protoindustrialization. What they ultimately could not agree on was a simple characterization of regions that protoindustrialized; the effects of protoindustrial employment on demographic behavior; the social and economic impact of protoindustrialization on families and, in particular, on women; and the relationship between protoindustrialization and industrialization. What became most controversial was the causal relationship implied in Mendels's identification of protoindustrialization as "the first phase of the industrialization process" (1972).

DEFINING PROTOINDUSTRIALIZATION

Mendels's first concern was to distinguish protoindustrialization from traditional cottage manufacturing. If this could not be done, the concept would be redundant and unnecessary. The difficulty of transporting manufactured goods and agricultural produce made cottage manufacturing a common feature of rural life. Fabric, household goods, and farm and building implements were produced everywhere, as was a panoply of crops. Regardless of terrain and climate, families raised everything from grain, to vines and

Rural Industry. Making wooden shoes. Engraving from the *Encyclopédie*, 1762.
©COLLECTION VIOLLET

fruit trees, to cows and other livestock. During planting and harvesting men, and to a lesser extent women, worked in the fields. (More generally, women cared for animals and men for the fields, except during the harvest, when everyone helped bring in the grain crops.) During the winter or dead season in agriculture, the same men and women produced fabric, clothing, baskets, stockings, ribbons, and other small items for themselves and for sale. Local artisans, who helped with the harvest but otherwise did not engage in farming, produced shoes, ropes, barrels, plows, bricks, and furniture for local use. If the raw materials were available, they also produced nails, tanned leather, and glass.

Sometimes entire families participated in the production of a single product. In the textile industries, for instance, women and children often cleaned, combed, and spun fibers for men to weave. In other cases women and men worked at unrelated tasks. Given the sexual divisions of labor throughout western Europe and Britain, women often spun thread, wove ribbons, made hats, or knit stockings for sale, while their husbands worked in the fields, forged iron, milled flour, and cut wood.

In the simplest form of these cottage industries, farm families produced the raw materials from which they made goods to sell in local markets. Linen weavers and cord or rope makers wove flax or braided hemp from their own plants. Wool spinners and weavers washed, carded, spun, and wove wool from their own sheep. In some places merchants distributed raw materials to farmers and artisans who turned them into finished products. Sometimes raw materials came from nearby villages or farms, other times they came from greater distances. All over Europe weavers who produced high-quality woolens worked with wool from Spain's merino sheep. Silk weavers throughout France worked with silk produced in the Rhône Valley, where mulberry trees and hence silkworms could be raised. Cotton spinners and weavers worked with cotton from Asia and North America.

Protoindustries resembled cottage industries in many ways. Rural families alternated work in cottage manufacturing with work in the fields. They worked in their own homes, using traditional technology (like spinning wheels and hand looms) or newer but still small machines (like knitting frames) to produce goods for putting-out merchants, who provided them with raw materials and paid them for completed goods. Thus they no longer worked with raw materials that they produced themselves. And the items they produced were no longer destined for local markets. Instead, they were sold in regional, national, and international markets. Perhaps most distinctively, protoindustries dominated local labor markets, employing a large number of rural residents (or, given the sexual division of labor, a large number of either the men or the women) in a region. For a region to qualify as protoindustrial, a majority of its population needed to be employed in cottage manufacturing.

The system was controlled by urban merchants whose desire to increase production (and profits) had led them to employ rural workers. (Before the technological innovations associated with the industrial

40

revolution, production could only be expanded by increasing the labor force.) To a certain extent, the decision to turn to rural workers was inevitable. Urban populations were relatively small, and new workers were hard to find; wages were higher than those of rural workers; and guilds continued to control the production and sale of manufactured goods. Potential rural workers existed in large numbers, produced much of their own food and therefore could work for low wages, and were often desperate for income; in addition, no one controlled the quality of the goods they produced. Such advantages outweighed the transportation and time costs involved in sending raw materials and finished products from town to country and back again.

The intensification of rural manufacturing did not occur in isolation from other economic changes. Sometimes dispersed cottage work was directly related to centralized workshops or protofactories. Even in the era of cottage industry fabric was always dyed and printed by urban craftsmen. The same was true of the fulling of wool fabric (Pollard, 1981, pp. 78–79). In the late eighteenth century, when spinning was mechanized and moved out of homes and into mills, textile merchants supplied rural weavers with mill-spun yarn (Gullickson, 1986; Levine, 1977). In the nineteenth century, when clothing and household linens began to be mass-produced, precut pieces were still sewn together by rural workers, who vastly outnumbered the factory labor force (Collins, 1991). In metal regions centralized operations produced copper and brass that were then put out into the countryside for the production of small items (Berg, 1994, p. 71).

In the short run the wages paid by the putting-out merchants improved life in rural villages, and other social changes resulted. Cafés and taverns began to appear in villages that had never seen such things before, a sign that those who combined farming and manufacturing now had some disposable income. Population grew, and more and more families became partially dependent on the merchants, even as it became increasingly unlikely that cottage workers would know the individual merchants for whom they worked. Their contact was with the porter who brought them materials to work and paid them for their labor. This development may have meant little to the peasants who worked for the merchants, as long as they were regularly paid, but anonymity was a step toward the impersonalization of work and the proletarianization of labor that is identified with industrialization.

As the invention of machines moved work into factories, peasant-workers' incomes declined precipitously. In some areas former cottage workers commuted on a daily or weekly basis to nearby mills. This strategy worked best when the mills employed women, who could walk to and from the mills, while their husbands and brothers continued to work in the fields. In the best-case scenario women might also bring home "out work" for other members of the family to do. In other places workers tried to hang on even in the face of mechanization, but the machines were hard to compete with, and even when workers like hand-loom weavers produced fine fabric, they still had to confront declining demand. In still other places entire families migrated permanently to cities, where men, women, and children sought work in a variety of occupations. Eventually, many protoindustrial regions became more purely agricultural than they had ever been.

LOCATING PROTOINDUSTRIES

While traditional cottage industries were ubiquitous, protoindustries were not. Initially, Mendels suggested that protoindustrialization occurred in areas of subsistence and pastoral farming, where bad soil made peasants very poor and in need of additional sources of income. Flanders was a classic case. In the interior regions, where peasants eked out a living on small plots of land, the linen industry became a major source of winter employment and income. In the maritime regions, where large commercial farms produced wheat, butter, and cheese for foreign and domestic markets, traditional cottage industries died out and were not replaced (Mendels, 1972).

In his 1960 study of eighteenth-century Switzerland (part of which appeared in English in 1966), Rudolf Braun had found a similar situation. The area of flat, fertile land that lay between Zurich and the Highlands had no cottage industry, while the steep and sparsely settled "back country" with "wood glens 'of forbidding aspect,' inconceivably bad communications, and a rude climate" produced large quantities of cotton thread or yarn for the Zurich merchants (p. 55). (Unlike in other textile regions, weaving was not done in the Zurich highlands because the transportation of warps and cloth up and down the mountains was far too difficult.)

Other studies bore out Mendels's predictions about the location of protoindustries. David Levine discovered that Shepshed, in Leicestershire, England, where the land was "rocky and stony," had a large framework knitting industry while neighboring villages with better land did not (1977, p. 19). James Lehning found that peasants living in the Stephanois mountains combined subsistence farming, sheepherding, and dairying with ribbon weaving for Saint-Étienne putting-out merchants who sold the ribbons

Linen Manufacture. Preparing flax for spinning into linen, County Down, Ireland, 1791. MARY EVANS PICTURE LIBRARY

in national and international markets (1980). Pat Hudson revealed that the Halifax area in the West Riding of Yorkshire, where the land was suited only to "livestock grazing and the cultivation of a few oats," became protoindustrialized, while the valleys and hills, where the soil was better and farms produced a variety of crops, did not (1981, p. 42–43).

What made the work offered by the putting-out merchants so desirable in these regions was the sheer poverty of the peasants, poverty made worse in some cases by the beginnings of a geographic sorting out of agriculture. Poor-soil regions found themselves unable to compete in the grain markets with richer-soil areas that were enclosing fields and intensifying production. As a result peasants in the poor-soil areas became even poorer than they had been and turned to cottage industry to prop up sagging income (see Jones, 1968).

Most historians were content with the notion that subsistence- and pastoral-farming areas were prime territory for the putting-out merchants. Mendels himself went further, moving toward a more determinist model than he had first proposed. By 1980 he was arguing that large-scale cottage industries were most likely to occur where commercial and subsistence agricultural zones abutted each other and lay near a city. He envisioned a three-way symbiotic relationship. Merchants could easily put work out into the countryside and increase production. Peasants in the subsistence area eagerly accepted their offers of work and wages. With their earnings they purchased food from the commercial zone. The farmers in the commercial agricultural zone acquired a market for some of their produce and did not have to search far for harvest labor.

While Mendels was developing this model, Peter Kriedte, working in conjunction with Hans Medick and Jürgen Schlumbohm, was suggesting that protoindustrialization was "relegated" to "harsh mountainous areas," although his subsequent discussion indicated that he did not mean this statement to be quite so categorical (pp. 14, 24, 26–27). Both of these predictive models had flaws, as historians quickly pointed out. Only Flanders seemed to fit Mendels's model. The Zurich Highlands certainly did not, nor did Shepshed, the Stephanois mountains, or the West Riding. And only the Zurich Highlands and the Stephanois mountains fit Kriedte's model. Worse yet, Gay Gullickson's work on the Caux in Upper Normandy revealed that the intensification of cottage industry was not confined to areas of poor soil. The Caux was a fertile area with large grain farms *and* a large cotton industry, a situation that most historians had thought would not occur. The same was true in Scotland, as Ian Whyte subsequently demonstrated. Rural textile production was concentrated not in the Highlands but in the Lowlands, where cereal crops were produced on large farms.

If protoindustries appeared in some but not all subsistence regions *and* if they appeared, at least occasionally, in zones of commercial farming, then subsistence and pastoral farming could not be the sole explanation for their presence. No one doubted that areas of poor soil and steep terrain were in desperate need of the work the putting-out merchants offered, but what determined the location of protoindustries was not just poverty. Other factors were decisive. Proximity to a merchant city advantaged some areas over others. A large landless or poor population made some regions more attractive than others. Weak communal or manorial controls made it possible for people to accept work from merchants and, as population grew, to clear land and build houses. Regions that were tightly controlled by lords or communal agreements could exclude merchants, restrict building, and force excess population to migrate. Partible inheritance customs that fragmented landholdings and impoverished regions could make industry attractive. Impartible inheritance that concentrated land in a few hands and created a poor landless population could do the same, as could enclosure. Any one of these phenomena could make cottage manufacturing an attractive proposition to peasants and merchants.

PROTOINDUSTRIALIZATION AND DEMOGRAPHIC BEHAVIOR

One of the first questions that interested historians about protoindustrialization was its relationship to population growth. The picture that emerged early on was that the income from cottage manufacturing led to considerable and often dramatic breaks in the "traditional" marriage and childbearing patterns of rural families. The traditional pattern was revealed by the work of historians like Micheline Baulant, John Hajnal, Olwen Hufton, and Peter Laslett. In the seventeenth and early eighteenth centuries the population of Britain and western Europe was fairly constant. This homeostatic demographic system resulted from high marriage ages for men and women and a relatively high percentage of both sexes who never married. These high marriage ages and celibacy rates were the results of economic constraints, cultural practices, and inheritance systems. The common pattern was for a man and woman to set up housekeeping in their own dwelling as soon as they married. To do so, they needed a place to live, some household goods, and a source of income. It took time to achieve these things. A woman had to work and save for years to acquire the requisite dowry of a mattress, pillows, sheets (one or two sets), eating and cooking utensils, and a storage chest. A man usually had to wait to inherit farmland or an artisan business. He also needed a place for the new family to live and rudimentary furniture. Not all sons inherited land or an occupation, and not all daughters were able to acquire a dowry. As a result the average marriage age for women was between twenty-four and twenty-six; for men it was between twenty-six and twenty-eight; and on average, 10 percent of adults never married. Even in the wealthy elite, as Laslett memorably pointed out, boys did not marry at age fifteen or sixteen or girls at twelve or thirteen as Shakespeare's Romeo and Juliet did.

Childbearing began quickly after marriage, but women bore only four to six children, and most people did not live long enough to know their grandchildren. Life in these small families was hard, and everyone worked—men, women, and children. If a husband or wife died young, the remaining spouse needed to remarry as quickly as possible to survive economically.

The employment and income provided by protoindustrialization, many have argued, made it possible for cottage workers to marry at younger ages and with greater frequency than their peasant counterparts. A woman no longer had to acquire a dowry and a man no longer had to inherit a small piece of land or occupation before they could take their wedding vows. When protoindustries provided employment for children as well as for adults, some historians have argued, cottage workers had an incentive to bear more children. Whether this was the case or not, the overwhelming majority of children born in the mid–eighteenth century were born to married women, and a decrease in women's marriage age or an increase in the number of women marrying would inevitably increase the number of children in these communities that did not practice contraception.

In many areas population growth entered an upward spiral. In Flanders, years in which the income provided by the merchants was high in comparison with the price of grain were followed by years in which the number of couples marrying increased. Perhaps most important for population growth, the reverse was not true. Bad economic years did not result in fewer marriages. Developments in Shepshed were even more dramatic. During the eighteenth century, when the vast majority of villagers knit stockings for London merchants, the average age at first marriage for both men and women fell by over five years. As a result population rose rapidly. In the Zurich Highlands marriages were more numerous and earlier than in purely agricultural regions. Contemporaries called these "beggar marriages" because the bride and groom had not acquired the dowry, economic skills, and property commonly regarded as prerequisites for marriage.

Other studies found less dramatic changes. Myron Gutmann and René Leboutte (1984) found that female marriage ages remained high and stable in three protoindustrial Belgian villages. Lehning discovered that protoindustrialization did not inevitably lead to lower marriage ages and higher marriage frequency in the Stephanois region of France (1983). Gullickson found that the number of women not marrying in the village of Auffay was very low when spinning occupied the majority of women and high in the subsequent era when spinning moved into factories and it became more difficult for women to find employment. Women's marriage ages, on the other hand, remained stable and high, dropping only from just above twenty-six to 25.3, while men's marriage ages fell from almost twenty-nine to just below 27.5. (1986, pp. 133–144). Many regions without protoindustries were also experiencing a decrease in women's marriage ages and population growth in this period (Houston and Snell, p. 482). Clearly, employment in rural industry was not the only factor affecting marriage behavior, but it certainly was a factor in many places.

WOMEN AND PROTOINDUSTRIALIZATION

Early in the discussion of protoindustrialization Hans Medick argued that the intensification of cottage manufacturing produced more egalitarian male-female relationships than had been the case before. The key developments, in his view, were the increasing importance of women's earnings and the return of men's work to the house. As a result, he argued, the sexual division of labor was eased, both in paid work and in the household. Women and men worked alongside each other, and men took over previously female housekeeping tasks. Being able to choose among the entire group of people who worked for the merchants increased the range of marriage partners. Moreover, Medick argued, working together within the confined space of the peasant house led to greater eroticism. As evidence he cited the lowering of marriage ages, middle-class observations about the "shameless freedom" of young men and women, and men's and women's joint participation in the consumption of alcohol and tobacco at home and in the taverns and cafés that followed in the wake of the putting-out merchants (1976, pp. 310—314). Medick might have added, but did not, that protoindustrialization also made it unnecessary for men to migrate during the winter months to find work (Collins, 1982, p. 140; Braun, 1966, p. 64).

Medick's statements addressed a question that women's historians had been asking for a long time: have economic changes improved or impaired women's lives and raised or lowered their status or power in the family, the workplace, and the community? Medick's answer was clearly that protoindustrialization improved women's lives and raised their status, but it is not an answer that further research has sustained, even though virtually all protoindustries provided jobs for women.

Women were employed in whatever manufacturing work was available in rural areas, although a sexual division of tasks was maintained in most, if not all, places. Women worked in large numbers across the English metal trades. They participated in the manufacture of buttons, toys, farm implements, cutlery, swords, and guns. In and around Birmingham they polished, japanned, lacquered, pierced, cut, and decorated metal. In the West Midlands they worked with hammers and anvils and pounded hot metal into nails (Berg, 1987, p. 85–). The industry in which they were most likely to be employed, however, was textiles in their many varieties. Textiles is the protoindustry about which we know the most and in which the importance of women's work is most clearly documented.

In the eighteenth century women spun and performed other preparatory tasks for men who wove. This division of labor produced more jobs for women than for men. The Flemish linen industry employed four female spinners and one and a half workers in ancillary tasks (performed by women and children of both sexes) for every male weaver (Mendels, 1981, p. 200). In peasant families of northwestern and western Ireland women spun and men wove flax for the merchants. The imbalance in labor demand for these tasks was so great that groups of single women moved around the countryside, working for one weaving family after another in return for room and board and a small amount of money. In those cases where the family grew its own flax, women were responsible for harvesting the plants, which further increased their workload. Children worked with their parents and often took responsibility for winding yarn onto shuttles for the weavers (Collins, 1982, pp. 130–134). In the Shepshed hosiery industry women spun yarn and men knit stockings. Boys and girls learned to perform ancillary tasks as young as age ten. There are no precise figures for the numbers of men and women who performed these tasks, but there is no reason to believe that the spinning-knitting labor ratio was lower than the spinning-weaving labor ratio, and it seems safe to assume that more women than men were working for the putting-out merchants (Levine, 1977, pp. 28–32). In the twenty-one villages in the canton of Auffay in Upper Normandy, 75 percent of adult women spun yarn for the cotton merchants. In contrast, only 15.6 percent of the men were employed in weaving (Gullickson, 1991, pp. 209–210).

The one place where a sexual division of labor was apparently not maintained in textiles was in the Zurich Highlands, although even here more women than men may have worked for the merchants. In the Highlands young men as well as young women spun yarn for the cotton merchants. (Both sexes also appear to have engaged in weaving, but their fabric was apparently sold only in local markets, which, by definition, means it was not a protoindustrial occupation.) Braun provides no count of the number of men and women who worked for the merchants, but because of the division of labor in agriculture, it is possible that women still were more likely than men to work for the merchants. This assumption fits with Braun's observation that in poor, but nevertheless landowning, families, daughters were more desirable than sons because they could produce more income (1966, p. 62).

When spinning was mechanized and moved into mills in the late eighteenth and early nineteenth centuries, much of the work that women had done for the merchants disappeared. The economic impact of the loss of these jobs was devastating in areas like northern Ireland and the Zurich Highlands, where they were not replaced by an increased demand for weavers. As one Swiss pastor observed in the eigh-

Linen Bleaching. Linen bleaching near Haarlem, the Netherlands. Drawing (1659–1665) by Gerbrand van den Eeckhout. Rijksmuseum, Amsterdam

teenth century, "These people came with cotton and must die with it." If they did not literally die, they confronted two basic choices—celibacy or migration (Braun, 1966, pp. 61, 64). In other areas like the Caux, north-central Ireland, Shepshed, and the Stephanois mountains, increased yarn production encouraged putting-out merchants to seek additional weavers and knitters, and women were able to move into occupations from which they had previously been excluded.

In Shepshed women continued to do ancillary tasks like winding and seaming, but they also became knitters. In the mid-nineteenth century 56 percent of the wives under age thirty-five were seamers or knitters (Levine, 1977, pp. 28–29). In many of the villages of the Caux the entry of women into weaving was far more dramatic. In the village of Auffay three times as many women as men were employed in weaving. In neighboring villages the ratios were as high as 8 to 1 (Gullickson, 1991, pp. 217–218). Farther south in the Stephanois mountains almost 88 percent of the ribbon weavers were women (Lehning, 1980, pp. 28–30, 40).

With the exception of north-central Ireland and perhaps the Zurich Highlands, the employment of women in protoindustries appears to have had little, if any, effect on their status within the family. In the eighteenth century the sexual division of labor made it easy to pay women less than men. In the nineteenth, when women entered weaving, the opportunity for

equal pay for equal work came into existence in at least some places. In north-central Ireland the availability of mill-spun yarn made it possible for almost everyone—girls, boys, the aged, and the infirm—to weave the coarse fabric desired by the merchants and to earn as much as adult men (Collins, 1982, p. 140). But in the Caux merchants hired women and men to weave different fabrics. Women were assigned to calico production, for which the demand was growing, and men to heavier fabrics, for which demand was not growing. The decision provided more employment for women, but it also made it possible for merchants to continue to pay women less than men. Despite the importance of women's earnings, there is little basis on which to argue that this work improved women's status within their families or communities. Sexual divisions of labor were maintained more often than not, and employing women to do "men's work" did not necessarily entail equal pay.

There also is no evidence, other than that of the contemporary observers cited by Braun and Medick, that men took over women's domestic tasks so women could work for merchants. The same is true for Medick's statements about the impact of protoindustrialization on the affective and erotic aspects of male-female relationships. The contemporary criticisms of the peasant-workers' behavior that led to Braun's and Medick's conclusions that protoindustrialization broke not only the homeostatic demographic system but also the constraints society had imposed on erotic behavior may reflect a change that actually occurred in many areas. But the observations may not apply broadly or, worse yet for historians, may be off the mark. What church and government officials represented as seductive and lewd behavior may have been common among peasant women and men regardless of whether they worked in cottage manufacturing, or it may have been rare. Unfortunately, there is no good way to find out what the emotional and affective lives of peasants and peasant-workers were like. The evidence, however, does not substantiate the argument that women's earnings led to dramatic behavioral changes or to greater gender equality.

PROTOINDUSTRIALIZATION AND INDUSTRIALIZATION

Protoindustrialization ended with the invention of machinery that was too large, too expensive, or too in need of a nonhuman source of power to be placed in people's homes. This development began, in essence, with the invention of spinning machines in Britain in the late eighteenth century and continued for at least a hundred years. Different tasks were mechanized at different times, and even when one task moved into a factory, associated tasks often continued to be put out into rural areas. But ultimately, anything resembling the massive putting-out industry known as protoindustrialization, where men, women, and children alternated agricultural and manufacturing work, came to an end.

In 1972 Mendels argued that protoindustrialization facilitated industrialization by creating a class with entrepreneurial experience, market contacts, and investment capital. These entrepreneurial merchants, he believed, became the builders of factories and the founders of industrialization proper. In some cases what Mendels and others (most notably, Kriedte, Medick, and Schlumbohm) expected did happen. The capital for building and equipping factories was often provided by the putting-out merchants, especially in textiles. They built textile mills and continued to compete for national and international markets and customers. The Rouen merchants who organized the rural cotton industry in the Caux are a case in point (Gullickson, 1981), as are the Manchester merchants who put work out into Lancashire (Walton, 1989).

But in many cases the urban merchants who had organized protoindustrial production did not succeed in transforming their putting-out businesses into modern industries. Instead, protoindustrialization was followed by deindustrialization. The mechanization of linen and cotton spinning destroyed both cottage weaving and cottage spinning in northwestern coun-

ties of Ireland (Collins, 1982, pp. 138–139). In the seventeenth and eighteenth centuries rural workers in the Weald of Kent, Surrey, and Sussex Counties in England produced large quantities of glass, iron, textiles, and timber products for markets in London and abroad. By the third decade of the nineteenth century all but the timber industry had died (Short, 1989). The same deindustrialization process occurred in early-nineteenth-century Silesia, which had been the scene of a thriving linen industry for two centuries (Kisch, in Kriedte, Medick, and Schlumbohm, pp. 541–564).

The deindustrialization of the towns and regions associated with protoindustrialization had many causes. In some cases, as Leslie A. Clarkson has pointed out, merchant capitalists invested their money not in the mechanization of their own trade but in other trades, some of them mechanized, some of them not. In East Anglia and western England merchants invested in farming, brewing, innkeeping, and retail trading, not textiles (p. 32). In other places a shortage of fuel, absence of raw materials, competition from other regions, and failure to keep up with intermediate developments prevented a transition to factory manufacturing. All of these factors spelled doom for manufacturing in the Weald (Short, 1989). In Silesia the Napoleonic wars disrupted markets, and local landlords refused to invest in the linen industry when mechanization called for it. In other places changes in fashion spelled doom to textile and lace industries (Coleman, 1983, p. 37).

CONCLUSION

Historical research has not upheld all aspects of Mendels's original notion of the role protoindustrialization played in the growth of the European and British population and economy, and debate about the concept continues. But the studies devoted to this topic have replaced the dichotomous pairings of rural and urban, traditional and modern, stagnant and dynamic that dominated historians' accounts of early modern Europe with a more varied and complex view. Industrialization seems a less abrupt development than it did before, as the Tillys predicted it would. We no longer see peasants as invariably devoted exclusively to farming, or manufacturing as an entirely urban activity. The urban and rural worlds no longer appear isolated from each other, and lines of influence no longer appear to have run in one direction only; developments in either place affected the other. Protoindustrialization may not have determined exactly where industrialization would occur, but it constituted a major transition in rural life and rural-urban relationships in the final decades of the old economic, social, and demographic regimes. It enabled regions to support a far larger rural population than agriculture alone could have done, cities to grow gradually rather than rapidly, and merchants to increase production for a long time without technological change. It made it possible for many rural men to cease short-term migrations in search of work, for women to make even larger contributions to the family's well-being than their work on farms and in small cottage industries had, and for many merchants to acquire the expertise and capital that would serve them well when it came time to build factories and increase production once again.

See also **The Population of Europe: Early Modern Demographic Patterns** *(in this volume);* **Artisans** *(volume 3);* **Gender and Work; Preindustrial Manufacturing** *(volume 4); and other articles in this section.*

BIBLIOGRAPHY

Agriculture, Cottage Industry, and Population

Braun, Rudolf. "The Impact of Cottage Industry on an Agricultural Population." In *The Rise of Capitalism.* Edited by David S. Landes. New York, 1966. Examines cottage industry in the Zurich Highlands. Forerunner of protoindustrial studies.

Hajnal, John. "European Marriage Patterns in Perspective." In *Population in History.* Edited by David Victor Glass and David Edward Charles Eversley. London, 1965. Identifies a unique western European marriage pattern.

Hufton, Olwen. "Women and the Family Economy in Eighteenth-Century France." *French Historical Studies* 9, no. 1 (1975): 1–22.

Jones, Eric. "The Agricultural Origins of Industry." *Past and Present,* no. 40 (1968): 58–71.

Laslett, Peter. *The World We Have Lost.* 1965. 2d ed., London, 1971. Uses demographic data to construct the early modern family, village, and society in England.

Tilly, Charles, and Richard Tilly. "Agenda for European Economic History in the 1970s." *Journal of Economic History* 31, no. 1 (1971): 184–198.

Protoindustrialization

Berg, Maxine. *The Age of Manufactures, 1700–1820: Industry, Innovation, and Work in Britain.* 2d ed. London, 1994. See pages 66–74 for overview.

Clarkson, Leslie A. *Proto-industrialization: The First Phase of Industrialization?* London, 1985. Important critical analysis.

Coleman, D. C. "Proto-industrialization: A Concept Too Many?" *Economic History Review,* 2d ser., 36 (August 1983): 435–448. Skeptical critique, especially of the marxist version of protoindustrial theory.

Collins, Brenda. "The Organization of Sewing Out Work in Late Nineteenth-Century Ulster." In *Markets and Manufacture in Early Industrial Europe.* Edited by Maxine Berg. London, 1991.

Collins, Brenda. "Proto-industrialization and Pre-famine Emigration." *Social History* 7, no. 2 (1982): 127–146.

Gullickson, Gay L. *Spinners and Weavers of Auffay: Rural Industry and the Sexual Division of Labor in a French Village, 1750–1850.* New York, 1986. Analyzes women's roles. Challenges connection between subsistence farming and protoindustrialization.

Gutmann, Myron P., and René Leboutte. "Rethinking Protoindustrialization and the Family." *Journal of Interdisciplinary History* 14 (winter 1984): 587–607.

Houston, Rab, and K. D. M. Snell. "Proto-industrialization? Cottage Industry, Social Change, and Industrial Revolution." *Historical Journal* 27 (June 1984): 473–492. Skeptical of explanatory power of protoindustrial theory.

Hudson, Pat. "Proto-industrialisation: The Case of the West Riding Wool Textile Industry." *History Workshop Journal* 12 (1981): 34–61.

Kriedte, Peter, Hans Medick, and Jürgen Schlumbohm. *Industrialization before Industrialization.* Translated by Beate Schempp. Cambridge, U.K., 1981. Marxist version of the theory. Includes articles by Franklin Mendels and Herbert Kisch.

Lehning, James. "Nuptiality and Rural Industry: Families and Labor in the French Countryside." *Journal of Family History* 8 (winter 1983): 333–345.

Lehning, James. *The Peasants of Marlhes: Economic Development and Family Organization in Nineteenth-Century France.* Chapel Hill, N.C., 1980.

Levine, David. "The Demographic Implications of Rural Industrialization: A Family Reconstitution Study of Shepshed, Leicestershire, 1600–1851." *Social History,* no. 2 (1976): 177–196. Reprinted in *Essays in Social History.* Vol. 2. Edited by Pat Thane and Anthony Sutcliffe. Oxford, 1986.

Levine, David. *Family Formation in an Age of Nascent Capitalism.* New York, 1977. A major case study of framework knitting. Focuses on demographic behavior.

Mathias, Peter, and John A. Davis, eds. *The First Industrial Revolutions.* Oxford, 1990. See especially articles by Davis and Mathias.

Medick, Hans. "The Proto-industrial Family Economy: The Structural Function of Household and Family during the Transition from Peasant Society to Industrial Capitalism." *Social History,* no. 3 (1976): 291–315. Reprinted in *Essays in Social History.* Edited by Pat Thane and Anthony Sutcliffe. Oxford, 1986.

Mendels, Franklin F. *Industrialization and Population Pressure in Eighteenth-Century Flanders.* New York, 1981. His published dissertation. Written in 1969.

Mendels, Franklin F. "Proto-industrialization: The First Phase of the Industrialization Process." *Journal of Economic History* 32, no. 1 (1972): 241–61. The article that established the field.

Mendels, Franklin F. "Seasons and Regions in Agriculture and Industry during the Process of Industrialization." In *Region und Industrialisierung.* Edited by Sidney Pollard. Göttingen, 1980.

Rudolph, Richard. "Family Structure and Proto-industrialization in Russia." *Journal of Economic History* 40, no. 1 (1980): 111–118.

Rudolph, Richard, ed. *The European Peasant Family and Society: Historical Studies.* Liverpool, U.K., 1995.

Short, Brian. "The De-industrialisation Process: A Case Study of the Weald, 1600–1850." In *Regions and Industries.* Edited by Pat Hudson. Cambridge, U.K., 1989.

Walton, John K. "Proto-industrialisation and the First Industrial Revolution: The Case of Lancashire." In *Regions and Industries.* Edited by Pat Hudson. Cambridge, U.K., 1989.

Whyte, Ian D. "Proto-industrialisation in Scotland." In *Regions and Industries.* Edited by Pat Hudson. Cambridge, U.K., 1989.

Women and Protoindustrialization

Baulant, Micheline. "The Scattered Family: Another Aspect of Seventeenth-Century Demography." In *Family and Society: Selections from the* Annales, Économies, Sociétés, Civilisations. Edited by Robert Forster and Orest Ranum. Translated by Elborg Forster and Patricia M. Ranum. Baltimore, 1976.

Berg, Maxine. *The Age of Manufactures, 1700–1820.* 2d ed. London, 1994. See chapter 7, "Women, Children, and Work."

Berg, Maxine. "Women's Work, Mechanisation, and the Early Phases of Industrialisation in England." In *The Historical Meanings of Work.* Edited by Patrick Joyce. Cambridge, U.K., 1987.

Gullickson, Gay L. "Love and Power in the Proto-industrial Family." In *Markets and Manufacture in Early Industrial Europe.* Edited by Maxine Berg. London, 1991.

Gullickson, Gay L. "The Sexual Division of Labor in Cottage Industry and Agriculture in the Pays de Caux: Auffay, 1750–1850." *French Historical Studies* 12, no. 2 (1981): 177–199.

Ogilvie, Sheilagh C. "Women and Proto-industrialisation in a Corporate Society: Württemberg Woollen Weaving, 1590–1760." In *Women's Work and the Family Economy in Historical Perspective.* Edited by Pat Hudson and W. Robert Lee. Manchester, U.K., 1990.

General Histories of Industrialization That Incorporate Protoindustrialization

Gutmann, Myron. *Toward the Modern Economy: Early Industry in Europe, 1500–1800.* Philadelphia, 1988.

Pollard, Sidney. *Peaceful Conquest: The Industrialization of Europe, 1760–1970.* Oxford, 1981.

Rule, John. *The Vital Century: England's Developing Economy, 1714–1815.* London, 1992.

THE INDUSTRIAL REVOLUTIONS

Patrick Karl O'Brien

Throughout history men and women manufactured commodities for use or for trade and sale. No society (family, village, urban, regional, or national) has operated without producing some range and levels of industrial output.

INDUSTRIALIZATION

Industrialization refers to economic change that is recent and different in scale and scope from the manufacture of artefacts. As a socioeconomic process, industrialization includes the rapid transformation in the significance of manufacturing activities in relation to all other forms of production and work undertaken within national (or local) economies. Following the seminal work of Simon Kuznets, economists, historians, and sociologists have measured and compared industrialization in statistical form as it appeared in national accounts and evolved historically for a large number of countries. Their data shows that as industrialization proceeds, shares of workforces employed in and national outputs emanating from primary forms of production (agriculture, forestry, fishing, and mining) decline, while shares of employment and output that is classified as industrial increase.

Output and employment emanating from the third macro sector of national production, services, can go up or down in relative terms. Services include all forms of noncommodity output that are sold (and/or supplied) either to consumers (for instance, health care) or utilized as "inputs" (e.g. distribution, legal advice, accountancy, etc.) in order to sustain both manufacturing and primary forms of production. Clearly, when industry grows more rapidly than other forms of commodity output then the allocation of services changes toward manufacturing and away from farming, fishing, forestry, and mining. Indeed macroeconomic analyses now emphasize the considerable degree of overlap between services and industry. Trends in the shares of services sold directly to consumers are,

however, difficult to explain. As development proceeds, final service output becomes a more important component of national product and employment but it can also increase in preindustrial economies as well, due to population growth, urbanization, and the slow growth of jobs in manufacturing. Thus, there is no exclusive correlation between industrialization and the service sector.

For sustained development there is no substitute for industrialization, which can also be measured as the reallocation of a nation's stock of capital (embodied in the form of buildings, machines, equipment, tools, infrastructure, communications, and distribution networks) away from primary and toward industrial production. Macro data, available for the foreign trade of nations, allows observers to track the progress of industrialization over the long run in the form of predictable shifts in the composition of a country's exports and imports. Sales of domestically produced manufactured exports normally grow in significance and purchases of foreign manufactures diminish as a share of total imports.

Thus economic data has been classified in heuristic ways and disaggregated into numerous activities and functions in order to expose the extent, pattern, and pace of industrialization over time across regions and among European and other countries. These essentially taxonomic exercises help to define and to make concrete a process that has proceeded on a global scale for nearly three centuries. They expose national variations from more general or regional patterns and contribute to the understanding of major economic variables that historically have fostered or restrained industrialization in Europe and other parts of the world.

Industrialization has been a highly important process for the welfare of mankind because the reallocation of labor, capital, and other national resources toward industry has usually been accompanied by technological and organizational change, which has led to higher levels of output per hour, rising living standards, population growth, urbanization, cultural changes, and shifts in the balance of power among nations. Thus, industrialization can also be defined in social, cultural, and political terms. For example, Parsonian sociology depicts the rise of industrial societies in terms of a set of interconnected characteristics, hegemonic values, and legal systems represented as functional for the development of modern industry. How, when, and why particular societies moved from preindustrial to industrial norms, motivations, status family systems, and modern institutions that characterize industrial society is not, however, explained in Parsonian models.

Other sociological taxonomies elaborate on the type of changes required in individual behavior and social institutions for modern industry to succeed. They contrast "traditionalistic patterns of action" that are defined as ascriptive, multidimensional, communitarian, familial, and authoritarian with the types of individualistic, achievement orientated, mobile, entrepreneurial attitudes and behavior that somehow became more dominant in national or local cultures as industrialization took hold. This approach to industrialization depends on the vocabularies and concepts drawn from sociology, psychology, and cultural anthropology and analyses, inspired by Max Weber, that continue to be preoccupied with value systems (derived ultimately from religions) that have "motivated" the "drive to industrialize" in different national and cultural settings.

Alas the historical record is not clear on whether social changes precede or accompany industrialization. Until recently, sociological approaches to industrialization have, moreover, been more concerned with its disruptive, dislocative, and potentially negative consequences for families, communities, villages, and regions, than with its nature, origins, and positive effects on living standards. Read as a social process, industrialization often leads to differentiation flowing from the division of labor, class formation, and uneven regional development. As industry diffuses from country to country, it becomes associated with diminishing returns, deindustrialization, unemployment, and the economic decline of some nations. The inspiration for writing in a pessimistic way about industrialization is often derived from Marx.

Fortunately, sociological understanding of industrialization is now changing to combine several schools of theory with historical inquiry and a more process-centered global perspective. Modern research has exposed how complex, multifaceted, and variable the process of industrialization has become since Marx, Comte, Durkheim, and other canonical social scientists wrote their critiques. There seem to be numerous

paths to an industrial society and no foreseeable end of capitalism. Several social sciences, as well as national historical narratives, are recognized as relevant, indeed as necessary, for the analysis of the process as a whole. Alas a "general theory" of industrialization at anything other than a meta level, focusing on structural changes in output employment and the allocation of resources (pace Kuznets) and obvious changes concerned with the "modernization" of societies (pace Parsons) still seems unattainable.

Vantage points on the industrial revolution vary. In the discussion that follows, emphasis is placed on issues of European versus global perspective and on related questions of causation. Many studies of industrialization emphasize technological change or measurements of economic growth. From the standpoint of social history, discussions of industrialization must include its impact on social culture and class tension and on gender and family life (including characteristic reductions in women's work roles and the removal of work from the family setting), as well as changes in work and leisure life. From whatever vantage point, discussion of industrialization is complicated by significant regional variations and also by the protracted quality of change. Industrialization was a revolutionary process (though some economic historians have disputed this point), but it stretched over many decades and might have also varied its shape in some crucial respects.

THE HISTORICAL PROCESSES AND STAGES

"Modern industry" (i.e. industrial activity concentrated in particular regions and towns, organized in factories, firms, and corporations, and using machinery and inanimate forms of energy) evolved gradually over the past five centuries. It appeared in some European economies before others. Industrialization, considered as a long-term process, has occupied generations of economic and social historians who have analyzed major forces that carried the growth of different national industrial sectors forward from one stage to another. In general their writings concentrate on the epoch that opens with the beginnings of the British industrial revolution in the mid-eighteenth century and closes with the end of the long boom after World War II (1948–73).

Nevertheless, a considerable literature has also been concerned with "preconditions" for industrialization that appeared in some regions of Europe over the centuries between the Renaissance and the first industrial revolution, while "late industrialization"

Industrial Plant. The Krupp iron works at Essen, Germany, c. 1878. Jean-Loup Charmet

characteristic of Russia, Eastern Europe, and the Balkans has generated another distinctive body of writing. For example, North and Thomas provide a succinct reminder about private initiatives and enterprise as structural preconditions for industrialization. The accumulation of capital in industry, the acquisition of skills needed for manufacturing, the diffusion of improved forms of organization for industrial production, and the funds needed for research and development into the scientific knowledge and technologies that raised productivity all required sustained private investment. That investment emerged as a response to incentives in the form of predictable material gains for the investors and entrepreneurs involved. It required politically enforced rules to mitigate the risks of instability, breakdown, and failure that often occurred during the buildup of modern industry. Such incentives, together with insurance against avoidable risks, rested in large part on institutions and laws for the conduct of all forms of economic activity (including industry) that were put in place and enforced more or less efficiently by some European governments and by private voluntary as-

sociations between the late Middle Ages and the era of the French Revolution, 1789–1815.

Once efficient institutions and legal systems were in place, protoindustrialization developed in many regions across the European continent. When it emerged after 1750, mechanized industry did not spread randomly across the map but located within established protoindustrial regions. Insights can be gained into industrialization by explaining the circumstances that led modern manufactures to grow and decay in some places before others, provided it is realized that there is no linear progression from proto to modern forms of industry.

Linear progression is too often the leitmotiv in writing about long-run economic development, an approach derived from Marx and scholars from the German Historical School, who explored the origins of European capitalism over several centuries from the High Middle Ages through to the nineteenth century. Rostow adhered to the basic position taken by that famous school, namely, that European economies had evolved in comparable ways but at different speeds through well-demarcated stages of growth.

In the early modern period an evolutionary accumulation of capital and knowledge carried them to the point of discontinuity, or "take-off," from which they industrialized at a speed and on a scale that took societies forward into "self-sustained" and irreversible growth. Critiques of Rostow's famous model are convincing; particularly Gerschenkron's essays, which represent European industrialization as a process of "unity in diversity." Unlike Rostow (and Kuznets) he is more interested in explaining variations than similarities across nations. Gerschenkron expected that the study of carefully delineated contrasts in the methods used by now affluent societies to build up modern industry could help to explain the time they took to converge toward the highest attainable (i.e. British) levels of industrialization and per capita income.

European industrialization might, at the cost of simplification, be represented as a homogeneous macroeconomic process, but differentiation in the composition of output, great diversity in methods of production, and variety in the modes and styles of organization actually characterized the development of European industry between the French Revolution and World War I. Viable alternatives to mass-mechanized production prospered not only in numerous regions on the mainland but also within Britain, the leading industrial economy of that period. They survived because technology only provided substitutes for handicraft skills within a constrained (if ever widening) range of industrial production and because markets, particularly the quality end of consumer and capital goods markets, required flexible adaptations to changes in demand. Mass, large-scale factory-based industrial production never became necessary and efficient for all manufactured artefacts. Considerable segments of traditional industry survived. Sharp discontinuities with more handicraft and proto forms of production never emerged. Instead, while industry became the dominant sector in economy after economy, change and expansion within industry continued to represent a process of continuous adaptation and redesign. New technologies, tools, forms of power, and modes of organization extended the range of skill required and qualities of products available. No American (or British) paradigm for industrialization based on large-scale corporate forms of organization producing homogenized products for sale on mass markets emerged across the industrial regions of Europe until after World War I. Even then that particular model only prevailed for five decades or so before Asian comparative advantages in small-batch, flexible, and differentiated production appeared in the late twentieth century.

PAST TENDENCIES, PRESENT TRENDS, AND FUTURE PROSPECTS DURING THE FIRST, SECOND, AND THIRD INDUSTRIAL REVOLUTIONS

After the onset of the first industrial revolution in Britain (c. 1750), global industrial output took more than a century to double. Between the mid-nineteenth century and World War I it quadrupled. Over forty years dominated by depression and war, 1913–1953, output trebled and then trebled again over the two decades that followed to the peak of the long boom in 1973. Thereafter, the annual rate of growth of global industrial output declined but it still remained rapid by historical standards. However, there are dramatic regional differences in this output.

Although industrial production in third world countries probably doubled over the two centuries after 1750, down to World War I, total output per capita may well have declined in both relative and in absolute terms as the population of Africa, Asia, and South America purchased a rising share of the manufactured goods they consumed in the form of imports from the industrializing countries of Europe and North America. Over the long run the share of world industrial output emanating from production located in Third World economies declined from around 70 percent, 1750–1800, down to the 10 percent range around 1950. It began to rise again during the last quarter of the twentieth century. Historically, for two centuries from 1750 onward, industrialization (particularly if it is measured as industrial output per capita) was essentially confined to Europe and its settlements overseas in North America (Bairoch, pp. 269–333).

Thus, until recently, discussions about the course and causes of industrialization have been overwhelmingly concerned with the scale, efficiency, and development of modern (i.e. technologically advanced) industries within Europe and North America. For a long time, indeed for roughly two centuries before 1900, Britain remained the world's leading industrial economy (conspicuously so when measured in terms of industrial output per capita) before it was superseded by the United States around 1900–1914 as a result of the "second industrial revolution," and then by other European economies and by Japan as the twentieth century progressed. European and North American industries attempted to converge toward and to surpass the standards of labor productivity, technological advance, and organizational efficiency displayed by many (but not all) British industries. After 1900–1914 (and during the second industrial revolution) the standards set for convergence shifted to the United States and to league tables, which ranked national industries and industrial sectors in terms of a battery of productivity indicators purporting to tell businessmen and governments how well or badly a particular economy was performing within global industry as a whole. Britain's relative decline, the rise of America, Germany, Russia, Sweden, Switzerland, Belgium, Italy, latterly Japan, and the newly industrializing countries of East Asia, can be traced and analyzed in relation to a range of indicators of industrial power and efficiency.

What stands out for most of the twentieth century is the overwhelming size of American industry and its persistent dominance, measured in terms of manufactured output per head of population, but less so in terms of productivity (i.e. manufactured output per man hour of labor employed in industry). That particular advantage, which the United States certainly retained for longer than would have been the case without two global wars (1914–1918 and 1939–1945), diminished during the long boom when productivity growth in several European economies exceeded that of the lead country. The history of this phase of "convergence" exposed how interactions between technological opportunities, social capabilities, scale economies, initial natural endowments, and underemployed labor operated as key variables behind the accelerated rate of industrialization achieved by European economies, and Japan, during and since the long boom, 1948–1973. Since 1950, within the developed market economies of Europe and North America industrialization has proceeded by exploiting and adopting the potential for productivity gains already embodied and clearly functioning in the technologies, organizational forms, and institutions of the lead (or leading) industrial economies.

Attempts to represent that process in terms of a rather bland conceptual vocabulary of convergence drawn from economics and sociology carry less conviction when transposed to the Asian and Latin American cultures of newly industrializing countries. For these so-called late industrializers, the roles their governments play and the strategies and organizational structures adopted by their firms, as well as distinctive processes of industrialization that have emerged, may represent a "new paradigm," or perhaps a "third industrial revolution." That paradigm embodies the adaptation to the opportunities provided by new technologies and to competitive challenges arising from the diffusion of industry to more and more locations and countries around the world. A new revolution in information technologies, high speed transportation, biochemicals, genetic engineering, robotics, and computerized control systems, as well as the relocation, diffusion, and integration of industries on a global scale, confront earlier (European and American) as well as late (Asian) industrialists.

For economic and social historians, who take a very long-run view, there may be little that seems novel in the current phase of restructuring, reorganization, and relocation of industry, or indeed in the rediscovery of sources of industrial innovation and of efficiency gains among the skills and motivations of workers on factory floors. It all seems reminiscent of the phase of regional economies and protoindustrialization in Europe between 1492 and 1756.

INDUSTRY'S LINKS TO AGRICULTURE, TRANSPORT, AND FINANCE

Although industry is usually represented as the "key sector" behind the long-run development of national economies, the history of when, where, how, and with what effect industrialization emerged to play that "leading role" depended on support from other sectors. Before nations industrialize, their resources are usually heavily concentrated within and upon agriculture. In the absence of inflows of foreign resources, the primary sector is called upon to supply much of the labor, capital, raw materials, and markets that industry requires for long-term growth. These connections have been formally modeled by economists but the basic linkages can be understood and their significance measured by comparing the experiences of particular countries (cases) during the early stages of industrialization when agriculture could nurture or constrain the development of towns and industries.

Forward and backward linkages between industry and transport are almost as important to appreciate. Demand for transportation widens and deepens when industries purchase inputs and sell final outputs over wider spaces. The coordination of specialized, regionally concentrated but spatially dispersed centers and sites for industrial production depended on the services supplied by an extended, and increasingly efficient, network of transportation. Industrialization has been accompanied and actively promoted by a long series of innovations in transportation (surfaced roads, canals, railed ways, steam, oil, and jet propelled engines), which lowered the costs, and speeded up and regularized the delivery of the final outputs and the inputs required for the expansion of manufacturing industry. Transportation declined in price and grew more rapidly than commodity production. It not only provided a final output, travel, but investment in transportation networks is connected through backward linkages to several major industries, including

Transportation. A cast-iron frame supports the glass roof of the train shed of the *Gare St.-Lazare, Paris,* painting by Claude Monet (1840–1926). BURNSTEIN COLLECTION/©CORBIS

iron and steel, engineering, and construction. Without rapid and continuous technological changes in transportation, industrialization on a regional, national, and global scale would have been severely constrained.

No set of institutions supporting industrial firms (particularly smaller firms) are as important as banks and other financial intermediaries. They collect savings and provide the loans that industrialists borrow as threshold capital, as well as the credits required to sustain the day-to-day operations of manufacturing enterprises. Industrial entrepreneurs and firms do not emerge and function unless they can be provided with ready and sustained access to finance. Unfortunately, the framework of rules and regulations promulgated by governments in order to avoid inflation and maintain the international value of currencies has operated to repress the emergence and distort the necessary activities of financial intermediaries. Regulating the money supplies and the national exchange rates, while providing for access to loans that are helpful for industry, presents governments with difficult choices as they try to balance the competing claims for industrial growth with price and balance of payments stability.

Monetary and fiscal policies cover an important subset of a whole range of connections between the state and the industrialization of national economies.

Famously for Russia and Eastern Europe, the creation of modern industrial sectors was actually planned and executed by their central governments. For most other European economies, states undertook a less comprehensive and dictatorial role. They financed and set up certain sections of industrial production, and subsidized others, but in general provided infrastructures of communications, energy supplies, education and training, information and technical advice, and security in order to promote private investment in and to support the private management of national industries.

Debates about connections between governments and industry have tended to become suffused with ideological preconceptions about the effectiveness of private compared to political initiatives and management for the promotion of modern industry. Thus, histories of industrialized economies have been written purporting to demonstrate the benign, as well as the malign, effects of state "interference" with the operation of market forces and private enterprise. Late (Cold War) industrialization also became a confusing battleground of claims and counterclaims for market failures versus bureaucratic ineptitude behind the performance of different countries in the late twentieth century. Fortunately, a more balanced view has emerged which seeks to analyze the kind of governmental strategies for industrialization that have proved either helpful, neutral, or hindrance for long-term industrial development; and to expose structural and historical conditions that have in large measure predetermined successes and failures in national economic policies. The intellectual discourse about the role of the state moved from mere ideology into the realism of empirically based histories, analyses, and theories.

THE INTERNATIONAL CONTEXT

Generalizations can also be drawn from a wide range of historical accounts of paths or patterns of industrial growth about the links between domestic industry and the international economy. While endogenous (internal) intersectoral connections matter, no country has ever industrialized without rather considerable recourse to assistance from societies beyond its borders. The buildup of national industrial sectors can often be traced to the stimulus of profits obtainable from the sale of manufactures on world markets; it also came from successful attempts to escape from the constraints of small or slowly growing home markets. In nearly every case some proportion of the inputs of raw materials, capital, skilled labor, professional know-how, and technology required to establish and sustain industries emanated (at least in the initial stages) from places beyond national frontiers. International flows of commodities (exports and imports), services (transportation, distribution, insurance, and other commercial assistance), and the factors of production (capital, credit, technology, and useful knowledge) have always been integral to the spread of industrialization around Europe and to the rest of the world, even before Britain emerged as the first industrial nation in the late eighteenth century.

The significance of trade and commerce across countries for the timing, pace, and pattern of industrialization can be captured by looking at a country's balance of payments accounts. International migrations of capital and labor have also been analyzed in order to reveal the pull and the push of foreign and domestic markets, as well as political and other forces involved in the diffusion of industrialization during the past three centuries and also (but alas, without much help from hard data) for several centuries before.

Between 1846 and 1914 globalization and industrialization went hand in hand, at least among European economies and European offshoots overseas in the Americas and Australasia. Dramatic declines in the costs of transportation integrated commodity markets and stimulated trade and specialization. Massive migrations of labor, followed by capital, reallocated resources efficiently across frontiers and sectors of national economies. In the absence of governmental impediments to trade or to labor and capital flows, underemployed and cheap labor moved out of the countryside toward the cities into employment in industry and related urban services. Alas, between 1914 and 1948, this benign process of globalization was restrained by tariffs, by immigration controls, and by two World Wars. It picked up again during the long boom, 1948–1973. At the end of the twentieth century, the diffusion of industrialization through trade, capital, and labor flows across frontiers was endangered by the resurgence of a "new protectionism."

Debate about the significance of "endogenous" versus "exogenous" forces in the industrialization of otherwise sovereign and ostensibly autonomous countries has persisted and covers the entire spectrum of national "cases" from Britain (site of the first industrial revolution) to the "Asian tigers" industrializing at far greater speed in the late twentieth century. Some commentators see commodity trade as the "handmaiden" rather than as the "engine" of growth, but the role of exports and imports probably varied from place to place and also depended from cycle to cycle on the underlying buoyancy of the world economy as a whole and upon the freedom of international economic relations.

Everywhere industrialization required high and increasing levels of investment not simply in buildings, machinery, inventories, and other assets that supported manufacturing activity, but, on a greater scale, in the infrastructural facilities needed for the transmission of energy, for urbanization, housing, transport and distribution networks, and public services that accompanied the buildup of modern industries. Internally generated savings could be inadequate, particularly when businessmen and governments wished to finance a rapid development of modern industry. Furthermore, the import content of local industrialization (particularly the machinery, but also raw materials, intermediate inputs, and the recruitment of foreign professional and skilled labor) had to be funded in the form of foreign exchange, which also became scarce and expensive when countries began to industrialize at any speed.

Loans and credit from abroad then became necessary to fill these two gaps, particularly in the early phases of industrialization, when local investors and financial intermediaries regarded industrial enterprises as risky, and/or when balance of payments constraints dominated the allocation of investable funds for industrial development.

Foreign capital often became available at prices that governments and local businessmen found exces-

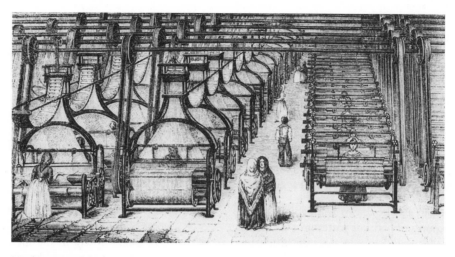

Machinery. Power-driven looms. *Ackroyd's Loom-Shed at Halifax (Worsted Goods),* engraving, eighteenth century. PRIVATE COLLECTION/THE BRIDGEMAN ART LIBRARY

sive and on terms they regarded as constrictive of national autonomy and as potentially prohibitive for longer-term industrial development. Before the era of decolonization (which occurred rapidly after World War II) an "imperial component" surely entered into payments made for inflows of metropolitan and foreign capital. Thereafter, bargains continued to be struck between investors and borrowers from more or less dependent, but nominally sovereign, economies, that the debtors have persistently regarded as intrusive and "exploitative." Yet most countries continued to rely heavily on international capital markets and in the twentieth century numerous industrializing economies in Eastern Europe (as well as the Third World) accumulated levels of foreign debt that reached crisis proportions in relation to their capacities to earn the foreign currency required to satisfy contractual obligations to creditors from overseas.

Long-term growth in output and productivity in manufacturing continues to rest upon the discovery, improvement, and development of scientific and technological knowledge that can be profitably applied to industrial production. Most industrialized and industrializing countries (and to some extent this observation applies even to first industrial nations) borrowed, emulated, adapted, and built upon manufactured products and industrial techniques initially developed outside their frontiers. Although there are certain competitive advantages to be reaped from being the locus of inventions and as a "first mover" in new product lines, industrialization as a global process depends more on adaptation, improvement, and further development of technically and commercially viable industrial technologies moved from place to place

and across countries. Thus it is the diffusion rather than the "discovery" of industrial technology that is at the "core" of industrialization.

Over the last half of the twentieth century multinational corporations (MNCs) assumed a leading role in facilitating the movement of investable funds and managing the transfer of industrial technologies around the world. These corporations and conglomerates were usually privately owned companies that were centrally controlled by an executive located in and recruited from a single country (overwhelmingly the United States, but including Britain, France, Germany, Switzerland, the Netherlands, and Japan). Multinational corporations produced and sold manufactured goods on a global scale, but in origin such organizations were not new. In form, structure, and purpose their antecedents can be traced back to Dutch, English, and French corporations trading with the Americas and Asia in the sixteenth and seventeenth centuries.

An impressive list of European and American corporations, making and trading in industrial commodities well beyond the frontiers of their own "national markets," certainly appeared well before 1914. Their range and reach spread between the wars. They soon encompassed the globe and assumed control over a large share of transnational trade, capital flows, and technology transfers before the end of the long boom, 1948–1973. American multinationals diffused modern technologies, new products, good managerial practices, and improved forms of industrial organization and thereby contributed positively to the recovery of European industries from World War II.

Yet the role of American, European, and Japanese multinational corporations in the development of industry in Asia, Africa, and Eastern Europe remains controversial. They stand accused of diffusing inappropriate products, exporting obsolete technologies, and recommending hierarchical, or culturally biased, managerial systems to underdeveloped countries. They are said to underinvest in the training they provide in order to upgrade local workforces. They are perceived to exploit cheap labor around the globe and retain monopoly rights over modern technologies and best-selling product lines. Even in developed countries of Europe and North America multinationals are regarded by some as unpatriotic agencies of deindustrialization and unemployment.

EUROPE'S INDUSTRIAL REVOLUTIONS

In earlier centuries Europe derived from Asia and the Middle East a considerable body of technological, scientific, and agrarian knowledge, which it adapted and embodied in commodities, artefacts, machines, and commercial practices, crops, and agrarian techniques, associated with the industrialization of the continent that occurred at an accelerated pace after 1750. Just as there has been considerable investigation into the extra-European origins and contributions of Asia, Africa, and the Americas to European industrialization as it evolved before 1815, so too the nature and antecedents of the British industrial revolution have been vigorously debated in interpretations of that famous transition to industrial society.

A key question for this illuminating discourse is why the Netherlands did not evolve into the first industrial nation. All the preconditions seemed to be in place: well functioning (competitive) factor and commodity markets, a productive agriculture, high levels of urbanization, a skilled workforce, good internal order, merchants poised to mature into industrial entrepreneurs, and so on. Yet during the eighteenth century the Netherlands entered into relative and perhaps into absolute economic decline and its interest as a case for students of industrialization resides more in the discourse of the rise and relative decline of a commercial and protoindustrial economy.

Nevertheless, that discourse remains as interesting to contemplate as Britain's protracted but still seminal discontinuity in global economic history. Thanks largely to the research and analysis of economists (who have encapsulated its major features and key variables in statistical form) modern conceptions of the first industrial revolution can now distinguish general from unique characteristics and allow us to clarify and to weigh the really significant determinants at work, which include: a productive agriculture, the slow accumulation of stocks of skilled labor, and military success in the competition for international commerce with its leading European rivals, including Holland, France, Portugal, and Spain.

National and particular contrasts in the pace and pattern of industrialization, as and when it occurred on the European mainland, are now perceived to be more analytically interesting than traditional accounts, based essentially on a British paradigm emulated in a chronological sequence (through a process of technological diffusion) by Belgium, France, Switzerland, Germany, Holland, Italy, Austria, Russia, and Iberia. For example, France, a much larger and more populous country than Britain, probably achieved higher rates of industrial growth down to the time of the Revolution and Napoleonic Wars, which then disrupted and delayed the industrialization of Britain's main rival, as well as other regions of western Europe such as Spain for some three to four decades. Less favorable natural endowments, a constricting heritage of agrarian property rights, and a persistent lack of military success in mercantilist competition with British commerce and industry for access to global markets in the Americas, Africa, and Asia seem to be the central components of modern explanations for France's different path.

Europe's "Mediterranean economies" (Italy, Spain, Portugal) also lost ground to British industry and commerce in the competition for international markets during the seventeenth and eighteenth centuries. Nevertheless, (and central to any understanding of their "failure" to undertake the structural changes required for industrialization over long stretches of the nineteenth and twentieth centuries) there was a lack of support from low-productivity agricultures; inadequate rates of investment in education and skill; and governmental policies that protected the cultivation of grain and failed to reform a constricting system of property rights and tenurial contracts within the agrarian economy. Agrarian preconditions, natural resources, and governments were not helpful in Italy or the Iberian Peninsula.

By contrast (and along with the Nordic countries) Germany included within its frontiers a range of skills and accessible supplies of coal and minerals, as well as concentrations of protoindustrialization within several regions that were economically integrated early in the nineteenth century and eventually politically united into a large and growing national market. Although modern industrialization cannot (in contrast to Russia) be presented as organized, managed, and funded by the state, in several ways the German process can be plausibly depicted as "stimulated" from above. That promotion by the state included: the very important project for the establishment of a railway system, the formation of the Zollverein (a customs union), the unification of currencies and prudential monetary policies, selective protection, and, to an outstanding degree for the times, public investment in education.

Like Japan later in the century, Germany started to industrialize from a basis of literacy, commercial sophistication, and technological know-how that added up to an accumulation of social capabilities that far exceeded anything available within, say, the Russian empire. By the 1860s German industrialists could call upon skills, professional management, scientific knowledge, as well as an infrastructure of transportation, financial intermediation, and public services that could not be taken for granted except within a few large cities and the western regions of the Habsburg empire to the east.

Recent and more optimistic interpretations of industrialization within that empire before its dismemberment in 1918 are surely a necessary corrective to the older history of stagnation. Nevertheless, regional variations remained pronounced and the kind of acceleration and diversification of industrial production achieved by Germany did not occur. After a good start in the eighteenth century, the Habsburg state seems to have failed to build up the efficient framework of laws and institutions required to promote a more impressive widespread process of industrialization over the succeeding century.

Within the spectrum of European powers, Russian industrialization started from a position of the greatest backwardness. Before the Revolution of 1917 the Romanov regime had, however, introduced a range of institutional reforms that facilitated the more efficient operation of that empire's labor and capital and commodity markets. In 1861, in the name of freedom, the tsar emancipated the workforce from serfdom, which thereafter allowed agriculture to make a more positive contribution to the growth of modern urban industry. Russian agricultural output increased at rather impressive rates. From a low base, industrial production responded and grew steadily from the 1840s down to World War I. With a substantial measure of assistance from overseas investment, from foreign managers, engineers, and technologies, a more diversified and capital-intensive structure of industrial production emerged in Russia between 1880 and 1914. At every stage the tsarist state, in partnership with foreign and local enterprise, attempted to force the pace of industrialization in order to overcome the empire's backwardness and geopolitical weakness.

That drive intensified under the Bolsheviks, who took over the ownership and control of the Russian economy in 1917. The new Communist regime erected the political and institutional structures required for a new style "command economy"; and in the face of an entirely hostile international political and economic order, succeeded in increasing the labor participation rate and the share of the country's resources devoted to fixed capital formation, particularly in heavy industry, to an extraordinary degree. Between 1917 and 1989 the domestic product of the Soviet Union multiplied by a factor of ten and its per capita product five times. Its record for state-inspired and driven industrialization is impressive but not that extraordinary and it might, counterfactually, have been achieved by a less authoritarian regime. The achievement is, moreover, one of "extensive growth" and owed very little to technological and organizational changes, which enabled rival economies to raise the productivities of labor and capital deployed to produce industrial output. The strategy and concomitant organizational and command structures meant that productivity gains became steadily more difficult to obtain. By the early 1980s, the Soviet economy had clearly run into sharply diminishing returns and by 2000 the Russian state was attempting to move the system toward some version of capitalism that could raise industrial productivity to levels that might gradually converge towards Western European and American standards.

EUROPEAN INDUSTRIALIZATION IN A LONG-RUN GLOBAL SETTING

Since Paleolithic times people have been engaged in making artefacts for use, decoration, and exchange. Supplies of industrial commodities increased in volume, range, and sophistication when settled agricultures emerged and generated the surpluses of food and raw materials required to support towns, specialization, trade, and the order associated with a succession of "empires" or "civilizations," which rose, flourished, and declined in Europe, the Middle East, Africa, Asia, and in Mesoamerica between the onset of the Neolithic era and the industrial revolution. Global historians periodize and divide this epoch of some five millennia from Sumerian civilization to the Middle Ages into a succession of ancient empires and have been preoccupied with the political, military, and cultural factors in their rise and decline.

For historians of industry (who tend to periodize in terms of the millennia before and the centuries after the industrial revolution in the eighteenth century), the interest in ancient civilizations resides in understanding the range, amount, design, and above all the costs or values in exchange of the manufactured artefacts these empires bequeathed to posterity. Archaeologists have collected and arranged a great deal of the evidence required to appreciate the evolving variety and volume of industrial production that originated from urban sites that seem to have been spatially concentrated and specialized in manufacturing as far back as the Sumerian Empire, which flourished in the Tigris and Euphrates Valley between 3800 and 2000 B.C.E.

They have classified and recorded the durable artefacts these empires produced and exchanged or acquired from other civilizations. The lists are long, variegated, and increasingly sophisticated, and testify to the existence of long-distance trade in manufactures within and across Asia, Europe, and Africa long before the heyday of the empires of Greece and Rome. Although diffusion of industrial products and the knowledge involved in their design and manufacture clearly occurred for millennia before the industrial revolution, it is impossible for historians to offer even conjectures about the amount of trade in manufactures or to begin to measure the volume of industrial production on national, let alone global, scales much before the beginning of the eighteenth century.

Yet industrial production and trade in industrial goods must have been important. Thus depictions of the industrial revolution in Europe as an unpredictable, sudden, and rapid transition from national or regional economies based overwhelmingly on agriculture to industrial economies are now regarded as simplifications. Not only were significant volumes of industrial products manufactured and traded in many parts of the world long before the industrial revolution, but machinery, some of it driven by windmills and waterwheels, had been used for centuries. Examples of concentrations of labor under the roofs of workshops and factories or within the walls of yards and organized in order to collaborate in the making of particular products can be found in numerous towns and cities of many empires and states in Europe, the Middle East, India, and China, as far back as Sumeria. Workmen, specialized and proficient in defined and evolving ranges of skills, crafts, techniques, or processes required to manufacture industrial goods, had formed a recognizable part of national and urban workforces in most ancient civilizations.

In short, features of industrialization that have transformed the potential for rapid economic growth over the past three centuries (including the manufacture of expanded ranges of useful artefacts, trade in industrial commodities, mechanical engineering, inanimate forms of energy, specialization, factories, and spatial concentration of industrial activity) can be found in archaeological and historical records that go back in many parts of the world to Neolithic times. Furthermore, and although such impressions cannot be validated with reference to hard statistical evidence, narrative histories of "rapid" and "impressive" growth in industrial production and trade that accompanied the rise of cities, towns, and regions in the Middle East, Europe, Asia, and Mesoamerica also convince us that the question of what may be new about "European" industrialization of the past three centuries has remained heuristic to contemplate.

That is why essential contrasts between the recent past and previous epochs can only reside in the pace, pattern, and the global diffusion and integration of industrialization. For example, since the late seventeenth century the volume and range of industrial commodities used, consumed, and enjoyed by masses of people in nearly every part of the world has increased at a rate that must simply be unprecedented in history. Before the modern era, upswings in the amount and variety of manufactured goods made for the affluent populations of particular empires and cities may well have been equally rapid but remained geographically confined, and the consumption of manufactures, even within favored sites and places, was restricted to minorities of their population with the money or the power to appropriate something more than the food, shelter, and clothing required for subsistence.

Furthermore, nearly all the towns and polities that contained significant concentrations of industrial activity remained vulnerable to political and natural disasters (including breakdowns of internal order, warfare, plague, disease, and natural disasters of every kind). Industry and trade could be destroyed and permanently depressed by exogenous shocks. Declines (serious and absolute), as well as dramatic accounts of the rapid rise of industry and commerce, seem to be omnipresent features of the histories of industrialized, commerical, urbanized societies right down to the sixteenth century. Short of a nuclear holocaust, nationwide vulnerability to political and natural disasters that afflicted the very survival of urban industry and commerce for past millennia seems to have been replaced by those altogether less catastrophic problems of shocks and relative economic decline that have punctuated the history of industrialization since the eighteenth century.

Thus, something akin to a major discontinuity seems to separate the history of industrialization considered as a global phenomenon from the growth of pockets of industrial activity as they appeared and disappeared around the world for millennia. That is why a distinguished succession of famous scholars from economics, history, sociology, and anthropology began to investigate the origins and to reflect on the positive and negative outcomes of the industrial revolution even before the first example of that famous transition had run its course in Britain and diffused onto the European mainland over the century after 1750.

Students are well advised to read these classical analyses of modern industrialization, referenced in the bibliography to this essay, before they turn to the more recent attempts to depict and explain the grand themes. Canonical texts are always instructive; they expose how many seminal concepts, insights, and approaches to the study of industrialization are included in the writings of the classics, but also how repetitious and circular many of the discussions that attempt to explain and to generalize about the long-run pace and pattern of modern industrialization in various parts of the world have now become. Nearly three centuries of empirical investigation and reflection by a succession of the very best minds in history and the social sciences have not produced any kind of general theory of industrialization.

As the leading sector in modern economic growth, accompanied by structural change, the process is, however, well understood. Sensible taxonomies and vocabularies defining the inputs and the intersectoral connections required to generate accelerated rates of industrial production have also been formulated and refined. Although the mechanisms through which these inputs' impact on growth are now understood, the sense in which they are separable and quantifiable components of a discernable historical process of sustained industrial development remains elusive. Net capital formation, the recruitment of better-skilled and more highly motivated labor, improved management, more efficient technology, optimal scale, and rational organization, aggressive marketing, and closer integration into a competitive international economy, an enhanced framework of supportive governmental policies, and so forth, will all be included in any discussion of the "preconditions," "requirements," or "proximate determinants" for industrial growth. Yet how, when, and why they all interacted and generated sustained industrial growth remain key questions for historians and social scientists pondering the very large fact that, after roughly three centuries of industrialization, the highest levels of industrial output per capita remain concentrated in roughly twenty to thirty national economies and support satisfactory standards of living for but a minority of the world's population.

Although several newly industrializing countries in the late twentieth century clearly entered the "club" of industrialized market economies and their levels of industrial productivity began to approach standards set by the leading industrial powers in Europe, North America, and Japan, there is no statistical evidence for any sustained worldwide process of convergence in levels of real wages or output per worker employed in manufacturing industry. On the contrary, divergence between an admittedly larger group of national economies that can be represented as industrialized and economically successful and those that are still "underdeveloped" may be increasing.

Given that a great deal has been revealed about the process of industrialization and the proximate factors required to promote it, the frequently posed question of why the whole world is still not industrialized deserves to remain high on the intellectual agenda; particularly as the industries of "follower countries" would seem to possess competitive advantages as and when they attempt to catch up. For example, countries with small and/or less efficient industrial sectors emulate and adapt the technologies and modes of organization that are demonstrably successful elsewhere in the world economy. They can borrow the funds and hire the technicians and managers required to establish modern industry on established international capital and labor markets. Their workers are cheap. Their natural resources are often underexploited. Their governments remain keen to promote and to subsidize the development and diversification of national industry. With misgivings they even welcome the plants and branches of multinational corporations. And yet, these advantages have not been enough.

It is now more than two to three centuries since Britain passed through the first industrial revolution, yet convergence has been slow, painful, and geographically constrained. Except at a rather banal level of generality, there is no short explanation of why many more countries are not industrialized. Students can and will be told that the small selection of national economies that followed Britain's lead (and particularly the twenty or so cases that eventually surpassed Britain's standards of industrial productivity) possessed or quickly built up something referred to as the "social capability" required to industrialize. Manifestly most other countries (which include within their borders the majority of the world's population) did not and have not acquired the requisite social capabilities.

Social capability is, however, little more than a portmanteau category that refers to cultures, values, family systems, political and legal institutions, religions, motivations, education, and skills embodied in national populations that, in combination, operated to inhibit or to facilitate the development of modern

Labor. *Leaving the Factory,* drawing (1908) by Barth Anthony van der Leck (1876–1958).
Rijksmuseum Kroller-Muller, Otterlo, Netherlands/The Bridgeman Art Library

and efficient industrial sectors. Obviously at any point in time they appear as a heritage of national and/or local histories. Social capabilities can be pushed in required directions by governments, by other institutions, such as churches, schools, and industrial firms, and altered by material incentives to invest, develop, and work in industry. As a result of this link to the particular historical context, there is no substitute for studying successful cases of industrialization country by country and contrasting them with cases that came later to the endeavor and found greater difficulty in converging toward the macroeconomic structures and productivity levels of leading industrial powers. That is, there is no substitute for history.

At a global level the general models (largely from economics and sociology) that claim to account for the limited spread of modern industrialization are schematic and taxonomic. Yet, even working inductively from individual case studies it is difficult to expect a functioning general model of industrialization.

That pessimistic reflection is strengthened, moreover, by the observation that difficulties for the formulation of any general theory of industrialization have been compounded because the international context within which regions and countries industrialized has changed profoundly since the eighteenth century. This has occurred first of all because the knowledge base and range of technologies used to manufacture industrial commodities has evolved at an accelerated rate since British industry pioneered the development of steam power, coke smelting, and mechanical engineering to raise the productivity of labor employed in the production of consumer goods, machinery, and transportation.

Secondly, the geopolitical parameters for industrial development based on trade, imports of investable funds from abroad, for the diffusion of technology, and for the hire of skilled and professional manpower on international labor markets has also changed dramatically. For example, a liberal international order from 1846 to 1914 succeeded the aggressive and war-prone mercantilism of previous centuries. Neomercantilism and the era of global warfare reappeared from 1914 through 1948. Thereafter, American hegemony, decolonization, and the rise of multinational enterprise reduced the obstacles to the spread and relocation of modern industry around the globe. Since 1989 the collapse of command economies, committed to forcing the pace of industrialization in Russia, Eastern Europe, and China, has severely further reduced the powers of states to control the geographical spread of industry.

Capitalism, assisted by positive help and incentives from governments, has triumphed as a so-called end to history. States everywhere seem committed to free enterprise, but it remains difficult to prescribe the right mix of policies for all national cases. Unless the current wave of protectionism intensifies, long-established trends in the interdependence and integration of industry on a global scale look set to continue, and industries will become ever more cosmopolitan and dispersed in their locations. Although the range of technologies now available to late industrializers provides opportunities for unprecedented rates of structural change and rates of increase in labor productivities, perhaps no particular illumination can be derived from labeling industrialization as it proceeded at the end of the millennium as qualitatively different, or as a third or fourth industrial revolution.

For more than three centuries modern industry has adapted to opportunities provided by flows of new knowledge. Telematics, biotechnologies, robotics, and other novel technologies are just the latest wave requiring industries to restructure, to relocate, and to readapt to possibilities to satisfy mankind's seemingly insatiable demands for manufactured commodities. In this current phase of technological development, knowledge, human skills, capacities for coordination, and flexible responses to volatile, global markets seem to carry the kind of competitive advantages required during an earlier phase of industrialization, before that process became synonymous with large-scale corporations, fixed capital, and mass production. Nowadays success involves new and different political and social capabilities that are already shifting the concentrations of industrial activity away from Europe and North America and back to Asia.

See also **Cliometrics and Quantification** *(volume 1);* **Agriculture** *(in this volume);* **Factory Work** *(volume 4); and other articles in this section.*

BIBLIOGRAPHY

Theoretical and General Studies of Industrialization

Frank, Andre Gunder. *ReOrient: Global Economy in the Asian Age.* Berkeley, Calif., 1998.

Gerschenkron, Alexander. *Economic Backwardness in Historical Perspective.* Cambridge, Mass., 1962.

Hoselitz, Bert, ed. *Theories of Economic Growth.* New York, 1960. Contains a good bibliography of classical writings from Adam Smith to Joseph Schumpter on industrialization.

Jones, Eric L. *Growth Recurring: Economic Change in World History.* Oxford, 1988.

Kuznets, Simon. *Modern Economic Growth: Rate, Structure, and Spread.* New Haven, Conn., 1966.

Landes, David. *The Wealth and Poverty of Nations.* London, 1998.

Maddison, Angus. *Dynamic Forces in Capitalist Development.* Oxford, 1991.

Mokyr, Joel. *Lever of Riches: Technological Creativity and Economic Progress.* Oxford, 1990.

North, Douglas C., and Robert P. Thomas. *The Rise of the Western World: A New Economic History.* Cambridge U.K., 1973.

Parsons, Talcott. *Structure and Process in Modern Societies.* Glencoe, Ill., 1960.

Pomeranz, Kenneth. *The Great Divergence: Europe, China, and the Making of the Modern World Economy.* Princeton, N.J., 2000.

Rostow, Walt. *The Stages of Economic Growth.* 2d ed. Cambridge, U.K., 1971.

Stearns, Peter N. *The Industrial Revolution in World History.* Boulder, Colo., 1998.

Weber, Max. *General Economic History.* New York, 1961.

Industrial Revolutions in a European Context

These works include bibliographies providing extensive reference to national case studies in English and other European languages.

Aldcroft, Derek H., and Anthony Sutcliffe, eds. *Europe in the International Economy 1500–2000.* Cheltenham, U.K., 1999.

Braudel, Fernand. *Civilization and Capitalism 15th–18th Century.* 3 vols. London, 1982–1984.

Cipolla, Carlo, ed. *The Fontana Economic History of Europe.* Vols. 1–6. London, 1972–1976.

Goodman, Jordan, and Katrina Honeyman. *Gainful Pursuits: The Making of Industrial Europe, 1600–1914.* London, 1988.

O'Brien, Patrick K., ed. *The Industrial Revolution in Europe.* Vols. 4 and 5 of *The Industrial Revolutions.* Edited by Roy A. Church and Anthony E. Wrigley. Oxford, 1994.

Pollard, Sidney. *Peaceful Conquest: The Industrialization of Europe 1760–1970.* Oxford, 1981.

Postan, M. M., and H. J. Habakkuk, eds. *The Cambridge Economic History of Europe.* Vol. 4–7. Cambridge, U.K., 1966–1978.

Sylla, Richard, and Gianni Toniolo, eds. *Patterns of European Industrialization: The Nineteenth Century.* London, 1991.

Teich, Mikulás, and Roy Porter, eds. *The Industrial Revolution in National Context: Europe and the USA.* Cambridge, U.K., 1996.

WAR AND CONQUEST

Jeremy Black

War has been central to European history and to the history of the European world. It is not a sphere separate from social history, remote in the details of operational activities, but rather an integral part of it, and the military itself has been a society of great interest and importance. Furthermore, military organization is an aspect of wider social patterns and practices, with which it intersects and interacts. Attitudes toward hierarchy, obedience, and discipline and the readiness to serve all partake of this interaction. The first crucial dimension of the dynamic of social change in and through war occurred when the military ceased to be coterminous with society, more specifically with adult male society. The origins of this process of specialization varied over time. The society of modern war can be understood primarily as a force of trained troops under the control of sovereign powers, with those powers enjoying a monopoly of such forces; the chronology and explanation of this development varies greatly from place to place depending on social and political circumstances.

The absence of developed statehood and powerful sovereign authority across much of the world from the beginning of the Christian era to about the year 1500 was such that it is generally more appropriate to think of tribal and feudal organization rather than a state-centric pattern. Yet, in areas of developed state power, such as imperial Rome and China, professional, state-controlled forces that reflected a functional specialization on the part of a portion of the male population were in place long before 1500. The relatively low productivity of agrarian economies was not incompatible with large forces at the disposal of such states, while the constraints that primitive command-and-control technology and practices placed on centralization did not prevent a considerable measure of organizational alignment over large areas. Thus, sophisticated military systems did exist in Europe prior to the second half of the second millennium, and there is no clear pattern of chronological development such that modernity can offer an appropriate theory or description. Aside from the analytical problem of assessing capability and change, there is also the more general moral issue, for the notion of "progress" toward a more effective killing and controlling machine is not one with which modern commentators are comfortable.

Any understanding of military organization must be wary of a state-centered, let alone Eurocentric, perspective, whether in definition, causality, or chronology. Many military organizations have not been under state control. Caution is advised before assuming a teleological, let alone triumphalist, account of state control of the military. It is questionable how far such a monopolization should be seen as an aspect of modernity.

Furthermore, modernity itself is a problematic concept, whether descriptive or prescriptive. Aside from the role of modernization as a polemical device in political debate, there is, in analytical terms, a difficulty in determining how best to define and dissect the concept. A series of critiques, from both within and outside the West, has eroded the triumphalist view of modernity as the rise of mass participatory democracy, secular or at least tolerant cultures, nation-states, and an international order based on restraint. Such critiques have a direct bearing on the understanding of military organization. Thus, for example, conscript armies could be seen in progressive terms in the nineteenth century as an adjunct of the extension of the male franchise. Both symbolized a new identification of state and people in countries such as France, Germany, and Italy, but not in Britain or the United States. Conscription was also important in the ideology of communist states; and after 1945, as a new politics was created in what had been fascist societies, conscription was seen, for example in Germany and Italy, as a way to limit the allegedly authoritarian and conservative tendencies of professional armies, particularly their officer corps.

In the more individualistic Western cultures of the 1960s, however, conscription as a form, rationale, and ideology for the organization of the military resources of society seemed unwelcome. Military service was presented less in terms of positive images, such as incorporating ideology and social mobility, and more as an unwelcome chore and a form of social control. Conversely, in Latin America, conscription had a more (though far from universal) positive image, in part because military service was seen as a means for useful training and for economic opportunity and social improvement, both for individuals and for society.

That the purpose of the military is to win wars is no longer a self-evident proposition; nor is the notion that military organization—the social systematization of organized force—is designed to improve the chances of doing so. Such propositions fail to note the multiple goals of military societies. Even if the prime emphasis is on war-winning, it is necessary to explain the processes by which such an emphasis affects the operation and development of such organizations.

THE PURPOSE OF MILITARY ORGANIZATIONS AND SOCIETIES

Military organizations and societies serve a number of functions, some of which are publicly defined and endorsed, while others are covert, implied, or implicit. One public function is national security, while an implied function is employing people and providing possible support for policing agencies. These functions did not develop uniformly, but rather varied, in an objective sense, by state, period, and branch of the military, and, in a more subjective sense, with reference to the views of leaders, groups, and commentators within and outside the military. Thus French army operations against large-scale smuggling gangs in the frontier region of Dauphiné in 1732 could be classed as policing or national security or both. The instrumentality of the military is not only a matter of defining its purposes but extends to the character of the military organization in a particular society. In other words, its purpose may not be that of achieving a specific military outcome; the prime objective of the creators of the organization may be the pursuit of certain domestic sociopolitical goals.

Political objectives. Military organization has two aspects: the internal structure and ethos of armed forces, and the relationship of the armed forces to the rest of society, specifically with reference to recruitment and control. Politicians may be more concerned to ensure "democracy" in the armed forces, or republican values, or revolutionary zeal, or commanders who will or will not automatically obey the government, than they are to consider the war-making potential and planning of the armed forces. Indeed the latter may be left to the professional military, provided the desired control culture and value system are in place.

The central feature of British military organization arising from British society was that it answered to civilian control and did so in war as well as in peace. Similarly, in 1924 the left-wing government that gained power in France was more concerned about the ideological reasons for shortening conscripts' terms of service than about preparing for war with Germany. In the modern West operational military control and political direction are largely disaggregated, although the distinction is hard to maintain, as was discovered in peacekeeping work, for example in Bosnia.

Opposite armies. A consideration of the chronological development of military society must be prefaced by a discussion of the sociology of different military systems. The evolution of specialized forces—of trained regulars under the control of states—occurred initially against the background of a world in which there was a general lack of such specialization. As has been noted, before 1500 there was an absence of powerful sovereign authority. A tribal pattern of organization lent itself particularly to a system of military membership, such that male membership in the tribe meant having warrior status and knowledge and engaging in training and warrior activity. Diversity was evidence of the vitality of different traditions rather than an anachronistic and doomed resistance to the diffusion of a progressive model. Diversity owed something to the interaction of military capability and activity with environmental constraints and opportunities. For example, cavalry could operate easily in some areas, like Hungary, and not in others, like Norway.

The prestige of imperial states, especially Rome and China, was such that their military models considerably influenced other powers, especially the successor states to the western Roman Empire. However, much of the success of both imperial states rested on their ability to co-opt assistance from neighboring "barbarians." Any account of their military organization that offers a systematic description of the core regulars is only partial. Indeed, both imperial powers deployed armies that were in effect coalition forces. Such was the case with most major armies until the age of mass conscription in the nineteenth century, and even then was true of their transoceanic military presence. Such co-option could be structured essentially in two different ways. It was possible to equip, train, and organize ancillary units like the core regulars, or to leave them to fight in a "native" fashion. Imperial powers, such as the British in eighteenth-century India, followed both methods.

The net effect was a composite army, and such an organization has been more common than is generally allowed. The composite character of military forces essentially arises both from different tasks and from the use of different arms in a coordinated fashion to achieve the same goal: victory on the battlefield. Such cooperation rested not so much on bureaucratic organization as on a careful politics of mutual advantage and an ability to create a sense of identification. In imperial Rome the native ancillary units commonly provided light cavalry and light infantry to assist the heavy infantry of the core Roman units. The Ottoman Turks were provided with light cavalry by their Crimean Tatar allies, their Russian enemies by the Cossacks and, in the nineteenth century, by Kazakhs also. Thus, cavalry and infantry, light and heavy cavalry, pikemen and musketeers, frigates and ships of the line, tanks and helicopter gunships combined to create problems of command and control that affect organizational structures. Indeed, "native" forces operated as a parallel force with no command integration other than at the most senior level. The frequent combination of "native" cavalry and "core" infantry suggests that, in part, such military organization bridged divides that were at once environmental and sociological. This linkage complemented the symbiotic combination of pastoralism and settled agriculture that was so important to the economies of the preindustrial world.

THE EARLY MODERN PERIOD

The period 1490–1700 was one of increased interaction among areas of the world. Most active in this process were the Atlantic European powers, along with a number of other expansive powers, including in Europe the Ottomans and Russia. Military success was as much a matter of political incorporation as of technological strength, and incorporation depended on the successful allocation of the burdens of supporting military structures. The raising of men, supplies, and money was the aspect of military organization most important to the states of the preindustrial world, and the ease of the process was significant to the harmony of political entities and thus to the effectiveness of their military forces. Organization must be understood as political as much as administrative, and indeed the political nature was paramount. Rulers lacking political support found it difficult to sustain campaigns and maintain military organization. This was a problem for Charles I in his conflicts with Scotland in 1638–1640.

The use of agencies and individuals outside the control of the state to raise and control troops and warships was so widespread that it cannot be seen simply as devolved administration. This point lessens the contrast between a medieval warfare based on social institutions and structures and an early modern system based on permanent organizations maintained and managed by the state. The notion of war and the military as moving from a social matrix—most obviously feudalism—to a political context—states in a states system—is too sweeping. In both cases the bellicose nature of societies was important, as was the accentuated role of prominent individuals that was the consequence of dynastic monarchy. A habit of viewing international relations in terms of concepts such as glory and honor was a natural consequence of the dynastic commitments and personal direction that a monarchical society produced. That view reflected traditional notions of kingship and was the most plausible and acceptable way to discuss foreign policy in a courtly context. Such notions also matched the heroic conceptions of royal, princely, and aristocratic conduct in wartime. Past warrior-leaders were held up as models for their successors: the example of Henry V was a powerful one at the court of Henry VIII of England, Edward III's victories over France were a touchstone, and Henry IV of France was represented as Hercules and held up as a model for his grandson, Louis XIV.

Similarly, aristocrats looked back to heroic members of their families who had won and defended nobility, and thus social existence, through glorious and honorable acts of valor. These traditions were sustained both by service in war and by a personal culture of violence in the form of duels, feuds, and displays of courage, the same sociocultural imperative underlying both the international and the domestic sphere. This imperative was far more powerful than the cultural resonances of the quest for peace: the peace-giver was generally seen as a successful warrior, not a royal, aristocratic, or clerical diplomat.

The pursuit of land and heiresses linked the monarch to his aristocrats and peasants. As wealth was primarily held in land, and transmitted through blood inheritance, it was natural at all levels of society for conflict to center on succession disputes. Peasants resorted to litigation, a lengthy and expensive method, but the alternative, private violence, was disapproved of by state. Monarchs resorted to negotiation, but the absence of an adjudicating body, and the need for a speedy solution once a succession fell vacant, encouraged a decision to fight. Most of the royal and aristocratic dynasties ruling and wielding power in 1650 owed their position to the willingness of past members of the family to fight to secure their succession claims. The Tudors defeated the Yorkists to win England in

The Battlefield. Squares of pikemen, mounted troops, and artillery fill the battlefield of Pavia, 24 February 1525. Woodcut by Hans Schäufelein. GRAPHISCHE SAMMLUNG ALBERTINA, VIENNA

1485, the Bourbons fought to gain France in the 1580s, the Austrian Habsburgs to gain Bohemia in 1621, the Braganzas to gain Portugal in the 1640s, William III to gain the British Isles in 1688–1691, and the Romanovs to hold Russia in the 1610s.

More generally warfare created "states," and the rivalries between them were in some fashion inherent to their very existence. Examples include the importance of the *reconquista* of Iberia from Islam to Portugal, Castile, and Aragon; of conflict with the Habsburgs for the Swiss Confederation and with England for Scotland; and the importance to the Dutch Republic of the threat from Spain and then France. State-building generally required and led to war and also was based on medieval structures and practices that included a eulogization of violence. War was very important, not only in determining which dynasties controlled which lands or where boundaries should be drawn but in creating the sense of "us" and "them," which was so important to the growth of any kind of patriotism.

From 1490 to 1700 professionalization and the rise of standing (permanent) forces on land and sea created problems of political and military organizational demand. Structures had to be created and co-operative practices devised within the context of the societies of the period. It is unclear how far professionalization and the rise of standing forces created a self-sustaining dynamic for change, in an action-reaction cycle or synergy, or to what extent effectiveness was limited, therefore inhibiting the creation of a serious capability gap in regard to forces, both European and non-European, that lacked such development. This is an important issue, given modern emphasis on organizational factors, such as drill and discipline, in the rise of the Western military.

Another important factor in change and professionalization was the development of an officer corps responsive to new weaponry, tactics, and systems and increasingly formally trained, at least in part, with an emphasis on specific skills that could not be gained in combat conditions. Although practices such as purchase of military posts limited state control (or rather reflected the nature of the state), officership was a form of hierarchy under the control of the sovereign. However, most officers came from the social elite, the landed nobility, and, at sea, the mercantile oligarchy. An absence of sustained social mobility at the level of military command, reflecting more widespread social problems with the recruitment of talent, was an important aspect of organization and a constraint on its flexibility.

European forces were not the only ones to contain permanent units and to be characterized by professionalism, but the degree of development in this direction in different parts of the world cannot be readily compared because of the lack of accurate measures and, indeed, definitions. Furthermore, it is necessary to consider how best to weight the respective importance of peacetime forces and larger wartime establishments.

In accounts of global military history, the early modern period is generally presented in terms of a European military revolution defined by the successful use of gunpower weaponry on land and sea. The onset of late modernity follows either in terms of greater politicization and resource allocation and an alleged rise in determination beginning with the French Revolution, or in terms of the industrialization of war in the nineteenth century, or in both. Such a chronology, however, due to its failure to heed change elsewhere, is limited as an account of European development and flawed on the global scale.

1700–1850

In searching for periodization, it is best to abandon a Eurocentric chronology and causation. The period 1700–1850, the age before the triumph of the West, closes as the impact of the West and Westernization was felt in areas where hitherto the effect was limited: Japan, China, Southeast Asia, New Zealand, inland Africa, and western interior North America. Beginning the period in about 1700 distinguishes it from that of the initial expansion of the "gunpowder empires." It also focuses on the impact of flintlocks and bayonets, which were important in India, West Africa, Europe, and North America. Furthermore, the sociopolitical contexts of war after the seventeenth-century general crisis affected much of the world's economy, with accompanying sociopolitical strains.

The study of war in the period 1700–1850 generally focuses on war within Europe under Charles XII (king 1697–1718), Peter the Great (tsar 1682–1725), the Duke of Marlborough (1650–1722), Frederick the Great (king 1740–1786), and Napoleon (1769–1821). However, conflict within Europe was less important in raising general European military capability than the projection of European power overseas, a projection achieved in a largely preindustrial world. To this end it was the organizational capacity of the Atlantic European societies that was remarkable. The Duke of Newcastle, secretary of state for the British Southern Department, claimed in 1758, "We have fleets and armies in the four quarters of the world and hitherto they are victorious every-where. We have raised and shall raise more money this year than ever was known in the memory of man, and hitherto at 3½%."

Warships themselves were the products of an international procurement system and of what were by the standards of the age massive and complex manufacturing systems. Their supply was also a major undertaking, as was their maintenance. Neither was effortless, and any reference to the sophistication of naval organization must take note of the continual effort that was involved and the problems of supplies. Naval supply and maintenance required global systems of bases if the navies were to be able to secure the desired military and political objectives. Thus, the French in the Indian Ocean depended on Mauritius and Réunion, the British on Bombay and Madras, the Portuguese on Goa, and the Dutch on Negapatam. When in the 1780s the British considered the creation of a new base on the Bay of Bengal, they acquired and processed knowledge in a systematic fashion and benefited from an organized process of decision making.

The globalization of European power was not solely a matter of naval strength and organization. The creation of powerful syncretic Western-native forces, especially by the French and then the British in India, was also important. A different process occurred in the New World. There the Western military tradition was fractured with the creation of independent forces. Their organizational culture and practices arose essentially from political circumstances. Thus, in the United States, an independent part of the European world, an emphasis on volunteerism, civilian control, and limited size, for both army and navy, reflected the politics and culture of the new state. This could be seen in Jefferson's preference for gunboats over ships of the line.

Within Europe there was also a process of combination. Armies were largely raised among the subjects of individual rulers, but foreign troops, indeed units, were also recruited; alliance armies were built up by a process of amalgamation. Furthermore, recruiting, in some cases forcible, extended to foreign territories. The Prussians were especially guilty of this process, forcibly raising troops for example in Mecklenburg and Saxony. Amalgamation could involve subsidies and could also be motivated by operational factors, specifically the recruitment of light cavalry from peoples only loosely incorporated into the state, such as Cossacks for Russia and Crimean Tatars for Turkey.

THE WEST AND THE REST

A notion of different and distinctive European and non-European military societies, and of their related effectiveness, is visually encoded in the art and im-

Napoleon. *Napoleon at the Battle of Austerlitz,* painting (1805) by Carl Vernet. CHÂTEAU DE VERSAILLES, FRANCE/THE BRIDGEMAN ART LIBRARY

agery of (European) empire. The image of the "thin red line," an outnumbered and stationary European force, drawn up in a geometric fashion and ready to fire, is meant to suggest the potency of discipline and the superiority of form. Charging the line—or, as the case may be, the square—of the European force is a disorganized mass of infantry or cavalry, lacking uniform, formation, and discipline. Such an image is central to a teleology of military society, a notion that organization entails a certain type of order from which success flows. As an account of the imperial campaigns of the second half of the nineteenth century and of European success, such an image is less than complete and is in some respects seriously misleading. The error is even more pronounced prior to the mid-nineteenth century. European forces won at Plassey, in India (1757), and the Pyramids (1798), but they lost on the Pruth River, then in Romania (1711). The organization of forces on the battlefield was only one element in combat; some non-European forces had sophisticated organizational structures, both on campaign and in battle, and European armies themselves frequently did not fulfill the image of poised, coiled power.

Organization and tactics. The nature of the Revolutionary and Napoleonic battle was traditionally presented by British historians as an object lesson in the superiority of disciplined organization. The traditional view of Wellington's tactics in his victory over Napoleon at Waterloo in 1815 is that his infantry, drawn up in line, simply blasted away at the oncoming French columns and stopped them by fire alone—in short that an organization geared to linear forma-

tions was most successful on the battlefield. The history of successful military organization in the nineteenth century is thus in part an extension of similar formations and practices of control by the Europeans to other parts of the world and emulation by local powers, although later in the century in Europe such formations were abandoned as they represented easy targets for opposing fire.

The conventional view of the interaction of organization, discipline, and tactics on the Wellingtonian battlefield has been revised. Wellington's favored tactic was for his infantry to fire a single volley, give a mighty cheer, and then charge. The key was not firepower alone but a mixture of fire and shock. This tactic was not as uncommon elsewhere in the world as might be believed. The role of morale comes into focus as an important element of shock tactics (and also, of course, where there is reliance upon firepower). Shock tactics were not simply a matter of an undisciplined assault in which social and military organization played a minimal role, as is evident from the columnar tactics of European forces in the period. They can be presented as the organizational consequence of the *levée en masse,* the addition of large numbers of poorly trained conscripts to the army of Revolutionary France.

Columns could also be employed on the defensive, a deployment on the battlefield that required a more controlled organization. The formation was appropriate in several ways. First, it was an obvious formation for troops stationed in reserve. Thus, infantry brigades and divisions stationed in the second line would almost always have been in column, this being the best formation for rapid movement, whether it was to plug a gap, launch a counterattack, or reinforce an offensive. Columns, it can be argued, were not merely the product of a relatively simplistic military organization, a regression from the professionalism and training of the army of Frederick the Great, but an effective improvement over what had come before. A sudden onslaught by a line of columns on an attacking force, and particularly an attacking force that had been shot up and become somewhat "blown" and disorganized, was likely to have been pretty devastating. Furthermore, columns could still fire, while they could also be placed side-by-side to present a continuous front. Columns gave a defender weight, the capacity for local offensive action and solidity, for troops deployed in line came under enormous psychological strain when under attack by columns.

The danger in presenting one form of tactical deployment as necessarily weaker than another is of obscuring what actually happened in combat. Organizational structure was clearly related to tactical deployment, although the extent to which there was a causal correspondence varied. Moreover, sources reveal the limitations of effective diffusion of tactics and weaponry, both within Europe and farther afield.

1850–1945

From the mid-nineteenth century the world was increasingly under the sway of the West, directly or indirectly. The organization of the Japanese army, in response first to French and then to German models, and of the navy, under the inspiration of the British navy, was a powerful example of this impact. Such emulation, however, was more than a matter of copying a successful military machine. There was also a sociopolitical dimension that focused in particular on the impact of nationalism but also on other aspects of nineteenth-century "modernization."

Nationalism and conscription. Although systems of conscription did not require nationalism, they were made more effective by it. Nationalism facilitated conscription without the social bondage of serfdom because conscription was legitimated by new ideologies. It was intended to transform the old distinction between civilian and military into a common purpose. Although the inclusive nature of conscription should not be exaggerated, it helped in the militarization of society and, combined with demographic and economic growth, provided governments with manpower resources such that they did not need to turn to military entrepreneurs, foreign or domestic. The political

and ideological changes and increasing cult of professionalism of the nineteenth century also made it easier for the states to control their officer corps and to ensure that status within the military was set by government.

Nineteenth-century national identity was in part expressed through martial preparedness, most obviously with conscript armies. These in turn made it easier to wage war because the states were always prepared for it, or at least less unprepared than in the past. The scale of preparedness created anxiety about increases in the military strength of other powers and a bellicose response in crises. The process of mobilizing reservists also provoked anxiety, for mobilization was seen as an indicator of determination, and once it had occurred, there was a pressure for action.

These factors can be seen as playing a role in the wars begun by Napoleon III of France, Bismarck's Prussia, and the kingdom of Sardinia during the Risorgimento (the nineteenth-century struggle for Italian unification). These regimes had policies they considered worth fighting for but that were to some degree precarious; it was hoped that the successful pursuit of an aggressive foreign policy and war would lead to a valuable accretion of domestic support. The regimes of nineteenth-century Europe were operating in an increasingly volatile milieu in which urbanization, mass literacy, industrialization, secularization, and nationalism were creating an uncertain and unfamiliar world. The temptation to respond with the use of force, to impose order on the flux, or to gain order through coercion was strong. A growing sense of instability encouraged the use of might to resist or channel it and also enabled "unsatisfied" rulers and regimes to overturn the diplomatic order.

Nationalism was both a genuinely popular sentiment and one that could be manipulated to legitimize conflict. It encouraged a sense of superiority over others. Politicians and newspapers could stir up pressure for action. In societies where mass participatory politics were becoming more common, public opinion played a role in crises; in 1870 in France and Germany it helped create an atmosphere favorable for war. A political leader profited from a successful war by gaining domestic prestige and support, although the desire for such support ensured that realpolitik was generally less blatant than in the eighteenth century. Napoleon III found it easier, more conducive, and more appropriate to seek backing by waging wars or launching expeditions in Russia, Italy, China, and Mexico rather than by broadening his social support through domestic policies. These expeditions coincided with a period of domestic peace after 1848; civil war in France, in the shape of the Paris Commune, did not resume until after serious failure in foreign war. Having demonstrated and sustained a role by leading the Risorgimento, Vittorio Emanuele II, king of Sardinia and then of Italy (1861–1878), found it useful to declare war on Austria in 1866 in order to head off pressure for reform from left-wing politicians. Similar domestic problems encouraged Wilhelm I of Prussia to press for war that year and had the same effect on Franz Joseph of Austria.

Indeed, Austrian policy can in part be viewed in terms of the relationship between domestic politics and war. Success in the latter encouraged a more authoritarian politics, as in 1849 and 1865. War in 1866 seemed the only solution to the domestic political and financial problems of the Habsburg state and the sole way to tackle fissiparous nationalism, most obviously in Venetia. In the case of Prussia, but not Austria, success in war encouraged a reliance on force, a repetition of the situation in France under Napoleon I.

In the twentieth century, because of nationalism and the attendant increase in the scale of mobilization of resources, war became a struggle between societies rather than simply armies and navies. This shift affected military organization. If society was mobilized for war, as was indeed the case in both world wars, then large sections of the economy were directly placed under military authority and became part of the organization of the militarized state. Other sections were placed under governmental control and regulated in a fashion held to characterize military organization. The ministry of munitions that was created in Britain in World War I was as much part of the military organization as the artillery. Other sections of society not brought under formal direction can be seen as part of the informal organization of a militarized state. World War I saw the expansion of universal military training and service, with conscription introduced in Britain (1916), Canada (1917), and the United States (1917). This pattern of military organization not based on voluntary service was central to the armed forces of the combatants in both world wars.

SINCE 1945

An account of military organization as a product of politics is not intended to demilitarize military history; but the notion and understanding of "fit for purpose" are essentially set by those who control the military. In some situations this control is vested in the military. That is the case when the political and military leadership are similar. This is true of military dictatorships, both modern ones and their historical progenitors, such as those Roman regimes presided over by a general who had seized power, such as Vespasian, and the regime of Napoleon I.

In some societies, such as those of feudal Europe, it may not be helpful to think of separate military and political classifications of leadership. In addition, in wartime generals may be able to gain control of the definition of what is militarily necessary, both in terms of means and objectives. On the whole, however, they have had only a limited success. In dictatorial regimes, such as those of the Soviet Union and Germany during World War II, the generals were heeded only if their views accorded with those of the dictator. In democracies generals have also been subject to political direction, although with less bloody consequences.

The demise of compulsion. The situation altered after World War II, largely in response to the impact of individualism in Western society. Other factors were naturally involved in the abandonment of conscription, not least cost and the growing sophistication of weaponry, but they would not have been crucial had there not been a major cultural shift away from conscription. This shift is the most important factor in modern military organization because it has opened up a major contrast between societies that have abandoned conscription and those where it remains normal. Again, however, it is necessary to avoid any sense of an obvious teleology. Thus the pattern in Britain was one of a hesitant approach toward conscription, even when it appeared necessary.

In the West, war in the twentieth century became less frequent and thus less normal and normative. Instead, war is increasingly perceived as an aberration best left to professionals. There has also been a growing reluctance to employ force in domestic contexts. Governments prefer to rely on policy to maintain internal order, and the use of troops in labor disputes is less common than earlier in the century. Britain phased out conscription in 1957–1963, and the United States moved in 1973 to an all-volunteer military that reduced popular identification with the forces.

It has become unclear whether a major sustained conflict in which such states were attacked would lead to a form of mass mobilization. That seems unlikely, for both political and military reasons; but were another world war to occur it might lead to mobilization designed to engender and sustain activism as much as to provide military manpower. The abandonment of conscription reflects the determination of the size and purpose of the military by political factors that are subject to political debate.

A Struggle between Societies. French troops board trains at Dunkerque, August 1914.
©ROGER-VIOLLET

Control and the military. Any theory of military organization must take note of problems of internal and external control. Organization is not an abstraction: the armed forces are too important in most societies to be left out of political equations. From 1500 to 2000 in the West, external control became less of a problem. The military became an instrument of the state, most obviously in the United States. There, the most powerful military in world history never staged a coup and had relatively little influence on the structure, contents, or personnel of politics. A cult of professionalism was central to the ethos of the American officer corps, and their training is lengthy. This model was influential in Western Europe after 1945, in part due to the reorganization of society (and the military) after World War II, especially in defeated Germany and Italy, and in part thanks to the influence of the American model through NATO (North Atlantic Treaty Organization) and American hegemony.

Eighteenth-century intellectuals struggling to create a science of society, or to employ what would be termed sociological arguments so as to offer secular concepts for analysis, understood the importance of political control over the military. The character and disposition of force within a society is integral to understanding that society's dynamics. In 1776, for example, the Scottish economist Adam Smith offered, in his *Inquiry into the Nature and Causes of the Wealth of Nations,* an analysis of the sociology of warfare in which he contrasted nations of hunters, shepherds, husbandmen, and the "more advanced state of society" in which industry was important. These were seen as providing a hierarchy of military organization and sophistication in which "a well-regulated standing army" was vital to the defense of civilization (Smith, 1976, p. 699). Smith argued that firearms were crucial in the onset of military modernity:

> Before the invention of fire-arms, that army was superior in which the soldiers had, each individually, the greatest skill in dexterity in the use of their arms. . . . Since the invention . . . strength and agility of body, or even extraordinary dexterity and skill in the use of arms, though they are far from being of no consequence, are, however, of less consequence. . . . In modern war the great expense of fire-arms gives an evident advantage to the nation which can best afford that expense; and consequently, to an opulent and civilized, over a poor and barbarous nation. In ancient times the opulent and civilized found it difficult to defend themselves against the poor and barbarous nations. In modern times the poor and barbarous find it difficult to defend themselves against the opulent and civilized. (p. 708)

Smith exaggerated the military advantages of the "opulent and civilized," but he captured an important shift. Those he termed "civilized" were no longer on the defensive.

See also **Military Service** *(in this volume);* **The Military** *(volume 3); and other articles in this section.*

BIBLIOGRAPHY

Scholarly interest in war has come to be seen as unsuitable, especially in the United States. This reluctance to engage the topic accounts for the limited number of works listed here. War may be repellent, but it is impossible to understand history without considering its nature and its impact on society, politics, economics, and culture.

Asch, Ronald G. *The Thirty Years War: The Holy Roman Empire and Europe 1618–48.* New York, 1997.

Black, Jeremy. *Cambridge Illustrated Atlas of Warfare: Renaissance to Revolution 1492–1792.* Cambridge, U.K., 1996. Historical atlas and supporting text.

Black, Jeremy. *European Warfare, 1660–1815.* New Haven, Conn., 1994.

Black, Jeremy. *War and the World: Military Power and the Fate of Continents, 1450–2000.* New Haven, Conn., 1998.

Black, Jeremy. *Why Wars Happen.* London and New York, 1998. Historical survey.

Black, Jeremy, ed. *European Warfare, 1453–1815.* New York, 1999.

Black, Jeremy, ed. *War in the Early Modern World, 1450–1815.* Boulder, Colo., 1999. Puts Europe in global context.

Blanning, T. C. W. *The French Revolutionary Wars, 1787–1802.* London and New York, 1996.

Downing, Brian M. *The Military Revolution and Political Change: Origins of Democracy and Autocracy in Early Modern Europe.* Princeton, N.J., 1991.

Elias, Norbert. *The Civilizing Process.* Translated by Edmund Jephcott. Oxford, U.K., and Cambridge, Mass., 1994.

Ertman, Thomas. *Birth of the Leviathan: Building States and Regimes in Medieval and Early Modern Europe.* Cambridge, U.K., and New York, 1997. Valuable account from perspective of a comparative-historical political scientist.

Glete, Jan. *Navies and Nations: Warships, Navies, and State Building in Europe and America, 1500–1860.* Stockholm, 1993. Best study of the naval dimension.

Howard, Michael. *War in European History.* London and New York, 1976.

Lynn, John. "The Evolution of Army Style in the Modern West, 800–2000." *International History Review* 18 (1996): 505–545.

Parker, Geoffrey. *The Military Revolution: Military Innovation and the Rise of the West 1500–1800.* 2d ed. Cambridge, U.K., and New York, 1996.

Porter, Bruce D. *War and the Rise of the State: The Military Foundations of Modern Politics.* New York and Toronto, 1994.

Tallett, Frank. *War and Society in Early-Modern Europe: 1495–1715.* London and New York, 1992.

Tilly, Charles. *Coercion, Capital, and European States, A.D. 990–1992.* Rev. ed. Cambridge, Mass., 1992.

Thomson, Janice E. *Mercenaries, Pirates, and Sovereigns: State-Building and Extraterritorial Violence in Early Modern Europe.* Princeton, N.J., 1994.

Wilson, Peter H. *German Armies: War and German Politics, 1648–1806.* London, 1998.

SCIENCE AND THE SCIENTIFIC REVOLUTION

John Henry

Although it remains to some extent a contested historiographical conception, most historians of science agree that the designation "scientific revolution" refers in a meaningful way to a period of comparatively rapid and radical change in the understanding of the natural world. During the scientific revolution the world picture shifted from a geocentric, finite cosmos of nested heavenly spheres, which allowed no empty space, to a heliocentric solar system in an infinite universe that was void except where it was dotted with stars. There arose a new worldview in which nature and all its parts were regarded as a giant machine, capable of being understood almost entirely in physical terms. Going hand in hand with this were new theories of motion and of the generation and organization of life, a revised human anatomy, and a new physiology. Use of the experimental method to discover truths about the natural world and of mathematical analysis to help in understanding it, led to the emergence of new forms of organization and institutionalization of scientific study. In particular this period saw the formation of societies devoted to the understanding of the natural world and the exploitation of natural knowledge for the improvement of human life.

THE RENAISSANCE AND THE SCIENTIFIC REVOLUTION

The scientific revolution resulted from such a huge range of causal factors that it is impossible to give a precise account of its causes. To speak in very general terms, however, it can be seen as a period in which the intellectual authority of traditional natural philosophy gave way to new conceptions of how knowledge is discovered and established with some degree of certainty. Accordingly, it is easy to see that the scientific revolution constitutes an important part of the wider changes in intellectual authority that were characteristic of the Renaissance, and so it can be said to share the same general causes as this major change in Eu-

ropean history. A full account of its causes would, therefore, have to encompass the decline of the old feudal system and the rise of commerce, together with the concomitant rise of strong city-states and national monarchies, during a period of increasing decline of the Roman Catholic Church and the Holy Roman Empire.

Also relevant was the discovery and exploration of the New World and other parts beyond Europe, producing the beginnings of an awareness of cultural relativism as well as a realization that traditional wisdom, such as the impossibility of life in the antipodes, could be, and was, misconceived. The invention of paper, printing, the magnetic compass, and gunpowder also had major cultural and economic repercussions, which can be seen to have had a direct bearing on changes in attitudes to natural knowledge. Furthermore, at a time when natural philosophy was seen as the handmaiden to the "Queen of the Sciences," theology, the fragmentation of western Christianity after the Reformation could hardly fail to have a major impact. Similarly, the recovery of ancient learning by secular humanist scholars, and the emphasis of the humanists themselves on the belief that knowledge should contribute to human dignity and the *vita activa* (active life) lived pro bono publico (which they held to be morally superior to the *vita contemplativa* or contemplative life), directly effected the acquisition of knowledge of nature and beliefs about how that knowledge should be used.

Skepticism and empiricism. The humanists' discovery of works like *The Lives of the Philosophers* by Diogenes Laertius (fl. 3d century A.D.) and *De natura deorum* (On the nature of the gods) by Cicero (106–43 B.C.) made it plain that Aristotle (384–322 B.C.), who had become the supreme authority in philosophy during the Middle Ages, was by no means the only philosopher, and was not even the most admired among the ancients themselves. Furthermore, the discovery of writings by other philosophers, including Plato (c. 428–347 B.C.), the neo-Platonists, Stoics,

HISTORIOGRAPHY AND THE SCIENTIFIC REVOLUTION

The historical reality of the scientific revolution has been vigorously contested. In some cases, however, the contention focuses merely on the suitability of the phrase "scientific revolution." Can a revolution take two centuries to be accomplished? Can it be called a revolution if it did not overthrow, against vigorous resistance, something that was there before? Since there was nothing corresponding to what we think of as science before this period in what way was it a *scientific* revolution? Objections of this kind can be dealt with simply by expressing a willingness to call it something else. But no other designation has ever caught on and, for all its faults, "scientific revolution" seems as good a name for this historical phenomenon as any. There is one much more substantial criticism, however, which claims that the term "revolution" is seriously misleading because of its implication that this period marks a disjunction with the past. Promoting what is called the "continuity thesis," critics who take this line argue that all the seemingly new developments in scientific knowledge were foreshadowed in the medieval period, or can be shown to have grown out of earlier practices or ways of thinking in an entirely continuous way. It seems fair to say, however, that subscribers to the continuity thesis tend to be concerned almost exclusively with developments in the technical and intellectual content of the sciences, where continuities can indeed be shown, and pay scant regard to the social history of science, where discontinuities with the past are much harder to ignore.

Indeed, the continuity thesis can be seen as an outgrowth of a major historiographical division between historians of science. During the early period of the formation of history of science as a discipline, from the beginnings of the cold war, historians of science formed into rival groups, dubbed internalists (who concentrated exclusively upon internal technical developments in science) and externalists (who looked to the influence of the wider culture to explain scientific change). Neither approach was satisfactory. The analyses of the externalists were often too far removed from the actual practice of science to fully understand historical developments. Internalists might have been right to suggest that we can learn more about Newton's work by looking at the work of Johannes Kepler or Galileo Galilei than we could by looking at the Puritan Revolution, but their analyses suggested that history was driven by great men, individual geniuses different from their contemporaries. Internalism completely failed to explain why change was seen to be necessary and how consensus was formed about the validity of new knowledge claims. It also suffered from a built-in whiggism, focusing on ideas or ways of thinking that clearly foreshadowed modern scientific ideas and failing to acknowledge the historical importance of blind alleys, misconceptions, and superseded knowledge.

In the later twentieth century there was something of a rapprochement, largely as a result of the influence of the historian and philosopher of science, Thomas Kuhn (1922–1997), and the new sociology of scientific knowledge that grew out of his work. The best of this work in the history of science pays proper attention to both the context within which the science in question is produced and the demands of technical and theoretical restraints and procedures. It is now possible to understand how even the most recondite and technical developments in science must owe something to the social context from which they emerge, although in many cases the relevant context will not be the wider context of the society at large, but the more local context of particular specialist or professional groups and their working milieu. From this perspective, the claims of the continuity thesis are much harder to sustain. Although technical developments in the early modern period can be shown to have a continuity with much earlier theories and practices, the contexts within which these ideas and practices were upheld and used, whether on the macrosociological or microsociological scale, can be seen to be radically different. In the end, then, whether we call it the scientific revolution or not, it remains undeniably true that the means used to acquire and establish knowledge of nature, the institutional setting within which that knowledge was validated and valorized, and the substantive content of that knowledge was vastly different in 1700 from the way it was in 1500.

and Epicureans provided a fund of alternatives to the all-pervasive Aristotelianism. One of the revived ancient philosophies was the skepticism of the later Academy, the much-admired school founded by Plato in Athens. Eclectic attempts to combine the best features of the ancient philosophies met with some success in moral and political philosophy, but were less successful in natural philosophy. One alternative, therefore, was to switch allegiance from Aristotle to Plato, or some other ancient sage. Other natural philosophers, however, perhaps more disoriented or more dismayed by the overthrow of traditional intellectual authority, or perhaps more sympathetic to the revived skepticism, tended to reject recourse to any authority

Surveying the Stars. The first transit instrument (used to measure the right ascension of a star, the celestial equivalent of longitude), built in 1684 by the Danish astronomer Ole Rømer (1644–1710). Engraving by Peter Horrebow, 1735. Rømer demonstrated the finite speed of light, estimating it to be 140,000 miles per second, and invented a thermometer that influenced D. G. Fahrenheit. He also held numerous government offices, serving as mayor of Copenhagen and a member of the royal council of Denmark. SCIENCE MUSEUM, LONDON/ SCIENCE AND SOCIETY PICTURE LIBRARY

and turned to personal experience as the best means of acquiring knowledge of nature.

This new attitude to the acquisition of knowledge gained further momentum, certainly among Protestant scholars, when Luther rejected the authority of the pope and the priest in religion, and encouraged everyone to read the Bible for themselves. The natural world was often regarded as God's other book, and just as the faithful were now expected to read the Book of Scripture for themselves, so it seemed to devout natural philosophers that God could be served by reading the Book of Nature. Where once natural philosophy had served as "handmaiden" to the doctrinal theology of the Church of Rome, it immediately became more important and more controversial when arguments raged as to who held the true faith. Although the traditional close affiliation between Aristotelianism and Roman Catholicism (brought about largely through the efforts of Thomas Aquinas, 1225–1274), meant that many, especially Catholics, continued to support Aristotelianism, for others it was seen as a Catholic natural philosophy, or a pagan one, and in either case was deemed unsuitable as a support for Christianity.

The time was ripe, therefore, for the development of a new experiential or empiricist approach to the understanding of the physical world. This new attitude was clearly exemplified by the radical Swiss religious, philosophical, and medical reformer known as Paracelsus (1493–1541). He not only wrote reformist works, developing a uniquely original system of medicine, but he also explicitly defended his new approach on empiricist grounds. In an announcement of the course he intended to teach at the University of Basel in 1527, for example, he rejected "that which those of old taught" in favor of "our own observation of nature, confirmed by extensive practice and long experience."

Another revolutionary empiricist was Andreas Vesalius (1514–1564), professor of surgery at Padua University. His reputation was based not only on his superbly illustrated anatomical textbook, *De humani corporis fabrica* (1543), but also on his new method of teaching. Where previously anatomy lecturers read from one of Galen's anatomical works while a surgeon performed the relevant dissections, Vesalius dispensed with the readings and performed his own dissections, talking the students through the procedure and what it revealed. It helped that Vesalius also had an anatomical lecture theater specially built with steeply raked tiers of seats, allowing all students a clear and not-too-distant view of the cadaver. It was easy to justify such detailed anatomical studies on religious and intellectual grounds. Human anatomy revealed the supreme handiwork of God, the great artificer of the world, and knowledge of it was important for the medical practitioner. A number of new discoveries by Vesalius and his successors at Padua, as well as their emphasis on the importance of comparative anatomy for the understanding of the human body, led to William Harvey's discovery of the circulation of the blood.

Harvey was a student at Padua between 1597 and 1602, and continued with the kind of anatomical study he learned at Padua upon his return to England. Although resisted at first, Harvey's experimental demonstrations of his discovery (published in 1628) were so elegant, and his audience so used by now to the relevance of experiment in revealing truths about nature, that his theory soon became accepted. This meant that the whole system of Galenic physiology, which was based on the assumption that the venous system and the arterial system were separate and unconnected (the former originating from the liver and the latter from the heart) had to be recast. The result was a marshaling of effort by anatomists and physiologists throughout Europe, leading to numerous new discoveries.

Perhaps the most significant outcome of this, from the point of view of the social historian, was an increased respect for medicine that seemed to be based on the latest specialist knowledge of the working of the body and of the physical world. Following Harvey, a vigorous movement known as iatromechanism sought to explain health and disease in terms of the body as a machine consisting of levers driven by hydraulic systems, and the like. Iatromechanism went hand in hand with the mechanical philosophy—the most successful system of natural philosophy developed to replace traditional Aristotelianism, which had become increasingly untenable throughout the seventeenth century. When the mechanical philosophy was subsequently revised in the light of Newton's doctrines, there developed a Newtonian version of iatromechanism. This clear foreshadowing of the more successful scientific medicine that began to be developed in the nineteenth century, essentially owed its origins to the demands of medical students in Padua and throughout Europe for better opportunities for anatomical study. These developments clearly suggest a belief among the early modern public that knowledge of nature is useful for improving medicine, and a willingness among doctors to exploit not only their knowledge of nature, but also their knowledge of public expectation.

Magic and pragmatism. We have seen how the Renaissance revival of skepticism, together with a new awareness that Aristotle was never the unique philosophical giant that the Middle Ages had taken him to be, led to a rejection of authority and increased attempts to establish the truth about things for oneself. The revival of magic during the Renaissance had a similar effect. As a result of church opposition to its more demonological aspects, magic tended to be excluded from the medieval universities and became widely separated from natural philosophy, both intellectually and institutionally. The only exception to this was astrology, which was taught in the medical faculties as an essential aid for the medical practitioner in prognosis and diagnosis. Unfortunately, as with the other aspects of natural magic (that is, magic supposedly based on the natural but occult powers of physical bodies), astrology also attracted the attentions of mountebanks and frauds seeking only to make money out of a gullible public. The result was that magic in general seemed disreputable to most natural philosophers. The image of magic dramatically changed, however, as a result of the Renaissance recovery of various ancient magical texts, especially the Hermetic corpus, a body of magical writings attributed to Hermes Trismegistus, who was taken to be an ancient sage, contemporaneous with or perhaps even older than Moses. It is now known that the Hermetic writings date from about the first century A.D. or later, but because they were held to be written at about the same time as the Pentateuch they were regarded as one of the earliest records of human wisdom. It seemed that magic was a respectable pursuit after all and its study enjoyed a huge revival in the Renaissance.

This in turn provided a further boost to the rise of empiricism. The natural magic tradition was always based on empirical, or trial and error, methods for bringing about particular effects. Critics of the magical tradition, indeed, decried its excessive empiricism and its lack of theoretical, explanatory grounding. According to Aristotelian natural philosophy physical phenomena should be explained in terms of the four causes and the four manifest qualities. Occult qualities were those which defeated efforts to reduce them to the manifest qualities and could not, therefore, be accommodated in Aristotelian explanations. The failure of occult qualities to fit in with Aristotelian theory was once seen as damaging criticism, but by the end of the sixteenth century it began to be seen as so much the worse for Aristotelian theory. From Francis Bacon's (1561–1626) suggestion that astrology, natural magic, and alchemy are sciences of which "the ends and pretences are noble," to Isaac Newton's (1642–1727) insistence that the cause of gravity remained occult in spite of his mathematical account of the universal principle of gravitation, natural magic came to be amalgamated with natural philosophy. The resulting hybrid is recognizable to us today as being closer to modern science than scholastic Aristotelian natural philosophy could ever have been. Certainly the empiricism and the practical usefulness which we regard as characteristic of science today were never features of traditional natural philosophy before the scientific revolution, but they were taken-for-granted aspects of the magical tradition. Traditional natural philosophy was concerned to explain phenomena in terms of causes, the new natural philosophy could forgo causative explanations in favor of a reliable knowledge of facts and how they might be exploited for human advantage.

If the rise of magic was made possible by its newly acquired respectability after the recovery of the Hermetic corpus, its adoption in practice owed more to its promise of pragmatic usefulness than to any Hermetic doctrine. The same concern for the pragmatic uses of knowledge can be seen in the increasing attention paid by scholars and other intellectuals to the techniques and the craft knowledge of artisans. Some notable individuals took pains to discover the secrets of specific areas of craft know-how and to communicate them to scholars, while others remained content to talk in general terms of the potential importance of craft knowledge. The Spanish humanist and pedagogue, Juan Luis Vives (1492–1540), for example, acknowledged the importance of trade secrets in his encyclopedia, *De disciplinis* (On the disciplines; 1531). Francis Bacon, lord chancellor of England, similarly, wanted to include the knowledge and techniques of artisans in a projected compendium of knowledge which was to form part of his *Instauratio magna* (*Great Restoration*), a major reform of learning. Bacon's influence in this regard can be seen not only in various groups of social reformers in England during the Civil War years and the interregnum, but also in the Royal Society of London for the Promotion of Useful Knowledge, one of the earliest societies devoted to acquiring and exploiting knowledge of nature (1660). The Society made a number of repeated attempts, using specially produced questionnaires, to ask its members to return information about local craft techniques and artisans' specialist knowledge in and around their places of residence. The idea was to produce a "History of Trades" to supplement the usual natural histories.

PATRONS, COLLECTORS, AND SOCIETIES

The emphasis upon the pragmatic usefulness of knowledge found further support from the increasing num-

SCHOLARS AND CRAFTSMEN

From the sixteenth century onward the Aristotelian natural philosophy, which dominated the curricula in university arts faculties all over Europe, came increasingly under attack. One focus of that attack was the contemplative nature of the Aristotelian philosophy (as it was taught), and the lack of any concern with practical knowledge. Some scholars sought to correct this by deliberately seeking out craft knowledge and reporting it to their fellow scholars. One of the major examples of this can be seen in the increasingly economically important area of mining and metallurgy. The first printed account of Renaissance mining techniques, including instructions on the extraction of metals from their ores, how to make cannons, and even how to make gunpowder, was *De la pirotechnia* (1540) of Vannoccio Biringuccio (1480–1539). Written in Italian by a mining engineer who rose to the rank of director of the papal arsenal in Rome, it was evidently intended as an instruction manual for others working in similar circumstances to Biringuccio himself. This can be compared with *De re metallica* (1556) of Georgius Agricola (1494–1555). Agricola was a humanist scholar who taught Greek at Leipzig University before turning to medicine. Practicing in a mining area, and initially interested in the medicinal uses of minerals and metals, he soon developed a compendious knowledge of mining and metallurgy. The fact that *De re metallica* was published in Latin shows that it was aimed at an audience of university-trained scholars, not at miners or foundry workers. Furthermore, the book's numerous editions and wide dissemination throughout Europe show that Agricola did not misjudge the audience.

A similar interest in the smelting of ores and the recovery of metals can also be seen in the first systematic study of magnets and magnetism, *De magnete* of 1600, published by a royal physician to Elizabeth I of England, William Gilbert (1544–1603). Although principally concerned to use the spontaneous movements of magnets to show how the earth itself might also move (Gilbert was the first to realize that the earth was a giant magnet), in order to support the Copernican theory, Gilbert also took the opportunity to report on all the practical know-how associated with magnets. As well as the metallurgical aspects, therefore, he also wrote at length on the use of the magnet in navigation, with a great deal of extra information on navigation besides. In this he explicitly drew upon the work of Robert Norman (fl. 1590), a retired mariner and compass maker who had recently discovered a way of using magnets to determine longitude even when the heavenly bodies were obscured by clouds or fog.

Although there undoubtedly was an increased awareness of craft know-how and a willingness to accept and exploit its practical usefulness, it is important to avoid overstating the case. During the 1930s and 1940s a number of marxist historians seemed to forget the role of the scholars in this and to suggest that modern science owed its origins to the working man. The historian Edgar Zilsel (1891–1944) even went so far as to argue that the experimental method was developed by artisans. This in turn led more conservative historians of science, no doubt concerned to deny the validity of marxist approaches, to reject the role of craft knowledge altogether and even to deny that early modern natural philosophers had any concern with practical matters. In the post–cold war age it is easier to see, however, that the knowledge of craftsmen and artisans was taken up by scholars during the scientific revolution but it was chiefly the scholars' idea to do so; it was not something that was imposed upon them by the craftsmen. This, and the fairly obvious fact that there was indeed very little of any immediate practical consequence that resulted from the new collaboration, suggests that the main concern of scholars was to discover new ways of establishing certain knowledge to replace the newly realized inadequacies of ancient authority.

ber of secular patrons in the Renaissance period. The earliest groupings of empiricist investigators of nature all seem to have been brought together by wealthy patrons, particularly by sovereigns and princes. Indeed the royal courts must have been one of the major sites for bringing together scholars and craftsmen, which we have already seen was one of the characteristic features of the scientific revolution. The amazingly elaborate court masques and festivals, conceived in order to display publicly the magnificence and glory of the ruler, required a huge team of facilitators. Learned scholars would devise appropriate themes, combining traditional notions of chivalry and honor with more fashionable lessons taken from newly rediscovered classical stories, while architects and engineers would design the elaborate settings intended to illustrate the moral themes, and a vast array of other artisans and craftsmen would be brought together to make it all a breathtaking physical reality. It is hard to imagine a comparable site during the period for the creative collaboration of scholars and craftsmen. Unless, of course, it was one of the many sites where the arts of war were conducted.

If festivals and wars were only occasional affairs, the offer of more long-term patronage to alchemists and other natural magicians, engineers, mathematicians, natural historians, and natural philosophers was obviously done with the aim of increasing the wealth, power, and prestige of the patron. Usually this meant that the patron was most concerned with some practical outcome from the work of these servants of his court. Even in the case of seemingly more remote and abstract physical discoveries, it is possible to see such practical concerns in the background. When Galileo Galilei (1564–1642) discovered the moons of Jupiter and called them the Medicean Stars, after the ruling Medici family of Florence, he was immediately associating his patrons with celestial and divine significance as well as putting them onto the star maps. But he did not stop there. By trying to produce tables of the motions of the moons of Jupiter, which he hoped would provide a means of determining longitude at sea, Galileo was potentially turning his discovery into one of the utmost practical benefit, from which the Medici could hardly fail to gain.

The political potential of natural knowledge was a major reason for Francis Bacon's concern to reform the means of acquiring knowledge and of putting it to use, as described in his various programmatic statements and illustrated in his influential utopian fantasy, *The New Atlantis* (1627). The most prominent feature of Bacon's utopia is a detailed account of a research institute, called Salomon's House, devoted to acquiring natural and technological knowledge for the benefit of the citizens. Charles II of England and Louis XIV of France clearly recognized the potential of this too, offering their patronage to what were to become the leading scientific societies in Europe, both of which were explicitly modeled on Salomon's House. In the French case at least, the Académie Royale des Sciences (1666) can be seen effectively as an arm of the state. The Royal Society, founded in the year of the restoration of the English monarchy, never gained direct state support from an administration that was preoccupied with more pressing matters. It had to be much more apologetic, therefore, in its attempts to demonstrate its usefulness to the state. Even so, it can be seen from the propagandizing *History of the Royal Society of London* (1667) and other pronouncements of the leading fellows that the most committed members of the Society, at least, saw their experimental method as a means of establishing truth and certainty and so ending dispute. This, in turn, was presented as a model which could be used to bring an end to the religious disputes that had divided England since before the Civil Wars, and to establish order and harmony in the state. The existence, to say nothing of the success, of the Académie and the Royal Society shows that the new natural philosophy was far more directly concerned with political matters than the natural philosophy of the medieval period.

Another important feature of the interest of wealthy patrons in natural marvels was the development of what were called cabinets of curiosities, collections of mineral, vegetable, and animal rarities and oddities, or of elaborate or allegedly powerful artifacts. Originally envisaged, perhaps, as nothing more than spectacles symbolizing the power and wealth of the collector, the larger collections soon came to be seen as contributing to natural knowledge, providing illustrations of the variety and wonder of God's Creation. The curator of Archduke Ferdinand of Tyrol's (1529–1595) collection, Pierandrea Mattioli (1500–1577), for example, became one of the leading naturalists of the age. Focusing particularly on the botanical specimens in the collection, Mattioli greatly superseded the work of the ancient authority on botany, Dioscorides (fl. 1st century A.D.), in the influential commentaries included in his Latin edition of Dioscorides's herbal (1554). Part of the success of this work derived from the accurate illustrations, supplied by craftsmen also under Ferdinand's patronage. The larger and more successful collections soon became early tourist attractions, drawing gentlemanly visitors on their "Grand Tours." Perhaps more significant for the spread of natural knowledge was the fact that acquisition of new specimens for the collections demanded extensive networks of interested parties, communicating with one another about the latest discoveries and where to acquire them. Eventually, of course, these collections and their obvious pedagogical uses inspired the formation of the more publicly available botanical gardens, menageries, and museums. Indeed in some cases, the larger collections formed the nucleus of the first public museums. The collection of the Tradescant family, acquired by Elias Ashmole (1617–1692), formed the nucleus of the Ashmolean Museum in Oxford, while Sir Hans Sloane's (1660–1753) collection

Cabinet of Curiosities. The *cabinet des curiosités* or *Wunderkammer* (collection of natural wonders) of the Neapolitan apothecary Ferrante Imperato (1550–1625). Etching from his *Historia naturale* (Naples, 1599). By permission of the Houghton Library, Harvard University

provided an impressive beginning for the British Museum in London.

The new appearance of formal societies or academies devoted to the study of nature is another characteristic of the scientific revolution. In what Bernard de Fontenelle (1657–1757), secretary of the Académie Royale des Sciences from 1697, called the "new Age of Academies," groups of thinkers came together to collaborate in the new understanding of the natural world. In some cases the group was called together by a wealthy patron with an interest in natural knowledge and its exploitation. One of the earliest of these was the group of alchemists, astrologers, and other occult scientists brought together at the court of Rudolf II (1552–1612) in Prague, another was the Accademia dei Lincei (Academy of the Lynxes), founded by the marchese di Monticelli, Federico Cesi (1585–1630). The evident attractiveness of such collaborative enterprises can also be seen in the astonishing interest shown by scholars all over Europe in the Brotherhood of the Rosy Cross, whose intended reforms of learning, based on alchemy, Paracelsianism, and other occult ideas were announced in two manifestos which appeared in 1614 and 1615. In fact, to the disappointment of those like René Descartes (1596–1650) who tried to make contact with them, the Brotherhood seems to have been as fictitious as Salomon's House. If Rosicrucianism came to nothing, however, Bacon's vision, as we have already seen, had profound effect.

The self-consciously reformist attitudes of the early scientific societies, and their public pronouncements of their methods and intentions in journals and other publications, mark them out as completely different from the universities. It used to be said that the universities during this period were moribund institutions, completely enthralled by traditional Aristotelianism, and blind to all innovation. This has now been shown to be completely unjustified, and the important contributions of some members of university arts and medical faculties to scientific change have been reasserted. Nevertheless, it seems fair to say that it was usually individual professors who were innovatory, not the institutions to which they belonged. If there were exceptions to this it was in the smaller German universities, where the local prince might hold greater control over the university by his patronage. A number of such universities introduced significant changes in their curricula. In particular, the introduction of what was known as *chymiatria* or chemical medicine (embracing Paracelsianism and rival alchemically inspired forms of medicine) as a new academic discipline radically transformed a number of German universities. Even so, for the most part European universities were slow to change and were institutionally committed to traditional curricula. In the case of the new academies or societies, however, the institutions themselves seemed innovatory, and they had a much greater effect on changing attitudes to natural knowledge.

MATHEMATICS, INSTRUMENTS, AND THE UNDERSTANDING OF NATURE

Another important aspect of the scientific revolution was the rise in status of mathematics and mathematicians, and the increasing use of mathematics to understand the physical world. There had always been mathematical practitioners of various kinds throughout the Middle Ages but their disciplines were regarded as inferior to natural philosophy. Mathematicians were able to dramatically revise their roles during the decline of Aristotelianism, capitalizing on their claims to be able to offer certainty at a time when previous intellectual authorities seemed unreliable, and on their claims to be able to fulfill the demand for practically useful know-how.

Like the occult arts, the use of mathematics was always intended to have practical consequences. With the increased opportunities provided by secular patronage, and demands for surveyors, military engineers, navigators, cartographers, and the like, mathematicians were increasingly admired, and held themselves in higher intellectual esteem. This provides the social background for even so technical an innovation as Copernican astronomy, in which the earth, previously held to be stationary at the center of the world system, was held to rotate around its own axis every twenty-four hours and to continuously revolve around the sun. For all but a tiny handful of people, when Nicholas Copernicus's (1473–1543) book appeared in 1543, it simply showed how the geometry of the heavens might be reimagined in order to facilitate the calculations of planetary position demanded for astrology, navigation, and the establishment of church feast days. For Copernicus himself, however, and a few mathematically minded followers, the mathematics was sufficient to reveal the truth of the way things are. For Aristotelians, the mathematics was incapable of explaining how the earth could move. Only physics could do that, and physics made it clear that the earth is incapable of motion through the heavens. Copernicus and his followers accepted that they could not provide a physical explanation of the earth's motion but insisted, against all reason as far as traditional nat-

ural philosophers were concerned, that the mathematics was sufficient to show that it must be moving.

The practical success of Copernican astronomy compared to the traditional geocentric astronomy, increasingly held sway and eventually led to the development of a new physics, developed by mathematicians like Galileo, Descartes, and Newton. It is important to note, however, that these developments cannot be properly understood without paying attention to the changing status of mathematics and mathematicians during the scientific revolution. Without those social changes, Copernican theory might have remained merely an instrumentalist way of calculating planetary movements, while the physics of the world system remained the intellectual province of the natural philosopher and, therefore, remained steadfastly geocentric.

The change in status of the mathematician was brought about not only by the mathematical superiority of the new astronomy over the old. Mathematicians were proving increasingly successful in many different areas, usually to great practical benefit. One aspect of this was the development of perspective techniques, which had such an impact on painting and bas-relief. Another was in the development of algebra, which allowed the solution of previously intractable problems. There seem to be two major strands to these developments. On the one hand, thanks to an increasing availability of elementary mathematical education, useful mathematical techniques increasingly found their way into the crafts. This in turn was picked up by those humanist scholars who recognized the importance of craft know-how and its techniques. On the other hand, more elite mathematicians, such as astronomers, increasingly sought to remove the barriers between mathematics and natural philosophy. The subsequent rapid development of algebra strongly suggests that these two strands easily came together. Elite mathematics tended to be concerned with classical geometry, while algebra, being an arithmetical art, seems to have developed first among more lowly practitioners coming out of the more arithmetical elementary abacus schools. It was not long, however, before algebra was increasingly taken up by elite mathematicians.

The difficulty and tedium of many mathematical procedures ensured the invention and promotion of numerous instruments intended to provide much-needed shortcuts for practitioners in the field. Some of these, like the astrolabe, had a long history, but new ones, some more successful and long-lived than others, were continually appearing. (The slide rule, for example, developed out of various calculating devices invented in the seventeenth century and was an essential element in any practical mathematician's kit until the advent of the pocket calculator in the late twentieth century.) Arising out of the mathematical instrument trade came what was called the philosophical instrument trade. The labeling seemed to perpetuate the old distinction between mathematics and natural philosophy but the evidence shows that these new instruments were developed by more elite mathematicians concerned to show the relevance of mathematical know-how to natural philosophy. The model was undoubtedly the magnetic compass, an instrument which worked by the occult power of the magnet but which was clearly an aid for the mathematical art of navigation. Perhaps the most powerful and exciting philosophical instruments were the telescope and the microscope, but there were others which proved to be extremely important, such as the barometer, the air pump, and the thermometer. In all cases the increasingly routine use of such instruments further reinforced the validity and superiority of the empirical approach to the understanding of nature. Similarly, they provided further dramatic evidence of the usefulness of the new science. The barometer, originally produced to demonstrate a theory about the nature of the void and the working of pumps, quickly became useful for indicating changing weather conditions, and the telescope was never confined to looking at the stars but was immediately put to more mundane uses.

SCIENCE IN A RELIGIOUS SOCIETY

The medieval belief that natural philosophy should be a handmaiden to theology thrived throughout the scientific revolution. For the most part, assumptions that natural truths and truths about religion could not be incompatible with one another (both being established by God) meant that natural philosophy and religion could keep a healthy distance apart. The Roman Catholic Church was unconcerned about the implications of Copernican astronomy, for example, until the highly ambitious Florentine mathematician, Galileo, made a public issue of its relevance to Church doctrine. The Church had been happy to regard Copernican astronomy as a hypothetical system used only to facilitate calculations, but Galileo's telescopic discoveries dramatically showed that the traditional Aristotelian world picture could not be physically true. Furthermore, Galileo was among the first to bring to the attention of other intellectuals that some mathematicians were upholding the physical truth of Copernicanism. If it was true, a number of Biblical statements which clearly implied the motion of the sun and the stillness of the earth would have to be cautiously reinterpreted. Since the Roman Catholic Church had recently taken a strict line on scriptural interpretation at the counter-reforming Council of Trent, this was bound to be a delicate matter. Galileo's own amateur efforts to show how these Biblical pronouncements should be treated, in his *Letter to the Grand Duchess Christina* (1615), only succeeded in getting him into bigger trouble with his church. The subsequent history of the "Galileo affair," up to his condemnation in 1633, must be seen as a series of unfortunate circumstances, often exacerbated by Galileo's own thoughtlessness and misjudgment of others. It cannot be seen, however, as a clear sign that religion and science were fundamentally opposed to one another. Galileo's condemnation by the Congregation of the Holy Office was the result of an unfortunate series of historical contingencies, not the inevitable result of some supposed inherent antagonism between a powerful church and the study of nature. For the majority of Renaissance and early modern thinkers, the study of nature continued to be a way of worshiping God.

In spite of the continuity of the science-as-handmaiden tradition and the continuing efforts of orthodox natural philosophers to show the usefulness of their natural philosophies for supporting religion, there can be no doubt that the new natural philosophies also contributed to the rise of atheism from the late sixteenth century. The first signs of the rise of atheism can be seen in the thought of a number of rationalist Aristotelian thinkers who, stimulated by the Renaissance recovery of more reliable texts of Aristotle's works than those known to the Middle Ages, denied God's providence and the immortality of the soul. The rediscovery of ancient Epicureanism, thanks to the discovery of a single copy of Lucretius's (c. 99–c. 55 B.C.) *De rerum natura* in 1473 and the three letters of Epicurus included in the edition of Diogenes Laertius's *Lives of the Philosophers* published in 1475, proved to be another major source for would-be atheists. This had major implications for subsequent developments, since the new mechanical philosophy was clearly based upon the atomistic theory of matter, which was the most prominent feature of Epicureanism. The mechanical philosophy of the seventeenth century rapidly came to be recognized as the only system of natural philosophy capable of replacing the compendious and comprehensive natural philosophy of Aristotle. Although there were subtly different versions of the mechanical philosophy, they were all based upon the atomistic materialism of Epicureanism.

Atheism and natural theology. All the promoters of the mechanical philosophy, with the possible ex-

Scientific Experiment. A traveling scientist demonstrates the formation of a vacuum by pumping air from a flask in which a bird is enclosed. The bird will die if the scientist is successful. *An Experiment on a Bird in the Air Pump,* painting (1768) by Joseph Wright of Derby (1734–1797). NATIONAL GALLERY, LONDON

ception of Thomas Hobbes (1588–1679), took pains to insist that their philosophy was based entirely upon theistic assumptions. There can be little doubt, however, that a significant number of their readers ignored these theistic claims and embraced a mechanistic philosophy that was to all intents and purposes atheistic. It is not easy, before the eighteenth century, to find individuals who can be singled out as atheists, but it seems clear from the vast anti-atheist literature emanating from the pens of churchmen and the more devout natural philosophers, that growing numbers of atheists seemed to the faithful to pose a threat to morality and social order. The mechanical systems of Hobbes and Descartes were usually seen to offer the easiest footholds for atheists. Hobbes was an extreme materialist and seemed to imply that God too must be a material being. This was usually taken at the time as a not-too-subtle way of hinting at atheism without actually putting one's head in the noose, but a few historians now claim that Hobbes was in fact a subscriber to a recognized form of radical Calvinism. Although Descartes's system was clearly based on theistic presuppositions, it no longer required God's intervention after the initial Creation. According to Descartes, God established the laws of nature which particles of matter had to obey, then set the whole world system

in motion. From then on, the system wheeled on and on as the result of the collisions and interactions of particles of matter in a vast cosmic clockwork. Given that a prominent argument of early-sixteenth-century Aristotelian atheists had been that, contrary to Judeo-Christian claims, the world has always existed throughout eternity, it was an easy matter for Cartesian atheists to dispense with the Creation and suppose that the Cartesian world had always been turning in accordance with the blind laws of nature.

Attempts to avoid, or scotch, these atheistic interpretations of the new philosophies account for numerous prominent characteristics of the systems and the way they were presented. Underlying the dispute between Newton and Gottfried Wilhelm Leibniz (1646–1716) about the nature of God's Providence, for example, were different sensitivities to the social threat of atheism. Leibniz was willing to uphold a rationally based Cartesian approach, in which God's omnipotence enabled him to create a cosmic clockwork that never needed subsequently to be wound up or adjusted. For Newton (represented in this clash with Leibniz by his friend, Samuel Clarke, 1675–1729), more conscious of the excesses of the interregnum period in England, which were often attributed to irreligion, this was to provide a hostage to atheists.

87

Newton, accordingly, insisted that God must occasionally intervene in his Creation, and be seen (by the right-thinking natural philosopher at least) to do so. Unappreciative of the political fears underlying Newton's position, Leibniz regarded Newton's vision of God as a scandal, seeing God as a cosmic tinker incapable of getting his clockwork to function smoothly.

Such examples could easily be multiplied. The general point to note is that, in all cases where theology seems to be playing a prominent role in early modern natural philosophy, what might seem like entirely abstract arguments of philosophical theology can be seen to reflect real social concerns about the threat to society supposedly presented by those who have no moral restraints imposed by religion.

It is easy to see, therefore, that throughout the period of the scientific revolution, natural philosophy had to take account of and often defer to religion and its institutions, and that this shaped the nature of early modern science. Some historians have gone further than this, however, and have suggested that it was religion itself which somehow stimulated an increased interest in and social sanctification of the study of the natural world. The active stimulation of religion can readily be seen in the work of very devout individuals, like Robert Boyle (1627–1691), and more generally in certain fields, such as comparative anatomy and other detailed extensions of more traditional natural history, especially those made possible with microscopy. For example, the entomological studies of Jan Swammerdam (1637–1680), based on the meticulous dissection of insects, were largely pursued for the glory of God. His studies of comparative anatomy appeared posthumously under the title *Biblia Naturae* (*Bible of Nature*) in 1737. The belief that nature was God's other book, the study of which was a religious duty equivalent to reading the Book of Scripture, found its fullest expression in the tradition of natural theology (using nature to prove the omnipotence and benevolence of God), an almost exclusively British tradition which originated in the seventeenth century and flourished throughout the eighteenth century and up to the advent of Darwinism in the nineteenth.

There is another more controversial aspect to this claim about the positive stimulus provided by religion, however, and that is the suggestion that the sudden burgeoning of science in seventeenth-century England was closely associated with, if not caused by, the rise of Puritanism. First suggested in the 1930s, most influentially by the sociologist Robert K. Merton (b. 1910), this has always been a highly contested thesis. The debate has certainly led to a vastly improved historical understanding of the relations between science and religion in seventeenth-century England but it is immediately obvious that it is too Anglocentric to provide a satisfactory account of the rise of science in general, which was a Europe-wide phenomenon.

AN ASSESSMENT OF THE SCIENTIFIC REVOLUTION

The scientific revolution was not a revolution in science, since there was nothing recognizable as science in the period before it. What has made the period seem revolutionary to historians of science is the fact that the beginnings of modern science could clearly be discerned for the first time. The use of the experimental method and the techniques of analyzing the world in mathematical terms are now entirely characteristic of science. It is now taken for granted that scientific knowledge is, or should be, useful for the amelioration of the human condition. Before the Renaissance, these features of modern science were not sufficiently closely allied to the study of natural philosophy to contribute to an understanding of the natural world. The goal of natural philosophy before the scientific revolution was to understand nature in abstract philosophical terms, *not* to exploit it. By contrast, the exploitative nature of naturalistic concerns during the scientific revolution is so marked that it has been singled out by feminist historians as a major feature of the revolution itself and the beginnings of another characteristic aspect of western science, its use for the subjection of women. What made the scientific revolution, then, was the bringing together of these separate elements and approaches to make out of traditional natural philosophy, the so-called mixed mathematical sciences, natural magic, and other more utilitarian concerns, something very like modern science. In the process, each of the ingredients became impressively extended and radically transformed, some beyond recognition, and the resulting combination formed something entirely new.

The major impetus for these changes can be seen to lie principally in the demand for practically useful knowledge from wealthy patrons or other clients, or the perception of that demand from would-be incipient professionals, seeking to make a living. It is important to note, however, that the promise of utility ran far ahead of what was achieved in practical terms. The major achievements of the scientific revolution, the establishment of heliocentric astronomy, Newton's laws of motion, the circulation of the blood, and the like, were not ones which could immediately be put to use in any practical way. This is one reason why some historians of science have denied the importance of the social changes underlying the scientific

PURITANISM AND SCIENCE

Alphonse de Candolle (1806–1893), a leading Swiss botanist, became a pioneer of quantitative social history in 1885 when he compared the proportions of Protestant to Roman Catholic scientists in the Académie Royale des Sciences and the membership of the British Royal Society with the proportion of Protestants to Catholics in the general population. He concluded that Protestantism was much more conducive to science than Catholicism was. A link between Puritanism and the encouragement of science was suggested as an explanation for the remarkable burgeoning of science in seventeenth-century England by two American historians, Dorothy Stimson (1935) and Richard Foster Jones (*Ancients and Moderns;* 1936). This claim was most influentially stated, however, by the sociologist Robert K. Merton (*Science, Technology, and Society in Seventeenth-Century England;* 1938), who presented it as a special case of the link between the Protestant ethic and the "spirit of capitalism," which had been proposed in 1904 by one of the founding fathers of the discipline of sociology, Max Weber (1864–1920). Although remaining a controversial thesis, it received influential support from the eminent historian of the Puritan Revolution, Christopher Hill (*Intellectual Origins of the English Revolution;* 1965), and perhaps its most powerful support in the work of the English historian of science and medicine, Charles Webster (*The Great Instauration;* 1976).

Proponents of the thesis are careful to deny a simple causal relationship between the rise of Puritanism and the rise of science. It is readily acknowledged that only a multicausal explanation can adequately account for the sudden rise of English science, and that the rise of Puritanism is only one factor. Indeed, it is generally acknowledged that the rise of Puritanism itself must be seen as being caused by a range of social and economic factors, many of which also stimulated increased interest in, and valuation of, scientific study. To some extent, therefore, wider changes led to the rise of both Puritanism and science, but this is not to diminish the relevance of Puritanism to the rise of science, since, as Merton pointed out, the dominant means of cultural expression at this time was through religious values. Inevitably, therefore, study of the natural world would tend to be directed by and justified in terms of religious beliefs. Stated in these general terms it seems impossible to deny that the rise of science in England paralleled the dramatic changes in English religion following the rise of English Calvinism from the reign of Edward VI (1547–1553) to the Parliamentary Rebellion of 1642, and continued to do so right into the Restoration period when English science could be said to have led the world.

revolution, preferring to look at the actual achievements and seeking explanations in purely intellectual terms. It is certainly true that erstwhile marxist claims, for example, that Newton wrote the *Principia mathematica philosophia naturalis* (1687) in response to economic demands for a better science of ballistics, are almost entirely overstated. Nevertheless, it remains impossible to understand Newton's scientific achievement without considering the social changes in the relationship between mathematics and natural philosophy, which were largely brought about by increasing awareness of the potential utility and certainty of mathematical results. In the age previous to Newton's there was natural philosophy, based on speculative principles of physical causation, and there was math-

ematics, based upon completely abstract principles of numbers and lines. By the time Newton wrote his great book, he could refer easily, even in his title, to the mathematical principles *of* natural philosophy, something that would have made no sense a century before. Those mathematical principles, together with other aspects of the scientific revolution, pointed the way to modern science.

Science and society since the seventeenth century.
The perceived success of Newtonian mathematical physics had astonishing and unprecedented effects. A new faith in the power of science led not only to major reforms of traditional subjects like alchemy and optics, but also to the formation of new branches of

WOMEN, SCIENCE, AND THE SCIENTIFIC REVOLUTION

Modern science has been a major focus of concern for feminist philosophers, sociologists, and historians. Once declared by a leading feminist philosopher to be "an unexamined myth," the belief that science was somehow an exclusively masculine pursuit has been exposed to extremely illuminating critical assessment by feminists since the 1980s. This scrutiny has been directed at three aspects of the relationship between gender and science. Feminist historians have looked on the one hand at the way women have been studied by male scientists, and on the other at the roles that women have managed to play in science as a vocation, a profession, or a pastime. Meanwhile, feminist philosophers of science have looked at the grounds for, and sought to correct, all-too-common assumptions that science is gendered, and that its gender is masculine.

One of the earliest historical treatments of these themes was Carolyn Merchant's profound historical attempt to trace the roots of the modern belief that science was an essentially masculine pursuit. Significantly, in her book *The Death of Nature* (1980), she traced those roots back to the origins of modern science itself during the scientific revolution. Although a number of aspects of her book are contested, it remains an important, groundbreaking work. In particular she was the first to point to the increased use of sexual metaphors by the new natural philosophers who wanted to insist that knowledge of nature ought to be exploited for the benefit of man. Standard masculine assumptions about sexual politics came to be applied figuratively to "Mother Nature." Those who wished to join the ranks of the new kind of natural philosophers were urged by the vanguard to capture and ravish Nature, to penetrate her inner chambers. One way or another, the relationship between man and knowledge of nature was likened to the relationship between man and woman. For Francis Bacon, lord chancellor of England and would-be reformer of knowledge, it was important "that knowledge may not be as a curtesan, for pleasure and vanity only, or as a bond-woman, to acquire and gain to her master's use; but as a spouse, for generation, fruit and comfort." Such talk clearly reinforced, if any reinforcement were needed, assumptions about the passive nature of women and their role in serving men, but it also engendered an influential view of the study of nature as a masculine enterprise.

Merchant's work was followed up by others, focusing on different aspects of the story. The close links between natural philosophy and theology, for example, led to claims that western science was always "a religious calling," pursued throughout the Middle Ages within a clerical culture, and maintaining the image of the scientist as a priest of the Book of Nature even into the modern era. Accordingly, just as women were excluded from the priesthood, they were also excluded from the ranks of those deemed fit to mediate between the commonalty and God's Creation. It seems that even the courtly origins of the new scientific societies were insufficient to overcome such prejudice against women. Although noble women seem to have played some minor roles in learned circles at court, when such informal groupings became academies or societies, women were excluded (except in the Italian academies at Bologna, Padua, and Rome, where a few exceptional women were admitted as fellows). If these were the beginnings of the exclusion of women from science, in succeeding ages, as other historians have shown, women came to be considered mentally and constitutionally unfit for scientific research. By the late eighteenth century, the science from which they were excluded had turned its attention to women as scientific subjects, and male scientists established, to their own satisfaction, that women did not, and could not, measure up to men.

In spite of the barriers raised against them, a few women did manage to make their mark in the scientific revolution. Although earlier suggestions that Lady Anne Conway (1631–1679) was an influence upon the great German philosopher G. W. Leibniz may be exaggerated, her credentials as a thinker are ironically suggested by the fact that it was once assumed that her book, *Principles of the Most Ancient and Modern Philosophies* (1690) was written by a man. The authorship of Margaret Cavendish (1623–1673), duchess of Newcastle, was never in doubt for any of the six books of natural philosophy that she wrote, but perhaps for that reason they were treated with condescension at best, and ridicule at worst. Émilie du Châtelet (1706–1749), a gifted mathematician who helped to introduce the work of Leibniz and Newton to French philosophical audiences by her translation of Newton's *Principia* into French (1759), and by her own popularizing *Institutions de physique* (1740), died of childbed fever before managing to overcome the diffidence that kept her from original work. Unfortunately, therefore, the remarkable achievements of these women, and one or two others like them, serve as impressive but only partial indicators of what women might have been able to do if the sociological and cultural position of women had been anywhere near comparable to men's.

science, such as the study of electricity, and even to new sciences, geology and biology for example. Biology was envisaged as an attempt to explain the workings of the organic world in accordance with laws of nature, analogous to Newton's laws of motion, and was completely different from the merely descriptive natural history that had gone before. Newtonianism even inspired the new sciences of man which developed in the late eighteenth century. Philosophers believed that morality and political economy could also be established in a mathematically certain lawlike way. It was no accident that the morality of utilitarianism, developed in Britain by Jeremy Bentham (1748–1832) and James Mill (1773–1836), was believed to derive from a "moral calculus" analogous to the mathematical calculus developed by Newton and others. In late eighteenth-century France, thanks to Voltaire (1694–1778) and other Anglophiles, even the much-admired constitutional monarchy established after the Glorious Revolution of 1688 was seen as an outcome of the rational empiricist tradition in English science heralded by Francis Bacon, and triumphantly established by Robert Boyle (1627–1691), Newton, and John Locke (1632–1704). Newtonianism or perhaps some rather more scientistic debasement of it can be seen, therefore, as a major aspect of the intellectual background to the French Revolution. Certainly by the nineteenth century, scientific knowledge was rapidly becoming the new intellectual authority in an increasingly secular world. Accordingly, the natural sciences took an increasingly large place in education at all levels and came to be recognized as having a major role to play in more and more aspects of life and culture. This in turn stimulated specialization in different fields of science and led to professionalization.

The culmination of increasing tension between secular science and the traditional authority of religion occurred with the announcement of the theory of natural selection by Charles Darwin (1809–1882) and Alfred Russel Wallace (1823–1913) in 1858. This theory grew out of the tradition of moral calculus and the inexorable workings of laws of nature which were inspired by eighteenth century Newtonianism. Darwin and Wallace independently arrived at the principle of natural selection after reading Thomas Malthus's (1766–1834) *Essay on the Principle of Population* (1798), a work of political economy in the Newtonian mold, which had been written to oppose a reform of the poor law proposed by Prime Minister William Pitt (1759–1806). Malthus warned that poor relief would only allow the poor to propagate and place an even greater burden on the state. Better to let the poor starve now, he suggested, than that

greater numbers should have to die later. The two experienced naturalists recognized straight away that the doctrine of "survival of the fittest"—a slogan first coined by Herbert Spencer (1820–1903), a Malthusian social theorist—fitted the natural world as well as human society.

Although meeting with vigorous opposition from a number of quarters, the theory was so closely linked to earlier traditions of Newtonian political economy, including the influential laissez-faire principles developed by Adam Smith (1723–1790) and his followers, and so well supported by data from the natural world that it eventually carried the day. The established religions for the most part had to accommodate themselves to Darwinian evolution, while a number of aggressively secular movements in the social sciences used the theory to promote Social Darwinism, eugenics, and other supposedly scientifically based means of social control. The intellectual authority of science was by now so powerful that the moral acceptability, even desirability, of eugenics was routinely embraced by both the left and right of the political spectrum.

The growth and success of the physical sciences took off exponentially after World War II when government organizations, especially the military, and large industrial concerns, particularly among the growing number of multinational corporations, began to fund scientific research. This was to lead to what has been called "Big Science," a massive change in the social organization and political significance of science. The result of this was not only that the late twentieth century became a period of incredibly rapid scientific advance, but also that science and scientific values permeated every aspect of daily life.

The ensuing tendency to let scientific values determine moral and political choices has certainly not been free from problems. Although the great success of the physical sciences led to the technological developments which have enabled Western culture and capitalism to dominate the world, it has also led to real fears as to whether the world as a whole can sustain these phenomenal changes. In the middle of the twentieth century humankind saw its very existence threatened by the nuclear weaponry which had developed indirectly out of Albert Einstein's (1879–1955) attempt to resolve problems in late nineteenth-century physics. By the end of the century, however, the danger seemed to come less from the threat of a sudden cataclysm and more from the gradual destruction of the ecological balance of the world system brought about by our thoroughly scientific society. The result of these developments is that an increasing amount of hostility has been directed towards science in recent decades. Those who wish to defend science, however, point to the obvious fact that it is science which has alerted us to the dangers of global warming and other ecological threats, and that if a solution to these dangers is to be found, it is as likely to come from science as from political economy.

See also **The Enlightenment; The Protestant Reformation and the Catholic Reformation; The Renaissance** *(volume 1);* **Medical Practitioners and Medicine** *(volume 4);* **Church and Society; Magic** *(volume 5); and other articles in this section.*

BIBLIOGRAPHY

General Works

Cohen, H. Floris. *The Scientific Revolution: A Historiographical Inquiry.* Chicago, 1994.

Cohen, I. Bernard. *Revolution in Science.* Cambridge, Mass., 1985.

Dear, Peter. *Revolutionizing the Sciences: European Knowledge and Its Ambitions, 1500–1700.* London and Princeton, N.J., 2001.

Henry, John. *The Scientific Revolution and the Origins of Modern Science.* New York, 1997.

Jacob, Margaret C. *The Cultural Meaning of the Scientific Revolution.* New York, 1988.

Jardine, Lisa. *Ingenious Pursuits: Building the Scientific Revolution.* New York, 1999.

Keller, Evelyn Fox. *Reflections on Gender and Science.* New Haven, Conn., and London, 1985.

Lindberg, David C., and Robert S. Westman, eds. *Reappraisals of the Scientific Revolution.* Cambridge, U.K., 1990.

Merchant, Carolyn. *The Death of Nature: Women, Ecology, and the Scientific Revolution.* San Francisco, 1980.

Porter, Roy, and M. Teich, eds. *The Scientific Revolution in National Context.* Cambridge, U.K., 1992.

Schiebinger, Londa. *The Mind Has No Sex? Women in the Origins of Modern Science.* Cambridge, Mass., 1989.

Shapin, Steven. *The Scientific Revolution.* Chicago, 1996.

Scientific Revolution and the Renaissance

Eamon, William. *Science and the Secrets of Nature: Books of Secrets in Medieval and Early Modern Culture.* Princeton, N.J., 1994.

Evans, R. J. W. *Rudolf II and His World: A Study in Intellectual History, 1576–1612.* Oxford, 1973.

Field, J. V., and F. A. J. L. James, eds. *Renaissance and Revolution: Humanists, Scholars, Craftsmen, and Natural Philosophers in Early Modern Europe.* Cambridge, U.K., 1993.

Popkin, Richard H. *The History of Scepticism from Erasmus to Spinoza.* Rev. ed. Berkeley, Calif., 1979.

Roper, Hugh Trevor. "The Paracelsian Movement." In his *Renaissance Essays.* Chicago, 1985.

Rossi, Paolo. *Francis Bacon: From Magic to Science.* Translated by Sacha Rabinovitch. London, 1968.

Rossi, Paolo. *Philosophy, Technology, and the Arts in the Early Modern Era.* Translated by Salvator Attanasio. Edited by Benjamin Nelson. New York, 1970.

Shapin, Steven, and Simon Schaffer. *Leviathan and the Air-Pump: Hobbes, Boyle, and the Experimental Life.* Princeton, N.J., 1985.

Webster, Charles. *From Paracelsus to Newton: Magic and the Making of Modern Science.* Cambridge, U.K., 1982.

Patrons, Collectors, and Societies

Biagioli, Mario. *Galileo, Courtier: The Practice of Science in the Culture of Absolutism.* Chicago, 1993.

Findlen, Paula. *Possessing Nature: Museums, Collecting, and Scientific Culture in Early Modern Italy.* Berkeley, Calif., 1994.

Hahn, Roger. *The Anatomy of a Scientific Institution: The Paris Academy of Sciences, 1666–1803.* Berkeley, Calif., 1971.

Hunter, Michael. *Establishing the New Science: The Experience of the Early Royal Society.* Woodbridge, U.K., 1989.

Impey, Oliver, and Arthur MacGregor, eds. *The Origins of Museums: The Cabinet of Curiosities in Sixteenth- and Seventeenth-Century Europe.* Oxford, 1985.

McClellan, James E., III. *Science Reorganized: Scientific Societies in the Eighteenth Century.* New York, 1985.

Martin, Julian. *Francis Bacon, the State, and the Reform of Natural Philosophy.* Cambridge, U.K., 1992.

Moran, Bruce T., ed. *Patronage and Institutions: Science, Technology, and Medicine at the European Court, 1500–1750.* Woodbridge, U.K., 1991.

Mathematics, Instruments, and the Understanding of Nature

Bennett, J. A. "The Challenge of Practical Mathematics." In *Science, Culture, and Popular Belief in Renaissance Europe.* Edited by S. Pumfrey, P. Rossi, and M. Slawinski. Manchester, U.K., 1991.

Biagioli, Mario. "The Social Status of Italian Mathematicians, 1450–1600." *History of Science* 27 (1989): 41–95.

Dear, Peter. *Discipline and Experience: The Mathematical Way in the Scientific Revolution.* Chicago, 1995.

Hadden, Richard W. *On the Shoulders of Merchants: Exchange and the Mathematical Conception of Nature in Early Modern Europe.* Albany, N.Y., 1994.

Helden, Albert Van. "The Birth of the Modern Scientific Instrument." In *The Uses of Science in the Age of Newton.* Edited by John G. Burke. Berkeley, Calif., 1983.

Westman, Robert S. "The Astronomer's Role in the Sixteenth Century: A Preliminary Survey." *History of Science* 18 (1980): 105–147.

Wilson, Catherine. *The Invisible World: Early Modern Philosophy and the Invention of the Microscope.* Princeton, N.J., 1995.

Science in a Religious Society

Brooke, John Hedley. *Science and Religion: Some Historical Perspectives.* Cambridge, U.K., 1991.

Cohen, I. Bernard, ed. *Puritanism and the Rise of Modern Science: The Merton Thesis.* New Brunswick, N.J., 1990.

Hooykaas, R. *Religion and the Rise of Modern Science.* Edinburgh, 1973.

Hunter, Michael, and David Wootton, eds. *Atheism from the Reformation to the Enlightenment.* Oxford, 1992.

Shea, William R. "Galileo and the Church." In *God and Nature: Historical Essays on the Encounter between Christianity and Science.* Edited by David C. Lindberg and Ronald Numbers. Berkeley, Calif., 1986.

Conclusion

Galison, Peter, and Bruce Hevly, eds. *Big Science: The Growth of Large-Scale Research.* Stanford, Calif., 1992.

Hankins, Thomas L. *Science and the Enlightenment.* Cambridge, U.K., 1985.

Kevles, Daniel J. *In the Name of Eugenics: Genetics and the Use of Human Heredity.* Cambridge, Mass., 1995.

Ospovat, Dov. *The Development of Darwin's Theory: Natural History, Natural Theology and Natural Selection, 1838–59.* Cambridge, U.K., 1981.

Smith, Crosbie. *The Science of Energy: A Cultural History of Energy Physics in Victorian Britain.* Chicago, 1998.

SECULARIZATION

Hartmut Lehmann

In his famous speech "Intellectual Labor as a Profession," delivered in Munich on 7 November 1917 and subsequently published as *Science as Vocation* in 1919, Max Weber explained that increasing intellectualization and rationalization, the hallmarks of the modern world, had caused not only the growth of science but also that of disenchantment (*Entzauberung*). In his 1954 Cambridge inaugural lecture, "De descriptione temporum" (Description of the course of the ages), C. S. Lewis spoke eloquently of the "un-christening" of Europe as a fundamental process of change that had occurred sometime between the age of Jane Austen and his own time and that surpassed the kind of change Europe had undergone "at his conversion," or, as he called it, the "christening." As a result, Lewis considered most of his contemporaries "post-Christian."

Weber introduced the term "disenchantment" as a synonym for "secularization," and Lewis used the term "un-christening" for the same phenomenon. Historically the roots of the term "secularization" are the Latin noun *saeculum,* which translates as "age," "epoch," or "century," and the Latin adjective *saecularis,* which means "long-lasting," that is, lasting for a whole century. In the Middle Ages, under the influence of the theology of St. Augustine, the meanings of *saeculum* and *saecularis* became more specific. Both terms were applied mainly to worldly or secular matters as opposed to the realm of the spiritual and the divine. As a result, "to secularize" began to mean to liberate certain areas of life from the influence of the church, of the clergy, of theology, or of an attachment to the divine. With these different and in some aspects vague meanings, the term "secularization" was used in a special sense to describe the transfer of property from ecclesiastical to civil possession. Specifically the term represented the view that public education and other matters of civil policy should be conducted without the introduction of religious elements or theological considerations. Moreover, between the sixteenth and the nineteenth centuries "secularization," in many similar linguistic variations, became an integral part of western European languages.

In the course of the twentieth century, "secularization" acquired new and specific meanings as it was linked to specific theories of modernization. As the terms used by Weber and Lewis indicate, "secularization" joined a distinct group of terms that try to define and describe the various aspects of the liberation of modern science from theology, modern ethics from the Ten Commandments, and therefore modern lifestyles from Christian tradition—in short, the modern world from a world shaped and governed by the teachings and examples found in the Old and New Testaments.

Many synonyms for secularization are closely related to terms that attempt to define the opposite. Therefore, the concept of secularization includes "sacralization." Accordingly, terms such as "christianization" or "rechristianization" are linked to the notion of "dechristianization," a term mainly used in modern French scholarship. "Anticlericalism" is a special term for opposition to the clergy, mainly within Catholicism, and "profanity" is a special word for disrespect for God and things holy. Furthermore, the verb "demythologize" characterizes skepticism vis-à-vis all things religious, and related verbs are "deconfessionalize," "despiritualize," and "desacralize." Terms describing the forces opposed to secularization include "revival," "awakening," "spiritual awakening," and "reawakening."

ORIGINS OF SECULARIZATION

The respective range of the synonyms for secularization has no precise definition, and to complicate matters further, the terms have somewhat different meanings in the various western European languages. This is true even for "secularization" itself, which cannot be translated into French or German without an additional specification of the precise meaning.

The rapidly changing scholarship on the processes of modernization in the fields of sociology, economics, and history accounts for the difficulty in defining secularization. For a scholar like Weber at the beginning of the twentieth century, secularization or disenchantment was mainly a topic of intellectual history; but research later in the twentieth century located the processes, causes, variations, and consequences of secularization in the everyday lives of common people as well as in economics and politics. What had been a problem of intellectual history, that is, the philosophy and the literature of the cultural elite, was transformed into a problem of the history of behavior and mentalities of all social strata. In the same manner, what had been defined as a matter related to theology and the church only became a matter of religiosity in a wider sense.

Interesting debates about the nature and the meaning of secularization emerge. First, where are the beginnings of this process? Leaving aside the view that Europe was never fully christianized in the early Middle Ages and remnants of a pre-Christian worldview were present in European society throughout the Middle Ages, two main theories address the origins of the secularization of Europe. Some scholars have argued that the Western world started to become more secular during the Renaissance, particularly in relation to Renaissance court life, the rise of modern science in the era of Francis Bacon, and the rapid changes in economic development, technology, and warfare in the Thirty Years' War. According to this view secularization commenced in the late sixteenth century, but other scholars have pointed to the eighteenth century and the enormous impact of the Enlightenment. For them secularization was caused by the new philosophical outlook propagated by thinkers such as Immanuel Kant, John Locke, and Voltaire, by new secular subjects introduced into university curricula, and by political theories that advocated the basic rights of the people over the divine right of kings. The first to argue explicitly that the modern world began in the eighteenth century was the theologian and philosopher Ernst Troeltsch, a friend and colleague of Weber at Heidelberg. In the years before 1914, almost all scholars, German and non-German alike, were convinced that Martin Luther and the Reformation had led the way to the modern world. Much to their dismay, Troeltsch insisted that the Middle Ages had lasted well into the eighteenth century and that it was the Enlightenment that had brought about the decisive change.

The causes and chronology of secularization are further complicated by the vantage point of social history. While the rise of science had some impact on popular views of religion even during the eighteenth century, other developments also competed with religious concerns. Thus growing interest in material consumption could be part of a popular secularization process. But other developments, like increased sexual activity, did not, in the minds of those who participated, necessarily indicate a renunciation of religion, even when clerics attacked the behaviors in question as irreligious. Working-class disaffection from formal churches during the throes of nineteenth-century industrialization did not always mean secularization. The transitions from religion to socialism were often complex and incomplete.

PROGRESS OF SECULARIZATION

After the 1950s scholarly opinion held almost unanimously that secularization, once started, had progressed continuously until its culmination in the twentieth century. By the end of that century another argument proposed that the theological view of secularization was much too simple, a self-assertion out of the mouths of secularized people. Instead of the steady progress of secularization, the argument suggested a complicated scenario of phases of secularization and sacralization or dechristianization and rechristianization. The forces that supported secularization coexisted with others that advanced sacralization in the Western world after the eighteenth century.

Understanding the impact of these forces requires complex models. According to this theory, secularization of European society and culture did indeed commence in the Renaissance, but early secularization met much resistance. The Renaissance and the baroque period that followed were also characterized by movements such as Puritanism in Britain, Jansenism in France and Italy, and Pietism in Germany, Sweden, the Baltic countries, and Switzerland. These revival movements were redefined in the context of this interpretation as the first major forces of the rechristianization of post-Reformation, pre-Enlightenment Europe. With the Enlightenment, however, another tidal wave of secularization swept through most countries of Europe, only to be countered by another wave of Christian revivalism in Methodism, the success story of the Moravians or *Herrnhuter,* and the First and Second Great Awakenings. In this sense early nineteenth-century missionary societies and Bible societies in Britain and elsewhere were Christian efforts to turn back the tide of radical rationalism in the late Enlightenment and to overcome the secularizing effects of the French Revolution. This struggle between pro- and anti-Christian elements continued throughout the nineteenth century and well into the second half of the twentieth century.

This interpretation has some major problems, however. Perhaps most vexing, secularization was vastly

96

different in most countries of Europe and North America. While in North America politics and culture seemed firmly in the grip of Fundamentalist pressure groups in the last decades of the twentieth century, in Europe the scales seemed to tip from interest in the sacred to interest in the secular. In contrast to North America, twentieth-century Europe appeared largely secularized if not dechristianized. Within the European context, forces such as urbanization and industrialization seemed to result in secularization. By contrast, the same factors seemed to support rather than hinder the triumph of Fundamentalism in the New World.

Without doubt, the juxtaposition of Europe and North America may be much too simple. Explanations of the variations of secularization in the Western world need a closer look at the development of individual European nations and even certain regions within those nations. The Netherlands, for example, became the most secularized country of Europe, but that occurred late in the twentieth century. All through the nineteenth century the Dutch people considered theirs a Protestant nation with a Catholic minority. By the end of the nineteenth century, most people in the Netherlands adhered to one of three political camps, neo-Calvinism, Catholicism, or socialism. In the 1970s these "columns," as they were called, dissolved, and at exactly that time secularization started to progress rapidly. In another instance, Ireland experienced rising religiosity in the nineteenth century, delaying secularization until the late twentieth century.

France seems to offer a different case. Following the French Revolution the French people divided into a progressive, anti-Catholic camp, with strong anti-clerical and laical feelings, and a conservative camp, with close ties to popular Catholicism and the Catholic hierarchy. Remarkably, for many decades neither camp made gains in relation to the other. Representatives of both camps attempted to occupy public spaces with prominent buildings and signs of symbolic value, and they tried to fill public time with processions and other rituals. But neither made advances over the other side. In Poland—which had been divided between Russia, Prussia, and Austria in the late eighteenth century—during the nineteenth century Catholicism and nationalism formed such a close union that it became almost synonymous to be Catholic and to be a Polish patriot.

VARIATIONS OF SECULARIZATION

In order to give some sense to what may otherwise appear as a play with casuistic distinctions, Hugh McLeod proposed a typology with five different categories distinguishing between

(1) "nations or regions with a dominant church, closely linked with traditional élites and conservative political parties," including France and Spain;

(2) "nations or regions with a pluralistic religious structure, but where ethnicity is relatively unimportant," including the Netherlands, Britain, and the Scandinavian countries;

(3) nations "with a pluralistic structure, where ethnicity is the main determinant of religious affiliation," such as the United States, Australia, and New Zealand;

(4) nations "where the population is polarized between two antagonistic religious communities," for example, Ireland and Germany in the *Kulturkampf* (cultural war); and

(5) nations "where the dominant church has become the major symbol of national or regional identity in the face of alien rule," such as nineteenth-century Poland (McLeod, pp. 21–33).

Each of these categories is a different form of secularization with a different story of the history of secularization.

Even though the typology developed by McLeod represented an important step forward, it was still far removed from a comprehensive explanation of the causes, variations, and consequences of secularization in Europe. Some problems deserve special attention as they have not yet been convincingly solved. Certainly the relationship between secularization and nationalism is the most sensitive issue, encompassing several aspects. First, one opinion is that nationalism is a kind of religion that, if fully implemented, replaces other forms of religion. Accordingly nationalism explains the past, defines the contours of the present, tells the people what the future holds for them, and spells out the sacrifices that will be necessary to achieve a brighter future. Through nationalism, with the help of rituals, episodes of the national past are sacralized, sites attain a sacred meaning, and persons appear to have performed sacred tasks for the cause of the nation. Interpreted this way, nationalism fulfills all the functions of religion. Disregarding the question of whether nationalism carries a certain amount of transcendental values and perspectives, one could call nationalism an "innerworldly" religion.

It is then a matter of further debate whether nationalism is the logical result of secularization, that is, the product of secularization carried to extreme conclusions, or nothing but a transformation or an *aggiornamento* of religion. This is a complicated issue that becomes even more so, considering the fact that in all European countries many people with strong religious feelings participated actively in national movements. This is true of people with progressive, liberal views and a critical distance from traditional Christianity as well as of people with strong conservative, orthodox feelings, that is, people who abhorred the ideas of 1789.

Similar difficulties confront attempts to interpret the relationship between Christianity and fascism and discussions of the role of religion in Adolf Hitler's Germany. On the one hand, the obvious pagan character of national socialism frustrates explanations of why Christians with some understanding of Christian tradition accepted the message of men like Hitler and Alfred Rosenberg, particularly why they accepted Nazi racism and anti-Semitism. On the other hand, most German church leaders, Protestant and Catholic alike, welcomed Hitler's rise to power and actively supported Hitler's regime well into the late 1930s, some even until 1945. The Catholic Church had special relationships with Benito Mussolini's Fascist Italy, Francisco Franco's Spain, Vichy France, and Fascist regimes in Portugal, Hungary, Romania, and other countries in Eastern and southern Europe.

The answer regarding communism, the other type of totalitarian rule, seems somewhat more simple. With few exceptions, under Communist rule churches were persecuted. It was only in the 1970s and 1980s that political pressure was reduced and that in some countries, like East Germany, attempts were made to develop a kind of coexistence between socialism, as it was called, and Christian churches. No doubt communism can be understood as an extreme form of secularization that possessed the qualities of an inner-wordly religion. It promised salvation to all who believed in the ideas of Marx, Lenin, and Stalin and who were ready to make sacrifices toward the victory of those ideas.

In all countries that had been under Communist rule for several decades, Christian traditions were weakened and in some cases severed. After 1989 the new generation of people in those countries knew practically nothing about Christian teachings. At the same time those people had a strong interest in all things religious, especially in esoteric doctrines and practices. Sectarian groups claimed impressive missionary successes. Therefore, secularization does not adequately describe these developments, but dechristianization is certainly appropriate for some aspects.

Another matter complicates a comprehensive theory of secularization. Secularization and sacralization attempt to describe processes of transformation,

that is, short-term and long-term linear change. While it is relatively easy to describe the transfer of property, the transfer of buildings and land, from the church or religious orders into nonecclesiastical possession, it is extremely difficult to analyze and interpret changes of religious mentality, that is, changes in worldview, belief, and conviction. How can religiosity be measured? What indicators provide insight into the degrees of religious belief and the variations of religious practice? Where is the historical material that is suited for quantitative analysis?

One strategy for finding answers is the analysis of the books people possessed. The assumption is that the more books with a religious content people owned, the more likely it is that they felt strongly about religion. But did people in fact believe in the contents of the books in their possession? Perhaps some of these books were given to them as gifts or were inherited. How can the people whose libraries were not preserved be included? Another possible measure is the analysis of religious formulas in the last wills of people. The assumption is that the more often such formulas were used, the stronger was the attachment of those people to the church. But last wills are a special kind of document, more defined by the notaries than by the persons who signed. Moreover, they are formalistic documents that, in view of impending death, are open to religious formulas.

Other scholars tried to measure secularization using the records of church attendance or the records of persons who took part in the holy communion. However, whether those materials are valid proof of the acceleration, slowdown, or reversal of the process of secularization is questionable. Furthermore, people who felt strongly about religion went to holy communion only very seldom, that is, only when they were convinced that their souls were pure enough to confront God. Those pious men and women are statistically in the same category as those who did not attend church regularly and who refused the Sacraments because they did not believe in their value. Each case lacks sufficient historical records to trace the rise and fall of secularization.

When David Martin published *A General Theory of Secularization* in 1978, sociologists of religion were convinced that they had successfully deciphered one of the major mysteries of modern history. That optimism was short-lived. Historians puzzled over why secularization advanced in a remarkable manner in the era of urbanization and industrialization in Europe while the opposite occurred in North America, where fundamentalism gained strength in the late twentieth century. Equally puzzling were the factors that trace and explain the success, failure, and variations of secularization. Religious energies that in the twentieth century were no longer firmly embedded in the Christian tradition might have transferred into other kinds of belief. Strong indications suggest that the mentalities and practices of "Western" men and women did not become more rational than they were, for example, in the eighteenth century.

Is secularization, therefore, one of the main characteristics of modern Europe or a temporary phase of European history? Immigration into Europe increased during the final decades of the twentieth century. Many of those immigrants came from non-Christian cultures and had strong attachments to religion. Even those immigrants who were "uprooted" from their native soil and were without a clear religious orientation did not convert to Christianity or embrace the blessings of a sceptical, enlightened world-view. Rather they rediscovered the value of their own indigenous religious tradition as a means of stabilizing their identity in an often hostile environment.

The secularized post-Christians of Europe did not react with a new religious fervor of their own. Europeans engaged in charitable activities based on enlightened humanism on the one hand and xenophobic behavior, sometimes even racism and violent hostility, on the other. The difficult path to a multi-ethnic, multicultural, and multireligious Europe has unpredictable cultural conflicts and confrontations and may result in the final triumph of secularization or a multifaceted coexistence of secular and spiritual norms and practices. A secularized Europe would be unique in a world dominated by several hegemonic cultures in which religion seems to play an ever more important part.

See also **Church and Society** *(volume 5).*

BIBLIOGRAPHY

Butler, Jon. *Awash in a Sea of Faith: Christianizing the American People.* Cambridge, Mass., 1990.

Davie, Grace. *Religion in Britain since 1945: Believing without Belonging.* Oxford, 1994.

Finke, Roger, and Rodney Starke. *The Churching of America, 1776–1900: Winners and Losers in Our Religious Economy.* New Brunswick, N.J., 1992.

Hutchison, William R., and, Hartmut Lehmann, eds. *Many Are Chosen: Divine Election and Western Nationalism.* Minneapolis, Minn., 1994.

Kirchliche Zeitgeschichte. Vol. 11, pt. 1: *Themenschwerpunkt, "Säkularisierung, Dechristianisierung und Rechristianisierung."* Göttingen, Germany, 1998. Special issue that includes contributions by Hugh McLeod, Peter van Rooden, Harry Lenhammer, Philippe Martin, Andreas Holzem, Stafan Plaggenborg, Paul Laverdure, Heinrich Schäfer, Hans-Jürgen Prien, William R. Hutchison, Jon Butler, Hartmut Lehmann.

Lehmann, Hartmut, ed. *Säkularisierung, Dechristianisierung, Rechristianisierung im neuzeitlichen Europa: Bilanz und Perspektiven der Forschung.* Göttingen, Germany, 1997.

Lübbe, Hermann. *Säkularisierung: Geschichte eines ideenpolitischen Begriffs.* Fribourg, Germany, 1965.

Martin, David. *A General Theory of Secularization.* Oxford, 1978.

McLeod, Hugh. "Dechristianization and Rechristianization: The Case of Great Britain." *Kirchliche Zeitgeschichte* 11(1998): 21–33.

McLeod, Hugh, ed. *European Religion in the Age of Great Cities, 1830–1930.* London and New York, 1995.

Nowak, Kurt. *Geschichte des Christentums in Deutschland: Religion, Politik und Gesellschaft vom Ende der Aufklärung bis zur Mitte des 20. Jahrhunderts.* Munich, 1995.

Schlögl, Rudolf. *Glaube und Religion in der Säkularisierung: Die katholische Stadt— Köln, Aachen, Münster—1700–1840.* Munich, 1995.

Weber, Max. *Wissenschaft als Beruf, 1917/1919.* Edited by Wolfgang J. Mommsen and Wolfgang Schluchter. Tübingen, Germany, 1994.

COMMUNICATIONS, THE MEDIA, AND PROPAGANDA

Thomas C. Wolfe

"Communications" has long been a subject of interest for historians of European societies: from the printing press to the Internet, technologies of communication have had a decisive impact on the politics, government, economies, and cultures of Europe. This essay will provide a framework for thinking about this enormous topic by discussing three distinct but related issues. First, it will make the obvious but important point that any history of communications relies on an idea of what communications "is." Historians have often—usually implicitly—understood communications as primarily a product of technology, something produced by a machine. But in recent decades social scientists have begun to argue for more anthropological understandings of communications, ones that stress how any act of communication takes place within a prior matrix of cultural meanings.

Second, it will present in compressed form what communications scholars have stressed when they look at the broad sweep of European and Western history. Such an account will be necessarily partial, but the goal is less to present a synoptic vision of historians' understandings than to view some of the dominant themes in modern history in light of communication as a cultural and social practice.

The third part of this essay will address an argument made by a number of philosophers and critics, that "communications" is by no means simply an academic subject, separated off behind the dense walls that seem to divide the present from the past, but is rather a crucial part of our present. Media institutions are intimately bound up with many of the predicaments that European societies, as well as those societies all over the globe shaped by "Western" ways of life, are facing today. Here we will consider just one of these predicaments, the problem of the public. Since the seventeenth century, the public has been a key idea in the evolution of democratic societies, and in order to think about the vicissitudes of the contemporary public, it is indispensable to have some idea of how the idea of the public appeared in Europe in the early modern period and what happened to it in the

course of the eighteenth and nineteenth centuries. In the European context, this history is particularly relevant now, as the leaders of the European Union seek to create a European public as the foundation of the single European state.

APPROACHING COMMUNICATIONS

If there is a foundational understanding of communications that has guided the research and thinking of many historians, it is that communications involves the transport of a message from a sender to a receiver. The message traverses time and space more or less intact, sent on its way by a mechanism that fixes language in mobile form. The history of communications thus addresses the evolution of means by which messages have been fixed and moved across time and space. This is a familiar history centered upon inventions and the inventors, businessmen, and patrons who developed and promoted them. In the temporal scope that is our interest here, the printing press stands out as the first in a long line of such machines, a line that culminates today in the latest software offered on the World Wide Web.

Many writers have argued that this model of communications is simply too narrow, and that communications history should not be a subfield of the history of technology. They stress that communication in its more general sense is a phenomenon of culture, and therefore communications history is in fact cultural history and should integrate the insights of anthropology, sociology, and cultural studies into its analytic vocabulary. For example, Armand Mattelart uses the term "communication" to denote broad social processes involving "multiple circuits of exchange." The objects exchanged include not only messages but also goods and people that together form a continuous kind of cultural "flow." This expansive definition makes the study of communications a vast field on which a multitude of seemingly disparate objects are mapped and related to each other, like the

Suez Canal and the utopian novel, nineteenth-century German anthropology and theories of naval power.

Another contemporary French writer, Régis Debray, criticizes the message-based model not for being narrow but for being simply mistaken. Building on the insights of many linguists and anthropologists, he argues that messages should not be considered as things separate from the social and cultural networks from which they emerge. Instead of being instantaneous, interpersonal, and peaceful—traits implied by the sender-message-receiver model—communication should be reconceived as acts of transmission that are historical, collective, and conflictual. The simplest text is but a moment in a historical process: no single person is ever the "author" of any message; rather, the message is the product of the social worlds to which individuals belong, worlds that are organized in terms of hierarchy and unequal power. Authors are certainly one part of the creation of messages, but it is a mistake to see them as the sole or even the most important part. Debray, like Mattelart, seeks a greatly expanded role for communication in organizing and in fact grounding our approaches to history, for the historical discipline's internal division in terms of military, diplomatic, social, and intellectual history is, he thinks, itself an artifact of the predominance of the sender-receiver model. The separation between social and intellectual history is particularly problematic: ideas and the social contexts that produced them are for Debray not separable, distinct phenomena; both need to be conceived as parts of the most concrete, material processes. "The Enlightenment," for example, "is not a corpus of doctrines, a totality of discourses or principles, that a textual analysis could comprehend and restore; it is a change in the system of manufacture/circulation/storage of signs" (p. 19).

Yet another group of historians has approached communication in culture by examining the connection between the dominant mode of communication in a society and the state or condition of consciousness of the members of that society. They work from the premise that the ways human beings experience themselves is in part a function of the nature of the communication mediums that define and connect them to their world. The Canadian writer Marshall McLuhan raised these broad questions most artfully and philosophically in the 1960s and 1970s, arguing that the history of media is the history of the transformation of the senses, first as space and time are overcome by writing and print, and then as new forms of presence are created by radio and television.

In terms of the long historical terrain that is our subject here, historians of communication and consciousness have described two significant shifts in Europe over the course of the last five hundred years. The first was the gradual movement from orality to literacy that occured in the modern period, and the second is the shift beginning in the twentieth century from print to visual culture or to a culture of the image. Historians of the transition from orality to literacy, such as Walter Ong and Michel de Certeau, have suggested that the printing press and the growth of communities based on literacy brought a qualitatively new kind of power to European societies in the seventeenth and eighteenth centuries. The capacity for imaginative thought and expression ceased to be conceived as being closely bound to and in some sense a part of nature, and became viewed as the possession of a creative self who writes from outside nature. Certeau suggests that printing involved the "discovery" of the blank page, upon which early modern scientific systems of astronomy, anatomy, and even music, could be written. This transformation made the concepts of imagination and creativity core cultural values for European civilization, and at the same time entailed a distancing from nature, from God, from an "enchanted" state in which all creatures were connected with each other in a harmonious universe.

With regard to the second transition mentioned above, a number of scholars have suggested that electronic technologies are today reshaping our consciousness in ways as profound as the print revolution reshaped the consciousness of Europeans centuries ago. In contrast to the disenchantment of the world caused by the systematizing nature of print, observers like the sociologist Michel Maffesoli today perceive the outlines of the reenchantment of the world, based on the ability of contemporary media to create new communities of faith. He argues that all kinds of cultural signs—industrial, personal, political, artistic—everything that is circulated as meaningful units of human culture, are taking the form of icons, of sacred images, which illustrate and concentrate belief, trust, and passion. He suggests that it is in the nature of the blank video screen to bring forth the proliferation of images and icons in the same way that it was in the nature of the blank page to demand systematic accounts of natural phenomena. The implication is that people are coming to know themselves and the world as images rather than as objects or ideas developed in the course of grappling with systems preserved and elaborated in print.

It is obvious that historians of communication and consciousness speak in a very different register from historians who study the details of communications technologies and the pace of their adoption in various societies. Social historians remind us, for example, that the movement from orality to print to image did not involve the supplanting of one medium by another, but rather the addition or overlaying of one by another. Similarly, they criticize simplistic claims about a second transition from print to image by arguing that electronic technologies since the nineteenth century have above all disseminated the printed word; in fact the computer and the Internet have brought about another print revolution, in which anyone with a personal computer becomes a printer and publisher. This is not quite fair, however, since at the heart of the interests of historians of consciousness is not the fabrication and circulation of the printed word but rather the creation of a subjective and affective power that shapes how readers and viewers interpret the world. Electronic technologies that transmit words and images have obviously not destroyed print, but they suggest that the printed word has itself become more powerful as an image than as a conveyor of verbal meaning. Paradigmatic examples are the ubiquitous logos of corporations, sports teams, and of commodities themselves.

A further point should be made concerning the messiness of the very concepts of orality and literacy. In the first place, anthropologists who have studied oral societies and historians who have studied the evolution of literacy in Europe show convincingly that neither orality nor literacy exist in any kind of pure state readable from the historical record. Members of oral cultures have many more means for knowing the world than simply what is told to them by their elders; these cultures encode knowledge in the nature world they inhabit as well as transmit meanings in the "written" form of art and design. Literacy is an equally difficult object to discern in the past. Even though the literacy rate has been a standard gauge for at least two centuries to mark the progress or stage of advancement of a society, historians remind us that the measurement of literacy is an extremely complex problem. Can we accurately call those farmers of an English county in the eighteenth century who managed to scratch out their name instead of simply marking an X in the parish register "literate"? In addition, they caution us against too rashly extrapolating literacy from the presence of educational institutions. There is little evidence, for example, that many young peasants in southern Italy who went to school for eight years at the end of the nineteenth century actually learned to read.

This condensed account of concepts of communications has been necessary to make the point that the historical study of communications includes a vast number of disparate topics and approaches. What follows will draw from a number of these approaches in order to describe how the printed word

became the chief solvent for breaking down the institutions of medieval society and the constituting medium for modern social and cultural forms.

COMMUNITIES AND CULTURES OF PRINT

Scholars of communications have contributed a great deal to our understandings of the major turning points in the broad sweep of European history. In particular they have furnished insights that help us understand two of the most important issues that historians have debated for several centuries: first, the dissolution of the medieval world and the rise of early modern society in the sixteenth and seventeenth centuries and, second, the later transition to the modern world in the eighteenth and nineteenth centuries. From the perspective of communications scholars, these questions concern the revolutionary impact of print on medieval society and secondly the place of media in the establishment of industrial, democratic, and capitalist states since the consolidation of absolutist regimes in the eighteenth century.

As to the first transformation, there is broad historical consensus that the invention of the printing press was one of the most significant events of the early modern era. While books had of course existed since antiquity, they were both expensive and rare, and they circulated within relatively small circles of the clergy and nobility. Yet by the middle of the sixteenth century, so many books, pamphlets, chapbooks, ballads, newsletters, newsbooks, and corantos (single-sheet collections of news items from foreign sources) began to appear that the scarcity of books seemed to contemporaries a thing of the distant past. Printed material poured from presses based on Johannes Gutenberg's design at a fraction of the cost of manuscripts, and these inexpensive books were adopted into the rapidly expanding networks of marketing and distribution that constituted the commercial revolution of the early modern period.

We can summarize the social impact of this process by saying that it enabled communities of print to compete with and eventually supplant the communities of kin and faith that comprised medieval societies. Most dramatically, these new kinds of communities founded in and by print challenged prevailing conceptions of religious faith and political governance. Printed works were sources of beliefs, arguments, and claims to fact that reconfigured the bonds of belonging to social, cultural, and political collectivities. Print made possible new forms of communities based not on social and cultural rituals but on the basis of agree-

A Reformation Broadsheet. Martin Luther, the German Hercules, slays the beasts of scholastic theology and philosophy, among them William of Occam, Thomas Aquinas, Aristotle, Avicenna, and Nicholas of Lyra. Broadsheet by Hans Holbein the Younger, 1522. Zentralbibliothek, Zürich, MS. A2, S. 150.
ZENTRALBIBLIOTHEK, ZÜRICH, SWITZERLAND

ment with views first put forth in printed form and then referenced in other texts. Books not only gave factual claims durability and longevity but also gave speed and momentum to ideas, as they were passed from hand to hand and from generation to generation. Contrasting accounts of reality could endure over time and be taken up by new readers, who then became new articulators of argument and belief. People separated in time and space could base their relationship on the stability of identical copies of texts, and through the printed word could feel a new kind of bond and imagine a new kind of sympathy.

In the area of religion, the Reformation—the central religious, political, and cultural event of the early modern period—can only be fully understood by noting the ways the leaders of the reform movement constructed radically new forms of Christian community by exploiting the unique characteristics of print. Cheaper Bibles, collections of sermons, and

prayer books enabled Protestant theologians to construct a style of worship based on direct access to the word of God as it was preserved on the printed page. Access to the divinity was no longer dependent on or a function of interactions with the human representatives of God on earth, who according to the reformers were members of a corrupt hierarchy, but was there for all those who could read. This was an early modern instance of a phenomenon that historians of communications have noticed repeatedly in the modern era: new forms of communication circumventing established hierarchies and thereby eroding the legitimacy of traditional institutions. In short, the printing press made possible a new kind of religiosity that absorbed and transformed existing religious institutions and ideas.

The printing press and the communities of print it made possible had an equally decisive impact on another major process in European history, the consolidation of the nation-state as the dominant political unit of the modern era. This appearance also dates to the sixteenth century, when the late medieval system of fluid political units based on the fluctuating fortunes of aristocratic families and alliances began to weaken, to be replaced by a system of nation-states. Scholars of communication have argued that the key trait of this new political unit was its dependence on networks of print culture that gave this abstract idea immense power. Historians of nationalism have referred to this new kind of cultural and political entity as an "imagined community"; they argue that any nation-state is above all an idea endlessly replenished by texts that restate and redefine its power over its "readers." In terms of the evolution of this idea, the scholar-bureaucrats of the seventeenth and eighteenth centuries gave European nation-states existence by disseminating in identical copies authoritative descriptions of these new bounded territories. They began in the seventeenth century to study the inhabitants of their territories; they began to think of occupants of territory as populations and went on to measure and decipher regularities and consistencies in matters of birth and death rates, agricultural production, and trade. Later, in the eighteenth and nineteenth centuries, the romantic movement produced writers whose philosophical essays, novels, plays, and poetry described the profound emotional tie between a state and its people, a tie so enduringly strong that it produced the virulent nationalisms of the nineteenth and twentieth centuries. In their works, nation-states became entities that, like people, suffered and triumphed, had ineluctable fates and unavoidable destinies. Other kinds of texts gave meaning to the nation-state as the bearer of political power; elite segments of society formed around the consumption of print began to think of states as possessing their own "national" interests that demanded brilliant statecraft on the part of leaders as well as the most noble sacrifices on the part of citizens. Viewed through the lens of communications, the entire history of national cultures and conflicts emerged because of the imaginary identifications made possible by print.

The importance of print communities to the process of secularization that steadily eroded medieval institutions and worldviews has led many writers to argue that the print revolution set Western civilization on a course of unending and limitless progress, and in the middle of the twentieth century many argued that for the rest of the world to join us on this path, they had to develop modern systems of communication. Progress depended on doing away with traditional forms of community and making new ones, and the European historical record showed there was no better solvent than print.

Scholars of communications have shown, however, that there is another side to this story. If it is possible to gloss the exit from the medieval world as unequivocally progressive, it is difficult to maintain that optimism in the face of another cultural entailment of print, which we might summarize with the observation that after the printing press, everything becomes a matter of opinion. The printing press made possible the growth of an international community of scholars dedicated to establishing the truth of their opinions by means of observation from experience; but it also made possible the establishment of a mode of social conflict in which communities of belief fought wars of words that led with depressing regularity to wars of cannons and bullets. No social group could defend itself or seek power for itself without the articulation of heresies and orthodoxies. In this sense the printing press early on took its place as one of the most effective weapons in European history.

The earliest manifestation of this new kind of conflict can be noted again in the sphere of faith. The Catholic Church's attention to threats to its authority posed by heretical texts of course predates Gutenberg, and yet it viewed the flood of written material that began in the sixteenth century with mounting alarm. The church felt an urgent need to keep back this tide of heretical texts from both inside and outside Christendom, and so promulgated more and more decrees defining and monitoring heresy in all its varied forms. The church paid attention to both the ideological side of things, enlarging the elaborate bureaucracy that scrutinized texts for the opinions they held, and the social side, increasing the surveillance of printers, booksellers, and authors who were in a position

to organize the creation and circulation of heretical texts. Thus we should remember how this new Protestant form of religiosity was itself influenced by the new kinds of responses it elicited on the part of the established religious authorities. There is nothing like being called heretical to give power to a text.

But scholars of communication have argued that this ambiguous and conflictual quality of print had its most enduring effects in the field of politics. The most famous early example of this was the upheaval in English society beginning in the 1640s that lasted for over four decades, culminating in the revolution of 1688. This was the first major political conflict in Europe in which the question of the control of print became itself a point of political debate and contestation. Beginning in the 1640s, pamphlets and broadsheets became the vectors of sustained political criticism of the monarchy, and the monarchy in turn introduced measures to control print, measures that bear striking similarities to the Catholic Church's innovations of the previous century. This restriction provoked John Milton's essay of 1644, *Areopagitica,* which attacked the Crown's action as an unjustified curtailment of a fundamental right. This essay has been read as a document founding the idea of freedom of speech and freedom of the press, although some scholars of communications history have pointed out that other readings are possible, ones that see Milton's text as itself partisan politics cloaked in high principle. Whatever Milton's own contribution to these events was, the upheavals in seventeenth-century English political life demonstrated how the printing press created new patterns of political conflict.

The English revolution was thus the first instance of what appears as a repeated pattern in the course of modern European history. First print helps to destabilize traditional political arrangements by fostering revolutionary actors who literally create their own forms of political power through print. Next these actors succeed in taking power, and as part of their new and more just vision of rule, they proclaim the liberalization of the sphere of print. Oppressive restrictions of the past are with much fanfare lifted and an era of freedom is inaugurated. But in the course of time the new regime generates a new opposition who themselves organize around print; clandestine networks of readers form, repressive measures are enacted, and the sphere of print becomes again a terrain of political conflict. Finally, what was once a revolutionary regime is denounced by new actors as traditional or feudal, a revolutionary situation emerges, and the cycle begins again.

The most conspicuous events that conform to this pattern are the French Revolution of 1789 and

Broadside of the English Civil War. *Mercurius rusticus* (Rustic Mercury) carrying the Royalist message to the countryside in the 1640s. BY PERMISSION OF THE BRITISH LIBRARY, LONDON

Selling the News. Paris newssheet vendor. Print (1791) made after a watercolor by Louis Debucourt. BIBLIOTHÈQUE NATIONALE, PARIS

the Russian revolutions of 1905 and 1917. In all these cases power flowed to those who organized themselves around print most effectively, articulating the most persuasive case against what they considered a stifling autocracy and establishing the most passionate conviction for change among their circles of readers. In both these cases, regimes that understood the proliferation of opinions in print as dangerous to the stability of the state were brought down by actors whose specialty was the dissemination of argument and belief in print. After these revolutions, the problem of tolerance and difference emerged again, as the revolutionaries attempted to control the very conditions that had made their seizure of power possible. In the French case this led to the autocracy of Napoleon, and in the Soviet case to the autocracy of the Communist Party. The harsh policies of these new governments then generated their own forms of critical, revolutionary politics, which themselves generated new instances of print insurgency. In this light, the print revolution was at the same time the propaganda revolution, for it was in the early modern period that idealism, censorship, and propaganda became welded together to form the unique cultural alloy that we still refer to today as "politics."

And yet an even stronger definition of propaganda is possible. Some writers have argued that the ambiguous legacy of the printing press is best seen not in these dramatic moments of revolutionary upheaval, but rather in the evolution of daily life over the course of the last three centuries. Sociologists like Jacques Ellul have argued that propaganda—the dissemination of one-sided messages intending to convince the reader or listener of the rightness of the sender's interests or opinions—is best understood as a cultural force whose ultimate effect has been to create distracted, decentered, unthinking publics, unable to tell the difference between philosophical principle and naked self-interest. The printing press was not primarily a vehicle of progress or upheaval, but rather the primary instrument by which powerful groups supplied common people with a steady diet of permitted thoughts. Ellul inverts the entire Enlightenment narrative of progress and improvement and sees the modern period as that era when Western societies gave themselves entirely over to the forms of unfreedom that derive from the sea of slogans, jingles, and images that compel us to behave in ways consonant with the powerful.

We do not have to look hard for evidence that seems to support this strong view of propaganda. In the first edition of Richard Steele's *Tatler* of 1709, the author writes that he is providing the paper for "the use of Politick Persons" because they, "being Persons of strong Zeal and weak Intellects," need to be told "*what to think*" (Steele's italics). The same view is unabashedly acknowledged by Edward L. Bernays, one of the pioneers of advertising and public relations in

Russian Revolutionary Poster. "We will not surrender Petrograd," Soviet poster, c. 1917–1922. THE DAVID KING COLLECTION

italist, democratic societies beginning in the middle of the nineteenth century, and the rise of mass political parties in the early twentieth century and their post-World War II versions today, the expansion of propaganda is unmistakable. For Ellul, who fought in the French Resistance and experienced firsthand the Nazi control of French journalism and broadcasting, it is imperative to realize that the term "propaganda" should not be restricted to the political programs, publications, and press of fascist or totalitarian regimes, but that it accurately captured the way that order is maintained in any modern state. No social or political group could constitute itself without propaganda, nor could it survive without engaging in intense propaganda struggles with other groups.

Ellul's argument was particularly disquieting in the context of the Cold War, when two political and economic systems appeared to be locked in mortal conflict. And given this struggle, his point that both Soviet and Western societies lived in conditions of unfreedom because in both the individual is conceived as an empty vessel to be filled with the interests of the powerful was not particularly welcome. Some concerned observers even took Ellul's history of propaganda as a prophetic kind of warning because in the 1960s the new technology of television was beginning to appear in both Western and Eastern parts of Europe as an even more efficient disseminator of messages than print. Television, after all, created a new social kind of interaction, an immediate but mediated co-presence, in which the voices of the powerful could be heard in your own living room appealing directly to your thoughts and manipulating your emotions.

THE PUBLIC PROBLEM

While the above discussion has argued that "communications" has a central place in both the positive and negative "grand narratives" about the modern era, another history cuts productively between these two polemical views, one that has provided a framework both for thinking about the past and for formulating approaches to contemporary political life, a history that takes up the evolution of European institutions as well as the shaping of consciousness by technologies of communication. This is the problem of the "public," one of the most intricate issues in Western culture, and a concept deeply bound up with the development of communications. If the Renaissance meaning of the word "public" still owed much to to the classical sense that referred to the male landowners of a given city-state gathered together to discuss public (i.e., their own) business, the early modern sense of

the United States, who had immense influence on the development of these disciplines in Europe. Bernays wrote in *Propaganda,* his 1928 primer of public relations, "The conscious and intelligent manipulation of the organized habits and opinions of the masses is an important element in democratic society. Those who manipulate this unseen mechanism of society constitute an invisible government which is the true ruling power of our country." Between these two writers was two centuries' worth of institutional growth dedicated to perfecting communications so that the people would act as they were told.

While this is certainly another "strong" view, polemical and critical of the way capitalist industrial societies took shape in the nineteenth century, there is plenty of evidence to suggest that propaganda is less a political than a cultural fact in European history. From the civil religion of the French Revolution and its postrevolutionary incarnations in the programs of Saint-Simon and Auguste Comte to the establishment of advertising agencies as essential institutions in cap-

Reading the Papers. Interior of a Viennese coffeehouse. "The Passion for Newspapers," engraving (1837) by Johann Christian Schoeller. HISTORISCHES MUSEUM DER STADT WIEN, ©DIREKTION DER MUSEEN DER STADT WIEN, VIENNA

the term was wrapped up in new forms of *publicity,* that is, in the new means of making something public in print. In the seventeenth century "the reading public" came to refer to the collectivity of readers who consumed the periodicals and newspapers available in the coffeehouses, taverns, and inns of Europe's major cities. Some historians have suggested that from this early reading public and from the discussions carried on in print about pressing issues of the day a "public sphere" came into being, an institution that was, according to Jürgen Habermas, absolutely vital for the creation of popular government. Print became a "place" where individuals could gather for the purpose of applying their reason to matters that affected them all. Crucially, the anonymity of print levelled all social differences so that arguments could be examined outside of the context of social hierarchy and status, and it enabled the emergence of a procedural base for democratic practice: the early newspapers and periodicals instructed the growing groups of literate businessmen, lawyers, bureaucrats and teachers how to deliberate about their own interests, how to consider the implications of social and political problems, and how to compromise.

The complicating factor present at the birth of this early modern society of letters was capitalism, and more specifically the tension between the survival of the medium—the newspaper or periodical itself—and the state of the cultural institution, the public sphere. In the early modern period, the public sphere was sustained by publications that were erratically published and short-lived, and by printers/writers/publishers who were often harassed and prosecuted by the authorities. Paradoxically, however, the ephemeral nature of these early newspapers gave vitality to the nascent public sphere as new printers and publishers joined the ongoing discussions, staking both their careers and their often meager resources on the growth of this peculiar public that constituted itself in the act of reading.

The problem, according to historians like Habermas, was that journalism and the entire public sphere became corrupted by the transformation of these publications into business enterprises that sought profits before they sought the public good. The public sphere was invaded by private interests to such a degree that by the end of the eighteenth century the stereotype of journalists as venal, self-interested scribblers who sold themselves to the highest bidders was fixed in popular culture. The public sphere's transformation was furthered with the industrial revolution and the growth of Europe's cities in the first half of the nineteenth century, when papers became intertwined with the promotion, advertising, and distri-

109

bution of a style of life based on the consumption of leisure goods and experiences. The problem was not only that the public use of reason took a back seat to the production of propaganda. Just as serious was that the strategies that newspapers used to compete with each other in the crowded, competitive sphere of periodicals ended up distorting readers' perceptions of the world. According to Richard Terdiman, print media was another site where we can note the imprint of the commodification of everyday life: in the press the world was broken up into the briefest items that were strewn across the page without order or reason, in exactly the same ways as early department stores jumbled together dresses and umbrellas, wallets and underwear. The readers of these mass newspapers were shown a world without order and were offered nothing to help them supply order to it. The readers no longer constituted a public but were rather treated as a *mass* whose opinions were to be supplied and whose consumption was to be molded.

Such a history of the public sphere does not aim to provide a full account of the development of journalism as a profession, much less the development of political institutions in democratic societies. It says nothing, for example, about other public spheres that appeared in the eighteenth and nineteenth centuries, like the proletariat public sphere formed by guilds, trade unions, and other working-class organizations. Neither does this story attend to the complex role played by women in both the formation of the public sphere and the processes that supposedly led to its transformation. The history of the public sphere is more like a framework that provides a useful starting point for thinking about the development of Western societies in the modern era, and it is a history that emerged again after World War II as particularly relevant to the task of rebuilding European societies. The question faced by European leaders in 1945 was how to give democracy a deep and enduring foundation so that the cataclysm of total war would never happen again. Propaganda systems and institutions were to be destroyed and broadcasting was to be decentralized; the press was to be democratized, and television was to serve the public as a new kind of pedagogical tool, teaching the viewing public Enlightenment values of tolerance, compromise, and respect.

In the 1960s and 1970s, however, many European intellectuals were still waiting for the creation of a responsive and effective public sphere. They argued that while the two sides in the Cold War held conflicting views about property and the creation of wealth, in one respect they were unmistakably similar: governments on both sides of the Iron Curtain had no interest in fostering the appearance of informed, active, and concerned publics. Governments in Eastern Europe refused to allow any kind of open political space in which the public's voices could be heard, and in Western Europe, postwar governments substituted economic priorities for political ones. Political debates were to be managed by technocratic experts, while the public devoted its energies toward consumption and the creation of national prosperity. By the 1980s, however, the postwar consensus was exhausted, and the public sphere appeared again as a useful idea with which to map out social change. The power of the idea was demonstrated most immediately in the revolutions in Eastern Europe of 1989, where socialist governments were brought down by groups claiming to act in the name of the public. The terms "public sphere" and "civil society" became catchwords of new governments in Czechoslovakia, Poland, and Hungary, and in the West too new groups appeared that shook up the conservative social landscape of the 1980s. Green parties challenged the political orthodoxy that states existed above all to foster economic growth; antinuclear activists challenged the common sense of international politics; and, in a considerably more ambiguous development, groups on the radical right appeared who villified the conservative, materialistic middle class with the same racist and violent messages used by the Nazis half a century before.

As the post–Cold War era has unfolded, however, the resurgence of the public sphere seems to have been of brief duration. Since the 1980s there has been a decisive push in a number of Western European states to privatize formerly state-run media institutions. These transnational media conglomerates tend to conceive of the public as a vast amalgamation of different market niches, while the major political parties turn steadily toward the American model of politics as entertainment heavily dependent on the orchestration in media of public debate and discussion. By contrast, in most Eastern European societies television remains under state control and in moments of political crisis is fought over as the only instrument that can guarantee political survival, as it did for the Russian president Boris Yeltsin on more than one occasion. Clearly the public sphere is still only a framework, valuable above all because it insists on a connection between the nature of a society's communication system and the quality of collective life lived by its citizens.

This essay has provided a sense of the diversity of ways to think about the history of communications in European societies, but it has also suggested how thinking about this history is a matter of some urgency, especially in the context of the remarkable social and technical transformations underway at the beginning of the twenty-first century. From advances in Internet and satellite technology that make more and more parts of the world visible and audible to other parts, to the steady progression of media mergers that produce enormous international conglomerates, communications institutions will continue to shape the lives not only of Europeans but of everyone who takes up media forms to explore the world around them. We participate in it, we observe it, but to change it we need to know how to think about it. And here histories are crucial.

See also **The Protestant Reformation and the Catholic Reformation** *(volume 1);* **Printing and Publishing; Literacy; Journalism** *(volume 5); and other articles in this section.*

BIBLIOGRAPHY

Anderson, Benedict. *Imagined Communities.* 2d ed. London, 1991.

Burchell, Graham, Colin Gordon, and Peter Miller, eds. *The Foucault Effect: Studies in Governmentality.* Chicago, 1991.

Certeau, Michel de. *Heterologies: Discourse on the Other.* Translated by Brian Massumi. Minneapolis, Minn., 1986.

Certeau, Michel de. *The Practice of Everyday Life.* Translated by Steven Rendall. Berkeley, Calif., 1984.

Curran, James, Michael Gurevitch, and Janet Woollacott, eds. *Mass Communication and Society.* London, 1977.

Debord, Guy. *The Society of the Spectacle.* New York, 1994.

Debray, Régis. *Media Manifestos.* London, 1996.

Ellul, Jacques. *Propaganda: The Formation of Men's Attitudes.* Translated by Konrad Kellen and Jean Lerner. New York, 1965.

Febvre, Lucien, and Henri-Jean Martin. *The Coming of the Book: The Impact of Printing, 1450–1800.* Translated by David Gerard. London, 1997.

Habermas, Jürgen. *The Structural Transformation of the Public Sphere.* Translated by Thomas Burger. Cambridge, Mass., 1989.

Hall, Stuart. "Encoding, Decoding." In *The Cultural Studies Reader.* Edited by Simon During. 2d ed. London, 1999. Pages 90–103.

Hall, Stuart, et al., eds. *Culture, Media, Language.* London, 1980.

Jansen, Sue Curry. *Censorship: The Knot That Binds Knowledge and Power.* London, 1991.

Lefort, Claude. *The Political Forms of Modern Society.* Cambridge, Mass., 1986.

Lippmann, Walter. *The Phantom Public.* New Brunswick, N.J., 1993.

Lippmann, Walter. *Public Opinion.* New York, 1922.

Maffesoli, Michel. *The Contemplation of the World.* Minneapolis, Minn., 1996.

Mattelart, Armand. *The Invention of Communication.* Translated by Susan Emanuel. Minneapolis, Minn., 1996.

Mattelart, Armand. *Mapping World Communications: War, Progress, Culture.* Minneapolis, Minn., 1994.

Mattelart, Armand, and Michèle Mattelart. *Rethinking Media Theory.* Translated by James A. Cohen and Marina Urquidi. Minneapolis, Minn., 1992.

McLuhan, Marshall. *The Gutenberg Galaxy.* New York, 1969.

Ohmann, Richard. *Selling Culture.* London, 1996.

Ong, Walter J. *Orality and Literacy: The Technologizing of the Word.* London, 1982.

Schramm, Wilbur. *Mass Media and National Development.* Stanford, Calif., 1964.

Sloterdijk, Peter. *Critique of Cynical Reason.* Translated by Michael Eldred. Minneapolis, Minn., 1987.

Smith, Anthony. *Books to Bytes: Knowledge and Information in the Postmodern World.* London, 1993.

Stephens, Mitchell. *A History of News.* London, 1988.

Terdiman, Richard. *Discourse/Counter-Discourse: The Theory and Practice of Symbolic Resistance in Nineteenth-Century France.* Ithaca, N.Y., 1985.

Williams, Rosalind. *Dream Worlds: Mass Consumption in Late Nineteenth-Century France.* Berkeley, Calif., 1982.

Section 6

POPULATION AND GEOGRAPHY

THE ENVIRONMENT

Richard H. Grove

The Renaissance marks a major watershed in the environmental history of Europe. It was itself at least in part a development inextricably intertwined with a new view of the world engendered by the maritime travels of Europeans far beyond the Pillars of Hercules. The literature about the Renaissance voyages permitted the evolution of a new self-consciousness among Europeans about themselves and the countries, landscapes, and societies they came from. In truth, we cannot really disentangle the history of landscape, environmental perceptions, and social history that go to make up the environmental history of the European landscape. All were transformed by the rapidly emerging new relationship between Europe and the rest of the world, philosophically, socially, and economically. Biologically, too, the encounter with the rest of the world after about 1300 was reflected in enormous transitions in Europe itself. From the Renaissance onward Europeans constructed themselves and their landscapes in terms of their new relationship with the non-European world. As Europe came increasingly to dominate a world economic system, the landscape of Europe was itself increasingly affected by the transformations that new economic forces and the concentration of capital brought about. These changes can be read, to varying degrees, in the evolving landscapes of Europe in the last half of the second millennium, five hundred years that saw much of the continent experience agricultural and industrial revolutions and a degree of urbanization that largely transformed the modes by which people used and shaped the landscape.

We should not, however, exaggerate the changes that took place in those five centuries. Arguably, and especially in Britain and France, much of the modern-day cleared agrarian landscape is in essence the landscape created during the Roman Empire. By 1300 a very high proportion of the original woodland cover of Europe had been cleared and, locally, resource shortages had stimulated the emergence of elaborate systems of management and common-property resource allocation. Some of these shortages may have helped to provoke the kinds of new fuel use that accompanied the beginnings of industrialization and protoindustrialization, especially in England. For this reason a careful examination of the historical geography and environmental history of England is especially relevant to understanding the changes that went on in the rest of Europe later on, as the effects of industrialization and urbanization made themselves felt. So too, the often hostile social responses to industrialization in England and France were pioneering and vital to the revolution in environmental perceptions that took place elsewhere in Europe after the mid-eighteenth century. These reactions, some of which took the form of a growing environmental concern and environmental consciousness, were strongly associated with physiocratic and romantic responses to capitalism and industrialization and are especially relevant in understanding the way in which environmentalism in the modern period has responded to contemporary European and global notions of environmental crisis.

Major environmental transformations took place in Europe between 1400 and 2000 in connection with six major phenomena: the clearance of woodlands and the draining of wetlands for agriculture, urbanization, and industry; changes in agriculture, field systems, crops, and the form of the landscape; urbanization and industrialization and pollution, especially during the nineteenth century; the impact of epidemic diseases and climate change; landscape design coupled with the growth of urban-stimulated environmentalism and pollution control; and roadbuilding and the industrialization of agriculture. In this period a demographic transition associated with agricultural and industrial revolutions and urbanization led to an intensification of resource use (especially fossil-fuel use) and agricultural production that was historically unprecedented, especially in the nineteenth and twentieth centuries. The period was also coterminous with the Little Ice Age, a distinct climatic period that lasted from 1250 to 1900, approximately, and which was characterized by an unusual frequency of extreme climatic events involving prolonged periods of cold or high temperatures, drought, and heavy precipitation events. The severest of these events, especially those which articulated with global El Niño and La Niña events, gave rise to periods of economic and social crisis in Europe that lasted several decades in some instances. The most dramatic environmental changes, however, involved the continued transformation or disappearance of the post–Ice-Age natural vegetational cover of the continent, as clearance for agriculture took place, and as a consequence of growing demand for wood for industrial and urban fuel.

THE LITTLE ICE AGE IN EUROPE AND ITS SOCIOECONOMIC IMPACT

The Little Ice Age was a period several centuries long during which glaciers enlarged. The term refers to the behavior of glaciers, not so much to the climatic circumstances causing them to expand. The Little Ice Age was not a period of prolonged, unbroken cold; in Europe certain periods within it, such as the years 1530–1560, were almost as benign as the twentieth century. European mean temperatures varied by less than two degrees centigrade, although particularly cold years or clusters of years occurred from time to time. Very cold decades in the 1590s and 1690s, for instance, saw prolonged snow cover, frozen rivers, and extensive sea ice around Iceland. The characteristics, meteorological causes, and physical and human consequences of this period, which was global in its impact, can be traced in most detail in Europe. Recently, the availability of historical data and concentrated field investigations have permitted reconstruction of many glacier chronologies. Documentary information ranging from ice cover around Iceland, sea surface temperatures, and the state of the fisheries in the North Atlantic to the timing of the rye harvest in Finland and the incidence of drought in Crete is unusually substantial.

The Little Ice Age has commonly been seen as occurring during the last three hundred years, during which glaciers from Iceland and Scandinavia to the Pyrenees advanced, in some cases across pastures or near high settlements. However, evidence is now accumulating that these advances, culminating in the seventeenth and nineteenth centuries, were preceded by others of comparable magnitude, culminating in the fourteenth century. The intervening period was not sufficiently long, or the effect of loss of ice volume great enough, to cause withdrawal to positions held in the tenth to early thirteenth centuries. It is therefore logical to see the whole period from about the mid-thirteenth century to the start of the recession in the late nineteenth century as one Little Ice Age. The Little Ice Age was in turn simply the most recent of several century-scale fluctuations to have affected Europe since the beginning of the Holocene ten thousand years ago.

The extent to which century-scale climatic events such as the Little Ice Age are manifestations of periodic adjustments in the interaction between oceanic and atmospheric circulation or responses of the global climatic system to external forcing caused by factors such as variation in geomagnetism or decreased solar input remain to be clarified. A full explanation must involve the combined influence of several factors, including the part played by volcanic eruptions, whose effects we know have been considerable, although generally short-lived, in European history. The end of the Little Ice Age cannot be attributed simply to anthropogenic warming following the industrial revolution, in view of evidence of comparable warming in the Medieval Warm Period. Just as the Little Ice Age consisted of decadal and seasonal departures from longer-term means, it was itself but one of several fluctuations within the Holocene, each lasting several centuries.

The physical consequences of Little Ice Age climatic conditions affected both highlands and lowlands, as well as coastal areas. Snow cover extended, and semipermanent snow appeared on midlatitude uplands, as in Scotland, and on high mountains in the Mediterranean, including the White Mountains of Crete. Snow lines fell, avalanches and mass movements increased greatly, as did floods, some caused by damming of main valleys by ice from tributary valleys. Periods of glacial advance were generally associated with increased flooding and sediment transport. Regime changes of streams and rivers flowing from glaciers led in the short term to both degradation and aggradation, according to the balance between meltwater load and stream competence.

In the longer term increased flooding and glacial erosion led to enhanced sedimentation rates and deposition of valley fills and deltas. Greater storminess caused flooding of low-lying coasts and the formation of belts of sand dunes, as at Morfa Harlech in northwest Wales. Little Ice Age climatic fluctuations were sufficient to have biological consequences, ranging from shifts in tree line altitude to changes in fish distribution in response to displacement of water masses. The disappearance of cod from the Norwegian Sea area in the late seventeenth century, associated with the expansion of polar water, is attributable to the inability of cod kidneys to function in water below 2 degrees centigrade. The northward extension of the range of European birds during the twentieth-century

The Little Ice Age. A fair on the frozen Thames River during the great frost of 1739–1740. Painting by Jan Griffier (died c. 1750). GUILDHALL ART GALLERY, CORPORATION OF LONDON/THE BRIDGEMAN ART LIBRARY

warming, such as the establishment of starlings in Iceland after 1941, implies that more substantial changes in the distribution of birds and insects must have occurred during the most marked phases of the Little Ice Age.

The consequences of the Little Ice Age for European populations ranged from ice advance onto farms and farmland, such as the obliteration in 1743 of Tungen Farm in Oldendalen, west Norway, and the overwhelming of sixteen farms and extensive farmland by the Culbin Sands in Scotland in 1694, to the fourteenth-century loss to the sea by Christchurch, Canterbury, in England, of over a thousand acres of farmland, together with many oxen, cattle, and sheep. The human consequences of the Little Ice Age climate were particularly marked in highland regions and areas near the limits of cultivation. When summer temperatures declined and growing seasons shortened, both grass and cereal crops suffered, and upper limits of cultivation descended. The viability of upland farming decreased as the probability of harvest failure

increased. If harvests failed in successive years, leading to consumption of seed grain, the results were disastrous. Failure of the grass crop limited the number of cattle overwintered, thus decreasing the quantity of manure, then essential for successful arable farming. Farm desertion was especially common in Iceland and Scandinavia, though it was not confined to such northern regions. In Iceland migration out of the worst-affected north, in the seventeenth century, caused increased economic impoverishment in the south. Gradual decline in resource bases could increase sensitivity to other factors, including disease and unrelated economic problems, making the impact of a sequence of particularly hard years, such as occurred in the 1690s, much more serious. Crop failure was most dire in its effects if several staples were affected simultaneously, or if alternative supplies were unobtainable.

The human consequences of the Little Ice Age climate were generally coincident with other social and economic factors from which they have to be dis-

117

entangled if they are to be assessed. In the early fourteenth century the impact was enhanced, even in lowland areas of southern England, by the population growth that had been encouraged by the rarity of harvest failures in the preceding Medieval Warm Period. Sequences of adverse weather in Europe between 1314 and 1322, coinciding with the rapid advance of Swiss glaciers, had major economic and social effects, including famine, their severity varying from place to place and class to class. More resilient societies or those in prosperous regions, such as the Netherlands, were less affected. Even so, throughout the Little Ice Age much of Europe was indeed affected by a variety of extreme climatic episodes, some of which lasted for several years, even up to a decade.

EL NIÑO EVENTS AND SOCIOECONOMIC CRISES IN EUROPE

Most of the severest of these episodes were, in fact, global climate events that also impinged on Europe. These global events took place when a weak phase of the North Atlantic Oscillation (bringing cold high-pressure weather to Europe and central Asia) coincided with and reinforced a strong El Niño event. Such articulation created climatic episodes (Mega-Niños) that in Europe typically produced a very cold winter followed by a long cold spring and a summer of alternating extreme wet and dry periods. In southern Europe El Niño episodes often produced very severe drought, sometimes leading to famine, especially in Spain, Greece, the Mediterranean islands, and Turkey. El Niño events were also linked to disease epidemics across Europe, which exacerbated or prolonged existing crises. So, for example, between 1396 and 1408 Europe experienced a series of very cold winters, with sea ice persisting in the North Atlantic and preventing trade with Iceland and Greenland. These coincided with major drought events in Egypt and India. In 1630 global El Niño-induced droughts affected southern Europe, while Italy experienced serious plague mortality.

These global El Niño-related climate crises were especially frequent and severe between 1570 and 1740 and again between 1780 and 1900. They appear to have led to the kinds of economic crises that have long been collectively referred to as the "seventeenth-century crises" in European and Asian economic history. Examples of other El Niño-related global climatic crises that affected Europe took place in 1578–1579, 1694–1695, 1709, 1769–1771, 1782–1783, 1812, 1877–1879, and 1941. All of these involved severe winters followed by late springs, unusual sum-

THE "GREAT EL NIÑO" OF 1788–1795, THE FRENCH REVOLUTION, AND THE CATALONIAN REVOLT OF 1787–1789

While further archival research is needed to characterize more fully the 1789–1793 event, the evidence of a strong global impact already indicates that it was one of the most severe El Niños recorded. In more temperate regions of the Northern Hemisphere, highly abnormal weather patterns were making themselves felt as early as 1788 in western Europe. There are some indications that an early precursor of the 1788–1793 event may have been an unusually cold winter in western Europe in 1787–1788, followed by a late and wet spring and then a summer drought, resulting in the severe crop failures that critically helped to stimulate the explosive social pressures that culminated in the French Revolution.

In France the hard winter and late, wet spring of 1787–1788 came at a time when free trade in grain had been allowed by an edict of the previous year, leading to empty granaries and a sharp increase in grain prices. Grain prices rose by about 50 percent—that is, the general price index rose from about 95 in late 1787 to 130 in the summer of 1789. The only peasants who profited from high prices were the big landowners and tenant farmers. The rest of the peasant population suffered severely from the rising price of bread. The small peasant who had to sell in order to pay his taxes and dues was short of grain by the end of the summer. The sharecropper, too, was hard-hit, and so was the day laborer who had to buy grain in order to feed his family. The dwindling of their resources also brought about a crisis in the vineyards of Champagne, Beaujolais, and the Bordelais: sales of wine were reduced because people gave up buying it in order to buy bread, and winegrowers were thus reduced to poverty. In fact, in many parts of France a previous drought, probably associated with an El Niño event of 1785, had already seriously damaged the vital winegrowing industry, especially in Normandy and Picardy. The drought of the summer of 1785 had resulted in heavy losses of livestock and a slump in the supply of wool. After 1785 the loss in disposable income led to a continuous slump in the sales of wine in parts of the country where much of the population had to buy its bread.

Warm, dry spring-summers are favorable to grain in northern France and northwestern Europe. But even in the northern areas of the Paris basin warmth and dryness can in certain cases be disastrous. A spell of dry heat at a critical moment during the growth period, when the grain is still soft and moist and not yet hardened, can wither all hope of harvests in a few days. This is what happened in 1788, which had a good summer, early wine harvests, and bad grain harvests. The wheat shriveled, thus paving the way for the food crisis, the "great fear," and the unrest of the hungry, when the time of the *soudure,* or bridging of the gap between harvests, came in the spring of 1789. No one expressed this fear better than the poor woman with whom Arthur Young walked up a hill in Champagne on a July day in 1789:

> Her husband had a morsel of land, one cowe, and a poor litte horse, yet they had 42 ibs. of wheat and three chickens to pay as a quit-rent to one seigneur, and 168 ibs of oats, one chicken and one sou, to pay another, besides very heavy tailles and other taxes. She had 7 children, and the cow's milk helped to make the soup. It was said at present that something was to be done by some great folks for such poor ones, but she did not know who or how, but God send us better, *car les tailles et les droits nous ecrasent.* (Young, 1950, p. 173)

These kinds of conditions led in late summer 1788 to what we can now see as the first serious rural unrest prior to the revolutionary movements of 1789. Serious unrest and small-scale rural revolts took place in the areas worst affected by the summer droughts, in Provence, Hainault, Cambresis, Picardy, the area to the south of Paris, eastward in Franch-Comte, around Lyons and Languedoc, and westward in Poitou and Brittany. So the extreme summer droughts and hailstorms of 1788 were decisive in their short-term effects. The conditions are well described in the journal of a peasant winegrower from near Meaux:

> In the year 1788, there was no winter, the spring was not favorable to crops, it was cold in the spring, the rye was not good, the wheat was quite good but the too great heat shrivelled the kernels so that the grain harvest was so small, hardly a sheaf or a peck, so that it was put off, but the wine harvest was very good and very good wines, gathered at the end of September, the wine was worth 25 livres after the harvest and the wheat 24 livres after the harvest, on July 13 there was a cloud of hail which began the other side of Paris and crossed all of France as far as Picardy, it did great damage, the hail weighed 8 livres, it cut down wheat and trees in its path, its course was two leagues wide by fifty long, some horses were killed. (Le Roy Ladurie, 1972, p. 75)

This hailstorm burst over a great part of central France from Rouen in Normandy as far as Toulouse in the south. Thomas Blaikie, who witnessed it, wrote of stones so monstrous that they killed hares and partridge and ripped branches from elm trees. The hailstorm wiped out budding vines in Alsace, Burgundy, and the Loire and laid waste to wheat fields in much of central France. Ripening fruit was damaged on the trees in the Midi and the Calvados regions. In the western province of the Beauce, the cereal crops had already survived one hailstorm on 29 May but succumbed to the second blow in July. Farmers south of Paris reported that, after July, the countryside had been reduced to an arid desert.

In much of France and Spain a prolonged drought with very high temperatures then took place. This was the followed by the severest winter since 1709, which had also been a severe El Niño year, when the red Bordeaux was said to have frozen in Louis XIV's goblet. Rivers froze throughout the country and wolves were said to descend from the Alps down into Languedoc. In the Tarn and the Ardeche men were reduced to boiling tree bark to make gruel. Birds froze on the perches or fell from the sky. Watermills froze in their rivers and thus prevented the grinding of wheat for desperately needed flour. Snow lay on the ground as far south as Toulouse until late April. In January Mirabeau visited Provence and wrote "Every scourge has been unloosed. Everywhere I have found men dead of cold and hunger, and that in the midst of wheat for lack of flour, all the mills being frozen." Occasional thaws made the situation worse, and the Loire in particular burst its banks and flooded onto the streets of Blois and Tours.

All these winter disasters came on top of food shortages brought on by the droughts of the 1787 summer and the appalling harvests of summer 1788. As a result the price of bread doubled between summer 1787 and October 1788. By midwinter 1788, clergy estimated that a fifth of the population of Paris had become dependent on charitable relief of some sort. In the countryside landless laborers were especially affected. Exploitation of the dearth by grain traders and hoarders made the situation steadily worse. It was in this context that the French king requested communities throughout France to draw up *cahiers* of complaints and grievances to be presented in Paris. From February to April 1789 over twenty-five thousand *cahiers* were drawn up. From these we can not only assess the accumulation of long-term grievances but also get some idea of the intense dislocation of normal economic life that the extreme weather conditions of the 1780s and especially 1788–1789 had brought about. Decreasing access to common resources, timber shortages, excessive taxes, and gross income dis-

(continued on next page)

THE "GREAT EL NIÑO OF 1788–1795" (continued)

parities were all compounded by bad weather, and together created the new political demands and anger that spilled over into active rebellion during 1789.

The excessive cold and food shortages of early 1789 soon overthrew any hesitation to break antipoaching laws or customs. Rabbits, deer, and other game were all slaughtered irrespective of ownership or regulation in many parts of France. Any gamekeepers or other symbols of authoritarian structures who opposed such actions were soon killed. Many sectors of the populace became accustomed to these kinds of resistance, which would soon develop into broader reaction and violent protest. Attacks on grain transports both on road and river followed the same pattern. Bakeries and granaries were also assaulted. Anger at the price of grain and bread in Paris soon found suitable targets for rioting and violence, particularly where the large population of rivermen and quayside laborers remained workless due to the Seine's still being frozen by April. The riots at the Reveillon factory, in which many hundreds of fatalities took place, were an example of this, and set the stage for a growing cycle of revolutionary violence in Paris. A number of pamphlets printed at this time made the very specific point that the supply of bread should be the first object of the planned Estates General and that the very first duty of all true citizens was to "tear from the jaws of death your co-citizens who groan at the very doors of your assemblies."

These connections between an accumulation of unusual and extreme weather events and popular rebellion were by no means confined to France. In Spain, the cold winter of 1788–1789 was, if anything, even more unusual than in France. Here too, persistent summer droughts were followed by a winter of intense cold and heavy snowfall. One observer wrote:

> Autumn this year was colder than normal . . . and noone alive has ever experienced the weather so cold in El Prat. It was extraordinary, both what was observed and the effects it caused. . . . On the 30th and 31st December the wash of the waves on the beach froze which has also never been seen or heard of before. Likewise it was observed that the water froze in the washbasins in the cells where the nuns slept at the Religious Order of Compassion. . . . The rivers channels froze and the carriages passed over the ice without breaking it.

Between August 1788 and February 1789, cereal prices in Barcelona rose by 50 percent, in spite of the city's being accessible by sea. Between February and March 1789 there was a revolt in the city, known as Rebomboris de Pa. Part of the population set fire to the municipal stores and ovens. The authorities attempted to pacify the population by handing out provisions and taking special measures so that supplies could be sold at reasonable prices. The privileged classes, it is said, also provided money and contributions in kind to pacify the underprivileged. The military and police authorities adopted a passive attitude, letting events run their course. The authorities then took refuge in the two fortresses that controlled the city, and powerful defenses were put up in case events got out of control. Despite these measures chaotic rioting took place, and in the aftermath six people were executed. Similar riots took place on other parts of Catalonia when the poor outlook for the 1789 harvest became clear and profiteers and hoarders made their appearance. Revolts and emergency actions by municipal authorities took place both on the coast and inland, with documentary reports being made in cities such as Vic, Mataro, and Tortosa. The fact that these social responses to cold and crop failure did not lead to the same degree of social turmoil and rebellion as in France should not disguise the fact that they were highly unusual.

In the summer of 1789 much of France rose in revolt, and crowds rioted in cities. How far the resulting course of revolution had its roots in the anomalous climatic situation of the period is open to debate, but the part played by extreme weather events in bringing about social disturbance during the French Revolution simply cannot be neglected. It may be, as Alexis de Tocqueville put it, that had these responses to anomalous climatic events not occurred, "the old social edifice would have none the less fallen everywhere, at one place sooner, at another later; only it would have fallen piece by piece, instead of collapsing in a single crash" (Tocqueville, 1952, p. 96). One of the advantages in trying to understand the French Revolution in terms of the succession of prior climatic stresses is that it contextualizes it, rather than isolating it as a historical phenomenon. To quote Tocqueville again, "The French Revolution will only be the darkness of night to those who see it in isolation; only the times which preceded it will give the light to illuminate it" (Tocqueville, 1952, p. 249). Today one can merely speculate. But the fact is that the whole social edifice of ancien régime France did collapse at a single blow, in the midst of one of the worst El Niño episodes of the millennium.

mer conditions, and harvest failures. Sometimes, as in the severe conditions associated with military retreats from Moscow in 1812 and 1941, the political consequences were incalculable. In 1878–79 El Niño conditions led to a series of crop failures in Europe that have sometimes been referred to as the "great agricultural depression." However, possibly the most extended and serious El Niño event to affect Europe in the last six hundred years was the "Great El Nino" of 1788–1795. Reconstruction of the effects of this climatic episode is instructive in understanding how other major El Niño events might have affected Europe in earlier periods.

THE CLEARANCE OF THE WOODLAND IN EUROPE AFTER 1300

The deforestation of the European plain after 1100 was, wrote Karl Gottfried Lamprecht, the great deed of the German people in the Middle Ages. In all its complexity it has attracted an enormous literature. But over most of central and western Europe agrarian effort had passed its maximum by 1300, and the great age of expanding arable land was succeeded in the fourteenth and fifteenth centuries by one of stagnation and contraction. Much of this decline may have been due to increasingly severe weather conditions after the onset of the Little Ice Age and to the associated incidence of famine (especially in 1315–1317) and episodes of disease, including the Black Death. During the hundred years between 1350 and 1450 this decline was still more marked. The causes of this recession are obscure and involved, and among the agencies invoked to explain it are the destruction caused by war, great pestilences, falling prices, and a basic decline in population. Abandoned holdings and depopulated or deserted villages were to be found not only in the "old lands" of the south and west but also in Mecklenberg, Pomerania, Brandenburg and Prussia. In the south and west of Germany the acreage of these abandoned lands, or *Wustungen,* has been placed as high as one-half of the area once cultivated; the statistical reduction for Germany as a whole has been placed at 25 percent. These figures probably overemphasize the contraction because some abandoned holdings may represent no more than temporary withdrawals or changes in use of land; but, when all reservations are made, the decline is still striking.

To what extent the woods advanced upon the untilled fields we cannot say, but there is no doubt that they did in many places, and traces of former cultivation are to be found in wooded areas even today. The abandonment took place at various dates, but in the main it is a medieval phenomenon. Comparatively recently it has been shown how many large forests in Germany have come into being since the Middle Ages. From such evidence as this we must not assume that the area under cultivation was at one time greater than it is today, because the phenomenon may in part be due to the more complete separation of forest and farmland. But more investigation is necessary before we can be clear about these matters. The ravages of war and pillage bore particularly hard upon some localities. The cultivated land that had been brought into being in Bohemia was very adversely affected by the Hussite wars (1419–1436), and it has been estimated that one-sixth of the population either perished or left the country. In the west Thomas Basin, the bishop of Lisieux, writing about 1440, described that vast extent of uncultivated land between the Somme and the Loire as all "overgrown with brambles and bushes." Population fell in places to one-half, even to one-third, of its former level. Some of the accounts may have been exaggerated, but there is no doubt about the widespread desolation and about the growth of wood on the untilled fields. In southwest France, in Saintonge, between the Charente and the Dordogne, for a long time people said that "the forests came back to France with the English."

The clearing that had taken place in the Middle Ages, epic though it was, still left western and central Europe with abundant tracts of wood. But soon, in the sixteenth century, in many places there were complaints about a shortage of timber, and the shortage developed into a problem that occupied the attention of statesmen and publicists for many centuries. It was not only that the woods were becoming smaller but that the demand for timber was growing greater. There had been signs toward the end of the fifteenth century that the recession in the economic life of the late Middle Ages was merging into a recovery and a new prosperity that brought with it an ever increasing appetite for wood. The pace of industrial life was quickening. Glassworks and soapworks needed more and more wood ash. The production of tin, lead, copper, iron, and coal depended upon timber for pit props and charcoal for fuel; the salt industry in the Tirol and elsewhere also needed wood for evaporating the brine. It was the iron industry that made the greatest demand, and, particularly in the wooded valleys of the upland blocks of France and central Europe, an endless series of small metal establishments were to be found, often run by men who divided their labors between forge and field. As the clearing progressed, the huts of the charcoal burners moved from one locality to another, and there appeared new mounds of small logs, covered with clay to prevent too rapid a combustion.

Woodcutters The month of December. Fresco in the Castello del Buonconsiglio, Trent, Italy.
SCALA/ART RESOURCE, NY

Early fears of timber shortage in England were expressed in a commission appointed in 1548 to inquire into the destruction of the wood in the ironmaking area of the Weald. But this commission and a number of parliamentary acts passed during the sixteenth century failed to slow the rate of destruction. The resulting shortages encouraged the search for a substitute, so that during the seventeenth century ironworkers were encouraged to turn to coal instead of charcoal, following the lead of domestic urban consumption, especially in London. In 1709 Abraham Darby started to smelt ore with coke at Ironbridge in Shropshire, and by 1750 the use of coal for smelting had become common. These kinds of transitions took longer to take place on the Continent, where the supply of wood was much greater and industry less developed. But shortages were being felt. In France, Jean-Baptiste Colbert introduced strictures on forest-cutting in 1669, and in 1715 attempts were made to limit the number of forges.

The increase in French and English trade and shipbuilding in the context of overseas expansion started to impose a new scale of demand for timber during the seventeenth century. The Dutch Wars of the seventeenth century, the maritime wars of the eighteenth, and then the Napoleonic Wars were a heavy pressure on timber resources. By the time of the English diarist Samuel Pepys in the second half of the seventeenth century, the crisis in supply had already developed and a worldwide search for new sources began in the Baltic and Scandinavia, India, North America, and South Africa. After the English Restoration the Royal Society commissioned John Evelyn to study the problem, and in October 1662 he presented his recommendations in *Sylva, or a Discourse of Forest Trees,* starting a series of attempts at replacement tree planting and encouraging attempts to slow down deforestation in Europe.

Throughout the period from about 1500 to 1900 agricultural production intensified, leading to several new phases of deforestation and wetland drainage. Some of this expansion led to soil erosion in upland regions, especially in central France and the Alps. However, in Germany the population losses resulting from the Thirty Years' War (1618–1648) may have prevented the level of deforestation that took place in much of the rest of Europe. By contrast, during the eighteenth century large clearances took place on the Polish plain, the Slovakian uplands, and the Carpathians. Despite this, the development of forest conservation systems in a number of countries meant that as late as 1900 substantial forested areas remained in Europe. In 1900 about 18 percent of Belgium was wooded, 19 percent of France, 27 percent of Germany, 23 percent of Poland, 37 percent of Austria, 33 percent of Czechoslovakia, 29 percent each for Yugoslavia and Bulgaria, and 28 percent for Romania. On the Hungarian plains the level was only 11 percent. However, the forest present in 1900 was very different in character from the dense natural woodland of a millenium before. It had been repeatedly cut over, managed, and replanted, much of it with conifer rather than deciduous species, and had become plantation rather natural woodland. Large areas of previously unforested sandy soils were reclaimed by artificial planting in the Kempenland of Belgium, the Landes region in France, Breckland in Britain, and on sand dune regions of the German Baltic coast.

In eastern and northern Europe, and in Russia, the transitional forest steppe was extensively deforested by colonists moving southward during the seventeenth century. After 1478 the expansion of the trading interests of Novgorod had ensured extensive deforestation. Even so, eighteenth-century Muscovy was still essentially one large forest, with infrequent clearings for villages and towns. Metallurgical industries founded under Peter the Great increased the rate of clearance. Further north, rotational burning and cultivation were practiced in Finland and parts of Sweden until World War I. After 1918 many of these northern forests were turned over to industrial wood production.

Since World War I the decline in forested area has largely been halted due to increasingly stringent forest reservation, the increased use of fossil fuels, and the decline in rural population and peasant agriculture. Since about 1960 some parts of Europe have actually experienced an increase in noncultivated marginal land and woodland as small-scale agriculture became less economic and state subsidies for upland and peasant agriculture fell away.

NEW CROPS AND SOIL EROSION

Much of the initial impetus for forest clearance after 1500 resulted from a demographic transition enabled to a large extent by an intensification of agricultural production fostered by new agricultural methods and the introduction of non-European crops, especially

Industrial Landcape. The Severn Gorge at Coalbrookdale, Shropshire, England. Iron works were built in the area after Abraham Darby developed the technique of smelting iron ore using coke in the early eighteenth century. Engraving by Wilson Lowry after a painting by George Robertson, nineteenth century. FROM "IRON BRIDGE TO CRYSTAL PALACE" BY ASA BRIGGS, PUBLISHED BY THAMES AND HUDSON LTD, LONDON

from the Americas. The most important of these were maize and the potato. Maize spread quickly after the Columbian voyages; in 1498 Columbus noted that "there is now a lot of it in Castile." By 1530 it was grown throughout Iberia, North Africa, and the Middle East, spread by Muslim refugees fleeing persecution. Population pressure in southern Europe may have encouraged the spread of maize in the sixteenth century, but it spread rapidly in France and elsewhere only during the climatic and economic crises of the seventeenth century. In Burgundy and southern France maize entered the food cycle in the same era, and by 1700 it was growing in every district south of a line from Bordeaux to Alsace and was the chief food of the poor peasant. In Italy the cultivation of maize rose after the plague and famine of the 1630s. Major rises in population in the eighteenth century in Spain (from 7.5 million in 1650 to 11.5 million in 1800), France, and Italy were accompanied by formidable rises in the areas of maize under cultivation. During the century maize production spread to eastern Europe in the Danube basin and into Russia. The population of Iberia, Italy, and the Balkans doubled to 70 million from 1800 to 1900, much of it sustained by a maize staple. These extraordinary expansions in maize plantings and population brought about widespread environmental damage and soil depletion throughout southern Europe.

The rise of the potato was even more dramatic than that of maize, especially in northern Europe. In the wetter maritime north, wheat and rye were at the northern end of their range and prey to molds and fungi, frequently producing ergotism and other diseases. Enormous population rises in such countries as Ireland and Norway were enabled by the potato. However, this kind of crop innovation, as well as encouraging a dangerous dependence on a single crop (a dependence that culminated in the Irish famines of the 1840s and 1850s), also produced severe soil degradation. As early as 1674 gullying and soil erosion were being reported from the Moravian states, leading to claims for tax remissions. Some of these instances may have been related to excessive heavy rains and snowmelt in and after severe Little Ice Age winters. But new crops such as maize and potatoes provided very little protection for soils and made them vulnerable to extreme rainfall events. A number of systematic surveys of soil conditions took place in France during the eighteenth century. Typically hundreds of *cahiers de doleances* written in the 1790s deal with soil erosion as a major hazard even in areas of relatively slight topography such as Champagne and Lorraine. Consciousness of erosion hazards also led to popular rural protests against private forest cutting. As con-

solidation of landholdings took place in many parts of France, Germany, and Britain during the late eighteenth century and large fallow fields were planted with new crops, the incidence of serious soil erosion quickly increased.

THE DEVELOPMENT OF CONSERVATION AND ENVIRONMENTALISM, 1600–1900

The environmental changes brought about in Europe by deforestation, agricultural intensification, industrialization, and urbanism after 1400 were unprecedented in world history. But the structured social reactions and narratives that those changes engendered were also remarkable. Regulations and legislation attempting to address smoke pollution problems in cities date back to the fourteenth century in a number of parts of Europe. In the seventeenth century John Evelyn was a vociferous critic of coal smoke pollution in London. Rapid urban growth was an initial reason for stress on the wider resources of the European countrysides, especially in the growing demands of cities for fuelwood in the period between 1500 and 1750, when fossil fuels started to become more important. Throughout Europe a variety of local regulatory systems governed the use of some woodland areas by local communities. In countries such as the Netherlands and England, where the proportion of wooded land had been small since late Roman times, these regulations were often elaborate and involved heavy penalties.

Statewide attempts at forest conservation were stimulated less by domestic demand and more by shortages of strategically important ship timber or by the needs of mines and metal, glass, or other mineral-working industries, especially in the context of what Joan Thirsk has called the protoindustrial revolution. Some early attempts at large-scale forest protection to ensure timber supply rather than for traditional hunting reserves were made in south Germany, especially in Nürnberg, as early as 1309 under the Nürnberg Ordinance. But it is was in the territories of the Venetian Republic that attempts at state forest conservation were first begun in Europe, especially after the Venetian defeat in the sea battle of Euboea in 1470. Shipbuilding and glassworking in Venice consumed huge amounts of wood. Venetians also recognized that deforestation and soil erosion were silting up the lagoon of Venice. However, attempts to restrict local timber cutting in the vital ship-timber forests of Montello brought the state into direct and long-term conflict with the local population. The failure of Venetian conservation measures contributed to the decline of

Venice and its displacement by maritime powers that had easier access to relatively unworked forests. The kind of crisis that Venice experienced was delayed in Britain, for example, as it started to draw on the Irish forests for industrial and naval sustenance, while the Netherlands, another precocious maritime power, drew on the Norwegian forests.

By the mid-seventeenth century even England, France, and the Netherlands were compelled to adopt much more stringent forest regulations for strategic reasons. In France Colbert was compelled to declare a temporary moratorium on timber getting in 1661 as a prelude to his famous Forest Ordinance of 1669. This ordinance set in place a governance for French forests that subsisted well into the nineteenth century and was widely imitated in Europe. By the mid-seventeenth century, too, the combined effects of population pressure, timber demands, and agricultural intensification were leading to serious social contests over lands and forests in many parts of Europe. In Cambridgeshire, England, riots broke out in the 1660s when attempts were made to fell local woodlands. Large-scale capital projects to drain the East Anglian Fenland were also vigorously opposed by those who saw their grazing and common-property rights threatened. These contests became sharper as states became more involved in attempts to conserve forests, enclose commons, and drain wetlands and marshes. In France, for example, the twenty-two thousand hectare Forêt de Chaux was the scene of increasingly savage battles after the 1750s between fifty-four villages that held customary forest rights and forest guards employed by the state to safeguard supplies for a growing number of rural industries. These contests, before and after the French Revolution, became increasingly violent, lasting until the 1870s and sometimes involving assassination attempts on forest guards.

The chaotic conditions of the French Revolution had themselves produced significant ecological changes. Believing themselves released from feudal and state regulation, rural people, especially in southeast France, embarked on an orgy of deforestation, much of it on steep mountain slopes. The disastrous torrents, floods, and landslides that this felling brought about led in turn to a body of conservationist and engineering literature and opinion that formed much of the foundation of the sophisticated French forest conservation movement of the nineteenth and twentieth centuries, reinforced by a German forest conservation ideology that was already well developed by the late nineteenth century in the works of men such as Jean Fabre (1797) and Michel Blanqui (1846). Similar moves toward both forest conservation and higher intensity of land use developed in most European countries during the period between 1670 and 1870, especially in the latter part of the period.

Landscapes were also increasingly transformed or modified for reasons of prestige and ornament, especially in England, France, and Italy. Some of them echoed the landscapes of tropical colonies and oceanic islands or romanticized wildernesses. In England and Italy artificially drained landscapes became the subject of elaborate planning projects and of early exercises in agricultural economic theory.

Interest in the aesthetics of the rural landscape in metropolitan France and Britain was already well developed by the end of the eighteenth century, as the writings of John Clare, Robert Southey, Thomas Gilpin, and others demonstrate. Poets such as Clare were deeply sensitive to the social and landscape traumas wrought by enclosure, while William Blake wrote of the "dark satanic mills" and William Wordsworth and the Lake Poets and their imitators fed notions of the romantic sublime to be found in wild landscapes to an increasingly receptive urban public. Much of the inspiration for these powerful sensibilities originated in the writings of Jean-Jacques Rousseau and Bernardin de St. Pierre, many of which were deeply hostile to the Enlightenment project and its implications and, in the case of the latter writer, were rooted in the circumstances of the colonial experience, specifically on the island of Mauritius. The rise of what the British literary critic Raymond Williams called the "green language" corresponded to the emotional commitment that had developed in relation to the threat perceived to the old landscape pattern in the context of the industrialization of agriculture, a phenomenon explored especially well in the novels of Thomas Hardy. As early as the 1840s what had been a minority interest at the time of John Clare had flowered into a major literary cult. Sir Robert Peel, for example, collected wild landscape paintings and frequently commented on the solace they offered him. In spite of this, when individuals did campaign against landscape despoliation by the forces of capital and the spread of railways, mines, and urban housing, they were largely unsuccessful, as the campaigns of William Wordsworth testify. Concerns about species extinctions in Europe developed much later than the preoccupation with rural landscape. The efforts made by Charles Waterton to turn his private estate into a nature reserve were an interesting precedent and an indication of the level of awareness of human destructive potential that had developed, in Britain at least, by the 1840s.

Embryonic worries about the destruction of rural landscapes and about species extinctions remained the concern of a largely ineffective minority until the 1860s, however. Only the cause of animal protection, strongly advocated by the Quakers, had resulted in serious legislation. This was a cause closely associated with antislavery campaigning and was strongly identified with an emerging urban public health and housing movement in several European countries. In 1842 the publication of Sir Edwin Chadwick's "Inquiry into the Sanitary Condition of the Laboring Population of Great Britain" highlighted the need to radically reform the environments of the new overcrowded, disease-ridden, and polluted cities. This and similar initiatives in France, Germany, and Italy helped to stimulate the growth of wider environmental reform movements, many of which took a long time to come to fruition. In the 1840s serious efforts also began to reduce the industrial pollution that was making many European rivers lifeless.

After the mid-nineteenth century the sheer scale of the transformation and modernization of the landscape invigorated an already nascent conservation movement that had many of its roots among French and English painters and artists as well as in statist moves toward forest and water conservation. The publication of two books, Charles Darwin's *The Origin of Species* (1859) and George Perkins Marsh's *Man and Nature* (1864), highlighted the role played by extinctions in the affairs of men and appear to have stimulated early environmentalism in a very profound way.

In England the first environmental lobby group, the Commons Preservation Society, founded in 1865, originated in a movement to protect the London Commons, threatened by enclosure, railway building, gravel extraction, and urban expansion. This group, headed by Quakers, biologists, urban liberals, lawyers, and feminists (among others), encouraged in turn the formation of the National Trust in 1891, an organization dedicated to the conservation of historic buildings and landscapes. The National Trust became a global model for future environmental organizations and provided much of the impetus for conservation in twentieth-century Britain. As far as species protection was concerned, the British Birds Protection Act of 1868 was a pioneer in Europe, and the brainchild of Alfred Newton, a close associate of Charles Darwin. Newton had made a careful study of the natural history of the great auk, a flightless seabird that had become extinct in the late 1840s. He had also been particularly influenced by the researches of his brother Edward Newton on the paleontology of the dodo, on Mauritius.

The nineteenth century saw important innovations in European environmental history, in two senses. First, new forms of environmental degradation occurred as a result of urban growth—with its attendant sewage and other issues—and industrial development, which created new levels of air and water pollution. These problems were particularly acute in areas around industrial cities, and urban waterways, especially, became increasingly foul. In the face of these developments, however, and due to independent cultural factors, a more explicit environmental concern arose as well. In the nineteenth century itself environmental reform was mainly associated with beautification movements such as those which promoted the establishment of urban parks. Though limited in scope and objectives, these reform movements provided a basis for the development of the more sweeping environmental regulations characteristic of the twentieth century, which managed to undo some of the worst consequences of industrialization in western Europe.

THE TWENTIETH CENTURY: RESPONDING TO OLD AND NEW HAZARDS

Although many of the environmental impacts of industrialization and agricultural intensification continued to develop in a more extensive way in the twentieth century, many aspects of artificially induced environmental change after 1900 were almost entirely new. So, necessarily, was the strength of the environmentalist reaction to the systemic changes that now appeared; small-scale environmental lobby groups became mass movements and eventually even political parties. Nevertheless, the twin sources of environmental change, especially destructive change, were the same as they had been in the previous two centuries. For the first half of the century, European human populations continued to expand. Second, human economic activity continued to accelerate and to substitute inanimate for animate energy. Since 1850 the burning of coal, oil, and natural gas has released some 270 billion tons of carbon into the air in the form of heat-trapping carbon dioxide. At least half of this amount derived from combustion that took place in Europe, although the relative European contribution since about 1980 has been somewhat reduced. Between 1900 and 2000 carbon dioxide outputs from Europe increased by approximately thirteenfold, and energy use expanded by about sixteen times. The atmospheric changes generated by the new scale of outputs of "greenhouse" gases are now thought to have substantially increased rates of global warming since about 1870. The end of the Little Ice Age in about 1900 has itself brought about a considerable natural cyclical warming, although the relative extents of these dynamics remain unknown. The twentieth century was also marked by the rapid industrialization of Russia and other parts of Eastern Europe through ambititious, often forced programs of industrial development. Lacking in capital but eager, for economic and military reasons, to bring their countries to Western levels of industrialization, communist regimes proved impatient with environmental concerns. The consequences for Eastern Europe included rampant pollution, chemical and otherwise.

Unlike most of the rest of the world, however, the noncultivated, especially scrub and forest, area of Europe has started to increase instead of declining. The switchover in this process took place just prior to World War II. From 1860 to 1919, 27 million hectares of land were converted to arable use, of which at least half was woodland and the other half grassland and wetland. But from 1920 to 1978, only 14 million hectares were converted to arable use, while 12 million hectares moved out of arable use, much of it back into forest, with a certain amount to industrial-urban use. Some of the most rapid parts of this reversal took place in marginal land in upland regions and in the economically marginal parts of southern Europe and the Mediterranean islands, as a rural-urban drift of peasantries took place to cities in Europe and outside it. The advent of the European Common Market and (later) Union may have temporarily slowed this move away from arable land use. Despite the slowdown in conversion to arable land, many old-growth forests were still clear-cut in Europe in the second half of the century, especially in England.

The two most destructive and significant kinds of environmental change have been the rise in industrial, chemical, and nuclear pollution of air and waters, and the deaths and pollution caused by the massive growth in vehicles powered by internal combustion engines. Indeed, it is the use of oil fuel that has created the most significant changes in environmental quality and quality of life in the twentieth century. The largest site of air and water pollution in Europe was the Ruhr basin in Germany, the biggest industrial region of Europe. Between 1870 and 1910 the region grew rapidly, both industrially and as a pollution source for both human and industrial waste. By 1906 the Emscher River had become an open sewage canal seventy miles in length. Industrial pollution, the worst in the world by 1914, was checked only by the impact of postwar reparations in 1923. It was then that the pioneering Siedlingsverband-Ruhrkohlenbezirk (Ruhr coal district settlement association) stepped in to try to save the remaining woods and trees from pollution damage and to attempt to control further growth of the region. In 1928

the damage caused by acid rain was first announced and propagandized, as the beginning of a long fight against acid rain and other industrial pollution in Germany that has lasted to the present day, but which was only revivified in the period since World War II by Chancellor Willy Brandt in 1969.

The spread of the automobile in western Europe in the 1920s and 1930s led to the development of arterial road systems and low-density urban sprawl that quickly reached into the countryside, along coasts, and beside seaside resorts. The growth was most rapid in Britain, where road-served suburbs spread rapidly west and south of London and along once beautiful parts of the Sussex coast. Similar developments took place on the outskirts of large cities such as Berlin, Paris, and Rotterdam. In England these unsightly and uncontrolled developments, driven jointly by car ownership and land speculation, soon led to an outcry in favor of planning control and "green belt" legislation, led by such organizations as the Council for the Preservation of Rural England and propagandized in books such as *Britain and the Beast,* edited by John Maynard Keynes in 1937. World War II temporarily ended these interwar conservation campaigns against the effects of the automobile. However, the impact of wartime planning psychology, especially in Britain, quickly led in the postwar period to the innovative and extensive growth of a government conservation and planning bureaucracy in the form of the Nature Conservancy and the Town and Country Planning Act, both legislated in 1949 to systematize a nationwide form of conservation and planning control.

Increasing anxieties over pesticide use and industrial pollution surfaced strongly in the late 1950s all over Europe, influenced to some extent by a parallel campaign against nuclear weapons, epitomized in England by the Aldermaston marches. Government and nongovernment organizations now started to collaborate to some extent in framing new legislation to control long-standing pollution risks. In England public anger at government failure to control London "smogs" peaked in the mid-1950s after a run of winters in which over four thousand people, mainly elderly, had died directly from the effects of air pollutants made from a cocktail of coal-fired power station emissions and petro- and diesel-chemical exhausts. The wholesale closure of the London tramway system in 1951 and the introduction of thousands of new diesel buses had seriously exacerbated the problem. Strict controls on coal burning and the Clean Air Acts of the late 1950s partially solved the problem; the episode also alerted European governments to a rising tide of public environmental awareness. In Germany a growing concern developed during the 1970s about

Nuclear Accident. A technician checks radiation levels at the Chernobyl reactor, Ukrainian S.S.R., June 1986. SOVFOTO/ EASTFOTO

developing in the 1960s. The risks from nuclear energy became a particular focus of attention for the emerging environmental movement. However, a very internationalist interest in saving endangered animal species, especially the whale, and in protecting tropical rainforests started to characterize European environmentalism. During the 1970s these preoccupations were transmuted into overtly political interests and specifically into the Green political parties, which by 1990 were present in every European country.

The Chernobyl nuclear disaster in the Ukraine in 1986 was a watershed in this respect. Green movements had been one of the few modes through which any form of political protest could take place behind the Iron Curtain. The failure of the state that the Chernobyl incident symbolized was a vital constituent of the decline in credibility of the communist governments in Eastern Europe and Russia during the 1980s. But the accumulation of evidence of the wholesale failure of the communist states to regulate pollution exerted an aftereffect that was not confined to the East. It also helped to destroy the last shreds of the popular European confidence in science that had flourished in the immediate postwar period in the West, and contributed to popular mistrust in the ability of conventional political parties and governments to protect the European environment, the climate, and the quality of life of European citizens. An initial result of this new level of distrust was the emergence of a far more confrontational style of radical environmental politics. Groups such as Earth First! (which had originated in the United States) and the loose coalitions that made up European antiroads movements began in the 1990s to fight through low-level, prolonged, and largely nonviolent direct actions against road-building and airport projects. These coalitions modeled themselves on activist animal protection groups and, more importantly, on resistance groups such as the Greenham Common Women, who had fought so apparently successfully against the installation of cruise nuclear missiles in eastern England. It remains to be seen whether these kinds of activist environmental groupings will be successful in encouraging European governments to move closer to the agendas of radical environmentalism. The failure of most European governments to move away from the established models of growth economies and continued erosion of habitats and biodiversity do not augur well in this respect.

the effects of acid rain. This kind of pollution had cross-border impacts throughout central Europe and crystallized many of the concerns of a powerful new green movement now headed, significantly, by a woman, Petra Kelly.

Europewide student and labor protests in 1968, associated partly with the anti–Vietnam War movement and partly with structural and political problems especially endemic to France, had already given a major boost to the environmental movement. In the years after 1968 such movements as Greenpeace and Friends of the Earth articulated European and North American environmentalist themes and reflected the growth of a mass movement that had already been

See also **The Annales Paradigm** *(volume 1);* **Protoindustrialization** *(in this volume);* **The Industrial Revolutions** *(in this volume);* **Urbanization** *(in this volume);* **Agri-**

culture *(in this volume);* **New Social Movements** *(volume 3); and other articles in this section.*

BIBLIOGRAPHY

Albion, Robert Greenhalgh. *Forests and Sea Power.* Cambridge, Mass., 1926.

Barrell, John. *The Idea of Landscape and the Sense of Place, 1730–1840; An Approach to the Poetry of John Clare.* Cambridge, U.K., 1972.

Bate, Jonathan. *Romantic Ecology.* London, 1991.

Blanqui, Michel. *Du deboisement des montagnes.* Paris, Chez Renard, 1846.

Brown, John Croumbie. *The French Forest Ordinance of 1669; with Historical Sketch of the Previous Treatment of Forests in France.* Edinburgh, 1883.

Brown, John Croumbie. *Forests and Forestry of Northern Russia and the Lands Beyond.* Edinburgh, 1884.

Braudel, Fernand. *The Mediterranean and the Mediterranean World in the Age of Philip II.* Translated by Siân Reynolds. Berkeley, Calif., 1995.

Braudel, Fernand. *The Structures of Everyday Life.* Translated by Siân Reynolds. London, 1981.

Brimblecombe, Peter, and Christian Pfister, eds. *The Silent Countdown: Essays in European Environmental History.* Berlin, 1990.

Butlin, Robin A., and Neil Roberts. *Ecological Relations in Historical Times: Human Impact and Adaptation.* London, 1995.

Buzard, James. *The Beaten Track: European Tourism, Literature, and the Ways to Culture, 1800–1918.* Oxford, 1992.

Charlton, D. G. *New Images of the Natural in France.* Cambridge, U.K., 1984.

Clapp, B. W. *An Environmental History of Britain since the Industrial Revolution.* London, 1994.

Cosgrove, Denis. *Social Formation and Symbolic Landscape.* London, 1984.

Crosby, Alfred W. *Ecological Imperialism: The Biological Expansion of Europe, 900–1900.* Cambridge, U.K., 1986.

Crosby, Alfred W. *Germs, Seeds, and Animals: Studies in Ecological History.* Armonk, N.Y., 1994.

Darby, Henry Clifford. "The Clearing of the English Woodlands." *Geography* 36 (1951): 71–83.

Darby, Henry Clifford. *The Draining of the Fens.* 2d ed. Cambridge, U.K., 1956.

Dietrich, B. F. A. "European Forests and Their Utilisation." *Economic Geography* 4 (1928) 140–158.

Fernow, Bernhard E. *A Brief History of Forestry: In Europe, the United States, and Other Countries.* Toronto, 1907.

Glacken, Clarence J. *Traces on the Rhodian Shore: Nature and Culture in Western Thought, from Ancient Times to the End of the Eighteenth Century.* Berkeley, Calif., 1967.

Goudie, Andrew S. *The Changing Earth: Rates of Geomorphological Processes.* Oxford, 1995.

Grove, Alfred Thomas, and Oliver Rackham. *The Nature of the Mediterranean.* New Haven, Conn., 2000.

Grove, Jean M. *The Little Ice Age.* London, 1988.

Grove, Richard. "Cressey Dymock and the Draining of the Great Level: An Early Agricultural Model." *Geographical Journal* 147 (1981): 27–37.

Grove, Richard. "The Global Impact of the 1789–1793 El Niño." *Nature* 393 (1998): 318–319.

Grove, Richard. *Green Imperialism; Colonial Expansion, Tropical Island Edens, and the Origins of Environmentalism.* New York, 1995.

Grove, Richard, and John Chappell. "El Niño Chronology and the History of Global Crises during the Little Ice Age." In *El Niño: History and Crisis.* Edited by Richard Grove and John Chappell. Cambridge, 2000.

Harvey, Graham. *The Killing of the Countryside.* London, 1997.

Lamprecht, Karl. *Deutsche Geschichte.* Vol 3. Berlin, 1893.

Lane, Fredric Chapin. *Venetian Ships and Shipbuilders of the Renaissance.* Baltimore, 1934.

Le Roy Ladurie, Emmanuel. *Times of Feast, Times of Famine: A History of Climate since the Year 1000.* Translated by Barbara Bray. Garden City, N.Y., 1971.

Lowe, Philip D. "Values and Institutions in British Nature Conservation." In *Conservation in Perspective.* Edited by Andrew Warren and Barry Goldsmith. Chichester, U.K., and New York, 1983.

McNeill, John R. *The Mountains of the Mediterranean World.* Cambridge, U.K., 1992.

McNeill, John R. *Something New under the Sun: An Environmental History of the Twentieth-Century World.* New York, 2000.

Mead, William R. *Farming in Finland.* London, 1953.

Perlin, John. *A Forest Journey: The Role of Wood in the Development of Civilisation.* New York and London, 1989.

Pyne, Stephen. *Vestal Fire: An Environmental History, Told through Fire, of Europe and Europe's Encounter with the World.* Seattle, Wash., 1997.

Quinn, William H., Victor T. Neal, and Santiago E. Antunez de Mayolo. "El Niño Occurrences over the Past Four and a Half Centuries." *Journal of Geophysical Research* 92 (1987): 14,449–14,461.

Schama, Simon. *Landscape and Memory.* New York, 1995.

Sclafert, T., "A propos du deboisement des Alpes du Sud." *Annales de Géographie* 42 (1933): 266–277, 350–360.

Skipp, Victor. *Crisis and Development: An Ecological Case Study of the Forest of Arden, 1570–1674.* Cambridge, U.K., 1978.

Soderquist, Thomas. *The Ecologists: From Merry Naturalists to Saviours of the Nation,* Stockholm, 1986.

Straker, Ernest. *Wealden Iron.* London, 1931.

Taylor, Bron Raymond. *Ecological Resistance Movements: The Global Emergence of Radical and Popular Environmentalism.* Albany, N.Y., 1995.

Te Brake, William H. "Air Pollution and Fuel Crises in Pre-Industrial London, 1250–1650." *Technology and Culture* 16 (1975): 337–359.

Thomas, Keith. *Man and the Natural World: Changing Attitudes in England, 1500–1800.* London, 1983.

Turner, B. L., ed. *The Earth as Transformed by Human Action: Global and Regional Changes in the Biosphere over the Past 300 Years.* Cambridge, 1990.

Tocqueville, Alexis de. *L'ancien régime et la Révolution.* Edited by J. P. Mayer. Paris, 1952.

Wall, Derek. *Earth First! and the Anti-Roads Movement: Radical Environmentalism and Comparative Social Movements.* London, 1999.

Wilcox, H. A. *The Woodlands and Marshlands of England.* Liverpool, 1933.

Williams, W. H. *The Commons, Open Spaces, and Footpaths Preservation Society, 1865–1965: A Short History of the Society and Its Work.* London, 1965

Worster, Donald. *Nature's Economy: A History of Ecological Ideas.* 2d ed. Cambridge, U.K., 1994.

Young, Arthur. *Travels in France.* Edited by Constantia Maxwell. London, 1950.

MIGRATION

Leslie Page Moch

Human mobility has been fundamental to European societies throughout their histories, yet the role it has played has changed with each era. By the eighteenth century, the social organization of migration took recognizable forms that remain useful in observing migration through to the twenty-first century.

Coerced migrations oust people from home against their will (for example, enslaved Africans and persecuted European Protestants) and forbid their return.

Settler migrations move people (like the English settlers in North America) far from home who were unlikely—but not completely unable—to return.

Career migrations move people at the will of their employers, who determine the movement and the possibility of return home (for example, Spanish and Portuguese Jesuit priests in Central America and Brazil).

Chain migrations link people from a common hometown or village with a particular destination. Operating through human contacts, especially people from home who, once settled at the destination, would help newcomers, this may be the most common organization of migration in peacetime history.

Circular migrations are undertaken by people who mean to return home after a period of time (such as their years as a servant or apprentice in town or their months away at seasonal harvest work).

Local migrations keep movers (like the bride from a neighboring village or worker born in the outskirts of the city) close to familiar faces and routines.

Although both men and women moved, migration was distinct for each sex. More men than women left Europe for the Americas until the twentieth century; moreover, men dominated the large teams of migrant harvesters that circulated through regions in the summers. Most migrants were young, single people, and men and women almost always worked at different occupations—this meant that they often chose different destinations, and even in a large city with work for all, young women were often domestic servants while young men were apprentices or laborers. Because women were more likely to travel short distances to marry or to work as servants, women may have actually been more likely to leave home than young men. In addition, noneconomic motives for migration, such as marriage, family difficulties, and a pregnancy to keep secret played a more significant role for women than for men.

LATE MIDDLE AGES AND THE RENAISSANCE

European society in the late Middle Ages and early Renaissance was primarily rural, yet people were not immobile. Indeed, inquiry into rural mobility has substantially changed our view of European rural history. Trade, exchanges of land, and human relations dictated certain kinds of movements. This remained the case for the coming centuries, to varying degrees. Beggars and pedlars brought news to isolated villages; peasants bought and sold property and moved in freeholding areas. In addition, merchants moved across long distances products that eventually reached elites everywhere: leather from central Spain, wool from England, cloth from Flanders, metals from central German areas, furs and timber from Scandinavia, grain from the north-central European plain, olive oil from the Mediterranean littoral. Finally, social life and church marriage regulations meant that men and women often sought mates outside the confines of their village.

The Protestant Reformation, beginning in 1517, opened a period of wars, repressions, and feuds that marked patterns of mobility. The Peasant Revolt of 1524–1525 marked the beginning of religiously based conflicts that developed into civil wars, the French Wars of Religion, the Dutch Revolt, and the Thirty

Assisting Migrants. Emigrants on their way to an emigrants' assistance office, Naples, c. 1920. TOURING CLUB ITALIANO/GESTIONE ARCHIVI ALINARI/ART RESOURCE, NY

Years' War (1618–1648), all of which emptied out regions, destroying farmlands and families. In addition, religious struggles led Protestant refugees—the Huguenots—to seek shelter in safe havens such as Calvin's Geneva, England, or the Netherlands. Intolerance moved people through the end of the seventeenth century; when Louis XIV terminated tolerance for Protestants by revoking the Edict of Nantes in 1685, for example, some 160,000 Protestants are estimated to have fled France.

With the European—initially Iberian—explorations of the sixteenth century, Spain and Portugal sent thousands of people (almost all men) across the Atlantic and Indian oceans as soldiers, seamen, priests, and traders. As the spice trade with India developed into the extraction of gold and silver in Mexico and Peru, more Europeans went to seek their fortune and many died abroad. These early explorations had two consequences for the mobility of European peoples. First, the seaports thrived; port cities such as Seville and Lisbon grew as they attracted seamen and potential expatriates from surrounding regions. In addition, men and women served as artisans and servants in these unusually prosperous cities; they came from the regions surrounding the seaports as well as from farther afield. Thus, even the earliest European explorations set off movements within Europe.

This is also true of the trade with Africa, which began as a gold trade under Portuguese auspices in the fifteenth century. This trade turned to a trade in enslaved Africans sold initially to work the mines and sugar plantations of the Americas. To date this was the largest single coerced migration in human history. About 8 million enslaved Africans arrived in the Americas before 1820, dwarfing the 2.3 million Europeans who by then had crossed the Atlantic. At least 9.5 million enslaved Africans arrived between the fifteenth and nineteenth centuries. About half of these went to the Caribbean, a third to Brazil, and only about 6 percent to what became the United States. Not until 1840 did more Europeans than Africans cross the Atlantic.

Nonetheless, the empires and explorations of early modern Europe increasingly affected seaports, small towns, and villages as the Iberian empires gave way in importance to those of the Dutch, English, and French. Both London and Amsterdam, for example, grew fivefold between 1550 and 1650, and more than doubled in the seventeenth century. Amsterdam was fed by people fleeing the Spanish Netherlands after 1550, and its imperial trade attracted immigrants from Germany and Norway as well as rural Dutch. A third of the people married in Amsterdam in the seventeenth century and one fourth of the eighteenth-century marriage partners were from outside the Dutch Republic. Many were Norwegian seamen, but German immigrants were most important: over 28,000 German men married in the city in these centuries, and over 19,000 German women. Many newcomers joined the ranks of seamen, but others—like the German women who were domestic servants—joined the labor force of the booming seaport. The same is true of London: it grew despite being the departure point for thousands of sailors, colonials, and indentured servants in the seventeenth century; moreover, it was the most important vocational training center for apprentices from throughout England as well as the workplace for young women servants and seamstresses from the surrounding regions. Thus, the early European empires affected not only world political and economic patterns, but also patterns of migration and settlement within the continent. Often, the number of people who entered the city far outnumbered its actual increase in population for two reasons: first, many subsequently went to sea as sailors, indentured servants, traders, or adventurers, never to return; second, many worked in the city and then left again to return home or to try another destination. Turnover and temporary migration were incalculably important to early modern cities.

Aside from the mobility affected by overseas exploration and settlement, the European continent was enlivened by continuing patterns of chain migration, circular migration, and local migrations that stirred the countryside and fueled cities. Many more people moved within Europe than left its shores. Chain migrations linked towns and villages to regional and national capitals as, for example, a sister joined her domestic servant sibling in town or village construction workers joined their experienced compatriots in a growing capital. Circular migrations not only sent workers—and elites—to cities and home again, but also organized harvest work. Local migrations characterized most marriage markets and land transfers.

THE EIGHTEENTH CENTURY

Two shifts modified the ongoing migration patterns in the eighteenth century. First, around 1750 the population began to grow throughout Europe in a trend that continued until the late twentieth century. In the 1750–1800 period alone, the population increased by 34 percent. Earlier marriage and fewer disastrous epidemics (such as the bubonic plague) meant that more children survived to need work and food; households and villages were fuller than they had been since the fourteenth century. At the same time, the production of goods in domestic settings—called rural industry, domestic industry, or cottage industry—expanded dramatically, increasing to unprecedented volumes as villagers produced products such as yarn, thread, silk, linen, cotton, ship nails, socks, watches, lace, and shoes in their homes. These fundamental

demographic and economic developments affected migration so that two distinct patterns of geographic mobility emerged.

On one hand, rural industry enabled villages, small towns, and certain urban centers to thrive—those that coordinated, finished, and exported domestic products. Precisely the small towns that coordinated this production were the kinds of urban areas to grow in this period, and industrial villages also attracted and retained people more than others. Many rural workers were women because the production of lace and fabric depended on women's work. The Austrian cotton firm Schwechat illustrates the size and composition of the labor force: in 1752, 408 workers worked in and around Vienna finishing cloth, 49 distributed raw material, 436 wove cloth (men's work), and 5,655 women were spinners. Rural production had the general effect of supporting people in industrial regions at home.

On the other hand, not all members of the new generations of the eighteenth century were supported by local economies. For more people, leaving home to work became routine. Indeed, by the end of the eighteenth century, seasonal, circular mobility expanded. In western and southern Europe, seven massive migration systems engaged at least 20,000 people each by 1800, most of whom were men. The greatest number of workers in the north traveled to the Paris basin where harvest work in the Ile-de-France and the city created a double attraction; they came from throughout France to work as laborers, traders, and harvest workers. The system that brought men to Holland was next most important, including up to 30,000 men at its peak; they came from Germany and France to work as sailors, servants, and harvesters. A third system in the north brought some 20,000 people to work in London and the home counties; from Ireland, Scotland, and Wales, they divided between urban laborers and harvest workers. The largest system in the south drew about 100,000 workers per year to Corsica, Rome, and Italy's central plain; harvest workers in vineyards and wheatfields and construction workers hailed primarily from Italy's mountainous provinces. The Po Valley engaged about 50,000 people; mountain-dwellers came to its rice fields and construction sites in Turin and Milan. Madrid and Castile attracted not only 60,000 workers from Galicia in northwest Spain, but also an army of upland French; these two groups of workers performed urban work as well as grain harvesting. Finally, the Mediterranean littoral, from northeastern Spain to Provence in eastern France, brought some 35,000 people out of the highlands every year to harvest grain and grapes, and to perform tasks in Barcelona and Marseille. These seven systems were essential to the workings of eighteenth-century European economies, and forecast future systems of circular migration by their size and importance.

THE NINETEENTH CENTURY

During the one hundred years between the fall of Napoleon and the opening shots of World War I (1815–1914), demographic and economic shifts again reshaped patterns of human mobility. The first of these is the astonishing growth of the population of Europe. The population of 187 million in 1800 grew to 468 million by 1913, increasing 42 percent in the first half of the century and another 76 percent by World War I. Behind this population growth lay high birthrates, a decrease in deaths from disease, and improved production and distribution of food. Consequently, European populations expanded more rapidly than those of Africa and Asia. In fact, Europeans and people of European origin were 22 percent of the world's population in 1800, and such people were 38 percent of the global population on the eve of World War I.

The second shift is the collapse of rural livelihoods, which began in Britain, to the west, and moved, unevenly, by region, to the east and south. Small farms and subsistence agriculture increasingly gave way to large-scale cash crops, such as the sugar beet. Crops failed: the potato famine in Ireland in the early 1840s is the most disastrous example of food shortages that were widespread, especially in the "hungry forties." Rural industries failed in region after region under the pressure of competition from mechanized industry; they had allowed hundreds of thousands of country people to survive.

Third, mechanized industry took hold in Britain, then on the continent, expanding not only industrial productivity and trade, but also the service sector of urban society. Relatedly, changes in transportation technology furthered long-distance movement, although much mobility, including urbanization, occurred in short regional moves. In the long run, these changes produced an urban society in Europe. By 1900, over half the British lived in towns of over 20,000, as did one-quarter of Belgians and Dutch and one-fifth of Germans and French. Urbanization, the growth in the proportion of people living in cities, is a central characteristic of this period when village society lost its preeminence as urban growth outstripped rural growth.

The collapse of rural livelihoods and the insecurity engendered by these collapses is at the heart of migration shifts, which left millions of people (particularly young people) with few alternatives to departure. Employment as farm hands (farm servants), which had engaged young men and women in annual contracts, was reduced as farm routines were increasingly dictated by the rhythm of cash crops; this meant that fewer people had year-round employment and more joined the teams of sugar beet workers, grain harvesters, and potato diggers that increasingly traveled to large farms to work for a period of weeks or months. The great systems of circular migration of 1800 described above gave way to larger systems of rural workers. For example, at midcentury 50,000 Irish per year worked in England between the time they planted their potatoes in February and harvested them in November. Over 264,000 male and 98,000 female agricultural workers in France moved in seasonal migration circuits, not counting the foreign harvesters like Belgians who harvested grain in northern France. The number of people working the vine harvest—intense, short-term work—reached nearly 526,000 men and 352,000 women. After 1850, when sugar beet cultivation became more important, 50,000 Belgians cut sugar beets in France and over 100,000 international workers (Russians, Poles, and Scandinavians) worked in Saxony. Poles—many of them women—from Galicia went east to Russia and west into German territories to work sugar beet and potato fields. Germany regulated the movement of its international workers to ensure their temporary status, especially Poles, who were required to return home from December to February. Thus, the agricultural labor force was international and mobile in 1914.

This is also true of the labor force that constructed the new transportation infrastructure of the nineteenth century, the railroad. Begun in England in the 1830s and 1840s, then Belgium, the Low Countries, then France, Germany, and Italy in the rest of the century, this was seasonal, outdoor work blasting out tunnels, building bridges, grading railroad beds, and laying rails. Railroad construction employed people willing to live in makeshift barracks in remote areas; these were often foreign workers: the Irish in England, Poles in Germany, and Italians in Germany, France, and Switzerland.

If temporary work was the hallmark of the countryside, it was also true for cities. Most important, the expanding cities of Europe were built by seasonal labor; housing, commercial spaces, public facilities, and urban infrastructures such as streets, sewer systems, tram lines, and subways were based on the summer work of men in the construction trades. Workers from Spanish Galicia and northern Portugal built Madrid, construction workers from Poland and Italy labored in the Rhine-Ruhr zone, masons from central France built Paris and Lyon. By 1907, over 30,000 Italians were at work in excavation and masonry in Germany, over 57,000 in construction—this in addition to the 14,000 German brickmakers from Lippe, whose migrant labor shadowed the construction season.

After the countryside, cities were the second great destination of the nineteenth-century European migrant. Millions of men and women moved to cities and—due to insecurity, a desire to return home, or a new opportunity—moved on. It is the net number of people who stayed on who ultimately created an urbanizing continent. Some cities mushroomed where there had only been small towns before; this enormous growth was the hallmark of the industrial age. Many newcomers were women, drawn to the textile towns that offered so much employment in spinning mills in the early industrial period. Manchester, for example, the first city of the industrial revolution, was home to over 41,000 people in 1774, nearly 271,000 by 1831, and over 600,000 in 1900. On the other hand, men outnumbered women in the metalworking and coal towns of the Ruhr Valley. Duisburg, at the confluence of the Rhine and Ruhr rivers, grew from 8,900 in 1848 to nearly 107,000 in 1904. Most cities with a longer history were commercial and administrative centers, and added some industry on their peripheries; their newcomers were proletarian laborers, domestic servants, dressmakers, artisans, clerks, and other service workers. Paris, for example, grew from 547,000 to over 2.5 million during the century; more typically, the provincial town of Nimes in southern France grew from 40,000 to 80,000.

The third great destination of nineteenth-century migrants lay beyond the Atlantic Ocean. Transoceanic migration was not new, but greatly expanded on previous trends. For example, about 1.5 million people had emigrated from Britain to North America in the eighteenth century; some 125,000 German settlers in North America had been increased by about 17,000 mercenaries who stayed on after the American Revolution. After 1815, 30,000 to 40,000 European migrants came to the Americas annually. Then in the 1840s, mass migrations began, fueled by two trends. On one hand, the demand for labor exploded in the farmlands and cities in North America and the sugar and coffee plantations of Latin America. Particularly in Latin America, the abolition of slavery was behind this demand for plantation workers. For example, Brazil, which had absorbed 38 percent of enslaved Africans since 1500, outlawed slavery in stages, from the abolition of the African slave trade in 1851 to the Golden Law of full abolition in 1888; consequently, it recruited Europeans (especially Italians) in hopes of replacing its field workers. On the other hand, Eu-

rope's "hungry forties," political struggles, and huge population growth exacerbated suffering and employment and thereby encouraged emigration. Transatlantic departures pushed into high gear as 200,000 to 300,000 Europeans departed in the late 1840s. Most dramatically, during the worst years of the potato famine in Ireland (1846–1851), a million Irish perished and another million set out for England and the United States; at this time the Germans and Dutch, also hard-hit, set out for the United States. Even this number increased so that an estimated 13 million embarked between 1840 and 1880 and another 13 million between 1880 and 1900. About 52 million migrants left Europe between 1860 and 1914, of whom roughly 37 million (72 percent) traveled to North America, 11 million (21 percent) to South America, and 3.5 million (6 percent) to Australia and New Zealand. About one-third of the emigrants to North American returned home.

THE TWENTIETH CENTURY

By the eve of World War I, mobile Europeans crossed the countrysides in work teams, entered the growing cities of the continent, and tried their fortunes abroad; at every destination, many men and women returned home or tried another destination. In many cases, they were part of an international labor force in city and countryside—whether in Europe or the Americas—laboring in factories, fields, offices, and middle-class kitchens. On the continent in 1910, there were over one million foreign workers in Germany, among them nearly 600,000 Poles and 150,000 Italians; foreigners were about 2 percent of the population. France, too, harbored over a million foreigners, over 400,000 Italians and nearly 300,000 Belgians; foreigners constituted about 3 percent of the population. Foreign immigrants were even more important in Switzerland, where nearly 15 percent of the population and 17 percent of the labor force were foreigners, with over 200,000 each of Germans and Italians. Most foreign laborers in western Europe were Polish, Italian, Belgian, or German, but the working reality of the immigrant labor force was more complex than that. Consider the frustrated foreman in the Ruhr Valley in 1901 who could not understand any of the thirty workers under his supervision—despite the fact that he spoke five languages! His work crew were Dutch men from the northwestern Netherlands, Poles from eastern German territories, and Croatians.

World War I. These vast flows of migrants changed suddenly with the outbreak of World War I, heralding a century of dramatic shifts in patterns of mobility

The Irish in England. "A Court for King Cholera," the Irish district in an English city. Drawing by John Leech in *Punch,* 25 September 1852. MARY EVANS PICTURE LIBRARY

and increasing state control—at least attempted control—of migration. With the outbreak of hostilities in the summer of 1914, overseas migrations nearly ceased, and in 1915, many Europeans returned home to fight. In Europe, the majority of Germans returned to their country. Not everyone was free to go home, however, and wartime meant labor recruitment and coerced migration. In the interests of the German state, over 300,000 Russian-Polish seasonal industrial and agricultural workers were kept on; where they had been forced to return home annually before the war, they were now forbidden to return. Russian Polish men of military age were retained so that they could not join enemy armies. Germany also used prisoners of war and recruited Belgian workers by force in the winter of 1916–1917, when over 100,000 Dutch and Belgians worked behind German lines. France used similar tactics, expanding its wartime labor force with prisoners of war and contract labor from Greece, Portugal, Spain, Italy, Algeria, Indochina, and China.

The twentieth century was an age of coerced migration for Europeans and for people worldwide. With the end of the war came the first great refugee movement of the century. The war, then revolution and civil war in Russia set off a stream of 500,000 refugees and exiles into Germany, 400,000 into France, and 70,000 into Poland; this stopped only when the border of the USSR closed in 1923. The years of war

had forced migration from Polish territories, so that about 700,000 Poles were repatriated by 1923. An estimated 200,000 Germans were repatriated, many from the eastern provinces of the Reich that were returned to a reconstructed Poland after the Versailles settlement. In the west, about 120,000 Germans from Alsace-Lorraine fled into the Rhineland, and 50,000 French moved into Alsace-Lorraine as it once again became part of France. This war, then, not only killed 10 million, but was also the impetus for the flight of Russians, Poles, and Germans to the west and the resettling of people around Alsace and the Rhineland.

After the war, the United States restricted immigration by passing laws in 1921 and 1924 that instituted restrictive national quotas on southern and eastern Europeans, especially cutting off the immigration of Poles and Italians that had been so significant before 1918. Immigration to Germany was reduced as well, since it was plagued by inflation and unemployment in the 1920s; the 2 million foreigners in 1918 were reduced to 174,000 by 1924. (Nonetheless, Germany continued to regulate foreign labor, especially in agriculture, where some 50,000 Polish workers came for the beet and potato harvests in 1920.)

By contrast, the state of France encouraged immigration. It allowed Russian and Polish political émigrés to build communities and also encouraged foreign workers for the rebuilding of war-destroyed areas and repletion of its labor force. The state eased the entry of a million reconstruction workers between 1919 and 1924; commercial recruiters brought many Poles—33,000 for sugar beet and wheat harvests, and 139,000 for the mines of northern France—who formed a cohesive and important minority. In addition, an increasing number of Spanish and Italians entered southern France. On the eve of the Depression, France had an unmatched number of foreign workers, 1.6 million, including, in order of importance, Italians, Poles, Spaniards, Belgians, Germans, Swiss, Algerians, Russians, Yugoslavs, Czechs, and Romanians.

With the Depression of the 1930s and the unemployment it engendered, the flow of workers throughout Europe altered dramatically. Most countries encouraged repatriation and restricted entries of foreigners. Germany closed its doors; by 1932, only 108,000 foreign workers remained, most of whom were longtime residents with permanent visas, and only 5,000 were agricultural workers. Only France was needy enough to require a significant bedrock of foreign workers, because its labor force had been so depleted by World War I and because its birthrate had long been low.

The movement of refugees began again between the wars, as fascist victories ousted political enemies and specific ethnic groups. For the victims of fascism in Italy, Germany, and Spain, France was the most important asylum on the continent. The first to exit were Italians who left in the wake of Mussolini's ascension to power in 1922. With Hitler's appointment as chancellor in Germany in 1933, 65,000 Germans left the Reich, about 80 percent of whom were Jews. Refugees of the 1930s faced restrictions, bureaucratic sluggishness, and anti-Semitism. Between 1933 and 1937, over 17,000 Germans, 80 to 85 percent of whom were Jews, found asylum in the United States. The Jews of Poland, Romania, and Hungary, who far outnumbered German Jews, were also in flight, because their home states increasingly persecuted Jews. As conditions in Central Europe deteriorated, Polish Jews predominated among the nearly 62,000 who found refuge in Palestine in 1935. By the eve of World War II, 110,000 Jewish refugees, many of whom were attempting to leave the continent altogether, were spread throughout Europe—about 40,000 in France, 8,000 in Switzerland, and many among the 50,000 people who found asylum in England in the 1933–1939 period. In 1939, France was literally awash in refugees, as some 450,000 Spanish republicans who came in the wake of Francesco Franco's victory in the Civil War joined those fleeing fascism in Italy, Germany, and Central Europe.

World War II. With the outbreak of war, the uprooting and displacement of peoples began on a monumental scale. On the western front, refugees fled before the German armies; by the end of May 1940, 2

War Refugees. Russian civilians flee the German advance as Soviet supply trucks head for the front, July 1941. M. SAVIN/ITR-TASS/SOVFOTO

million French, 2 million Belgians, 70,000 Luxembourger, and 50,000 Dutch were displaced and destitute in northern France. One-fifth of the French population fled toward the south. That summer, 100,000 French left Alsace-Lorraine as Germany repossessed this territory.

These upheavals in the West were less severe than those in the East, where masses of people were deliberately uprooted by Nazi policies and Soviet displacements. For example, Germany divided Poland into a western zone that was incorporated into the Reich and an eastern zone (the "General Government") for unskilled slave labor. Quickly, 1.5 million Poles, including 300,000 Jews, were deported to the General Government to make room for the favored German ethnics, like those from the Baltic states, who were uprooted with equal speed. European Jews who were trying to flee were caught in two forces by the end of 1941, when the final solution became defined as the murder of all European Jews: on one hand, avenues of escape dried up as the United States and Palestine both resisted entrants; on the other, Nazis began to round up Jews and send them to the General Government.

Other Europeans were pulled into the German Reich to be part of its wartime labor force. Early on, two million workers from the defeated nations and two million prisoners of war were coerced or persuaded to work in German fields and factories; by 1944, one worker in five was a foreign civilian or prisoner of war and Germany's forced laborers numbered over 7 million, primarily Soviets, Poles, and French.

With the war's end in 1945, millions of people took to the road. Forced laborers and prisoners of war returned home, and by the time the winter of 1945–1946 closed in, most of 11 million people moving west were repatriated. With the German retreat from the east, came two major, permanent shifts of European people and the second great refugee crisis of the century. The first shift was a move from east to west, as the advance of the Soviet army sent Germans fleeing into Germany—even long-established German minorities in central and eastern Europe. This marked the end of the historic eastward movement of Germans. The second shift was the destruction of European Jewry. The Allies anticipated that at least a million Jewish refugees would be found at the end of the war, but the number fell far short of that; for example, of Poland's Jewish community of greater than 3 million people, only some 31,000 (2.4 percent) survived. (Of those remaining, many Jews chose to leave Europe after the war, including some 340,000 who settled in Israel in the 18 months after its founding.) All told, the number of people displaced by the 1939–1945 war in Europe amounted to 30 million—men, women, and children of Eastern, Central and Western Europe who were displaced, deported, or transplanted in wartime.

The dramatic coerced migrations of wartime and large-scale prewar labor migrations occurred against a backdrop of ordinary movements that had long animated the lives of Europeans, such as moves to another village, regional city, or capital. By the end of World War II, however, fundamental changes at work in Europe since about 1880 altered the nature of migration for the second half of the century: levels of education and literacy had increased; European birthrates had declined; and European states were regulating foreigners with greater care. After 1950, the continent increasingly sought foreigners for unskilled jobs in agriculture, production, and services. Such people were in demand especially as smaller generations came to maturity. States sought them out, recruited them, and attempted to control their movements.

The immediate postwar period marked a fundamental shift in migration patterns that endured for the remainder of the twentieth century: there was adequate work in Europe for its people so that relatively few departed; indeed, the days of mass labor migration to the Western hemisphere had definitively ended. Concomitantly, Europe became a continent of immigration, and northwestern Europe a core attraction for Asians and Africans, as well as for Europeans from the south and east. The work of postwar rebuilding occupied the surviving population—and much of the new population. In the case of Germany, newcomers included 12 million *Volksdeutsch* refugees, who reached western Germany between the end of the war and 1950. From farther away came Asian Indians, members of now-independent nations of the New Commonwealth who numbered 218,000 by 1951; they joined England's immigrants of long standing, the Irish. These immigrants of the late 1940s and 1950s signal two demographically vibrant sources for newcomers to northwestern Europe: former colonies (which increased with decolonizations in the 1960s and 1970s), and the nations of southern Europe and the Mediterranean basin.

The foreign workers of postwar Europe echoed historical patterns and processes. These men and women entered the labor market at times when the deaths and low birthrates required new workers to substitute for a demographic lacuna; the twentieth-century migrants filled places left by the World War II dead and by the low birthrates of the depression just as previous migrants filled places left by the Thirty Years' War and other disasters. The newcomers complemented the place of the native-born in the labor force by taking the difficult, low-status jobs that Europeans avoided. Like the migrants in eighteenth- and nineteenth-century Europe, most postwar immigrants came from regions short on capital and long on population, regions much poorer than northwestern Europe. Moreover, the migration processes were similar to those of the past: most postwar migration streams were pioneered by men, but came to include a significant proportion of women. Like earlier migrants, the men who founded these migration streams to northwestern Europe intended to maintain or enhance their lives at home with money earned abroad; they came for months or years, but they did not intend to remain in Europe. As they had in the past, however, many stayed, sent for their families, and became a permanent part of European society.

Immigration into northwestern Europe increased dramatically between 1950 and 1972 as postwar rebuilding gave way to a prolonged economic boom. Like the 1880–1914 period, the postwar economic success created a time of intense capital formation, which engendered massive international migration. New Commonwealth nations (former British colonies in the Caribbean, the Indian subcontinent, and Africa) and East Germany both sent a flood of immigrants until they were cut off by the Commonwealth Immigrants Acts of 1962 and the construction of the Berlin wall in 1961. Western Germany (the Federal Republic of Germany, FRG) recruited workers through bilateral agreements with Italy and then with Turkey, Morocco, Portugal, Tunisia, and Yugoslavia. By 1971, over 3.2 million residents of the FRG, about 5 percent, were foreign born. These included over a million Turks, nearly 750,000 Yugoslavs, and over 500,000 Italians. At the same time, France housed about 3.3 million immigrants, approximately 6.7 percent of its population. The largest group of new arrivals were Algerians (nearly 850,000) who came to France in the wake of Algerian independence in 1962, in addition to 1.8 million southern Europeans from Italy, Spain, and Portugal. Although their numbers were fewer, foreigners also flocked to Switzerland, where 750,000 immigrants made up 16 percent of the population; the majority (500,000) came from Italy, but also from Spain, Yugoslavia, and Turkey.

All in all, the northwestern European countries of the FRG, France, Switzerland, Belgium, and the Netherlands hosted nearly 8 million nationals from Italy, Spain, Portugal, Greece, Yugoslavia, Turkey, Tunisia, Algeria, and Morocco in the early 1970s. With the exception of Algerians in France and other former colonials, most foreign nationals were thought of as temporary residents by host nations, or "guestworkers" (*Gastarbeiter*) as they were called in Germany.

The majority were men who had come to work, and especially in Switzerland (where foreign workers from the south lived in barracks as they rebuilt the infrastructure of Geneva) had limited rights to stay. There the language problem on work sites could be like it was in 1910 because labor teams combined men of different nationalities; ironically, although the city of Geneva specialized in international communications and hosted a well-educated corps of diplomatic, professional, and clerical employees, the construction workers—from central Spain, from southern Italy, from Bosnia—shared only a few words.

The expectation that foreign residents were temporary migrants was tested—and proven wrong—in the wake of the oil crisis, inflation, and recession that began in 1973. Over half of the eight million foreigners in northwestern Europe were wives, children, and other relatives who were not working (or did not report employment). Like circular, temporary, migrants in past centuries, the workers of the 1960s were willing to distort their lives considerably—to work at difficult, demeaning, and dangerous jobs; to tolerate very bad housing—as long as these conditions were temporary. However, migrant workers had not been willing to forego all hope of a family life. They had arranged periodic returns home, married at destination, or had sent for their wives. Some wives had been recruited as laborers in their own right, and many children were brought along or born in the host country. In any case, migrant communities had changed, and their demographic structure by 1973 more resembled immigrant communities than temporary labor groups.

Nonetheless, host countries made vigorous efforts to stop immigration altogether. In November of 1973, the FRG banned entries of workers from non–European Community nations and within a year several other governments did the same. France banned the entry of dependents as well as of workers, then offered a repatriation allowance. The Netherlands and Germany began assistance plans for Yugoslavia and Turkey to increase employment in workers' home countries. No country except Switzerland, however, instituted the stringent measures necessary to keep foreigners out, efficaciously barring the entry of dependents. The attempt to shut off immigration was fundamentally unsuccessful, and more dependents joined their relatives in northwestern Europe. The absolute number of foreign residents increased by 13 percent in the FRG between 1974 and 1982, by 33 percent in France (1969–1981) and by 13 percent in Britain (1971–1981). Although the flow of newcomers was reduced from the 1960s, the total numbers of foreign residents did not diminish and they appeared to be "guests come to stay."

Algerians in France. Immigrants in Marseille protesting against the killing of an Algerian in Avignon, France, in 1985. ©RICHARD KALVAR/MAGNUM PHOTOS

The economic crises of the early 1970s sharpened hostility to foreign workers and gave birth to several anti-immigrant political movements that retained their energies through the end of the century. European prejudices—irritated by the phenotypical distinctiveness of many foreigners, their visibility in local labor markets, and their numbers in many cities—fed off social stress and fueled antiforeign incidents. Algerians were murdered in southern France and their wives were denied residence permits in the north. Similar actions against Pakistanis in Britain and against Turks in Germany reflected growing hostility to immigrants, particularly to those who were distinct in race or ethnicity. Resentment was fueled as foreigners became more visible as their children entered school systems, social welfare programs attended to their families, and public housing attempted to eradicate the shantytowns that had spread on the edge of many a metropolis. Organized racist groups such as the National Front in Britain, and neo-Nazis in the FRG, and anti-immigrant political parties such as the Front National in France, and the Centrum Partij in the Netherlands, expanded in the anti-immigration politics of the 1970s. The large proportion of Muslims among newcomers in Europe called forth a particularly strong response, as an anti-Muslim bias was

deep-rooted and of long standing in Europe. Like many migrants throughout history, Muslims who entered European urban society brought distinct patterns of gender relations, fertility, and labor force participation.

Migration to Europe of significant, but stable, ethnic minorities and immigration patterns shifted again shortly before the European Union was to be finalized in 1992. The opening of the Berlin Wall in 1989, followed by the unification of Germany in 1990 and the collapse of the Soviet Union in 1991, put Germany at the center of a host of migration streams, including East-West movement of labor migrants, asylum-seekers, and ethnic Germans from the former Soviet Union, Poland, Romania, and other Eastern European countries. Under German law, ethnic Germans have rights to citizenship; 397,000 of these *Aussiedler* arrived in 1990, 148,000 from the Soviet Union, 134,000 from Poland, and 111,150 from Romania. Fears proved groundless that an open Europe, shut off from the East by Cold War policies, would become a "Fortress Europe" implementing exclusionary policies to keep out East Europeans; although Germany received great numbers of ethnic Germans and refugees, by the end of the twentieth century there was no great flood of Eastern Europeans to the west. Rather, Poland and Hungary were becoming nations of immigration. Refugees from the Balkan wars of the 1990s were part of a formidable contingent of asylum-seekers from countries such as Eritrea, Afghanistan, Chile, Argentina, and Vietnam, as well as from eastern and southern Europe.

The close of the twentieth century, then, found Europe transformed by the human mobility of the century, which showed no signs of slowing in a global age of migration. The foreign-born, and their children, were an important contingent in the increasingly diverse societies of this continent. In 1990, there were 1.9 million foreign citizens in the United Kingdom (3.3 percent of the total population). European Community nationals made up nearly half the foreign-born, signaling the fruits of free movement among members of the European Union; the largest single groups in Britain were the 638,000 Irish, followed by 155,000 Asian Indians. Foreign residents made up 6.4 percent of France's total population, where the most significant groups were 646,000 Portuguese, 620,000 Algerians, and 585,000 Moroccans. The 4.6 percent of the Dutch population that was foreign came largely from Turkey (204,000) and Morocco (157,000). In Switzerland, where 16.3 percent of the population was foreign born in 1990, the largest groups were the 379,000 Italians, 141,000 Yugoslavs, and 116,000 Spaniards. It is difficult to discern the foreign-born in

Germany, where newcomer Germans are counted as citizens, but in 1990, Turks remained the largest immigrant group at 1.6 million people, followed by Yugoslavs.

The reception of newcomers continued to be ambivalent at the opening of the twenty-first century. Although Europe needed laborers, the parties set against immigration, such as France's Front National and Austria's Freedom Party, were political forces to be reckoned with, German conservatives urged people to have more children rather than to accept immigrants, and Britain marshaled laws against the tide of asylum seekers. On the other hand, some children of immigrants enrolled in universities and others held skilled positions. Human mobility and intrepid migrants were, as ever, at the heart of European society.

See also **Emigration and Colonies; Immigrants; Nineteenth Century** *(volume 1);* **Urbanization** *(in this volume);* **Gender and Work** *(volume 4).*

BIBLIOGRAPHY

Berger, John, and Jean Mohr. *A Seventh Man: Migrant Workers in Europe.* New York, 1975.

Bretell, Caroline. *Men Who Migrate, Women Who Wait: Population and History in a Portuguese Parish.* Princeton, N.J., 1986.

Brubaker, Rogers. *Citizenship and Nationhood in France and Germany.* Cambridge, Mass., 1992.

Canny, Nicolas, ed. *Europeans on the Move: Studies on European Migration, 1500–1800.* Oxford, 1994.

Castles, Stephen, and Mark J. Miller. *The Age of Migration: International Population Movements in the Modern World.* New York, 1993.

Castles, Stephen, Heather Booth, and Tina Wallace. *Here for Good: Western Europe's New Ethnic Minorities.* London, 1984.

Clark, Peter. "Migration in England during the Late Seventeenth and Early Eighteenth Centuries." *Past and Present* 83 (1979): 57–90.

Cross, Gary. *Immigrant Workers in Industrial France: The Making of a New Laboring Class.* Philadelphia, 1983.

De Vries, Jan. *European Urbanization, 1500–1800.* Cambridge, Mass., 1984.

Hochstadt, Steve. *Mobility and Modernity: Migration in Germany, 1820–1989.* Ann Arbor, Mich., 1999.

Hohenberg, Paul, and Lynn Lees. *The Making of Urban Europe, 1000–1994.* Cambridge, Mass., 1995.

Hollifield, James. *Immigrants, Markets, and States: The Political Economy of Postwar Europe.* Cambridge, Mass., 1992.

Hoerder, Dirk, and Leslie Page Moch, eds. *European Migrants: Global and Local Perspectives.* Boston, Mass., 1996.

Jackson, James H., Jr. *Migration and Urbanization in the Ruhr Valley, 1821–1914.* Altantic Highlands, N.J., 1997.

Kofman, Eleonore. "Female 'Birds of Passage' A Decade Later: Gender and Immigration in the European Union." *International Migration Review* 33, no. 126 (1999): 269–299.

Koser, Khalid, and Helma Lutz, eds. *The New Migration in Europe: Social Constructions and Social Realities.* New York, 1998.

Kulischer, Eugene. *Europe on the Move: War and Population Changes, 1917–1947.* New York, 1948.

Kussmaul, Ann. *Servants in Husbandry in Early Modern England.* Cambridge, U.K., 1981.

Lees, Lynn. *Exiles of Erin: Irish Migrants in Victorian London.* Ithaca, N.Y., 1979.

Lucassen, Jan. *Migrant Labour in Europe, 1600–1900: The Drift to the North Sea.* Translated by Donald A. Bloch. London, 1987.

Lucassen, Jan, and Leo Lucassen, eds. *Migration, Migration History, History: Old Paradigms and New Perspectives.* Bern, Switzerland, 1997.

Marrus, Michael. *The Unwanted: European Refugees in the Twentieth Century.* New York, 1985.

Moch, Leslie Page. *Moving Europeans: Migration in Western Europe since 1650.* Bloomington, Ind., 1992.

Noiriel, Gérard. *The French Melting Pot: Immigration, Citizenship, and National Identity.* Translated by Geoffroy de Laforcade. Minneapolis, Minn., 1996.

Ogden, Philip, and Paul White, eds. *Migrants in Modern France: Population Mobility in the Later Nineteenth and Twentieth Centuries.* London, 1989.

Pooley, Colin, and Jean Turnbull. *Migration and Mobility in Britain since the Eighteenth Century.* London, 1998.

Tilly, Charles. "Migration in Modern European History." In *Human Migration: Patterns and Policies.* Edited by William McNeill and Ruth Adams. Bloomington, Ind., 1978. Pages 48–74.

Weber, Adna. *The Growth of Cities in the Nineteenth Century.* 1899. Reprint, Ithaca, N.Y., 1963.

Yans-McLaughlin, Virginia. *Immigration Reconsidered: History, Sociology, and Politics.* New York, 1990.

THE POPULATION OF EUROPE:
EARLY MODERN DEMOGRAPHIC PATTERNS

David Levine

Most of what is known about the early modern demography of Europe is derived from the analysis of parish registers. The following discussion primarily relates to the northern and western parts of Europe, and even then it is not exhaustive. Scandinavia and the northern Netherlands are completely neglected, as is the "Celtic fringe" of the British Isles. Rather than look at any particular example in detail, this article explains how parish register studies assist interpretations of reproductive patterns in the period 1500–1800.

Parish registers were the products of Renaissance and Reformation state formation. The earliest ones date from the fifteenth century, but the longest series comes from England, with some surviving from 1538, the year in which Henry VIII made it mandatory for all parishes to maintain registers of vital events celebrated in the local branch of the state church. These parochial records have been the subject of two main forms of analysis: aggregative analysis, which provides an overview of the total numbers of baptisms, burials, and marriages; and family reconstitution, which examines demographic statistics in fine detail but is limited by the reliability of the registration of vital events as well as the necessity of having long, unbroken series of primary data.

While the English record series are the longest, they are by no means the most complete. Indeed Belgian, French, and German parochial registers provide much greater detail, although these continental documents are rarely available in continuous series from much earlier than 1660. The relatively short time span of the continental documents means that the demographic profiles of only two or three cohorts can be successfully reconstituted from them for the early modern period. This is a problem because the secular trend in population growth poses difficulties in interpreting the continental results, but bearing this point in mind, it is possible to make use of the family reconstitution evidence.

Looking at the subject from another perspective, it is probably most useful to adopt a heuristic framework, in which the uniqueness of any particular study is sacrificed in getting at an understanding of the organization of the larger system to which the various national and subnational components belonged. The elements of demographic history must first be placed in a broader perspective so that the unique characteristics of the northwestern European system of family formation can be appreciated.

POPULATION GROWTH

Between 1500 and 1750 the European population doubled from about 65 million to around 127.5 million. Most of this growth occurred before 1625. After 1750 a new cycle of expansion began, and the European population more than doubled to almost 300 million in 1900. It should also be noted that the 1750 to 1900 figures underestimate growth because they take no cognizance of mass emigration from Europe. Perhaps 50 million Europeans went overseas from 1840 to 1914. Migrants, their children, and their children's children were removed from the demographic equation. If they had stayed to contribute their fecund powers, quite likely Europe's population would have been more than 400 million in 1900. Thus, a study of early modern demography begs some important definitional questions about chronological boundaries. This discussion is confined to the period 1550–1800, but these boundaries are neither hard nor fast.

This early modern epoch includes two periods of rapid growth that bookend the several generations who lived between 1625 and 1750, when population levels were stable or, as was the case for short periods in some places, even falling. Generalized statistics are the product of a compromise, which sees compositional complexity as an essential part of the nature of early modern population dynamics.

While debate about the mechanisms of growth has been considerable, it is evident from even the briefest perusal of demographic statistics that the experience of life in the modern world is radically different from that prevailing in, to use the historian

Peter Laslett's phrase, the "world we have lost." The premodern life cycle was compressed by the weight of reproductive imperatives. People born in 1750 had a life expectancy of around thirty-five years. Of 100 children born alive, almost one-half either died before marrying or never married. Survivors spent most of their adult lives with little children underfoot, so the typical woman was usually either pregnant or nursing a child from marriage right through menopause. People born in 1750 expected to die about twelve years before the birth of their first grandchild, whereas in the late twentieth century people usually lived twenty-five years after the birth of their last grandchild.

For women in particular changes in life expectations radically altered experience. In contrast to the eighteenth-century world in which women were continually a part of a family, about two-thirds of late-twentieth-century women's adult years were spent in households without children, while for nearly 60 percent of their adult years women lived without a husband.

The early modern social system adjusted to compensate for unwieldy dependency ratios. Children began working at an early age, and they and their labor were often transferred away from their family of origin around the time they reached puberty. Leaving home was a more protracted process that started earlier and ended later than in the late twentieth century because children did not move out to found their own households before they married. But they did move away from their parental homes. Perhaps one-quarter of the fifteen-year-old males born as late as 1850 lived in someone else's household, whereas in the 1990s that applied to about one in twenty. At all ages between seventeen and twenty-seven, more than 30 percent of all males were classified as neither dependent children nor household heads. It would appear that teenaged females were as likely as their brothers to leave their natal homes, some going into domestic service but most leaving to work as farm servants, apprentices, or janes-of-all-work. Initially at least, girls rarely moved outside networks described by family, kin, and neighborhood. As they grew older, women strayed farther afield. Social class and local employment opportunities also played significant roles in determining the ways in which individuals experienced systemic structures.

The demographic keystone of the early modern system of marriage and family formation was that, uniquely, northwest Europeans married late. More precisely, the link between puberty and marriage was dramatically more attenuated in northwestern Europe than elsewhere. The identification of this austere, Malthusian pattern was the greatest achievement of the first generation of scholarship in early modern historical demography. Basing his conclusions on fifty-four studies describing age at first marriage for women in northwest Europe, Michael Flinn showed that the average fluctuated around twenty-five. While Flinn did not provide measurements to assess the spread of the distribution around this midpoint, other studies determined that the standard deviation was about six years, which means that about two-thirds of all northwest European women married for the first time between twenty-two and twenty-eight. The small number of teenage brides was counterbalanced by a similar number of women who married in their thirties. Perhaps one woman in ten never married; in the demographer's jargon, that tenth woman was permanently celibate. These statistics provide a single measure which distinguishes the creation of new families in northwestern Europe from that in other societies.

THE ADJUSTMENT OF POPULATION AND RESOURCES

Perhaps the closest analogy to the European experience is nineteenth-century Japan, where a fault line divided the early-marrying eastern half of the country from the later-marrying western parts. Marriage among young Japanese women was not linked to puberty. In the eastern region Japanese women married in their late teens and early twenties, while in the west brides were more likely to be in their early to middle twenties. The control of fertility in early modern Japan was, however, only partly the result of this gap between puberty and marriage; it was also partly the result of deliberate infanticide. Taken together the slightly later ages at marriage and stringent controls within marriage kept the population from overwhelming a slow incremental gain in per capita income. A larger proportion of the Japanese population was released from primary food production to work in rural, domestic industries than in any other preindustrial social formation outside northwestern Europe. In contrast, historical demographic studies of pre-1900 China established that the age at first marriage for Chinese women was close to puberty.

A uniquely late age at first marriage for women, that is, in relation to puberty, seemingly was a part of northwestern European family formation systems for most of the millennium. The origin of this system of reproduction is the key unanswered question arising from several decades of intensive statistical studies. Yet paradoxically, further statistical studies cannot yield an answer. Rather, the answer lies within the social contexts of marriage and family formation.

The early modern marriage strategy was vitally important for two reasons. First, it provided a safety valve or margin of error in the ongoing adjustment between population and resources that characterized the reproduction of generations and social formations. Second, it meant that women were less dependent and vulnerable insofar as they were marrying as young adults, not older children.

As noted above, early modern Europe experienced not one constant rate of population growth but an oscillation, that is, fairly rapid growth of about 1 percent per annum between 1500 and 1625 and again after 1750 interrupted by more than a century of rough stability. Yet it is not likely that the outer limits of growth were ever approached. Even during the periods of fastest growth, a prolonged period of celibacy existed between puberty and marriage; premarital intercourse and pregnancy were the experience of a minority, albeit a large minority at the end of the eighteenth century; and the cultural practice of prolonged breast-feeding (which is associated with anovulation during the first six months after giving birth) meant that intervals between pregnancies were hardly shorter than in the intervening generations of population stability or decline.

The safety margin may have bent, but it never came close to breaking. In comparison with what we know is humanly possible in terms of reproductive rates, the fastest early modern growth levels pale into insignificance, around 1 percent per annum as opposed to over 3 percent per annum in parts of the Third World at the end of the twentieth century. The early modern population grew, but it grew slowly.

In a stable population, about three-fifths of all families were likely to have an inheriting son, while another fifth had an inheriting daughter. About one-fifth of all niches became vacant in the course of each generation. In a growing population, marginal groups, such as noninheriting children, felt the full force of the nonlinear implications of population growth. This is a crucial point. Increasing population produced a disproportionate rise in their numbers. In a schematic way, this fact suggests that villagers who were over and above replacement were presented with two stark alternatives: they could either wait in the hopes of marrying into a vacated niche, or they could emigrate, that is, they could move socially down and physically out of their native land. This second alternative was the stark reality presented to generations of their predecessors, for whom noninheritance meant downward social mobility and demographic death.

Cottage industries were a godsend for these noninheriting, marginal people. The luckiest ones subsidized the formation of a new household without having to leave their native hearths. Others not as lucky moved to the villages and towns where proto-industry was located. There they set up on their own and supported themselves with income derived from their labor and with common rights to keep a cow, a pig, and perhaps even a garden where, after 1700, they grew potatoes. With a little money they built their new homes, usually one-room shacks called "one-night houses" because they sprang up overnight.

Many marginals moved to the cities, where charitable endowments were concentrated. But early modern urban migration was something of a zero-sum strategy because the urban counterweight played a significant role in the early modern demographic equation. Early modern cities ate up the surplus population of the countryside because they consistently recorded more deaths than births. The seventeenth-century London growth, for example, consumed more than one-half of the surplus sons and daughters produced by the rural population of England. Only in the second half of the eighteenth century did London replenish its native population without immigration. As cities cleaned up and virulent epidemics lost their potency, the urban populations of the industrial era grew by leaps and bounds.

In the early eighteenth century, London's population was about equal to the population of all other English cities combined. By the second quarter of the nineteenth century, sprawling conurbations existed in the West Midlands around Birmingham, on Merseyside around Liverpool and Manchester, in the West Riding of Yorkshire, and on Tyneside. These new conurbations sprouted up in hitherto rural areas. Manchester, for example, had 2,500 inhabitants in 1725, when Daniel Defoe rode through, and nearly 1 million in 1841, about the time that Friedrich Engels moved there. In addition many older cities, like Leicester, Nottingham, Bristol, and Norwich, doubled or trebled in size. This broadly based growth was possible because the urban death rate began closely to approximate its birthrate. By the end of the eighteenth century, indigenous populations grew not only in the cities but also in the countryside, whose surplus population had previously been the sole source of urban population increase. The push from the countryside and the pull of the cities were as important as the ability of the cities to nurture their native populations and free themselves from their dependency on immigrants.

For marginal people lifetime moves into the proletariat comprised the dominant social experience. While their actions may have consisted of efforts to retain or recapture individual control over the means of production, they were swimming against a powerful historical current that ultimately pulled most of them down into the ranks of the landless. If boom times were like a siphon sucking population out of rural cottages, then protoindustrial communities were like sponges soaking up these footloose extras. Overall, with a few notable exceptions like Amsterdam and London in the sixteenth and seventeenth centuries or the industrializing regions in the eighteenth century, the rate of urbanization was not much greater than the overall rate of population growth. On the eve of the French Revolution in 1789, for example, Paris contained about 3 percent of the French population, which was hardly different from its proportional significance at any point in the previous 250 years.

WOMEN'S INDEPENDENCE AND FAMILY FORMATION

The second aspect of this early modern system of family formation to some extent has been doubly obscured, first by a scholarly emphasis on early modern prescriptive literature and later by the historiographical concern with the gendering actions put into discursive practice by historical patriarchs. While it is true that all women were denied equality with men in early modern society, an emphasis on this inequality has eclipsed a comparative appreciation of the relative independence and self-control northwestern European women experienced. Their marriages were almost never arranged; their choices of partners resulted from courtship and negotiation rather than parental dictates. A large proportion of the population was landless and therefore unlikely to need parental approval except insofar as those people retained connections with their families. Furthermore, most of these landless young women moved away from the parental home after reaching puberty, and many lived away for a decade or longer before marrying. While landless women were not freed from either poverty or a dependent status, they were independent in the sense that parental authority was neither a constant nor a supervening day-to-day reality in their lives. They were not masterless to be sure—almost all such women lived in man's household—but it stretches credulity to assert that men unrelated to them took a paternal interest in their courtship activities.

Women were theoretically free to choose their mates according to the dictates of their consciences, as was the rule of the Christian church, but they were also free to choose within the dictates of the social reality of their lives. They were not subject to the veil, nor were their public movements kept under surveillance by chaperones. They largely controlled their own destinies by deciding on their own partners. The

prescriptive literature of the time took cognizance of this dimension of early modern women's independence only so as to castigate those who prenuptially became pregnant and to blame the victim for the crime. The literature regarded these women with a mixture of fear and loathing because their independence threatened to turn the patriarch's domestic world upside down. Prescriptive literature is always a better guide to the concerns of the social controllers than to the social reality of control. The well-attested fact that early modern women were courting and marrying when they were adults means that the prescriptors' discursive vision of helpless dependency is an inadequate guide to social behavior. Furthermore that vision tells us nothing about the motivation of the women in question. Women were proactive in deciding whom they married, where they married, and at what age they married. This proactivity is strikingly different both from the marital arrangements common for most women in most other parts of the world and from the more restricted range of actions allowed their social betters, whose marriages were often social alliances in which they were not always willing players.

The early modern demographic system turned on women's late age at first marriage, and like the spokes on a wheel, other aspects of early modern demography were arrayed in relation to the hub. Geographic mobility was largely a premarital matter. Fertility was largely a postmarital matter, as was mortality in that one-half of all deaths were those of infants and young children. Of course, epidemic mortality was unconnected to this system of family formation, while density-dependent mortality, characteristic of urban areas and rural regions with polluted water supplies, was only indirectly linked to it. Before unraveling the interconnections between marriage, fertility, and infant mortality, it is helpful to examine the issue of mortality in more detail.

EPIDEMIC MORTALITY: DISEASE, FAMINE, AND WAR

For more than half of the early modern period, epidemic mortality was directly connected to the recurrent outbreaks of plague that had been a deadly scourge since 1348. The final plague visitation occurred in southern France at the beginning of the 1720s. The plague did not simply peter out; its destructiveness persisted at a high rate almost until the eve of its disappearance. The great London plague of 1666 bears witness to the continuing impact of the bacillus more than three centuries after its first appearance. Quarantine was effective, but seemingly bacteriological

In Memory of the Plague. English broadside (1636) commemorating visitations of the plague in 1603, 1625, and 1636, with appropriate prayers and suggestions of preventive measures.

changes were even more important in its disappearance, just as similar bacteriological mutations between the plague bacillus and its host had signaled its onset in southern Asia in the 1330s.

Plague was the most prominent and most deadly epidemic disease. But a veritable portfolio of epidemic diseases—"ague," bronchitis, chicken pox, convulsions, croup, infantile diarrhea, diphtheria, "dropsy," dysentery, "fevers" of many types, "flux," gonorrhea, influenza, malaria, measles, pneumonia, smallpox, syphilis, tuberculosis, typhus, and whooping cough, to mention some of the worst offenders—attacked the population of early modern Europe. What is most peculiar about this onslaught is that peaks in mortality occurred unpredictably. Unlike the plague, which killed its victims, most of these other diseases undermined people's general health, with relatively few deaths attributable to their direct impact. Still the population's resilience was severely tested. When infectious epidemics occurred in tandem with famine or warfare—conditions of social disintegration—death rates skyrocketed.

The Black Death was the worst microparasite in early modern times, but warfare was the most deadly form of macroparasitism. Nowhere was this more true than in Germany, where the Thirty Years' War brought spectacular devastation. Estimates vary, especially locally, but the carnage appears to have been especially intense in the duchy of Württemberg, where the population dropped from 450,000 in 1618 to 166,000 in 1648. No single experience can be generalized to the German population as a whole; rather, different regions suffered different disasters at different times. Analysis of local studies from early modern Germany explains how the causal arrows flowed from mortality to family formation and therefore structured the operation of the demographic system.

In the Hohenlohe district the net loss of 33 percent during the Thirty Years' War underestimates the massiveness of population movements. By 1653 few families could trace their ancestors back to the sixteenth century in their native villages. Some fell victim to war-related plague and famine, while others were bled white by taxation and their farms bankrupted, causing them to flee from the region. While the upper sections of the rural social structure remained intact, the social pyramid lost its massive base. The marginal elements in society played a key role in the first cycle of early modern population movements. Growth was concentrated at the bottom of the social pyramid in the century after 1525, and during the Thirty Years' War, when this excess population was lost, the marginal lands on which they had squatted reverted to waste.

Another Württemberg village, Neckarhausen, was similarly devastated during the Thirty Years' War. Its population was over five hundred at the beginning of the seventeenth century, but by 1650 it had fewer than one hundred villagers. The early-seventeenth-century level was not reached again until the 1780s. In fact Neckarhausen's post–1648 evolution was a reversal of pre–1618 Hohenlohe. Late-seventeenth-century Neckarhausen was dominated by respectable *hausvaters,* or heads of families, but the systemic tendency for growth to create a subpeasantry and a significant number of wage laborers became the hallmark of its eighteenth-century population. This systemic tendency gave free rein to the emergence of "minifundia" (dwarf holdings) because subdivision of the land had created a pool of surplus labor. To some extent this labor was engaged in land reclamation projects and was deployed on the commons, but mostly it was drawn into rural weaving and other crafts. These people were progressively marginalized. Although they were fully integrated into the village power structure in 1700, by 1780 only two of twenty-three officers were petty commodity producers, and all local officials were in the top quartile of taxpayers.

Indirectly, then, disease and warfare created or took away opportunities for family formation. The system tottered but never cracked. Indeed, this play within the system is the crucial point. Late age at first marriage for women made it possible to adjust the population and resources equation in the face of massive devastation without abandoning the prudential character of delayed marriage. No evidence suggests that German patriarchs responded to these massive population losses by marrying off their daughters at puberty or that German matriarchs abandoned their practice of prolonged breast-feeding.

The population dynamic was kept in an exquisite balance through the prudential check of delayed marriage. If circumstances warranted, that is, if age at first marriage for women dropped a year or two or if more women ultimately married, then over the course of a couple of generations small shifts could lead to monumental changes in the rate of growth. Who decided if circumstances warranted? Not makers of social policy or prescriptive patriarchs. Anonymous women and men for their own reasons decided to marry a few months or a few years earlier than their parents had. On an individual level this was small stuff. On a broader level, when individual behaviors in warranted circumstances are aggregated, the scales on the balances shift to search out a new equilibrating point. But those involved in this social drama made choices consciously without cognizance of their demographic implications. Moreover their choices were

War. "The Beast of War"—made up of the body parts of a wolf, a horse, a human being, a lion, and a rat—in a German broadsheet (c. 1640) offering an allegory of the devastation of the Thirty Years' War. STADTBIBLIOTHEK ULM, GERMANY

essentially traditional in the sense that they were made with reference to expectations that depended upon the contingencies of the time.

At the end of the early modern period, Germans policed the marriages of the poor. The poor continued to court and to initiate sexual relations at much the same ages as their parents and grandparents, but while their relationships were consummated, they were not consecrated. Consequently the rate of illegitimacy rose sharply. By the next generation the meddling ceased, and the illegitimacy rate plummeted. The rate of reproduction was hardly changed by the administrative dynamics, which were significant to policymakers but were largely ignored by the objects of their policies.

FERTILITY AND THE BIRTHRATE

Birthrate is itself the product of length of marriage and fertility rates per year of marriage. Even small changes in those variables, when aggregated and allowed to multiply over several generations, had profound implications.

The most astonishing aspect of the early modern system of family formation comes from the evidence pertaining to fertility. In analyzing fertility, fe-

cundity, and sterility, historical demographers use the concept of "natural fertility," which is at best a tendentious abstraction. It is also misleading. Louis Henry's original formulation of the concept was aimed at determining a precontraceptive equilibrium, but he emphatically recognized that this equilibrium had almost nothing to do with maximum fertility levels. According to Henri Léridon, the biological maximum for women who remain fecund and exposed to risk from their fifteenth to their forty-fifth birthdays and who do not breast-feed their children is seventeen or eighteen children. Any population would have some sterile women. But most of the difference between Léridon's biological maximum and observed total fertility rates can be accounted for by referring to cultural and historical factors, such as the age and incidence of nuptiality; breast-feeding practices; abortions, both spontaneous and calculated; starvation-induced amenorrhea; coital frequency; rates of widowhood; remarriage; and separation or desertion.

So-called natural fertility in early modern Europe was the product of starting and spacing methods of regulation. This measurement is better called "cultural fertility," since the historical demographers' statistics show that childbearing was well within the calculus of conscious choice throughout the quarter-

151

millennium of the early modern period for which demographic statistics are available.

Starting and spacing are also important methods of fertility control. In premodern populations stopping, that is, contraception, was probably the least-chosen method. Indeed, little evidence of the practice of systematic contraception exists. On the other hand, the early modern period yields a great deal of evidence of deliberate attempts to control fertility through starting at later ages. It seems age at marriage was consistently a decade or more later than menarche. Absolutely no evidence confirms the onset of puberty among early modern women, which presents a problem in discussing early modern marriage and fertility patterns, especially the hiatus between puberty or menarche and marriage. Most people writing on the subject simply ignore their own ignorance.

Historical demographers' statistical analysis of fecundity and birth intervals testifies to the fact that spacing was widely practiced as fertility control. A crucial component of this spacing behavior, the lengthening of birth intervals, was prolonged breast-feeding, which, as has been noted, inhibits ovulation during the first six months after a woman gives birth. While its contraceptive protection declines thereafter and unexpected pregnancies become increasingly more common, it is a fairly reliable method of birth control for the group if not for individuals. The demographic implications of breast-feeding have rarely been studied outside the narrow confines of statistical measurements, particularly regarding connections between early modern breast-feeding practices and the exercise of domestic power by women. Curiously, historians of nineteenth-century women have been more interested in this subject as it pertains to arguments about the principles and practices of "domestic feminism."

The early modern population, therefore, tended to control its fertility by means other than stopping, which is not to say that this population had no stoppers. Fecundity ratios measure the proportion of fecund women who bore a first child, a second, and so on. Some women stopped bearing children before they reached age forty, which is considered the average age of menopause, although evidence for the physiological end of fecundity is as scarce as for its beginning at menarche. Why did these women stop bearing children? In most family reconstitution studies that have investigated fertility profiles, women who married in their early twenties were on average under forty when they gave birth to their last child, whereas women who married for the first time when they were over thirty gave birth to their last child when they were several years older. Was this difference a matter of physiological sterility or cultural choice?

MODEL POPULATION DYNAMICS

Demographers employ complex formulas to analyze population dynamics. For historians it is enough to know that a given rate of population growth can be the result of a number of different combinations of marriage rates, fertility, and life expectation at birth. For example, an early modern population with a total fertility rate of 5.5 and a life expectation at birth of thirty yields the same growth rate as a modern one with a total fertility rate of 2.1 and a life expectation at birth of seventy-five. In both cases births and deaths cancel one another, resulting in neither growth nor decline.

After a reasonably long period of time, even a minute shift in the birthrate, which includes marriage ages for women, marriage frequencies, and premarital and postmarital fertility, or the death rate could yield significant results. Substantial shifts could have explosive results in the short term. In another example, an unchanging total fertility rate of 6.0 combined with a doubling of life expectation at birth from 24 to 48 would instantaneously transform a population from no-growth into doubling every thirty years. Such is the prolific power of compound interest.

Two model populations, peasant and proletarian, illustrate the dynamics of population growth. No allowance is made for illegitimacy in these model populations. In the observed conditions of the 1750–1880 period, the proletarian population was supercharged by the additional impetus for growth provided by premarital births and bridal pregnancies.

The main characteristic of the peasant population was that the age at first marriage for women was almost a decade after puberty, 25. Their husbands were usually about the same age. In this peasant population model, life expectation at birth ["e°"] was 39.32 years, which corresponds to an infant mortality rate of 188 per 1,000 and a 61 percent survival rate from birth to the average age at first marriage for women. The "life expectation at birth," "age-specific mortality rates," and "survival ratios" draw information from Sully Ledermann's collection of life tables (Ledermann, 1969, p. 155).

The average woman and man, having survived to marry at 25, could expect to live to about 60. For calculating the rate at which these populations reproduced, adult survival is nearly as important as the fertility of those who remained in fertile conjugal unions. The prospect of a marriage being broken by death was the product of two adult mortality experiences, those of the woman and the man, interacting with each other. The result was far greater than would at first seem to be the case. Of course, the actual situation was immeasurably more complicated since desertion cannot be measured but obviously represented a form of "marital death." Anything that kept husbands and wives together had a stimulating impact on the birthrate.

In each of the five-year marriage intervals, about 5 percent of women and a similar number of men died. Combining male and female chances of survival produces an estimate that 90.7 percent of marriages survived this first five-year period. Of these survivors, 95 percent of both men and women survived the next five-year period, so 81.8 percent of the original marriages remained intact for ten years, until the woman was 35. In the third five-year period, 89.1 percent of the surviving marriages made it through, so 72.9 percent of the original marriages remained intact after fifteen years.

The implications of this mortality regime are apparent when connected with fertility levels. In this peasant population married life is divided into three five-year stages, from marriage at 25 to menopause at 40. Demographers usually calculate marital fertility as the number of live births per thousand years lived by women in each age cohort. Thus, among 1,000 women aged over 25 and under 30, the expectation is for 450 live births, which is translated as an age-specific fertility rate of 450/1000. Among the next two stages the potential age-specific fertility rates are as follows: 30–34 = 340/1000; 35–39 = '167/000. As with all the demographic information set forth, these age-specific fertility rates are guesses based on reported results from family reconstitution studies, with the following points in mind. The women between 25 and 29 presumably breast-fed their children, and the contraceptive effects of suckling combined with other factors to yield a birth spacing of three years. Further arbitrary adjustments to the age-specific fertility of more mature women gave weight to the duration effect that had an impact on coital frequency and secondary sterility. For this reason, fertility in the second and third cohorts was lowered by 25 percent and 50 percent respectively.

If this average woman lived in a fecund conjugal union from marriage to menopause (from 25 to 40), she had the potential to give birth to 4.79 children. However, the above exercise in survivorship suggested that not all women lived from marriage to menopause in a fecund conjugal union. Allowances for the impact of adult mortality on marital fertility can be made first by establishing a midpoint marital survival for each five-year cohort and second by adjusting the potential age-specific fertility by allowing for fertility depletion caused by adult mortality and the interruption of a fecund conjugal union. Remarriage is not considered

in this schema because men were more likely to remarry than women, and the salient issue in this exercise is the experience of adult women. In addition, no allowance is made for children born out of wedlock. The adjusted fertility is:

Age	Potential Fertility	Marital Survival Ratio	Children Born
25–29	2.25	.943	2.13
30–34	1.70	.849	1.44
35–39	.84	.755	.64
25–39	4.79		4.21

In this peasant population mortality not only cut deeply into the potential fertility of adults but also sharply curtailed the life expectations of those children born to surviving married couples. Almost 61 percent survived to twenty-five, reducing the adjusted fertility figure of 4.21 to 2.56 surviving children. No allowance is made for the fact that men were less likely to survive to their average age at marriage, twenty-six. In a certain sense, ignoring the sex-specific character of survival compensates for not incorporating some allowance for remarriage into the algorithm. Of these survivors, 90 percent probably married, suggesting that 2.30 children in the next generation would marry.

Given the parameters of mortality, nuptiality, and fertility outlined above, at what rate did this peasant population reproduce? The length of each generation can be determined by finding the midpoint in an adult woman's fertility career, that is, her median birth, which was somewhat earlier than the middle of her childbearing years. Each first-generation couple had 2.3 marrying children, so every 30 years this model population grew by 15 percent. The first generation of 1,000 marriages, that is, 2,000 adults, had 2,020 children after 24.5 years (2020/2000 = 101 percent = 1 percent above replacement). In turn this suggests an annual rate of growth of something on the order of 0.47 percent and a doubling of the original population every 150 years.

In contrast to the peasant population, the proletarian population married earlier and more frequently and remained in stable fecund unions longer, so that they had more children. These differences are important because marriage was the linchpin in the demographic system of early moderns, although it was a flexible system that could accommodate divergent interpretations. Why did proletarians marry earlier, or why did European peasants marry at late ages? For both proletarians and peasants living in northwestern Europe, marriage was decisively separated from puberty, even though marriage continued to be closely connected with the formation of a new, independent

TABLE 1
HYPOTHETICAL EFFECTS OF DEMOGRAPHIC CHANGES ON RATES OF POPULATION GROWTH

	Peasant	Proletarian
e° (Ledermann)	39.32 (153)	39.32 (153)
Marriage age ♀	25	22
Marriage–Menopause ♀ Survival Ratio	.85	.84
Potential Fertility (Rate per Thousand)		
15–19	n/a (n/a)	n/a (n/a)
20–24	n/a (n/a)	1.40 (450)
25–29	2.25 (450)	2.25 (450)
30–34	1.70 (340)	1.70 (340)
35–39	.84 (167)	1.25 (250)
Total Fertility	4.79	6.60
Marital Survival Ratio		
15–19	n/a	n/a
20–24	n/a	.975
25–29	.907	.887
30–34	.818	.798
35–39	.729	.710
Children Born		
15–19	n/a	n/a
20–24	n/a	1.365
25–29	2.04	2.000
30–34	1.39	1.355
35–39	.61	.890
Total 15–39	4.04	5.61
Survival Ratio (Birth– ♀ Marriage)	.61 = 2.56	.62 = 3.48
% Marriage	90% = 2.30	95% = 3.30
Generational Replacement	115%	165%
Generational Interval	30	27.5
Annual Growth Rate	0.47%	2.4%
Doubling (in Years)	150	29.1

household. So both peasants and proletarians married as young adults, and they married as independent individuals. It is imperative to connect these cultural parameters with the opportunities for household formation so as to understand the factors that made marriage relatively difficult for peasants, who had to wait to inherit a niche in the local economy, and relatively easy for proletarians, who married earlier and more frequently because wage laboring afforded them freedom from patriarchal intervention. The vast secular boom of the late eighteenth century, the product of industrialization and population growth, radically increased the demand for wage labor. Hence the likelihood increased that a young couple could begin life together without hindrance from patriarchal authorities. If young people waited until they were in their twenties to begin courtship, they did not have to wait to inherit a niche. Proletarians were better able to take advantage of opportunities to begin their married lives according to the dictates of their own reason and social experience.

Table 1 represents a highly schematic simulation exercise that demonstrates the massive shifts in annual rates of growth resulted from relatively small demographic changes. The exponential power of compound interest is so cumulatively overwhelming that, had the annual rate of reproduction of the proletarian population prevailed from the Neolithic to the industrial revolutions, the human population of the world in 1750 would have been far greater than the ants on the earth, the birds in the air, and the fish in the seas. In fact the rates of growth suggested by the proletarian population model have approximated reality during only two periods in human history. The first was in Europe and its overseas colonies during the first half of the age of mass modernization, between 1750 and 1870, and the second was in the late-twentieth-century Third World. Possibly something similar occurred in the two centuries before the Black Death.

If in 1750 the European population had shifted completely from the peasant model to the proletarian one with its propensity to double in number every 29.1 years, the original 127.5 million Europeans living in 1750 would have been replaced as follows:

1750	127.5
1779	255
1808	510
1837	1,020
1866	2,040
1895	4,080

Obviously not all Europeans conformed to the model, and only 70 percent might be classified as proletarians. Even if only the proletarian component of the 1750 population had conformed to this model, the replacement would have occurred in the following way:

1750	89
1779	178
1808	356
1837	716
1866	1,432
1895	2,864

Many European proletarians changed their behavior. The study of Shepshed captured one such community (Levine, 1977). It would be a mistake to generalize, but even if only a fraction of the original 89 million proletarians completely took on these characteristics or if all took on some of the changes outlined in the two simple models, that would explain the observed growth within the parameters of the model propounded by the so-called theory of protoindustrialization.

In Shepshed the age at first marriage for women dropped more than in the simulated populations. Seventeenth-century brides in this Leicestershire village were, on average, almost 28.1 years old, whereas their great-granddaughters, who married framework knitters in the early nineteenth century, were 22.3 years old. This 5.8-year fall in the age at first marriage for women is almost twice the size of the drop suggested in the simulation exercise. Furthermore age-specific fertility rates rose slightly, while illegitimacy levels skyrocketed. On the other side of the vital equation, adult mortality levels improved in the period after 1750 over those before 1700. Infant and child mortality rates rose noticeably, so life expectation at birth dropped from about 49 before 1700 to 44 after 1750.

Franklin Mendels and others argued for the "prolific power" of protoindustrial populations. Not all the European peasants who were displaced from their *pays* or *heimat*—their land, their home—took on the characteristics suggested by this simple model. But even if only some of them did so it would account for the impact of new forms of social production on systems of reproduction and family formation, which by itself completely explains the growth of the European population. That is all Mendels claimed, in a modest version.

Finally, the crucial lesson of this schematic simulation is that the key issue confronting the student of early modern demography concerns the ways in which population growth was thwarted by its imbrication in the social world. Therefore, rather than adopting a modernist perspective that focuses on growth and studies its individual components at the expense of understanding the operation of the whole mechanism, early modernists would do well to give attention to the interaction of late marriage, culturally controlled fertility, the urban counterweight, recurrent warfare, and swinging bouts of epidemic mortality. Those factors combined to keep population and resources in a rough balance during the early modern period.

See also **Protoindustrialization; The City: The Early Modern Period** *(in this volume);* **Patriarchy; The Household; Courtship, Marriage, and Divorce; Illegitimacy and Concubinage** *(volume 4); and other articles in this section.*

BIBLIOGRAPHY

Abbott, Andrew. "Transcending General Linear Reality." *Sociological Theory* 6 (1988): 169–186.

Anderson, Michael. "The Emergence of the Modern Life Cycle in Britain." *Social History* 10 (1985): 69–87.

Appleby, Andrew. "Epidemics and Famine in the Little Ice Age." *Journal of Interdisciplinary History* 10 (1980): 643–663.

Davis, Kingsley, and Pietronella van den Oever. "Demographic Foundations of New Sex Roles." *Population and Development Review* 8 (1982): 495–511.

De Vries, Jan. *European Urbanization, 1500–1800*. Cambridge, Mass., 1984.

Drake, Michael. *Population and Society in Norway, 1735–1865*. London, 1969.

Dupâquier, Jacques, et al. *Histoire de la population française*. Vol. 2: De la renaissance à 1789. Paris, 1988.

Durand, John D. "Historical Estimates of World Population: An Evaluation." *Population and Development Review* 3 (1977): 253–296.

Fildes, Valerie. *Wet Nursing: A History from Antiquity to the Present.* Oxford, 1988.

Flinn, Michael W. *The European Demographic System, 1500–1820.* Baltimore, 1981.

Flinn, Michael W. "The Stabilization of Mortality in Pre-industrial Western Europe." *Journal of European Economic History* 3 (1974): 285–318.

Goldstone, Jack A. *Revolution and Rebellion in the Early Modern World.* Berkeley, Calif., 1991.

Gordon, Linda. *Woman's Body, Woman's Right: A Social History of Birth Control in America.* New York, 1976.

Hanley, Susan B., and Kozo Yamamura. *Economic and Demographic Change in Pre-industrial Japan, 1600–1868.* Princeton, N.J., 1977.

Hareven, Tamara K. "The History of the Family and the Complexity of Social Change." *American Historical Review* 96 (1991): 95–124.

Hayami, Akira. "Another *Fossa Magna*: Proportion Marrying and Age at Marriage in Late Nineteenth-Century Japan." *Journal of Family History* 12 (1987): 57–72.

Henry, Louis. "Some Data on Natural Fertility." *Eugenics Quarterly* 18 (1961): 81–91.

Herlihy, David. "Family." *American Historical Review* 96 (1991): 1–16.

Hohenberg, Paul M., and Lynn Hollen Lees. *The Making of Urban Europe, 1000–1950.* Cambridge, Mass., 1985.

Kamen, Henry. "The Economic and Social Consequences of the Thirty Years' War." *Past and Present* 39 (1968): 44–61.

Knodel, John. "Breast Feeding and Population Growth." *Science* 198 (1977): 1111–1115.

Knodel, John. "Natural Fertility in Pre-industrial Germany." *Population Studies* 32 (1978): 481–510.

Knodel, John, and Etienne Van de Walle. "Breast Feeding, Fertility, and Infant Mortality: An Analysis of Some Early German Data." *Population Studies* 21 (1967): 109–131.

Ledermann, Sully. *Nouvelles tables-types de mortalité.* Paris, 1969.

Lee, James Z., and Wang Feng. *One Quarter of Humanity: Malthusian Mythology and Chinese Realities, 1700–2000.* Cambridge, Mass., 1999.

Léridon, Henri. *Human Fertility.* Chicago, 1977.

Lesthaeghe, Ron. "On the Social Control of Human Reproduction." *Population and Development Review* 6 (1980): 527–548.

Levine, David. *Family Formation in an Age of Nascent Capitalism.* New York, 1977.

Levine, David. *Reproducing Families: The Political Economy of English Population History.* Cambridge, U.K., 1987.

Levine, David. "Sampling History: The English Population." *Journal of Interdisciplinary History* 28 (1998): 605–632.

Lorimer, Frank. *Culture and Human Fertility.* Paris, 1954.

Lynch, Katherine A. "The Family and the History of Public Life." *Journal of Interdisciplinary History* 24 (1994): 665–684.

McEvedy, Colin, and Richard Jones. *Atlas of World Population History.* Harmondsworth, U.K., 1978.

McLaren, Angus. *Reproductive Rituals: The Perception of Fertility in England from the Sixteenth to the Nineteenth Century.* London, 1984.

McNeill, William H. *Plagues and Peoples.* Garden City, N.Y., 1976.

Mendels, Franklin F. "Industrialization and Population Pressure in Eighteenth-Century Flanders." Ph.D. diss., University of Wisconsin, 1969.

Mendels, Franklin F. "Proto-industrialization: The First Phase of the Industrialization Process." *Journal of Economic History* 32 (1972): 241–261.

Robisheaux, Thomas. *Rural Society and the Search for Order in Early Modern Germany.* Cambridge, U.K., 1989.

Sabean, David Warren. *Property, Production, and Family in Neckarhausen, 1700–1870.* Cambridge, U.K., 1990.

Smith, Daniel Scott. "Family Limitation, Sexual Control, and Domestic Feminism in Victorian America." *Feminist Studies* 1 (1973): 40–57.

Smith, Daniel Scott. "A Homeostatic Demographic Regime: Patterns in West European Family Reconstitution Studies." In *Population Patterns in the Past.* Edited by R. D. Lee. New York, 1977. Pages 19–51.

Smith, Thomas C. *Nakahara: Family Farming and Population in a Japanese Village, 1717–1830.* Stanford, Calif., 1977.

Tilly, Charles. "Demographic Origins of the European Proletariat." In *Proletarianization and Family History.* Edited by David Levine. Orlando, Fla., 1984. Pages 1–85.

Tilly, Louise. "Women's History and Family History: Fruitful Collaboration or Missed Connection?" *Journal of Family History* 12 (1987): 303–315.

Wall, Richard. "The Age at Leaving Home." *Journal of Family History* 3 (1978): 181–202.

Watkins, Susan Cotts, Jane A. Menken, and John Bongaarts. "Demographic Foundations of Family Change." *American Sociological Review* 52 (1987): 346–358.

Weir, David. "Rather Never Than Late: Celibacy and Age at Marriage in English Cohort Fertility, 1541–1871." *Journal of Family History* 9 (1984): 340–354.

Wrigley, E. A. "Fertility Strategy for the Individual and the Group." In *Historical Studies of Changing Fertility.* Edited by Charles Tilly. Princeton, N.J., 1978. Pages 135–154.

Wrigley, E. A. "A Simple Model of London's Importance in Changing English Society and Economy, 1650–1750." *Past and Present* 37 (1967): 44–70.

Wrigley, E. A., and R. S. Schofield. *The Population History of England, 1541–1871.* Cambridge, Mass., 1981.

Wrigley, E. A., R. S. Schofield, Ros Davies, and Jim Oeppen. *English Population History from Family Reconstitution, 1580–1837.* Cambridge, U.K., 1997.

THE POPULATION OF EUROPE:
THE DEMOGRAPHIC TRANSITION AND AFTER

Michael R. Haines

Every modern, high-income, developed society has undergone a shift from high to low levels of fertility and mortality. This is known as the demographic transition, and it has taken place, if only partially, in many developing nations as well. It is part of the more general process of modern economic growth and modernization, which includes other features such as rising levels of education and skill (human capital); structural transformation from low-productivity, predominantly agrarian societies to high-productivity manufacturing and service economies; increasing innovation and application of new technologies; significant relocation of the population from rural to urban and suburban places; and increasing political and administrative complexity, accompanied by deepening bureaucratization.

Europe and its direct overseas offshoots (the United States, Canada, Australia, and New Zealand) were pioneers of the demographic transition. An immediate result of this process was the acceleration of population growth. Table 1 presents data on the size of the population of Europe (not including Russia) and selected European nations at dates between 1750 and 1990 and calculates the implied growth rates for the subperiods. Especially notable was the acceleration of population growth in the nineteenth century, with a slowing down in the twentieth century. Consequently, the population of Europe rose from about 16 percent of the estimated world total in 1750 to about 20 percent in 1950. But slower European growth relative to most of the rest of the world (especially many developing nations) after 1950 had reduced that share to 14 percent by 1990.

In the nineteenth century several nations that underwent rapid industrialization and urbanization also experienced high population growth rates, most notably England and Wales and Germany. But this was not always the case, as the example of France shows. Rapid growth sometimes preceded industrial and urban development, as in Germany and the Netherlands. The slower population growth in the first half of the twentieth century (relative to the nineteenth

century) was due especially to declining birthrates but also to the effects of two catastrophic wars. Europe suffered almost 8 million battle deaths (including Russia) and over 4 million civilian casualties in World War I. World War II was even worse, with over 10 million battle deaths and over 25 million in civilian losses.

The acceleration of population growth in the nineteenth century was a direct consequence of declining death rates and stable or even rising fertility rates. In England rising birthrates produced much of the growth, and these were, in turn, the consequence of increased incidence of marriage and earlier age at marriage and not of rising marital fertility. Birthrates rose in Germany in the nineteenth century as well. In other cases declining mortality played a more central role.

The standard model of the demographic transition has four stages. First is the premodern era of high fertility (for example, a crude birthrate [births per 1,000 population per year] in the range of 45 to 55) and mortality that is both high (for example, a crude death rate [deaths per 1,000 population per year] in the range of 25 to 35) and fluctuating. This is the world that Thomas Robert Malthus depicted in his *Essay on the Principle of Population* (1798), in which population growth was checked by periodic mortality crises caused by famine, disease, and war. The second stage is the mortality transition, in which death rates stabilize and fall but birthrates remain high. The effect is a significant rise in natural increase (the excess of births over deaths) and population growth. The third phase is the fertility transition, leading finally to a decline in natural increase and population growth. The final stage is that of the demographically mature society with low birth and death rates.

There are a number of problems with this model, not the least of which is that it predicts poorly the timing and speed of both the mortality and fertility transitions in many cases. Whether the mortality tran-

TABLE 1
ESTIMATED POPULATION (000s) AND IMPLIED GROWTH RATES (%) IN EUROPE, 1750–1990 (CONTEMPORARY BOUNDARIES)

Approximate year	Europe (without Russia)	England and Wales	Germany	France	The Netherlands	Italy	Spain	Sweden	Russia
Estimated Population									
1750	125,000	5,739[a]	15,000	25,000	1,900	15,700	8,400	1,781	42,000
1800	152,000	8,893	22,377	27,349	2,047	17,237	10,541	2,347	56,000
1850	208,000	17,928	33,413	37,366	3,057	24,351	15,455	3,471	76,000
1900	296,000	32,588	56,637	38,451	5,104	32,475	18,594	5,137	134,000
1950	393,000	44,020	68,376	41,736	10,114	47,104	28,009	7,047	180,075
1990	498,000	50,719	79,364	56,735	14,952	57,661	38,969	8,558	281,344
Implied Growth Rates[b]									
1750/1800	0.39	0.81	0.61	0.18	0.11	0.19	0.78	0.55	0.58
1800/1850	0.63	1.40	1.11	0.62	1.22	0.66	0.64	0.78	0.61
1850/1900	0.71	1.20	1.10	0.06	1.03	0.59	0.43	0.78	1.13
1900/1950	0.57	0.61	0.38	0.17	1.34	0.76	0.82	0.63	0.59
1950/1990	0.59	0.35	0.37	0.77	0.98	0.51	0.83	0.49	1.12

Source: Durand, 1967; Mitchell, 1998; United Nations, 2000; McEvedy and Jones, 1978; Livi-Bacci, 1992.
(a) England only. Implied growth rate 1750/1800 also computed for England only.
(b) Growth rates adjusted for differences in census or population estimate dates.

sition precedes or occurs simultaneously with the fertility decline is also debated. It fits the historical experience of Europe well in only some cases, and it does not deal with migration. Nonetheless, it does provide a convenient framework for discussion.

THE FERTILITY TRANSITION

The fertility transition in Europe is now well documented by a substantial study, the European Fertility Project, completed in the 1980s. The study provides a set of standard measures of fertility and nuptiality for over twelve hundred provinces of Europe from the middle of the nineteenth century to 1960. The standard measures are the indices of overall fertility (I_f), marital fertility (I_g), nonmarital fertility (I_h), and the proportions of women married (I_m). The indices compare the actual number of births in a nation or geographic subunit with the number that would be pro-

duced if all the women had the birthrates of the highest fertility population ever observed—married Hutterite women (members of an Anabaptist sect) in North America in the 1920s. Specifically, I_f gives the ratio of actual births for a given population of women to the births that the same group of women would have experienced if they had had the fertility of married Hutterite women. I_g measures the same for married women in the given population, and I_h provides an index for unmarried women. The fertility indices thus furnish a form of indirect standardization with a value of 1.0 being historically close to maximum human reproduction. I_m is different, being ratios of the weighted age distributions of married women in the given population to the weighted age distribution of total women in the given population. While these indices are merely a form of indirect standardization, their modest data requirements, easy intuitive interpretation, ease of calculation, and current wide utilization are real advantages. Also, it is useful to note that when nonmarital fertility is low (as it was in most of Europe in the late nineteenth and early twentieth centuries), I_f is approximately equal to I_g multiplied by I_m.

Table 2 provides measures of fertility and mortality for a set of European nations selected because of their size, historical importance, and regional representativeness. The table gives one measure of marital fertility (I_g), one measure of nuptiality (I_m), and two commonly used measures of mortality, the infant mortality rate (infant deaths per thousand live births per year) and the expectation of life at birth ($e[0]$). The upper three panels describe the fertility transition. Several things are noteworthy. First, the transition in overall fertility (I_f) was due to declining marital fertility (I_g) and not changes in nuptiality (I_m). Marriage actually increased, at least after 1900. Second, France by 1870 already had relatively moderate levels of overall and marital fertility (with an I_g of .494). In contrast, other nations still had high levels, such as Germany (.760), Sweden (.700), and the Netherlands (.845). Third, Russia (and most of eastern Europe and the Balkans) had a delayed decline, though not by too much. Finally, although not seen in this table, there was a nuptiality "frontier" in Europe in the late nineteenth century, running from southwest to northeast from around Trieste at the northern end of the Adriatic to the eastern end of the Baltic. Areas north and west of this line were dominated by what John Hajnal has called the "western European marriage pattern." It was characterized by late ages at first marriage (23 to 28 years) and high proportions of the population never marrying (often above 10 percent of the population aged 45 to 54 years). South and east of the line, first marriage was much earlier (18 to 22 years) and the rate of permanent nonmarriage significantly lower (below 10 percent of the population aged 45 to 54 years).

Summarizing the main results of the European Fertility Project, John Knodel and Etienne van de Walle (1982) drew six major conclusions. First, the modern fertility transition in Europe was caused proximately by reductions in marital fertility and not by changes in marriage or nonmarital fertility. Second, prior to the transition, Europe's populations were characterized by natural fertility, that is, by fertility not subject to deliberate limitation. Third, once under way, the decline was irreversible. Fourth, with the exception of France, the irreversible decline commenced roughly in the period 1870 to 1920. Fifth, the transition took place within a wide variety of social and economic conditions. Sixth, cultural settings exercised a significant influence.

Socioeconomic and cultural explanations. These data raise the issue of what causes families to decide whether, when, and how to have fewer children. The conventional explanations emphasize structural factors associated with socioeconomic development. The decline of infant and child mortality reduced the need for as many births to generate a target number of surviving children. The costs of children rose and their direct economic benefits fell for a variety of reasons, including the relative decline of agriculture and self-employment, the improved status of women (increasing the opportunity cost of their time, including the care and rearing of children), increased female employment outside the home, laws restricting child labor, compulsory schooling laws, the rise of institutional retirement insurance (reducing the value of children for that end), and rising housing and subsistence costs associated with urbanization. As more education brought higher returns, parents were led to invest in more quality per child and to reduce the numbers of children to make this possible. In addition, the cost, availability, and technology of family limitation methods improved from the late nineteenth century onward.

There is now evidence, however, that these explanations are insufficient. One finding of the Euro-

Thomas Malthus. ©Bettman/Corbis

TABLE 2
FERTILITY AND MORTALITY IN EUROPE, 1870–1980 (CONTEMPORARY BOUNDARIES)

Approximate year	England and Wales	Germany	France	The Netherlands	Italy	Spain	Sweden	Russia
Index of Overall Fertility (I_f) [a]								
1870	0.369	0.396	0.282	0.384	0.389	—	0.319	—
1900	0.273	0.373	0.228	0.347	0.369	0.383	0.302	0.540
1930	0.154	0.157	0.182	0.227	0.255	0.291	0.152	0.428
1960	0.214	0.202	0.222	0.252	0.200	0.228	0.172	0.207
1980	0.154	0.122	0.165	0.133	0.135	0.217	0.137	0.145
Index of Martial Fertility (I_g) [a]								
1870	0.686	0.760	0.494	0.845	0.646	—	0.700	—
1900	0.553	0.664	0.383	0.752	0.633	0.653	0.652	0.755
1930	0.292	0.264	0.273	0.446	0.471	0.540	0.303	0.665
1960	0.289	0.293	0.323	0.394	0.338	0.403	0.241	0.356
1980	0.209	0.170	0.235	0.203	—	0.351	—	—
Index of Proportions of Women Married (I_m) [a]								
1870	0.509	0.472	0.529	0.438	0.568	—	0.409	—
1900	0.476	0.513	0.543	0.450	0.549	0.559	0.411	0.696
1930	0.503	0.534	0.613	0.499	0.513	0.504	0.422	0.628
1960	0.699	0.644	0.646	0.630	0.578	0.553	0.626	0.581
1980	0.656	0.615	0.626	0.632	—	0.605	0.461	—
Infant Mortality Rate [b]								
1870	158	232	189	210	224	200	131	266
1900	156	217	155	151	165	195	105	255
1930	67	88	88	53	115	119	57	173
1960	22	36	28	18	43	38	17	36
1980	12	13	10	9	15	13	7	27
Expectation of Life at Birth [c]								
1870	40.8	37.0	41.4	39.6	35.3	—	45.0	27.7
1900	47.4	46.5	46.8	49.0	42.8	34.8	52.9	31.8
1930	60.2	61.3	57.2	64.0	54.9	50.3	63.1	44.4
1960	69.0	69.7	70.5	73.5	69.8	69.6	73.4	68.3
1980	72.1	72.6	74.4	75.6	74.4	75.6	75.8	69.4

Source: Coale and Treadway, 1986; Keyfitz and Flieger, 1968; Dublin, Lotka, and Spiegelman, 1949; United Nations, 2000.
(a) For a description of the index, see text.
(b) Infant deaths per 1,000 live births. Three-year averages when possible.
(c) In years. Both sexes combined. For Russia before 1960, data given for European Russia only; for 1960 and 1980, data given for the Russian Federation.

pean Fertility Project was that the irreversible decline in marital fertility began under a wide variety of socioeconomic conditions. For example, England and Wales, taken as a single nation, was the most modernized nation in Europe in the late nineteenth century, but its sustained decline in marital fertility only began around 1890. At that time it had an infant mortality rate of 149, 15 percent of the male labor force in agriculture, 72 percent of the population urban (and 57 percent living in cities of twenty thousand or more), and low illiteracy. In sharp contrast, Bulgaria began its sustained transition around 1910 (merely twenty years later) with a similar infant mortality rate (159), but at a much lower level of socioeconomic development: 70 percent of the male labor force in agriculture, only 18 percent urban (and only 7 percent in cities of twenty thousand or more), and 60 percent of the adult population illiterate. France, the most unusual case, began its transition very early (from at least 1800), with an infant mortality rate of 185, 70 percent of the male labor force in agriculture, 19 percent urban (and 7 percent in cities of twenty thousand or more), and high illiteracy. These examples can be multiplied. In other words, the standard structural variables did not predict when the European fertility transition would set in.

Furthermore, this process occurred in different ways for different groups, and other factors could be involved. Middle-class groups were often among the first to reduce birthrates because of their early commitment to higher levels of education and therefore to the ensuing costs. Too many children jeopardized the fairly high standard of living that middle-class families sought to maintain. Peasants usually made the turn to lower fertility later, for children's work continued to seem useful. But in special cases where concern for the preservation of property against inheritance divisions was a factor, as in France, peasant birthrate reductions could begin early. Urban workers, under pressures of economic insecurity, usually began to reduce birthrates after the middle class.

Another finding of the European Fertility Project was that cultural settings made a difference. This is illustrated by several examples. Belgium is divided by a linguistic boundary, with Flemish predominantly spoken on one side (roughly northern and western Belgium) and French on the other (roughly south and southeast Belgium). Along that boundary, socioeconomic conditions were similar, but fertility was demonstrably higher on the Flemish-speaking side. It was also found that excellent predictors of early fertility decline among the arrondissements of Belgium were the proportion voting socialist in 1919 (a positive predictor) and the proportion making their Easter

duties in the Roman Catholic Church (a negative predictor). This phenomenon was titled "secularization" by Ron Lesthaeghe. In France, also, areas of religious fervor long displayed higher-than-average birthrates. Similarly, a map of marital fertility in Spain around 1900 bears a strong resemblance to a linguistic map of the same country. The rapid spread of the idea of family limitation in the late nineteenth and early twentieth centuries across a variety of socioeconomic settings supports the notion that it was as much a change in worldview as a change in underlying material conditions that initiated the fertility transition. Ansley Coale (1967) has noted that three preconditions are necessary for a fertility transition: first, fertility control must be within the calculus of conscious choice; second, family limitation must be socially and economically advantageous to the individuals concerned; and third, the means must be available, inexpensive, and acceptable. Much of the research has focused on the second condition. But the cultural explanation asserts that the first condition was not fulfilled in most of Europe until the late nineteenth or early twentieth centuries.

In the long run, of course, birthrate reductions also responded to the drop in infant mortality, but the latter usually occurred after the former had begun. Some historians argue that, having fewer children, families became more alert to protecting the health of those who were born.

Birthrate reductions were often initially based on sexual restraint (this was true for workers into the twentieth century, in places like Britain). In some cases women may have taken the lead, out of a concern for their own health and also because, since they were responsible for household budgets, they were particularly aware of children's costs. The impact of this part of the demographic transition on family life and on the self-perceptions of mothers and fathers have stimulated further analysis. The process was clear, but not necessarily easy.

Declining reproduction rates. Birthrates by the end of the twentieth century had declined to the point that many populations in Europe were not, in the long run (fifty to seventy years), reproducing themselves. The gross reproduction rate is a measure of that reproductive capacity. A value greater than 1.0 indicates that, in the long run, natural increase (the surplus of births over deaths) will be positive; a value of 1.0 means that natural increase will eventually be zero; and a value less than 1.0 points to eventual negative natural increase. The gross reproduction rate by the 1990s was below 1.0 in most western European nations: England and Wales (.856 in 1985), Germany

(.629 in 1996), France (.828 in 1996), Italy (.581 in 1994), the Netherlands (.730 in 1996), Spain (.552 in 1995), Sweden (.916 in 1994), and the Russian Federation (.633 in 1995). In several cases (Germany, Italy, the Russian Federation, Bulgaria, the Czech Republic, Hungary, the Ukraine) natural increase is already negative. Without net immigration, these nations will have declining populations (and several do). This decline has occurred despite the "baby boom" that many of these countries experienced after World War II. Peak gross reproduction rates came in the early 1960s: England and Wales (1.66), West Germany (1.18), France (1.37), Italy (1.22), the Netherlands (1.52), Spain (1.38), Sweden (1.18), and the Russian Federation (1.21).

The reasons for this fertility "boom" and "bust" since 1945 are complex, and consensus is still not fully achieved. But the small age groups (age cohorts) of young adults in the prime childbearing years (ages eighteen to thirty-five) experienced very favorable labor market conditions in the 1950s and early 1960s: high wages, low unemployment, growing real incomes. This interacted with their modest consumer aspirations, created during the lean years of depression, war, and postwar recovery in the 1930s and 1940s, to produce a desire for more goods and services as well as more and better-educated children. The result was rising birthrates from the late 1940s to the early 1960s in many European societies (as well as in the United States, Canada, Australia, and New Zealand). The "baby bust" began in the mid 1960s as real wages and income failed to keep pace with consumption aspirations and has continued to the present.

There are now strong concerns about possible population declines and also about the rapidly aging population. A proportionately older population creates greater strains on currently funded retirement systems as it adds more recipients and fewer net contributors. The systems of medical facilities and insurance are also burdened with greater care for the elderly and similar erosion of the tax base. Population analysis shows that the demographic age structure depends (in the absence of significant international migration) largely on fertility and not on mortality. Although mortality does have some effect, especially in the last decades of the twentieth century as death rates declined rapidly among the elderly, it really operates at all levels of the population age pyramid. Fertility, in contrast, works only at the bottom of the age pyramid, among the youngest age cohorts. Low and declining birthrates produce a proportionately older population. For example, in 1861 Italy had 5.7 percent of its population aged sixty and over. By 1951 this figure was 12.2 percent, and it had risen to 20.9 percent in

1991. It is projected to be about 30 percent in 2025. Similarly, England and Wales had an elderly population (aged sixty and over) of 7.3 percent of the total in 1851. This had risen to 15.9 percent in 1951 and 20.9 percent in 1991. The projection for the United Kingdom for 2025 is about 27 percent. Approximately the same is true for all other European nations. One of the most important population welfare challenges of the twenty-first century will be to find ways to fund retirement and health care for these aging populations despite a relatively shrinking tax base.

THE MORTALITY TRANSITION

The mortality transition is the other part of the European demographic transition. This has become known as the "epidemiological transition," following Abdel Omran (1971), who divides the history of mortality into three broad phases. The first is the "age of pestilence and famine," in which the expectation of life at birth ($e[0]$) is in the range of about twenty to forty years and the annual death rate is quite variable. This was true for Europe before about 1750 or 1800. The great variability is characteristic of a Malthusian world in which population growth is checked by periodic mortality crises caused by epidemics, famines, wars, and political disturbances. However, not all areas experienced these crises. France did in the seventeenth and eighteenth centuries, for example, but English population growth was more often checked by adjustments to fertility via marriage in the same period. The second period is the "age of receding pandemics," in which the $e(0)$ rises to the range thirty to fifty years and during which the extreme mortality peaks diminish in both frequency and severity. This era began in Europe in the late eighteenth century and predominated by the late nineteenth century. Finally, we are now in the "age of degenerative and man-made diseases," in which the $e(0)$ rises above fifty years. Europe entered this period in the twentieth century. Similarly, work by Richard Easterlin (1999) dates the modern mortality transition in Europe from the late nineteenth and early twentieth centuries: England and Wales from 1871 with an $e(0)$ of 41 years, Sweden from 1875 with an $e(0)$ of 44.9 years, and France from 1893 with an $e(0)$ of 45.4 years.

Mortality rates. The course of the modern mortality transition in the eight countries used as examples here is outlined in the last two panels of table 2. They present the infant mortality rate (deaths in the first year of life per thousand live births per year) and the $e(0)$ for both sexes combined. Although mortality had already been declining from the eighteenth century, the modern transition commenced in the late nineteenth and early twentieth centuries. So, for example, $e(0)$ rose from about thirty-seven years around 1780 in Sweden to about forty-five years around 1875. But it then increased to approximately seventy-five years by 1975. Sweden thus gained only 4.6 years of $e(0)$ in the fifty years prior to 1875 but 17.2 years in the fifty years thereafter. England and France also experienced accelerations in the rate of mortality decline in the late nineteenth century, England from about 1870 and France from about 1890.

The transition in the infant mortality rate accompanied this decline, although the modern transition was often delayed by several decades. (Note that infant mortality is an important component of $e[0]$.) The basic factors affecting infant mortality were often quite different from those affecting general mortality rates: practices of infant feeding (including breast-feeding), weaning, and infant care as well as the types of diseases were wholly or significantly unrelated to the factors affecting survival for older children, teenagers, and adults. The infant mortality transition was truly dramatic. Around 1870, between 13 and 30 percent of all infants did not survive their first year of life. By 1980 this was down to between .7 and 2.7 percent, and it has continued to improve. But it is also apparent that in some countries (England and Wales, Germany, Spain) little progress was made until after 1900. Interestingly, a country's level of development was not decisive in predicting either the initial level or the timing of decline: England and Wales and Germany were quite economically advanced but did poorly. Sweden was not especially developed by the 1870s but did quite well in terms of lower levels of infant mortality and an early transition. England and Germany were impeded to some degree by their high and growing levels of urbanization.

Causes of death. The model of the epidemiological transition emphasizes causes of death. The earliest period is dominated by infectious and parasitic diseases, whether epidemic or endemic. These would include smallpox, measles, scarlet fever, diphtheria, cholera, malaria, typhoid fever, typhus, whooping cough, tuberculosis, pneumonia, and such generic conditions as bronchitis, gastritis, and enteritis. Causes of death then progressively shifted to so-called degenerative diseases such as cancer, heart disease, cerebrovascular disease (of which stroke is the most prevalent), and diabetes. Unfortunately for historical research, cause of death information is neither abundant nor often of good quality. Systematic collection of cause of death data did not commence until the mid-nineteenth century, and then medical theories most often suggested

causes based on symptoms rather than on underlying disease processes. Some designations were uninformative or even absurd (such as senility, teething, failure to thrive). The First International List of Cause of Death (ICD-1) was not accepted until 1899. Since then there have been eight revisions, moving more in the direction of disease processes rather than symptoms. Thus the categories have had shifting boundaries over time.

Nevertheless, a pioneering effort to look at the modern mortality transition from the perspective of cause of death was undertaken by Samuel Preston, Nathan Keyfitz, and Robert Schoen (1972; also Preston, 1976). They documented two of the earliest populations in Europe with acceptable data: England and Wales from 1861 and Italy from 1881. For England and Wales, the share of diseases demonstrably caused by pathogenic microorganisms (respiratory tuberculosis; other infectious and parasitic diseases; influenza, pneumonia, bronchitis; and diarrheal diseases) declined from 69 percent of known causes (for both sexes combined) in 1861 to 13 percent in 1964. Correspondingly, the share of degenerative diseases (neoplasms [cancer], cardiovascular, and certain other degenerative diseases) rose from 17 to 80 percent over the same period. For Italy, the decline in the share of infectious disease was from 70 percent in 1881 to 11 percent in 1964 (of known causes), and the increase in the share of degenerative disease was from 16 to 78 percent for the same time span. Some of this shift was due to the aging of the population, but most of it was a change in the underlying cause structure of mortality. (As an indicator of problems with the data, however, the share of causes in the category "other and unknown" fell from 31 percent of all deaths in 1861 to only 8 percent in England and Wales over the hundred years from 1861 to 1964. Italy experienced a similar improvement in data quality, with a decline in the share of "other and unknown" causes from 23 to 11 percent from 1881 to 1964.)

Causes of the transition. The causes of the mortality transition are complex and operated over a longer time period than the factors affecting fertility decline. Prior to the middle of the nineteenth century, some changes did take place that improved the chances of human survival. The bubonic plague ceased to be a serious epidemic threat after the last major outbreak in southern France in the years 1720–1722. The reasons are unclear, but exogenous changes in the etiology of the disease probably occurred (that is, the rat population changed its composition). The role of effective quarantine made possible by the growth of the modern nation-state and its bureaucracy must also be considered. Another development was the progressive control of smallpox, first through inoculation in the eighteenth century (which gives the patient a case of the disease under controlled conditions) and then vaccination in the late eighteenth and early nineteenth centuries.

But gains in longevity from medical and public health advances and improvements in the standard of living were often offset by the growth of urban environments that accompanied modern economic growth. In England and Wales and in France, the expectation of life at birth was about ten years lower in cities than it was in rural areas in the early nineteenth century. Although the underlying relationship between development (and especially real income per capita) and mortality was probably positive by the early nineteenth century, the correlation might not have been very strong, partly because of urbanization and also because extra income could not "buy" much in terms of extra years of life. Urban mortality rates did not converge with rural death rates until the interwar period, although today cities often have better longevity because of superior health care.

The origins of the "epidemiological transition" in Europe were influenced by a variety of factors. They may be grouped into ecobiological, public-health, medical, and socioeconomic factors. These categories are not mutually exclusive, since, for example, economic growth can make resources available for public-health projects, and advances in medical science can inform the effectiveness of public health. Ecobiological factors were generally not too important. Although there were favorable changes in the etiology of a few specific diseases or conditions in the nineteenth century (notably scarlet fever and possibly diphtheria), reduced disease virulence or changes in transmission mechanisms were not apparent. One important new epidemic disease, cholera, made its appearance in Europe for the first time in the 1820s and early 1830s.

The remaining factors—socioeconomic, medical, and public-health—are often difficult to disentangle. For example, if the germ theory of disease (a medical-scientific advance of the later nineteenth century) contributed to better techniques of water filtration and purification in public-health projects, it is not easy to separate the role of medicine from that of public health. Thomas McKeown (1976) has proposed that, prior to the twentieth century, medical science contributed little to reduced mortality in Europe and elsewhere. His argument basically eliminated alternatives: if ecobiological and medical factors are eliminated, the mortality decline before the early twentieth century must have been due to socioeconomic

factors, especially better diet and nutrition, as well as improved clothing and shelter (that is, standard of living). These conclusions were based particularly on the experience of England and Wales (and the available cause-of-death data back to the mid-nineteenth century), where much of the mortality decline between the 1840s and the 1930s was due to reductions in deaths from respiratory tuberculosis, other respiratory infections (such as bronchitis), and nonspecific gastrointestinal diseases (such as diarrhea and gastroenteritis). No effective medical therapies were available for these infections until well into the twentieth century. However, to cite an example of the problems with this account, the bronchitis death rate in England and Wales actually rose while that for respiratory tuberculosis was falling, indicating better diagnosis. Such results certainly vitiate McKeown's contentions.

Impact of medicine and public health.
It is true that medical science did have a rather limited direct role before the twentieth century. In terms of specific therapies, smallpox vaccination was known by the late eighteenth century and diphtheria and tetanus antitoxin and rabies therapy by the 1890s. Many other treatments were symptomatic. The germ theory of disease was arguably the single most important advance in medical science in the modern era. It was put forward by Louis Pasteur in the 1860s and greatly advanced by the work of Robert Koch and others in the late nineteenth century. But it was only slowly accepted by what was a very conservative medical profession. Even after Koch conclusively identified the tuberculosis bacillus in 1882 and the cholera vibrio in 1883, various theories of miasmas and anticontagionist views were common among physicians. Hospitals, having originated as pesthouses and almshouses, were (correctly) perceived as generally unhealthy places to be. Surgery was also very dangerous before the advances in antisepsis and technique in the 1880s and 1890s. Major thoracic surgery was rarely risked and, if attempted, patients had a high probability of dying from infection or shock or both. Amputations were best done quickly to minimize risks. Although anesthesia had been introduced in the 1840s and the use of antisepsis in the operating theater had been advocated by the British surgeon Joseph Lister in the 1860s, surgery was not considered reasonably safe until the twentieth century.

Although the direct impact of medicine on mortality in Europe over this period may be questioned, public health did play an important role and thereby gave medicine an indirect role. After John Snow identified polluted water as the cause of a cholera outbreak in London in 1854, pure water and sewage disposal became important issues for municipal authorities. William Budd correctly identified the mode of transmission of typhoid fever in 1859. The specific causal agents for a number of diseases were found from about 1880 onward, and therapies and immunizations were developed. A notable example was a diphtheria vaccine (in 1892 by Emile Adolph von Behring). And the twentieth century saw the development of specific therapies (such as Salvarsan for syphilis) and general antimicrobial drugs (sulfanomides and broad-spectrum antibiotics) from the 1930s onward.

A pattern was emerging in the late nineteenth century: massive public-works projects in larger metropolitan areas provided clean water and proper sewage disposal. But progress was uneven. As time went along, filtration and chlorination were added to remove or neutralize particulate matter and microorganisms. This was a consequence of the acceptance of the findings of the new science of bacteriology. Public-health officials were often much more cognizant of the need to use bacteriology than were physicians, who sometimes saw public-health officials as a professional threat. Marshaling resources and political support to pay for many of these public-works and public-health projects could slow their development. Much of the development was locally funded, leading to uneven and intermittent progress toward water and sewer systems, public-health departments, and so on. A famous case that convinced many of the skeptics took place in Hamburg during the cholera epidemic of 1892. The city of Hamburg, which had a somewhat antiquated water system not equipped to protect the city from water-borne disease, experienced a devastating epidemic, while the adjacent Prussian city of Altona, which had a sanitary system, had no dramatic increase in deaths.

Progress in public health was not confined to water and sewer systems, though they were among the most effective weapons in the fight to prolong and enhance human life. Simply by reducing the incidence and exposure to disease in any way, public-health measures improved overall health, net nutritional status, and resistance to disease. Other areas of public-health activity from the late nineteenth century onward included vaccination against smallpox; use of diphtheria and tetanus antitoxins (from the 1890s); more extensive use of quarantine, as more diseases were identified as contagious; cleaning urban streets and public areas to reduce disease foci; physical examinations for school children; health education; improved child labor and workplace health and safety laws; legislation and enforcement efforts to reduce food adulteration and especially to obtain pure milk; measures to eliminate ineffective or dangerous medications; increased knowledge of and education concerning nutrition; stricter licensing of physicians, nurses, and midwives; more rigorous medical education; building codes to improve heat, plumbing, and ventilation in housing; measures to alleviate air pollution in urban settings; and the creation of state and local boards of health to oversee and administer these programs. The new knowledge also caused personal health behaviors to change in effective ways.

Public health proceeded on a broad front, but not without delays and considerable unevenness in enforcement and effectiveness. Regarding the case of pure milk, it became apparent that pasteurization (heating the milk to a temperature below boiling for a period of time), known since the 1860s, was the only effective means of ensuring a bacteria-free product. Certification or inspection of dairy herds was insufficient. Pasteurization was resisted by milk sellers, however, and it only came into common practice just before World War I.

Public health and public policy can thus be seen as having played an indispensable part in the mortality transition. The role of nutrition and rising standards of living cannot be discounted, but applied science was much more important than allowed by McKeown. Work by Preston (1976, 1980) has demonstrated that up to three-quarters of the improvement in $e(0)$ in the twentieth century was not due to economic development (that is, improvements in real income per capita) but rather to shifts in the relationship of development to mortality, much of which can be attributed to public-health and medical intervention.

But there were interactions between reduced incidence of infectious and parasitic disease and improvements in general health. An indicator of health status is final adult stature. A population may have reasonable levels of food intake, but a virulent disease environment will impair net nutritional status—the amount of nutrients available for replacement and augmentation of tissue. Repeated bouts of infectious disease, especially gastrointestinal infections, impair the body's ability to absorb nutrients and divert calories, proteins, vitamins, and minerals in the diet to fighting the infection rather than to tissue construction or reconstruction. Research in the 1980s and 1990s indicated increases in stature (based largely on military records) since the nineteenth century. For example, between the third quarter of the eighteenth century and the third quarter of the nineteenth, adult male heights increased by only 1.1 centimeters on average in six European nations (Great Britain, France, Norway, Sweden, Denmark, and Hungary). But after the mortality transition had begun, stature grew by an average of 7.7 centimeters in the following century.

Migration. Hungarian refugees arriving in Switzerland, 1956. ©RENÉ BURRI/MAGNUM PHOTOS

MIGRATION

An issue not usually addressed by the demographic transition is migration. Historically, the movement of peoples was very important in Europe. By the early nineteenth century, large numbers of Europeans began leaving their countries, in many cases destined for the United States and other overseas areas (Canada, Australia, New Zealand, Argentina). This was a major factor in reducing population growth rates. Between 1820 and 1970, Europe sent approximately 36 million people to the United States alone. After the potato famine of the 1840s Ireland lost so many people to migration (4.5 million to the United States between 1840 and 1970) that the population declined for over a century, from over 8 million in 1841 to about 4.3 million in 1951. Lesser known is the fact that Norway had the second highest out-migration rate in Europe. By 1910, 14.7 percent of the population of the United States (and 22 percent of the Canadian population) was foreign-born.

By the late twentieth century Europe had changed from a region of net emigration to one of net immigration. People from the Third World and from areas of Europe outside the foci of rapid economic growth (the Balkans, eastern Europe, Russia) migrated to western Europe in substantial numbers. Besides exacerbating a number of social issues, it made more difficult the maintenance of the modern welfare state. But these new residents provided what the receiving nations needed—their labor. And the trend will continue as long as sharp wage and income gaps exist between the prosperous nations of Europe and these sending areas, as long as serious economic and political dislocations continue in the former East European bloc, and as long as the receiving nations do not close their borders to migrants.

CONCLUSION

In the past two hundred years, Europe has undergone the demographic transition from high levels of fertility and mortality to low, modern levels of birth and death rates. This led to lower rates of population growth and the aging of the populations. Increased longevity, very low infant and child mortality, and remarkably improved education and health have all been part of this modernization process. Nonetheless, the low population growth rates and progressively older populations now pose new challenges for public policy.

See also **Modernization** *(in this volume);* **Public Health** *(volume 3);* **Medical Practitioners and Medicine** *(volume 4);* **Standards of Living** *(volume 5); and other articles in this section.*

BIBLIOGRAPHY

Alter, George. "Theories of Fertility Decline: A Non-Specialist's Guide to the Current Debate on European Fertility Decline." In *The European Experience of Declining Fertility, 1850–1970*. Edited by John R. Gillis, Louise A. Tilly, and David Levine. Oxford, 1992. Pages 13–27.

Chesnais, Jean-Claude. *The Demographic Transition: Stages, Patterns, and Economic Implications*. Translated by Elizabeth and Philip Kreager. Oxford and New York, 1992.

Coale, Ansley J. "Factors Associated with the Development of Low Fertility: An Historic Summary." In *World Population Conference: 1965*. United Nations, Department of Economic and Social Affairs. Vol. 2. New York, 1967. Pages 205–209.

Coale, Ansley J., and Roy Treadway. "A Summary of the Changing Distribution of Overall Fertility, Marital Fertility, and the Proportion Married in the Provinces of Europe." In *The Decline of Fertility in Europe*. Edited by Ansley J. Coale and Susan Cotts Watkins. Princeton, N.J., 1986. Pages 31–181.

Coale, Ansley J., and Susan Cotts Watkins, eds. *The Decline of Fertility in Europe*. Princeton, N.J., 1986.

Davis, Kingsley. "Cities and Mortality." In *International Population Conference: Liège, 1973*. Report of the International Union for the Scientific Study of Population. Vol. 3. Liège, 1973. Pages 259–282.

Dublin, Louis, Alfred Lotka, and Mortimer Spiegelman. *Length of Life: A Study of the Life Table*. Rev. ed. New York, 1949.

Durand, John. "The Modern Expansion of World Population." *Proceedings of the American Philosophical Society* 111 (1967): 136–159.

Easterlin, Richard A. *Growth Triumphant: The Twenty-first Century in Historical Perspective*. Ann Arbor, Mich., 1996.

Easterlin, Richard A. "How Beneficent Is the Market? A Look at Modern Mortality History." *European Review of Economic History* 3 (1999): 257–294.

Fogel, Robert William. "New Sources and New Techniques for the Study of Secular Trends in Nutritional Status, Health, Mortality, and the Process of Aging." *Historical Methods* 26 (1993): 5–43.

Johansson, Sheila Ryan. "Food for Thought: Rhetoric and Reality in Modern Mortality History." *Historical Methods* 27 (1994): 101–125.

Keyfitz, Nathan, and Wilhelm Flieger. *World Population: An Analysis of Vital Data*. Chicago, 1968.

Knodel, John, and Etienne van de Walle. "Fertility Decline: 3. European Transition." In *International Encyclopedia of Population*. Edited by John A. Ross. New York, 1982. Pages 268–275.

Lesthaeghe, Ron. "A Century of Demographic and Cultural Change in Western Europe: An Exploration of Underlying Dimensions." *Population and Development Review* 9 (1983): 411–435.

Livi-Bacci, Massimo. *A Concise History of World Population*. Translated by Carl Ipsen. 1992. 2d ed., Malden, Mass., 1997.

McEvedy, Colin, and Richard Jones. *Atlas of World Population History*. New York, 1978.

McKeown, Thomas. *The Modern Rise of Population*. New York, 1976.

Mitchell, Brian R. *International Historical Statistics: Europe 1750–1993*. 4th ed. New York, 1998.

Omran, Abdel. "The Epidemiologic Transition: A Theory of the Epidemiology of Population Change." *Milbank Memorial Fund Quarterly* 49 (1971): 509–538.

Preston, Samuel H. "Causes and Consequences of Mortality Declines in Less Developed Countries during the Twentieth Century." In *Population and Economic Change in Developing Countries.* Edited by Richard A. Easterlin. Chicago, 1980. Pages 289–341.

Preston, Samuel H. *Mortality Patterns in National Populations.* New York, 1976.

Preston, Samuel H., Nathan Keyfitz, and Robert Schoen. *Causes of Death: Life Tables for National Populations.* New York, 1972.

Szreter, Simon. "The Importance of Social Intervention in Britain's Mortality Decline ca. 1850–1914: A Reinterpretation of the Role of Public Health." *Social History of Medicine* 1 (1988): 1–38.

United Nations. *Demographic Yearbook: Historical Supplement.* New York, 2000.

Weir, David R. "Life under Pressure: France and England, 1670–1870." *Journal of Economic History* 44 (1984): 27–47.

Williamson, Jeffrey G. "Was the Industrial Revolution Worth It? Disamenities and Death in Nineteenth Century British Towns." *Explorations in Economic History* 19 (1982): 221–245.

Wrigley, E. A., and Roger S. Schofield. *The Population History of England, 1541–1871: A Reconstruction.* Cambridge, Mass., 1981.

THE EUROPEAN MARRIAGE PATTERN

David Levine

The demographic keystone of the northwestern European system of family formation was the prolonged hiatus between puberty and marriage. Certain statistics provide a measure which distinguishes the creation of new families in northwestern Europe from that in other societies: Only a tiny minority of girls married as teenagers, and an even smaller number of all brides were mature women who married for the first time in their thirties. Perhaps one woman in ten never married. The identification and description of this particular pattern of family formation is among the great achievements of scholarship in historical demography. The marriage system is called "neo-Malthusian" advisedly. Thomas Malthus (1766–1834) theorized that population grows at a faster rate than its resources; if that growth is not checked in some way—disease, war, moral strictures—disintegration and poverty follow. Malthus stressed the prudential check as a factor of crucial importance. In Malthus's eighteenth-century England, the check was late marriage: women usually married for the first time when they were in their mid-twenties.

Much of the force of H. J. Hajnal's pioneering 1965 study came from his singular insight that northwestern Europe was different, although he reminded his readers that the idea was hardly novel. Indeed Malthus had made that idea one of the cornerstones of his *Essay on the Principle of Population* (1798), which itself built on the arguments of previous commentators. Hajnal's achievement, though, was to subject the Malthusian rhetoric to systematic analysis using statistical information. In so doing he opened a doorway to new research and theorizing.

Historical demographers have provided evidence regarding the northwestern European practice of deferred marriage among women. Secondarily, the northwestern European family apparently lived in nuclear households without kin. Marriage was almost always the occasion for forming a new household. Family formation, therefore, was a double-sided process in which the new couple not only left their parents' residences but also founded their own household.

This system of family formation was quite unlike the systems that prevailed among Mediterranean, eastern European, or non-European populations. Few girls in these other populations seem to have delayed their marriages much beyond puberty, and residences often contained joint families composed of two or more married couples. The families sometimes extended horizontally, as when brothers lived in the same household, and sometimes they extended vertically, as when fathers and sons lived together under the same roof.

Hajnal noted that early ages at first marriage for women continued to be a characteristic of eastern Europe as late as 1900. Three-quarters of western European women were unmarried at age twenty-five, whereas east of a line running from Trieste to St. Petersburg three-quarters of the women were married by age twenty-five. Alan Macfarlane suggested that it is impossible to explain the differences between demographic zones in Europe before the nineteenth century by physical geography, by political boundaries, or by technology. Where the age at first marriage for women was high, the northwestern and central regions, that later age correlates with a low proclivity for living in complex, multiple-family households. In contrast, where the age at first marriage for women was early, the Mediterranean and eastern zones, the propensity was high for residential complexity.

Macfarlane thus rejected a materialist explanation of the relationship between family formation and household organization or modes of reproduction and modes of production. Instead, he concentrated on the role of broad cultural and ethnic regions that coincided with the spatial distribution of distinctive family systems. Macfarlane derived his explanation by grafting Hajnal's studies of household formation, which stressed an east-west division, onto Jean-Louis Flandrin's findings about a similar north-south line that split France in two. Macfarlane recognized that this tripartite cultural division seems to find a deep resonance in Peter Burke's 1978 sketch of the geography of popular cultural regions in early modern Europe.

In the 1970s Peter Laslett, who pioneered work on household structure, suggested another partition. He added a fourth region comprising central Europe, where female marriage was late but household structure was complex rather than nuclear as in northwestern Europe.

These divisions in systems of domestic organization, Hajnal's two, Macfarlane's three, and Laslett's four, have clarified that the age at first marriage for women is the keystone in the arch of family formation strategies. They also ask another question: What happened to the young women who did not marry at puberty? Adolescent and young adult servants were common in the later-marrying northwestern and central regions but were uncommon in the Mediterranean and irrelevant in the east. The age at first marriage of women, therefore, not only had profound demographic implications but was also a pivot on which the reproduction of different cultural systems turned.

How did this distinctive family culture of nuclear households and deferred marriage take root in the northwestern corner of Europe? While research has uncovered much about the distribution and shape of this system of reproduction, its origins remain an unanswered question. Paradoxically, this key question cannot be answered with more statistical studies. Rather, its answer lies in the social-historical contexts of marriage and family formation and nonstatistical sources.

FROM SLAVERY TO FEUDALISM

Ancient concepts of family and household reflected the social realities of a slaveholding society that was also fundamentally sexist. Patriarchal dominance was characteristic of the immensely influential Aristotelian tradition, which envisaged a hierarchically ordered body whose highest form was an independent, property owning, adult male. The rise of Christian society brought changes in domestic life, but the break with antiquity was by no means complete in terms of the moral economy of patriarchy since, in the New Testament, the father of the house is the despot or absolute lord over the house. Paul, in particular, was outspoken in his misogyny. In combination with the demise of slavery, the Christian model of marriage created a social mutation of profound importance. Christianity broke away from its Judaic and pagan inheritance in separating descent from reproduction. As a religion of revelation, it linked salvation neither with lineage nor with ancestral achievements. Christians were not enjoined to maintain the patriline as a

religious task, nor were they expected to continue the cult of the dead through physical or fictitious descendants. However, Christianity's negative view of human sexuality developed into a new set of taboos regarding marriage and incest.

In contrast with the decentralized organization of the ancient church, the Carolingian church embarked on a new ecclesiastical strategy that touched on every aspect of conduct, especially with regard to economic, family, and sexual relationships. The Carolingians' ambitious plans to remodel Christian society in the image of a secular monastery failed, but this model provided the inspiration for the Gregorian Reformation, which occurred in the eleventh century when the Carolingian Empire disintegrated and power slipped from the central monarchy into the hands of the territorial nobility. In feudal families, unlike in their Carolingian predecessors, primogeniture and the indivisibility of the patrimony became the keys to their lineage strategy.

Georges Duby has argued that the man responsible for a family's honor tried to preserve its prestige by exercising strict control over the marriages of the young men and women subject to his authority. He handed over the women quite willingly but allowed only some of the men to contract lawful marriages, thus forcing most of the knights to remain bachelors. Of particular importance in this process was the shift from horizontal to vertical modes of reckoning kinship. The male line was imagined to stretch back to reach a single progenitor. Kings and great feudal princes further tightened the bond of vassal friendship by using marriage to make alliances and to provide their most faithful followers with wives. Above all marriage was a way of striking out on one's own. Some knights, by taking a wife or receiving one at the hands of their lords, escaped from another man's house and founded their own. A new organization of family life was thus a major characteristic of the feudal revolution that turned the ruling class into small rival dynasties rooted in their estates and clinging to the memory of the male ancestors. In this political disintegration, mirrored in the sexual and dynastic tensions that circulated through the great houses, ecclesiastical reformers sought to enhance the social role of the church and make it the arbiter of legitimation. Elevating marriage into a sacramental status removed men and women from the sphere in which unions were free, unregulated, and disorderly. Marriage was seen as a remedy for sexual desire, bringing order, discipline, and peace.

While much attention inevitably devolves upon the marital alliances and strategies of the upper class, the post-Gregorian church's marriage policies had a significant resonance for the lower orders, too. In establishing the centrality of consent in a Christian marriage, the canon law of marriage made the marital union easy to create, endowed it with serious consequences, and made divorce difficult. This was exactly the opposite of the situations in Roman and barbarian law. The Christian desire to evangelize the servile population, drawing it into the cultural domain of the church, was founded on a remarkably democratic principle, that all men and women, whether free or servile, were morally responsible agents whose sins were an abomination in the sight of God.

The preeminent meaning of *familia* in the early Middle Ages did not refer to "family" in the twentieth-century sense but rather to the totality of the lord's dependents. It was in relation to the orderly maintenance of stable domestic government among his dependent population that a lord extended regulation beyond the immediate tenant to include the peasant family. However, it is important to note that surveillance was most likely not conducted on a daily basis but rather as a more generalized maintenance of frontiers and boundaries within the social formation. In 1967 Marc Bloch pointed out that the slave was like an ox in the stable, always under a master's orders, whereas the villein or serf was a worker who came on certain days and who left as soon as the job was finished.

Around the year 1000 the rural population in northwest Europe consisted mostly of peasant farmers who lived in nuclear families. A marriage joined two individuals, not their families, and created a conjugal family, not a family alliance. In northwest Europe, marriage was tied to household formation, which was in turn connected to the young couple's ability to find an available niche in the local economy. By no means a homogenous social group, these nuclear families differed among themselves in the amount of land to which they had access. Additionally, over the course of their lives their households changed according to the rhythms of their family cycles. It seems that, when a household had too many mouths, it brought in servants as extra hands. According to Hajnal's analysis of spatial variation in household formation systems, the northwestern European households characteristically included a large number of coresident servants.

Because households in northwestern Europe were nuclear, youthful marriage on the Mediterranean model (the creation of joint households) was not an option. Why did peasant men marry women who were well past puberty, often in their mid-twenties? Why did they not marry teenagers, as in Mediterranean Europe? The answers require consideration of the socially constructed characteristics of a good wife

and the role and responsibilities of a housewife. The deeper expectation was that a peasant woman would be more than a breeder. It may have been the case that a married woman's fecundity was her most valuable asset, but it is a different matter to suggest that her fecundity was more valuable than the labor she might contribute to the maintenance of the household or the property she brought into the marriage. From an early time a majority of the population was either landless or free from seigneurial control. Among this group, subsistence rather than feudal modes of patriarchy was the main impediment to the marital freedom of young women and men.

MALTHUSIAN MARRIAGE

Scholars working on English feudal documents, called manorial court rolls, of the thirteenth and fourteenth centuries denote an age at first marriage for women that was as much as a decade after puberty. The revisionists further suggest that the post–Black Death (after 1348) age at first marriage for women was a continuation of an earlier system of marriage and family formation whose essential outline is detectable in the populations surveyed in the manorial court rolls. The social world of marriage that the revisionists espouse is a "low-pressure" demographic regime that continued for centuries and that has been identified in demographic studies of parish registers. This low-pressure demographic regime was the same one that Malthus associated with the prudential check that he believed was the primary method of population control in his society. Indeed, he took that regime's existence for granted, never asking how or why it came into being.

A parochial system of vital registration began in the Renaissance. From this point forward the statistical record is reasonably complete and quite irrefutable in its conclusions regarding age at first marriage for women. Surviving parish registers from early modern northwestern Europe have been analyzed according to a method known as family reconstitution to provide a large database. Michael Flinn analyzed fifty-four village studies describing age at first marriage for women. They showed that the average fluctuated around twenty-five. The standard deviation in this sample was about six years, which means that about two-thirds of all northwest European women married for the first time between twenty-two and twenty-eight.

In the sixteenth century it was widely understood that an appropriate age at first marriage was well beyond puberty. In the "hometowns" of Reformation

Protestant Marriage. *Pastor Blessing a Couple,* painting (1768) by an anonymous Alsatian artist. MUSÉE DES TRADITIONS POPULAIRES, PARIS/©PHOTO RMN–J. G. BERIZZI

Germany, craft guilds limited access to marriage among their apprentices and journeymen and also linked marriage to acquisition of the skills and material resources that a master controlled. Young men's personal freedoms were formally regulated, and their energies were displaced into youth groups, *Wanderjahre,* and male sociability centered on the alehouse. Matriarchs kept respectable females under domestic surveillance. These practices were not peculiar to Germany or small towns, however. It is evident from the 1563 English "Statute of Artificers" that similar concerns were part of the Elizabethan state formation initiative:

> Until a man grows unto the age of 24 years, he (for the most part though not always) is wild, without judgement, and not of sufficient experience to govern himself, nor (many times) grown unto the full or perfect knowledge of the art or occupation that he professes, and therefore has more need still to remain under government, as a servant and learner, than to become a ruler, as a master or instructor.
>
> Some take wives and before they are 24 years of age, have three or four children, which often they leave to the parish where they dwell to be kept, and others fall to chopping, changing, and making of many unadvised bargains and more than they are able to en-

compass, so that by one means or another they do utterly undo themselves, in such wise that most of them do hardly recover the same while they live. Of all and which things many mischiefs and inconveniences do rise, grow, and daily increase in the common wealth, which might be easily avoided by binding young apprentices until their ages of 24 years.

Access to marriage was thus a part of an interconnected ensemble of social relations in which life-cycle stage, political entitlement, and material resources were poised in a fine balance.

People who deviated from these rules were identified and punished for their transgressions to prevent beggar-marriages based on nothing more than the fleeting attraction of two people. This, too, was the subject of legal attention. In 1589 an English statute prohibited the erection of cottages with less than four acres of attached land, which spoke directly to the patriarchal concern that feckless, landless youths would take serious matters of family formation into their own hands. Ministers of the state church alerted poor-law authorities whenever they were approached to perform marriages between such youths, and in a number of instances, the couples were forcibly separated. In a great many cases such marriages were prevented as the forces of patriarchal discipline closed ranks against the star-crossed lovers. If the young woman was pregnant, she was disowned and severely punished. Underlying these disciplinary actions was a pre-Malthusian sense that marriage was not only a noble estate but a socially responsible one not to be entered into lightly. These unspoken assumptions orchestrated the surveillance of marriage and family formation and remained unspoken because they were considered natural and right.

Parish register studies or family reconstitutions have revealed oscillations in the ages at which women first married. In England, for example, women's age at first marriage fell from an early eighteenth-century high point of over twenty-five to an early nineteenth-century low point of under twenty-three, coincidental with the expansionary phase of the first industrial revolution. The later period never experienced a preponderance of teenaged brides even though illegitimacy rates skyrocketed and bridal pregnancies became very common. The long hiatus between puberty and marriage, the central characteristic of the northwestern European family system, was not seriously challenged.

TWENTIETH-CENTURY RESEARCH CONTRIBUTIONS

During the twentieth century researchers relegated explicit statistical comparisons to a secondary role and inquired into the motivations for behaving in the manner identified. In postfamine Ireland, for example, the decision to marry was the result of a complex interplay between the wider family network and socioeconomic opportunities related to the operation of the family holding, the provision of security, and the need for support in old age. Thus in postfamine Ireland the rising number of people who never married included those who controlled households and were tied down by obligations and also their siblings, who would have renounced their claims upon marriage. Each subgroup, for its own reasons, was more likely to remain permanently celibate. In balancing all the various aspects of their social stations, their decisions concerned whether or not they wanted to marry instead of whether or not they could afford marriage.

Understanding the social actors' own reasons is of crucial importance, and one person's reasons were not necessarily the same as another's. Hardly an earthshaking concept, it does, however, demonstrate that the northwestern European marriage system deserves further study. Such a revisionist approach complements Hajnal's original strategy rather than subverting it.

In an original approach, Wally Seccombe in 1992 developed a scenario in which marriages among landholding peasants were negotiated freely by the four sides in the exchange, that is, the couple acting in their own interests and for their own reasons and the two sets of parents, who were trying to cement intrafamily alliances as matchmakers. In Seccombe's

account each actor had a veto over the choices of others. This double veto dovetailed with the clerical concern that couples freely enter into marriages. Seccombe's scenario is perhaps less compelling in accounting for the marriage strategies of the landless sectors of the population, for whom parental agreement was of emotional but not economic importance, and, even in the heyday of feudalism the population included a substantial landless component. In the sixteenth century these landless people significantly outnumbered landholding peasants, and during the eighteenth and early nineteenth centuries the ratio rose yet again.

Expanding economic opportunities made it possible for landless people, who had to live by their wits and by their labor, to contemplate early marriage, whereas stagnation left them on the outside looking in. External contingencies were in this way incorporated into the internal dynamics of family formation. The preindustrial epoch experienced a labor surplus, and wageworkers usually married later and married older women than did peasants. During the industrial revolution these proletarians frequently were able to found independent households much earlier than their forebears had. For this reason above all others, a few generations of northwestern Europeans reinterpreted the prudential check during the first industrial revolution. At exactly this time women's age at first marriage fell to the lowest level recorded in English family reconstitution studies. Was it merely coincidental, then, that in 1798 Malthus published his famous *Es-*

Marriage Contract. The engaged couple make a contract before a notary. French drawing, eighteenth century. PAUL-DUPUY MUSEUM, TOULOUSE

say extolling the restraint inherent in the prudential check and bemoaning its recent weakening?

The marriages of the landless represented a degree zero of the system's deep-rooted cultural hold. The landless were essentially free agents who conformed to the practices of deferred marriage and nuclear household formation, but the system left room for interpretation. Social change led the landless proletarians to reinterpret deferred marriage and nuclear household formation without abandoning the cultural heritage of family life. The changes are statistically interesting, yet the landless proletarians did not marry at puberty or form extended, multiple-family households. This corollary reemphasizes Malthus's original arithmetic argument that small changes, when aggregated over a long period of time, can have massive structural implications.

While an increase in residential complexity accompanied massive urbanization in the nineteenth century, the larger social ambition to found nuclear-family households at marriage was essentially unchallenged. Urban-industrial proletarians were likely to live in consensual, common-law unions only because they were unwilling or unable to pay the various taxes on marriage demanded by the church and the state. Those consensual, common-law unions mirrored the nuclear households formed by their more respectable contemporaries in all essential statistical parameters. The only exception was that many new urban industrial centers had such serious housing problems that sometimes single men and women or poor young couples were forced to spend some time as lodgers in the households of established families. But as soon as they could afford to, these youngsters conformed to the cultural type and established their own nuclear-family households.

Rural and urban differences also resulted from sex-specific migration processes. Capital cities filled with female domestic servants, while mining towns and heavy industrial towns had a huge surplus of young males. Overseas emigration left some regions with an overabundance of females. Between and within local social systems a fair bit of heterogeneity developed in the ways the so-called Hajnal-Laslett rules were incorporated into daily life. Some subgroups clustered around earlier marriages, some were more likely than others to defer marriage longer, others lived in more residentially complex domestic units.

The Hajnal-Laslett thesis has also been fruitfully explored by those who study marginal regions, places that were arrayed along the borders between one system and another. Late nineteenth- and early twentieth-century Spain, for example, exhibited the widest range of marriage patterns in western Europe. Demographic

Wedding Ceremony. *The Arranged Marriage,* painting (1862) by Vasili Vladimirovits Pukirev (1832–1890). TRETYAKOV GALLERY, MOSCOW/BRIDGEMAN ART LIBRARY

and economic variables did not efface the strong cultural differences between Spanish regions. In areas of partible inheritance, marriage was earlier and more universal. Impartible inheritance was associated with later marriage and male out-migration, which left the remaining females in the parlous situation of outnumbering their potential mates.

North-cental Italy was a stronghold of sharecropping, which during the Renaissance was associated with its own peculiarities of family formation in the hinterland of Florence. At the beginning of the twentieth century when the death rate was plummeting, survival of extra mouths and extra hands put new pressures on the traditional system of social reproduction. For centuries sharecroppers had lived in multiple-family households, but their children's marriages were now connected with other avenues of employment. Some continued as sharecroppers, others became agricultural proletarians, others worked in the factories that were attracted to the large pools of available labor, and still others emigrated to Florence, Bologna, Milan, or overseas. Each of these new subgroups had its own reasons for embarking on family formation. Within each of these sociological categories were familial factors that made marriage more or less likely, but in contrast to their Renaissance fore-bears, the north-central Italians of 1900 married long after puberty.

The Italian case is interesting because the documentary record traces its evolution over a half-millennium. The censuslike enumerations, such as the fifteenth-century Florentine *catàsto* or land registry, show that age at first marriage for women was the mid-teens, which was about ten years earlier than in the northwestern European parish register populations. Tuscan men were on average ten years older than their brides. In the cities this difference was more marked than in the countryside, but the essential ten-year gap was still evident along with the link between the female age at first marriage and puberty. Among the Florentine upper crust, grooms were often in their middle thirties, and they married nubile girls who had just reached puberty. The identified difference between rural and urban populations stemmed from the fact that male sharecroppers seem to have married earlier than other peasants and townsmen, but their wives were still likely to have been pubescent teenagers.

Seeing matters in this long-term perspective, Richard Smith in 1981 raised questions about the Renaissance system. Was it "Mediterranean" or "medieval" in the sense that early female marriage ages and residential complexity were responses to the conjuncture occasioned by the Black Death, which hit the Tuscan population savagely and repeatedly? If the Re-naissance family system described in the Florentine *catàsto* was "medieval," why was it so different from the English response that Smith and his revisionist colleagues inferred from their analysis of the fourteenth-century poll tax registers?

CONCLUSION

Hajnal and Laslett developed the basic parameters of the northwestern European marriage system in the 1960s. Apparently the system's hegemony stood uncontested for the best part of a millennium and this deeply entrenched system of marriage and household formation was very supple. It bent but did not break during the nineteenth-century urbanization and industrialization. Twentieth-century scholarsip, however, notes profound structural changes. Marriage and reproduction were no longer tightly conjoined. Marriages were broken by divorce, and in some places more than half of all children were not living with their biological parents, even when both were still alive. Furthermore, the definition of "family" was stretched so far that a twentieth-century sociologist in England counted 126 different patterns. The ideological carapace of family life proved extremely durable, but close inspection has revealed profound redefinitions taking place as the patriarchal powers of fathers, subjected to legal challenge, disintegrated.

See also other articles in this section and the section **The Family and Age Groups** *(volume 4).*

BIBLIOGRAPHY

Alter, George. "New Perspectives of European Marriage in the Nineteenth Century." *Journal of Family History* 16 (1991): 1–6.

Bailey, Mark. "Demographic Decline in Late Medieval England: Some Thoughts on Recent Research." *Economic History Review,* 2d ser., 49 (1966): 1–19.

Bloch, Marc. "How and Why Ancient Slavery Came to an End." In *Land and Work in Medieval Europe.* Berkeley, Calif., 1967.

Brown, Peter. *The Body and Society: Men, Women, and Sexual Renunciation in Early Christianity.* New York, 1988.

Burguière, André. "Pour une typologie des formes d'organisation domestique de l'Europe moderne (xvi–xix siècles)." *Annales: Économies, societés, civilisations* 41 (1986): 639–655.

Burke, Peter. *Popular Culture in Early Modern Europe.* New York, 1978.

Duby, Georges. *The Knight, the Lady, and the Priest: The Making of Modern Marriage in Medieval France.* New York, 1983.

Duby, Georges. *Medieval Marriage: Two Models from Twelfth-Century France.* Baltimore, Md., 1978.

Flandrin, Jean-Louis. *Families in Former Times: Kinship, Household, and Sexuality.* Cambridge, U.K., 1979.

Flinn, Michael W. *The European Demographic System, 1500–1820.* Baltimore, Md., 1981.

Foucault, Michel. *The History of Sexuality.* 3 vols. New York, 1978–1990.

Gillis, John R. *For Better, for Worse: British Marriages, 1600 to the Present.* New York, 1985.

Gillis, John. *A World of Their Own Making: Myth, Ritual, and the Quest for Family Values.* New York, 1996.

Goitein, S. D. *A Mediterranean Society.* Vol. 3: *The Family.* Berkeley, Calif., 1978.

Goldberg, P. J. P. "Introduction" and "For Better, for Worse: Marriage and Economic Opportunity for Women in Town and Country." In *Woman Is a Worthy Wight.* Wolfeboro, N.H., 1992. Pages 1–15, 108–125.

Goldberg, P. J. P. *Women, Work, and Life Cycle in a Medieval Economy.* Oxford, 1992.

Goody, Jack. *The Development of the Family and Marriage in Europe.* Cambridge, U.K., 1983.

Guinnane, Timothy. "Re-thinking the Western European Marriage Pattern: The Decision to Marry in Ireland at the Turn of the Twentieth Century." *Journal of Family History* 16 (1991): 47–64.

Hajnal, H. J. "European Marriage Patterns in Perspective." In *Population in History.* Edited by D. V. Glass and D. E. C. Eversley. London, 1965. Pages 101–143.

Hajnal, H. J. "Two Kinds of Pre-industrial Household Formation System." In *Family Forms in Historic Europe.* Edited by Richard Wall. Cambridge, U.K., 1983. Pages 1–64.

Hammer, Carl I., Jr. "Family and *Familia* in Early-Medieval Bavaria." In *Family Forms in Historic Europe.* Edited by Richard Wall. Cambridge, U.K., 1983. Pages 217–248.

Herlihy, David. "The Making of the Medieval Family: Symmetry, Structure, and Sentiment." *Journal of Family History* 8 (1983): 116–130.

Herlihy, David. *Medieval Households.* Cambridge, Mass., 1985.

Herlihy, David, and Christiane Klapisch-Zuber. *Tuscans and Their Families: A Study of the Florentine Catàsto of 1427.* New Haven, Conn., 1985.

Homans, George Caspar. *English Villagers of the Thirteenth Century.* New York, 1941.

Hopkins, Keith. "The Age of Roman Girls at Marriage." *Population Studies* 18 (1965): 309–327.

Kertzer, David, and Dennis Hogan. "Reflections on the European Marriage Pattern: Sharecropping and Proletarianization in Casalecchio, Italy, 1861–1921." *Journal of Family History* 16 (1991): 31–46.

Ladurie, Emmanuel Le Roy. *Montaillou: Cathars and Catholics in a French Village, 1294–1324.* Translated by Barbara Bray. London, 1978.

Laslett, Peter. "Family and Household as Work Group and Kin Group: Areas of Traditional Europe Compared." In *Family Forms in Historic Europe.* Edited by Richard Wall. Cambridge, U.K., 1983. Pages 513–563.

Laslett, Peter. *The World We Have lost.* London, 1965.

Laslett, Peter, ed. *Household and Family in Past Time.* Cambridge, U.K., 1972.

Lerner, Gerda. *The Creation of Patriarchy.* New York, 1986.

Levine, David. *At the Dawn of Modernity: Biology, Culture, and Material Life in Europe after the Year 1000.* Berkeley and Los Angeles, 2000.

Levine, David. "Education and Family Life in Early Industrial England." *Journal of Family History* 4 (1979): 368–380.

Levine, David, " 'For Their Own Reasons': Individual Marriage Decisions and Family Life." *Journal of Family History* 7 (1982): 255–264.

Levine, David. "Illiteracy and Family Life during the First Industrial Revolution." *Journal of Social History* 14 (1980): 25–44.

Levine, David. *Reproducing Families: The Political Economy of English Population History.* Cambridge, U.K. 1987.

Little, Lester K. "Romanesque Christianity in Germanic Europe." *Journal of Interdisciplinary History* 23 (1992): 453–474.

Lynch, Joseph H. *Godparents and Kinship in Early Medieval Europe.* Princeton, N.J., 1986.

Lynch, Katherine. "The European Marriage Pattern in the Cities: Variations on a Theme by Hajnal." *Journal of Family History* 16 (1991): 79–95.

Macfarlane, Alan. "Demographic Structures and Cultural Regions in Europe." *Cambridge Anthropology* 6 (1981): 1–17.

Macfarlane, Alan. *Marriage and Love in England: Modes of Reproduction, 1300–1840.* Oxford, 1986.

McNamara, JoAnn, and Suzanne Wemple. "The Power of Women through the Family in Medieval Europe, 500–1100." In *Women and Power in the Middle Ages.* Edited by Mary Erler and Maryanne Kowaleski. Athens, Ga., 1988. Pages 83–101.

Mitterauer, Michael. "Christianity and Endogamy." *Continuity and Change* 6 (1991): 295–334.

Murray, Alexander Callander. *Germanic Kinship Structure: Studies in Law and Society in Antiquity and the Early Middle Ages.* Toronto, 1983.

Pagels, Elaine. *Adam, Eve, and the Serpent.* New York, 1988.

Poos, L. R. "The Pre-History of Demographic Regions in Traditional Europe." *Sociologia Ruralis* 26 (1986): 228–248.

Poos, L. R. *A Rural Society after the Black Death.* Cambridge, U.K., 1991.

Poos, L. R., and R. M. Smith. " 'Legal Windows onto Historical Populations'? Recent Research on Demography and the Manor Court in Medieval England." *Law and History Review* 2 (1984): 128–152.

Poos, L. R., and R. M. Smith. " 'Shades Still on the Window': A Reply to Zvi Razi." *Law and History Review* 3 (1985): 409–429.

Rappaport, Steve. *Worlds within Worlds: Structures of Life in Sixteenth-Century London.* Cambridge, U.K., 1989.

Razi, Zvi. "The Demographic Transparency of Manorial Court Rolls." *Law and History Review* 5 (1987): 523–535.

Razi, Zvi. *Life, Marriage, and Death in a Medieval Parish.* Cambridge, U.K., 1980.

Razi, Zvi. "The Myth of the Immutable English Family." *Past and Present* 140 (1993): 3–44.

Razi, Zvi. "The Use of Manorial Court Rolls in Demographic Analysis: A Reconsideration." *Law and History Review* 3 (1985): 191–200.

Reher, David Sven. "Marriage Patterns in Spain, 1887–1930." *Journal of Family History* 16 (1991): 7–30.

Seccombe, Wally. *A Millennium of Family Change: Feudalism to Capitalism in Northwestern Europe.* London, 1992.

Segalen, Martine. "Mean Age at Marriage and Kinship Networks in a Town under the Influence of the Metropolis: Nanterre, 1800–1850." *Journal of Family History* 16 (1991): 65–78.

Shaw, Brent D. "Funerary Epigraphy and Family Life in the Later Roman Empire." *Historia* 33 (1984): 457–497.

Sheehan, M. M. "Theory and Practice: Marriage of the Unfree and the Poor in Medieval Society." *Mediaeval Studies* 50 (1988): 457–487.

Shorter, Edward. *A History of Women's Bodies.* New York, 1982.

Shorter, Edward. *The Making of the Modern Family.* New York, 1975.

Smith, Daniel Scott. "A Homeostatic Demographic Regime: Patterns in West European Family Reconstitution Studies." In *Population Patterns in the Past.* Edited by Ronald Demos Lee. New York, 1977. Pages 19–51.

Smith, R. M. "The People of Tuscany and their Families in the Fifteenth Century: Medieval or Mediterranean?" *Journal of Family History* 6 (1981): 107–128.

Smith, R. M. "Some Reflections on the Evidence for the Origins of the 'European Marriage Pattern' in England." In *The Sociology of the Family.* Edited by Chris Harris. Keele, U.K., 1979. Pages 74–112.

Tacitus, Cornelius. *The Agricola and the Germania.* Translated by H. Mattingly. Harmondsworth, U.K., 1971.

Todd, Malcolm. *Everyday Life of the Barbarians.* London, 1972.

Todd, Malcolm. *The Northern Barbarians: 100 B.C.–A.D. 300.* London, 1975.

Toubert, Pierre. "Le moment carolingien (VIIIᵉ–Xᵉ siècle)." In *Histoire de la famille.* Vol. 1: *Mondes lointains, mondes anciens.* Edited by André Burguière, C. Klapisch-Zuber, and M. Segalen. Paris, 1986. Pages 340–341.

Wrigley, E. A. et al. *English Population History from Family Reconstitution, 1580–1837.* Cambridge, U.K., 1997.

Wrigley, E. A., and R. S. Schofield. *The Population History of England, 1541–1871.* Cambridge, Mass., 1981.

BIRTH, CONTRACEPTION, AND ABORTION

John M. Riddle

Historians long avoided analyzing private lives, partly because matters of conception and birth were just that—private. Even if such knowledge were to be regarded as worth the effort, what went on in peasant and burgher bedrooms was believed to be beyond possible scrutiny. How people were conceived and born escaped scholarly attention, but, in avoiding the investigative enterprise, questions arose that urgently needed reflection. Prior to the advent of the modern era in the nineteenth century did people (in distinction to the elites who were presumed to know what they were doing) reproduce like rats in hay or did they engage in practices that resulted in control of their reproduction? How can we explain the low birth rates in the early modern periods and the attention that leaders gave to population increase incentives? Was the corpus of common obstetrical knowledge safe, natural, effective, and practiced by women whose arts were separate from male inspections and influence? How do we evaluate the processes of modernization by which women were increasingly pushed away from controlling birth and even their pregnancies?

Most Europeans in the early modern period were born in an overheated room, their parents' room, with neighboring women and female relatives hovering in the background, while an experienced midwife assisted the parturition process. If rural and poor, the husband may very well have eschewed a midwife's service, either unwilling or unable to pay the relatively small fee. In those cases, an experienced neighbor or friend would substitute. In almost all cases, the mother-to-be would be either seated on a birth stool brought for the occasion by the midwife, especially if they were in central Europe, or on a chair or squatting on the floor or even, infrequently, on another woman's lap. Depending where they were geographically, few women remained in bed once the water burst and the contractions began. Known since classical antiquity, the birth stool received extensive usage among German midwives, but its use extended over most of Europe. A familiar scene was the midwife with her bag of instruments and drugs hurrying to her next delivery and carrying her stool with her.

Many of the women present at childbirth helped in various ways, such as making sure that the birth amulet—eagle stones, haemites, agate, and oriental or occidental bezoars being common—remained on the stomach. Meanwhile, the expectant father was apt to be with male friends in a nearby room or tavern awaiting congratulations. Some fathers practiced the couvade, an ancient, bizarre ritual of posing as the woman in labor by going through the moans, contortions, and ordeal of birth and, when the birth parody was over, pretending to suckle a newborn. Anthropologists and historians disagree over the couvade's meaning, offering such interpretations as sympathetic magic, aversion of dangers, and protection for the newborn. The entire birth scene raises a number of questions about early modern society.

EARLY MODERN MIDWIVES AND OBSTETRICS

As idealized in historical perspective, midwives were schooled through the experienced guidance of an older practitioner and generally knew more about obstetrics and even gynecology than male physicians. During the parturition process, they assisted the natural course whenever intervention was necessary. Recent interpretations modify this image. Up until approximately 1750, midwives generally provided safer and better services than physicians could have done given their training and knowledge. Still, midwives intervened from the moment of arrival and in ways modern science considers either harmless superstition or dangerous interference. Examples of meddling included breaking the waters with nails or a pointed instrument, massaging the vagina with an herbal preparation, widening the birth canal with manipulations even before the cervix opened, and placing women on birth stools before the water broke. The overheated room dates back to pre-Christian notions that cold

181

Birth. A midwife washes the newborn baby while the mother rests in bed and the husband and his cronies drink. From the title page of *De conceptu et generatione hominis* by the Zürich doctor Jakob Rueff (Frankfurt, 1580). [For another scene of the birth chamber, see the article "Childbirth, Midwives, Wetnursing" in volume 4.] BIBLIOTHÈQUE DE L'ANCIENNE FACULTÉ DE MÉDECINE, PARIS

drafts are harmful to the newly born. The medical skills of early modern midwives were substantially unchanged from classical times, save for additional Germanic folk practices whose utility from the modern perspective was confined to the psychological province. Few received training or experience in handling obstetrical emergencies or in when to call a physician. All too often, when a physician arrived it meant the death of either the baby or the mother.

Another form of intervention now considered harmful was the retrieving of the placenta immediately after birth. Normally the placenta will be expelled naturally within a half hour, but often midwives, perhaps desiring to conclude the ordeal, entered and pulled it out, causing an occasional hemorrhaging or inverted uterus, sometimes fatally. Following a delivery the woman was prescribed bed rest for nine days. Even bed linens were not expected to be changed during this period for fear of disturbing the mother. Reports of foul and smelly rooms were standard. Economic and family circumstances did not always allow what was considered to be the best therapy. When physicians in the late twentieth century supported "natural

births," the historians followed by stressing the wisdom of old midwives who witnessed and helped natural processes unfold. Clearly such romantic notions were overdrawn because midwives and experienced older women were not reluctant to intervene. This attitude, however, has another side: western European birth practices called for intervention in obstetrical emergencies, unlike some other traditional societies, and many a mother and child were saved by skillful applications of therapeutic procedures.

Medieval terms for midwives, such as *rustica* (rustic), *vetula* (old woman), *mulier* (woman), *obstetrix* (midwife), and *herbala* (herbalist), reveal their informal origins. As late as the eighteenth century, a French word for midwife was *sage-femme* (wise woman). By the second half of the fifteenth century, various attempts were begun throughout Europe to control by an oath abuses of midwife behavior. Oaths varied according to time and region, but three elements were essential: helping any patient, rich or poor; preventing the murder of a neonatal; and dispensing no miscarriage or abortion medicines. Women received from other women advice and direction concerning the entire regimen of women's health and reproduction, including irregular menstrual cycles, breast-feeding, sterility, rape, venereal diseases, fertility enhancement, contraception, and abortion. Barbers, physicians, and, less frequently, midwives bled women at least three times per pregnancy in the fifth, seventh, and ninth months. But the knowledge and practices of women outside the birth scene also caused many troubles for women who knew about women's health and reproduction.

The diagnoses of pregnancy were little changed from antiquity. The signs of pregnancy were explained, mostly for the benefit of men, in a seventeenth-century work attributed to Albertus Magnus, called *Aristotle's Masterpiece:* they included cessation of menstruation; fullness and milk in the breast; strange longings, especially for foods; a slight greenness of veins under the tongue; swollen veins in the neck; and a tightly closed cervix. Urine examination, so-called uroscopy, took account of smell, sediments, suspensions, color, and taste. Because a pregnant woman's albumen in her urine is highly elevated, it is possible that skilled practitioners were detecting a sign. Midwives claimed abilities to detect the sex of the unborn. Until the witchcraft suppressions, women seemed to have trusted midwives, as judged by their prestige in their communities.

The seventeenth century saw the beginnings of bringing the "secrets of women" to the high medical and learned culture through developments in gynecology. Ambrose Paré (1510–1590) described one development, a manipulation to shift the fetal position for a feet-first movement through the birth canal. Paré was first to record the procedure but said he learned of it from two Parisian barber surgeons. Eucharius Rösslin (c. 1500–1526) published, first in German, a work entitled *The Pregnant Woman's and Midwife's Rose Garden,* in which he disclosed much that had been mysterious to men. He recommended abortion only for cases where the woman's life would be imperiled through delivery. More information, perhaps none innovative, was disclosed in works in German by Walter Ryff (1545); in Italian by Scipione Mercurio (1595), a practicing obstetrician; in Spanish by Luis Mercado (d. 1611), who wrote four large books on diseases of women; and in French by François Rousset, whose description of a cesarean section in 1581 was outstanding. Thus what happened in birth rooms was becoming the subject for academic examinations. The primary question facing historians is to what degree were the sixteenth-century gynecology and obstetrics writers innovative and how much critical modification they made to traditional knowledge. Even though women orally transmitted much information, there are sufficient medical and anecdotal writings to analyze early modern popular knowledge, as social and medical historians are beginning to do.

EARLY MODERN BIRTH CONTROL

The subject of birth control is a complex one in early modern Europe. Prior to the beginning of the eighteenth century, the birthrates were low even considering external factors, such as wars, celibacy, famine, plagues, land use, and nutrition. Birthrates were well below the biological potential, even leaving aside the probably 20 percent of all couples in which one person was infertile. We know from other data that, if left unchecked, average per-couple birthrates will total sixteen to eighteen children from the onset of female puberty to menopause. European rates were well under half this total. The precise reasons are complex and ultimately escape historical confidence. Assuredly important factors include a delayed marriage age, relatively prolonged lactation after the birth of each child, probably a decrease in sexual activity within marriage as couples reached their mid-thirties, and bastard infanticide. Of these, delayed marriage age is best documented and undoubtedly an important element. The medical and anecdotal data from the early sixteenth through the eighteenth centuries indicate artificial birth control on top of these arrangements. The effectiveness of birth control and even family planning is the subject of debate among historians, demographers, and scientists.

The nature of artificial birth control on top of these arrangements is debatable, though there were definitely a number of methods (some linked to beliefs in magic) and probably some successes. Until recently historians and demographers believed that, prior to the late eighteenth century, women did not possess sufficient knowledge for dependable birth control, although midwives, witches, and old women were accused of engaging in practices that led to fewer children. Older historians such as Henry Lea regarded these kinds of accusations as a vast conspiracy by the inquisitors to accuse innocent people. In contrast, Margaret Murray, Thomas Forbes, and Barbara Ehrenreich observed that a disproportionate number of those accused of witchcraft were midwives. Murray said that "in the sixteenth and seventeenth centuries, the better the midwife the better the witch." An English midwife oath, typical in its sentiments, prohibited not only the administration of birth control drugs but the giving of counsel about "any herb, medicine, or poison, or any other thing, to any woman being with child whereby she should destroy or cast out that she goeth withal before her time." A church dictum stated, "If a woman dare to cure without having studied she is a witch and must die." Witches and midwives, whether the same or different, were accused of engaging in various practices, usually involving "poisons," that interfered with reproduction, ranging from impotency for men to contraception, abortion, and sterility for women and death for the newly born, notably those born and not yet baptized. Social historians and historians of science are more inclined toward accepting the accusations, at least to the degree that women possessed knowledge that allowed them to exercise effective and relatively safe birth control.

Clearly, various forms of artificial birth control were known or attempted, but primarily drugs were used. Coitus interruptus was seldom employed as a contraceptive measure, to judge by the paucity of references to it, although in Italy there are a number of anecdotal allusions to it. The act requires strong male cooperation and, in general, males are less strongly motivated in restricting conceptions. Those few references, however, indicate that the procedure was known. Barrier methods were not known. Some pessaries prepared as drug prescriptions with specific ingredients and administered on wool pads could possibly have resulted in mechanical blockage of sperm progression. Gabriel Fallopio is credited with the first medical description of the condom, in a publication in 1563. The name of the device comes from a Dr. Condom, physician in the court of Charles II of England (ruled 1660–1685), and it was popularized by Casanova (1725–1788), who called it "the English riding coat." In its original form, made of animal skins, it did not receive widespread usage.

The primary means of contraception and abortion were drugs, mostly herbal. A number of plants that, usually taken orally, contracepted and/or aborted were known from classical times and recorded by medical writers such as Hippocrates, Dioscorides, and Galen. Prominent among the contraceptives were white poplar, *asplenium* (a fern), juniper, barrenwort, the chaste plant, squirting cucumber, dittany, and artemisia; among the abortifacients were rue, pennyroyal, tansy, and birthwort. Modern scientific studies, especially in the realm of animal science, have shown that these plants interfere hormonally in a variety of ways with the reproduction processes. The chaste plant (*Vitex agnus-castus*) affords an intriguing example. Not only was the plant used historically as a female contraceptive but, in modern testing on dogs, the bark of this small tree reduces spermatogenesis to infertility. The opposite of the new drug Viagra, it was taken by ancient priests to prevent erections. Witches or midwives were accused of tying a ligature, or invisible string, around the penis to prevent erections. Formerly we assumed these allegations to be either malicious or illusionary. Now, on the basis of scientific data, we can reassess entire aspects of sexually related charges related to old women, witches, and midwives.

Interspersed with pharmaceuticals were amulets, charms, and various practices that we today consider superstitious. Medical, ecclesiastical, and municipal authorities sought to eliminate these vulgar practices. A part of a Parisian midwife oath in 1560 was "I will not use any superstitious or illegal means, either in words or signs, nor any other way." As with the fertility-enhancing medicines, modern evaluators of the early modern period give various explanations of the role of magic and the occult and the importance that psychological factors could have played. Modern investigators' uncertainty about that role applies to the entire spectrum of fertility, gestation, and birth.

Credence can be given to the substance of some of the accusations aimed at midwives or supposed witches, but many questions are unanswered. Among them, if women possessed effective means of birth control, why did early modern medicine not recognize what was happening? How could knowledge once widely held be diminished and restricted to a few marginalized practitioners, most of whom were women? If the birth control agents were effective, what about the fertility-enhancing herbal preparations that were perhaps even more prominently mentioned in midwifery and medical accounts? The short answer to the last question is that modern science has not sufficiently studied the actions of these preparations to begin addressing the question historically.

A large factor in the loss of knowledge was how birth control learning was transmitted. As medical education became formalized within the universities, the curriculum did not include "women's medicines." Practicing physicians working within their guilds eschewed folklore while combating irregular, informally trained practitioners. That distrust continued throughout the twentieth century.

WITCH-HUNTS AND CONTRACEPTIVE "POISONS"

Another reason for the diminution in birth control information is that such knowledge was dangerous in the sixteenth and seventeenth centuries. As a woman revealed before the Inquisition in Modena in 1499, "Who knows how to heal knows how to destroy." A version of Pseudo-Aristotle's *Secrets* in 1520 advised men "never to confide in the Works and Services of Women" and to "beware of deadly poison, for it is no new thing for Men to be poison'd." And what did these poisons do? They were said to destroy a fetus or to make men either impotent or sterile and women unable to conceive. Thus the focus of witchcraft persecutions on midwives came to center on birth control "poisons" and other preparations that to some were poisons and to others medicines.

Two German investigators, Gunnar Heinsohn and Otto Steiger, connect the poisons, witches, and midwives with economic policy and demography. Heinsohn and Steiger see a direct relation between the women persecuted as witches and the steady increase in population that began in the sixteenth century. As proof they provide statistical evidence that in areas where virulent witch-hunts were conducted there followed a population upswing. Juxtaposing their thesis with the evidence for a decline in effective birth control measures, we can hypothesize that the targets were women who knew the "poisons" that were contraceptive and abortifacient plants. Town and ecclesiastical leaders who promoted witch-hunts may genuinely have been concerned with devilish activities by "weisen Frauen" (wise women) that they saw as preventing babies from being born and baptized.

Critics of Heinsohn and Steiger are not persuaded by their data. The medical and pharmaceutical literature, especially from the official dispensaries employed by apothecaries, indicates that the preparations were still known and sold but in a different form. The herbs and minerals were compounded, mixing twenty or more "simples," for retail distribution. Early modern women became dependent on purchased drugs, rather than gathering the plants for themselves. In order to know the plants, harvesting, morphology of site for extraction, amounts, frequencies, and when to take them, they needed information formerly taught by their mothers and the "wise women" of the community. To gather the plant "simples," or even to know how, was dangerous because it would make one a suspect in procedures where proving innocence was difficult and failure to do so was often fatal. Approximately half a million people died at the stake, the overwhelming majority being women, most of whom were old. Heinsohn and Steiger's thesis has challenged social historians to view birth and population controls during the early modern period in a different way.

Laws on infanticide were tightened throughout most of Europe in the early modern period. Between 1513 and 1777 in Nürnberg eighty-seven women were executed for killing their babies, and all but four were single. Nürnberg's town council enacted an ordinance that prohibited midwives from burying a fetus or stillborn child without informing the city council. In Essex, England, between 1575 and 1650 fifty-one women were tried for the offense, and two-thirds were convicted and executed. In comparison, during the same period in Essex 267 women were tried for witchcraft, and only one-fourth were found guilty. Clearly, these figures are relatively low, so that infanticide cannot be considered a major factor in population size, even acknowledging that many crimes were undetected by authorities.

ABORTION AND THE BEGINNING OF LIFE

Knowledge of effective birth control measures continued to appear in medical, pharmaceutical, and anecdotal accounts, but normally it was carefully circumscribed.

Abortifacients were referred to in early modern medical literature as menstrual stimulators. When a woman took an emmenagogue (menstrual stimulant) because of a delayed monthly period due to pregnancy, she would have committed an abortion in modern terms but not in the early modern era. Based on classical Greek concepts, it was thought that the male sperm remained in a woman's body until her womb accepted it and a fetus was formed. This period was not defined but could be a number of weeks. The question of "when does life begin" was not examined in the way it is today prior to the nineteenth century in European society, either in high learning or popular culture.

Knowing that an accident or cesarean section could result in a live birth, Aristotle asked when the fetus developed independent life. When the fetus had all of its form, Aristotle said that it had *psyche,* meaning "life." The Stoics developed the notion of "soul," and, by employing the word *psyche,* they altered its meaning. Learning from the Stoics, the Christians read Aristotle's question about the beginning of independent life as a discussion of ensoulment. The only explicit reference to abortion in the Bible or Torah occurs in Exodus 21:23, in answer to a question about the fault of a person assaulting a pregnant woman and causing a miscarriage. The question's answer was "life is for life." The Hebrew word for life, *nefesh,* was translated by the Greek Septuagint as *psyche,* thus suggesting that a "soul for a soul" was the punishment decreed for the act. Most of the church fathers adapted Aristotle's views and agreed that ensoulment came at that point in a pregnancy when there was fetal movement. The popular term in English, with equivalents in other vernaculars, was "quickening." They envisioned the soul to have come from God, not the parents, and the divine act came when the fetus was formed. Christian doctrine ultimately incorporated Aristotle's assertion that there was a single act (or, as Aristotle said, a relatively short period) from which time the fetus goes from "unformed" to "formed." Prior to ensoulment a woman was free to terminate her fertility by returning to her menstrual cycle. There was a notable restriction to this freedom, however. Roman law, Judaic pronouncements, and early medieval law codes held that a woman did not have the right to deny a child conceived in wedlock if the husband wanted the child.

The medieval and early modern churches, Greek Orthodox and Roman Catholic alike, condemned abortion, contraception, and, indeed, any agent or means that interfered with fertility. In practice, however, as John Noonan has demonstrated, both contraception and abortion were practiced prior to fetal movement or quickening. But several trends in the early modern period began to restrict even more reproductive practices and so-called rights.

Following the Black Death and the resultant economic distresses, medieval town councils recognized a connection between population growth and economic prosperity. Consequently medieval towns on the Continent became more involved in legislation declaring pregnancy terminations criminal by punishing those who assisted a woman. To rectify abuses medieval towns first regulated and licensed midwives. The laws of the Holy Roman Emperor Charles V in 1532 essentially took the provisions of some towns and promulgated them into state law. The Caroline laws regarded one who assisted a woman in an abortion as guilty of homicide and a woman who performed the act on her own as guilty of a lesser although severely punished felony. A woman who terminated a fetus "not yet living" (not formed or quickened) or a person who assisted her was to be punished by penance, a physical punishment (such as pillory), or exile. In 1556 French law condemned as a criminal any woman who concealed her pregnancy and allowed a fetus to be killed or a child to die prior to baptism. In contrast, a review of English common law in a relatively few trials reveals that juries would not punish anyone, assistant or woman, who aborted a fetus prior to birth.

The strongest stance against abortion came in a bull issued by Pope Sixtus V (1585–1590) that condemned abortion of a "conceived fetus" with "severe punishments" for both the woman and anyone who advised or assisted her. It is unlikely that the bull had any effect on European practices and may have been intended primarily for prostitution in the city of Rome. Some Catholic theologians, such as Thomas Sanchez (1550–1610), argued for a woman's right to terminate a pregnancy in cases of rape or threat to her life. Nonetheless, a woman sinned who terminated a pregnancy to protect her reputation or prevented conception in order to protect an estate from being divided among too many heirs. In response to liberal views by some theologians, Pope Innocent XI (1676–1689) reaffirmed the medieval church's stance against any interference with fertility and birth but left vague the so-called therapeutic abortion to save the life of a woman. Few differences regarding birth or birth control practices appear in Protestant communities. Luther and Calvin both spoke out against the "sin of Onan," a biblical passage, Genesis 38:8–10, now considered misinterpreted as a condemnation of contraception and masturbation.

MARRIAGE AND PREGNANCY

Studies comparing marriage dates and birth or baptism dates in England and Germany have shown that roughly one-fifth of the brides between 1540 and 1700 were pregnant at marriage. In later centuries the number rose to two-fifths. A major reason was the delayed marriage age in the early modern period. These data indicate that women engaged in premarital sexual relations as a marriage strategy.

Surprisingly few illegitimate births occurred in early modern Europe, however, which greatly reduced pressures for abortion or infanticide. Community controls discouraged young adults to engage in outright sexual intercourse before marriage. The effectiveness of these controls is surprising, given late average age at marriage. Some cities even sponsored prostitution houses, especially for foreign, single workers (or so they said), so that their daughters would receive fewer pressures for favors. Some women who did not marry would deliver a child out of wedlock, but they were too few for demographic significance. One set of figures shows that illegitimate births were 2 percent of total births in 1680 and rose to 6 percent by 1820, a trend that may have horrified the contemporary custodians of morality but, in comparison to modern times, is startlingly low. Given the data on the number of brides pregnant at the time of marriage, what happened to those women who were rejected for marriage? Given the low illegitimacy rates, some must have resorted to abortion.

Anecdotal information portrays women who failed to receive a bridal offer and who then had to seek clandestine means to procure abortions. Because surgical abortions were considered more dangerous than chemically induced abortions, most of the anecdotal and medical data emphasize drugs taken orally. For example, a woman reproved another because she had delivered a "base child," thus soiling her reputation and the community's as well, all because she was "not acquainted with it [the medicine] in time." As late as the nineteenth century, a man commented that juniper had saved the reputation of many young women.

Many factors affected childbearing in the early modern period: late marriage ages, time intervals for births, wars, immigration and migration, economic opportunities to establish work and living space, infanticide, famines, diseases (especially in the sixteenth century), illegitimacy, and altered life styles (such as the rise of factory workshops, wet-nursing, prostitution).

CHANGES IN MODERN EUROPE

The eighteenth through the twentieth centuries saw the development of several broad themes: attention of formal, "high" medicine to obstetrics and gynecology; numerous technical improvements; scientific developments in the understanding of physiology, pharmacology, and the mechanics of reproduction that altered age-old concepts and attitudes toward contraception and abortion; diminished importance and involvement of women in birthing procedures and decisions; dependence upon apothecaries for birth control drugs; intervention by secular governments in abortion laws; and revised Christian and, to a lesser degree, Judaic canons concerning sexuality and reproduction.

Women and male medicine. Changes in birthing procedures and the involvement of newer kinds of experts were gradual. The movement that ultimately led to less control for women can be ascribed to a woman, Jane Sharp, who in 1671 wrote *The Compleat Midwife's Companion,* with the aim of helping women: "I have often sat down sad in the consideration of the many miseries women endure in the hands of unskillful midwives." She sought to correct abuses, but in doing so she disclosed practical information unknown to men of science, thereby making the issues of the birth scene a matter for public view.

In 1668 the French physician Francis Mauriceau published a book on obstetrics in French that was translated into English, Dutch, German, and Italian. Among his achievements were the treatment of *placenta previa* (expulsion of the placenta), the condemnation of cesarian section (as too dangerous to be performed), and the assertion that fetal development is gradual, with no difference in male and female development times. Women who enjoy sexual intercourse, he claimed, are less fertile because their orifices are more closed to seminal fluid. In England Nicholas Culpeper wrote a *Directory for Midwives* in 1651, whose purpose was to take away the mysteries of reproduction and correct abuses. Culpeper followed this work with an immensely popular pharmaceutical guide because he lambasted the proprietary control of drugs by druggists. Growing in yards, parks, and woodlands were the sources for drugs that people needed, and, strangely, he included thinly disguised contraceptives and abortifacients.

One technological invention greatly assisted women in childbirth but, at the same time, opened the birth scene more to males. In 1647 Peter Chamberlen constructed a practical obstetric forceps based on an earlier instrument made by a family member. The manufacture of the cleverly designed instrument remained a monopolistic secret for about 150 years. The two halves could be separated, inserted, and reassembled inside the pelvis, allowing the fetal head to be grasped safely and extracted. The Chamberlen family said that when a doctor was called, they did not want him to make the decision on whether to save the mother or the child. Probably the most critical technological innovation was the invention of the stethoscope in 1816 by René-Théophile-Hyacinthe Laënnec because it enabled a physician to hear the heartbeat. There are individual variations in when the heart can be heard, but by the 1840s and 1850s physicians could determine pregnancy by no later than the fourth month. Heretofore pregnancy was either determined and declared by the woman or, late in the pregnancy, obvious to all. With the now familiar stethoscope around their necks, physicians declared when a woman was pregnant.

Prior to around 1720 most births involved exclusively women as attendants and supporters. After that time male midwives, formally trained and licensed, began to appear and gain popularity. Heretofore males were called for obstetrical emergencies, but as the eighteenth century progressed, males, as midwives and physicians, were increasingly involved at the beginning of the birth process. Adding to the loss of prestige as a result of the association with witchcraft, the publication of many new works on the subject vulgarized midwifery "secrets." Women were being pushed aside in a world that they had controlled for thousands of years. Changing attitudes toward sexuality contributed to women's losses. Seventeenth-century English works on pornography portrayed women as eager and aggressive for sexual contacts, but when intercourse was described, the man jumped on the woman and pushed her around. The new industrial order altered vocabulary. A new term "opposite sex" implied that women were opposite, separate, unequal, just not men.

Scientific discoveries and technical innovations such as the vaginal speculum, introduced early in the nineteenth century to allow more effective examinations before childbirth, encouraged expanded roles for physicians in the birthing process. (Fathers, too, were

Male Physicians in the Birth Chamber. A male doctor makes notes after the birth as the father comforts the mother. Painting (1908) by Victor F. Lecomte. MUSÉE DES BEAUX-ARTS, NANTES, FRANCE

more likely to be present at births beginning in the late eighteenth century, at least in upper-class households.) The introduction of anesthetics in the mid-nineteenth-century greatly increased the benefits physicians might offer to women. Childbirth increasingly became a physician-dominated event, and then in the twentieth century, a hospital-based event. Infant and maternal mortality rates did drop in the process, though there was a period in the 1860s and 1870s when physicians, scorning sanitary procedures, actually introduced new infections. But the big mortality reductions after the 1880s were due in part to improved medical knowledge and the new interventions. Whether the cultural experience of giving birth suf-

fered in the same process is something historians and feminists have debated.

Science and abortion. In 1651 William Harvey (1578–1657) discovered the "eggs" in deer and declared that "all living things come from an egg." To this he added that the fetus developed "gradually," not in stages, as Aristotle implied. Marcello Malpighi (1628–1694) and Jan Swammerdam (1637–1680) examined fetal development in eggs, and Swammerdam declared that the black spot in a frog's egg is "the frog itself complete in all its parts."

The hypothesis was that each ovum contains the individual seed of the entire species that is to come

188

afterward. The preformationists regarded the egg as central to reproduction, while the male triggered the process. But with the invention of the microscope, the debate was enriched. Antonie van Leeuwenhoek (1632–1723) saw first that each drop of seminal fluid contained millions of "worms" or, in the less dramatic term, "animalcules." Contemporaries were fascinated by the news, but they were baffled by all those worms. The preformationists and epigenecists—the egg-people and the sperm people—debated what they saw murkily. The debate spilled from the drawing rooms to the public arena. Europeans saw that older theories about fetal life were wrong, and the new ideas caused them to reexamine their positions on abortion. Even though it was not until 1876 that Oskar Hertwig actually saw a sperm fertilizing an egg, the event was known to science and to much of the public.

France made abortion criminal in 1792 with words based on the provisions of medieval town ordinances. In 1803, through Lord Ellenborough's bill, Britain declared anyone who administered an abortion a criminal, specifying only drug-induced abortions. The same act defined abortion as a procedure performed on any woman "being quick with child." In 1810 Napoleon's Penal Code declared criminal any act whereby someone gave "food, beverage, medicines, violence or any other means" to procure an abortion. By the 1830s it was recognized that the concept of quickening, based on Aristotle, was untenable. The question was when was an abortion an abortion? In 1837 abortion was defined as eliminating pregnancy at any period, thereby dropping reference to quickening. In 1851 Pope Pius IX declared as subject to excommunication anyone who procured "a successful abortion." Even though conception per se was not specified, gone were concepts such as ensoulment and "formed fetus" (quickened). One by one the nation-states of Europe defined abortion as occurring anytime after conception that pregnancy was deliberately terminated: Austria, 1852; Denmark, 1866; Belgium, 1867; Spain, 1870; Zürich Canton, 1871; Netherlands, 1881; Bosnia/Herzegovina, 1881; Norway, 1885; Italy, 1889; and Turkey, 1911.

The actual history and context of abortion both explained and defied legal patterns. Sexual activity was rising, particularly among young people and the lower classes. Many women found themselves pregnant before marriage, and while rates of illegitimacy increased, there was also a new desire to terminate pregnancy. Wives might also seek means of reducing the threat of unwanted children in overcrowded, impoverished families. The desire for abortion increased, at least in some quarters. This helps explain the new efforts at legislation, but also their considerable inef-

fectiveness. Many women exper
tions—one estimate held that a
class women in Berlin had had a
by the 1890s. Even in the twen
more effective birth control limite
tion within marriage in Western
sexual activity among youth main
demand. In Eastern Europe, wh
control devices remained limited c
the late twentieth century, aborti
common, serving as a basic mean
even though here too it was frequ
in the later twentieth century di
countries move to legalize abortion
often dangerous gap between law a

Birth control. Even so, and fa
abortion, there were huge gaps betv
tural prescriptions on the one han
velopments in the nineteenth and ea
turies on the other. Need for and rat
both increased.

The need was clear. Beginnin
classes in the late eighteenth and earl
turies, European families redefined t
nuses of children. Middle-class pare
vide some education for boys and
were hard-pressed to meet their obl
reducing the birthrate. A bit later, w
ilies, affected by child labor laws and t
that reduced the earning power of c
tion to schooling requirements and f
also discovered the desirability of redu
birthrates. Peasant families varied in
in this direction. Overall, however,
rapid population increase plus change
that, during the nineteenth century,
western Europe found children becc
economic liability than an asset and re
accordingly. Similar patterns set in
southern Europe by 1900.

Methods of birth control varied.
were few new methods available and w
and cultural contraints on artificial m
families resorted to coitus interruptus
this was true in working-class families
tieth century. In the long run howeve
made possible and affordable by devel
as the vulcanization of rubber (1840s)
artificial means available and permitted
reational rather than procreational sex
marriage and without. Middle-class fam
turned to the use of diaphragms (calle
the nineteenth century), while worker

sed condoms. Knowledge spread gradually; condoms were seen as exotic—called "Parisian articles"—by German laborers as late as the 1870s. But the development of new levels of artificial birth control was steady and involved major changes in family life and sexuality alike.

Well into the twentieth century, most governments, whether communist, fascist, or democratic, continued to promote population growth and oppose birth control. The gap between policy and widespread practice widened. Even in Nazi Germany, birth control levels receded only briefly. By the 1960s, faced with new levels of adolescent sexual activity, most European governments moved toward legalizing the availability of birth control devices. Concerns about disease supported this move. One result was a far greater decline in adolescent pregnancy in Europe than in the United States, where the legislative framework differed considerably and where programs to promote abstinence won greater favor.

The control of birth. In the nineteenth century a woman's body was opened to the public in ways held private in early centuries. To learn whether she was pregnant a woman would go or be sent to a physician, whose eyes would observe the darkening of the areola and view her vagina. His hands would feel her breasts and his fingers the cervix for the so-called Hegar's sign, enlargement and softening of the uterus and cervix. Male midwives increased in numbers and importance, partly because they received formal education for licensing. In eighteenth-century France male *accoucheurs* (midwives) were said to be driving women from the profession. In England it was said that female anatomy was designed to fit the male midwives' fingers.

The late nineteenth century witnessed important events for birth in what Angus McLaren calls the medicalization of procreation. Increased attention on germ theory made the environment of the birth chamber increasingly important. The result was the move to hospitals for delivery. The "lithotomy position" (the woman on her back) for childbirth replaced the standing or squatting position. "Twilight sleep," or the use of anesthesia, pioneered by Bernhard Krönig in Germany in 1899, promised the removal of pain. These gains, undeniably beneficial for women, brought with them the price of men and the state controlling their reproductive processes. The womb was made public.

Birth control drugs once known by women, learned from mother to daughter, came to be dispensed by druggists, many of whom did not know proper preparations or even the correct plants and their amounts. Proprietary menstrual regulators were peddled and some women relied on them. The concerns by nineteenth-century political and ecclesiastical leaders about declines in birthrates resulted in more rigorous legislation and enforcement about birth control laws relating to contraceptive and abortion drugs and surgical procedures for abortions. Thomas Malthus, famous for his dismal pronouncement about population increase, said that he was even more worried about dangers of population decreases. Reproduction was too important to be left in the control of women.

By the twentieth century, in what Barbara Duden calls the iconography of pregnancy, the fetus was spoken as having "life" and as being "human." The question of theologians about when ensoulment occurs was altered to when does life begin, and the answer was at conception. The controversies swirled around these issues of the age-old right of women to employ birth control techniques and the right of society to protect its newly formed definition of life. Procreation was safer for women, but safety was purchased with freedom.

See also sections 15, 16, and 17 (volume 4), and other articles in this section.

BIBLIOGRAPHY

Banks, Amand Carson. *Birth Chairs, Midwives, and Medicine.* Jackson, Miss., 1999.

Duden, Barbara. *Disembodying Women: Perspectives on Pregnancy and the Unborn.* Cambridge, Mass., 1993.

Eccles, Audrey. *Obstetrics and Gynaecology in Tudor and Stuart England.* Kent, Ohio, 1982.

Gélis, Jacques. *History of Childbirth: Fertility, Pregnancy, and Birth in Early Modern Europe.* Translated by Rosemary Morris. Boston, 1991.

Heinsohn, Gunnar, and Otto Steiger. *Die Vernichtung der weisen Frauen: Beiträge zur Theorie und Geschichte von Bevölkerung und Kindheit.* Munich, 1985.

Jacobsen, Grete. "Pregnancy and Childbirth in the Medieval North: A Topology of Sources and a Preliminary Study." *Scandinavian Journal of History* 9 (1984): 91–111.

McLaren, Angus. *A History of Contraception from Antiquity to the Present.* Oxford, 1990.

Musacchio, Jacqueline Marie. *The Art and Ritual of Childbirth in Renaissance Italy.* New Haven, Conn., 1999.

Noonan, John T., Jr. *Contraception: A History of Its Treatment by Catholic Theologians and Canonists.* Enlarged ed. Cambridge, Mass., 1986.

Oakley, Ann. *Women Confined: Toward a Sociology of Childbirth.* New York, 1980.

O'Dowd, Michael J., and Elliot E. Philipp. *The History of Obstetrics and Gynaecology.* New York, 1994.

Riddle, John M. *Eve's Herbs: A History of Contraception and Abortion in the West.* Cambridge, Mass., 1997.

Shorter, Edward. *A History of Women's Bodies.* New York, 1982.

Speert, Harold. *Obstetrics and Gynecology: A History and Iconography.* Rev. ed. San Francisco, 1994.

THE LIFE CYCLE

Sherri Klassen

A society's vision of the life cycle plays a major role in determining the life choices individuals make and how they portray these choices to others. Drawing together social and cultural history, a history of the life cycle examines both behavior and its relationship to ideas about aging and the structure of life. Demographic, economic, political, religious, and technological change all influenced the way Europeans understood their lives. The experiences Europeans anticipated in their various life stages and the relationships they formed with their contemporaries and with people in differing life stages depended on their life-cycle expectations.

Between the Renaissance and the late twentieth century, three major changes occurred in Europeans' perception of the life cycle. First, the passage of time within a human life came to be viewed less as cyclic than as progressive: whereas once life and lives were imaged as continuous, following cyclic patterns through time, lifetimes came to be seen as finite and involving an individual's passage through rising and declining status. Second, Europeans saw a growing stratification of the stages of life and an effort to define these stages more precisely. This feature of the life cycle developed slowly over the course of the early modern period, reaching its apogee in the late nineteenth and early twentieth centuries. Finally, European history has seen a slow disappearance of diversity in life-course patterns, a trend that began reversing itself in the latter half of the twentieth century.

THE LIFE SPAN: FROM A CIRCLE TO A STAIRCASE

In both the early modern and modern eras, Europeans recognized that the span of human life involved some elements that were best understood in terms of repeating cycles and others that were better understood as linear development. While the two models coexisted, the circular model predominated until the seventeenth century, after which the model of linear progress and decline came to the fore. These developments are apparent in artistic representations of the life cycle, narratives of individual lives and biography, and behavior as seen in demographic and notarial records.

Circles and stairs in art and theory. The term "life cycle" reflects an understanding of life as continuous and circular. Seen in late medieval pictorial representations of the life cycle, this appreciation of life depicts all ages as equal before God and influenced more by divine intervention than by the sheer passage of time. Paintings and prints from before the sixteenth century show different epochs of life along the spokes of a wheel with no apparent hierarchy of ages. Predictable differences exist between the epochs, but the differences are not shown as essential and do not appear to have emerged from experience or development. The appearance of Christ in the center of some of these wheels confirms the place of Providence in holding together the different ages of the life cycle. Other paintings feature women and men of different ages brought together to demonstrate contrast and also the continuity and fullness of time.

Theoretical writings of the Renaissance toy with the meaning of cycles as well. Niccolò Machiavelli's writings, for example, discuss cycles in political lives. Other prevalent notions show fortune as a wheel in which periods of prosperity follow upon periods of misfortune. Fortune governs both the individual's life course and the course of human history. These cycles allowed premodern thinkers to draw analogies between the individual and the societal.

Prints portraying the life cycle became both more common and more linear after the sixteenth century. Rather than the purely circular image, these representations display the increasingly familiar image of the life cycle as an ascending and descending staircase. Middle age stands firmly at the apex of the staircase, showing a clear indication of the hierarchy of ages—individuals ascend through time to middle age and then descend toward death.

The Wheel of Life. The cycle of life moves clockwise from birth in the lower left to death at the bottom; Christ is in the center. Illustration from a psalter, 1339. British Library MS. Arundel 83, fol. 126v. BY PERMISSION OF THE BRITISH LIBRARY, LONDON

By the time prints of the life cycle gained widespread popularity, they had also become much more secular in their content. The images show domestic and professional developments up and down the stairway, only occasionally portraying spirituality. Divine orchestration no longer controls the life cycle. Instead, each step follows upon the earlier in a progression determined by the passage of time, accumulated human experience, and biological change.

The secular life cycle as portrayed in these prints gained popularity in the eighteenth century as Enlightenment thought began to see aging as a primarily biological process. As fascinated as their forebears with the passage of time, the Enlightenment writers saw the distinctions between life-course stages as rational and natural distinctions that contrasted with the irrational social distinctions of rank. The secular life cycle emerging in the eighteenth century saw life's turning points as predictable and rational, as necessarily following one another, and as developing not

from divine intervention but from human experience or laws of nature.

Scientific developments over the course of the nineteenth century show a tension between the tendencies to see the life course as linear progression and as cyclic continuity. Medical science before the eighteenth century accepted elements of progression alongside the cyclic reversals of human aging. The hope for progress in the medicine of the Enlightenment at once encouraged a more linear vision of the life course and set medical minds seeking a cure for aging. Theorists intent on overcoming aging emphasized the regenerative capabilities of the body, seeing life not as one large cycle but as a conglomeration of many small cycles of decay and regeneration. In 1788 James Hutton described the geological notion of deep time by comparing the earth's history with the human body and claiming that both followed continuous cycles of decay and regeneration—evidenced in the body by the circulation of the blood and the body's capacity to heal itself after injury. In commenting on Hutton's theories, the evolutionary biologist Stephen Jay Gould was able to mock them since twentieth-century approaches to the life cycle assert that aging brings necessary, and irreversible, elements of change.

Cycles and progression in narrative forms.

Biographical writings were rare before the modern era, but those extant, especially the lives of the saints, demonstrate the circular-life course model. The thirteenth-century collection of saints' lives known as the *Golden Legend* contains two major life-course patterns. One pattern shows a lack of change. The saint's miracles and unusual virtue begin at an early age and continue throughout his or her life. Neither the passage of time nor the saint's many experiences effect either growth or regression. The second life course pattern involves conversion from a life of sin to one of sanctity. One such case of a major change in lifestyle is St. Mary of the Desert, a woman who converted from a prostitute to a hermit because of a miraculous act of the Virgin Mary. The change in her life occurs not out of accumulated experience, tempered by the passage of time, but rather from providential revelation. St. Mary of the Desert's life fits with an awareness of life as a circle of redemption where a soul is brought from a state of sinfulness back into one of grace. The saint's life is embedded within a circle of grace that began with creation rather than with the saint's life on earth and frequently continues after the saint's bodily death.

Although these patterns remained evident after the sixteenth century, the linear model of the life course grew more common in various forms of biographical writings. Thomas Cole (1992) traces these developments to a competing ideology in Christianity that envisioned life as a pilgrimage or journey. As the idea of the pilgrimage gained popularity in the later middle ages, so did the idea of life as a pilgrimage. Written in 1678 by John Bunyan, *Pilgrim's Progress* represented the fruition of this development by depicting life as a spiritual journey in which an individual achieved salvation by learning from experiences along the pathway. Saints' lives written after the sixteenth century likewise demonstrate an awareness of personal development, often portraying a more gradual progression toward sanctity.

Emerging narrative forms such as novels, memoirs, and biographies also demonstrate a growing appreciation of life as structured by development across time. Starting in the seventeenth century, these genres depicted individual lives that changed as a result of influences and human experiences. The narrative form itself came to force a structure onto the telling of human lives such that life stories became chronological arrangements of events with clear beginnings and conclusions (a structure that had very rarely been in place in pre-Reformation life stories). The trend toward life narratives structured to show linear development across time continued with the explosion of publishing in these genres in the nineteenth century. While biography writing, and to a large degree memoirs, continued to hold to this structural form in the twentieth century, fiction showed a greater latitude in its portrayal of time's role in the life cycle.

Linear growth in lived experiences.

The full impact of an ideological switch from life as composed of recurring patterns to life as composed of linear progression was not felt by the majority of Europeans until the early twentieth century. Many of the changes were gradual, affecting child-rearing practices, the regard for seniority in work environments and institutionalized retirement, the treatment of the elderly, and consumption habits.

The growth of the social welfare state facilitated the spread of some of these changes. Mandatory primary schooling for children, first introduced as legislation in seventeenth-century Germany, instilled the notion that childhood was a period for growth. The idea of legislation of this sort spread well before it could truly be implemented or enforced. By the mid-nineteenth century, however, such legislation existed in most of Europe and dictated childhood education as a life-cycle choice for whole populations. Through pension legislation, the state also spread the notion that old age represented a period of decline. Poor laws from at least as early as the seventeenth century had recognized old age as a condition precipitating want, but age was only one of many factors. Universal old-age pensions affirmed a belief that old age in and of itself marked decline.

The effects of industrialization on the life course are still debated. They were most certainly gradual, as older patterns persisted despite the demands of a new work schedule that drew workers out of a familial setting. Elements of progression in working lives had been prevalent in some aspects of the economy well before the modern age. A successful master artisan developed from a lowly apprentice and was rewarded for skill and hard work. As industrial enterprises began to specialize the tasks performed, workers could move from one position to another along a progressive career path. The industrial workplace may have discouraged older workers because the tasks could not be modified to fit individual needs, but at the same time industrial employers sought to reward seniority as a means of retaining workers. Autobiographies of

Linear Model of the Life Course. The stages of life, from birth to death. Color lithograph published at Metz, France, between 1852 and 1858. (For an earlier interpretation of the linear model of the life course see the article "The Elderly," in volume 4.) BIBLIOTHÈQUE NATIONALE, PARIS, TD 24 FOLIO

working men and women from the industrial era suggest that men quickly saw their lives as containing progressive career trajectories whereas women saw their working lives as containing different but non-progressive segments.

The changing perceptions of life-cycle patterns affected the tenor of family dynamics as well. A model of life emphasizing cycles and repetition encouraged a sense of reciprocity between parents' care of young children and the care of parents by those children as adults. A common folk tale told of a young child observing his father mistreat an elderly parent. The child then innocently proclaims his intention to follow his father's example and the father, chagrined, mends his ways. Popular as a moral tale, the story also demonstrates the cycles upon which care for the elderly rested. Individuals cared for their elderly parents because the next turn of the cycle would require that they receive care. Likewise, parents instilled in their children a sense of indebtedness that would be called upon when they required care as elders.

By the end of the eighteenth century, duty toward children and the elderly came to be based less on indebtedness than on personal attachment. Treatises on education and child rearing attest to the belief that care of children was important in that it affected their developmental capacities. A parent, therefore, had the important task of steering the child's development into a responsible adult. Child-rearing beliefs in the eighteenth and nineteenth centuries heightened the role of personal attachment; this emotional context then grew as the basis for filial duty toward the elderly. Only this context of personal attachment could serve the needs of the family within the paradigm of the linear life course as perpetual generational indebtedness had once served those needs in a world-view based on cycles and repetitions.

The linear life course, in addition to revamping the family and workplace, also created new consumer preferences. A fascination with youth was not new in the modern era, but previously Europeans were more interested in seeking elixirs that would allow them to return to a period of youth after old age than in forestalling the affects of aging. Tales of fountains of youth or special elixirs that could transform an elderly individual into a youthful one reflect a popular dream of perpetuating the cycles within a single lifetime. Common from the Middle Ages through the seventeenth century, the dream of repeating the cycle of youth inspired both serious inquiry and fantasy. By the twentieth century, neither medical science nor fantastic literature was exploring the possibility of returning an old body to its youthful state. Beginning in the eighteenth century, elixirs claimed more fre-

MME DE GENLIS
ON REJUVENATION

Stéphanie Felicité Ducret de St.-Aubin, comtesse de Genlis wrote her memoirs shortly after the French Revolution. Here she remembers her encounter with a man she believed to have found a cure for aging. She was twelve years old at the time of her meeting.

> I was persuaded—and my father believed it firmly—that M. de Saint-Germain, who appeared to be forty-five years old at most, was in fact over ninety. If a man has no vices, he can achieve a very advanced age; there are many examples of this. Without passions and immoderation, man would live to be a hundred years old and those with long lives would live to one hundred and fifty or sixty. Then, at the age of ninety, one will have the vigor of a man of forty or fifty. So, my suppositions regarding M. de Saint-Germain were in no way unreasonable. If one admits as well the possibility that he had found, by means of chemistry, the composition of an elixir (a particular liquor appropriate to his temperament), one would have to admit that even without belief in a philosopher's stone, he was older than I had thought. During the first four months I knew him, M. de Saint-Germain said nothing extraordinary. . . . Finally, one night, after accompanying me to some Italian music, he told me that in four or five years I would have a beautiful voice. And, he added, "And when you are seventeen or eighteen, would you like to remain fixed at that age at least for a great number of years?" I answered that I would be charmed. "Well then," he replied seriously, "I promise it to you." And immediately spoke of other things.

Source: *Mémoires inédits de Madame la Comtesse de Genlis, sur le 18ème siècle et la Révolution Française.* (Paris, 1825), 109–110. (Translation is my own.)

quently to prevent the onset of old age than to reverse the process. The twentieth-century cosmetics industry continued a tradition of selling a dream of postponing the linear process of aging. With the ascendancy of the linear life-course model, the idea of complete rejuvenation lost credibility. Yet the dream did not completely fade; while many of the "anti-aging" cosmetics are aimed at postponing the affects of age on the skin, others claim to reverse the process. Furthermore, drugs that induce hair growth or stimulate male virility reflect a hope of returning to an earlier phase rather than simply preventing the onset of age.

STRATIFICATION OF THE LIFE STAGES

As conception of the life cycle grew linear, it also became more highly stratified in the eighteenth century. Placed along a hierarchy, each life stage grew more distinct from any other and the transitions that marked the changes more highly ritualized. Numerical age grew more significant in determining life patterns as the modern era advanced, and in combination, the separation of life stages and the heightened importance of age led to a shift from communal and task-related rites of passage to familial and age-related ones.

Age awareness. Age grew more important in signaling transitions from one life stage to another as Europeans grew more aware of their own ages. The simplest means of gauging the extent of this awareness is to analyze the precision of ages, which individuals were asked to supply, reported in census, civic, and church records. Research in this area has been less than systematic, but it suggests that both governments and individuals increasingly valued precise numerical ages from the seventeenth century onward. Previously, ages were reported infrequently in death and marriage records. Through the course of the seventeenth century, ages came to be recorded regularly in death registers, and in the course of the eighteenth century, marriage registers began to include the precise ages of the spouses.

Even in the eighteenth century, however, the numbers supplied in the records were often inconsistent and imprecise. Demographers use the term "age heaping" to describe the pattern of age recording that could be found in premodern Europe (see figure 1). Examined in the aggregate, each year shows certain ages being reported far more frequently than others. Premodern Europeans appear to have rounded their ages to the decade, half decade, or less. While the ages reported might have approximated the chronological age, they may also have been used as an indication of status. If this was the case, the numerical age was descriptive rather than causative: one did not become old by turning sixty years of age; by turning old, one became sixty. A decrease in age heaping over the course of the eighteenth century suggests that Europeans had begun to award greater significance to age and were interpreting it more literally.

Not only were Europeans reporting their ages to bureaucrats with greater precision in the eighteenth century, they were also making note of the ages of their friends and relatives. Individuals writing memoirs in the late eighteenth and early nineteenth centuries show a fascination with chronological age, making special note of the specific ages of their friends

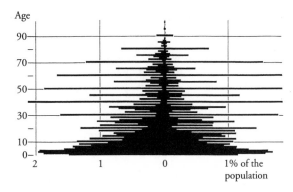

Figure 1. Age pyramid showing ages as recorded for over 250,000 individuals in fifteenth-century Tuscany. The long lines out in either direction from the center are the "heaps" of ages that demonstrate a lack of concern over precise age keeping. With precise recording of age, the pyramid would show a clearer approximation to a pyramidal shape. From David Herlihy and Christiane Klapisch-Zuber, *Les Toscans et leurs familles,* (Paris, 1978).

and family members. They frequently commented on individuals who appeared younger than would be expected for their age and on people who acted "inappropriately," and took care to mention the exact age of the person they were either deriding or praising. Numerical age had a meaning apart from, and sometimes at odds with, the physical and social characteristics of aging.

Age awareness emerged unevenly across the European landscape. Both France and England saw heightened age awareness in the course of the eighteenth century. Russian documentation, on the other hand, suggests that age awareness there was spotty even at the end of the nineteenth century. Regions with high levels of age awareness also displayed high levels of literacy and stronger government bureaucracies than the parts of Europe with low levels of age awareness.

Atomized life stages and age grading. Europeans combined their earlier notions of a life cycle composed of many equal stages with their new awareness of precise age differences by envisioning the stages of life as composed of categories of precise ages. Age became the determining factor for passage between a rapidly increasing number of stages.

The prints of the life cycle that portrayed a double staircase not only show the move from a cyclic to a progressive life course but also demonstrate the growing stratification between stages. As a step along the life span, each life stage was as distinct as it was dependent on the one before it. In the nineteenth century these prints showed a greater number of distinct life stages and greater distinctions between the life patterns of men and women.

Developments in medicine helped to partition the population according to age. As physicians developed specialties in the nineteenth century, they created two—pediatrics and geriatrics—that were defined by the age of their patients. Pediatrics emerged as its own discipline in the early nineteenth century, with children's hospitals opening in Paris, Berlin, St. Petersburg, and Vienna. While geriatrics did not develop as a discipline with the same speed as pediatrics, treatises, booklets, and pamphlets devoted to medical discussions of the ailments of the elderly proliferated in the late eighteenth and nineteenth centuries.

Even more than medicine, the national schooling systems that emerged in the nineteenth century encouraged stratification according to age group. Two models of education dominated the European public schools in the eighteenth and nineteenth centuries. The first, the monitorial system, mixed ages of children in a classroom, utilizing the skills of the more advanced students to assist in teaching the others. This model was largely overtaken in the nineteenth century by schools modeled on the theories of the Swiss educational reformer Johann Pestalozzi (1746–1827). Pestalozzi argued that children developed in clearly definable stages and that an educational system should anticipate these stages. Rather than mixing children of various ages and achievements, Pestalozzi proposed placing all pupils of the same stage together and separating them from other children. Given the same educational influences, the children would develop as a cohort from one stage to the next. Compulsory ages for school attendance quickly linked age to academic developmental stages. The Prussians were the quickest and most diligent pupils of these theories, and the Prussian school system became a model that other European states emulated.

If age grading within the schools defined the ages in childhood, old age pensions and retirement legislation instilled age grading at the other end of the life cycle. Entitlement to the earliest pension schemes depended on work status and disability as much as old age. The pensions became strictly age graded when governments universalized the pensions in the early twentieth century. Once the pensions included middle-class as well as working-class recipients, need and ability to work were dropped from the qualifications for receipt, and age alone stood as the definition of the appropriate time for retirement.

While many of the trends in age stratification accelerated throughout the nineteenth and early twentieth centuries, a number of novelists, scientists, and theorists at the turn of the century critiqued atomized life stages and universalistic understandings of time. In literature, the works of Marcel Proust, James Joyce, and Virginia Woolf saw an individual's personal past conflated with the present and portrayed the passage of time as elastic rather than rigidly divided into parcels. The writings of Sigmund Freud, on the one hand, theorized universal stages of human development but, on the other, weighed the stages disproportionately. Instead of neatly ordered, equal divisions of time, Freud saw the first step in the double staircase of the life course as overshadowing all the others that would follow it. Education reformers in the early twentieth century saw the stages as highly variable, arguing that individual children progressed along their own paths of development, which could not be easily compiled into universal stages of educational development.

Life course transitions and rites of passage.

Rituals marked life-stage transitions in both the premodern and modern European experience, but in the nineteenth century age played a heightened role in defining the timing and content of the rites of passage—a trend that began to be reversed only in the last three decades of the twentieth century. Rituals of life-course transition also became family occasions rather than religious or institutional rituals in the course of the nineteenth century.

The rituals of pre-Reformation Christianity marked several of the life-stage transitions. Baptism marked the entrance of a child into the world and into the Christian community of souls; marriage marked adulthood for the majority of Europeans. Extreme unction and funeral rites marked death as a transition in the spiritual life cycle. With the exception of extreme unction, both Protestant and Catholic churches retained religious rituals to mark these life-stage transitions. Confirmation grew in importance as a ritual in seventeenth-century Catholicism and in the Church of England, marking a transition into youth.

In addition to church rites, work status played a role in defining life-course transitions. Both peasants and city dwellers passed from youth to adulthood when they either inherited land or accumulated enough wealth to allow them to establish independent households. In many areas marriage marked the transition to adulthood largely because it had marked the couple's economic independence. The life-course transitions of artisans also grew out of guild and city regulations. City and later royal governments dictated the minimum age for apprenticeship in the early modern period. The duration of apprenticeship varied more widely. Rituals marking the passage from apprentice to journeyman or journeyman to master signaled

work transitions. Retirement was generally ad hoc and frequently gradual; the transition out of the workplace often blended physical infirmity with plans to prepare the next generation for its inheritance.

In the nineteenth century, religious work, and education rites developed a more familial character than had previously been the case. Marriage, for example, remained a religious occasion but developed a very strong family component in the nineteenth and twentieth centuries. Weddings emerged at this time as events of enormous emotional and financial expenditure on the part of families. Likewise, graduations and retirements became occasions for family celebration as they became more regular, predictable, and associated with specific ages.

Work and family life-cycle transitions became occasions for family rituals especially when they represented movement from one sphere of activity to another. The life cycle that emerged in the nineteenth century placed different spheres of activity clearly in different epochs of the life cycle. If early childhood was nurtured within the private, domestic sphere, the next phase of childhood and adolescence was assigned to education. Work for economic gain in the public sphere, rather than marriage, marked adulthood for men while the older pattern of marriage as a transition marked adulthood for women through the nineteenth and into the twentieth century. Age marked numerous transitions that signaled acceptance into diverse spheres of social and occupational activity. Once property and gender qualifications were eliminated, voting rights became a strictly age-graded transition. Limitations on child labor caused the beginnings of paid employment to stand as an age-graded transition as well. While these two cases show transitions allowing youths to move out of the domestic sphere and into the public, the age of retirement signified a move out of commercial space and into the private sphere.

The celebration of the birthday is perhaps the most illustrative of life-course rituals in that it demonstrates both the importance of chronological age and the value of the family as the site for modern rituals of life-stage transitions. The birthdays of kings and nobles were celebrated from at least as early as the seventeenth century as festivals that reiterated the honor due to the individual and reinscribed the loyalty of the subjects. Before the eighteenth century, nonruling people rarely celebrated their birthdays; the events were not occasions on which to dwell upon the passage of time and levels of accomplishment.

For many Europeans before the modern era, only one birthday—that which marked the age of majority—held significance. In a land-based econ-

Birthday. *Many Happy Returns of the Day* by William Powell Frith (1819–1909).
Harrowgate Museums and Art Gallery, North Yorkshire, U.K./The Bridgeman
Art Library

omy, this age marked the date of inheritance, allowing the young adult to establish an independent household. The passage of inheritance could depend upon proof that a minor heir had come of age. The proof came in the form of testimony from village elders. In these cases elders oversaw the passage from youth to adulthood within their communities. The age of majority was important as a rite of community recognition of adulthood as much as it was recognition of age as relevant in defining status.

In the eighteenth century literary works first began to mention ordinary birthdays. Johann Wolfgang von Goethe thought enough of the coincidence of sharing a birthday with his rival in love to refer to the birthday in his novel *The Sorrows of Young Werther* (1774), in part based on his experiences. Goethe apparently celebrated his birthday together with his rival in 1772. In her memoirs of her bourgeois Paris girlhood, Mme Roland recounts celebrating the birthdays of her grandparents with visits and gift exchanges in the 1760s. Gifts passed in both directions at the elders' birthdays, but she makes no mention of her own birthdays. Queen Victoria is credited with having brought the custom of family celebrations of the birthday from her German relations to England and with popularizing it there, but the origins of the traditions in France and Germany remain obscure.

THE CAUSES OF CHANGE

The conditions that prefigured these developments in the meaning of age and the life cycle were gradual and manifold. Altered perceptions of time, religious change, a growing state bureaucracy, and the spread of literacy in European society all contributed to the emergence of a linear life course stratified by age. Developments in the perceptions of time can be traced back to the invention of the mechanical clock in the fourteenth century. The growing efficiency and mass production of the clock beginning in the seventeenth century accelerated the process whereby Europeans thought of time as finite, composed of uniform parcels and proceeding in a uniform manner.

Religious change and the invention of the printing press are the most plausible causes for the distinct shift toward a life-course model emphasizing linear rather than cyclic patterns. The message of religious reformers in sixteenth-century Germany was heavily laden with eschatological references that stressed the apocalypse as the completion of a linear development of history rather than the fruition of a cycle. Protestantism, moreover, argued against a vision of the individual's life as composed of cycles of sin followed by absolution. In arguing that good works were irrelevant to grace, Martin Luther removed the cycles involved in human salvation. The printing press prop-

BIRTHDAYS AND UN-BIRTHDAYS

By the end of the nineteenth century, the celebration of birthdays was an established ritual for marking the passage of time, especially in childhood. At the same time, scientists and literary figures alike were questioning the nature of time and its impact on human lives. When Lewis Carroll created a world with inverted temporal and spatial laws, he included several discussions of the meaning (or lack of meaning) of age and one discussion of birthday gifts. In the looking-glass world, one particular day could have no more meaning than any other; dividing time in this fashion was, in itself, complex mathematics.

> "They gave it to me—for an un-birthday present."
> "I beg your pardon?" Alice said with a puzzled air.
> "I'm not offended," said Humpty Dumpty
> "I mean what *is* an un-birthday present?"
> "A present that's given when it isn't your birthday, of course."
> Alice considered a little. "I like birthday presents best," she said at last.
> "You don't know what you're talking about!" cried Humpty Dumpty. "How many days are there in a year?"
> "Three hundred and sixty-five" said Alice.
> "And how many birthdays have you?"
> "One."
> "And if you take one from three hundred and sixty-five, what remains?"
> "Three hundred and sixty-four, of course."
> Humpty Dumpty looked doubtful.
> "I'd rather see that done on paper," he said.
> Alice couldn't help smiling as she took out her memorandum book, and worked out the sum for him:

$$\begin{array}{r} 365 \\ 1 \\ \hline 364 \end{array}$$

> Humpty Dumpty took the book and looked at it carefully. "That seems to be done right—" he began.
> "You're holding it upside down!" Alice interrupted.
> "To be sure I was!" Humpty Dumpty said gaily, as she turned it around for him. "I thought it looked a little queer. As I was saying, that *seems* to be done right—though I haven't the time to look it over thoroughly just now—and that shows that there are three hundred and sixty-four days when you might get un-birthday presents—"
> "Certainly," said Alice.
> "And only *one* for birthday presents, you know. There's glory for you!"

Source: Lewis Carroll, *The Annotated Alice* (New York, 1974), 267–268.

agated Protestant thinking as well as the pictorial representations of the life cycle, stimulating thought and awareness of life cycle images.

The printing press also encouraged the spread of literacy, which seems to have influenced the development of age awareness. A correlation between the two developments has been found in numerous societies, and early modern Europe was no exception. The reasons for this correlation have not been explored extensively; it may be that age awareness relied more on an ability to read numbers than actual literacy but that this ability accompanied literacy in the cultures studied.

Some of the credit for a heightened awareness of age of the populace as a whole must also go to the record keepers themselves, who made strong efforts at keeping accurate records that included precise ages. The growth and rationalization of state bureaucracies ensured that the population was frequently asked to report ages and, thus, that specific chronological age entered more deeply into the consciousness of the European population.

DIVERSE PATHWAYS

The dominant shifts in life-cycle attitudes reflect the dominant sectors of society. Both individual life-cycle patterns and the ideology that frames them vary for peoples who were not dominant in their societies because of gender, class, or race. Research has begun to look at the impact of gender or class on attitudes toward aging and life-cycle decisions in Europe's past. Historians of twentieth-century Europe will need to pay greater attention to racial diversity to understand the development of life-cycle patterns in Europe's increasingly multicultural population. The late twentieth century marked a growing awareness of diverse life patterns. This awareness may break apart the notion of a dominant life-course pattern that had become seemingly less diverse in the early twentieth century.

Until the mid-twentieth century, the female life cycle held certain marked differences from the male. Evidence of women's life-cycle patterns from the eighteenth and nineteenth centuries shows a divergence from the vision of a progressive life-course pattern. Rather than advancing to midlife and then retreating, women slowly increased their activities and social networks into advanced old age. Neither cyclic nor linear, this pattern reflects a vision of the life course as expansive or elastic. Nineteenth-century women defined their life-cycle transitions more frequently by biological events such as childbirth and menopause than by strictly age-graded events. Supported by scientific biases that emphasized the power of the physiological on women, women developed their own rituals surrounding female biological transitions. The life-cycle patterns of working women were functions of both gender and class. Working women tended not to see movement in and out of the workplace as marking significant life-course transitions. The significant points, instead, were related to family dynamics and composition: marriage, the death of parents, or the activities of children among the transitional life-course events.

The life cycles of the working classes and peasantry were consistently more variable and less age stratified than the pattern set by the bourgeoisie and elites. Adult family life for members of all classes before the nineteenth century involved the presence of small children for approximately twenty years—between a relatively late marriage and the woman's menopause. Middle-class patterns over the nineteenth century abbreviated the childbearing period by limiting family size at the same time as they lowered the age of marriage. Working-class women and men also got married at lower ages when industrialization opened up new avenues of independence, but they bore larger families, each member contributing to the family economy. Childbearing, then, became a trait associated with youth for middle class women and remained more variable for peasants and working-class women until the twentieth century. Economic prosperity relied on a smaller number of children for the middle classes and a larger number for the workers since, in all stages of childhood, children in middle-class households were economic dependents, whereas older children were economic assets in working-class families. Working-class families, thus, deeply resented the introduction of child labor laws.

While middle-class couples passed from youthful parenthood into a period of childless independence, working-class couples saw their households expand to include both young children and much older unmarried offspring. Education drew middle-class adolescents from the family hearth to boarding schools that offered discipline but independence from parents. Working-class youths, on the other hand, remained in their parents' homes longer in industrialized Europe than before as apprenticeship and domestic service declined in the late nineteenth century. Previously, youth employment in these two sectors had required the youth's residence in the place of employment. Once industrial labor offered better opportunities, youths resided with their parents. The spread of mandatory education had a much smaller effect on working-class and peasant adolescents than on the members of the bourgeoisie. Though they complied with the law, children of both the peasantry and the urban working classes ceased studies at the earliest legal age. Though mandatory school attendance lengthened childhood by delaying work, economic employment, rather than schooling, continued to define the life-stage transition. While the middle class recognized adolescence as a period of transition between childhood incompetence and adult work responsibility, working-class youths assumed adult work responsibilities as soon as they were able. The creation of adolescence occurred for the working class only after World War I, half a century after the middle class had initiated it.

On the other hand, working-class autobiographies demonstrate patterns consistent with a linear life-course model. Workers aimed at advancing their careers and generally present their lives as cohesive narratives. Turning points in their lives acted as catalysts for linear growth rather than revelations resulting in a cyclic return or rebirth. By the mid-twentieth century, the working class and the middle class accepted the same basic traits in the life course, both agreeing on the various life stages—that they were based on chronological age, that the family life course was distinct from the workplace, and that life progressed along a trajectory. For a brief period, one model prevailed.

The late twentieth century, however, heralded the onset of the postmodern life course, which is defined not by any unifying factors but by a diversity of patterns and a shift away from using age as a criterion for status. Ages of first marriage and childbearing grew more variable, and work involved less a single career trajectory than several trajectories following upon each other. Early retirement practices and a resistance to mandatory retirement resulted in an increasingly imprecise definition of retirement age. Rejecting sharp stratification, the postmodern life course is neither linear nor cyclic. It defies the temporality of the life span by dismantling the chronological, socially constructed stages of life upon which both the life cycle and the life course models have for so long rested.

See also other articles in this section.

BIBLIOGRAPHY

Abbott, Mary. *Life Cycles in England, 1560–1720.* London and New York, 1996.

Bell, Rudolph, and Donald Weinstein. *Saints and Society: The Two Worlds of Western Christendom, 1000–1700.* Chicago, 1982.

Cole, Thomas R. *The Journey of Life: A Cultural History of Aging in America.* New York and Cambridge, U.K., 1992. Chapter 1 discusses European material.

Day, Barbara Ann. "Representing Aging and Death in French Culture." *French Historical Studies* 17 (spring 1992): 688–724.

Foner, Anne. "Age Stratification and the Changing Family." *American Journal of Sociology* 84 supp. (1978): S340–S365.

Gillis, John. *A World of Their Own Making: Myth, Ritual, and the Quest for Family Values.* New York, 1997.

Gould, Stephen Jay. *Time's Arrow, Time's Cycle: Myth and Metaphor in the Discovery of Geological Time.* Cambridge, Mass., 1987.

Herlihy, David, and Christiane Klapisch-Zuber. *Tuscans and Their Families.* New Haven, Conn., 1985.

Jalland, Pat. *Women from Birth to Death: The Female Life Cycle in Britain, 1830–1914.* Brighton, U.K., 1986.

Kern, Stephen. *Culture of Time and Space, 1880–1912.* Cambridge, Mass., 1983.

Klassen, Sherri. "The Domestic Virtues of Old Age: Gendered Rites in the Fête de la Vieillesse" *Canadian Journal of History* 32 (December 1997): 393–403.

Kohli, Martin, et al. "The Social Construction of Aging through Work" *Ageing and Society* 3 (1983): 23–42.

Rosenthal, Joel T. *Old Age in Late Medieval England.* Philadelphia, 1996.

Rosenthal, Joel T. *Patriarchy and Families of Privilege in Fifteenth-Century England.* Philadelphia, 1991.

Sears, Elizabeth. *The Ages of Man: Medieval Interpretations of the Life Cycle.* Princeton, N.J., 1986.

HEALTH AND DISEASE

Kenneth F. Kiple

Studies centered on political, economic, military, or church affairs are very old avenues of historical investigation in Europe. By considerable contrast the study of disease and history is quite new.

In part this is because until the beginning of germ theory in the late 1800s, people did not know what caused them to be sick and to die. When court chroniclers and historians felt pressed to account for the presence of diseases, "God's will" was a handy explanation—a "will" that was routinely credited with epidemics that delivered misery and death to thousands, even hundreds of thousands, of individuals. Perhaps because God might be credited but never blamed, this explanation was also generally laden with the suspicion that divine will had gotten a helping hand from secular sources such as the ragged and dirty poor, or outsiders, or Jews, all of whom came to comprise the usual scapegoats during epidemics.

However, the study of disease in history is also a phenomenon of the last two centuries or so because the writing of history was an enterprise that tended to deal with the affairs of a highly visible elite as opposed to the murky masses. Hence epidemics—the most dramatic manifestation of disease—which as a rule fed on those masses while sparing the elite (whose wealth separated them physically and nutritionally from the masses and permitted flight from epidemic sites), were often not counted as very noteworthy events for those in a position to record them.

It was the birth of both germ theory and social history that changed this state of historiographical affairs by clearing the way for twentieth-century historians to focus on the role of human health in history. These historians, in turn, have made the study of the impact of disease on societies indispensable to any holistic understanding of those societies. This article looks at the march of a number of diseases across Europe from the Renaissance to the present. It attempts to do so in chronological order, but sections of the article sometimes overlap because an effort has also been made to present diseases in categories. Most of these categories feature diseases of an epidemic or pan-demic nature. However, the less dramatic endemic diseases are also discussed, as are those caused by foods and nutritional deficiencies.

As for nomenclature, "epidemic" is defined as a disease suddenly appearing to attack many people in the same region at roughly the same time and "pandemic" as an epidemic disease that becomes widely distributed throughout a region, continent, or the globe; "endemic" refers to a disease that is always present in a population.

DISEASE AND THE RENAISSANCE

Somewhat ironically, given its connotation of "rebirth," a distinctive feature of the Renaissance was widespread death, much of it caused by bubonic plague, which had become pandemic. It is generally said (but not without dispute) that the disease originated east of the Caspian Sea, then followed the caravan routes westward to burst upon Europe in 1347–1348, just as the Mediterranean Renaissance was getting under way. The disease, however, apparently failed to establish an endemic focus in Europe, meaning that it had to be reintroduced if Europe was to experience another epidemic; indeed it was reintroduced with an awful regularity, reappearing somewhere every quarter of a century or so until 1720—almost four hundred years of plague that began in the Renaissance and ceased only in the modern period.

The initial wave of plague, which we call the Black Death, lasted a terrible seven years, beginning with its appearance in Sicily in 1347. It subsequently reached the Italian peninsula, then marched through the Iberian Peninsula in the summer of 1348 and northward to reach Paris and the ports of southern England. The following year saw the British Isles devastated; then plague plunged into northern Europe and by 1350 was moving through eastern Europe. This first European tour of the plague culminated with an assault on Russia that saw Moscow under siege in 1353.

205

The Black Death. The black death at Tournai, by Gilles de Muisit, 1349. BIBLIOTHÈQUE ROYALE DE BELGIQUE, BRUSSELS/THE BRIDGEMAN ART LIBRARY

Although its trajectory was such that no region suffered plague for more than a few months, historians generally agree that the mortality it inflicted was in the 20 to 50 percent range. In the Mediterranean, in urban areas where people lived in close proximity to one another, such as Florence, Venice, Rome, Milan, and Barcelona (which were nurturing the early Renaissance), mortality rates were probably the highest. But it was in the myriad towns, villages, and hamlets, which contained the vast bulk of the population of a Europe still lingering in the late Middle Ages, that the plague harvested the overwhelming majority of its victims.

The impact of the Black Death, combined with that of the recurrent plague epidemics that followed, is difficult to comprehend in both breadth and magnitude. Populations that had been enjoying a period of sustained population growth were drastically pruned practically overnight, and a Europe that had been relatively crowded was so no longer. Whole villages were empty and fields deserted save for equally deserted sheep, cattle, and hogs. A great shortage of labor meant that patterns of landholding and land use had to change. Although not always without strife, landlords became easier to deal with, and many peasants became landowners. Population pressure on food supplies was reduced, and prices fell because of a lack of demand. Animal protein—suddenly abundant—began to grace even the tables of the poor, and the pace of urbanization quickened as individuals no longer needed in the countryside found nonagricultural jobs in cities and towns.

In addition to these significant changes, the onset of plague seems to have wrought some curious microparasitic alterations in Europe's disease ecology beyond the obvious introduction of the rodent disease *Yersinia pestis,* which we call bubonic plague. For reasons not fully understood, leprosy—a disease present in Europe since at least the sixth century— went into an abrupt recession while, at the same time, pulmonary tuberculosis began an ever increasingly prosperous career that would elevate it to the status of a major plague by the eighteenth century. One explanation offered by the American historian William McNeill for the decline of leprosy at this time takes note of the fact that the arrival of plague coincided with climatic change that saw average temperatures falling precipitously in Europe. Prior to the Black Death, with most of Europe put to the plow, firewood was scarce, and people doubtless kept warm on cold nights by huddling together, thereby increasing the ability of leprosy to spread. But in the wake of the Black Death there would have been less need to huddle, with some 40 percent fewer individuals putting pressure on the firewood supply; such a population reduction also meant that wool (and hence clothing) was more readily available. All of these factors may have acted in concert to interrupt leprosy's pattern of skin-to-skin transmission. As for the rise of tuberculosis (TB), the growth of crowded urban areas encouraged by the plague would have proven a fine incubator for this illness, which most frequently spreads from person to person by infected droplets from the lungs.

Populations did begin to recover with the improved conditions of life ushered in by the plague, and despite renewed appearances of this disease, urban areas did grow to support still other illnesses. Indeed, although it is difficult for historians to put a name to most epidemic diseases prior to the sixteenth century, there is no question that their pathogens were ricocheting about inside the walls of the swelling cities and towns, whose rivers and wells festered with human waste, whose markets swarmed with flies, whose dwellings were alive with rodents, and whose human inhabitants avoided bathing and seldom changed woolen clothing and bedding even though they harbored lice, bedbugs, and other assorted vermin.

EPIDEMIC DISEASE DURING THE EXPANSION OF EUROPE

While Europeans were cultivating pathogens at home, they were also importing them from abroad. The Crusaders have been suspected of returning home with some novel microorganisms as well as exciting new plants and an enhanced weltanschauung, but it was the Portuguese, in leading the expansion of Europe with their century of African exploration, who brought many in Europe into contact with tropical ailments for the first time. Yaws—a disease caused by treponemas, a genus of spirochetes—may or may not have been present in an earlier and warmer Europe, but the illness began regularly reaching Iberia via a Portuguese–run slave trade and, according to epidemiologist E. H. Hudson, could have evolved into the syphilis that would soon engulf the Continent.

Falciparum malaria was another African contribution to Europe's pool of pathogens. Europeans had suffered from other types of malaria that were widespread during the Middle Ages; but falciparum malaria is by far the most lethal of the malarial types, so deadly in fact that it summons genetic defenses against it through the process of natural selection—defenses such as the sickle-cell trait and blood enzyme deficiencies that hold down the level of parasitization in the human body. The disease had been present in the eastern Mediterranean for thousands of years—long enough to have encouraged the development of such defenses (as discovered by the Crusaders, who did not possess them)—and in some nearby Greek and southern Italian populations as well. But the Iberians had had no opportunity to develop protection against this illness now arriving directly from Africa, which took root in the peninsula and even depopulated the Tagus Valley for a time. Indeed, the extent of that root can be seen in the fact that today, like Italians and Greeks

of the Mediterranean, some southern Iberians also carry evidence in their blood of the beginnings of genetic defenses against falciparum malaria.

Meanwhile, typhus is thought to have first reached Europe via Granada in 1489–1490 with Arab reinforcements for those Moors locked in combat with the forces of Ferdinand and Isabella—the final spasm of centuries of a reconquest that saw Spain ultimately triumphant in 1492. Typhus, however, proved a staunch ally of the Moors by killing some seventeen thousand Spanish soldiers—six times more than the Moors themselves managed to dispatch. And this was only the beginning of a series of typhus epidemics erupting on European battlefields throughout the centuries that followed.

It was in the same year that the Moors were defeated by the Catholic monarchs that their emissary Christopher Columbus and his men arrived at the New World. Shortly thereafter syphilis turned up in Naples, where the French and Spanish armies were contesting control of that kingdom. Initially known as the "disease of Naples," syphilis burned with such a fury among the French forces—ecumenically recruited from all corners of Europe—that they were compelled to withdraw, and the disbanded soldiers carried this new pox to all of those corners. It was now called the French disease (by most everybody but the French); yet some took note of the coincidence of its outbreak with the return of Columbus and suggested that it might better be called the Spanish disease.

Many medical historians and bioanthropologists lean toward the view that syphilis was probably a relatively mild New World treponemal infection that became virulent when transferred to the Old World (perhaps by fusing with other treponemas), and thus it was, technically, a new disease for the Europeans. Certainly it seemed like a new disease loosed on a people with little in the way of immunological defenses. It spread with such extraordinary speed that it was reported from all over Europe by 1499; it was also extraordinary in its virulence, producing hideous symptoms and high rates of mortality. Yet a few decades later, syphilis began to relent in its ferocity and to lose its epidemic character, evolving into the relatively mild disease known in the late twentieth century. But it is worth noting that what the disease lost in malignancy it gained in its ability to stigmatize those who contracted it; the syphilitic came to personify vice itself.

In England, however, as the fifteenth century came to a close, people had more in the way of pestilence to contend with than just syphilis. In 1485 a mysterious disease dubbed *sudor anglicus,* the "sweating sickness," or simply the "Sweat," swept parts of that country and killed up to a third of the populations of the towns and villages it visited. The Sweat made return visits to England (but not Scotland or Ireland) in 1506, 1517, 1528, and finally, 1551. Then it apparently vanished forever, leaving one of the most intriguing mysteries of historical epidemiology in its wake. What was the disease and where did it come from?

The 1485 outbreak took place during the War of the Roses, which changed the status of the victorious Henry Tudor, duke of Richmond, to that of Henry VII, king of England, and it was suspected that the Sweat had entered the country with some of Henry's mercenaries returning from France. But no single factor, including military movement, seems able to account for the other outbreaks. Only once did the Sweat apparently strike outside of England, when in 1528–1529 it was reported as epidemic across northern Europe all the way to Russia. However, in an area also under siege by syphilis and typhus, it is difficult to disentangle Sweat morbidity and mortality from that caused by these other two epidemics (not to mention the myriad other infections afoot). Influenza, malaria, typhus, and streptococcal infection have all been put forward as candidates, and in 1981 the medical historians John Wylie and Leslie Collier proposed that the disease was caused by an arbovirus (any of a group of viruses transmitted to humans by mosquitoes and ticks) harbored by small animals and carried to humans by insects. Since arboviruses are generally tropical in residence, this raises the intriguing (but probably epidemiologically remote) possibility that the close connection of the English with the Portuguese during the years of the Sweat outbreaks had put them in touch with some virus of tropical Africa.

One reason for dismissing typhus and influenza as candidates for the Sweat is that the English, like the rest of the Europeans, had become painfully familiar with both of them and thus were not likely to view them as novel. Beginning in 1522 at Cambridge, typhus had started making courtroom appearances and became the scourge behind the famous Black Assizes. The disease—also known as "jail fever"—was carried by prisoners into the courtroom, where it infected spectators, judges, and jurors.

Typhus made its second great battlefield appearance in 1528—this time in Naples—and became the second disease within thirty-two years in that disputed kingdom to wreck great French plans of state. The troops of the Holy Roman Emperor Charles V, which were under French siege near Naples, had been decimated by bubonic plague to the point where a French victory seemed assured, and all of Italy stood ready to acknowledge the rule of Francis I. But then the power of pestilence suddenly sided with imperial ambition as typhus launched a counterattack that destroyed some thirty thousand soldiers in the French army. Like syphilis before it, typhus engineered a French defeat that opposing troops could not.

Given that bubonic plague was now intermingling with the new plagues of syphilis and typhus, sixteenth-century Europe was a pathogenically perilous enough place without smallpox, an old disease now suddenly acting like a new and virulent one. There were two types of this disease, which medicine believes it finally killed off in the last half of the 1970s. One was variola major (major, because it produced mortality rates of up to 25 to 30 percent); the other was the much milder variola minor, with mortality rates of 1 percent or less. Doubtless, there were strains intermediate between the two, but until the first decades of the sixteenth century, it seems to have been mostly a relatively mild smallpox that Europeans had known. Yet, beginning in that century, smallpox increasingly became one of Europe's biggest killers, so that in the seventeenth and eighteenth centuries it accounted for 10 to 15 percent of all deaths in some countries and as much as 30 percent in some cities.

There is no satisfactory explanation for this mysterious increase in virulence, only intriguing speculation that involves the Americas on the one hand and Africa on the other. Smallpox reached the Caribbean by at least 1518 and was carried onto the American mainland in 1519, where it began a devastating march north and south that brought demographic disaster to Native American populations wherever it appeared. The deadliness of smallpox for them has generally been explained in terms of their lack of experience with the malady and thus their lack of resistance to it. But it is also possible that in this human crucible the smallpox virus became increasingly venomous as it passed through tens, even hundreds, of thousands of inexperienced bodies and was thus transformed into the virulent disease that would soon replace plague as the most important check on European populations.

Alternatively, it could be that the smallpox unleashed on Native Americans was already a killer. It is generally assumed that India was the cradle of smallpox, but long ago August Hirsch, the great German epidemiologist, pinpointed regions of central Africa as other foci. The year 1518, when smallpox entered the Caribbean, was also the year that Charles I of Spain permitted the beginning of the transatlantic slave trade, and it is not impossible that the smallpox that fell on the Native Americans was a malignant disease of Africa rather than the relatively mild one of Europe.

Certainly it was the case that later explosive smallpox epidemics appear to have reached the Americas from Africa via the Atlantic slave trade. But either way, as a new strain of smallpox from Africa or a newly mutated disease that had incubated in the New World, this "new" smallpox easily reached the European Old World to settle in there as well.

EUROPEAN ENDEMIC AND FAMILIAR EPIDEMIC AILMENTS

These major plagues were regularly joined by other diseases to prune continental populations. Influenza made sufficiently regular appearances in the fifteenth century to precipitate detailed descriptions of the disease, and three large-scale epidemics ravaged Europe in 1510, 1557–1558, and 1580. The latter was actually a pandemic that made itself felt in Asia and Africa as well, and the high rates of morbidity and mortality it produced among young adults suggests a strain similar to that which caused the world-shaking pandemic of 1918.

Typhoid, which travels the oral-fecal route, generally in water, was obviously widespread in Europe's fouled water supplies, where there was little or no separation of sewage and drinking water. Indeed, because in the absence of effective antibiotic treatment, typhoid (or putrid malignant fever, as it was called) can kill 10 to 20 percent of those it infects, one might wonder why anyone was alive to experience the other diseases under discussion. One ready answer, however, is that exposure to the typhoid bacillus provides a relative immunity to future attacks. Another is that, on the whole, people drank water that had been processed into alcoholic beverages and thus purified. Later they added nonalcoholic beverages to the list, such as coffee, tea, and cocoa—all of which were generally made with boiling water.

Measles, which was often confused with smallpox and frequently operated in concert with it, also struck alone, and numerous measles epidemics were reported in the seventeenth and eighteenth centuries. Scarlet fever, diphtheria, rheumatic fever, and mumps were other diseases to be endured, especially by the young, which brings us to the issue of urbanization and childhood illnesses.

THE DECLINE OF THE OLD EPIDEMICS

Perhaps paradoxically, even though Europe was awash in a sea of pathogens, the continued growth of cities slowly began to stem that pathogenic tide. It is not that cities and towns were healthy places. Quite the contrary, they were, as already described, squalid strongholds of pestilence. But as they grew larger they rendered themselves capable of taming some of that pestilence by transforming epidemic diseases into endemic diseases. Epidemic diseases such as smallpox and measles tended to roll over an area, either killing or immunizing victims as they did so. Then they disappeared because of a lack of suitable hosts and only reappeared when these were again present in the form of a new generation of nonimmune individuals. But as urban populations grew larger, they eventually produced a sufficient number of new hosts through births to retain diseases on a year-round basis and keep them from disappearing, whereupon they became essentially childhood diseases. In other words, pathogens that had periodically slaughtered young and old indiscriminately were now confined mostly to the young. Much life was saved by this arrangement because many diseases tend to treat the young more gently than they do adults while providing them with immunity against a future visitation.

FOODS, NUTRIENTS, AND ILLNESSES

Europeans also suffered from ailments that were food and nutrition related. One was ergotism—a fungal poisoning caused by the ergot fungus, which can form on cereal grains and especially on rye ears to poison heavy consumers of breads and porridge made from affected grains. Needless to say these consumers were usually the poor. August Hirsch listed 130 epidemics of the disease in Europe between 591 and 1879, while acknowledging that these were only a fraction of the ergotism outbreaks that had taken place. Also known as St. Anthony's fire, when the disease affected the central nervous system it was called convulsive. In its other, gangrenous form, the cardiovascular system is affected. Either form could and did kill relentlessly. Data has revealed, for example, that during ten ergotism epidemics in nineteenth-century Russia, those who were afflicted experienced a mean mortality rate of 41.5 percent. But ergotism is also of interest because the convulsive type of the disease causes victims to experience hallucinations and convulsions. Interestingly, research has linked years favorable to the growth of ergot with the hallucinations and convulsions that were a part of religious revivals and even with the "Great Fear" that swept the French countryside in 1789, just prior to the French Revolution.

Europeans also had their share of deficiency diseases. Scurvy, arising from a lack of vitamin C, must have seemed like another new disease as the maritime nations of Europe put together the technology to keep ships away from shore long enough for it to develop. In 1498 Vasco da Gama lost perhaps as many as half of his crew to the affliction, and from that time until about 1800, estimates would have as many as a million sailors dying from scurvy—probably more deaths than were generated by naval warfare, shipwrecks, and all other shipboard illnesses combined. Yet scurvy was not confined to seamen. It tormented the inmates of prisons, workhouses, hospitals—indeed anyone without access to foods containing vitamin C. People living in Europe's northernmost regions, characterized by long winters, in early spring began searching out the first green shoots of those various plants they called "scurvy grass" to heal their bleeding gums. Scurvy was also a regular visitor to battlefields, especially when a siege was under way. But despite the experiments of James Lind, James Cook, and others, which had shown the efficacy of lime juice in preventing or treating the disease, and despite the British navy's making lime juice a part of the rations of its seamen (hence the name "limeys"), scurvy continued to break out among other navies and especially armies, from Napoleon's army during its retreat from Moscow to those forces engaged in the Crimean War, right up to the combatants in the Franco-Prussian War of 1870–1871.

Another deficiency disease, pellagra, arose in northern Spain, Italy, southern France, and the Balkans, where the peasants had planted maize from the Americas and then centered their diets on the grain. Native American populations had lived for millennia on maize but treated it with lime (calcium oxide), which not only made the kernels pliable but broke the chemical bond to release the niacin they contained. Without such processing, a consumer whose diet rests heavily on maize will become niacin deficient and pellagra prone. The disease produces diarrhea to aggravate malnutrition, dermatitis, and dementia, finally resulting in death. In France, where a physician successfully urged his government to curtail maize production and encourage the peasants to cultivate other crops and eat more animal foods, the disease was virtually wiped out by the end of the nineteenth century. Elsewhere, it continued to haunt the poor in maize-growing areas well into the twentieth century.

Rickets occurs when the growing bones of the young (the adult form is called osteomalacia) do not receive sufficient calcium—generally because of a lack of vitamin D, so necessary for the utilization of calcium. The bulk of our vitamin D is the result of bodily production that takes place when the skin is stimulated by the ultraviolet rays of sunlight reflecting from it. Thus, the bowed legs and bossed skulls left in the wake of bouts with rickets were especially

prominent in northern Europe and England, which frequently experienced long, overcast winters. In fact, the disease was such a feature on England's medical landscape during the seventeenth century that in 1650 it received what has been called its classic description in the book *De rachitide* (On rickets) by Francis Glisson. A few years later, in 1669, another physician, John Mayow, followed with his own *On Rickets*, claiming that the affliction had first appeared in England only around 1620. Whatever the reasons for its abrupt appearance, rickets was not likely to wane as England began the industrialization process, filling the air with coal smoke and smog that screened out the sun's ultraviolet rays and closed off working-class children in urban slums hardly constructed with healthy exposure to sunlight in mind. In 1789 an English physician discussed the efficacy of cod-liver oil in curing and preventing rickets, but another century and a half would elapse before science, in discovering the vitamins, would learn why it was effective.

The year 1789 also effectively marked the end of a curious practice begun half a millennium before, when Louis IX, newly returned from the Crusades, began administering the "king's touch" to cure scrofula. Outward symptoms of scrofula were swellings in the neck. When these swellings were enlarged neck glands that frequently became putrid, they were mostly the result of primary tuberculosis of the cervical lymph nodes caused by the ingestion of milk from tubercular cows. Because most cases of primary tuberculosis resolve themselves over time and the unsightly symptoms disappear, the king's touch must doubtless have seemed miraculous—not only to the king's subjects but also to the monarch himself, through whose hands supposedly passed the healing power of the Almighty.

Not to be outdone, monarchs in England soon followed suit to show that they, too, were ruling by divine right, and the touch was increasingly used and then widely administered by the Stuart kings. Indeed, in 1684 there was such a mob of applicants for the touch that many were reportedly trampled to death in a vain attempt to reach the hand of a restored Charles II. Perhaps the record for touching, however, belongs to Louis XV of France, who reportedly touched more than two thousand individuals at his coronation in 1722.

Scrofula could also mean goiter—an enlargement of the thyroid gland caused by iodine deficiency—and since these cases do not resolve themselves, they would not have been good advertisements for the king's touch. Both England and France seem to have had goiter sufferers, but fortunately for the reputation of the royal touch in the latter country, the

The King's Touch. The ill and infirm line up to be touched by the king in hopes of a cure. Engraving by Frederick Hendrick van Hove (c. 1628–1698). PRIVATE COLLECTION/THE BRIDGEMAN ART LIBRARY

real centers of goiter were far from the throne in the remote mountains and valleys with their iodine-leached soils in and around the Alps and the Pyrenees.

MORTALITY AND ITS DECLINE

In the seventeenth century typhus continued to stalk Europe and especially its battlefields so that during the Thirty Years' War (1618–1648) battle casualties were minimal when compared with the ravages of typhus, not to mention those of plague, scurvy, and dysentery. But typhus was also carried to civilian populations: Germany was said to be so devastated in some places that wolves roamed empty streets. Typhus entered Scandinavia during the Baltic wars, was in the thick of the struggle between Crown troops and Huguenots in France, and became a major player in the English civil wars, reportedly converting the island into one huge hospital by 1650.

By this time tuberculosis mortality also had begun to increase considerably in countries undergoing urbanization, such as England, where at midcentury, despite typhus, TB was accounting for some 20 percent of all deaths and London was contributing a disproportionately large percentage of the victims. Perhaps by way of compensation, the Great Plague of London in 1665 marked the final visit of this pestilential scourge to Britain, and by the beginning of the

eighteenth century, all of northern Europe was protected by the famous Cordon Sanitaire—the Austrian barrier manned by 100,000 men to keep plague from reaching Europe from the Ottoman lands. To the south, however, plague seemed unrelenting. It besieged Naples in 1656, where it reportedly killed some 300,000 people, and Spain, which had been buffeted by epidemics of plague in 1596–1602 and 1648–1652, continued to suffer from it during the nine long years from 1677 to 1685. Mercifully, however, plague's career also came to a close in the European Mediterranean countries after a last furious parting shot, between 1720 and 1722, that killed tens of thousands in Marseilles and Toulon. Eastern Europe and Russia were the last areas of the Continent to become plague free, following severe epidemics in Kiev in 1770 and Moscow in 1771.

Prior to the nineteenth century, medicine was powerless against plague and other epidemic pestilence, and any success people enjoyed against disease was because of measures undertaken by health boards. The quarantine was invented in Ragusa (Dubrovnik) in 1377 and was subsequently employed from time to time by cities, with varying degrees of success, against potentially infected outsiders and especially against maritime shipping. The pest house, or *lazaretto*, provided a way of isolating the sick and the poor (regarded as purveyors of pathogens) during an epi-

211

demic while the wealthy followed the path of flight—
"flee quickly, go far, and return slowly."

Despite their heavy burden of disease, as the eighteenth century got under way, some European populations were beginning to experience what the English physician Thomas McKeown (1976) terms "the modern rise of population." The reasons why this occurred—why an age-old cycle of population growth spurts, brutally reversed by soaring mortality, followed by demographic collapse, came to an end— has been and still is vigorously debated. Factors like the recession of plague and some positive steps in public health seem straightforward enough. Other factors put forth, such as a change in the nature of warfare, are a bit less convincing—especially in a century that began with Europe at war over the question of the Spanish succession and closed with France and England locked in a global struggle, with a series of almost countless struggles in between. One can grant that, up to a point, armies were more disciplined than in the previous century, that they were frequently more isolated from civilian populations (which better distanced the latter from typhus and other diseases carried by armies), and even that advances were made in military hygiene, and yet still wonder if what has been granted might represent any significant decline in mortality.

McKeown, who sorts through the various possibilities, argues that improved nutrition was the key to understanding the process of mortality decline— an argument that has summoned numerous detractors, most of whom concede that this might be part of the answer but hardly the whole story. Undeniably, nutrition did improve for many, in no small part because of crops from America. Potatoes, introduced to Europe in the sixteenth century, had caught on (also squash to a lesser extent) by the end of the seventeenth century in Ireland and England and would soon do the same on the Continent. They not only provided a rich source of calories for the peasants along with a year-round supply of vitamin C, but were also an important hedge against famine. Maize, as we saw, brought pellagra to southern and eastern Europe where the grain was consumed by humans. In northern Europe, however, it became an important crop for feeding livestock, permitting more animals to be carried through the winter and thus ensuring a greater availability of animal protein year round in the form of milk, cheese, and eggs, as well as meat.

Among other things, more protein in the diet, so crucial to combating pathogenic invasion, would have helped in significantly reducing infant and especially child mortality in an age that had previously seen between a third and a half or more of those born

fail to reach their fifth birthday—often because of protein energy malnutrition (PEM). This comes about when malnutrition and pathogens work together, as they frequently do, in a process called synergy, whereby the pathogens enhance a protein-deprived (and hence malnourished) state, which, in turn, leaves the body even more defenseless against the pathogens. Thus the greater availability of protein would have altered one side of the synergy equation, while a general reduction of pathogens would have done the same for the other.

The protein intake of a population can be judged, to some extent, by the average height of that population, and although there is dispute over places and times at which populations began to grow taller in Europe, there is no argument that European populations of the eighteenth century would have towered above their predecessors of a couple of centuries earlier. The armor of the warriors of those chivalrous days was, as a rule, constructed for much smaller people, suggesting that nutrition (especially protein intake) had, indeed, improved as Europe passed through its century of Enlightenment.

The Enlightenment was an age of increasingly strong states, a factor that affected the other side of the synergy equation because strong states were frequently able to compel pathogen reduction, albeit often serendipitously. Strong states, for example, were better able to regulate maritime commerce, and such regulation, with its delays and red tape, often became a quarantining device in itself, even when quarantines were not officially imposed—although, of course, strong states were better able to accomplish these as well. They were also able to insist on cleaner cities, not because monarchs and their officials were ahead of their time in grasping the nature of pathogens and their vectors, but rather because clean cities without raw sewage in the streets alongside decaying bodies of dead animals were considerably more pleasing aesthetically. The consequences, however, would have been a substantial reduction in disease vectors—especially flies, with their dirty feet. Such measures, along with the attention of the state to other matters such as drainage, could only have had a positive impact on public health.

This was also the case with more efficient agricultural practices that released more and more individuals from the countryside to enter the rapidly growing cities, where ever greater portions of populations became immunized in the process of converting epidemic and pandemic diseases to childhood ailments. And then, at the end of the eighteenth century, with the advent of the Jenner vaccine to replace haphazard and often downright dangerous variolation techniques, medicine finally made a significant contribution to population growth that would ultimately lead to the eradication of smallpox (save for that which remains in laboratories) some two centuries later.

IMPORTED PATHOGENS: THE EIGHTEENTH AND NINETEENTH CENTURIES

Two more new plagues struck Europe during the late eighteenth and early nineteenth centuries. One of these was yellow fever, a tropical killer to which Europeans had already proven themselves remarkably susceptible in Africa and the West Indies. The same susceptibility was apparent at home during periodic epidemics that had first begun striking Europe during the eighteenth century and continued to do so in the nineteenth. Yellow fever reached the Continent circuitously, moving first from Africa (via the slave trade) to the New World, whereupon Europeans carried it back to the Old. During the nineteenth century, however, after the legal slave trade had been abolished, the focus of the now contraband slave trade was narrowed to just Brazil and Cuba, and the mother countries of the Iberian Peninsula became especially vulnerable to yellow fever. The coastal cities of Oporto, Lisbon, and Barcelona bore the brunt of its assaults, although the disease did venture inland, even reaching Madrid in 1878. England, France, and Italy also saw yellow fever outbreaks on occasion as the disease radiated outward from Iberia.

A few yellow fever epidemics, however, were insignificant when compared with Asiatic cholera, which was by far the biggest epidemic news of the nineteenth century. Just as yellow fever was an African plague with which Europeans had no prior experience, cholera was an Indian disease that had been confined to the Indian subcontinent, where it had festered for some two thousand years or more. The Portuguese in India had described it as early as 1503, but a number of conditions had to be met for Europeans to confront epidemic cholera—a usually waterborne disease—on their own soil. Among these were transportation improvements in the form of railroads and steamships that could whisk cholera pathogens from city to city and port to port after another requirement had been met: an increased movement of people who could carry the disease away from its cradle on the Ganges. Still another condition had already been satisfied. The ever increasing crush of people in Europe's cities meant a huge demand for water from nearby lakes, rivers, and reservoirs, and in an age before san-

itation procedures, such demand was generally met with water fouled by those swelling populations—an ideal situation for pathogens that traveled the oral-fecal route and were easily transmitted in water.

In 1817–1818 British troop movements in India widened the range of cholera within India, and in the 1820s the disease was extended beyond that subcontinent and into Russia, where it reportedly killed over two million individuals. This time cholera spared the rest of Europe, but in 1830–1831 it again reached Russia and, instead of pausing, marched across most of Europe by 1832. In Paris, gravediggers threw aside their shovels and fled, letting bodies pile up in the streets; in England, frantic mobs assaulted authorities attempting to enforce sanitation regulations and destroyed hospitals, even attacking physicians they suspected of somehow engineering the epidemic to ensure a better supply of bodies for dissection. From Europe cholera hurdled the Atlantic to reach the Americas even before it invaded the Iberian Peninsula in 1833 and Italy in 1835.

Cholera reached Europe again in 1848, 1852, 1854 (the disease was sufficiently widespread to make this the worst of the cholera years), and yet again in 1866. During the fifth pandemic (1881–1896) cholera at first only touched the Mediterranean shores of Europe, but it later became widespread in Russia and Germany. During the twentieth century, however, only eastern and southern Europe experienced the disease, and these outbreaks were sporadic.

In terms of overall mortality, cholera was not so great a killer as the bubonic plague that preceded it or the massive influenza epidemic that followed it. But it did spur important developments in public health, especially in the area of sanitation, and with the arrival of germ theory at the end of the nineteenth century, the causative organisms of many diseases, including cholera, became known.

PLAGUES OF THE MODERN ERA: THE NINETEENTH AND TWENTIETH CENTURIES

In the case of tuberculosis, however, knowing the pathogen that caused it did little to slow the course of this illness, which was already in decline. TB had become epidemic in Europe in the seventeenth century, beginning to peak at about midcentury and continuing at a high level of activity for the next quarter century or so. Then it receded until the following century, when it again surged around 1750 to become the major cause of death in most European cities for the next hundred years. About 1850, however, the

Cholera the Harvester. *Le choléra* cuts down victims during the First Balkan War, 1912. Lithograph from *Le Petit Journal*, 1 December 1912. PRIVATE COLLECTION/ROGER-VIOLLET, PARIS/THE BRIDGEMAN ART LIBRARY

disease began a decline that (save for a surge during World War I) continued until chemotherapy was introduced after World War II, finally giving medicine its "magic bullet" against this plague that had already been so mysteriously tamed.

In the eighteenth century, according to Hirsch, scarcely a year elapsed without typhus epidemics in one part or another of the Continent. It marched with troops, who scattered the disease about in the wars of the Spanish, Polish, and Austrian successions during the first half of the century, and in the Seven Years' War and the French Revolution during the second half. It was in 1812 at the battle of Ostrowo that typhus once again became decisive in warfare by joining the Russians and the weather in decimating Napoleon's forces. Of the close to 500,000 soldiers that marched on Moscow, only 6,000 made it home again.

Following this epidemic, typhus seems to have deserted the west and settled into the eastern portion of the Continent for good. The Franco-Prussian War of 1870–1871, for example, spawned no typhus ep-

idemics, but the disease was omnipresent in the eastern European revolutions of 1848 and the Crimean War of 1854–1856. Similarly, during World War I there was no typhus on the western front, but it was absolutely rampant in the east among soldiers and civilians alike. During the first six months of the war, Serbia alone experienced some 150,000 typhus deaths—a horrendous toll, but nothing like the two and a half million typhus deaths estimated to have occurred during Russia's retreat of 1916, the revolutions of 1917, and the subsequent onset of civil war.

It was at this juncture that influenza also began to play a considerably larger role in world affairs. Barely active in the seventeenth century, the disease swept Europe with three pandemics in the eighteenth century (1729–1730, 1732–1733, and 1781–1782), along with several epidemics. In the nineteenth century, there were at least three more pandemics in Europe—those of 1830–1831, 1833, and 1889–1890—with the latter killing at least a quarter of a million people. This pandemic was diffused swiftly by the ongoing transportation revolution, providing something of a preview of what was to come; but none of this was preparation enough for the wave of influenza that began to roll in the late winter and spring of 1918.

The 1918 influenza seems to have arisen first in the United States but soon swept over Europe and its battlefields, and then reached out to almost all corners of the globe. The morbidity it produced was staggering, as hundreds of millions were sent to their sickbeds, but it was an ability to kill young adults as well as its usual victims—the very young and the old—that made this disease so deadly for so many. Global mortality has been estimated at over 30 million, of which Europe's share was placed at a little more than 2 million. Then, just two years later, another wave of the disease washed across the globe, after which it somehow dissipated.

The next apparent epidemic threat to a world badly shaken by influenza was poliomyelitis. It is very difficult to spy polio in the distant past because its major symptoms—fever and paralysis—are hardly distinctive. Many individual cases were described in the eighteenth century that could have been polio, and one is mentioned in England in 1835. However, the first clearly recognizable victims of epidemic polio are said to have hosted the disease in Norway in 1868. But cases that were regularly reported throughout the nineteenth century in Scandinavia as well as in Italy, France, Germany, and the United States are now understood to have been polio. At the turn of the century polio reached epidemic proportions in Scandinavia and continued to surge in these proportions well into the twentieth century. England, too, began to experience polio cases and by 1950 was second only to the United States in case incidence.

At this point, however, medicine began to assume its well-known role in the matter with first the Salk and then the Sabin vaccines; once these became available, in 1955 and 1960, respectively, they were widely administered throughout the United States, Europe, and much of the rest of the world, and fears of a global epidemic such as the influenza of 1918 quickly subsided. Humankind seemed to be entering a new era in which epidemic disease was no longer to be an important health factor. Antibiotics were controlling venereal diseases, tuberculosis appeared on the verge of extinction along with smallpox and most other killers of the past, and death rates from all causes had plummeted throughout the century, even though those subsumed under the rubrics of "diseases of the circulatory systems" and "malignant neoplasms" had more than doubled. The chronic diseases were seen to have replaced epidemic diseases as the real enemy, and medicine began training its guns on them, especially lung cancer, breast cancer, and heart related diseases, which, although not contagious, appeared to be assuming epidemic-like proportions.

Part of this development was explicable in terms of medicine's success against contagious illnesses: people were living longer, and many more than ever before were reaching ages when such illnesses were most likely to develop. In no small part longer lifespans were attributable to preventive medicine, which had been remarkably successful in fostering good general health, especially among infants and children. But in addition to lifespan, lifestyle was also implicated, and the concept of risk factors was introduced following epidemiological studies that established a causal relationship between the inhalation of tobacco smoke and both lung cancer and heart disease. A positive relationship was also found between high blood cholesterol, triglyceride levels, and coronary events (with high blood pressure and diabetes also risk factors), and the high fat content of Western diets was linked not only to elevated rates of heart disease but to some cancers as well—especially breast cancer.

Lifestyles, however, change slowly. Many people keep an eye on their diets, but many do not, especially those who find frequent comfort in traditional, often fat-laden, regional cuisines. And tobacco smoke has continued to spiral upward into European air. Something of an anomaly, however, has been discovered in the diet of people in Mediterranean countries, which is based on olive oil and wine and little in the way of animal fat; consumers of this diet enjoy relatively low levels of the chronic diseases despite cigarette smoking—suggesting that medicine, having identified risk

Influenza Epidemic. A British public-health worker wearing a surgical mask carries a pump with anti-flu spray for use on buses, March 1920. HULTON DEUTSCH/CORBIS

factors, may still have much to learn about their modification.

Medicine also learned abruptly that it was not done with epidemic disease, for in 1977, at just the time when that profession was congratulating itself for apparently snuffing out smallpox forever, another global epidemic was in the making. The acquired immune deficiency syndrome (AIDS) began to surface during the late 1970s, as physicians in the United States reported a number of unusual disease conditions among otherwise healthy homosexual men. By 1981 the illness had been formally described, and by 1983 research in laboratories in the United States and France had identified its cause as a previously unknown human retrovirus, HIV-1. It was determined that the virus passes from person to person through bodily fluids. The disease had seemed at first to be an exclusively American problem that was centered in the country's gay communities and among injection drug users who shared needles, but it quickly became apparent that Caribbean populations and Africans south of the Sahara were also afflicted with this horrifying ailment, which causes the immune system to collapse. Then in 1985 a related virus, HIV-2, which passes through heterosexual activity, was discovered to be widespread in Africa.

With many of its citizens having contacts in the United States, the Caribbean, and Africa, Europe had no chance of escaping AIDS; in addition, many of its hemophiliacs were infected with blood from America. By the early 1990s the disease had spread throughout the world, and in 1996 the number of cases was estimated to exceed 22 million. In 1997 the European

Russian Anti-Smoking Posters. "96 percent of people who get lung cancer are smokers" *(left)* and "Stop smoking. There's poison in cigarettes." *(right).* The poster on the right is by Vladimir Mayakovski (1893–1930). WORLD HEALTH ORGANIZATION/NATIONAL LIBRARY OF MEDICINE, BETHESDA, MARYLAND

Centre for the Epidemiological Monitoring of AIDS pointed out that the fifteen countries of the European Union had 93 percent of Europe's AIDS cases and predicted a rapid case increase in the rest of Europe, with much of this the result of heterosexual contact.

Although about 90 percent of the more than 22 million cases in the world are in developing countries, some 2 million are not—and these patients have found themselves subjected to the same kind of cruel stigmata that plague and syphilis victims experienced centuries before. Indeed this latest plague, which at one time was regarded as the Black Death of the twentieth century, came not only at a time of medical complacency but also at a point when any social or political experience in confronting such a widespread public health crisis had long since been forgotten. In the West medical science at the turn of the century began at last to have some success in grappling with the disease—at least in increasing survival time—and the din of stigmatism faded somewhat. But the epidemic is far from over, and sequels such as a sharp increase in the incidence of tuberculosis also remain to be dealt with.

AIDS administered a number of brutal lessons, and one stands out starkly. The disease showed how, in an age when one can travel to almost any place on the globe in a matter of hours, the West is now vulnerable to diseases that break out anywhere in the world. Globalization of pathogens seems as inevitable as the globalization of food and economies, and as a consequence, it appears doubtful that we can hope to experience any reprieve from epidemics of the kind that ranged from the influenza of 1918 to AIDS.

See also other articles in this section.

BIBLIOGRAPHY

Arrizabalaga, Jon, John Henderson, and Roger French. *The Great Pox: The French Disease in Renaissance Europe.* New Haven, Conn., 1997.

Benedek, Thomas G., and Kenneth F. Kiple. "Concepts of Cancer." In *The Cambridge World History of Human Disease.* Edited by Kenneth F. Kiple. New York, 1993. Pages 102–110.

Biraben, Jean-Noël. *Les hommes et la peste en France et dans les pays européens et méditerranéens.* Paris, 1975–1976.

Brandt, Allan M. "Acquired Immune Deficiency Syndrome (AIDS)." In *The Cambridge World History of Human Disease.* Edited by Kenneth F. Kiple. New York, 1993. Pages 547–551.

Carmichael, Ann G. *Plague and the Poor in Renaissance Florence.* New York and Cambridge, U.K., 1986.

Carmichael, Ann G., and Arthur M. Silverstein. "Smallpox in Europe before the Seventeenth Century: Virulent Killer or Benign Disease?" *Journal of the History of Medicine and Allied Sciences* 42 (1987): 147–168.

Carpenter, Kenneth J. *The History of Scurvy and Vitamin C.* New York, 1986.

Crosby, Alfred W. *Ecological Imperialism. The Biological Expansion of Europe, 900–1900.* New York, 1986.

Crosby, Alfred W. *Epidemic and Peace.* Westport, Conn., 1976.

Hayes, J. N. *The Burden of Disease.* New Brunswick, N.J., 1998.

Hirsch, August. *Handbook of Geographical and Historical Pathology.* Translated by Charles Creighton. 3 vol. London, 1883–1886.

Hopkins, Donald R. *Princes and Peasants: Smallpox in History.* Chicago, 1983.

Howell, Joel D. "Concepts of Heart-Related Diseases." In *The Cambridge World History of Human Disease.* Edited by Kenneth F. Kiple. New York, 1993. Pages 91–102.

Kiple, Kenneth F. *The Caribbean Slave: A Biological History.* New York and Cambridge, U.K., 1985.

Kiple, Kenneth F. "The History of Disease." In the *Cambridge Illustrated History of Medicine.* Edited by Roy Porter. Cambridge, U.K., 1996. Pages 16–51.

Kiple, Kenneth F. "Scrofula: The King's Evil and Struma Africana." In *Plague, Pox, and Pestilence.* Edited by Kenneth F. Kiple. London, 1997.

McKeown, Thomas. *The Modern Rise of Population.* New York, 1976.

McNeill, William H. *Plagues and Peoples.* Garden City, N.Y., 1976.

Matossian, Mary Kilbourne. *Poisons of the Past: Molds, Epidemics, and History.* New Haven, Conn., 1989.

Patterson, K. David. *Pandemic Influenza, 1700–1900: A Study in Historical Epidemiology.* Totowa, N.J., 1986.

Roe, Daphne A. *A Plague of Corn: The Social History of Pellagra.* Ithaca, N.Y., 1973.

Speck, Reinhard S. "Cholera." In *The Cambridge World History of Human Disease.* Edited by Kenneth F. Kiple. New York, Pages 642–649.

Wylie, John A. H., and Leslie H. Collier. "The English Sweating Sickness (*Sudor Anglicus*): A Reappraisal." *Journal of the History of Medicine and Allied Sciences* 36 (1981): 425–445.

Zinsser, Hans. *Rats, Lice, and History.* 1935. Reprint, New York, 1965.

DEATH

David G. Troyansky

Death is a phenomenon both universal and profoundly personal. Its history takes many forms. It may be written in terms of a familiar presence in people's lives, a series of catastrophes resulting from epidemics and wars, a challenge to be overcome by science and medicine, a private event giving meaning to life, and an occasion for religious or secular ritual. It is about humanity at its most vulnerable and life at its most meaningful—and meaningless. Approaches range from historical demography and family history to the history of disease, religion, and the state. Histories of death tell tales of horror, medical triumph, continuity and discontinuity of religious belief, and shifts in the relationships between individuals, families, and communities.

In the last three decades of the twentieth century, social historians and historical demographers contributed mightily to the body of knowledge on certain aspects of the history of death. Much of the quantitative work, illustrating a remarkable demographic triumph over mortality, is summarized in Jean-Pierre Bardet and Jacques Dupâquier's three-volume *Histoire des populations de l'Europe* (1997–1999), from which some of the demographic data in this essay is drawn. The field of the history of death, however, has been dominated by two French historians whose writings of the 1970s and early 1980s combined social and cultural history and remain the only European-wide overviews from the late Middle Ages to the contemporary era. The better-known work remains that of Philippe Ariès, but perhaps more influential among specialists, both in terms of argument and method, is the scholarship of Michel Vovelle. Ariès told a story of growing individualism and large-scale sociocultural change. Vovelle identified changes in mentalities associated fundamentally with secularization. Historians working in the 1980s and 1990s have developed variations on those themes. This essay addresses those fundamental works as well as the themes raised by a generation of social-historical scholarship. It first provides an overview of demographic knowledge of death since the Renaissance.

DEMOGRAPHY

The most notable demographic feature in the long history of death from the Renaissance to the twenty-first century is the reduction in mortality rates and the increase in life expectancy from birth. Death rates in sixteenth-century cities fluctuated around 35 to 46 per thousand, exceeding 100 in periods of epidemic disease. In 1996 the rate for most European countries was between 8 and 11 per thousand. The timing of the mortality change varied from place to place, but the most dramatic improvements occurred from 1880 to 2000. Some reduction in mortality was seen beginning in the eighteenth century, but even then rates of death fluctuated in a range that was reminiscent of medieval conditions; and in the contemporary period, for reasons that have to do with politics and warfare, it would be fair to say that Europe's history has been played out against a background of death.

Beginning in the 1340s the Black Death decimated the European population. Even a century later, Europe was without one third of its preplague population, having fallen from 73.5 million inhabitants in 1340 to 50 million in 1450. Plague mortality in England ranged from 35 to 40 percent. Its 1310 population of 6 million was not seen again until 1760. Cities were devastated. Hamburg lost 35 percent of its master bakers and 76 percent of its town councillors in the summer of 1350. Florence lost 60 percent of its population, Siena 50 percent. The population of Paris fell from 213,000 in 1328 to 100,000 in 1420–1423, that of Toulouse from 45,000 in 1335 to 19,000 in 1405. People fled the cities, but large areas of the countryside were touched as well. Upper Provence saw a 60 percent decline in numbers of households from 1344 to 1471; eastern Normandy lost 69 percent of its households from 1347 to the middle of the fifteenth century; and Navarre lost 70 percent from the 1340s to the 1420s. Most villages in some territories of the Holy Roman Empire were deserted.

Burial at Ornans. Painting (1849) by Gustave Courbet (1819–1877). MUSÉE D'ORSAY, PARIS/GIRAUDON/ART RESOURCE, NY

Population decline was actually multicausal, with increased mortality documented even before the arrival of the Black Death, but plague was terrifying, as it hit rich and poor, young and old. Historians disagree about the cultural impact of the Black Death. Some describe a religious turn, others document a release in sensuality, but the next wave of plague in the 1360s seems to have led to a morbid literary and visual culture. Fear led to assault on those considered "other," especially Jews. Survivors saw an increase in per capita wealth and a weakening of feudalism in western Europe. Some historians describe the plague as putting an end to a demographic and economic deadlock and forcing the renewal of intellectual and spiritual life.

Recovery began in the period 1420–1450 and was even more dramatic after 1500; but until the eighteenth century, plague was endemic in Europe, and it joined famine and warfare as a major cause of death. Several outbreaks decimated local populations and terrorized survivors. The 1651 plague in Barcelona was particularly well documented. Nonetheless, Europeans had learned a lesson from the Black Death and limited population growth to a generally manageable level. They lived in greater equilibrium with the environment than they had done in the late Middle Ages.

Such equilibrium did not rule out great demographic shocks. Early modern Europe was characterized by broad fluctuations in mortality due especially to epidemic disease. Mortality rates (per thousand) in England in the mid-sixteenth century provide a good example (Table 1). In the eighteenth century, fluctuations were less dramatic, and gradual improvement was evident in the nineteenth (Table 2). Famines still occurred in the early modern period (and as late as the 1840s in Ireland, and even later in Russia), but they tended to be local and often prompted by war. There was not a year without war in Europe from 1453 to 1730. The Wars of Religion of the sixteenth century and the Thirty Years' War (1618–1648) were particularly deadly, but even then more people died of disease than of battle wounds. Movement of troops across Europe spread disease with alarming speed and destroyed crops and homes. An army of fewer than ten thousand could cause more than a million deaths by plague.

Population growth stagnated during the various crises of the seventeenth century but then continued in a significant way after 1720. From 1400 to 1800 the European population tripled, from 60 to 180 million inhabitants. Indicative of that progress is the emergence of scientific thinking about mortality and life expectancy in the late seventeenth and eighteenth centuries. John Graunt and Edmund Halley in the seventeenth century and Nicolaas Struyck, Willem Kersseboom, and Antoine Deparcieux in the eighteenth were among the founders of the modern demographic study of mortality; their work gave the lie to the early modern truism, appearing in many testaments, that the moment of death is completely unpredictable.

aphic transition, or Vital
.orians describe it, life expec-
..ed from 25 to 35 years. It was
..rn and western Europe than southern
.urope. Until the eighteenth century, 40
.rcent of children did not reach the age of 5.
..s of survival varied geographically. In the 1750s
life expectancy at birth was 28.7 in France, 38.3 in
Sweden; the difference was narrower at age 10: 44.2
in France, 46.7 in Sweden. "National" figures, however, are misleading, as regional variation was striking.
Within France, among those born between 1690 and
1719, 61 percent of children in the southeast failed
to reach age 10, while the figure was only 46 percent
in the southwest. Mary Dobson (1997) finds great
mortality differences among southeastern English parishes separated only by ten miles and by elevations of
four and five hundred feet. Even as late as the 1870s,
infant mortality ranged from 72 per thousand in a

TABLE 1
MORTALITY RATES IN ENGLAND
(PER THOUSAND)

1555	25.8
1556	24.4
1557	42.5
1558	53.9
1559	47.3
1560	31.6
1561	25.9
1562	24.2
1563	34.6
1564	26.3
1565	23.7

Source: B. R. Mitchell, *British Historical Statistics* (Cambridge, U.K., and New York, 1988), p. 52.

FROM *A JOURNAL OF THE PLAGUE YEAR*

And as I have written above, God took our little girl the day after her mother's death. She was like an angel, with a doll's face, comely, cheerful, pacific, and quiet, who made everyone who knew her fall in love with her. And afterwards, within fifteen days, God took our older boy, who already worked and was a good sailor and who was to be my support when I grew older, but this was not up to me but to God who chose to take them all. God knows why He does what He does, He knows what is best for us. His will be done. Thus in less than a month there died my wife, our two older sons, and our little daughter. And I remained with four-year-old Gabrielo, who of them all had the most difficult character. And after all this was over I went with the boy in the midst of the great flight from the plague to Sarrià to the house of my mother-in-law. I kept quarantine there for almost two months, first in a hut and then in the house, and would not have returned so soon had it not been for the siege of Barcelona by the Castilian soldiers, which began in early August 1651.

James S. Amelang, ed. and trans. *A Journal of the Plague Year: The Diary of the Barcelona Tanner Miquel Parets, 1651.* New York, 1991, p. 71.

rural area of Norway to 449 per thousand in the most deadly districts of urban Bavaria.

During the demographic transition, the greatest shift in death rates concerned infants and children. The farming out of babies to wetnurses often had disastrous consequences. Among infants kept by their mothers, mortality was lower for those who were breast-fed than those who were fed by bottle, but the choice of method sometimes depended upon the mother's work environment or upon regional and cultural patterns that are still poorly understood. In the nineteenth century, central and northern German mothers tended to nurse, while Bavarians often had recourse to the bottle. Religion was one of the factors at work, and higher infant mortality rates were often found among southern European Catholic populations than among their northern European Protestant counterparts. Some historical demographers explain such divergences by positing a Catholic resignation about death and a more active Protestant, particularly Calvinist, pattern. But it would be hazardous to argue for such a simple explanation.

Differential mortality rates resulting from social inequality were greater in cities than in the countryside. They would be dramatic in the era of industrialization, but they were already visible in the early modern period. Table 3 illustrates life expectancy at

TABLE 2
MORTALITY RATES IN ENGLAND
(PER THOUSAND)

1700	27.9	1800	26.7
1710	26.4	1810	27.9
1720	32.4	1820	24.0
1730	36.2	1830	20.7
1740	31.1	1840	23.3
1750	27.5	1850	21.0
1760	26.4	1860	21.2
1770	28.6	1870	22.8
1780	29.0	1880	20.5
1790	25.8	1890	19.5

Source: B. R. Mitchell, *British Historical Statistics* (Cambridge, U.K., and New York, 1988), pp. 52–53, 57–58.

birth and at age thirty in Geneva according to the social status of the father.

Industrialization in the nineteenth century made cities even more dangerous, particularly for the laboring classes. Insalubrious living conditions, inadequate nutrition, and dangerous workplaces, combined with unprecedented concentrations of people, increased mortality rates for a generation or two. Among the Danish working classes in the period 1820–1849, mortality rates in Copenhagen were 230 per thousand, in provincial cities 160 per thousand, in rural regions 138 per thousand. But eventually municipal authorities, often with the collaboration of the medical profession, addressed problems of drinking water and sewage.

DISEASE

Historians have debated the causes of the demographic transition, from general improvement in health resulting from greater nutrition and resistance to infectious diseases to medicine and public health measures. Quarantining populations worked effectively in responding to plague. Environmental factors and more effective provisioning may have caused the early decline in mortality in the period 1750–1790. Greater decline occurred from 1790 to the 1830s and 1840s, when the smallpox vaccine, discovered by the English physician Edward Jenner in 1798, had an important impact. There followed a period of stagnation until the 1870s and 1880s, with dramatic changes coming from Louis Pasteur's research into infectious disease in the 1880s. Still, different parts of Europe were on different schedules. Western and central Europe saw progress in the early part of the century, southern Europe registered change by the middle of the century, and eastern Europe entered the transition around the end of the nineteenth century.

For Europe as a whole, 1895–1905 represented a great turning point in infant mortality. But causes of death still varied geographically. Southern Europe had many deaths from diarrhea and gastroenteritis. In industrialized England tuberculosis was the more pressing problem. Historians have offered both ecological and climatic explanations and socioeconomic ones for the timing of the mortality change. Lower temperatures seem to have encouraged lower mortality. The turn of the century saw a combination of better climatic conditions and improvement in public and private hygiene.

Causes of death shifted from infectious diseases to cardiovascular illness and cancer. The nineteenth century as a whole saw an epidemiological and sanitary transition. Plague was gone, smallpox was greatly reduced, and public health measures eventually dealt with epidemics of cholera, typhoid, measles, scarlet fever, diphtheria, whooping cough, and gastroenteritis. Cholera coming from Asia reached central and eastern Europe in late 1830 and early 1831. It continued west to Poland, Germany, Scandinavia, and

TABLE 3
LIFE EXPECTANCY AT BIRTH AND
AGE 30 BY SOCIAL CLASS IN GENEVA

Period of Marriage	Notables		Artisans		Workers	
	0	30	0	30	0	30
1625–1644	36.8	30.7	25.3	25.5	19.1	24.4
1650–1684	36.8	32.1	26.0	28.0	20.5	27.0
1687–1704	39.9	35.2	30.3	30.3	27.8	30.3
1725–1772	44.8	36.5	35.1	33.3	32.5	33.0

Source: Bardet and Dupâquier, vol. 1, p. 300.

Great Britain, reaching Belgium and France in early 1832 and southern Europe by 1833. More pandemics hit in 1848, 1865, and 1883. Intervention by public health officials protected cities by the late nineteenth century. The great exception was the cholera epidemic of 1892 in Hamburg, the destructiveness of which, killing almost ten thousand in about six weeks, was a result of the failure of the municipality to filter the city's water. As presented in Richard Evans's massive study (1987), it was a classic example of resistance by the business class to medical intervention. Cholera affected young and old more than adults. It was a shock to European opinion, as Europeans imagined they no longer had to fear epidemic disease. The quick progress of the disease and its high rates of mortality were terrifying, and the experience of 1892 indicated the importance of clean water and effective sewer systems.

A major triumph for medicine was the defeat of smallpox, a disease of childhood that was painful to behold. Mandatory vaccination had its impact, yet as one disease was conquered, another seemed to take its place. Tuberculosis, the most deadly epidemic disease in the nineteenth century, became endemic, with cases doubling in cities in the first half of the century. Curiously, the disease took on a fashionable image in the European upper and middle classes, who portrayed its victims, slowly wasting away, as romantic sufferers. The reality was greater incidence among the working classes and the poor, who lived in crowded conditions and suffered from poor nutrition. Suburbanization and improved nutrition probably helped reduce the incidence of the disease at the end of the nineteenth century.

THE TWENTIETH CENTURY: MASS DEATH AND A NEW VITAL REVOLUTION

The twentieth century began and ended with significant reductions in mortality. It might be said to constitute a second Vital Revolution, but the twentieth century also witnessed the death of 80 million Europeans as a result of war, deportation, famine, and extermination. World War I had at least 8 million victims, with another 2 million succumbing to the influenza epidemic of 1918–1919. World War II saw 43 million deaths in Europe and the Soviet Union, including 30 million civilians. The Soviet Union lost 26.6 million, 7.5 million of whom were soldiers. Poland lost 320,000 soldiers but 5.5 million civilians, including 2.8 million Jews. Germany lost 4.7 million people. The bloodletting was unprecedented, but declining mortality accelerated after the war. Progress was continuous in western Europe. In the east mortality rates actually went up after the collapse of communism.

Death took on a different meaning with the genocides of World War II. The ghettos, to which many Jews were confined, were already places of very high morbidity and mortality rates; then the Nazis moved to mass shootings and mass extermination by gas. Some 60 percent of Europe's Jews were killed. One third of the Roma (Gypsy) population was killed. The Eastern Front saw racial war, as 3.3 of 5.7 million Russians imprisoned by the Germans died in captivity. Central and Eastern Europe were more touched than the West. Poland lost 15 percent of its population. Whereas World War I had killed young men, World War II killed men and women of all ages.

Mass death—the influenza epidemic of 1918–1919, the Soviet famine of 1933, and, of course, the world wars—has been one of the major characteristics of the twentieth century. It was an essential part of the political processes of the era. The idea of the two world wars' constituting Europe's second Thirty Years' War brings to mind the way in which the events of 1618–1648 represented a major crisis in European history. The resolution of that war saw the achievement of stability and rationality. The resolution of the conflicts of 1914–1945, even if it took the rest of the century and a cold war, also represented the achievement of a kind of stability and, in the history of death, an unprecedented turn.

Mortality had declined in Europe since the eighteenth century, and the process accelerated in parts of Europe in the 1880s. The two postwar periods saw even greater progress, especially the antibiotic revolution after World War II. The most common age for dying was displaced. Death had always clustered in childhood and youth and then been fairly evenly distributed across the life course. By the second half of the twentieth century, it clustered in advanced age, and thus the image of death was transformed.

Life expectancies around 1900 still varied greatly from one part of Europe to another. Over the course of the twentieth century, they increased by 50 and even 100 percent, and by the end converged, for most of Europe, around ages in the late 70s and early 80s. Death rates were cut in half. Infant mortality fell from 190 per thousand in 1900 to 9 per thousand in 1996. Causes of death also changed. Respiratory infections were defeated by medicine, gastrointestinal ailments by public health measures, climatic change, and better nutrition. Tuberculosis had been a major killer of young people; it was surpassed after 1960 by violent death in traffic accidents. The emergence of AIDS proved that infectious disease was not thoroughly defeated.

It is clear that the medical triumph over death has left inequalities. Women's life expectancy continues to increase faster than men's. The female advantage, having disappeared completely for a time in some nineteenth-century cities, was 3 years in 1910, 5.1 years in 1960, and 8 years in 1995. Socioeconomic inequalities before death were noticeable in early modern cities but increased with industrialization. The spread of health insurance and public health measures reduced such inequality, but continued differences in standards of living, dietary habits, exercise, and the use of tobacco are among the factors encouraging inequality. Regional inequalities have evolved. At the start of the twentieth century, northwestern Europeans were used to living longer than southeastern Europeans, for the north and west had begun the sanitary transition relatively early. That distinction was reduced by 1960, but soon the major difference occurred between east and west, as life expectancy continued to increase in the west but stagnated in the east.

SOCIAL AND CULTURAL HISTORIES OF DEATH

The history of death requires measures of mortality, but numbers alone do not tell us how people faced death. The historical literature on death has examined a huge variety of sources and addressed a wide range of questions, from cultural representations and social attitudes to ritual, ceremony, and bedside practices. Ritual tends to resist change, but even traditional patterns undergo significant modifications over time and reveal social and cultural transformations.

Ariès's work on the history of death came after his influential history of childhood and before his project on the history of private life, and it shared a major concern of those works: an emphasis on individualism and its relationship to families and communities. He observed that contemporary European society, greatly influenced by developments in the United States, had increasingly serious problems dealing with death but could learn much from historical experience. He borrowed the English author Geoffrey Gorer's notion of the "pornography of death"—the idea that death replaced sex as the great taboo subject—and looked for the various ways premodern people seemed to face death more successfully. Of course, they had more experience with death, but for Ariès changes in mortality were not as important as changes in culture. In four essays (1974) that appeared before his magnum opus with individualism as his great theme, he laid out the argument that medieval and some fortunate modern people saw death as "tamed," something to be approached with equanimity and in public and to be managed comfortably by the dying individual surrounded by others. He used cultural representations of the deaths of knights and monks, along with an assortment of literary characters, to paint a picture of death as an event provoking little anxiety. Death then became less tame, and Ariès claimed that a new religiosity, beginning in the High Middle Ages but developing significantly in the era of the Reformation, encouraged a new focus on "one's own death."

Death, as Ariès saw it, came to be governed by religious concerns, by the struggle between God and the Devil, by a shift from a cultural focus on Final Judgment and the end of time to concern for the individual soul and its separation from the body. The cultural fascination with death prompted a widespread literature of the *ars moriendi* (art of dying). Guides for dying well proliferated in the sixteenth and seventeenth centuries and indicated a new sense of individual fear and responsibility. Out of that individualism emerged a concern for the death of loved ones, what Ariès called "thy death." It included an eroticization of death as early as the Renaissance, but it developed more fully and in a more secular fashion in the eighteenth and nineteenth centuries, especially in the culture of romanticism and a Victorian cult of death. A subsequent rejection of that cult followed, according to Ariès, and developed into a profound discomfort around reminders of mortality, the "forbidden death" that he thought marked the second half of the twentieth century.

Ariès's larger work employed the same basic argument as the four essays on death. Yet whereas the essays proceeded with elegant simplicity, the book amassed a weight of evidence demanding a more complicated structure. Archaeological sources, artistic, literary, religious, and philosophical representations, scientific and medical treatises, and sheer interpretive daring made *The Hour of Our Death* the benchmark against which subsequent works would be measured. Ariès's sometimes naive use of a limited sample of high cultural sources led him to propose cultural changes more dramatic than those subsequent scholars could identify, but his ideas have continued to appear in the scholarly literature.

Have people died comfortably or anxiously? Have they died alone or in public? Have they spent long periods of time in preparation for death? Have they been accompanied by religious or medical authorities? Have they been buried with great pomp or simplicity? Has the body been treated individually or buried in mass graves, the bones dug up and placed in ossuaries? All such questions sprang from the pages of his book, and his answers have served as hypotheses for subsequent historians of death.

BETWEEN RENAISSANCE AND ENLIGHTENMENT

The question of pomp versus simplicity and the related issue of secularization lay at the heart of Michel Vovelle's investigations into the history of death. His first major work (1973) was essentially a study of testaments in Provence in the seventeenth and eighteenth centuries. It took secularization or, as he put it, de-Christianization as its major theme and proposed a transition from a time of baroque piety to one of Enlightenment simplicity and secularism. It also represented a major methodological contribution to modern historiography, for it brought a "serial" method from social and economic history to the study of culture. Vovelle understood that Enlightenment thinkers doubted the received wisdom of religion and found medical and public health issues in the realm of death, but he wondered how far down in French and European society new ideas, beliefs, and practices might be found. The serial study of testaments permitted such analysis. The testament is a document that expresses religious faith and property concerns. Clauses invoking the Virgin Mary or the various saints went into decline, and religious bequests gave way to more secular directives, making the testament a more profane document in a world in which property took precedence over matters of the soul. By employing large numbers of wills that represented a broad area of Provence and a socially diverse population, Vovelle could trace the spread of new mentalities and social practices across space and time.

Vovelle had used archival traces of preparation for death to explore popular beliefs and practices, but his study of wills was limited to one part of southern France and one period, from the end of the Catholic Reformation to the end of the Old Regime. A literature developed concerning other times and places. Pierre Chaunu (1978) demonstrated a somewhat earlier cultural shift in Paris, Bernard Vogler (1978) explored differences between Catholics and Protestants in Alsace, and Jacques Chiffoleau (1980) discovered significant changes in the uses of wills in Papal territories in southern France in the late Middle Ages. Chiffoleau identified the creation of the culture of death that Vovelle saw unraveling. In other words, he wrote of the Christianization of death, describing residents of Avignon who, cut off from traditional village solidarities and family lineages, forged new ways of dealing with death. Against a background of devel-

FROM THE WILL OF A SIXTEENTH-CENTURY SPANISH NOBLEMAN

I, Don Martín Cortés, Marquis of the Valley of Guaxaca, residing in this city of Madrid, beset by infirmities and lacking in health, but unaffected in my intellect, fearing that since death is a certainty but its hour an uncertainty, I might be taken while I am unprepared in those things that are necessary for salvation, and wishing to make perfectly clear to my wife and children how they are to inherit my belongings, so that there will be no discord or quarreling among them, do hereby order and execute this my last will and testament in the following manner.

Quoted in Eire, p. 19.

oping trade and urban growth, people of Avignon spent their wealth on "flamboyant" funerals and religious bequests, the cultural practices that Ariès had called "one's own death." The most ambitious work on testaments was undertaken by Samuel Cohn, who in one book (1988) traced them over the course of six hundred years (1205–1800) in the city of Siena, finding dramatic changes in attitudes and practices, and in another (1992) compared testamentary practices in six Italian cities from the twelfth century to the fifteenth. In the Siena study, Cohn found late medieval testators dividing their wealth among pious causes, practicing a selfless religious devotion in preparation for death, until the second wave of plague in the fourteenth century, when they concentrated their donations and made long-term demands of their heirs. The dying were using their wealth to make a lasting impact on earth. Late Renaissance donations turned secular and familial, and subsequent Counter-Reformation and Enlightenment-era trends corresponded with some of Vovelle's findings. Vovelle's use of serial sources was also taken up by his own students, including Bernard Cousin (1983), who studied votice paintings of life-threatening events.

Critics of Vovelle, including Ariès, argued that he may have mistaken privatization of religious belief and practice for full-blown de-Christianization. Vovelle supplemented his work on long-term change with a study of de-Christianization in the French Revolution. He demonstrated the importance of sudden

Christianization of Death. *Funeral Procession at the Door of the Church.* Anonymous French engraving, eighteenth century. PRIVATE COLLECTION/THE BRIDGEMAN ART LIBRARY

death and political death, and other scholars have followed that path. In his own synthetic study of death since the late Middle Ages, Vovelle offered a picture that was somewhat more complicated and more careful than that of Ariès, but, unlike the latter, it never had great impact on the broader public, perhaps because it never appeared in English translation. Both synthetic works told a story of secularization and individualism, but subsequent scholarship recognized no simple transition from medieval to modern attitudes.

The study of testaments was one approach to the topic of religion and death. Historians have also looked at the twists and turns of religious ritual, the idea of death as a rite of passage, and the ways in which Europeans faced death, disposed of the dead, and mourned. Some of those practices had to do with religious doctrine. Even during times when much evidence indicates change in religious attitudes, traditional religious practices provided solace.

Most Europeans for most of the period approached death with an arsenal of Christian ideas, beginning with the notion that death was the consequence of original sin. They learned to expect a separation between body and soul, to prepare for an individual judgment, and to hope for Final Judgment at the end of time. Catholics were encouraged to see the time before death as a trial, and the last rites, including prayer, anointing with oil, the administering of Communion (the viaticum), and the commen-

dation of the soul, were essential parts of the process. Multiple editions of the *Ars moriendi* warned against the five temptations of the dying: unbelief, despair, impatience, spiritual pride, and excessive attachment to things of this world. Illustrations show competition between terrifying devils and an inspiring Christ. The passage from life to death involved changing patterns of emotional and financial investment by family and ritual behavior by community. Sharon Strocchia's study (1992) of Renaissance Florence described a double agenda for the death ritual, which recognized the honor of individuals and families, distinguishing them from others, and the need to reaffirm the community's sense of order. The funeral was the setting for demonstrating an individual's or family's power and status; the funeral procession demonstrated and legitimated the city's social hierarchy. Their increasing flamboyance revealed competition among old and new elites. On the other hand, the requiem was designed to bring people together. It affirmed communal and spiritual ties, as friends, neighbors, coworkers, kin, and public officials joined together in commemorating the dead.

The flamboyance of Renaissance funerals had social and political functions, but the culture of death evolved in religious contexts. Charitable bequests, processions, masses, and prayers eased the journey of the soul in Catholic Europe, as the actions of the living were thought to shorten the stay in purgatory and encourage the passage to heaven. Carlos Eire's book on sixteenth-century Madrid (1995) is the most detailed study of the testament, of ways of approaching death, and of cultural models for dying. Eire described how, when someone was thought to be dying, the notary and priest would be called for, kin and neighbors would arrive to help the dying person, and members of religious confraternities would attend. All those participants would help the dying person in the final battle. The testament itself narrates a process of identification before God and one's neighbors, supplication, meditations on death and judgment, profession of faith, deliverance into God's hands, and then instructions concerning the disposing of the body, the saving of the soul, and the dividing up of the estate. In sixteenth-century Madrid one was buried in a parish church, a monastery chapel, or occasionally a cloister. Clergy to be buried wore their religious garb, but so did many in the laity. The Franciscan habit was the most popular item of clothing for the dead laity in Madrid. Some even wore two habits and called explicitly for the advocacy of Francis. Early in the century the vast majority of testators provided detailed instructions for the funeral. Later many left the planning to their executors. A similar evolution had occurred a century earlier in Valladolid, and it might be interpreted as an increased codification of ritual by status rather than a loss of interest. The funeral procession began with the clergy; the coffin followed, with family, friends, and acquaintances next, and the poor and orphans, who were paid for their trouble, taking up the rear. Processions became more elaborate over the century; in the second half large numbers of mendicant friars joined the cortege, and participation by confraternities grew. Demands for masses in perpetuity (literally forever) increased as well. Eire concludes that people of Madrid pawned their earthly wealth to shorten their stay in purgatory.

Eire also presented two elite models of Catholic death: Philip II (1527–1598) and Teresa of Ávila (1515–1582). Philip, who built the Escorial as his place of death and as a gathering place for religious relics, taught a lesson in how to die. His was a slow, painful death, one that demonstrated publicly that even a king could not escape mortality; it affirmed also the centrality of the sacred in public life in Catholic Spain. The saintly paradigm was even more important than the royal one, and Saint Teresa of Ávila became the great exemplar of Counter-Reformation death. As a mystic she combined ecstasy and death. Her body after death was said to have become smooth as that of a child and to emit a healing fragrance. The buried body was associated with miracles. After nine months it was dug up and described as uncorrupted. But it was then cut up and parceled out for relics and

the continued working of miracles. As the example of Saint Teresa suggests, Catholic approaches to death had grown more intense during a time when the Church was being challenged by Protestantism.

PROTESTANT DEATH

Protestantism rejected the Catholic emphasis on the last hours—the outcome had already been decided—but important elements of the "good death" carried over. Preparations mattered, and the behavior of the dying might indicate where the soul was headed, but confession, absolution, and extreme unction disappeared. The Protestant on his or her deathbed played an active role, offering good advice to family and demonstrating acceptance of the inevitable. The good death survived as a familial event for the bereaved. The Protestant Reformation, by eliminating purgatory, whose existence Martin Luther denied in 1530, focused attention on the faith of the dying individual and the grace of God, and Protestant thinkers claimed that the passage to heaven was immediate. It called into question and indeed placed limits on efforts by the living to intercede. Prayers for the dead would be of no use.

Such a dramatic change in doctrine had major repercussions for the ways in which people behaved when in mourning. As described in Craig Koslofsky's study (2000) of early modern Germany, a separation was made between the living and the dead both in terms of the decline of purgatory and the relegation of cemeteries to less populated areas. That process had to do with interpretation of doctrine but also the practical problems of residing in growing cities. The rejection of Catholic tradition, which Luther described as trickery, did not automatically result in the elaboration of a Protestant model. Radical Reformers buried their dead with utter simplicity, but Lutherans developed a new ritual that eventually included communal processions, funeral hymns, and honorable burial in a communal cemetery rather than a churchyard. Funeral sermons became the central element by 1550. Religious and secular authorities valued the use of ceremony to reinforce social hierarchies. Burial at night, reserved for criminals, suicides, or dishonorable people, or any burial without the participation of pastor and community was seen as irreligious. The possibility of denying Christian burial meant an emphasis on the individual's relationship to the living rather than to the dead. The sermon was the occasion to use the dead to honor the living.

The Lutheran model did not hold for all Protestants. Lutherans and Calvinists battled over matters of ritual, and by the late seventeenth century Lutheran nobles opted for nocturnal interment, which now was seen as honorable, and by candle-lit processions. Pietism and the preference for private devotion provided a context in which non-noble people also participated in nocturnal burial, which remained a common way of dealing with death throughout the eighteenth century. When daylight funerals once again became common in Germany, they retained a private, familial nature.

David Cressy (1997) has demonstrated that in England men and women maintained long-standing death rituals long after the Reformation. Traditional ways of dealing with the dead, such as sprinkling with holy water, wakes, the ringing of bells, and elaborate processions, continued in some parts of Protestant England into the seventeenth century; but vestiges of Catholic practice began to be seen as heathen superstition, and memories of purgatory may have survived in the form of belief in ghosts. Elaborate ceremony certainly continued, as the wealthy dressed and coffined their dead in more ostentatious fashion, but it may have been a necessary substitute for the older actions on behalf of the soul. What had previously been done for the dead had obviously functioned effectively for the grieving. The proliferation of individual graves provided new sites for such activities. Inscriptions had more to do with earthly memory than with old beliefs in resurrection. The era of the Protestant Reformation saw a separation of life-course ritual from participation by the entire community, an assertion of privacy. Ralph Houlbrooke's study (1998) of early modern English death demonstrated that family and neighbors replaced clergymen at the deathbed and, as ritual support diminished, had more to do. Some traditional practices, including of course rites and gestures associated with belief in purgatory, were strongly reaffirmed in Catholic Europe, but even there elites gradually moved away from a public culture of death. The poor were no longer invited. In the seventeenth and eighteenth centuries, communal care for the dead in some places even began to give way to the professional services of undertakers, although their dominance would not come until the nineteenth century.

ENLIGHTENMENT

Seventeenth-century thought played on fears of damnation, but belief in hell fell into decline among significant numbers of Catholics as well as Protestants. In the eighteenth century, Enlightenment thinkers sought a non-Christian way of dying and ridiculed

their fellows who opted at the last minute for a Christian exit. Stories circulated of the deaths of philosophes, the French Enlightenment thinkers and writers; Voltaire's managing to die (in 1778) "in the Catholic religion" but not of it and not as a Christian represented an Enlightenment triumph. Form and dignity mattered; serenity and the metaphor of sleep replaced the agony of the religious death; in response to the question of whether he recognized the divinity of Jesus Christ, Voltaire said, "Let me die in peace." Belief in a non-Christian Supreme Being, the emergence of a protoromantic cult of melancholy, the development of more secular funerary sculpture, and public health concerns about overcrowded urban cemeteries led to new ways of thinking about death. The pilgrimage to the tomb was itself an important activity even as faith in reunion after death was shaken. A late-eighteenth-century cult of death encompassed deists, agnostics, and Christians.

Posterity, an earthly form of immortality, replaced heaven in much Enlightenment thought. Practical contributions to society and expressions of public virtue would yield a post-Christian form of immortality. Serving the nation or even humanity became the new ideal. Late Enlightenment and French Revolutionary funereal architecture, with its neoclassical plans and structures, embodied a secular and often nationalized way of death. The draped urn, the willow, the broken column, and the veiled mourner were all part of the neoclassical vocabulary of death. Secular ceremonies honoring revolutionary martyrs replaced Christian practices in the 1790s; hymns, processions, and eulogies emphasized civic virtue rather than Christian spirituality. The citizen's political death provided a new model for a republican public.

THE NINETEENTH CENTURY

Secularization was hardly complete. High cultural sources indicate a Romantic turn that involved a good deal of spirituality. Sentiment and sorrow replaced the serenity of the previous period. New levels of attention were devoted to grief and to mourning rituals. Romantic burial grounds and a literature evoking them provided an alternative to the neoclassicism of the eighteenth century. The afterlife made a comeback, but the new emphasis was on a heaven where loving families would reconstitute themselves. Religious and secular beliefs and ritual combined in the nineteenth century. Alternative cults of the dead proliferated; their creators included the liberals Victor Cousin and Charles-Bernard Renouvier and the socialists Charles Fourier and Pierre Leroux. Less po-

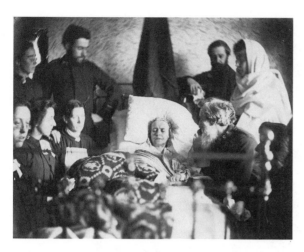

Victorian Deathbed. William Booth, founder of the Salvation Army, at the deathbed of his wife, Catherine Booth (1829–1890). ©HULTON-DEUTCH COLLECTION/CORBIS

litical but equally mainstream was the spiritism of Allan Kardec and Camille Flammarion, encouraging communication between the living and the dead. Spiritism, like the occult more generally in Europe, was largely a middle-class phenomenon, a response to the decline of formal religious practice and an expression of enthusiastic hopes for science.

A focus on the legacy of the Enlightenment, on declining church attendance, and on movements toward separation of church and state may lead one to disregard the survival of religious practices for the majority, particularly when marking life-course events. In Victorian England, a continuity can be detected until the 1870s in the Evangelical style of dealing with death, which perpetuated the notion of the good death but added great intensity in the expression of grief. But there was already a good deal of secular influence. Throughout Europe the doctor played a more important role at the bedside. His administration of opiates eased the passage. The doctor's bedside presence in nineteenth-century votive paintings demonstrates his intervention in even the most devout Catholic contexts. Large suburban cemeteries took the burial ceremony away from the churchyard and into secular space. The cemeteries came to resemble cities of their own, with streets, alleys, and addresses. Burials increasingly fell into the hands of commercial enterprises.

When twentieth-century Europeans looked back at the nineteenth century, they criticized what they took to be elaborate Victorian rituals of death. They assumed that what appeared to be excessive mourning by Queen Victoria for Prince Albert was considered normal by her contemporaries. Scholarship of the 1990s calls that assumption into question. Victoria was, in fact, criticized for excessive mourning; her own subjects saw her as depressed. But formal mourning practices, rules, and schedules certainly were important in Victorian society. In France widows mourned for a year and six weeks in Paris, two years in the provinces; men mourned six months in Paris, a year in the provinces. Fashionable widows spent the first months in the black woolen dress, hood, and veil of high mourning, the next stage in black silk, and the last in alternate colors. In high society mourners wrote on black-bordered paper, widows continuing the practice until remarriage or death.

THE TWENTIETH CENTURY

Nineteenth-century formality was already giving way before World War I, but the mass slaughter that ensued transformed the setting if not the content of the cult of death. The difficulty of finding bodies and, once found, of transporting them raised practical problems. Bereavement in some ways became more difficult, and recovery from a loved one's death was seemingly more challenging. Such developments occurred across Europe, and in every country monuments sprang up quickly. Monuments to the war dead placed local contributions within a national narrative, and the key to their success was the listing of names. Whereas previously war memorials had honored rulers and officers, now they were democratized. Veterans' groups were often heavily involved, thus taking some responsibilities out of the hands of families. Sometimes local sculptors crafted original monuments, but most towns and villages opted for mass-produced works which they ordered out of catalogs. In some cases the meaning of memorials was contrary to the received wisdom. Among a few small pacifist monuments that stand in rural France, one shows a schoolboy in Gentioux with raised fist and the inscription, "Cursed be war." But most monuments of that era represent the soldier or an allegorical female embodying the nation.

World War II called for further commemoration of mass death, but the working out of memory and the design of monuments were in some ways more difficult. Death in the Holocaust, in particular, was long described as unrepresentable. Yet as survivors reached old age at the end of the century, efforts were made to collect their stories, to encourage them to speak, and to create monuments and memorials not only in Europe but in countries all over the world. Commemorating the deaths of those who fought in colonial and postcolonial wars involving Europeans

Twentieth-Century Funeral. *Funeral in Agunnarud, Småland* (Sweden), painting (1969) by Sven Hagman. NORDISKA MUSEET, STOCKHOLM/THE BRIDGEMAN ART LIBRARY

also took some time. In France, the Algerian War of Independence (1954–1962) began to be memorialized in a serious way that recognized French defeat and Algerian victory only in the 1990s.

After World War II, European countries moved against the death penalty. The Nuremburg tribunals in the war's immediate aftermath resulted in the executions of Nazi war criminals. But 1948 saw the adoption of the Universal Declaration of Human Rights, which proclaimed a right to life. Although the declaration did not explicitly call for the outlawing of the death penalty, it served as the basis for a series of international covenants. The death penalty was abolished in Italy in 1948, in West Germany in 1949, in Britain in 1965, and in France in 1981. In 1989 the European Parliament adopted a Declaration of Fundamental Rights and Freedoms, which announced the abolition of the death penalty.

The post–World War II period also saw the transformation of the cultures of death in the most traditional regions of rural Europe. In Brittany Catholic ceremony and Breton folklore coexisted with modern individualism. Until the 1960s traditional notions of purgatory predominated, mourning was still a communal experience, and supernatural connections between the living and the dead were central to people's worldviews. But by the end of the century,

even Brittany participated in the more general "denial of death."

In the twentieth century people chose alternative methods to the traditional disposal of the body by burial. By the latter part of the century, 72 percent of English people in 1998 opted for cremation. For some religious and ethnic minorities that choice was more difficult to make, as it raised the question of assimilation. Some immigrant communities also engaged in reflection on the meaning of being buried in Europe rather than in their countries of origin. Generations born in Europe questioned their elders' attachments.

SUICIDE AND EUTHANASIA

Suicide and euthanasia, specialized themes in the history of death, offer perspectives on the processes of secularization and medicalization. In English the word for suicide did not exist until the seventeenth century. Until then the act was called self-murder, and those who committed it were assumed to be criminals, madmen, and sinners. Suicide was an affront both to God and to the social order. Suicides were tried posthumously, their property was forfeited, and their bodies, denied Christian burial, were buried away from the community. In England suicides were buried face-down with wooden stakes driven through them so as to prevent their ghosts from wandering. The incidence of suicide is difficult to measure, but it has elicited scholarly interest during the Renaissance and serious investigation during the Enlightenment. The Renaissance saw the revival of classical cases of elite suicide. Taking one's own life could be construed as an act of freedom. Literary representations of suicide proliferated in the period 1580–1620, notably in the 1600 example of *Hamlet*. Seventeenth-century thinkers tried to repress the practice, but the numbers seem to have been fairly constant. By the late seventeenth century, as officials and the public grew more sympathetic, attitudes toward suicide had begun to change; evidence suggests that in England after 1750 suicide was seen not as diabolical but as the result of mental illness. Coroners' juries increasingly refused to punish severely; where they did convict, they undervalued self-murderers' goods. Among Enlightenment thinkers, the right to commit the act was supported by those favoring individual liberty, but the fact of suicide was seen as an attack on social solidarity. Although the French Revolution decriminalized the act and Romantic suicide in the wake of Goethe's *Sorrows of Young Werther* (1774) gave it some cachet, Enlightenment ambivalence toward it continued. Self-sacrifice for political reasons might be seen as an ideal or, alternatively, as an act of cowardice. In the first half of the nineteenth century, suicide became less a philosophical subject than a social scientific one. The practice, of course, continued, but by the second half of the twentieth century attempted suicides were seen as calls for medical help, not acts requiring legal responses.

Euthanasia represents a related phenomenon. It originally meant a gentle death, such as that which may be the desire of suicides seeking to end unendurable pain. Since the work of the English philosopher Francis Bacon in the seventeenth century, the assumption has been that euthanasia, as the alleviation of the suffering of the dying, must be administered only by a doctor, although doctors have ethical obligations not to end life. Beliefs about euthanasia began to change in the 1890s, when Adolf Jost wrote of voluntary euthanasia (a right to die) and the idea of negative human worth. In 1920 Karl Binding, a professor of jurisprudence, and Alfred Hoche, a professor of psychiatry, developed the idea of "life unworthy of life." What began as a discussion of psychiatric reform in line with cost-effectiveness ended up as a program for the killing of the mentally and physically handicapped. Euthanasia came to be seen as a eugenic method for "improving" the population and eliminating those deemed unworthy of life. The early euthanasia program in Nazi Germany focused on the young. In 1940–1941 70,273 people were killed, many in gas chambers. Some of the killers would soon use the same methods on the Jews of Europe.

Postwar opinion recoiled at the crimes of the Nazis. Yet as long life became the norm in subsequent generations, and the incidence of degenerative diseases in old age increased, doctors and patients returned to the issue of mercy killing. Questions of the withholding of medical care that would prolong the lives of the terminally ill accompanied debates over medical coverage in the world of the welfare state. Rationing of medical care and notions about the overconsumption of medicines were on the public agenda in the turn to neoliberalism in the 1980s and 1990s.

CONCLUSION

The contributions of social history have challenged the understanding of changes and continuities in the experience of death. It is not always easy to pinpoint the relationship between physical and cultural change. For example, nineteenth-century grief, particularly over the death of children, may have contributed to greater attention to measures designed to reduce mortality levels; but shifts in mortality levels affected attitudes toward death and mourning practices in turn.

The history of death is about the present as much as it is about the past. It permits us to address painful issues at a distance. Yet clearly those issues are not in fact all that distant. Some historians seem to be looking for a better way of dying and dealing with uncertainty. In that spirit, the German historian Arthur Imhof (1996) turned from historical demography to the kinds of cultural and religious questions raised by Ariès. He asked why life had become so difficult despite a dramatic medical triumph over death, and devised a chart that illustrated the history of life expectancy as a decline from hope of heavenly immortality to knowledge of earthly mortality. Like Ariès, he claimed that as Europeans have conquered death, they have lost the ability to deal with it. For example, the response to the death of Diana, Princess of Wales, on 31 August 1997 prompted studies of the hunt for new ways of mourning. In that case, mass mourning became a media event and vice versa, as multicultural mourners, in the role of both participants and spectators, explored new ceremonies and rituals. Death was far from hidden, and the ways in which media death might influence ordinary Europeans' approach to dying remained to be seen.

See also other articles in this section.

BIBLIOGRAPHY

Anderson, Olive. *Suicide in Victorian and Edwardian England.* Oxford and New York, 1987.

Ariès, Philippe. *The Hour of Our Death.* Translated by Helen Weaver. New York, 1981.

Ariès, Philippe. *Images of Man and Death.* Translated by Janet Lloyd. Cambridge, Mass., 1985.

Ariès, Philippe. *Western Attitudes toward Death: From the Middle Ages to the Present.* Translated by Patricia M. Ranum. Baltimore, 1974.

Badone, Ellen. *The Appointed Hour: Death, Worldview, and Social Change in Brittany.* Berkeley, Calif., 1989.

Bardet, Jean-Pierre, Patrice Bourdelais, Pierre Guillaume, et al. *Peurs et terreurs face à la contagion: Choléra, tuberculose, syphilis: XIXe–XXe siècles.* Paris, 1988.

Bardet, Jean-Pierre, and Jacques Dupâquier, eds. *Histoire des populations de l'Europe.* 3 vols. Paris, 1997–1999.

Burleigh, Michael. *Death and Deliverance: "Euthanasia" in Germany, c. 1900–1945.* Cambridge, U.K., and New York, 1994.

Chaunu, Pierre. *La mort à Paris: XVIe, XVIIe, et XVIIIe siècles.* Paris, 1978.

Chiffoleau, Jacques. *La comptabilité de l'au-delà: Les hommes, la mort et la religion dans la région d'Avignon à la fin du Moyen Âge (vers 1320–vers 1480).* Rome and Paris, 1980.

Cohn, Samuel K., Jr. *The Cult of Remembrance and the Black Death: Six Renaissance Cities in Central Italy.* Baltimore, 1992.

Cohn, Samuel K., Jr. *Death and Property in Siena, 1205–1800: Strategies for the Afterlife.* Baltimore, 1988.

Cousin, Bernard. *Le miracle et le quotidien: Les ex-voto provençaux, images d'une société.* Aix-en-Provence, 1983.

Cressy, David. *Birth, Marriage, and Death: Ritual, Religion, and the Life-Cycle in Tudor and Stuart England.* Oxford, 1997.

Dobson, Mary J. *Contours of Death and Disease in Early Modern England.* Cambridge, U.K., and New York, 1997.

Eire, Carlos M. N. *From Madrid to Purgatory: The Art and Craft of Dying in Sixteenth-Century Spain.* Cambridge, U.K., and New York, 1995.

Etlin, Richard A. *The Architecture of Death: The Transformation of the Cemetery in Eighteenth-Century Paris.* Cambridge, Mass., 1984.

Evans, Richard J. *Death in Hamburg: Society and Politics in the Cholera Years, 1830–1910.* Oxford and New York, 1987.

Gillis, John R., ed. *Commemorations: The Politics of National Identity.* Princeton, N.J., 1994.

Houlbrooke, Ralph. *Death, Religion, and the Family in England, 1480–1750.* Oxford and New York, 1998.

Imhof, Arthur E. *Lost Worlds: How Our European Ancestors Coped with Everyday Life and Why Life Is So Hard Today.* Translated by Thomas Robisheaux. Charlottesville, Va., 1996.

Jalland, Pat. *Death in the Victorian Family.* Oxford and New York, 1996.

Jupp, Peter C., and Clare Gittings, eds. *Death in England: An Illustrated History.* New Brunswick, N.J., 2000.

Jupp, Peter C., and Glennys Howarth, eds. *The Changing Face of Death: Historical Accounts of Death and Disposal.* New York, 1997.

Kear, Adrian, and Deborah Lynn Steinberg, eds. *Mourning Diana: Nation, Culture, and the Performance of Grief.* London and New York, 1999.

Koslofsky, Craig M. *The Reformation of the Dead: Death and Ritual in Early Modern Germany, 1450–1700.* New York, 2000.

Kselman, Thomas A. *Death and the Afterlife in Modern France.* Princeton, N.J., 1993.

Lebrun, François. *Les hommes et la mort en Anjou aux 17e et 18e siècles: Essai de démographie et de psychologie historiques.* Paris, 1971.

MacDonald, Michael, and Terence R. Murphy. *Sleepless Souls: Suicide in Early Modern England.* Oxford and New York, 1990.

McDannell, Colleen, and Bernhard Lang. *Heaven: A History.* New Haven, Conn., and London, 1988.

McManners, John. *Death and the Enlightenment: Changing Attitudes to Death among Christians and Unbelievers in Eighteenth-Century France.* Oxford and New York, 1981.

Minois, Georges. *History of Suicide: Voluntary Death in Western Culture.* Translated by Lydia G. Cochrane. Baltimore, 1999.

Schofield, Roger, David Reher, and Alain Bideau, eds. *The Decline of Mortality in Europe.* Oxford and New York, 1991.

Strocchia, Sharon T. *Death and Ritual in Renaissance Florence.* Baltimore, 1992.

Vogler, Bernard, ed. *Les testaments strasbourgeois au XVIIIe siècle: Textes et documents de M. M. Mager, M. Pierron et B. Spor.* Strasburg, France, 1978.

Vovelle, Michel. *La mort et l'Occident: De 1300 à nos jours.* Paris, 1983.

Vovelle, Michel. *Piété baroque et déchristianisation en Provence au XVIIIe siècle: Les attitudes devant la mort d'après les clauses des testaments.* Paris, 1973.

Walker, D. P. *The Decline of Hell: Seventeenth-Century Discussions of Eternal Torment.* Chicago, 1964.

Whaley, Joachim, ed. *Mirrors of Mortality: Studies in the Social History of Death.* New York, 1982.

Woods, Robert, and Nicola Shelton. *An Atlas of Victorian Mortality.* Liverpool, U.K., 1997.

Section 7

CITIES AND URBANIZATION

URBANIZATION

Alexander Cowan

The key to much of the social change experienced in Europe between the Renaissance and the present lies in the process of urbanization. This may be defined in three separate but linked ways. It is the process by which individual urban centers grew larger, both in terms of numbers of inhabitants, and in terms of the total space occupied. Secondly, urbanization is the process by which the proportion of the population of a given region engaged in urban economic activities and living in urban centers increases. Lastly, it is the process by which the urban becomes the dominant feature of all landscapes: physical, economic, political, social, and cultural.

The process of European urbanization was neither new in the sixteenth century nor did it progress at the same rate and in the same way in every part of Europe. Much depended on economic and demographic change, and on the size, character, and location of individual urban centers. Some general trends can be identified. By contrast with conditions in 1500, when a relatively small proportion of the European population lived in urban centers and carried out activities that were identifiably urban (with the exception of northern and central Italy and the Netherlands), the map of Europe at the end of the twentieth century was dominated by networks of urban centers, whose collective populations represented a high proportion of the continent's total inhabitants. Most of this change had taken place since the middle of the nineteenth century and was linked in some way with the economic growth associated with industrialization.

Since the middle of the twentieth century, however, two developments may be said to have signaled the end of the urbanization process in the classic sense. The first is the development of metropolitan areas. These were first seen around the great European capital cities, London, Paris, and Berlin, toward the end of the nineteenth century, but later came to characterize whole regions, within which individual urban centers close to each other expanded to such a degree that their economic functions, and sometimes even their individual identities, merged to become part of a greater urban whole. The Ruhr valley in Germany, the agglomeration around Lille-Roubaix-Tourcoing in France, and the region based on the Rivers Tyne and Wear in the northeast of England all exemplify this trend.

The second development is associated with the first and may be called de-urbanization. This process is a form of reversal of the urban growth of earlier periods, which had taken place in the form of an expansion of the urban core within a rural context. De-urbanization, by contrast, places the focus on the simultaneous expansion of urban housing and economic activity in a number of locations that are related to the old urban center but are no longer part of it. Suburbs, industrial estates, science parks, and new out-of-town shopping centers designed to meet demand from regional customers with their own transport have all changed the role of the classic urban center. Population figures for the urban core have signaled a downturn, while those for the outer suburbs continue to rise. Between 1921 and 1931, the population of Paris fell from 3 million to 2.89 million. It is now more appropriate to refer to an urbanized society rather than to urban society, and for this reason, this article will focus largely on the period between the Renaissance and the middle of the twentieth century.

Social historians have approached the urbanization process in several different ways. Many have chosen to emphasize a break between the premodern and the modern urban center, brought about by industrialization. In these terms, all sense of community was lost when the majority of the urban population was subjected to the disciplines of capitalism, the scale of the urban area had grown to such an extent that it was no longer possible to conceive of the town as a single entity, and the leadership of the social elite and organized religion no longer exercised a strong influence over townspeople. Others have sought to identify the aspects of urban society that have persisted in spite of changes in the scale and organization of industrial production, particularly in their exploration of changes in urban culture.

Some of these contrasting approaches may be explained by the comparative speed with which industrialization affected urban centers in different parts of Europe. It began intensively in Britain and the Low Countries at the turn of the eighteenth century, extended more slowly to France and Germany during the nineteenth century, and reached Italy, Spain and central Europe only toward the end of the 1800s. As a result, changes to social organization, social interaction, and the use of space in individual urban centers varied according to the size of the population, the scale and timing of economic and political pressures, whether or not a center carried out a specialized rather than a generalized urban function, and where a particular center belonged within its regional hierarchy. In many urban centers, some of which had been at the forefront of economic development between the fifteenth and the eighteenth centuries, little changed in terms of their size, their use of space, and their prevailing architectural appearance until the later twentieth century or until they experienced extensive damage during World War II. They had been left to one side by industrialization.

THE URBAN CENTER
IN A BROADER CONTEXT:
NETWORKS AND SPECIALIZATION

The organization of any urban society is shaped by the size of the urban center and by its role within a wider urban network. This applied as much to the twentieth century as it did to the sixteenth, with two important differences. The first is one of scale. A small town in the 1500s could have a population as low as two thousand or less, but, like the Sicilian town of Gangi, still house a range of artisans, shopkeepers, rentiers, and merchants, all of whom provided the basic elements of industrial production and commercial exchange necessary to define it as an urban center. A modern equivalent, Carpentras, in the south of France, with twenty-four thousand inhabitants in the late twentieth century, may have been many times larger but offered little more in terms of economic functions. The same contrasts of scale can be seen by comparing Venice (190,000 at the end of the sixteenth century), with Birmingham, at present England's second city (roughly 1 million in 1991). In terms of its economic complexity, and still more of its international cultural importance, Venice ranks far higher than Birmingham, but on a much smaller demographic base.

The second difference in context relates to the organization of urban networks. All urban centers in premodern Europe were part of urban networks, usually local or regional. Within these networks, towns were placed in a hierarchy, usually determined by their size, the complexity of their economic activity, and their distance from other centers of similar size. Towns at the head of regional networks belonged in turn to looser collections of international trading centers through which they exported and imported goods, money, ideas, and people. They were the intermediaries between the rural hinterland, the population of smaller towns, and other parts of Europe and beyond. The role of hierarchies and networks differed little in the twentieth century, except for their scale, now worldwide, the speed of communications, and the size of urban hierarchies, which often extended far beyond the traditional region across national boundaries. Differences in the quality of facilities and the range of opportunities within these groupings remained.

The experience of individual towns was also shaped by specialization levels. While commercial exchange, supported by some industrial production, remained the raison d'être for all urban centers throughout the period, many towns belonged to specific categories, which, at different times, contributed to their rapid growth or stagnation, and by requiring particular kinds of labor force not only engendered particular kinds of elites, but also gave a specific character to their economies. Some categories remained important, such as port cities like Genoa and Hamburg, and administrative centers like Toulouse, once the home of one of France's regional parlements, now the capital of the region of Midi-Pyrénées. Other categories grew in importance: centers of industrial production such as Hondeschoote in the Netherlands were comparatively rare before industrialization, but came to typify the towns of the later nineteenth and twentieth centuries. Others were quite new. Spa towns, such as Evian-les-Bains (France), Baden-Baden (Germany) and Spa (Belgium), where the wealthy from town and countryside came to settle for the season under the pretext of taking the mineral waters for their health, flourished in the later nineteenth century.

Changing patterns of tourism moved the focus away from cultural visits to the big city such as Vienna, Venice, Paris, or London, to new centers dependent for their economic well being on the seasonal arrival of visitors. From the 1930s, resorts catering to a working-class market, such as San Sebastian and Blackpool, joined Nice and other towns on the Côte d'Azur, which had become a source of winter sun and entertainment for the wealthy of northern Europe two generations earlier. Finally, capital cities, which brought together almost all these specialized functions, not only grew in proportion to the expansion of the territorial states of which they were the administrative and political centers, but in many cases came to dominate the urban organization of the entire state. Berlin, which became the German capital only in 1870, exceptionally shared some of this power with other cities which earlier had exercised a dominant regional role.

THE CHANGING USE OF SPACE

The process of urbanization was frequently expressed by changes in the use of urban space. Naturally, the overall surface occupied by urban activities expanded as a response to demographic growth and changes to the economy, but the most striking changes in the use of space took place in the old medieval urban core.

Changes to the medieval core, sixteenth to eighteenth centuries.

The medieval core was frequently defined by the presence of fortifications, both walls and waterways, separating the physical concentration of urban housing and activity from the countryside. Within this core, street patterns had developed in a haphazard way, interrupted by occasional attempts at formal planning. People and goods moved between marketplaces, gates, and harbors and between their homes and key buildings such as churches, civic buildings, and guildhalls as best as they could. There was much competition between livestock, the transport of goods and people, and the appropriation of spaces outside shops and workshops as extensions of places in which to work, store goods, or sell commodities. Occasionally, this could lead to violence, as in the case of a Barcelonan silversmith who was arrested in 1622 for throwing a knife at the driver of the inquisitor's coach because the latter had brushed against him as he worked in a very narrow street. Larger spaces, such as market squares and the areas in front of public buildings, accommodated multiple activities which either overlapped, or monopolized the spaces at predetermined times, such as the annual assembly of burghers to take the civic oath in German towns, or the twice-yearly race of the *palio* in Siena.

Social zoning was partial at best. Some preindustrial cities largely conformed to Gideon Sjoberg's model, in which the wealthy lived in the center, close to a concentration of markets and religious and political institutions, while the artisans lived in their own quarter, often close to a river, which provided them with motive power, washing, and waste disposal, and the poor lived on the periphery. Other cities did not follow this model. The wealthy lived cheek by jowl with the poor, differentiated not only by the spaciousness of their housing but also by their presence on the first and second floors of buildings, while those below them in the social hierarchy lived higher up, or behind the main streets in a labyrinth of alleys and courtyards. Spatial discrimination was vertical, not horizontal. Timber buildings with straw roofs, interspersed by the occasional structure in stone, roofed with tiles or slates, remained the norm, with the consequent dangers of fire, such as the conflagration of 1666, which destroyed 13,700 houses in London. These buildings remained relatively low, giving prominence to those few structures whose height could be seen from outside the walls: churches, castles, and civic buildings.

Early pressures arising from the demographic increase of the "long sixteenth century" created few changes to urban spatial organization. Traffic became worse. Buildings were subdivided, and there were attempts by jerry-builders to accommodate tenants in unsafe structures. The main forces of change were not demographic. Demand for housing from the poor brought little income to entrepreneurs.

On the other hand, the individual demands of the wealthy, and the collective needs of the urban authorities and of the developing territorial states from the 1600s succeeded in introducing changes of some importance, even if they did not alter much of the fabric inherited from the Middle Ages. The demand for more comfortable housing in brick or stone with slate or tiled roofs in a style that would convey high social status and enable its inhabitants to travel by coach or on horseback with ease was met by the construction of new quarters, often on land made available by the extension of urban fortifications or, increasingly through the eighteenth century, in areas where the threat of military attack was a distant memory, in suburbs. These new houses were particularly favored by members of the administrative elite. It took much longer for wholesale merchants to give up the traditional links between their homes and their places of work, something graphically illustrated by the spatial distribution of merchant and administrator subscribers for seats in the major theater of eighteenth-century Lyon.

The ideas expressed in the new urban quarters were also superimposed on the old, in the form of new streets cut through the medieval fabric to link key buildings with gates, ports, or barracks, such as the Via Toledo in Naples, constructed to enable soldiers from the Spanish garrison to move into the city at times of unrest, or the construction of the Uffizi palace in Florence by the Medici grand dukes of Tuscany. These new streets were interrupted by squares decorated with neoclassical monuments and statues,

A Town Square in the Eighteenth Century. A horserace (the *palio*) in the Piazza del Campo in Siena during the visit of Francis, grand duke of Tuscany, and Maria Theresa of Austria in 1739, the year before they became emperor and empress. Engraving by Giuseppe Zocchi. BANCA DEL MONTE DEI PASCHI, SIENA, ITALY/©ARCHIVO ICONOGRAPHICO, S.A./CORBIS

whose main purpose was to increase the visual impact of the imposing buildings beyond. All commercial activity was rigorously excluded.

Turin experienced this kind of redevelopment on the largest scale, but these developments were gradually introduced all over Europe, first in capital cities and major trading and administrative centers, later in smaller towns on a scale determined by the ability of the municipal authorities to finance their aspirations. Most towns and cities therefore entered the nineteenth century with a combination of the old medieval core, increasingly inhabited by the poor, and more spacious buildings set along broader streets, interspersed with squares. Early attempts at street lighting and the provision of reliable water supplies had met with only limited success.

The nineteenth century: City planning and Haussmanization.
The demographic expansion of Europe's capitals and commercial centers later in the nineteenth century placed strains on the urban fabric of a kind hitherto unknown. Most of the surplus population was housed in new suburban areas, some of which were also initially places of refuge for the wealthy from the smell, congestion, and disease of the old town centers, but the biggest changes to the use of space took place within the centers of towns themselves. This reflected two trends. The first was the gradual adoption of the urban core as a central business district, in which residential housing and small-scale industry gave way to buildings associated with commerce (banks, stock exchanges, shops, and offices), entertainment and cultural improvement (theaters, music halls, cinemas, restaurants, museums, and art galleries), and, usually to one side of these other services, railway stations, whose architecture signaled their high economic and social importance. Within this complex, many of the old public buildings inherited from the past—churches, cathedrals, town halls, and guildhalls—retained their place, if not their centrality.

The second trend reflected a new interest in town planning, which brought together moralists, architects, engineers, and the urban authorities in a common project to create a center that could accommodate the new needs of the economy and society. They were driven both by fear and by ambition. The rapid rise in the population of cities like London,

240

Paris, and Berlin created a spectre of unrest and social upheaval. The new industrial workforce, mostly living and working on the edge of the urban area, not only outnumbered the wealthier members of society, but had demonstrated its power in unrest across Europe from the end of the eighteenth century. Epidemic disease (bubonic plague from the Middle Ages until the early eighteenth century, and cholera for much of the nineteenth) was a constant worry, not only because of the high mortality levels during outbreaks, but also because of its capacity to spread throughout the urban area. In two successive days in July 1835, 210 and 173 cholera victims were buried in Marseilles alone.

This ambition to create a new urban environment to match the wealth and power of its rulers was shared throughout Europe, but found its greatest expression in the Paris of Emperor Napoleon III, whose prefect, Baron Haussmann, transformed the city. Haussmann's guiding principle was to facilitate the circulation of people, money, goods, and traffic. This required the construction of broad new streets, the boulevards, to link key points in the city, cutting through old residential areas and leveling inclines in

order to bring this about. These new streets were designed to create better circulation of the air to combat disease and pollution, to introduce more greenery, and, below ground, to ensure an effective system of fresh water and sewers. They also opened up the possibility of building comfortable new housing for the wealthy.

Haussmann's plans were emulated elsewhere, with varying degrees of success. Often the money, the political will, and the willingness of landowners and investors to participate were lacking. New streets such as Kingsway and Oxford Street in London were driven through older housing to open up the area to commercial development. In many smaller centers, the Parisian model was only realized in the form of a square or a single new street. Even in Paris, the overall plan was never fully effective. The areas between the boulevards, such as the district of the Arts-et-Métiers in the third arrondissement, retained much of their earlier form.

The movement to "clean up" the old town centers also elicited a response around the end of the nineteenth century, which can now be seen as the

A Town Square in the Twentieth Century. Parade preliminary to the annual horserace (*córsa al palio*) in the Piazza del Campo in Siena, summer 1983. ©DAVID LEES/CORBIS

241

Urban Transportation Hub. Paddington Station, London, depicted in *The Railway Station,* painting (1862) by William Powell Frith (1819–1909). ROYAL HOLLOWAY AND BEDFORD NEW COLLEGE, SURREY, U.K./THE BRIDGEMAN ART LIBRARY

birth of heritage awareness. A major debate was opened in Florence in 1900 by an open letter to the municipality, signed by the heads of leading British museums and art galleries and drawing attention to the dangers to the city's cultural heritage and the potential loss of income from a growing tourist industry if the construction of new streets and buildings continued to bring about the loss of its architectural glories.

The twentieth century. New responses to the continued growth of the urban population developed in the 1920s and 1930s. Late-nineteenth-century developments in iron-framed building design were extended as a result of the widespread use of reinforced concrete. The work of the French architect Le Corbusier popularized the concepts of concentrating the population into tower blocks surrounded by green spaces and served by roads linking different parts of the city. It was not, however, until the widespread destruction caused by bombing by both sides during World War II that these new ideas were put into practice on a large scale. In England alone, the centers of Coventry, Plymouth, Exeter, Hull, and Southampton required complete reconstruction.

From the 1960s, one of the most important factors in altering the use of space was the increasing use of the car to move into and around town centers. New buildings were planned to incorporate underground parking spaces for residents and office workers. Many of London's squares retained their external appearance while masking car parks below. Additional tunnels,

expressways, and elevated motorways were also constructed to increase traffic flow through town centers, such as the expressway constructed along the right bank of the Seine in Paris.

The planners' dream of separating pedestrians from wheeled traffic, which had been first considered in sixteenth-century projects for ideal cities by Leonardo da Vinci and Serlio, came several stages nearer to reality with the introduction of pedestrianized shopping precincts. The initial concrete plazas set back from the older street plan at different levels were followed by extensive covered precincts, which attempted to reproduce the atmosphere of the marketplace while retaining all the benefits of air-conditioning. Later, motor traffic was excluded from large parts of town centers, and the streets paved over in order to encourage undisturbed shopping in competition with large out-of-town developments. Often, it was those remains of the preindustrial center which had fortuitously survived, such as the quarter of St.-Georges in Toulouse, which became a new pedestrian focus of recreational shopping.

SOCIAL HIERARCHIES

Social historians define the composition of European urban society in several overlapping ways. Statistical analysis of taxpayers provides the evidence for a hierarchy of wealth and for a partial correlation between sources of income and income levels. Occupational analysis offers a measure of economic and social complexity, but its utility is limited by the superimposition of categories by government and municipal agencies, by the use of similar terms over long periods of time to describe forms of work that had changed in terms of both the technology used and dependence levels of the worker, and by the absence of distinctions between one practitioner and another.

Changing definitions of citizenship. Contemporary perceptions of the nature of urban society constantly prove their value but require an understanding of the ideological basis within which they evolved. Between the sixteenth and the eighteenth centuries, it was members of urban elites, with a patriarchal and top-down view of society, who uniformly generated perceptions of urban society. Consequently, there is a mismatch between the idea of "society" developed by the early sociologists, who attempted to provide models of the entire urban population, and the view of urban society inherited from the medieval jurists, which limited its membership to the citizens or burghers of a particular urban center. These citizens were all part of a corporate body. They not only belonged to the town, and demonstrated this by paying taxes, taking part in the urban militia, and participating, at least in name, in the political process; collectively they were the town.

A definition of this kind excluded large numbers of the urban population, who by modern conventions would conventionally be considered to be part of the urban society. Very few women were allowed to take up citizen status. When they did so, this was frequently for a limited period of time, until a widow's son came to the age of majority, for instance. In any case, women were only given limited citizen status. They could pay taxes, but they were excluded from the political process, did not swear oaths of allegiance to the city, and could not bear arms in its defence. Many others did not or could not become citizens. It was necessary to be economically independent. Apprentices and servants had neither the means nor the autonomy to fulfill this criterion. The poor and the indigent were socially invisible and often exposed to expulsion in times of crisis. Foreigners were suspect and required lengthy residence before being accepted as citizens. Many, particularly merchants, showed little interest in becoming citizens, whether or not their involvement in their host community was long-term. Religious sensitivities during the Reformation also placed a barrier before outsiders practicing a different faith from the official religion of each town or region. In Strasbourg, non-Lutherans were prevented from becoming burghers. Jewish communities in particular were excluded from full engagement in urban economies, for fear that they would compete with local artisans. Many towns, particularly in Germany and Italy, reinforced this by enclosing Jews in ghettos.

The fiction that urban society comprised only those adult males who had been granted the privileges of citizenship was eroded still further by demographic growth and by a shift in urban government from consensus to authoritarianism, characterized, in many German cities at least, by a change in vocabulary distinguishing members of city councils from other burghers. Pamphlets published during the constitutional crisis in Lübeck in the 1660s now spoke of "rulers" and "subjects," replicating the terms of the ancien régime state. While the concept of citizen unity remained a powerful influence well into the nineteenth century, as urban populations grew larger, the realities of political power led to a tripartite view of society. As before, this emanated from the elite, but was often driven by external value systems shared by all parts of the state. In general terms, the elite feared the threat represented by the poor, many of them recent arrivals, whose behavior and numbers potentially lay outside well-tried systems of control and whose

Pedestrianized Shopping Precinct. Shopping and entertainment street in the Montmartre district, Paris, 1994. BOB KRIST/AKG LONDON

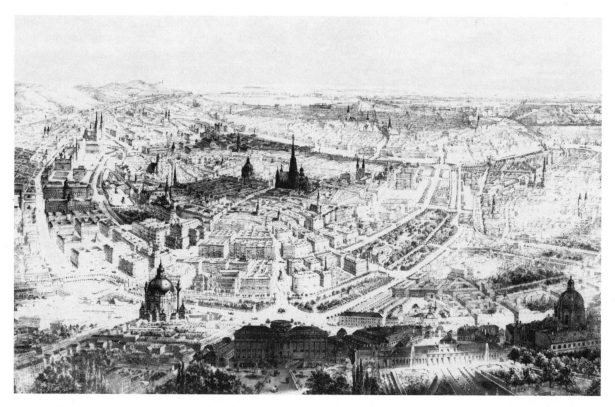

Imperial Vienna. Vienna in 1873. St. Stephen's Cathedral is in the center of the old city, which is surrounded by the Ringstrasse. Colored lithograph. ©MUSEEN DER STADT WIEN, VIENNA

location on the edge of the urban area as well as in its center placed the wealthy in a vulnerable position. The third group identified by the elite was never well defined, using values such as respectability and reliability to associate them with the forces of stability. Such individuals were believed to have a stake in the well-being and peace of their towns, expressing a willingness to oppose the forces of instability, without threatening the position of the elite. The introduction of universal male suffrage in the course of the second half of the nineteenth century was believed to reinforce this role. In the course of the twentieth century, the growing sophistication of social analyses, coupled with the disappearance of a visible elite, and the growth of the middle classes modified views of urban society to an extent that they do not lend themselves easily to clearly identifiable models.

The role of urban elites in urban society. The impact of urban elites, small groupings of wealthy families at the top of the social hierarchy, was considerable on all sizes of urban center until the early years of the twentieth century. Collectively and as individuals, they were responsible for the economic and political organization of each town, the organization of

space and the buildings around it, the setting of cultural and charitable norms through patronage, and the integration of each urban center into wider national and international cultural networks. Initiators of substantial change at times, urban elites could also marshal the forces of social conservatism, both in the face of perceived internal threats, such as drinking, gambling, and prostitution, and external threats, such as the railway. A newspaper in Bordeaux, which closely reflected elite opinion, pronounced in 1842 that railway construction was "too advanced for France." The first station opened in the city only in 1902.

Europe's cities experienced many political changes after the Middle Ages but there was substantial continuity in the persistence and organization of urban elites. There were regional variations. The participation of the landed nobility was always much stronger in the towns of Italy, France, and the Iberian Peninsula than it was in the Netherlands or the British Isles. The role of merchants and entrepreneurs in urban elites reflected the extent to which individual urban centers owed their economic expansion to commerce and industry. Mercantile elites were prominent in seventeenth-century Amsterdam and Hamburg, while in those cities whose earlier commercial success they had overtaken, such as Lübeck and Venice, there was a growing rentier element, based on income from land and housing. Some similar comparisons can be drawn from France in the nineteenth century, where merchants dominated Marseilles and Caen, but Nice moved in the opposite direction from its earlier German counterparts, changing from a rentier town to a wine-exporting port and tourist center.

New administrative centers, such as Valladolid, Dijon, and Barcelona, brought lawyers and other officeholders to prominence in the sixteenth and seventeenth centuries, relegating merchants to a subsidiary position within the elite. In the case of the capital cities, this process was both stimulated and distorted by the presence of princely courts, whose members comprised a kind of parallel elite. Their role within the city as consumers, patrons, and trendsetters is not to be underestimated. In seventeenth-century Paris it was preeminent. The new quarter of the Marais was constructed to meet the housing needs of leading members of the French aristocracy who attended on the Bourbon kings. Much the same could be said of the Paris of Haussmann, where the courtiers of Napoleon III joined the city's bankers and entrepreneurs to construct new houses along the city's boulevards, and of Habsburg Vienna, where the old ramparts were replaced by the stately splendor of the Ring.

Less complex urban elites acted in order to safeguard their economic and social interests by ensuring that outsiders were excluded or only allowed in according to strict criteria. Unrestricted access was bad for business. Much occupational and professional solidarity was buttressed by a network of intermarriage, a pattern which gave rise to long-standing dynasties, like the Sicilian Muscatello family of Augusta, notaries for five generations between 1774 and 1904, and the merchants and lawyers of the Hamburg Ausinck family, active between 1752 and 1831. Social and economic power was maintained through inheritance by ensuring that the patrimonies of elite families remained within the same circles as much as possible. Certain cultural practices also ensured that only a small minority of newcomers could join the elite. These varied from one century to another. The *Tanzstatut* (dance law) passed by the Nürnberg city council in 1521 established a list of the families whose members were permitted to attend the dances in the basement of the Town Hall, and whose younger members were consequently admitted to a restricted marriage market. In early-nineteenth-century Sicilian towns, certain cafés, clubs, and reading groups were established, whose membership was open only to the descendants of men whose social privileges had once been established by law. Social unity within urban elites was not always paralleled by political uniformity. In many towns, politics was colored by factional divisions on local—or, in the case of England, national—lines. The long-standing monopoly of the right to participate in politics, however, ensured the exclusion of others.

Such a concentration of social, economic, and political power could not survive the triple processes of industrialization, rapid demographic growth, and electoral reform. The early twentieth century was marked by the introduction of widespread municipal socialism. In any case, urban government had become far too complicated to be undertaken by the representatives of a few wealthy families. They found new roles, or developed existing nonpolitical positions as the leaders of philanthropic or cultural organizations. The rising costs of building and the reorganization of industrial, financial, and commercial enterprises also transferred the role of dominant urban builders from members of the elite to anonymous banks, insurance companies, and industrial conglomerates.

URBAN CULTURE: THE CULTURE OF THE DAY AND THE CULTURE OF THE NIGHT

The growing scale of urban life and its impact on the population brought two contrasting cultural responses. One, identified by Émile Durkheim as anomie, was the loss of any sense that the individual was part of a larger community, leading ultimately to a loss of shared values and to an emphasis on day-to-day survival.

Associational culture. The other response was the growth of associational culture. Associational culture never embraced everyone—its participants were predominantly male and from the stable core of society—but it was an important feature of urban society from the later seventeenth century until the television age. Its roots lay even further back in guilds and religious organizations. Guilds, confraternities, and parishes had provided their members with a sense of common identity, a sense that they differed from nonmembers, a focus, usually a meeting place, rules that regulated their lives, a hierarchy within which they could hope to advance over time, and a set of rituals, which included communal eating and drinking. But membership in a guild or confraternity was also a link with the community as a whole. Both organizations took part in processions and were recognized as part of either the body politic or the ecclesiastical organization of the town.

An overlap between these groups and more specific forms of associational culture began in the seventeenth century. One did not replace the other, unless the journeymen's organizations are included, which developed as a response to the concentration of power among master craftsmen. Early groups developed among the elite and those with aspirations to be seen as gentlemen. They met at coaching inns, where the latest newspapers and pamphlets were first delivered, in order to talk about politics, literature, and science. Others took over the administration of charity from guilds, whose resources had declined, and from the church, particularly in Protestant areas. Religious fragmentation and the growth of secularism also gave rise to groups exhibiting the characteristics of a common focus, rituals, common meeting places, and a sense of distinctive identity. Often these were part of much larger networks, such as the freemasons.

The expansion of the industrial city brought an explosion in associations. Seventy-two patriotic and military groups alone were listed in the eastern French center of Nancy in 1938. There was some correlation between the social status of association members and the extent to which groups emphasized local concerns. The further up the social scale, the more associations embraced members from different parts of the city, with central meeting places. Local meetings were more convenient for those who did not wish to travel. Hence we find the Cercle de la Treille, founded in a restaurant in the Parisian suburb of Bercy in 1881 by a group of wine and spirit retailers, who declared that they wished to meet in the evenings close to their businesses. Employers' organizations were only one type of association. As before, one could join philanthropic groups, some of which were focused on helping the needy, while others, such as the English Literary and Philosophical Societies, organized lecture series and developed libraries in the hope of acculturating the working class. Common interests in sports—cricket, tennis, fishing, and, in the early twentieth century, cycling—engendered other groups. And of course trade union organizations appealing to workers formed dense associational networks that brought members together for everything from entertainment to education. Each association depended on voluntary leadership and on the willingness of its members to devote time to meeting and common activities. Such culture remained an element of urban society throughout the twentieth century, but the increasing competition of other forms of recreation eroded its base. Consumerism had taken over from voluntarism.

Informal and alternative cultures.
Associational culture was only one dimension of the urban culture or cultures to which townspeople belonged and which gave them a sense of belonging. There were many other cultural foci with unwritten rules, whose rituals were as recognizable to their members as the dinners celebrated by churchwardens in sixteenth-century London, the initiation rites of the masons, or the minutiae of the annual general meetings of gardeners' clubs or chambers of commerce. The exclusion of women from politics, organized labor, and much religious activity for most of the period was compensated for by other kinds of informal association. Many of these centered on key gendered tasks: childbirth, washing clothes at the communal laundry, collecting water from the well, and shopping at the market or, later on, at the corner shop. While each activity had its own immediate importance, its cultural importance cannot be exaggerated. By engaging in practical activities which led to meetings at a given focus—the bed of the woman giving birth, the river or laundry, the well, the market, or the corner shop—women exchanged information and reinforced given social values just as effectively as all the sermons given to confraternities or the moral blackmail practiced by journeymen and apprentices on their fellow guild members. As economic organization changed so did some of these foci. Middle-class women, in particular, whose main occupations were associated with the home, but for whom the presence of live-in servants provided more leisure, met in each other's houses, in cafés, and in the new department stores.

Immigrant groups provided a constant alternative cultural focus to the cultures of established townspeople. Most of the demographic growth of the urban population, whether in the sixteenth century or the twentieth, was dependant on in-migration. Mortality levels were too high to permit natural replacement, let alone sustained growth. New arrivals often congregated in the same districts as others from the same region and engaged in the same occupations. This contiguity of home and employment reinforced preexisting similarities of language, culinary customs, dress, courtship, religious observance, and daily routine. If migration was intended to be temporary, there were few incentives to alter these practices. The men from the Limousin in central France who came to Paris in the early nineteenth century to work as builders continued to maintain an agrarian routine, rising at five or six in the morning and walking to their place of work. Even when they spoke French instead of their own dialect, they punctuated their words with long silences.

On the other hand, there was a constant tension between the persistence of immigrant customs brought into a town and the integrative mechanisms enabling newcomers to be accepted. Intermarriage with partners of different origins, economic success, and opportunities to live away from immigrant areas all contributed to the dilution of specific immigrant cultures, particularly where there were comparatively few contrasts between the immigrants and the host community. New waves of postcolonial migration to European urban centers during the last third of the twentieth century replicated both patterns of integration and of segregation, with one important difference. The integrative mechanisms came to operate in two directions, enabling elements of immigrant culture, primarily music, dress, and food, to become accepted as part of mainstream urban culture.

The distinction between popular culture and the culture of the wealthy and literate, which had developed during the sixteenth and seventeenth centuries, widened still further as a result of industrialization. At the time when "high culture" (classical music, painting, books, scientific collections, and ideas) was moving out of the private houses of the wealthy into buildings dedicated to the edification of the general public, the conditions of factory work, the location of more and more housing away from the central business district, and a general absence of possibilities for self-improvement prevented more than a minority of workers from taking advantage of the new cultural institutions. Free time was at a premium. There were few incentives for a Viennese jeweller's apprentice working in the suburb of Friedrichsstadt in the early twentieth century, for instance, to make the journey into the center of the city to view the shops in the Kärntner Strasse or to admire the works of Klimt and Schiele in the galleries. It was only when the regulations in Berlin that required all shop windows to be shuttered on Sundays (in order not to disturb the Sabbath) were relaxed that thousands of workers walked in from the suburbs in order to window-shop and visits to city centers became common again.

Night culture. During the Renaissance, the Venetian Republic created a magistracy, the *signori della notte,* with special responsibility for keeping order between dusk and dawn. This action was a recognition that there were important distinctions between the activities that took place in the city by day and those by night, and consequently between the culture of the day and the culture of the night. The distinction has continued to be one of considerable importance. To its detractors, the culture of the night has always been illicit. The day was to be devoted to work, both practical and intellectual, while the night was to be spent in sleeping or in domestic tasks. Only Sundays and feast days were open to alternative forms of behavior,

and these were strictly circumscribed. In the absence of reliable street lighting, travel by night was dangerous and unusual. Any nocturnal activities were consequently beyond the usual social norms and required control. The Venetians arrested men for brawling in the streets, kidnap, rape, and even suborning nuns during Carnival. This suspicion of the culture of the night remained even when working hours had become shorter and many streets were illuminated by gas or electricity. Some anxiety was justified. The night was a time for crime—theft, murder, and prostitution—but as the case of prostitution shows, the illicitness of the culture of the night owes much to its role as a meeting place between the respectable and the suspect. Without the complicity of the young and wealthy, who derived a thrill from visiting certain "dangerous" parts of the city after nightfall, much of the culture of the night, with its drinking haunts, market stalls, and places of entertainment, would not have developed. On the other hand, although the culture of the night can be easily distinguished from the culture of the day, the culture of the day was most important in breaking down differences between the sexes, between people of different social status and origin, or at least to facilitate a common cultural experience, which did much to create a single urban culture in the later twentieth century.

The process of European urbanization serves to emphasize the contrasts between urban and rural social organization both before and after industrialization. Within urban centers, however, the continuities between the sixteenth and the twentieth centuries dominated the urban experience. For most of the time, urban dwellers lived in a society whose scale was too large for them to relate to in its entirety, but whose composition enabled them to belong to multiple groupings based on neighborhood, occupation, place of birth, gender, religious affiliation, political or sporting allegiances, or voluntary activity. Each created its own cultural constructs but shared enough of them with others to enable society to function effectively except in times of crisis. This society was constantly shaped on the one hand by the immigrants whose arrival helped to fuel the demographic increases associated with urbanization, and on the other by organs of local and national government, whose priorities reflected the concerns of dominant urban elites. Urbanization reached its peak in the course of the twentieth century, leading to conditions of social overload in terms of population density, demand for services and housing, and an erosion of long-standing social relationships. Since then, urban centers have become even more socially confused as a process of formal or informal deurbanization takes place.

See also **Housing** *(volume 5); and other articles in this section.*

BIBLIOGRAPHY

General

Bairoch, Paul. *Cities and Economic Development: From the Dawn of History to the Present.* Translated by Christopher Braider. Chicago, 1988.

Braunfels, Wolfgang. *Urban Design in Western Europe: Regime and Architecture, 900–1900.* Translated by Kenneth J. Northcott. Chicago, 1988.

Cowan, Alexander. *Urban Europe, 1500–1700.* New York, 1998.

De Vries, Jan. *European Urbanization, 1500–1800.* London, 1984.

Friedrichs, Christopher. *The Early Modern City, 1450–1750.* New York, 1995.

Sutcliffe, Anthony, ed. *Metropolis, 1890–1940.* Chicago, 1984.

Social Organization

Blackbourn, David, and R. J. Evans, eds. *The German Bourgeoisie: Essays on the Social History of the German Middle Class from the Late Eighteenth to the Early Twentieth Century.* London, 1991.

Crossick, Geoffrey, ed. *The Artisan and the European Town, 1500–1900.* Aldershot, U.K., 1997.

Crossick, Geoffrey, and Heinz-Gerhard Haupt. *The Petite Bourgeoisie in Europe, 1780–1914: Enterprise, Family, and Independence.* London, 1995.

Malatesta, Maria, ed. *Society and the Professions in Italy, 1860–1914.* Cambridge, U.K., 1995.

Morris, Jonathan. *The Political Economy of Shopkeeping in Milan, 1886–1922.* Cambridge, U.K., 1993.

Morris, R. J., and Richard Rodger, eds. *The Victorian City: A Reader in British Urban History, 1820–1914.* London, 1993.

Wakeman, Rosemary. *Modernizing the Provincial City: Toulouse, 1945–1975.* Cambridge, Mass, 1997.

Culture

Certeau, Michel de, et al. *The Practice of Everyday Life.* Vol. 2: *Living and Cooking.* Translated by Timothy J. Tomasik. Minneapolis, Minn., 1998.

Cowan, Alexander, ed. *Mediterranean Urban Culture, 1400–1700.* Evanston, Ill., 2000.

Gee, Malcolm, Tim Kirk, and Jill Steward, eds. *The City in Central Europe: Culture and Society from 1800 to the Present.* Brookfield, Vt., 1999.

Schlor, Joachim. *Nights in the Big City: Paris, Berlin, London, 1840–1930.* London, 1998.

THE CITY: THE EARLY MODERN PERIOD

Christopher R. Friedrichs

Throughout the early modern era, cities and towns played a vastly greater role in shaping the character of European society than the number of their inhabitants might suggest. European society in the early modern era was predominantly rural. At the beginning of the sixteenth century, only about one-tenth of the total population of Europe inhabited urban centers, and by the end of the eighteenth century this proportion was not substantially larger. Yet cities and towns (the terms are almost interchangeable, with American usage generally preferring "cities" and British usage favoring "towns") had an economic, political, and cultural impact out of proportion to their collective size.

Cities were bigger than villages. What defined them as cities, however, was not mere size, for they had specific characteristics and functions that made them fundamentally different from the rural communities in which most Europeans lived. Cities were centers of exchange. They always had frequent markets that served the needs of the surrounding region and often had annual or semiannual trade fairs that attracted merchants from much farther away. They were also centers of production, for handcrafted goods were manufactured and sold in every European town. Often this craft production was highly specialized. Distinct trades with their own techniques and traditions were devoted to the production of particular varieties of textiles, clothing, leather goods, metalware, ceramics, and wooden products. Larger urban centers also played an important role in organizing long-distance trade and providing financial services. Often the inhabitants of cities enjoyed the exclusive right to carry out these various urban functions.

The special character of the European city had emerged gradually during the Middle Ages, when feudal rulers granted charters that gave town dwellers special economic and political privileges in return for benefits, usually financial, that the towns could offer the rulers. A typical privilege was the right to hold markets and fairs. Another was the right to construct a wall, which would enable the town to regulate the flow of people and goods through its gates. Often towns also obtained rights of self-government, under which interference by the ruler's officials was sharply restricted. Only a few cities were fully independent city-states, but many enjoyed a high degree of political autonomy.

The social organization of towns was also distinctive. Each European city had a body of adult male householders—citizens, burghers, freemen, bourgeois, or the like—who collectively embodied the political community. Membership in the citizenry was passed on to male descendants, though newcomers might also be admitted. In theory, though not always in practice, only citizens could participate fully in the city's economic life as merchants or craft masters. Economic life was organized largely around guilds, which were typically but not always made up of individuals who practiced the same occupation. Membership in the relevant guild was often a prerequisite for engaging in a particular trade or craft. Authority in all its forms was exercised on a collective basis. Virtually every city was governed by a council or group of councils made up of prosperous male citizens. Power was always gendered. Women could inherit and own property and engage in certain forms of economic enterprise, but they were excluded both from decision making in the guilds and from membership in any of the governing councils.

These basic parameters of urban life remained largely constant during the early modern era. Yet urban society was by no means static. Some cities acquired an entirely new role in the early modern era, as hitherto minor towns like Madrid or Berlin turned into major administrative capitals for the absolutist states which emerged in the seventeenth and eighteenth centuries. Even cities whose functions remained largely commercial also underwent significant changes between the end of the Middle Ages and the eve of the industrial era. But urban historians continue to debate the pace, extent, and character of these changes.

FUNDAMENTAL THEMES

Writings on the history of cities in early modern Europe can be grouped into three main categories. The first group examines cities from the perspective of urbanism. This approach emphasizes changes in the design and layout of cities and the character of buildings and urban infrastructures. Though drawing heavily on the history of architecture and urban planning, the urbanist tradition is ultimately concerned with the relationship between the physical structures of cities and the quality of urban life. The most influential work in this tradition is Lewis Mumford's *The City in History* (1961). Mumford valued what he perceived as the organic and intimate character of the medieval city and viewed the attempts by early modern rulers to redesign cities along more grandiose lines as alienating—a view adopted, with modifications, by some of his disciples.

A second approach looks at cities from the point of view of urbanization. This approach is concerned less with specific cities than with the relationship among cities within broader urban networks and attempts to delineate or measure changes in the size and economic importance of urban society as a whole. Notable works within this group include the important survey by Paul M. Hohenberg and Lynn Hollen Lees, *The Making of Urban Europe, 1000–1950* (1985), and the pioneering summary and analysis of demographic data by Jan de Vries, *European Urbanization, 1500–1800* (1984).

The third approach, which might be called urban history as such, is founded on the description and analysis of the social, political, economic, or cultural history of particular cities. The earliest publications in this tradition belong to the genre of local history, works whose main purpose is to inform inhabitants or visitors about the history and heritage of individual cities. But the most important works of urban history are those whose authors examined individual cities as case studies to cast some light on the character of urban society as a whole. French historians of the early postwar era established a benchmark for such studies with their attempts to study the *histoire totale* of particular cities. Only a few historians have attempted to achieve the same breadth that Pierre Goubert did in his pioneering study of Beauvais and its region, but many have emulated his commitment to understanding early modern society by examining individual urban communities in depth.

In fact most of the great themes of early modern European history are closely linked to the urban experience. Inevitably, then, urban historians have striven to determine both the extent to which cities played a

role in causing fundamental changes and the extent to which the cities themselves were transformed by these changes.

One major theme involves the religious division of Europe brought about by the Protestant Reformation of the sixteenth century. Cities played a key role in the emergence of Protestant ideas, and some cities became arenas of bitter religious conflict. But cities also served as templates for religious compromise when Europeans began to experiment with the concept of confessionally divided communities.

A second theme relates to the growing power of centralized states, especially in western and northern Europe. Cities inevitably felt the impact when monarchical regimes tried to expand their administrative reach. But the process of state expansion was irregular, and the way in which cities responded was far from uniform. In some cities local elites firmly resisted any attempts to diminish local autonomy, but in other cases urban leaders cooperated with state officials and welcomed the opportunity to integrate themselves into broader structures of authority.

A third great theme has to do with the cluster of economic changes generally referred to as the growth of capitalism. Historians have debated exactly what capitalism is or was. To some, notably those in the marxist tradition, capitalism is an economic system in which the dominant form of production is manufacture and the means of production are mostly owned by bourgeois entrepreneurs. To others, influenced by Max Weber, capitalism is a system of economic practice characterized by the rational pursuit of sustained profit. To yet others, capitalism is virtually synonymous with market relations, the free exchange of goods and services, with prices and wages determined by supply and demand rather than traditional expectations or state controls. Yet no matter which of these definitions is preferred, substantial evidence indicates that economic transactions in early modern Europe increasingly took place in a capitalistic way. Less self-evident is the role that cities played in this process. Traditional marxist historiography presupposed that capitalist enterprise was based in cities and was controlled by members of the urban bourgeoisie. Yet analysts emphasized the extent to which capitalist practices were also applied to agricultural production. Some also argued that the emergence of large-scale rural manufacturing during the early modern era—the process generally referred to as protoindustrialization—diminished the importance of cities in the transition to a modern industrial economy. There is little question, however, that even if dramatic increases in production took place in the countryside, cities continued to supply much of the capital invested

The City Celebrates. Entrance of King Ferdinand IV and Queen Barbara of Braganza into Seville, 1747. Painting (1783) by Juan de Espinal. MUSEO PROVINCAL, SEVILLA/INSTITUT AMATLLER D'ART HISPANIC

in rural enterprises. Of course cities, especially strategically located ports, were the conduit through which the profits generated by European conquests in the New World were funneled back to the Old.

Some historians have posited a fourth major theme of early modern social history, the growth of what is generally labeled "social discipline." This refers to the efforts by social elites to impose habits of obedience and regularity on the rest of society to make members of the lower orders more pliant to the authorities and more accustomed to the work routines required by the capitalist system. The pervasiveness of this program and the degree to which cities were involved have been matters of dispute, but attempts by urban magistrates to streamline systems of poor relief and to diminish the number or visibility of people they regarded as social undesirables have been cited as manifestations of this undertaking.

Finally, the early modern era was characterized by cultural transformations in which cities played an important part. High culture—literature, music, theater, and the visual arts—continued to depend heavily on royal or aristocratic patronage, but artists, composers, and writers were generally of urban origin. Throughout the early modern era cultural consumption was broadened to include many patrons among the urban bourgeoisie. Even more important, however, were the invention of printing in the fifteenth century and the explosive diffusion of printed matter from the sixteenth century onward, which in turn stimulated and reinforced the spread of literacy among ever larger circles of the European population. Almost

all printed matter was produced in cities, and much of it was consumed there as well. Literacy rates varied sharply between regions and countries, but almost everywhere literacy was higher in cities than in the rural hinterland. Though firm measurements are lacking, it is apparent that by the end of the eighteenth century, at least in northwestern Europe and Germany, the great majority of men and women in cities were able to read and write. Cities were thus the pacesetters for the diffusion of print culture throughout Europe as a whole. Beginning in the mid-seventeenth century, European cities also experienced a proliferation of organizations, societies and clubs devoted to the presentation of scientific findings or the discussion of political, cultural, and literary topics. All of these typically urban institutions, which ranged from scientific academies established by royal charter to informal salons run by aristocratic hostesses, eventually contributed to the ferment of new thinking associated with the Enlightenment of the eighteenth century.

CHARACTERISTICS OF THE EARLY MODERN CITY

Nobody knows exactly how many cities existed in early modern Europe or exactly how many people lived in them. Comprehensive census data did not exist before about 1800. Furthermore, despite the generally clear distinction between cities and villages, the legal status of a number of market communities remained ambiguous. The overall picture, however, is

DONAUWÖRTH

Donauwörth, situated at the junction of the Danube and Wörnitz Rivers in southern Germany, was by any measure a small town. At the beginning of the seventeenth century the city had about 4,000 inhabitants, and the population declined to less than 3,000 as a result of the Thirty Years' War (1618–1648). But the city's physical layout, depicted in the 1640s by the celebrated topographer Matthäus Merian, had many elements characteristic of European cities large and small. The city was surrounded by a wall and some additional fortifications, which enabled it to keep out unwanted visitors and fend off small-scale raiders. The wall was not adequate, however, to discourage a truly determined foe, as the citizens discovered in 1607, when the city was seized by the duke of Bavaria. The city did not have a formal market square, but it did have an unusually wide central street, the *Reichsstrasse* or Imperial Way, which served as the marketplace and the site of ceremonial events. At the eastern end of this street stood the relatively modest city hall. Toward its western end was the large Fugger House, from which the powerful South German dynasty of the Fuggers administered its properties in the surrounding region. Far more imposing than these secular buildings, however, were the city's major ecclesiastical structures, notably the parish church in the city center and the large monastery of the Holy Cross in the southwestern corner. One of the major trades of Donauwörth was the production of woolen cloth. After the cloths were woven and fulled, they were hung out to dry on huge racks just outside the city's western wall. Gardens and orchards were located both within and outside the walled area. The city retained this appearance until it began to raze the walls in the early nineteenth century.

Matthäus Merian and Martin Zeiller. *Topographia Bavariae: das ist, Beschreib: vnd Aigentliche Abbildung der Vornembsten Stätt vnd Orth, in Ober vnd Nieder Beÿern, der Obern Pfaltz, vnd andern, zum Hochlöblichen Baÿrischen Craisse gehörigen Landschafften.* 2d ed. Frankfurt am Main, Germany, 1657. Illustration facing page 106.

---

clear. Most cities were small by modern standards. In 1500 only three or four cities in Europe had populations of more than 100,000, and by 1800 the number remained less than twenty. Jan de Vries estimated that in 1500 Europe had about 500 cities with populations over 5,000 and by 1800 Europe had roughly 900 such places. But the pace of urbanization was uneven, with more growth in the sixteenth century, a slower rate in the seventeenth century, and a sharp increase in the eighteenth century. Many cities experienced only a moderate increase in size during the early modern era, and some even lost population as their economic importance declined. Yet a few cities, especially national capitals that were also major centers of commerce, experienced spectacular growth. Naples, whose population of about 150,000 made it the largest city in Europe in 1500, almost tripled in size by 1800. Paris grew from about 100,000 to 600,000 during the same three centuries. By far the most dramatic increase, however, was experienced by London, which went from less than 50,000 in 1500 to almost 900,000 by the end of the eighteenth century.

The factors that accounted for the growth of cities have long been the subject of debate by historians. In the long run many cities must have experienced some natural increase caused by an excess of births over deaths. But the balance was precarious, for cities were often subject to sudden increases in mortality as a result of harvest crises or epidemic diseases. Until the late seventeenth century, for example, cities all over Europe faced periodic visitations of the bubonic plague, which could wipe out a third or more of a community's population within a matter of months. A key element in the growth of cities was undoubtedly immigration from the surrounding hinterland or more distant regions. But not all immigrants contributed to the demographic growth of the city, for many of them were ill-paid laborers or servants who never accumulated enough resources to get married and establish families. Altogether, despite the exceptional growth of a few major cities, the pace of urbanization in Europe during the early modern era was modest compared to what occurred in the nineteenth and twentieth centuries.

At the beginning of the early modern era towns of every size had certain structural characteristics in common, and many of these features remained intact until the end of the eighteenth century. Inevitably some of the great metropolitan centers began to diverge from the general norms, but even in cities like London or Paris much of the institutional and physical legacy of earlier times remained firmly entrenched.

Almost every early modern city was surrounded by a wall punctuated by gates and watchtowers. If a city grew, the new districts were supposed to be enclosed by extensions of the wall. This did not always happen, for the fastest-growing cities were ringed by suburbs and faubourgs outside the walls, often populated by newcomers who were only partially integrated into the city's administrative system. In cases like these, the walls became increasingly irrelevant and were gradually broken through or allowed to decay. In other cities, especially in areas that faced sustained military activity, the walls were not just preserved but were transformed into elaborate systems of fortifications, with bastions and outerworks designed to thwart all but the most determined siege.

The internal layout of almost all cities had certain elements in common. The typical city had an array of gently curving streets supplemented by a confusing network of hidden alleys, lanes, and courtyards. Every city had a number of open squares or wider streets that served as marketplaces. In ports and riverside cities the streets were generally intersected by a system of moats and canals. The largest buildings were usually ecclesiastical. At the beginning of the early modern era this category included parish churches, chapels, monasteries, and nunneries. If the city was the seat of a bishop, it also had a cathedral. In cities that went Protestant the monastic houses disappeared, but the churches remained. Major public buildings included city halls, granaries, warehouses, hospitals, and almshouses. A few cities also had castles left over from medieval times. Larger cities often had mansions or palaces occupied by particularly prominent families. No matter what other structures a city might have, most of the building stock consisted of houses. Virtually every house served a dual function as a residence and as a workshop or place of business. The later differentiation between industrial, commercial, and residential zones was unknown, but generally the very center of the city was considered the most desirable neighborhood. The city's greatest merchants typically lived in houses clustered around the main marketplace or near the largest church. Poorer inhabitants were more likely to live farther from the center or even outside the walls. Sometimes a city's unique topography created its own rules. In canal-webbed Venice, for example, streets were used only by pedestrians, while vehicular traffic was exclusively waterborne. The grandest palazzi were not clustered in the city center but stretched out along both sides of the Grand Canal. But most cities conformed to a more familiar pattern of spatial organization.

This traditional pattern, however, was not attractive to Renaissance theorists of urban planning or

Fortified City. Plan of Antwerp by Virgilius Boloniensis, 1565. MUSEUM PLANTIN-MORETUS, ANTWERP/STEDELIJK PRENTENKABINET

absolutist rulers whose vision of perfect cities involved broad avenues radiating uniformly from great central plazas. Not many new cities were founded in early modern Europe, so few opportunities to apply notions of urban planning to entire communities arose. But these visions did find increasing expression in the seventeenth and eighteenth centuries, when, in contrast to the usual haphazard growth of suburbs, carefully planned neighborhoods were laid out on the peripheries of existing towns. By the end of the eighteenth century, many of Europe's larger cities thus had a modern district with elegant new squares and broad boulevards awkwardly conjoined to a more traditional city center.

SOCIAL ORGANIZATION OF CITIES

Despite regional variations and the inevitable differences between large and small communities, the basic social structure of most European cities followed a common pattern. Every city had a core group of established householders. In some places almost all of these householders were citizens; but even where the formal rights of citizenship were confined to a more exclusive group, noncitizen householders still had a recognized status with clearly defined rights. The adult male householder was likely to be the master of some craft and thus a full member of the relevant guild. The master carried out his trade with the assistance of his journeymen and apprentices and some help from family members and unskilled servants. In theory each master was economically independent, buying raw materials and selling finished products on the open market. In practice things were never so simple, for poor masters often found themselves doing piecework for wealthy entrepreneurs on whom they were economically dependent. Furthermore the master's wife, or sometimes even the master himself, might seek to supplement the household income by engaging in retail activity or other work outside the home. Some householders were not artisans but worked in the service sector, for example as innkeepers, teachers, or clerks. Nevertheless, the traditional image of the urban community consisting largely of households headed by artisans who plied their own trades under their own roofs never lost its validity.

Every city, large or small, also had a highly visible social elite. The wealthiest craftsmen or practitioners of the most prestigious trades might belong to the lower fringes of this elite group. The core of the elite, however, was normally made up of merchants and some professionals, notably lawyers. The largest cities might also have an even higher stratum of patrician families, whose members were no longer active in trade but lived off their investments and strove to be regarded as members of the aristocracy. Some towns attempted to define formally who belonged to the social elite, usually by specifying which families had the right to be represented in the city's highest political bodies. Such cases were rare, however. Most cities required some flexibility in defining membership in the elite, if only to replace old families that had died out. Even those municipal elites whose members made the most stringent attempts to bar any newcomers from joining their ranks, such as the patriciates of Venice or Nürnberg, eventually found it necessary to bend the rules and admit a few particularly wealthy or well-connected families.

At the other end of the social spectrum, every city harbored a large population of individuals who were too dependent, poor, or transient to be counted among the regular householders. Many of these people lived as journeymen, apprentices, or servants in the households of their employers. Others were unskilled laborers who lived in small rented quarters and supported themselves by performing the menial tasks that abounded in a premechanized society, such as carrying, digging, transporting, and animal tending. Even further down the scale was a floating population of paupers and thieves with no fixed homes or legitimate means of sustenance. Some Iberian cities also had slaves, both white and black. A special social niche was occupied by people regularly employed in occupations that placed them outside the margins of respectable society, such as executioners, carrion removers, and dung porters. The status of prostitutes declined in the early modern era. In the late Middle Ages prostitution was an acknowledged occupation, and its practitioners generally lived in carefully supervised establishments. By the end of the sixteenth century, however, almost all of those houses had closed, and prostitutes unavoidably slipped into the urban underworld.

The presence of ethnic or religious minorities complicated the social structure of some communities. Occasionally ethnicity determined a resident's legal or social status. In some cities in the Baltic region, for example, people of Slavic origin were barred from political rights and occupations that remained open to people of German descent. Religious minorities were even more common. Most of these religious subgroups arose during the Reformation, when some town dwellers insisted on adhering to a religious faith different from the one approved by the authorities. Sometimes adherents of a persecuted religion arrived as refugees in cities and were given rights of residence. In many cases members of religious minorities were

allowed or even encouraged to participate in lucrative economic activities even though they were not accepted as full members of the community. Often this meant that members of a religious subgroup became quite wealthy while remaining socially and politically marginalized.

The most extreme case involved the Jews. By the early sixteenth century Jews had long since been barred from living in England and France and had more recently been banished from various places in central Europe and from the Iberian Peninsula. But Jews were allowed to live as members of self-contained, socially isolated communities in cities in Italy, Germany, and much of eastern Europe. Some Jews became wealthy as moneylenders and merchants, and by the eighteenth century "court Jews" were deeply involved in helping European princes finance their regimes. Even so, wherever they lived the Jews remained socially segregated until the beginning of emancipation in the late eighteenth or early nineteenth century.

Early modern government officials were assiduous record keepers, and in many cities substantial data survived, making possible statistical reconstructions of urban social structure. Among the most informative sources are the records of property taxes paid by citizens or other established householders. Despite significant differences between various types of communities, wherever these data survive they demonstrate huge disparities in wealth among the householders of any given city. The great south German city of Augsburg is typical. In 1618 just under 9,000 citizen households were inscribed in the tax registers of Augsburg. Almost half of the householders were listed as "have nots," meaning not that they were entirely without resources but that their real and liquid property was not substantial enough to be taxable. Another quarter of the citizens paid an annual tax of not more than 1 *gulden,* corresponding to taxable assets worth up to 400 *gulden.* Above them were ranged an ascending scale of ever wealthier taxpayers. At the pinnacle were ten merchant princes, whose annual tax payments were over 500 *gulden,* representing fortunes of 100,000 *gulden* and up.

Disparities like this help explain why urban elites were so insistent on seeing the social structures of their communities in hierarchical terms. Some cities issued tables of ranks showing who could march where in public processions or clothing ordinances specifying what forms of adornment could be worn by which social groups. Yet no attempts to perpetuate the existing social hierarchy were ever able to resist the ceaseless pressure of social mobility. Urban patricians sometimes pretended they constituted a virtual caste, but in fact they belonged at best to an unstable status group. The upper reaches of urban society were constantly replenished by new families made rich by marriage, inheritance, or success in business. Prosperous immigrants from other communities also had to be accommodated and shown the respect that their wealth commanded. Some experienced downward mobility too, as the fortunes of wealthy families decayed or even, in some spectacular cases, rich men went bankrupt. In fact movement up and down the ladder of wealth and prestige took place throughout all ranks of urban society. Significant change often occurred within one or two generations. It was not unheard of for poor men to have rich grandchildren or, conversely, for rich men to have poor descendants.

URBAN GOVERNMENT

Urban government was always conciliar in structure. Cities often had a number of councils, but most of them were merely consultative. Real power was typically invested in a single council that combined executive, legislative, and judicial functions. Cities like Venice or Strasbourg with complex systems of interlocking councils were rare. Mayors might rotate in and out of office, but council members generally served for life. Occasionally the councilmen were elected, and sometimes a certain number of seats were reserved for particular constituencies, such as guilds or neighborhoods. In most cases, however, when a seat on the council became vacant through death or retirement, the existing members chose the replacement themselves. Thus many city councils were in effect self-sustaining oligarchies. On the whole urban constitutions were highly conservative. Occasionally changes were introduced, most often when rulers intervened to restructure the municipal government or to install their own clients in positions of authority; but whenever possible the magistrates resisted such changes and preserved the form of government that had been established during the Middle Ages.

Research on the composition of councils in European cities has shown that, no matter how the members were chosen, the end result was almost always the same: council members tended to be drawn from among the wealthiest members of the community. This was already the case in the late Middle Ages, but the tendency was steadily reinforced during the early modern era, when city councils became increasingly exclusive in their memberships. Yet the fact that wealth rather than pedigree was the most common ingredient in appointing new councilmen insured that political power could become available to emerging members of the social elite. Some changes occurred in the occupational profile of councils. Late medieval councils were typically composed of merchants and wealthy craftsmen, but during the early modern era craftsmen gradually disappeared from councils except in the smallest cities. At the same time more seats were held by rentiers who were not active in trade. The role of the legal profession in urban government shifted. In the late Middle Ages lawyers were influential in municipal affairs as advisers to the magistrates, but in the course of the early modern era more lawyers actually came to occupy council seats. By contrast, members of the clergy did not hold municipal office, though in some Protestant cities they sat with council members on consistories that formulated and enforced policies about marriage arrangements and personal conduct.

Changes in the composition of the urban political elite were closely linked to a gradual transformation in the relationship between cities and broader political structures. In the Middle Ages urban leaders struggled to assert their autonomy from kings and princes. By the sixteenth and seventeenth centuries, however, greater financial and military resources made it easier for rulers to assert or reassert their authority over cities. A few cities, such as Venice, Geneva, and the free cities of the Holy Roman Empire, managed to resist this trend. Other cities struggled against the rulers' power only to be forced into submission by military action. Most urban oligarchies soon perceived the advantages of cooperation with princely governments. Often the traditional municipal elite and the corps of royal officials slowly merged into a single urban oligarchy of wealthy and well-educated men whose families were intermarried with each other and increasingly isolated from the rest of the community.

Yet although civic leaders were drawn from an ever narrower fraction of the population, a number of factors prevented them from becoming entirely self-serving. City governments never commanded police power in the twentieth-century sense. They employed a few beadles or constables, but in attempting to maintain order the council depended chiefly on the cooperation of civic militias and neighborhood watches made up of the citizens themselves. The existence of an armed citizenry aware of its latent rights as members of the political community was a significant constraint on the exercise of arbitrary power. From time to time, when excessive taxes or unwelcome policies suggested that the magistrates had too blatantly ignored the wishes of their fellow citizens, uprisings flared. Sometimes council members were actually deposed, but more often they got a serious fright. Magistrates did not have to wait until they faced an armed crowd in the marketplace to know that they could govern ef-fectively only by heeding the interests of the established citizen householders.

GUILDS AND THE URBAN ECONOMY

Numerous groups in urban society voiced the concerns of adult male citizens, including militia companies and parish councils. But the most significant interest groups in European cities were generally the guilds. Although guilds sometimes had religious and social functions, their major purpose was always economic, that is, to guarantee the uniformity and quality of the goods and services their members provided and to protect their members' livelihoods by regulating the process through which apprentices became journeymen and journeymen became masters. A persistent objective of the guilds was to prevent the manufacture of goods by nonmember craftsmen in the surrounding countryside or in the city itself. This occasionally brought the guilds into conflict with aristocrats who patronized rural craftsmen or with entrepreneurial merchants who employed the cheap labor of nonguild artisans. But guilds also experienced internal conflict, typically between poorer masters, who might want to limit the number of journeymen permitted to work in any one shop, and richer masters, who wanted no restrictions.

The tensions between guild artisans and merchants or among the craftsmen themselves arose largely from developments associated with the spread of capitalism. When merchant entrepreneurs gained control of the sources of raw materials or the markets for finished goods, they made it impossible for masters to function as independent economic actors and effectively reduced the masters to wage laborers. Such trends were by no means new to the early modern era, having already become evident in some late medieval cities. But the trends accelerated in early modern times and triggered in turn more aggressive efforts by craftsmen to preserve their traditional rights.

In the struggle to protect their interests, guild members often voiced their faith in the legitimacy of economic monopolies, but this faith was by no means confined to traditional artisans. For urban capitalism in early modern Europe was also largely dependent on monopoly rights. Certainly some merchants in the sixteenth and seventeenth centuries tried to break guild monopolies by articulating the case for freedom of exchange in particular branches of production. But many of the most significant capitalist enterprises in early modern Europe, notably the overseas trading companies that pioneered in the extraction of wealth from the New World or the Indies, depended on royal charters or other privileges that granted their members the exclusive right to deal in specific goods or to trade in specific regions.

To the liberal or physiocratic thinkers of the eighteenth century, guilds, like chartered trading companies, were obstacles to economic freedom that stood in the way of economic growth. The assumption that guilds were backward-looking organizations that hindered social and economic progress persisted through the twentieth century. Many historians have recognized, however, that this is an oversimplification. Guilds never uniformly opposed technological innovation or entrepreneurial activity, though they consistently protected the ability of their members to earn a living as independent economic actors. In fact the guilds often played an effective and useful role in promoting the interests of their members and preserving the autonomy and integrity of skilled craft production throughout the early modern era.

Journeymen were integral to the guild system of production without being actual members of the guilds. A young journeyman was expected to spend some years traveling from town to town, enriching his experience and honing his skills by working on a contract basis for a succession of masters. Eventually the journeyman would hope to settle down in one city, often his town of origin. In theory journeymen were thought of as masters in the making who could ascend to full mastership once they met such customary requirements as the payment of a fee, presentation of an acceptable masterpiece, and engagement to a suitable bride. But often masters attempted to limit their own ranks by imposing stiffer fees or tightening the standards for admission. Journeymen had organizations of their own—*compagnonnages* in France and *Gesellenvereinigungen* in central Europe—whose importance increased as more of their members faced the prospect of never ascending to mastership. These organizations not only helped the journeymen to locate work and lodgings when they arrived in a new town but also provided the fellowship and solidarity that emboldened journeymen to protest or strike against inadequate wages or unfair conditions. Guilds are occasionally but inaccurately described as an early form of trade unions. In fact it was the journeymen's associations rather than guilds that served as prototypes for the labor unions that emerged in the nineteenth century.

RELIGIOUS AND SOCIAL ISSUES

Though urban magistrates were repeatedly called upon to adjudicate the disputes that arose among various groups with conflicting economic interests, the challenge of settling even the most bitter economic disagreements often paled before some of the other problems confronting urban rulers. Beginning in the sixteenth century, many of these problems had to do with religion. Religious tensions had not been unknown in medieval cities, especially when the authorities faced destabilizing outbursts of religious enthusiasm fueled by charismatic preachers. But an entirely new situation was introduced by the Protestant Reformation, which began when Martin Luther issued his Ninety-five Theses in 1517. The Protestant cause, which challenged some of the most fundamental beliefs and practices of the traditional church, found early support in the cities of central Europe, where widespread anticlerical sentiments merged with the humanist values of some educated citizens. The changes the early reformers demanded—a transformed structure of worship, a married clergy, an end to monasteries and nunneries, and a rejection of the traditional veneration of saints—required not just a new religious outlook but also a different relationship between the institutions of secular and religious authority. Some municipal leaders bowed to popular pressure and openly embraced these changes, while others adamantly opposed them. But many urban authorities took a more cautious line and ended up simply implementing the religious policies and preferences formulated by their princes.

By the middle of the sixteenth century, Protestant ideas in various forms had spread from Germany and Switzerland to much of the rest of Europe. In some areas, especially in northern Europe, Protestantism was imposed by royal or princely fiat. Authorities in Italy and the Iberian Peninsula prevented it from ever taking root. Communities in some countries, notably France and the Netherlands, were split by religious differences that led to bitter tensions and occasional riots. Historians have struggled to find a social basis for the religious allegiances of Protestants and Catholics in sixteenth-century cities, usually with little success except to note that urban men and women with some degree of education were more likely to be attracted to the new faith than those with no education. Municipal leaders, themselves often divided along religious lines, struggled to retain their authority while balancing the conflicting demands of their fellow citizens or of rulers and other powerful outsiders. Mostly the magistrates succeeded in retaining power, though sometimes new elites representing a different religious outlook took their place.

By the seventeenth century the confessional complexion of European cities was generally stabilized. There were numerous exceptions—notably En-

Municipal Leaders and Religion. The Antwerp burgomasters and aldermen in session with members of the Broad Council, 12 April 1577. The Antwerp magistrates requested Calvinist preachers to leave the city; one of them, Johan Saliger (standing behind the rear bench, in front of the fireplace) delivers his protest. Engraving by Frans Hogenberg. MUSEUM PLANTIN-MORETUS, ANTWERP, BELGIUM/STEDELIJK PRENTENKABINET, ANTWERP, BELGIUM

gland, where religious and political struggles within the Protestant camp in the mid-seventeenth century divided many cities into Puritan and Anglican factions. But sooner or later in most cities one confession came to predominate, and through a process of steady "confessionalization," the differences between Protestant and Catholic cities became fixed and permanent. Protestant communities, for example, had a small core of highly educated pastors primarily concerned with preaching and religious leadership. Catholic cities, by contrast, continued to have large ecclesiastical establishments with substantial numbers of priests and members of religious orders who provided spiritual, educational, and charitable services. Religious practices not just in churches but also in schools and households assumed distinctly Protestant or Catholic forms.

Although only a handful of cities, mostly in Germany, formally granted equal status to members of more than one Christian confession, the tumults of the sixteenth century left a residue of religious minorities in many communities. Often the members of a minority developed far-flung business contacts within their own subgroup or became noted practitioners of a particular craft. Some urban leaders, especially in dynamic port cities that tended to attract religious refugees, tried to take advantage of the economic services such groups provided while still upholding the concept of religious uniformity. In the great north German entrepôt of Hamburg, for example, the Lutheran clergy struggled throughout the early modern era to keep the city solidly Lutheran, while the more pragmatic, business-minded leaders of the municipal government repeatedly extended residential rights and even some religious freedoms to Calvinist, Catholic, Mennonite, and Jewish subcommunities. Although the number of religious subgroups in Hamburg was particularly large, the presence of such groups and the issues they raised for the urban authorities were far from unique.

The capacity of some urban leaders to put economic interests ahead of religious purity was linked, at least in some cases, to their mounting concern with an issue that confronted the authorities in every European city, namely the problem of poverty. Of course there had been poverty in the medieval city, but it was generally viewed in religious rather than social terms. Guided by the biblical maxim "the poor are always with us," lay and religious leaders of the Middle Ages stressed the obligation to help the poor but never felt challenged to eliminate poverty as such. Good Christians were encouraged to perform acts of charity more for the sake of their own souls than for the benefit of those whom they helped. The sixteenth century, however, witnessed a markedly heightened concern with poverty as a social issue, particularly in cities. A widespread notion emerged that the number of poor people in cities was increasing. In fact the demographic upsurge of the sixteenth century seems to have caused more men and women who could not sustain themselves in their own villages to head for urban centers. There was also a shift in attitudes. Beginning in the early sixteenth century, one city after another adopted ordinances to outlaw begging in the streets and replace it with centralized mechanisms to collect and distribute charity. In theory only the "deserving" poor, local inhabitants who had fallen on hard times, were to be aided, while "sturdy beggars" from outside were to be excluded. These ordinances owed something to the new Protestant doctrines that rejected good works as irrelevant to salvation; but the new approach to urban poverty was adopted, with some modifications, in Catholic cities as well. The real mainspring was the growing conviction among Protestants and Catholics alike that idleness in general and begging in particular were contrary to divine command and to earthly productivity. Those who could no longer work should be given assistance, but everyone who could work should be required to do so.

By the seventeenth century institutions such as orphanages, workhouses, and hospitals, in which people who did not belong to households would be provided for and the able-bodied among them would be put to productive labor, proliferated. To some historians this development amounted to a "great confinement" of the urban poor as part of a grand program to subject them to social discipline. In fact these institutions housed only a small fraction of those in need, and many of the inmates, resentful of having to work long hours for negligible pay, chose the first opportunity to escape. For most of the poor the first line of assistance in times of trouble was the informal system of self-help provided by family and friends supplemented, especially in Catholic cities, by church-based philanthropy. Only when these means were inadequate would they turn to municipal charity or, despite all prohibitions, resort to open begging. Unified schemes to deal with urban poverty on a citywide basis almost always failed because their proponents repeatedly confronted an unbridgeable gap between the extent of the need and the amount of available resources. Despite their unremitting attempts to deal with the problem, urban leaders always found it impossible to eliminate poverty or even sweep it off the streets. The poor were indeed always with them.

CONCLUSION

By the end of the early modern era, significant changes had taken place in European urban life, yet the elements of continuity were still preponderant. Though a few cities were approaching a size unknown in Europe since Roman times, the spatial organization and even the physical appearance of most cities were little changed from what had prevailed in the Middle Ages. The urban skyline was still dominated by steeples. Most cities were still walled, though progressive-minded thinkers increasingly urged that the walls be razed so as to integrate suburbs more effectively into the urban core.

The basic structure of economic life also showed significant continuities. Early modern Europeans were enthusiasts for technological innovation, and the early modern era saw the introduction of numerous improvements and refinements in the way goods were manufactured or transported. Yet the basic processes of production and distribution in the key sectors of the economy, including food, textiles, and metalworking, changed little. Except in England, where they steadily lost importance during the eighteenth century, guilds remained influential in the organization of economic life. Capitalist entrepreneurs who engaged in long-distance or overseas trade or who found ways to circumvent guild restrictions by organizing large-scale production continued to make huge fortunes. Rural manufacture of goods by peasants outside the guild system expanded significantly during the early modern era, but the capital that made this production possible normally came from wealthy men in the cities. Urban craftsmen continued to dominate the production of more complex, delicate, or refined goods.

The social organization of cities also remained fundamentally constant. Urban society was still strongly patriarchal. Men exercised authority in the community, shop, and family, though women had some influence over the property they inherited and some opportunities to earn an independent living. Power in cities belonged to a small oligarchy of wealthy men who dominated municipal councils, but places were always available for "new men" whose families had recently become rich. The old antagonisms between cities and princely regimes were largely forgotten as members of the urban elite worked with officials of the regime and the regional aristocracy and their families socialized or even intermarried. The broad mass of ordinary householding citizens, though generally excluded from real political decision making, exercised some influence through their seats on lesser councils, their participation in guild affairs, or their membership on parish or neighborhood committees.

Urban society in the early modern era was never static. The city offered endless opportunities for ambitious men and, in a more limited way, ambitious women to move up the social ladder by increasing their wealth or by finding useful patrons or spouses. The city offered pitfalls as well, for misfortune or miscalculation could cause rapid downward movement. The overall contours of urban society were modified as new forms of capitalistic enterprise and changing visions of culture and comfort created new occupations and opportunities. Religion, which had generated intense hopes and fearful conflicts in cities of the sixteenth and seventeenth centuries, began to play a slightly less dynamic role as it competed for allegiance with the rationalist culture of the eighteenth century. Yet none of the changes in urban life during the early modern period could rival the transformations that lay ahead in the nineteenth and twentieth centuries. The emergence of modern industrial society would transform urban life in ways that could never have been envisioned or imagined during the three centuries of the early modern era.

See also **Marxism and Radical History; The Protestant Reformation and the Catholic Reformation** *(volume 1);* **Capitalism and Commercialization** *(volume 2);* **Charity and Poor Relief: The Early Modern Period; Social Class; Social Mobility** *(volume 3); and other articles in this section.*

BIBLIOGRAPHY

General Works

Clark, Peter, and Paul Slack. *English Towns in Transition 1500–1700.* London, 1976. A slightly dated but still highly effective overview of the topic.

Cowan, Alexander. *Urban Europe, 1500–1700.* London, 1998. A useful survey that stresses the ways in which European cities coped with change during the early modern era.

De Vries, Jan. *European Urbanization, 1500–1800.* Cambridge, Mass., 1984. Uses extensive demographic data to delineate the contours of urban growth in the early modern era.

Friedrichs, Christopher R. *The Early Modern City, 1450–1750.* London and New York, 1995. A broad survey of the social history of early modern European cities that stresses the elements of continuity in urban life.

Garnot, Benoît. *Les villes en France aux XVIe, XVIIe et XVIIIe siècles.* Gap and Paris, France, 1989. A brief overview with useful references.

Gerteis, Klaus. *Die deutschen Städte in der Frühen Neuzeit: Zur Vorgeschichte der "bürgerlichen Welt".* Darmstadt, Germany, 1986. The best one-volume overview of early modern German urban history.

Hohenberg, Paul M., and Lynn Hollen Lees. *The Making of Urban Europe, 1000–1950.* Cambridge, Mass., 1985. A broad overview of European urbanization that treats the early modern era as a "protoindustrial age."

Jack, Sibyl M. *Towns in Tudor and Stuart Britain.* New York, 1996. Covers cities in both Great Britain and Ireland.

Konvitz, Josef W. *Cities and the Sea: Port City Planning in Early Modern Europe.* Baltimore, 1978. An important analysis of state-directed city planning.

Le Roy Ladurie, Emmanuel, ed. *La ville classique de la Renaissance aux Révolutions.* Vol. 3, *Histoire de la France urbaine,* edited by Georges Duby. Paris, 1981. A survey of French urban history during the early modern period.

Mackenney, Richard. *The City State, 1500–1700.* Atlantic Highlands, N.J., 1989. A short but useful overview of the relationship between cities and states.

Mumford, Lewis. *The City in History: Its Origins, Its Transformations, and Its Prospects.* New York, 1961. The central work in the urbanist tradition of urban history.

Selected Case Studies

Amelang, James S. *Honored Citizens of Barcelona: Patrician Culture and Class Relations, 1490–1714.* Princeton, N.J., 1986. A brief but penetrating analysis of the elite in one city.

Boulton, Jeremy. *Neighbourhood and Society: A London Suburb in the Seventeenth Century.* Cambridge, U.K., 1987. An admirably detailed investigation of social relations in one London parish.

Brady, Thomas A. *Ruling Class, Regime, and Reformation at Strasbourg, 1520–1555.* Leiden, Netherlands, 1978. A classic treatment of the urban Reformation approached through the collective biography of one city's leaders.

Cowan, Alexander Francis. *The Urban Patriciate: Lübeck and Venice, 1580–1700.* Cologne, Germany, 1986. An important comparative study of elites in one northern and one southern European city.

Dinges, Martin. *Stadtarmut in Bordeaux 1525–1575: Alltag, Politik, Mentalitäten.* Bonn, Germany, 1988. A conceptually pathbreaking analysis of the dimensions of urban poverty and the strategies for coping with it.

Friedrichs, Christopher R. *Urban Society in an Age of War: Nördlingen, 1580–1720.* Princeton, N.J., 1979. Uses tax registers and other records to analyze social structure and social mobility in a German city.

Goubert, Pierre. *Beauvais et le Beauvaisis de 1600 à 1730: Contribution à l'histoire sociale de la France du XVIIe siècle.* 2 vols. Paris, 1960. A pioneering attempt to encompass the total history of one city and its hinterland that influenced many subsequent studies of French cities.

Le Roy Ladurie, Emmanuel. *Carnival in Romans.* Translated by Mary Feeney. New York, 1979. Draws on anthropology and other disciplines to interpret the violence that beset one French city in 1579–1580.

Lottin, Alain. *Chavatte, ouvrier lillois: Un contemporain de Louis XIV.* Paris, 1979. Uses the personal journal of an obscure weaver as the basis for a broad analysis of the society of one French city.

Pullan, Brian. *Rich and Poor in Renaissance Venice: The Social Institutions of a Catholic State, to 1620.* Cambridge, Mass., 1971. A thorough treatment of social values and the administration of charity in a major city.

Robbins, Kevin C. *City on the Ocean Sea, La Rochelle, 1530–1650: Urban Society, Religion, and Politics on the French Atlantic Frontier.* Leiden, Netherlands, 1997. A masterly integration of urban social and political history.

Roeck, Bernd. *Eine Stadt in Krieg und Frieden: Studien zur Geschichte der Reichsstadt Augsburg zwischen Kalenderstreit und Parität.* 2 vols. Göttingen, Germany, 1989. A massive analysis of the society of one German city before and during the Thirty Years' War.

Underdown, David. *Fire from Heaven: Life in an English Town in the Seventeenth Century.* New Haven, Conn., 1992. A lucid description of the social impact of religious change.

Whaley, Joachim. *Religious Toleration and Social Change in Hamburg, 1529–1819.* Cambridge, U.K., 1985. Shows how urban authorities coped with religious pluralism.

Wunder, Gerd. *Die Bürger von Hall: Sozialgeschichte einer Reichsstadt, 1216–1802.* Sigmaringen, Germany, 1980. An outstanding example of a methodologically sophisticated work in the local history tradition.

THE CITY: THE MODERN PERIOD

Josef W. Konvitz

The modern world is an urban one. Within a few years after the beginning of the twenty-first century, more than half the world's population will be living in cities. Because Europe was the first region where the transformation from a predominantly rural to an overwhelmingly urban society occurred, the modern European city since 1800 has a wider significance. Will massive urban growth in many developing countries, given conditions of poverty and political instability, recapitulate the worst in the European experience of urbanization? Historians are justly suspicious of models which blur the specificities of time and place. There is no simple model or series of stages of urban development which every society recapitulates. Progress is neither linear nor cumulative but is rather the result of economic circumstances, social values, and political choices which necessarily vary according to place and time. But an emphasis on the differences between countries and periods which emerges from the multiplication of local studies can also obscure some of the recurring patterns associated with urban development, patterns which give some policy relevance to a better understanding of urban history.

FROM EARLY MODERN TO MODERN CITY

The biggest differences between the early modern and modern eras of urban development are the easiest to measure, namely demographic growth and the increase in economic production. But even the sense of rupture which accompanies the industrial revolution belies a continuity with an older pattern of urbanization. Of course the economic differences between the preindustrial, early modern city and the city since the onset of industrialization are dramatic and have had far-reaching social and environmental consequences. However, the explosive growth in productive capacity did not represent the emergence of fundamentally new urban functions, but rather elevated the importance of economic activity as an urban function. Because the industrial economy was itself located predominantly (but not exclusively) in cities, it can be said that the expansion of urban economic capacity, which has sustained urban growth more generally, was itself organized and rooted in cities.

The most important continuities are also the most difficult to measure, namely, cultural attitudes and social systems broadly open to novelty and change, migration, and defense of the rights and responsibilities of citizenship. The fact that the historic cores of many European cities have survived successive economic and political regimes is itself symbolic of what was carried over from the early modern to the modern era. Today, the identity of Europe is being shaped explicitly as a civilization of cities, symbolized by the selection each year of one or more cities as a City of Culture, and by the growing recognition on the part of the Commission of the European Communities (which does not have legal competence on urban policy according to the Treaty of Rome, 1957) that urban issues must be addressed if progress toward European unification is to be made.

URBAN STUDIES

Given the high degree of urbanization characteristic of Europe in the modern era, the study of the modern city is inseparable from a dozen or more topics covered elsewhere in this encyclopedia. If the city touches on everything, then what is its specificity? Urban specialists try to isolate the urban variables, those factors which appear to explain how and why certain events or trends evolved as they did because they took place in cities. This task is inherently difficult, not only because it is difficult to disentangle cause and effect when so many factors are in play, but also because urbanization itself has made urban life and behavior normative in society at large.

It is no surprise that many of the scholars who study urban phenomena have disciplinary roots in literature, sociology, economics, cultural studies, history, and the like. Support for research on urban issues is irregular, and university departments of urban studies often have an uncertain status, neither fully assimilated into the social sciences and humanities nor entirely independent as a professional field. The study of the city is essentially an interdisciplinary effort, but the integration of different disciplinary perspectives, and especially of the economic and the social, is elusive. Moreover, urban spatial phenomena are often marginalized in urban studies, treated as a branch of architecture and physical planning rather than as an independent factor of change. As a result, cities and urban phenomena more generally are not well integrated into larger syntheses of economic and social studies, which continue to focus on the nation-state as the unit of analysis. The national census collects vast amounts of data, but if one looks for information about social and economic conditions in a region as large as Paris-Île-de-France, with a population smaller than that of the Netherlands but with a gross domestic product as large, the gap between national and regional data collection becomes stark.

Antiquarian studies of individual cities began to be written in the nineteenth century, and local history remains an important aspect of scholarship. The major journals are *Urban History Yearbook, Journal of Urban History,* and *Urban Studies.* Broad interpretive syntheses are often organized thematically, with evidence coming from any of a score or more of cities. Important examples with a spatial-social focus are by Sir Peter Hall and Lewis Mumford. They are concerned with explaining the interaction between individuals and the urban milieu, and therefore, with a sense of optimism based on the potential for collective action without coercion, they also try to identify those aspects of urban development which promote better social outcomes. In this they echo many of the great novelists who have tried to show how the lives of people in cities are interconnected by physical pathways and by invisible social networks, thereby emphasizing the ability of individuals to shape their identity in relation to the rest of society. The English novels of Charles Dickens and John Galsworthy, the French novels of Honoré de Balzac, Victor Hugo, Émile Zola, and Jules Romains, and the German works of Theodor Fontane and Thomas Mann come to mind. Given the parallel growth of photography as a medium and of cities, it is not surprising to find that some of the greatest and most innovative photographers were also some of the most important recorders and interpreters of cities: Charles Marville, Eugene Atget, August Sander, Berenice Abbott, Bill Brandt, Robert Doisneau.

SOCIALIZATION AND THE CITY

In the early modern city, major events such as wars, even revolutions, and such cultural movements as the Renaissance, the Reformation, and the Enlightenment left basic social structures intact. The very mode of life in cities in the mid-eighteenth century would have been broadly familiar to anyone who could have stepped back in time to the early sixteenth century. By contrast, there can be a debate about the relative rate of change today compared to, say, the 1820s or 1910s, but not about the impact of change, nor about the importance of cities as places which make change manifest.

The ability of successive generations of people—most of them migrants from the countryside or small towns—to adapt to life in cities helps to explain the survival of the city as the most complex social unit in the history of civilization. Because cities are so dynamic, even after a society reaches a high degree of urbanization, the capacity of people to adjust to change remains important. Indeed, one of the functions of the modern city involves facilitating the adjustment of individuals and groups to change. Cities do this by supporting formal institutions such as schools and libraries and informal ones such as philanthropic and community organizations, by making information widely available at minimal cost, by providing a context for social interaction and consumerism which fosters fluidity and the appreciation of novelty, and above all, by supporting large labor markets which give people opportunities to use and improve their skills as technologies evolve. Adaptability is a complex phenomenon, involving the ability of people to learn, to improvise, to innovate, and to imagine how things could be different. It is culturally contextual, because people are not sensitive to the same things—a change which is easily accepted in one place at one moment may be resisted elsewhere. What matters is that the mental and social habits of people be sufficiently flexible to accommodate changes which are often profound and irreversible in such things as technology, scientific concepts, social relationships, political institutions, and economic regulations and norms.

Until the late nineteenth century, much of the discourse about cities was part of a larger cultural undertaking to describe and define the social and cultural workings of civilization. Urban sociology emerged from this mode of thought when Ferdinand Tonnies, Max Weber, Émile Durkheim, Georg Simmel, and Robert Park began to dissect the workings of social systems in cities by interpreting behavioral patterns against a model of urban society. A major theme of this work involved how large social systems cohere and function given the high rate of individual mobility, meaning that the population of any group in a given place is unstable. Their explanatory framework tended to emphasize abstract value systems and role models which diffused expectations of normative behavior in respect to personal and social goals. In this context they explored how the city, as a social and spatial environment, affected individual behavior. Paradoxically, therefore, the greater autonomy of the individual in a city was explained, not as a reaction against or as independence from large social systems, as was the case in the romantic era of the early nineteenth century, but as a reflection of very powerful sets of ideas and pressures to conform which emphasized individuality as compatible with social goals such as enterprise, cooperation, professional ethics, and public service.

The debate today about what is happening in cities, and to cities, often appears in the media in articles about "the urban crisis" which lack a historical perspective. If cities become less able to help people acculturate, then the likelihood of social problems on a wider scale increases. Concern about crime, terrorism, and drug trafficking are responsible for the spreading use of closed-circuit television cameras and electronic surveillance, instruments of control more passive but more pervasive than anything known before. The potential for centralizing control over urban populations, which was limited in the past by the fluidity in urban society which overwhelmed systems of information and communication, has been strengthened by the introduction of networked systems linked to huge data bases that operate in real time. Urban problems emerge unexpectedly; urban policy, which evolves slowly, is more often remedial than proactive. Cities are more diverse than before: places with 500,000 inhabitants may have immigrant groups from a hundred different nations. But lacking the administrative capacity and resources of nation-states, cities are often hard-pressed to promote cohesion and integration. The balance between freedom and constraint has always been difficult to set in cities, even if their scale, density, and complexity make the issue unavoidable.

THE HISTORY OF THE MODERN CITY

In contrast to the early modern city, the history of the modern city is one of dynamic change which requires a chronological framework to be understood in its broad pattern.

Before 1800, with the possible exception of the Netherlands and parts of northern Italy where the spread of cities was greater, only about 20 percent of Europe's population was urban. That figure rose to over 50 percent in England by 1850 and in France by the early twentieth century. The post-1945 era has seen the level of urbanization reach 80 percent on average across Europe. A comparably high degree of urbanization can be found today in North America, Australia, and Japan, raising questions about the degree to which generalizations about the modern city in Europe can be extended to other continents. In countries with an indigenous urban tradition, such as Japan, the European city was seen in the nineteenth century as the model to be imitated; in countries colonized by Europeans (particularly Canada, the United States, and Australia), European cultural and legal influences had a major influence on urban spatial form, social structure, and economic functions. In the twentieth century non-European cities (principally American) have influenced European ideas about architecture, social welfare, culture, and so on, sometimes negatively, sometimes positively. But the status of Paris, London, and Rome at the top of the list of the most visited cities in the world, and indeed the importance of cities as a category of tourist destination across Europe, are signs that European cities are still admired as unique environments, even in a world of cities.

Given the high population density of cities, as much as 80 percent of the land of Europe has remained rural, even though as little as 3 percent of national employment involves people engaged in agriculture. Urban regions are characteristic of the British Midlands and southeast England, of a broad band extending from the North Sea coast of the Low Countries and France across the Rhineland to northern Italy, a Mediterranean crescent from Catalonia across France to Italy, and a Baltic archipelago including parts of Sweden, Norway, and Denmark. Most Europeans have easier access to more than one city than do most Americans: on average, the distance between cities in Europe is only 16 kilometers, against an average distance of 29 kilometers in Asia, 53 kilometers in America, and 55 kilometers in Africa.

The largest European city in 1800 was London, with over 1 million inhabitants; Paris, which had been larger than London from the Middle Ages until about 1700, had a population of about 900,000. Most cities were smaller, however, and the gap between the largest and the smallest (five thousand inhabitants) in cultural terms was enormous. At the end of the twentieth century, the largest cities—taking account of their metropolitan area—were again London and Paris, with about 16 million. (By then, however, the largest cities in the world, with populations of 20 million or

London, 1827. St. Paul's Cathedral dominates the City. View across the Thames from the southwest. Engraving (1827) by William Wallis after a drawing by Thomas H. Shepherd.
MARY EVANS PICTURE LIBRARY

more, were all in Asia or Latin America). Put in other terms, 20 percent of the people live in cities larger than 250,000 inhabitants, 20 percent in medium-sized cities of between 50,000 and 250,000 inhabitants, and 40 percent in smaller cities of between 10,000 and 50,000. Life in very large cities is still more often the exception than the rule, which should make us beware of generalizations based on conditions in them. The sheer size of large cities, combined with an interest in local history which is very widespread in more modest places, means that historians have studied small and medium-sized cities more than their individual importance in urban history might suggest.

1800–1880. The history of the modern city can be divided into four periods, all shaped by the interaction between cities and larger political and economic events. From the late eighteenth century until around 1880, the outlines of the modern city emerged in two different kinds of places, the new industrial cities such as Manchester and older capital centers such as London. The industrial cities were strikingly different due to a large number of factories and the associated pollution and slum housing. At this time, however, the older centers did not acquire heavy industry; their change was more a function of their growth in size and of the ways of life of people. Capitals retained, and indeed enlarged, monumental spaces which conformed to their elite functions, but they also supported large numbers of small workshops, some devoted to the luxury trade which was both local and

for export. What emerges from a survey of London or Paris is the sheer range or diversity of skills and crafts practiced in the city. It is this period which is studied in depth when the transition to the industrialized economy and a society of classes is investigated.

1880–1914. From 1880 to 1914, heavy industry based on a new wave of innovations (electricity, automobiles, chemistry, media) settled in capital cities (Berlin, Budapest, London, Paris); cities in many parts of Europe such as Italy, Hungary, Austria, and Sweden which had grown modestly before began to grow at a very rapid rate; and new modes of planning and management—as well as new urban technologies such as the streetcar and modern systems for water and waste—became widespread regardless of the size and age of the city. During this period, academic departments for planning and architecture were established; frequent meetings and a stream of publications created an international, transatlantic culture about cities. At this time, widespread concern about crowd control and criminality lead to the introduction of modern, scientific methods of identification of individuals (measurement and photography). Many of the problems of rapid industrial urban growth came under control as new professions in public health, education, engineering, and administration applied scientific methods and developed new institutions.

1914–1950. The era of the two world wars, 1914–1950, was characterized by the role of the city in war production and in the control of large social systems. This period is less well understood than other periods of urban development, notwithstanding its enormous importance for the second half of the twentieth century. Increasingly, the city was the arena of conflict, either when directly attacked or when torn by the struggle between totalitarian and democratic ideologies. From the uprisings of St. Petersburg of 1917 and of Vienna and Berlin in 1919 through such events as the Popular Front in France in 1936 and the wave of destructive attacks on synagogues in Germany on 9 November 1938, cities were the sites of riots which had the potential to provoke revolutionary change. Not since the seventeenth century had riotous activity been so widespread and intense; with good reason, this era can be called the second Thirty Years' War. The trauma of violence and sacrifice among civilian populations (including severe malnutrition and epidemics) and the profound scale of political and social change gave rise to the construction of many major monuments, provoked debates about historic preservation and reconstruction, and created new myths of civic survival for the epicenters of conflict (Verdun, Ypres, Louvain in World War I; Rotterdam, Hamburg, Leningrad, Warsaw, Berlin, Coventry, Dresden, Hiroshima in World War II).

Dependence of urban populations on technological infrastructure for daily living made cities appear vulnerable if the level of physical destruction was high enough, or attacks precise enough, to destroy the complex systems providing clean water, removing waste, generating power, and supporting communication. The assumption of strategic bombing was that modern city dwellers are so dependent on sophisticated technology that they are no longer capable of initiative if disoriented and displaced. However, this negative judgment of urban society was contradicted by the behavior of people in almost every city subject to annihilation—for the most part, people coped within the boundaries of civilized life. Although on the margins black markets, thievery, and rape were evident, the destruction of cities did not bring about a collapse of civilization.

The era of world war was decisive in several respects. It brought about a period of inflation which lasted virtually for the rest of the twentieth century, shifting influence from creditors to debtors and wiping out the savings of small investors in the short run; it caused the disappearance of such social groups as the Jews from many cities in Germany, Austria, Poland, Hungary, and Czechoslovakia, where they had lived in large numbers, often in communities that were centuries old; it gave rise to large migratory movements as prosperous northern economies recov-

ered by absorbing surplus labor from eastern and southern Europe and, increasingly, from former European colonies as well. And it gave rise to the movement for European unification, which has been the basis for peace and growth since the 1950s and for the growing importance of supranational institutions on domestic matters which had previously been the monopoly of the nation-state.

The economic and political pressures of the world wars, and especially of World War I, had other effects which often go unrecognized for their urban significance: the collapse of the small family firm in many medium-sized commercial cities due to rapid changes in world economic conditions and to inflation, thereby encouraging people to seek careers in government or in large corporations, and the enormous wartime expansion of productive capacity, which helped to validate scientific management and large capital-intensive factories as the model of production. Only in the 1970s and after has this been corrected by the growing emergence of small and medium-sized firms and by the growth of the service sector, both of them predominantly urban in character, which have created new job opportunities for people.

The economic crises of the 1920s and 1930s limited the extent to which popular demands for a better quality of life could be satisfied in terms of improved housing, transport, and public services. During this period, control over urban economies passed decisively from the local to the central level. The imperatives of social and economic control during wartime, justified during the emergency, and the difficult adjustment to peacetime propelled central governments to expand their influence into spheres of domestic policy from which they had often stood apart in the past.

1950 to the present. The era 1950–1990 involved reconstruction along two different lines, the welfare state in Western Europe and centrally planned economies in communist-controlled Eastern Europe. As a result, the pattern of convergence in urban society which had been characteristic of the 1880–1914 period, and which made life in Budapest and in Stockholm fairly comparable, mutated into two different trajectories. In both East and West, cities had to cope with massive rural-to-urban migrations and with a lack of resources to add social facilities on a scale envisioned by enlightened planners. But it is the contrasts which matter more. Freedom and prosperity leading to the consumer revolution of the 1950s through the 1970s in the West stood in contrast to the uniform and repressed system of life in the East. The fracture line in Europe no longer ran within urban societies, separating classes and parties, but between them, along the Iron Curtain.

While the West had more freedom, its cities were faced with a growing burden of national regulation and with an inadequate tax base and limited borrowing power, making them dependent on provincial and central governments for an appreciable proportion of their finances. National trade, tax, transport, health, and especially economic policies have far more influence over cities than any strategy designed at the city level, or even any explicit urban policy at the national level. Although most people live in cities, provincial and national legislatures often are overrepresented by rural areas. In a hierarchy of national administration, the city may be the lowest level, but to many citizens it is the highest level of government with which they have regular contact.

The symbols of municipal office, the debates in the city council, the routine functions of civic administration, and mayoral elections play a vital, irreplaceable role in democracy. This role, however, is under pressure due to decreasing participation in local elections. Increasingly, cities are exploring the limits of their freedom of action, especially in the international arena, through developments such as the twin city movement, direct representation abroad, international marketing, and positions on issues of international importance. Decentralization in the 1990s was not so much a response to demands from cities for more autonomy as a response by central governments to pressures in the financial markets to reduce their expenditures and limit their exposure to potentially very high levels of social transfers and welfare payments. Cities are taking advantage of the opportunities provided by decentralization and globalization to develop cooperative international networks, economic development strategies, and local environmental initiatives.

Three issues highlight a positive trend toward an urban renaissance in Europe: sustainable development, which calls attention to social cohesion and environmental quality in cities; decentralization, which highlights the importance of strong regional and local institutions capable of guiding the development of cities; and civil society, which calls for greater public participation in decision making, a role for community and nonprofit organizations, and a culture of trust and understanding in an increasingly diverse society. The survival and reinforcement of cities is a more conspicuous objective of public policy in western Europe than in Australia, Canada, or the United States. The pursuit of a more balanced form of development, a priority in Europe, is increasingly accepted as the objective for cities everywhere.

BUILDING AND REBUILDING THE MODERN CITY

No one foresaw the rate of urban growth or its consequences. The gap between the goals set to improve cities and the means applied to meet those goals has often been very wide. At first, urban conditions had a bigger impact on society, depressing living standards. Only from the mid-nineteenth century onward has society made substantial progress in remaking the city. In the final analysis, however, the burden of urban problems associated with rapid urban growth and with the management of very large cities has not undermined the city.

The modern city differs from the early modern in the nature of its physical expansion, which had enormous consequences for social organization. (The importance of city building in economic terms is captured by the percentage of a country's capital stock that is invested in urban buildings and infrastructure, which often reaches 25 percent.) The early modern city (with rare exceptions, such as Paris after the 1660s) was enclosed by walls which provided defense and served as a fiscal barrier. New districts within or without the city were realized only when the city walls needed to be modernized, new public squares built, or when part of a city destroyed by fire needed to be reconstructed (all too frequent a phenomenon until fire regulations and insurance spread in the most commercially sophisticated cities during the eighteenth century). There was always a tendency toward social segregation within the early modern city based on wealth and family or ethnic affinities, but it was never total in a given area or along a particular street. Cities in the nineteenth century were refortified, and remained so until after 1918 (Paris regained walls after the 1840s), and population growth quickly filled in whatever open land was left. Population pressure on housing therefore maintained a pattern of social heterogeneity, with the exception of the worst tenements and rooming houses, often in areas already known to be unhealthy or adjacent to industrial facilities. The breach in the walls was the railroad, whose construction toward the center of the city and whose capacity to absorb land brought irreversible change. Efforts in the twentieth century to provide an outer limit to a city, through regional planning measures such as new towns and a green belt, have been of limited success, partly because they are difficult to sustain over long periods of time, and partly because development can leapfrog around them.

The rebuilding of the city is most often associated with Baron Georges Haussmann (1809–1891), whose administrative control over Paris for nearly

Tenements for the Poor. "Over London—by Rail," engraving by Stephane Pannemaker after a drawing by Gustave Doré. The engraving appeared in William Blanchard Jerrold's *London, a Pilgrimage* (1872). CENTRAL ST. MARTINS COLLEGE OF ART AND DESIGN, LONDON/THE BRIDGEMAN ART LIBRARY

twenty years gave him the opportunity to execute redevelopment projects on an unprecedented scale. These projects called for the rebuilding of the center to accommodate more people and activities, the construction of new linear traffic arteries, and new building codes allowing larger buildings while creating an impression of uniformity at the street level. Haussmann also annexed many suburban communities, thereby extending the limits of the city far beyond its then current needs in 1860, a model for management which has been followed elsewhere. The transformation and enlargement of Paris, and of other cities on this model such as Vienna, Berlin, and many smaller provincial centers, led to more homogenous residential areas; the creation of functional zones devoted to retailing, wholesaling, legal and administrative activities, and cultural and leisure facilities; the construction of new broad, long avenues for circulation (which often involved the demolition of much of the existing urban fabric along their path); and the extension, through engineering on a large scale, of urban facilities into the countryside, to meet urban needs (canals, reservoirs, etc., as well as places for relaxation, such as parks and forests). The organization of agriculture to supply cities, the construction of modern transport,

and the growth of large markets in cities as distribution points were parts of a single process by which commerce and government worked to assure a supply of food at low cost to a large urban population.

Imagination and considerable managerial skill were needed to build water supply and sewer systems, underground or elevated inner-city rail networks, electricity generation and distribution facilities, and so on. Indeed, some of the modern techniques of large-scale organization management, including personnel policies, differential pricing to consumers, in-house research laboratories, market research, and the like either originated in or were developed on a large scale in relation to these networked systems by which technology reshaped not only the city and its environmental impact but also the daily lifestyles and temporal rhythms of its inhabitants. These interrelated technological networks compressed space, permitting densities to rise and buildings to soar, but they also expanded the use of time, enabling people to undertake more activities stretched over more hours. A key result, visible in European cities by the 1870s, was a marked decrease in urban death rates, thus breaking the dependency of cities on in-migration for growth—a truly historic change.

The specialization of architecture accompanied this process. New structural forms were based on iron, steel, glass, and concrete, thereby giving rise to debates about whether traditional structures such as churches and theaters could be given radically new architectonic expression. Factories were often monumental structures, dominating urban form and the cityscape. The debate between traditional and modern views of architecture was often linked to broader political, ideological divisions.

In the nineteenth century the vast majority of urban residents, whatever their incomes, were tenants; most landlords were small investors, though some were large-scale property developers whose ambitions often created spectacular fortunes but could lead just as easily, when a downturn in the economy came, to bankruptcy. Row houses for the middle and upper classes were built by the same methods as tenements for the poor, the difference being the quality of construction and space per inhabitant. Because the quality of housing was linked to incomes, many poor people were condemned to overcrowded and unsanitary conditions, which prevailed until the post-1945 era. Suburbs connected to cities by rail lines (beginning with Bedford Park in London) gave middle-class people a wider range of options, but until the 1920s and the expansion of mass transit and the construction of social housing on a large scale, cities continued to grow faster than suburbs. Rising levels of home ownership are only characteristic of the post-1945 era, and are associated with a decline in the population size of cities relative to suburbs.

The principal civic structures of the modern city mix opulence with utilitarian purposes: libraries and museums, department stores, theaters, hotels, hospitals. The proliferation of such facilities has been accompanied by the expansion in numbers of people working in the cultural and service sectors (health, education, and culture are often the largest single employment sectors in cities today), and it reflects the capacity of strong local cultures to survive and modernize, often with an impact felt far away (theater in Munich, music in Milan, architecture in Glasgow and Barcelona). The growth of dedicated vacation towns by the sea (Brighton, Deauville) or of spas (Vichy, Aix-les-Bains, Baden-Baden) also represented a form of specialized urban space, produced to stimulate a certain kind of consumption, in this case fashion, health, and entertainment. Civic art, especially in the form of decorations on the facades and in the interiors of buildings, gave visual delight and beauty a pervasive presence in many parts of the city, whereas before aesthetic design had been associated only with churches and great public buildings, which people did not frequent on a daily basis.

MODERN URBAN SOCIETY

Although social segregation increased in housing, the city streets remained a part of the public realm, characterized by great heterogeneity. For most of the nineteenth and early twentieth centuries, even after the introduction of mass transport (horse-drawn omnibuses, cabs, streetcars, rapid-transit trains), people walked considerable distances daily, and walking remained the most common form of movement. People also mingled in concert and music halls, pubs and cafés, parks and churches. The nighttime illumination of the city, first by gas and then by electricity, coupled with the extension of police patrols, transformed the hours after dark into a time of recreation. But as literature and drama reveal, the interaction in the city at night was often an occasion for lonely people to witness others enjoying a good time from which they were excluded. Émile Durkheim, in his famous study of suicide, found that the people who were most likely to take their own lives were those who had the fewest connections or networks with other individuals. Solitude led to death. Today, however, people are increasingly likely to live in cities alone, either as a lifestyle choice when young or as a circumstance of old age. Is this a sign of greater individuality? Or a failure of social communication and organization? Whatever the answer, this is a novelty in urban society, leading in turn to a need for more dwelling units for a population of a given size, and for more social and commercial services outside the home.

Social mixing in the nineteenth century, when associated with high density, and at a time when contagious diseases such as cholera, tuberculosis, and syphilis accompanied a lack of sanitation and considerable overcrowding, also gave rise to public debates about promiscuity. The ability of strangers to meet—a cultural pattern promoted by so many migrants coming to the city—was linked to the ease with which people in the city could become anonymous or create a new identity. This was a factor in the rise of racist ideology designed to keep people apart in separate ethnic groups. Debates about whether city living enhanced civilization or lowered morals—debates which had their origin in the Enlightenment—were carried forward in an urban culture in which religion appeared to be declining.

Thus the city has been depicted by some as a place where society fragments and by others as a place where individuals can come together into a larger, more unified body. Disaggregation or unity? Individual autonomy or collective solidarity? Is the city a fluid, dynamic environment which can be shaped by individuals, or a rigid, structuring container which imposes choices and limits options? These pairings represent, not judgments on cities as a whole, but a range of social choices which the city, more than any other settlement, can provide.

CITY PLANNING AND SOCIAL DEVELOPMENT

The problem for city planners has been that the scale on which they work is far greater than the scale which individuals inhabit and use on a daily basis. As a result, the techniques for giving form to urban space, to prepare them for development, have tended to shade the differences between people, to standardize around the average. This was above all typical in the Fordist era of mass production, when building and planning by rules and norms made possible the progressive expansion of the city while eliminating a range of environmentally unsound and unsanitary practices. The result, however, was a city zoned into single-purpose districts, each of which lacked the diversity to evolve as circumstances changed. Uniform monofunctional buildings and land use patterns on this scale risk becoming prematurely obsolete, expensive to modernize but difficult to use otherwise. In recent years, the concept of mixed-use planning (which always survived for historic urban cores) has become a goal. This involves new problems of combining different uses, and buildings and spaces created and modified over time. Many historic urban cores, a product of the preindustrial, early modern era, have characteristics more suitable to the postindustrial, knowledge-based service sector economy than areas built to serve a manufacturing labor force and urban economy twenty or even sixty years ago.

Modernism emerged during this period (approximately 1880–1960) and was often applied to city planning. Modernism was grounded in the assertion that there are principles and rules by which buildings and cities can be ordered. One can in fact talk of a tradition of modernity: a spirit of reform linked to an architectural and planning vocabulary suitable in a great variety of places and at many different scales, based on principles of reason and the criterion of meeting human needs. From this perspective, the Gothic revival of the mid-nineteenth century was just as much a phase of modernism as was the neoclassical revival of the late eighteenth. The most common understanding of modernism, however, which relates most clearly to the period from the late nineteenth to the mid-twentieth century, involved a strenuous dismissal of decorative elements, especially if superimposed on a structure, and a celebration of a form which expresses its function and structure.

The problem is now how to change the city as it exists to meet the social and economic opportunities and needs of the twenty-first century. The lessons of the modernists are often forgotten now that technology provides many of the physical elements needed to make life in cities comfortable, but the historical effort to renew modernism is still important: modernism emphasized the need to improve environmental conditions and to give people access to light and space; it created public spaces appropriate to large urban crowds yet still often intimate enough for people to be alone; and above all, it asserted that people must understand the city to make best use of it—hence the pursuit of a visual language designed to communicate clearly and meaningfully. Postmodernism, by contrast, rejects the very idea that design can meet the needs of different people in a coherent manner, based on the argument that people are too diverse, and that any effort to develop a coherent style involves a relationship of power.

This discussion about modernism raises the question of for whom the city is made. This is an important issue because many of the problems of sustainable development, including social disparities and environmental degradation, require a high level of technical expertise to solve. How much will people be willing to learn, in order to participate in decision making? If decision making is centralized, how can it remain democratic? What decisions and investments should be taken today, to assume better living conditions in ten or twenty years? These questions are not new, but animated political and community life during much of the nineteenth and twentieth centuries. The debates around critical planning issues and urgent social problems are now read by historians to better understand the distribution of power within urban societies, the role of gender and class in decision making, and the social construction of technology and space.

There are those for whom the city is, in effect, a residual, the product of social and economic forces. This argument is frequently coupled with an assertion that in the market economy, the spatial structure of cities represents what people want. From this point of view, there is nothing necessary about a city center: centers may have been important for technological and economic reasons during certain phases of economic development, but they can be dispensed with in the current era of globalization and information technology. Taken to an extreme, this approach to urban development does not consider the location of economic activity to be a significant variable in national economic performance. Planning has fallen into disfavor, largely, no doubt, because it is perceived as a bureaucratic exercise devoid of imagination, and because it is associated with an economy of scarcity, not of abundance.

The opposing view is held by people who believe that the future of cities is not to be shaped entirely by market forces and technological trends, but should rather be guided by an understanding of what they contribute to economic life and democratic society, and by a vision of what cities can become. This approach is far more sensitive to the contribution of different kinds of urban spaces and networks to economic innovation and production, and to the interrelationship among social, environmental, and economic conditions. Increasingly, economic development strategists recognize that the best investment cities can make in their own economic development is to enhance the quality of life that they offer. This is linked to an understanding of the role that city centers play as places necessary to the well-functioning of the city as a whole, and thus to its sustainability.

The perfect society, ever since the days of Plato and Thomas More, has commonly been represented in urban terms. Utopian writers have tried to show perfection in cities as a matter of a regular street pattern, buildings of uniform shape and with a high standard of comfort, and an adequate disposition of civic spaces and cultural facilities. In the perfect city, different groups would all find their place, without pressuring one another. As a mirror image of reality, utopian representations showed that the urban norm was overcrowded and conflictual, that living conditions were inadequate, streets uneven, and civic culture weak—in other words, dystopian. There was a tension implicit in the exercise of writing and drawing utopian cities, however: how to get from the way things are to the way we want them to be. Was it necessary to reform society to build a better city? Or if a better city could be built, would the environmental and social conditions in such a place improve individuals, communities, and the state? During the Renaissance and Enlightenment, the physical means to build better cities were quickly exhausted on a small number of princely towns of very modest size, or on a few distinguished urban squares or complexes. In the nineteenth and twentieth centuries, however, the sheer rate of urban growth as well as the increasingly large role of the state (or in some cases, of benevolent industrialists) made possible the design and construction of large residential and commercial areas which were very progressive in style and quality. It was only a short step further to argue that a reallocation of resources could transform cities. The economic failure of the centrally controlled economies, together with the sheer cost and complexity of building planned

towns in western Europe after each world war, have damaged the utopian aspects of planning.

THE URBAN ECONOMY IN SOCIAL TERMS

A brief examination of the urban economy is needed, not only because the modern city is devoted to economic production and consumption to an unprecedented extent, but also because the creation of wealth has been one of the foundations of efforts to improve quality of life. Given the fact that the wealth of European cities was at a much lower level than it is now—and that wars and depressions have destroyed capital—how can a poorer society become richer? The neomarxist argument holds that capitalism exploits the city, first by using speculative investment in land to accumulate capital but also by promoting a lifestyle based on the consumption of commodities and prematurely obsolete fashion. Development theory, on the other hand, calls attention to saving, investment in education and in improvements which lengthen the average lifespan and improve health in the productive years, and institutions of trust which reduce conflicts and enhance problem solving—all factors found first in European cities, and often well developed by the middle of the nineteenth century. Countries undergoing the transition from rural to urban accompanied by a rise, not a fall, in living standards include Sweden in the interwar era and Spain after the 1970s—both influenced by atypical policy environments, the former by a countercyclical economic policy, the latter by integration into the European Union. In these cases, redistribution mechanisms helped to overcome a situation which in the nineteenth century had been marked by immiseration. A virtuous cycle may even exist: when wealth is applied to the creation and diffusion of knowledge and the improvement of living standards, health, and housing, people are more productive and social capital is enriched, thus enabling society to achieve further economic growth. This cycle is difficult to initiate and difficult to sustain. It does not just happen by chance.

This cycle implies three points: first, that the modern economy rests on an essentially urban way of life; second, that efforts to make cities more efficient and productive have always given rise to questions about how wealth is distributed and shared; and third, that the solution of urban problems related to power, sanitation, communications, etc., have led to significant innovations in services and technology which have become the basis of major industries on their own. In other words, not only was society being reshaped to serve economic systems, it can also be said that social processes have influenced economic growth.

For example, the classic narrative of industrialization omits the fact that urban growth impelled many facets of industrialization, beginning with the manufacture of building supplies and the raising of agricultural productivity. From the perspective of social history, what matters is that the organization of the city's own economy to meet the daily needs of people, as well as the production of goods and services to pay for goods imported from other places, involved the creation of opportunities based on individual initiative in an economic system that absorbed migrants. Fear of a vicious circle—that success of a city will lead to its growth, adding to the scale of problems which must be solved if the city is to remain viable—has sometimes led to efforts to limit city size, but these have always failed. Instead, we need to talk of a virtuous cycle, whereby urban problems generate innovations and solutions which improve efficiency and the quality of life.

Communication between people from different walks of life and professional fields (cross-fertilization) has long been, and remains, an ingredient in economic development. Examples of cross-fertilization which helped to solve urban problems include the growth of the insurance industry, which grew out of fire prevention codes in London in eighteenth century; electrification, as a response to the pollution associated with coal and gas; and telephony, as a response to the traffic congestion and sprawl of the late nineteenth century. A socially grounded element of the modern city which was fundamentally shaped by its economic needs is therefore the reliance on coordination and cooperation rather than on command and control systems of organization. Coordination and cooperation depend on the ability of people to trust one another and to rely on unwritten rules or norms as well as on formal modes of communication such as books and newspapers to solve problems.

Cities therefore provide markets where standards of quality, price, and availability promote trade and innovation. The management of urban density is itself a factor in making markets work, helping to reduce the risks and costs of doing business in cities, expanding capacity, and eliminating bottlenecks. The introduction of new modes of production and of better methods of financing credit and identifying risks all implied a flexibility in organization which stood in contrast to the formal and rigid order of guild-based economic activity in the early modern era.

It is possible to categorize cities by their economic functions, not only because their spatial structure may reflect these differences but because their social structure may as well (affecting the relative distribution of professional, managerial, employed, and unskilled workers). With the emergence of the post-industrial, service economy, categories which proved useful in the past no longer apply. In the past, however, seaports, provincial capitals, and manufacturing cities were all very different kinds of places.

The port city as a type can illustrate this phenomenon. Because ports were connected to wider networks of trade, they were places where exotic goods—and contraband—could be found more easily and visibly. They were also places where foreign foods could be sampled, where zoos displayed the animals of Africa and Asia, where the flags and shields of consulates were visible in the city center, and where hospitals had specialists who could treat tropical diseases. Ports were cosmopolitan in ways that other cities, even capitals, were often not. The imperatives of freight handling and warehousing gave them a distinctive appearance (London docks, Hamburg warehouses)—highly congested. This specificity has now been lost. The commercial buildings of the port—now vacant because containerization has displaced port functions to huge, capital-intensive sites, often far removed from the city center, where large volumes of containers can be moved between ship, rail, and truck efficiently—have been reclaimed as leisure centers and as housing and office space. The river, once polluted and crowded with ships, is now often clean, but barren of human use.

The specialized functions of different cities, once reflected in a unique blend of institutions, buildings, social categories, and cultural patterns, have now been dissolved. Cities still specialize economically to varying degrees, but their specializations no longer lead to differences which are so visible to visitor and resident alike. When the famous market "les Halles" was torn down in 1972, a victim of the huge growth of Paris and congestion in the city center, which had made the distribution of foodstuffs difficult, it was replaced by an underground shopping center directly accessible to suburbanites by a series of high-speed rail links.

In this context, speculation has begun about the impact of information and communication technology and of the new networked economy on the social, economic, and spatial characteristics of cities. One early concern relates to the phenomenon of exclusion, whereby some individuals or groups lack the skill or access to participate in the new economy. Another concern relates to the possible relocation of people and activities far outside cities as the cost of communicating over distance diminishes. On the other hand, the networked economy highlights the importance of creativity and innovation in cities as an element in economic growth, cultural change, and new modes of social life.

The specificity of the city has been raised in connection with the study of innovation and creativity. Why, in a largely urbanized world, and one in which cities are more alike than different, are some places uniquely more important as creative "milieus"? This is a social and spatial phenomenon—spatial because interaction, especially unplanned and spontaneous, is often a matter of how people interact in public places, and social because new ideas often emerge when people of different backgrounds observe each other and find opportunities to meet. The key factors seem to include migration, a social mix, and some pressures in the form of mild political constraints, economic limitations, and so on which lead to polarized debates and anxiety about the future. The most important cities for cultural creativity are not necessarily those where economic innovation is strongest, and vice versa, although the distinction between commerce and culture is breaking down now that cultural activities are themselves recognized as a major source of employment. Still, the network or map of creative cities does not reproduce a single urban hierarchy, but multiple ones. Where will the creative urban centers of tomorrow be?

CONCLUSION

The modern city, in terms of social history, shows urbanization to have been a process based on the interaction between material circumstances and economic conditions, on the one hand, and social aspirations and political objectives on the other. Synchronization between what people wanted and what they could achieve has been elusive. But over time, and certainly from the perspective of the present, enormous progress has been made, especially in terms of living conditions and the formation of social capital (health, education, safety). Social cohesion, even in favorable economic circumstances, still appears fragile, giving rise to retrospective assessments of community life in the past, which can take on the aura of a golden age. Life in cities has never been easy, in part because the city is itself the largest and most complex social unit developed by man. Cultural creativity—long held to be the final measure of the potential of urban life—is perhaps the most problematic basis by which to measure change. On the one hand, there has been of late a marvelous expansion in the number of patents and in the number of titles of books in print; on the other hand, questions can be asked about the endur-

ing value of what is produced. Comparisons with 1900 are not flattering to ourselves.

Ultimately, the problem of urban policy is a problem about how political advances can keep pace with economic change. Each of the three major periods of urban development since the Renaissance expanded political rights and economic opportunities, albeit through a process of change that was often highly conflictual. The late eighteenth and nineteenth centuries witnessed the creation of capital and commodity markets for the first major metropolitan centers of the Atlantic world, but also checks on arbitrary government and on the dominion of the military over cities, as well as the emergence of individual rights enshrined in law. Urban growth in the period 1880–1920 accompanied the introduction of modern telecommunications, urban infrastructures, electrification, mass production, and retailing, as well as modern social welfare systems and universal suffrage. The economic opportunities of our era, combining globalization, environmental gains, high technology, and urban growth, are fairly clear to see. But their implications for the exercise of democratic rights and for the protection of the rights of the individual are difficult to grasp. Without a concerted effort to strengthen representative government at the local and regional levels, however, it is difficult to see how the competitiveness and sustainability agendas can be implemented.

The role of the city in a highly urbanized society is unclear today. Against what point in time should progress be measured? And according to which criteria? The number of millionaires in a city, or the percentage of adolescents completing secondary school? The murder rate, or the rate of bankruptcy? Why should people want to live in cities? Traditionally, the existence of cities has been justified on the basis that they allow individuals and groups to fulfill their social and intellectual potential in ways that no other social environment can. This potential can be expressed in commerce and the economy just as well as in the creative and performing arts, or in the conduct of civic and public affairs. The past is full of examples of people who have engaged themselves with their city as much or more than with any other unit of social organization. The beginning of the twenty-first century, however, appears to mark the end of the era of the modern city as much as the end of the eighteenth century marked the end of the early modern city. A time of transition has clearly begun: its outcomes depend in part on whether people still care to shape the cities in which they live according to their aspirations and values.

See also **Civil Society** *(volume 2) and other articles in this section.*

BIBLIOGRAPHY

Agulhon, Maurice, ed. *La ville de l'age industriel.* Vol. 4 of *Histoire de la France urbaine.* Edited by Georges Duby. Paris, 1983.

Berry, Brian J. L. *Comparative Urbanization: Divergent Paths in the Twentieth Century.* 2d ed. New York, 1981

Brun, Jacques, ed. *La ville aujourd'hui.* Vol. 5 of *Histoire de la France urbaine.* Edited by Georges Duby. Paris, 1985.

Dyos, H. J., ed. *The Study of Urban History.* New York, 1968.

Dyos, H. J., and Michael Wolff, eds. *The Victorian City: Images and Realities.* 2 vols. London, 1973.

Evans, Richard J. *Death in Hamburg: Society and Politics in the Cholera Years, 1830–1910.* New York, 1987.

Fishman, Robert. *Urban Utopias in the Twentieth Century: Ebenezer Howard, Frank Lloyd Wright, and Le Corbusier.* New York, 1977.

Graham, Stephen, and Simon Marvin. *Telecommunications and the City: Electronic Spaces, Urban Places.* London and New York, 1996.

Hall, Peter. *Cities of Tomorrow: An Intellectual History of Urban Planning and Design in the Twentieth Century.* Updated ed. Oxford, 1996.

Hall, Peter. *Cities in Civilization: Culture, Innovation, and Urban Order.* London, 1998.

Mumford, Lewis. *The City in History: Its Origins, Its Transformations, and Its Prospects.* New York, 1961.

Olson, Donald J. *The City as a Work of Art: London, Paris, Vienna.* New Haven, Conn., 1986.

Pevsner, Nikolaus. *A History of Building Types.* Princeton, N.J., 1976.

Relph, Edward. *The Modern Urban Landscape.* Baltimore, 1987.

Schlor, Joachim. *Nights in the Big City: Paris, Berlin, London, 1840–1930.* Translated by Pierre Gottfried Imhof and Dafydd Rees Roberts. London, 1998.

Sharpe, William, and Leonard Wallock, eds. *Visions of the Modern City.* Baltimore, 1987.

Sutcliffe, Anthony. *The Metropolis, 1890–1940.* London, 1984.

This article presents the author's own views and not those of the OECD.

THE URBAN INFRASTRUCTURE

Nicholas Papayanis and Rosemary Wakeman

The urban infrastructure is analogous to the internal frame of a building: as the frame is the underlying structural support for the building, the urban infrastructure is the underlying structural foundation of a city. Cities from the earliest times have had infrastructural amenities—roadways and sewers, for example—and all infrastructural development involves the provision of public services and the use of public spaces that are deemed essential for the ability of people to live in the city. Over time an increasingly accepted notion was that circulation of air, sunlight, commerce, vehicles, water, waste matter, people, and even knowledge was as essential to the healthy operation of the city as, to employ another analogy, blood circulating through the human body. What marks the development of the modern infrastructure since the nineteenth century is its close association with technological development, industrialization, and the dramatic growth of city populations. While definitions of the urban infrastructure may include any and all public services, the essential elements of the urban infrastructure during the nineteenth century, the formative period of the modern city, consist of new streets and boulevards, mass transit, new sewage systems, and the provision of gas, water, and electricity. The net effect of these infrastructural developments is the creation of the modern city as a circulatory system designed to move people and material products rapidly and efficiently, both above- and belowground.

THE STREET

Streets are the most basic element of the urban infrastructure. Traditionally they are designed to carry vehicular and pedestrian traffic, transport merchandise, and provide public spaces for social interaction. They also function as conduits for waste matter and, in modern times, house sewage, gas, electrical, and water systems below their surface. On a more fundamental level, streets are essential for access by city dwellers to work sites, markets, and homes. Because streets are public spaces, political, social, and ideological considerations figure in their construction and control. Government authorities are always concerned with street activities as a function of public order and safety. The health of the city is closely related to the street: for example, narrow streets do not permit the circulation of air or the diffusion of sunlight, and streets without effective drains breed disease from stagnant water and waste matter. Thus, whether the construction of streets is financed privately or by the government, control over the street rests with public officials.

Beginning in the mid-eighteenth century, London set the standard for street improvements. The Westminster Paving Act of 1762 shifted responsibility for street maintenance from home owners to paving commissioners. The latter had a paid staff and the right to tax abutters for street improvements. By 1800 London had extensive gutters, paving using smooth stones rather than pebbles, sewers, storm drains, piped water, and sidewalks. Street planning also involves aesthetic considerations and social consequences. This is evident in the construction of London's Regent Street, a south-north thoroughfare designed by John Nash and built mostly from 1817 to 1823. The most significant visual transformation of London at that time, Regent Street was cut in the West End, extending from Portland Place in the north to the Carlton House at the south end. Regent Street was conceived essentially as a magnificent formal street for rich strollers and shoppers, a physical conduit for the wealthy. Thus its placement conformed to existing patterns of social division in London. Given the limited access routes to Regent Street from the poorer East End, the latter was cut off from the more elegant West End, thereby reinforcing social separation. Only between 1832 and 1851, following a series of parliamentary reports, did London planners and government officials begin to address health issues and working-class morals when cutting new streets as part of slum clearance programs.

French government administrators were impressed with English infrastructural advances, and in

1823 G. J. G. Chabrol de Volvic, the prefect of the Seine Department from 1812 to 1830 and the official in charge of administering Paris, paid an official visit to London to study that city's water distribution system, sewers, and sidewalks. In France he proposed the extension, widening, and paving of Paris streets and roads. His first aim was the creation of a communication network linking all parts of Paris. His second priority was to reform those streets that were important, in his words, "to public security, to sanitation, or to the needs of commerce." Beautification was his last consideration. He also devised a system for delivery and distribution of water throughout Paris that would assure, he correctly believed, the health of the city. The French government lacked the resources or the political will at that time to implement Chabrol's vision of a modern Paris. Nevertheless, as Nicholas Papayanis observed in *Horse-Drawn Cabs and Omnibuses in Paris* (1996), that vision must rank as an important forerunner of Georges Haussmann's sweeping reforms of the urban infrastructure and therefore of the idea and shape of the modern city.

Although not much progress was made during the French Restoration (1814–1830) in building sidewalks, sixty-five new streets were opened during this regime. The prefect of the Seine Department under the July Monarchy (1830–1848), Claude Rambuteau, began applying English reforms to the rebuilding of the Avenue of the Champs-Elysées and other large boulevards. The pace of street construction accelerated with a total of 112 new streets, including the rue Rambuteau in the center of Paris and intense building speculation on the Right Bank. It remained for the authoritarian empire of Napoleon III and for Haussmann, his chief planner and prefect of the Seine Department, to construct the modern network of Paris roads. Haussmann completed the "great cross" of Paris boulevards that bisected the city in a north-south (the boulevards Saint-Michel and de Sébastopol) and east-west (the rue de Rivoli and the avenue Doumesnil) direction. Built to address strategic, health, economic, and aesthetic considerations first anticipated by Paris intellectuals and administrators before the Second Empire, Haussmann's neobaroque boulevards also reinforced spatial segregation in Paris. Slum clearance forced workers out of the city center toward the eastern and northern parts of Paris and its suburbs, while the well-to-do concentrated in the northwest of Paris and neighboring suburbs.

By the mid-nineteenth century the link between narrow streets and the health of the city was widely recognized in Europe. At this time Germany, too, adopted the principle of the wide boulevard. Aesthetic and symbolic considerations, however, were the primary factors in the construction of Vienna's most famous road, the Ringstrasse. As Austria industrialized during the nineteenth century, Vienna, whose upper classes had never abandoned the capital, remained a city for the well-to-do; industry and workers occupied the suburbs. When Austria adopted a constitution in 1860, the bourgeoisie replaced the aristocracy as the governing elite of the country and of Vienna and, as Carl E. Schorske noted in *Fin-de-Siècle Vienna* (1981), proceeded to shape the capital in its own image. The medieval walls that had surrounded the old city were destroyed. Central to the new image was the city's first grand boulevard, the Ringstrasse, whose monumental public buildings (the opera house, the university, the courts of justice, the houses of parliament, the municipal theater, and the art history and natural history museums) were linked symbolically and architecturally to secular liberal ideals. The massive and ornate apartment houses that occupied the greater length of the Ringstrasse were intended by the Viennese middle classes to suggest the opulent life of the aristocracy. Middle-class planners gave no consideration to social programs for workers.

Two other developments transformed European streets. From the late 1880s streets throughout Europe (and the United States) were paved with asphalt, a smooth, water-resistant surface ideally suited to the automobile. The increased use of automobiles on city streets was a major factor in the demise of the mixed use of streets (for strolling, shopping, and the like), as the requirement for rapid vehicular movement became the street's principal function. This in turn promoted new forms for streets closely associated with modernism, the urban expressway and the multilevel interchange. The modernist aesthetic was summed up by the architect Le Corbusier in his famous dictum that the street had become "a machine for traffic, an apparatus for its circulation."

URBAN TRANSPORT

The street as an instrument for vehicular circulation has a long history. From the seventeenth century on, horse-drawn cabs and private coaches became a common feature of urban life in capital cities. Their increased use in Paris and London, the two leading capitals of early and modern Europe in terms of infrastructural advances, corresponded to the physical expansion of the European city, the increase in its population, and the desire of the well-to-do for greater comfort in their daily rounds. The first hackney coaches appeared on London streets in significant numbers in the 1620s. The first regular Paris horse-

Boulevards. The Ringstrasse, Vienna, late nineteenth century. The Ring, a series of boulevards that replaced the old city walls and glacis, was begun in 1859. Museen der Stadt Wien, Vienna

drawn cab service began operating around 1630. In both cities municipal authorities established strict regulations governing the operation of coaches for hire. Early modern Paris even had a kind of omnibus service briefly. Between 1662 and 1677 a Paris firm owned by three court nobles operated a vehicle, whose invention is commonly ascribed to the philosopher Blaise Pascal, designed for the transportation of a large number of unrelated people. This rectangular coach, the *carrosse à cinq sols* (five-penny coach), so called because of the price of a single ride, traveled along fixed routes, cost relatively little, and had regular departures whether full or not. Unlike the modern omnibus, however, the law expressly forbade common people to ride in this coach. The cost of all forms of urban transportation limited their regular use to the upper classes until well into the nineteenth century. For the most part the lower classes worked and socialized within walking distance of their homes.

Although the circulation of people and vehicles was becoming a quintessential element of modern urban life, it was only during the eighteenth century that a sophisticated theory of urban communication flow emerged, related both to Adam Smith's writings on the necessity of capital circulation for a healthy economy and William Harvey's discovery that blood freely circulates through the healthy body. Urban intellectuals and public officials increasingly saw the ability of people and commerce to circulate freely through the city as a mark of its health.

The great age of public transportation was the nineteenth century, however. New and dramatic urban demographic pressures, significant industrial and commercial expansion, and the continued physical expansion of the city increased the demand for and the supply of public transportation. In Europe, including Great Britain, France led the way in the organization of urban public transit in the first half of the nineteenth century. The number of horse-drawn public cabs in Paris increased from 2,542 in 1819 to 13,655 in 1907. After 1907 the number of horse-drawn cabs began to decline significantly as the number of motor cabs increased. But the first substantial transformation in urban transit in Europe during the horse-drawn era was the introduction in France of the omnibus, a closed, rectangular vehicle with seating capacity initially for fourteen people. Designed to travel along fixed routes for relatively low fares, the modern omnibus admitted people from all classes without restrictions except for those rules governing proper behavior. Omnibuses began to operate in the French provinces before they did in the capital. Nantes had omnibus service in 1826, Bordeaux in 1827. Paris officials, having determined the safety of the vehicle, permitted omnibuses on the central streets of the capital in 1828. In June 1854, in a move later copied in London, Second Empire officials created a unified municipal transit operation by placing all omnibuses under the control of one firm, the Compagnie Générale des Omnibus. In February 1855 they also created a virtual monopoly, which lasted until 1866, of cab service under the control of the Compagnie Générale des Voitures à Paris.

Not everyone was served equally by public transit in Paris. Cabs, with their high fares and small car-

Urban Transportation. Horsedrawn omnibus, Paris. Illustration by Victor Adam, c. 1840.
BIBLIOTHÈQUE DES ARTS DECORATIFS, PARIS/©GIANNI DAGLI ORTI/CORBIS

rying capacity, were never intended for the general populace; but they were ideal vehicles for tourists or the Parisian bourgeoisie. The omnibus initially served the middle classes more than Parisian workers. The first omnibus routes ran in the heart of the well-to-do residential parts of Paris, the Right Bank center and the Left Bank just opposite. At mid-century omnibuses did not begin operating until eight o'clock in the morning, too late for most workers to start off to work, and the two-zone fare of central lines made the omnibus too expensive for most workers. Workers did benefit, however, from increased working opportunities in urban transport.

For urban transport Parisians also had a small circular rail line, *la petite ceinture,* that tied together the disparate rail stations, none of which penetrated the city center. Beginning in 1867 steam-powered boats operated on the Seine River for travel outside Paris. A small number of horse-drawn trams began running in the 1870s, and one cable car line opened in 1891. Public coaches in France and elsewhere in Europe began converting to motor traction in the 1890s.

London was just behind Paris in the development of mass urban transport. George Shillibeer, who had worked for a Paris coach maker, was impressed with Paris omnibus service. Returning to London, on 4 July 1829 he began operating an omnibus route between Paddington and London. Only after 1832, when the hackney coach monopoly that had governed the operation of London coaches for hire ended, were omnibuses permitted to service the center of London. In 1855 French financiers, along with English associates, took the lead in forming a concentrated omnibus firm that ran about six hundred of the approximately eight hundred omnibuses in London at the time. It was replaced by a largely English firm, the London General Omnibus Company, in 1858. Concentration of urban transport in London, as in Paris, became a characteristic of the industry. Also in Paris, initial fares in London were too high and starting times too late for the omnibus to be of use to workers. Until the 1850s, when fares on larger omnibuses began to drop, it was a vehicle largely for the middle classes, tradespeople, and clerks, allowing them to live farther out from the center of London. People could also get about or to and from London by steamships on the Thames, although these were not all-weather vehicles, by railroads, and, from the 1870s, by horse-drawn trams. Trams ran from the inner suburbs to the London periphery and were prohibited in the central London districts; but because they could carry more people, they charged low fares.

In an additional breakthrough with respect to mass urban transit, tram service throughout Europe was electrified during the last two decades of the nineteenth century. By the early twentieth century the technology had spread unevenly but had become widespread on the Continent and in Great Britain, with important social consequences. As John P. McKay demonstrated in *Tramways and Trolleys* (1976), the electric tramcar marked a genuine revolution in urban mass transit, as electric trams covered far greater distances than horse-drawn trams and were far less expensive to operate. These trams contributed far more dramatically than their horse-drawn counterparts to suburbanization, reduced fares, and the opening up of leisure activities for all classes outside the city. They were also important instruments for highly concentrated capital investment.

A second important development in urban transit occurred in London on 10 January 1863, when the line of the world's first underground urban railway opened. Within six months over 26,000 passengers were riding the underground daily. Fast and comfortable, the London underground railroad also provided special fares for workers. Budapest and Glasgow became subway cities in the 1890s. The Paris Métro, after the London Underground the second most important and extensive European subway, opened on 19 July 1900. Its construction was delayed by a political dispute, between the central government and railway companies on one side and municipal officials on the other, over whether it would be linked to the national rail system or serve only Paris, and by public debates over whether it should be above- or belowground. The city won, but as a result the Paris Métro did not begin to service suburban communities until the late 1920s. Its primary function was to transport all classes quickly and cheaply within Paris. Between the beginning of the twentieth century, the inaugural era of European rapid mass transit, and the 1960s, many more European cites, among them Berlin, Madrid, Rome, Leningrad (now St. Petersburg), Kiev, and Frankfurt, also became subway cities.

STREETLIGHTS

Not only did electricity power Europe's subways after 1900, it was also the means by which the darkness of night was illuminated by powerful, permanent, artificial light. Street lighting, like other infrastructural developments, was a characteristic of the early modern city. Lighting streets and home exteriors by candle was common in the sixteenth century. By the seventeenth century street lanterns, as Wolfgang Schivelbusch showed in *Disenchanted Night* (1988), became a matter of government policy. This development coincided with the formation of the centralized state and points to a cardinal function of street lighting, namely the state's control and surveillance of public spaces. Gas lighting, in use in English factories by 1800, moved out onto London streets by 1814. Paris first experimented with gas lighting for streets in 1829, but only after the 1840s did its use become general. German cities began using gas lighting in the 1820s, but its extensive use there dates from the 1850s. Electricity as a source of lighting was introduced in the late 1880s, a great improvement over gas in that it did not consume oxygen, was odorless, and could be turned on and off at will. As Schivelbusch observed, electricity's use also coincided with and was made possible by the great concentration of capital at that time. Only huge capitalist enterprises could construct and operate the central power stations needed for the city's supply of electricity for streetlights, homes, and factories. The circulation of electricity throughout the city became a key element, therefore, in creating the circulatory network of infrastructural amenities aboveground, in stimulating the capitalist economy, and in linking homes to central power sources. It integrated those elements more deeply into the urban fabric and opened the night to shopping, theatergoing, and other leisure activities pursued in safety and under the watchful eye of the state.

THE UNDERGROUND CITY

Water, in the urban setting closely associated with health, also circulated in the city. In 1850 basic urban utilities and sanitary conditions were about the same as they had been for centuries. Water was a precious resource, available only to those who could afford it. The overwhelming majority of urban inhabitants were dependent on river or pump water for domestic use. The London water supply, for example, came mainly from the heavily polluted Thames River. Inadequate amounts were supplied by private companies to wealthier households through rudimentary, leaky wooden pipes that extended only into the basements of houses. The poor took what they could get from local wells or outside taps, which ran only a few hours or a few days each week. In the new industrial towns whole neighborhoods were sometimes without water even from local wells. Most of the water for Paris originated from the Ourcq Canal and was used to supply public wells and fountains. In 1840 neither the kitchen nor the privy in a middle-class Parisian flat had running water. Water carriers sold from the streets, but the poor filled their pails from public outlets or scooped water from the gutters. In Vienna, Moscow, and St. Petersburg, insufficient water remained a serious prob-

Urban Transportation. Directors and engineers of the Metropolitan Railway Company, London, inspect the world's first underground line, between Paddington and the City of London, 24 May 1862. Chancellor of the Exchequer W. E. Gladstone is seated in the front row, near right. The line began service in January 1863. ©HULTON-GETTY/LIAISON AGENCY

lem. Street sellers hawked bucketfuls to residents until well into the nineteenth century. In Moscow water was so scarce that it was rationed to institutions. Only in Berlin, where the groundwater level was a few meters below the surface, did inhabitants easily supply themselves with well water.

Cities did not have adequate waste removal systems until the second half of the nineteenth century. Few towns had sewers, and storm water mixed with animal excrement and other wastes flowed through street gutters directly into rivers. The most commonly employed methods of disposing of human waste products were the belowground privy and the cesspool system. Night soil was carted beyond the town limits and used as fertilizer on nearby farms, or it was dumped into watercourses or onto vacant land. Even along the most elegant streets of Berlin, such as the Leipzigerstrasse, the contents of privies were emptied at night by brigades of women, filling the air with appalling odors. London and Paris had rudimentary disposal

systems that had originally been constructed only for the drainage of storm water. While solid waste stored in cesspools or casks was carted away, liquid waste was emptied directly into the street gutters. In Paris the twenty-six kilometers of drainage ditches kept up by private contractors often overflowed in a downpour. The city's stench and filth invariably horrified visitors. Enterprising businessmen appeared with planks during rainstorms and charged pedestrians a small fee to cross open sewers on their boards. London's sewer system was composed of a hodgepodge of gutters, underground drains, and open drains administered by eight different commissioners. Even in the capital cities with rudimentary utilities, the size and quality of drains varied widely. Large drains emptied into smaller ones, and few were built with any incline. The plans and locations of ancient networks of conduits and water pipes were often long forgotten or lost. Europe's towns and cities fell into a crisis of basic services with every storm or dry spell.

Waste Removal. In Lille, France, waste was removed by men who purchased it from households, collected it in barrels, and sold it to farmers to use as fertilizer. The practice continued until 1889. Cartoon from *Le Lillois,* 7 July 1889. ARCHIVES DEPARTMENTALES DU NORD, LILLE, FRANCE/PHOTO BY JEAN-LUC THIEFFRY

THE URBAN HYGIENE MOVEMENT

The modern underground circulatory system of the European city began to take shape with the urban hygiene movement of the mid-nineteenth century. Chronic cholera and typhoid epidemics during the late eighteenth and early nineteenth centuries had thoroughly shaken both the public and the authorities. In particular the cholera epidemic that swept through Europe's cities in 1832, claiming 5,300 victims in London and 20,000 in Paris, provided the impetus for sanitary reform and prodded the redesign and expansion of underground drainage systems dur-

ing the 1850s and 1860s. The increased interest in urban hygiene was also stimulated by massive increases in population. Between 1800 and 1850 the population doubled in some cities. The population of Paris went from 547,000 to 1,053,000, that of London from 1,117,000 to 2,685,000, and that of Berlin from 172,000 to 419,000. It was difficult to supply the growing population with services from wells, river water was increasingly polluted, and sewer systems were already inadequate and overtaxed. Cesspools overflowed. Common drainage ditches became elongated cesspools filled with uncovered, stagnant excrement. With industrialization, factories along the water's edge in-

283

creased the demand for pure water used in manufacturing but at the same time pushed water pollution to the extremes of crisis.

Perhaps the most important reason for the increased awareness of hygienic problems in Europe was the sanitary movement in Great Britain. Edwin Chadwick's reports on hygienic conditions in urban areas, published as *Report on the Sanitary Condition of the Labouring Population of Great Britain* in 1842, brought to light the inadequacies in the provisioning of basic urban utilities. The streets, courts, and alleys where cholera and typhoid first broke out and were most deadly were invariably in the immediate vicinity of open sewers, stagnant ditches and ponds, gutters filled with putrefying waste, and privies. Disease and ill health in Chadwick's opinion were a major cause of destitution and pauperism and a burden on the taxpayer. Conditions could improve only with investments in urban sanitation, the removal of waste, and an improved water supply.

Chadwick and his group of social reformers known as the "sanitary school" argued that clean springwater could be steam pumped, as the heart of a new urban circulatory system, through pipes or veins into every tenement, which would be supplied with a water closet. Each tenement would be connected to a sloped sewer system that used gravity to flush out waste. The sewers or arteries would then conduct their contents to sewerage farms for fertilizer. Filtered through the soil, the waste would be collected by a drainage system that flowed to the nearest river and eventually to the sea. Chadwick's urban reformers believed that their arterial sanitation system—decades ahead of its time—was a cure-all for the social question.

Within the next few decades a complete reconsideration of the dual questions of water supply and waste removal led to a revolution in public utilities. By the beginning of the twentieth century, most towns and cities in northwestern Europe had comprehensive water systems under public ownership that supplied the urban population with clean water. Sewer systems, built at enormous cost and designed for the removal of storm water, wastewater, and human waste products, had been built or were being planned.

However inadequate and overtaxed, London remained the standard against which continental cities measured their own shortcomings. Early urban renovation projects, such as the construction of Regent Street and Regent's Park, provided opportunities to open the underground and install new networks of drains and sewers, waterworks, and a canal. The City Commission of Sewers constructed some forty-four miles of huge sewers. With the manufacture of cheap metal water pipes and improved methods of steam

pumping, private companies supplied water from the Thames to first- and second-story water closets. Running water and the invaluable new water-closet appliance made dwellings in London's favored districts an unimaginable luxury in comparison to contemporary Vienna and Paris. Fixed baths came somewhat later, but as early as 1840 they were frequently found in London's newer houses. Nonetheless, tens of thousands of the city's poorer inhabitants remained without access to any services at all, even communal water spigots. Long lines of people, pails in hand, stood for a turn at the nearest outdoor faucet the few hours the water supply was turned on. In winter the faucets froze. Private companies had no obligation to provide piped water to the poor, and few landlords were willing to invest in utility improvements. Only half the buildings in London were connected to sewers in 1848.

The City Sewers Act of 1848 required installation of water cisterns and drains connected to sewer lines in all new houses in London. The city could also compel owners of existing buildings to provide them. The Metropolitan Water Act of 1852 required that private water companies obtain their water supplies from unpolluted sections of the Thames River, cover their reservoirs, filter their water, and furnish a constant supply of water in those districts that demanded it. In 1855 the indirectly elected Metropolitan Board of Works was established with responsibility for managing public works, and sewering, paving, cleansing, and supplying water came under general public control. Joseph Bazelgette, leader of the board's engineers, designed a sewer system that relied on underground sloping conduits connected to the old drainage pipes that would flush waste west to east across London and then deposit it into the Thames far below the built-up area. However, during the very hot summer of 1858 the board deadlocked over the location of the sewer outlets. The pollution in the Thames became so intolerable that it was known as the "great stink" of 1858 and became a national scandal, eventually pushing the government into breaking the impasse. Bazelgette's metropolitan sewer system, completed in 1865, was one of the greatest engineering feats of the nineteenth century. Sewers eighty-two miles in length were built in or tunneled beneath London and washed away 420 million gallons of waste and rainwater daily almost entirely by gravity. Circular or oval in shape, the brick sewers varied from four to twelve feet in diameter. The most notable addition was the Victoria Embankment along the Thames, built essentially as a lid to cover both the main sewer conduit and the underground Metropolitan Railway. The ongoing excavations for Bazelgette's work, which continuously dis-

Bazelgette's Metropolitan Sewer System. Victoria Embankment, London, from Waterloo Bridge, c. 1895. Somerset House is to the left, St. Paul's Cathedral in the distance. Below the roadway is a sewer and the Metropolitan Line of the London Underground. AKG LONDON

rupted the streets and traffic of London, provided visible evidence of the radical transformation taking place underground.

THE SUBTERRANEAN ORGANS OF PARIS

Spurred by the shock of cholera and the example of the British public health movement, a new approach to sanitation practices took shape in Paris as well. The city began building new systems to distribute water and evacuate waste that would help, according to urban reformers, cleanse the city not only of its sewage but of the underlying causes of social and revolutionary turmoil. H. C. Emmery, the head of the Paris sewer system from 1832 to 1839, placed fountains at the heads of streets in northeastern, working-class districts. Water from the fountains washed into new gutters under sidewalks and emptied into sewer drains. While traditionally sewers had been built with hewn stone, engineers began substituting millstone and cement mortar, which allowed the introduction of curved sewer floors that made flushing easier, as did construction on a regular incline. Like all later sewers, they were large enough to allow a man to move around standing up. The conduits flowed into central collec-

tors that drained directly into the Seine River. In 1852 the Paris prefecture ordered installation of direct sewer hookups for wastewater in all new buildings. When the last open sewer was covered in 1853, Paris already had 143 kilometers of sewer lines. But serious problems remained. New building construction strained even these improvements, and the sewers continued to overflow into the streets with every downpour. Twice daily, after the public fountains opened and the sewers emptied into the Seine, the river darkened, and the two pumps that siphoned water from the river for Parisians' use were clogged with fetid liquid.

During the Second Empire, Napoleon III saw the continued modernization of the sewage and water systems as fundamental to the transformation of Paris into an imperial city. According to Haussmann, the excavations for street building were an unparalleled opportunity to construct an underground urban circulatory system free of blocked arteries and foul orifices. They would function like the organs of the human body, and fresh water, light, and heat would circulate like the fluids that support life. He proposed an expanded dual water-supply system for the city. Water for domestic consumption would be brought via aqueducts from distant springs. New waterways and portions of ancient Roman aqueducts were in-

Subterranean Organs of Paris. The sewers of Paris, c. 1860. Photograph by Nadar (Gaspar-Félix Tournachon, 1820–1910). ©HULTON-GETTY/LIAISON AGENCY

corporated into the extensive system that brought water to Paris from the Dhuys, the Vanne, and the Marne Rivers. Water from the Ourcq Canal and the Seine River would be used only for industrial purposes and to supply public fountains.

While the length of Paris streets doubled during the Second Empire urban renovation projects, the sewer system grew more than fivefold. Old sewers were rebuilt to meet new standards. Haussmann's engineers continued the earlier practice of making the sewers large enough to permit workmen to repair and cleanse them. In the plan developed by the government engineer Eugène Belgrand, the narrower drains flowed into three main outfall collectors (five by the turn of the century) that served as the large intestine of the system and discharged waste into the Seine northwest of Paris rather than in the city. Belgrand realized that a constant flow of water would be far less effective as a means of cleansing than periodic concentrated purgings. Water for this purpose was trapped in small reservoirs fed with river water throughout the system. The reservoirs numbered more than four thousand at the turn of the century, and sluice carts and boats in the collectors facilitated the flushing.

Between 1788 and 1907 the length of sewer per inhabitant increased eighty-fourfold. The extension of the sewer system contributed significantly to the decline of waterborne epidemic disease in Paris. The sewer tunnels housed two sets of water mains, one for drinking water and one for water from the Seine River used to clean streets and to water city parks. Telegraph and telephone wires, pneumatic tubes for the postal service, tubes carrying compressed air, and later the traffic control electrical system stretched across the roofs of conduit galleries. By the turn of the century, tours of the sewers were offered every two weeks during the summer; six hundred curious visitors took the voyage each time.

In the early 1850s modern urban hygiene also began in Berlin. In 1852 a privately owned water supply system was constructed, although no facilities were provided for sewer drainage. The sewage question was turned over to a municipal commission, which after years of study recommended the plan of Police President James Hobrecht, a German engineer whose social ideas closely matched those of Chadwick. Hobrecht's plan included a combined water-carriage system, dividing the city into small drainage areas, and pumping urban sewage through an underground pipe system to numerous sewerage farms on the city's outskirts. Work on the project began in 1873, and plans were also made for a new, municipally owned water supply. The Hobrecht plan remained in force virtually unaltered until 1919.

Throughout the nineteenth century Europe's capital cities, especially London and Paris, led the way in sanitation reform. National governments cared more about their capital cities, which more easily found money for the massive investments required for sanitation improvements. Other towns and cities lagged far behind, especially in southern and eastern Europe. At a time when Paris had already built new water and sewerage systems, the population of Marseille still drank polluted water from the Durance River. As a result Marseille was the site of the last major cholera epidemic in France in 1884. Lyon began to construct modern water and sewage facilities in the 1880s. Even in Vienna running water, central heating, and fixed baths reached only a small proportion of residential buildings in the late nineteenth century. In 1910 no more than 7 percent of all dwellings had bathrooms, and only 22 percent had private water closets. Kitchens in all but luxury flats rarely had a water supply but instead depended on the water basin in the public corridor. Italian cities, including Naples, Turin, Bologna, and Venice, in the 1880s began civic improvements such as street renovations, sewer systems, and slum clearance. Not until the 1930s were water and sewage taken over by public management in Italy.

EXTENDING SERVICES TO THE SUBURBS

The later reform programs were also shaped by the vast processes of suburbanization that drastically changed the form and landscape of the city. The great underground networks of services that were constructed during the nineteenth century transformed the central districts of Europe's great cities. But little was done to alleviate the dearth of services in the slum districts and squatter settlements spreading from densely built, working-class quarters into the outlying districts. Water supplies from wells and latrine services were shared at common sites far from dwellings, and residents were at the mercy of speculators. Although cholera and typhoid fever had largely been conquered, tuberculosis, which was directly linked to squalid living conditions, remained a major scourge. Slum clearance was consistently offered as the solution to the continued public health and social crisis.

During the first half of the twentieth century, the garden city ideal was promoted by architect-planners, such as Ebenezer Howard in England, Tony Garnier and Henri Sellier in France, and Ernst May in Germany, as slum replacement. Garden cities, made up of cottages and modest apartments outfitted with gas, electricity, and modern kitchen and bathroom facilities and surrounded by green space, would create a utopian working-class environment. The ideal emphasized gas and water municipal reform that would provide utilities on a nonprofit basis. Engineering systems were to constitute the largest set of municipal services in new towns designed for working-class suburbs. Although only a small number of garden cities were constructed, they provided the model for the extension of the vast underground gas, water, and sewer systems later deemed a vital part of urban life. Public housing projects along the peripheries of London, Paris, and Berlin carried out the ideal in the 1920s with solidly built structures supplied with modern utilities. But the extension of the underground services was long and costly and required the incorporation of vast suburban areas under a unified administrative jurisdiction. The difficulties involved in providing basic services to the growing suburbs was one important reason why planners turned away from the garden city ideal. Instead, by the 1940s Le Corbusier's vision of vast apartment towers

Corbusian Apartment Building. Cité Radieuse, Marseille, France, designed by Le Corbusier (Charles-Édouard Jeannret, 1887–1965); built 1947. ©ARS, NY/GIRAUDON/ART RESOURCE, NY

and complexes was seen as a more efficient way to build and provision the water, sewage, gas, and electricity networks required for the growing numbers of families calling metropolitan regions their home. The inner workings of the human body no longer served as the metaphor for urban infrastructure and planning. The new image was the Corbusian machine for living, the the efficient, geometrically designed and engineered corridors and networks of the harmonious city.

See also **The Environment; Health and Disease** *(volume 2);* **Public Health** *(volume 3);* **Cleanliness** *(volume 4); and other articles in this section.*

BIBLIOGRAPHY

Agulhon, Maurice, et al. *La ville de l'âge industriel: Le cycle haussmannien.* Vol. 4 of *Histoire de la France urbaine.* Edited by Georges Duby. Paris, 1983.

Anderson, Stanford, ed. *On Streets.* Cambridge, Mass., 1978.

Barker, T. C., and Michael Robbins. *A History of London Transport: Passenger Travel and the Development of the Metropolis.* 2 vols. London, 1963.

Benevolo, Leonardo. *The European City.* Translated by Carl Ipsen. Oxford, 1993.

Balfour, Alan. *Berlin: The Politics of Order, 1737–1989.* New York, 1990.

Brun, Jacques, et al. *La ville aujourd'hui: Croissance urbaine et crise du citadin.* Vol. 5 of *Histoire de la France urbaine.* Edited by Georges Duby. Paris, 1985.

Caron, François, et al., ed. *Paris et ses réseaux: Naissance d'un mode de vie urbain, XIXe–XXe siècles.* Paris, 1990.

Çelik, Zeynep, Diane Favro, and Richard Ingersoll, eds. *Streets: Critical Perspectives on Public Space.* Berkeley, Calif., 1994.

Dyos, H. J. *Exploring the Urban Past: Essays in Urban History.* Edited by David Cannadine and David Reeder. Cambridge, U.K., 1982.

Dyos, H. J., and Michael Wolff. *The Victorian City: Images and Realities.* 2 vols. London, 1973.

Evenson, Norma. *Paris: A Century of Change, 1878–1978.* New Haven, Conn., 1979.

Fyfe, Nicholas R., ed. *Images of the Street: Planning, Identity, and Control in Public Space.* London and New York, 1998.

Gaillard, Jeanne. *Paris, la ville, 1852–1870.* Paris, 1997.

Hall, Peter. *Cities in Civilization.* New York, 1998.

Hall, Peter, *Cities of Tomorrow.* Oxford, 1996.

Hammarström, Ingrid, and Thomas Hall, eds. *Growth and Transformation of the Modern City.* Stockholm, Sweden, 1979.

Harvey, David. *Consciousness and the Urban Experience: Studies in the History and Theory of Capitalist Urbanization.* Baltimore, 1985.

Hietala, Marjatta. *Services and Urbanization at the Turn of the Century: The Diffusion of Innovations.* Helsinki, Finland, 1987.

Hohenberg, Paul M., and Lynn Hollen Lees. *The Making of Urban Europe, 1000–1950.* Cambridge, Mass., 1985.

Jordan, David P. *Transforming Paris: The Life and Labors of Baron Haussmann.* Chicago, 1996.

Kostoff, Spiro. *The City Assembled: The Elements of Urban Form through History.* Boston, 1992.

Lees, Andrew. *Cities Perceived: Urban Society in European and American Thought, 1820–1940.* New York, 1985.

Lucan, Jacques, ed. *Eau et gaz à tous les étages: Paris, 100 ans de logement.* Paris, 1992.

Masur, Gerhard. *Imperial Berlin.* New York, 1971.

McKay, John P. *Tramways and Trolleys: The Rise of Urban Mass Transport in Europe.* Princeton, N.J., 1976.

Morris, A. E. J. *History of Urban Form: Before the Industrial Revolutions.* 3d ed. New York, 1994.

Mumford, Lewis. *The City in History.* New York, 1961.

Olsen, Donald J. *The City as a Work of Art: London, Paris, Vienna.* New Haven, Conn., 1986.

Papayanis, Nicholas. *The Coachmen of Nineteenth-Century Paris: Service Workers and Class Consciousness.* Baton Rouge, La., 1993.

Papayanis, Nicholas. *Horse-Drawn Cabs and Omnibuses in Paris: The Idea of Circulation and the Business of Public Transit.* Baton Rouge, La., 1996.

Papayanis, Nicholas. "Les transports à Paris avant le métropolitain." In *Métro-cité: Le chemin de fer métropolitain à la conquête de Paris, 1871–1945.* Edited by

François Gasnault and Henri Zuber; Compiled by Sheila Hallsted-Baumert. Paris, 1997. Pages 15–30.

Pinkney, David H. *Napoleon III and the Rebuilding of Paris.* Princeton, N.J., 1958.

Pinol, Jean-Luc. *Le monde des villes au XIXe siècle.* Paris, 1991.

Pinol, Jean-Luc, and Denis Menjeot, eds. *Water and European Cities from the Middle Ages to the Nineteenth Century.* Brookfield, Vt., 1998.

Porter, Roy. *London: A Social History.* Cambridge, Mass., 1995.

Rabinow, Paul. *French Modern: Norms and Forms of the Social Environment.* Cambridge, Mass., 1989.

Ratcliffe, Barrie. "Cities and Environmental Decline: Elites and the Sewage Problem in Paris from the Mid-Eighteenth to the Mid-Nineteenth Century." *Planning Perspectives* 5 (1990): 189–222.

Reid, Donald. *Paris Sewers and Sewermen: Realities and Representations.* Cambridge, Mass., 1991.

Schivelbusch, Wolfgang. *Disenchanted Night: The Industrialization of Light in the Nineteenth Century.* Translated by Angela Davies. Berkeley, Calif., 1988.

Schorske, Carl E. *Fin-de-Siècle Vienna: Politics and Culture.* New York, 1981.

Sennett, Richard. *Flesh and Stone: The Body and the City in Western Civilization.* New York, 1994.

Sheppard, Francis. *London, 1808–1870: The Infernal Wen.* Berkeley, Calif., 1971.

Simson, John von. "Water Supply and Sewerage in Berlin, London, and Paris: Developments in the 19th Century." In *Urbanisierung Im 19. und 20. Jahrhundert: Historische und geographische Aspekte.* Edited by Hans Jürgen Teuteberg. Cologne, 1983. Pages 429–439.

Summerson, John. *Georgian London.* Cambridge, Mass., 1978.

Sutcliffe, Anthony. *The Autumn of Central Paris: The Defeat of Town Planning, 1850–1970.* London, 1971.

Sutcliffe, Anthony, ed. *Metropolis, 1890–1940.* Chicago, 1984.

Sutcliffe, Anthony, ed. *The Rise of Modern Urban Planning, 1800–1914.* London, 1980.

Sutcliffe, Anthony. *Towards the Planned City: Germany, Britain, the United States, and France, 1780–1914.* New York, 1981.

Tarr, Joel A., and Gabriel Dupuy, eds. *Technology and the Rise of the Networked City in Europe and America.* Philadelphia, 1988.

Wakeman, Rosemary. *Modernizing the Provincial City: Toulouse, 1945–1975.* Cambridge, Mass., 1997.

Wohl, Anthony S. *Endangered Lives: Public Health in Victorian Britain.* London, 1983.

SHOPS AND STORES

Montserrat M. Miller

One of the most pervasive structures in the history of retail commerce has been the small urban shop. With origins dating back to the classical period and before, small shops have been a characteristic feature of the geography, economy, culture, and sociopolitical fabric of towns and cities since the eleventh-century revival of urban life in the West. Eastern Europe's towns and cities, while following a somewhat distinct economic and historical pattern, also featured shops as one of the main vehicles for the retail sale of goods even during communist rule. The term "stores" is generally used by historians to denote larger retail entities that sold a wider variety of goods. Department stores, known in France as *grands magasins,* first became established in the mid-nineteenth century, introducing important changes in the way many city dwellers acquired clothing, textiles, and other household and personal articles. Likewise, self-service grocery stores and supermarkets, appearing in European cities in the post–World War II period, have over the course of the last half of the twentieth century profoundly altered the way in which most households are provisioned.

European social historians have mainly been interested in shops and stores because their past is deeply intertwined with that of the guild system and the emergence of the bourgeoisie, because they reveal much about how municipal corporations controlled economic exchange, because they are crucial institutions for the study of consumerism, because they raise important questions about the nature of women's work in the past, and because of the range of political and economic responses to industrialization and the emergence of mass consumer society that their owners exhibited. Thus the history of shops and stores is particularly significant to historians concerned with urban life, social structures, work and gender, retail business, and political movements in the industrial era.

THE RISE OF THE SHOP

The rise of shops in Europe was deeply intertwined with the revival of urban life in the eleventh century.

Throughout western Europe, the growth of towns involved increases in the numbers of artisans and traders. At first finding room within existing town walls, the expansion in numbers of artisans and traders was soon accompanied by the growth of new neighborhoods, frequently known as burgs, outside of the increasingly limited fortified space. Most items were sold to the urban populations of eleventh-century western Europe at markets, usually located in church squares and long regulated by ecclesiastical authority; the new commercial districts of towns were the site of the first actual shops. Most frequently, these early shops consisted of windows through which artisans such as blacksmiths, butchers, cobblers, and bakers could sell to passersby on days and at times when the town's periodic markets were not in operation. It appears that in many areas, local authorities discouraged such commerce because it was more difficult than open-air markets to regulate on behalf of the consumer. Still, through the twelfth and thirteenth centuries more and more artisans sold from their windows, thus increasing the amount of commerce taking place in the burgeoning towns and establishing the legitimacy of the workshop as a point from which retail trade could be conducted.

These early artisanal shops, many of which featured shutters that folded down by day to serve as sales counters but whose windows eventually became doorways through which customers passed in order to make their purchases, were distinct from the retail merchandise shops that would appear and proliferate later on. The earliest artisanal shops only sold goods that were made on the premises and linked consumers directly with producers. These shop owners frequently offered their wares at the town's markets as well and, along with other prosperous townspeople, participated in guild organizations and the development of local commercial codes. The earliest artisanal shop owners, then, were among the groups central to the formation of the urban polity. Attached to individual residences, these shops were family operations with both husbands and wives participating in the commercial enterprise.

Artisanal Shop. The fish vendor, from the sign of Aries. Anonymous fifteenth-century fresco in the Palazzo della Ragione, Padua, Italy. PALAZZO DELLA RAGIONE, PADUA/SCALA/ART RESOURCE, NY

From approximately the thirteenth century forward these first shop owners began to be joined by a new group: itinerant traders eager to settle in towns and engage in retail commerce. These newcomers were distinct from the artisanal shopkeepers in that they were essentially middlemen, selling goods they had purchased elsewhere, sometimes second- or third-hand. The successful among these new merchants joined town guilds and imitated artisanal shop owners by establishing points for the retail sale of merchandise that were part of a permanent residence and that had an opening on the street, either a window shutter sales counter or a door through which customers could pass in order to make a purchase. Few members of this new group participated in town markets, preferring instead to concentrate their sales in the vibrant burgs and take advantage of the lively flow of foot traffic that characterized urban spaces through the high Middle Ages. So while markets of various types remained important elements of the urban retail structure in most areas until the late nineteenth century, shops began to compete effectively with markets for customers from at least the early twelfth century forward, becoming a crucial part of town commerce.

Shops quickly caught on in the new urban centers of Europe, and their numbers and variety proliferated. The generally favorable individual living standards of the mid-fourteenth through the mid-

sixteenth centuries contributed to this growth. In addition to grocers (who tended to sell by weight), tailors and drapers (who generally sold by measure), shops that sold artisinal objects, and shops that sold secondhand goods, a plethora of shops that offered services were added. Scribes, notaries, pawnbrokers, apothecaries, wine merchants, and tavern keepers of numerous varieties all opened shops in large towns and cities and added to the expansion of urban commerce. Steep hierarchies accompanied this growth in retailing. At the top of the economic order were wealthy merchants concentrating in profitable long-distance trades while at the bottom were peddlers without so much as a market stall from which to sell. Small shop owners occupied a vast middle ground and succeeded in consolidating their position within the urban polity.

While municipal authority in many western European cities was dominated by wealthy merchants who formed a patriciate, the interests of modest shopkeepers were reflected in commercial law and, of course, in the corporate regulation of the guilds. Most of the rules governing exchange were designed to prevent unbridled competition, maintain quality, and control prices. Both the nature of the product being sold and the process of retail exchange were also governed by municipal codes and/or guild rules. Shop owners were authorized to sell particular goods and could not expand their line without a new permit. Purity, weight, price, and workmanship were also frequent targets of regulation. Hours of operation, weights and measures, and working conditions were all subject to corporate controls. Even the nature of communication between shopkeepers and customers fell under the regulatory purview of municipal and guild authority. Craftsmen, for example, were sometimes forbidden to call out to passersby or engage in any other method of attracting consumers to their wares. The history of shops shows quite clearly that western European urban polities of the Middle Ages offered opportunities to accumulate capital through the profits derived from small-scale retail commerce, although enterprises that sought to do so certainly operated within a context that maintained relatively tight controls over the act of economic exchange.

Still, it would be erroneous to conceptualize shops as isolated and autarkic enterprises operating within towns characterized as closed systems. Urban history has in recent years emphasized the dynamic relationship between medieval towns and cities and the regions within which they were located. Studies of individual shops illustrate the complexity of the relationships linking urban and rural areas in the Middle Ages. Shopkeepers, and especially grocers of virtually all varieties as well as market vendors, had to maintain ties with rural suppliers in order to serve their urban customers. Town life may have been quite distinct from country life in the Middle Ages, but as the relationship between shops and their sources of supply clearly indicates, the boundaries were permeable.

The history of shops can also reveal much about the emergence of the bourgeoisie, the relationship of work to family life in preindustrial cities, and gender divisions of labor. At the core of the earliest bourgeoisie was the population of urban artisans and shopkeepers. The growth and development of their enterprises and their efforts at self-regulation and self-government illustrate how this crucial urban social group carved out a place for itself in the hierarchy of classes. Examining the way that shops operated allows us to understand how central family labor was to the emergence and economic consolidation of the bourgeoisie. Shops, attached to households, were family enterprises, and often a simple curtain was the only barrier that separated living from retail spaces. Husbands, wives, and children each contributed to the economic survival of the family, and thus boundaries between work and home were blurry indeed. Though the precise nature of the gender divisions of labor appear to have changed somewhat over time, with women losing ground in terms of artisanal production as the Middle Ages waned, shops were clearly business enterprises in which women's labor was ubiquitous and essential. Whether women were engaged in some element of production, in providing food and lodging for workers, or serving customers who came through the doors, the social history of shops sets in bold relief their very active and direct participation in the economy of preindustrial cities.

By the close of the Middle Ages shops had become a tremendously important element of the urban morphology of western Europe. Frequently arranged by specialty, shops of given varieties lined particular streets, giving them distinct flavors and personalities. Avenues dotted with jewelers and silk merchants, for example, exuded a greater air of prestige than did streets whose shops specialized in cheese and other edibles. These arrangements certainly shaped the lives of urban residents. One of the legacies of this pattern is that many western European cities still have, in their old quarters, street names and a certain flavor derived from the types of commerce that municipal authorities allowed. On the other hand, some types of shops, such as bakers, butchers, and greengrocers, were seldom grouped together and were more frequently distributed by authorities throughout the urban landscape in order to provision more efficiently the city's distinct quarters. However distributed in specific instances, shops and the nature of the commerce taking place in them gave town and city districts distinct characters.

RETAILING IN THE SEVENTEENTH AND EIGHTEENTH CENTURIES

The numbers of shops in many areas of western Europe, including England, France, Germany, Spain, and Italy, grew dramatically in the seventeenth and eighteenth centuries. This growth appears to have occurred throughout the retail hierarchy: luxury shops became more abundant but so too did marginal secondhand shops, as did crude inns and taverns catering to lower-ranking members of society. In many cities, the conversion of residential buildings into shops on prominent streets caused a shortage of rental property for the wealthy. Such a proliferation of retail outlets, while both contributing to and reflecting the growth in complexity of the distribution network, was not indicative of any sort of golden age of shops in the early modern period. In fact, shopkeeper bankruptcy became quite common in the seventeenth and eighteenth centuries. In some places the number of retail outlets proved to be larger than the economy could sustain.

The widespread use of credit was one factor that contributed to the growth in the number of shops but also increased economic precariousness. By the seventeenth century shops were using credit extensively: they frequently relied on the extension of credit to them by wholesalers, paying for their stock in installments over time, and they extended credit to their customers, wealthy and humble alike (although the rich were always extended credit more generously and leniently than the poor). Failure to receive credit from suppliers and delays or customer refusals to settle outstanding accounts were typical ongoing fears for shop owners. While allowing the economically marginal to obtain materials to sell, the increasing reliance upon credit by shops could, and frequently did, prove disastrous to the survival of small retail enterprises.

But the growing reliance upon credit was only one of numerous changes occurring in this period: it now appears that the eighteenth century in particular witnessed a transformation in the way that many shops presented and displayed their goods. A great many shops in the towns and cities of western and central Europe became more elaborate. Shops selling luxury goods led the way by adding crystal chandeliers, mirrors, and elegant furnishings. The use of glass increased tremendously, both in the fixtures holding merchandise and in display windows, which became the objects of competition between shop owners. In

Seventeenth-Century Shops. Shops in the gallery of the Palais de Justice, Paris, c. 1625.
ARCHIVE PHOTOS

addition, shop signs began to incorporate greater elements of artistry with the use of new materials chosen to announce more explicitly the elegance and prestige of the enterprise in question. More humble establishments imitated these changes as best they could, while shops on main thoroughfares gave increased attention to aesthetic issues. Such transformations only reinforced the already existing hierarchy of shops, more firmly differentiating so-called backstreet shops, whose resources and pretensions were more limited, from elegant shops in fashionable districts.

The early modern period also featured, first and most notably in England, the emergence and growth of a new type of retail shop catering to the increasing consumption of sugar, caffeine drinks, and tobacco between 1650 and 1750. The growing demand for these items, imported from abroad and not traditionally available in village markets, contributed to the appearance of small general grocery stores, mostly in rural areas. In addition to the new stimulants and various provisions, these retail outlets tended to sell semidurables such as clay pipes, glass, and ceramic tableware. While preexisting shops in large towns and cities took up the sale of these items, new retail outlets came into existence in the countryside to meet growing demand for groceries and housewares, and became quite common in rural England and America by the close of the eighteenth century.

Alongside these physical and structural changes, and the overall growth in the number of shops in the early modern period, social historians have identified a shift in the attitudes of ordinary people toward the act of purchasing and consuming material goods. From their outset shops had been sites for more than just economic exchange: literary and artistic evidence along with extant personal testimony illustrate the lively and ongoing sociability between shopkeepers and customers that took place as part of the process of buying and selling. But the research on this subject now shows quite clearly that something new was afoot as early as the seventeenth century: a form of consumerism was emerging among the popular classes in many areas of western Europe long before industrialization. Consumerism, social historians maintain, involves new levels of personal satisfaction from acquiring goods, as well as new assertions of social standing through purchasing and displaying material objects. The early modern variant of consumerism seems to have focused on clothing and housewares. Though the bulk of the research deals with England, studies indicate that other areas also became increasingly consumerist, thus helping to explain the expansion in the number of secondhand clothing shops and shops selling semidurable household goods. Changes in the way that shops presented and displayed merchandise, the growth in their numbers, and the new financial arrangements through which they operated are all of significance because they constitute one of the external manifestations of the early emergence of consumerism. In the seventeenth and eighteenth centuries, shopping began to take on new meanings, beginning its transformation into an important new leisure-time activity for the middle and working classes alike.

THE AGE OF THE DEPARTMENT STORE

Building on early modern shifts, considerable changes also occurred in the nineteenth- and early-twentieth-century history of shops and stores. It was in this period that guild controls over urban commerce came to an end in most places, thus lifting impediments to organizational innovations in commerce. With industrialization maturing and urbanization advancing, the long nineteenth century witnessed the emergence of large-scale, highly capitalized retail structures along with an enormous increase in the variety of manufactured goods for sale. With wages and leisure time gradually increasing and mass advertising becoming more common, the second half of the nineteenth century in particular featured the spread and deepening of consumerist values. From the early modern focus of demand on clothing and housewares, nineteenth century consumerism widened to include children's toys, novels, holiday decorations, items such as oriental rugs, pianos, and bicycles, plus popular entertainment such as dance hall performances. Department stores, chain stores, and mail-order companies emerged and expanded rapidly to meet the new mass demand for manufactured goods and commercial services.

Of all the new forms of highly capitalized large-scale retailing, the department store has received the most systematic scholarly attention. Originating in the 1850s and 1860s, the *grands magasins* of Paris were the first real department stores. These grew in size and number until the eve of World War I, quickly spreading to England and then other parts of Europe, including tsarist Russia. In many ways department stores could not have been more different than the small family shops that had long dotted the urban landscape. Scale was the most obvious characteristic distinguishing department stores from shops. These new stores offered expanding and diversified lines of merchandise that drew, by the 1880s, some ten thousand customers a day into the Bon Marché alone. By 1911 the twelve largest department stores in Paris employed more than nine hundred persons each, contrasting sharply with the vast majority of retail enterprises whose average number of employees was ten or less. In some instances, nineteenth-century Parisian department stores offered on-site dormitories as well as organized and respectable leisure activities for their employees. It was not uncommon for department stores also to provide free medical services, accident insurance, and pension plans. In terms of sheer volume of customers and employment of wage labor, small family shops had little resemblance with *grands magasins* in the nineteenth century.

Another sharp point of contrast between small shops and department stores can be found in the manner in which stocks and supplies were acquired for sale. Nineteenth-century shops tended to order their merchandise on credit through intermediaries and frequently used sample books from which customers could select items to be ordered. Markups were high and volumes were low. Department store merchandise ordering was on a much larger scale, so much so that they could frequently dictate production schedules. Selling directly to department stores for cash on delivery, manufacturers could save warehousing costs by timing production to coincide with delivery commitments. These savings could be passed on to consumers, who found a wide a array of goods in the department stores on sale at relatively inexpensive prices.

Department stores featured important innovations in retailing. Customers were encouraged to enter the building even if they had no intention of making a purchase; managers considered browsing to be perfectly acceptable. The bulk of the merchandise was displayed in such a way that consumers could directly inspect it for quality and workmanship. In the event of some dissatisfaction with a purchase, returns could be easily effected. Department store clerks were trained to distinguish themselves from the sales techniques of shopkeepers: customers were not to be needled into making a purchase, and clerks were to offer information about the products for sale without the concomitant pressure that took place in small shops. The social relations that accompanied shopping assumed a distinct form in these new retail outlets.

Still, it is important to note that not all of the department stores' most salient features were original innovations in retailing. Often laden with luxury fixtures and featuring elaborate decors, department stores were not the first to use fantasies about wealth and opulence to promote sales. Early modern shops had certainly moved in this direction prior to the nineteenth century, and glass and iron arcades, similar in form to train stations and covered markets, had become common in a number of cities well before the appearance of the department store. Shopping arcades typically housed small upscale boutiques and featured gas—later electric—lighting that lent an air of fantasy to enclosed shopping promenades. Department stores merely elaborated on the techniques that shopkeepers had earlier devised to add an exciting and dreamlike quality to the experience of material acquisition. And neither did the *grands magasins* invent the concept of

A *Grand Magasin*. Interior of the Bon Marché department store, Paris, c. 1850. GENERAL RESEARCH DIVISION, THE NEW YORK PUBLIC LIBRARY, ASTOR, LENOX AND TILDEN FOUNDATIONS

department shopping itself. This, too, was an innovation traceable to small and medium-sized family shops. With guild control over commerce suppressed, new shops featuring fixed prices and expanded lines of merchandise began to appear as early as the late eighteenth century and became relatively common by the 1830s in Paris. Known as *magasins de nouveautés,* these commercial entities emphasized turnover and volume, an approach quite different from that of traditional shops. Department stores seized upon these innovations in retailing, implementing them on a grand scale and developing new managerial systems appropriate for their dimensions.

SHOPS AND SHOPKEEPERS IN THE AGE OF THE DEPARTMENT STORE

Social historians have been especially interested in the emergence of new forms of retailing such as department and chain stores because of the reactions of shopkeeping populations to this change. While many small nineteenth-century shop owners perceived department stores as a threat to their livelihood, the nature of the competition between these two forms of retailing is less clear. Many small shops thrived in the immediate environs of department stores, and sales of upscale items such as jewelry and haberdashery were quite slow to shift away from small family firms. The wealthiest shoppers usually disdained the environment of the department store, designed to enthrall the consuming masses, and preferred instead the exclusivity of traditional shops. In the face of department store competition some shops turned toward greater emphasis on luxury merchandise, some expanded their lines and adopted new retailing strategies, while others, especially ones dealing in increasingly mass-produced items such as gloves, umbrellas, and underwear, struggled to survive. The relevant point is that while the emergence of new forms of large-scale retailing posed a significant challenge, small shops were not necessarily reluctant to adapt to changing economic circumstances or even slow to embrace new commercial strategies.

In some respects the nineteenth century offered new opportunities for small family-owned retail shops, and in many places the expansion in their numbers outpaced population growth. Rapid urbanization made new space available for shops as well as increasing the pool of potential customers. Gradually rising wage levels after 1850 meant that working-class families had more to spend in the market economy, with small shops taking their share of consumer dollars along with department stores. And throughout northern Europe, municipal governments ceased constructing food markets to provision the urban population in the late nineteenth century. As existing urban market halls decayed and fell into disuse, neighborhood shops increased their share of the retail distribution of provisions. With food having become the fastest-growing sector of the nineteenth-century economy, small neighborhood shops stepped in where markets had once dominated, establishing themselves as crucial venues for the sale of provisions through the next century. So while both the early modern period and the nineteenth century featured considerable innovations in the retailing sector of the economy, small shops survived these changes as important elements of the retail distribution structure of European towns and cities.

One of the main reasons that historians study the relationship between shops and new larger-scale forms of retailing has been to explore the cause and nature of shopkeeper activism. Initial interpretations holding that shopkeepers embraced nationalist, conservative (and often anti-Semitic) ideologies in the late nineteenth century have given way to more nuanced and variegated assessments of their political ideologies and impulses. Likewise the presumption that shopkeepers, because they longed for a return to protectionist policies of the preindustrial economy, were everywhere at the heart of fascism's popular support has also come under increasing scrutiny. Small retail organizations and institutions in Barcelona, for example, strongly supported the Republican municipal government in the final days before the outbreak of rebellion, and were not drawn toward the fascist organic model of the state offered by the Falange. And in Italy and Germany, support for or acquiescence to fascist authority now appears to have been more a result of calculations of opportunism than blind obedience. The overgeneralized conservative proclivities of the European petite bourgeoisie had largely been predicated on a presumption of desperation and dupability. Crucial to the reevaluation of late-nineteenth- and twentieth-century shopkeeper political ideologies has been a growing recognition that small retail and artisanal enterprises were not necessarily doomed to extinction by the process of industrialization, and indeed possessed a considerable amount of historical agency. Thus, much of the twentieth-century work on the history of shops and stores seeks to explain how small and medium-sized firms have remained viable and have achieved, as the cases of Italy and Germany so clearly illustrate, an important degree of political power.

New large-scale forms of retailing continued their expansion in Europe over the course of the twentieth century. The pre–World War I years mainly featured the growth of chain stores, mail-order concerns, consumer cooperatives, and, of course, the further spread of department stores. The pace of change was not even, though. Consumer cooperatives, which were in many ways a creative reaction to the capitalization of commerce, came into existence virtually everywhere but took hold especially in England and the Scandinavian countries, where they came to make up a considerable part of the retail provisioning sector. Mail-order companies were particularly successful in Germany, quite possibly due to the economy of the postal service and the facility of its COD collection. Department and chain store growth prior to World War I was somewhat slower in central Europe than in England and France, though all major European capitals featured their own variants of the *grand magasin* on the eve of the Great War.

THE AGE OF THE SUPERMARKET

While the 1919–1945 period brought a disruption to the expansion of the retail sector, the postwar period featured a renewed surge in its growth as well as the appearance of a distinctively twentieth-century retail innovation: the self-service supermarket. The National Cash Register Company, an American firm, played an active role in promoting the adoption of self-service across western Europe in the 1950s and beyond. While many food shops that converted to self-service never increased their size, others grew into supermarkets and supermarket chains. The European country quickest to adopt American-style supermarkets was Switzerland. By 1955, the Swiss Migros chain, founded by Gottlieb Duttweiler, had in operation 150 self-service food stores, including seven large supermarkets. Consumer cooperatives in Britain and Scandinavia were also among the earliest and most eager converts to this new form of retailing, most likely because of the economies of scale and consequent reduction of prices that nearly always accompanied the shift.

Still, the spread of supermarkets in western Europe was distinct from that of the United States. Beginning somewhat later in the 1950s than in America, self-service supermarkets became established in European cities where space was at a tremendous premium and where individual establishments tended to be smaller and parking space much more limited than in their North American counterparts. Essentially dependent on the consumer use of the automobile to transport multiple bags of groceries from the point of retail to the point of residence, supermarkets could not expand to North American dimensions without large parking lots and widespread automobile ownership. Instead, though car ownership continued to increase through the postwar decades, supermarkets took their place in western Europe in the 1950s, 1960s, and up to the mid-1970s within a preexisting retail provisioning structure that featured a balance between neighborhood food shops, chain stores such as the British company Lipton's, consumer cooperatives, and, in parts of southern Europe, networks of public or private covered markets. Industry analysts in the immediate postwar period cited a number of other factors that slowed the spread of supermarkets in Europe. Among the impediments they perceived were inadequate refrigeration and packaging facilities, inadequate brand consciousness, and the (presumably negative) force of deeply seated commercial traditions.

European retailers were accustomed in the mid-twentieth century to much higher levels of competition than their American counterparts. In contrast to the 2½ food retailers per 1,000 population in the United States in the mid-1950s, Europe ranged from a low in France of 6 per 1,000 to a high of 26 per 1,000 in Belgium. In addition, American supermarket missionaries to Europe complained about the pervasive commercial organizations with local, regional, and national units that pursued policies of trade and territorial protection. As had been the case at the end of the nineteenth century, large-scale, heavily capitalized retail firms made significant inroads in the first

three decades of the postwar period, though without eliminating more traditional forms of commerce such as small family-owned shops.

Though their density varies according to region, with southwestern Europe seemingly leading, small and medium-sized retail enterprises have fared well over much of the second half of the twentieth century. To an important degree this can be attributed to the ability of these firms to adapt to changes in both demand and production, but shop owners' effective political activism within their national polities also helped maintain their viability. Here the Italian and German cases are both noteworthy and most clearly outlined in the social history literature. German artisans in the post–World War II period adapted successfully to the industrial capitalist system, as evidenced by the fact that in 1994, 17.4 percent of the economically active population there was employed in independent *Handwerk* shops. Forty-seven percent of those firms employed five or fewer persons. Recent work has shown that the continued viability of *Handwerk* within the advanced industrial economy of Germany has in no small part been due to the connections between its institutions and the major political parties, to its maintenance of training programs and systems, its organization of purchasing and retailing cooperatives, its investment in research and development, and to its functioning as an effective organ of interest-group representation. Likewise in Italy, a national commercial organization established in 1946 and known as the *Confcommercio* has succeeded in defending the interests of firms engaged in retail commerce. Representing roughly one-seventh of the electorate, the postwar Italian retail sector mobilized to maintain commercial licensing policies because of the protection they offered to small and medium-sized enterprises. Especially in comparison with other regions of the world, the interests of small shops have tended to carry considerable weight within the electoral constituencies of several western European polities in the postwar period.

More recent trends have indicated a shift in the closing years of the century. Large-scale, heavily capitalized retailing enterprises have made new inroads since 1975. One indication of this has been the appearance of hypermarket stores in peripheral urban areas of western Europe. Larger than most Walmarts and K-Marts in the United States, the hypermarket combines provisions, clothing, housewares, furnishings, and heavy appliances on a heretofore unknown scale. A single enterprise under one roof, the hypermarket began draining consumer dollars away from small urban supermarkets and shops as early as the 1980s. In the 1990s western European cities also be-

Urban Department Store. Interior of Galleran department store, Stockholm. MACDUFF/
CORBIS/BETTMANN

came the sites of large-scale, multistoried commercial malls. In some ways resembling their American counterparts, these retail centers often include hypermarket anchor stores and have posed a significant threat to older forms of neighborhood-based retail activity.

Since the revival of urban life in the eleventh century, privately owned retail firms have constituted a ubiquitous presence in western European cities. Though only some portion of the sector has undergone revolutionary changes in scale, organization, and potential for profitability, the political power wielded by the owners of retail concerns has remained considerable. Essential to the maintenance of urban populations, retail shops and stores continue to represent a crucial part of the economy and morphology of western European cities.

The history of shops and stores in eastern Europe has followed a somewhat different trajectory but has received remarkably little attention from social historians. While experiencing both urban growth and an expansion of retail commerce, eastern Europe did so somewhat later on account of the greater strength of rural aristocrats and the Tatar suzerainty in Russia, which extended into the fourteenth century. Urban shop owners never developed the political power in eastern Europe that they established in the west during the Middle Ages. Still, in the nineteenth century, most eastern European cities experienced growth in the number of shops and the establishment of new large-scale, highly capitalized stores, similar to their western counterparts. The communist period, quite obviously, represents a stark departure from western patterns, though political authorities did use both shops and stores to distribute what consumer goods the state-controlled system of production made available, rather than devising a new conceptual model for retail distribution. Scholars from the fields of political science, marketing, and to some degree urban planning are turning their attention to eastern European cities and raising important questions about the economic and political cultures that best foster commercial enterprises. Eastern Europe remains a fertile field for social historical inquiry into the nature of retail distribution.

See also **Capitalism and Commercialization** *(in this volume);* **Fairs and Markets** *(in this volume);* **The Lower Middle Classes** *(volume 3);* **Gender and Work** *(volume 3);* **Consumerism** *(volume 5); and other articles in this section.*

BIBLIOGRAPHY

Braudel, Fernand. *The Structures of Everyday Life: The Limits of the Possible.* Translated by Siân Reynolds. New York, 1981.

Braudel, Fernand. *The Wheels of Commerce.* Translated by Siân Reynolds. New York, 1982.

Coles, Tim. "Department Stores as Innovations in Retail Marketing: Some Observations on Marketing Practice and Perception in Wilhelmine, Germany." *Journal of Macromarketing* 19 (1999): 34–47.

Crossick, Geoffrey, and Heinz-Gerhard Haupt. *The Petite Bourgeoisie in Europe, 1780–1914: Enterprise, Family, and Independence.* London, 1995.

Glennie, Paul. "Consumption, Consumerism, and Urban Form: Historical Perspectives." *Urban Studies* 35 (1998): 927–952.

McKitrick, Frederick L. "An Unexpected Path to Modernisation: The Case of German Artisans during the Second World War." *Contemporary European History* 5 (November 1996): 401–426.

Miller, Daniel. *A Theory of Shopping.* Ithaca, N.Y., 1998.

Miller, Michael B. *The Bon Marché: Bourgeois Culture and the Department Store, 1869–1920.* Princeton, N.J., 1981.

Morris, Jonathan. "Contesting Retail Space in Italy: Competition and Corporatism 1915–1960." *International Review of Retail Distribution and Consumer Research* 9, no. 3 (July 1999): 291–305.

Morris, Jonathan. *The Political Economy of Shopkeeping in Milan, 1886–1922.* Cambridge, U.K., 1993.

Mui, Hoh-Cheung and Lorna H. Mui. *Shops and Shopkeeping in Eighteenth-Century England.* Kingston, Ontario, 1989.

Nord, Philip G. *Paris Shopkeepers and the Politics of Resentment.* Princeton, N.J., 1986.

Shammas, Carole. *The Pre-Industrial Consumer in England and America.* Oxford, 1990.

Stearns, Peter N. "Stages of Consumerism: Recent Work on the Issues of Periodization." *Journal of Modern History* 69 (March 1997): 102–117.

Zimmerman, Max Mardell. *The Super Market: A Revolution in Distribution.* New York, 1955.

URBAN INSTITUTIONS AND POLITICS:
THE EARLY MODERN PERIOD

Christopher R. Friedrichs

The institutional structure and political practices of European cities during the early modern era were products of the Middle Ages. The framework of institutions and customs by which European town dwellers regulated both their internal affairs and their relations with the broader society took shape roughly from the eleventh to the fourteenth centuries. Despite significant pressures for change, this framework remained relatively constant throughout the early modern era. Only with the gradual emergence of mass politics following the French Revolution (1789) and the acceleration of urban growth following the industrial revolution did this framework fully fall apart.

Not only was the institutional structure of European cities during the early modern era highly stable, it was also remarkably uniform. The names of urban institutions and the details of their organization varied enormously from place to place, but the fundamental forms and functions did not. In many ways Europe had a common urban political culture.

The institutional structure of early modern European cities is well documented and widely known. By contrast, the character of political interaction within European cities is less well understood. Because city councils normally conducted their deliberations in secret, exactly how urban rulers arrived at their decisions is often hard to reconstruct. But historians are increasingly aware of the complexity of urban politics. Cities were normally governed by a small stratum of wealthy men who expected deference and obedience from those over whom they ruled. Yet even the most well entrenched urban elites always had to respond to pressures exerted by an array of rival authorities and interest groups inside and outside the city.

INSTITUTIONS

The most fundamental urban institution was the citizenry. Whether known as freemen, burghers, bourgeois, *Bürger,* or even (as in Rome) the *populo,* the citizens represented an identifiable segment of every city's total population. They were that portion of the adult male householders who comprised the city's political community. In almost every city, membership in the citizenry could be obtained in two ways: by inheritance or by purchase. Typically citizenship was activated when a young man married and established his own household. At that point he paid the necessary fees and took an oath of allegiance to the community. As a citizen he had the right to live and practice a trade in his city and the obligation to pay taxes and to bear arms in the city's defense. Citizenship was gendered: only an adult male could fully hold this status, though wives and daughters of citizens might enjoy a latent form of citizenship, which protected their right to live in the city and to carry on certain businesses. Many—often most—of a city's adult inhabitants were not citizens at all: the broad mass of servants and unskilled or unemployed laborers generally had no political status and lived in the city only as temporary or tolerated residents with no recognized rights.

Although in formal juridical terms citizens formed the city's political community, their actual level of involvement in political decision making was often limited. An assembly of all citizens might meet from time to time to hear decrees or voice opinions, but the actual power to rule the community was normally invested in a small council or, in certain cities, a group of councils. Occasionally the citizens played some role in the election of council members, but in many cities the council simply filled any vacancy in its ranks without broader consultation.

The political structure of cities was not democratic. But at the same time it was not autocratic, for political power in cities was almost always collective, exercised by councils rather than individuals. Most cities had mayors, but their powers were usually limited. Typically they were senior or former council members who held the highest office on a rotational basis. Even in Venice, where the elected prince, or doge, served for life and enjoyed enormous prestige, real decision-making authority was still exercised primarily by the senate and its various committees.

The council (or councils) typically regulated almost every conceivable aspect of the city's economic, social, and cultural life. Yet the council was normally answerable to some higher authority—the overlord who had granted or confirmed the city's charter of rights and privileges. Only a handful of cities were truly autonomous city-states. Almost every city owed allegiance and taxes to its overlord—typically an emperor, king, or prince, but sometimes a bishop or even a collective entity like the council of a larger city. Relations with the overlord were rarely stable. During the Middle Ages urban leaders had struggled to expand their own powers and to limit the role of the ruler's officials in administering the city's affairs. But as the feudal states of the Middle Ages gave way to the absolutist states of the seventeenth and eighteenth century, sovereigns steadily reasserted their authority over cities and their officials intruded ever more deeply into the day-by-day details of urban administration.

Every city had an administrative structure of municipal officials appointed by the council. At the pinnacle were the city's legal advisors. Then came the clerks and scribes who codified the council's decisions and an array of market inspectors, constables, beadles, and watchmen who regulated economic activities and maintained order. Some administrative functions were carried out by the citizens themselves, often on a part-time basis in their capacity as neighborhood or parish officeholders. Citizens everywhere were expected to participate in defending their city from intruders or invaders. In some cities, the structures for maintaining civic self-defense evolved into highly organized militia companies, whose members gathered regularly for purposes of drill or conviviality.

For many town dwellers, the institutions that had the most significant impact on their everyday lives were the guilds. The medieval origins of these organizations are somewhat obscure, though they seem to have filled a combination of economic and devotional functions. By the early modern era, guilds had assumed a clear form in almost every part of Europe. The guild was typically an association of all the adult male householders engaged in a particular craft or branch of trade. These masters ran their own home-based shops, often supervising the labor of a few journeymen and apprentices. Though economically independent, each master was bound by his own guild's collective decisions about the way in which shops should be run, goods produced and new members trained. Each guild, in turn, was answerable to the city council, which confirmed the craft's by-laws and issued decrees about prices, wages, and the quality of goods.

Other institutions of urban life reflected the city's connections to broader systems of authority. In many cities one might find representatives of the overlord, though the number of such officials and the degree to which they were involved in urban administration differed substantially from one country to another or indeed from one town to the next. In France, for example, a handful of major towns had royal courts of justice known as *parlements,* which often intervened directly in running the affairs of the cities in which they were located. In other French cities the council might have to share its authority with a royal governor or *intendant.* Yet there were many cities, in France and elsewhere, where the overlord's involvement was far less heavy-handed. In a few cities, especially in Germany, Switzerland, and northern Italy, the overlord's authority had become greatly attenuated or even—as in Geneva after the 1530s—disappeared altogether.

A universal presence in European cities was provided by the institutions of the Christian church. Every city in Europe had parish churches. In the late Middle Ages larger cities also had monasteries and convents, and any city that served as the seat of a bishop had an episcopal bureaucracy. Often the ecclesiastical institutions enjoyed administrative autonomy: their property and buildings within the city functioned as enclaves over which the city officials exercised little or no control. This changed radically in certain parts of Europe in the sixteenth century, for in those cities that underwent the Protestant Reformation monasteries and convents were dissolved and the parish clergy came under the direct authority of the secular officials. In Catholic countries and communities, however, the autonomous status of ecclesiastical institutions was largely preserved. Indeed, the intense spiritual revival of the Catholic Reformation led to the establishment of new religious orders and lay organizations, which were added to the institutional structure of Catholic cities.

In some cities, notably in Italy, Germany, and parts of eastern Europe, a parallel set of urban institutions emerged: the self-administrative structures of Jewish communities. Only in economic affairs were the Jews allowed to interact with the surrounding Christian community; in every other sphere of life, the Jewish community was expected to remain separate. If Jews were granted residential rights, they not only lived in their own neighborhoods and maintained their own religious, educational, and welfare institutions, but they also had their own council, their own officials, and their own mechanisms for resolving conflicts.

City Militia. *A Banquet of the Officers of the St. George Militia Company,* Haarlem, the Netherlands, painting (1616) by Frans Hals (between 1581 and 1585–1666). FRANS HALS MUSEUM, HAARLEM, THE NETHERLANDS/THE BRIDGEMAN ART LIBRARY

POLITICS

The mainspring of the urban political system was always the city council or, in some large cities like Venice or Strasbourg, the cluster of interconnected councils. In modern urban politics, a city council is typically a body in which representatives of different parties or viewpoints openly debate the issues that divide them and then arrive at decisions by majority vote. In early modern Europe, discussions and votes were held in secret. Occasionally there was some evidence of factional disputes among the council members; more often, however, the magistrates papered over their differences so as to appear to contemporaries as a unified body that embodied supreme authority within the community.

A significant element in the political system of any city was the process by which individual citizens became council members—a process whose importance was heightened by the fact that once they were chosen, the successful candidates often served for life. Every city prided itself on maintaining its own customs for the nomination or selection of council members. Some cities had rules or traditions according to which only the members of certain families were eligible for seats on the council. Sometimes guilds or neighborhoods had a constitutional right to council representation. Often, however, the only formal criterion for council membership was status as a citizen. In some cities the selection process involved vigorous public contests between hostile families or factions. More often choices were made behind closed doors in a carefully orchestrated process of consultation and compromise. Yet despite these differences, the analysis of urban elites in early modern Europe has shown that in the end council members in almost every city were drawn from the ranks of the community's wealthiest families. In a deferential society, people expected to be ruled by their superiors.

Urban magistrates were proud of their rank. They wore robes of office to denote their authority and filled town halls and other public buildings with portraits of themselves to perpetuate their memory. Sometimes they voiced sweeping claims of complete authority over their communities. Yet in actual fact the magistrates were constrained in their powers, and they knew it.

In the first place, most city governments were subordinate to the authority of a king or some other overlord. If he was dissatisfied with a city's response to his demands for revenue or political cooperation, an angry sovereign might send troops or arrive in person to compel obedience or install more pliable magistrates. Ecclesiastical institutions or members of the regional nobility might also enjoy rights and privileges that restricted the magistrates' freedom of action. Though less likely than overlords to use military means to enforce their will, bishops or nobles might apply economic pressure or engage in litigation to achieve their aims. And no matter how proud the magistrates might be of their city's legal autonomy, they generally knew that it was wiser to respond to pressures of this sort than to resist.

Yet the most important forms of political pressure exerted on the magistrates often came not from outside the community but from within. Most city

Aldermen of Toulouse. The *capitouls,* or civic officers, of Toulouse, France. Painitng by Jean Chalette (1581–1645). MUSÉE DES AUGUSTINS, TOULOUSE, FRANCE/GIRAUDON/ ART RESOURCE, NY

councils had very limited means at their disposal to enforce their decisions. Typically the magistrates commanded only a small number of soldiers or constables. The maintenance of order depended largely on the cooperation of the inhabitants themselves—especially the citizens, who were often armed and always opinionated. For even when citizens were excluded from direct participation in decision making, they retained a strong sense of their identity as part of the political community and they rarely hesitated to give expression to their point of view.

Almost any aspect of urban life could become politicized, but certain issues were recurrent sources of contention. Economic issues were perpetually on the council agenda. The city council regulated every aspect of economic life and was often called upon to adjudicate between the competing claims of different economic actors: craft masters versus merchants, journeymen versus masters, artisans in one trade versus artisans in another, visiting traders versus local retailers, consumers versus producers. At certain times, however, religious issues became paramount. During the sixteenth century, for example, the Protestant groups that emerged in countless cities often pressured magistrates to accept or adopt the new religion. At such times the magistrates were often faced with agonizing choices, for they had to consider not only the religious passions of the city's own inhabitants but also the preferences of the city's overlord and of other powerful political and ecclesiastical stakeholders outside the community.

Often the citizens' dissatisfaction with the way in which the magistrates had dealt with economic, religious, or other issues led to deeper conflicts over the way the city was being governed. Suspecting the magistrates of mismanaging the city's finances or endangering the city's well-being, the citizens might insist that the council be made more accountable for its actions. They might even call for changes in the constitutional arrangements under which the council exercised its powers. In modern cities dissatisfaction with the current administration is often resolved by elections, which can put new people into office. This option hardly existed in a system under which council members would often remain in office until they died. But there were other means by which the citizens— and other inhabitants—could put pressure on the magistrates. These included petitions, litigation, agitation, or, in extreme cases, violence.

The one political right shared by all inhabitants of the community was the right to submit petitions to the council for the granting of some benefit or redress of some grievance. All petitions had to receive due consideration, but special attention had to be paid to those submitted by members of the citizenry. Women or servants or laborers whose petitions were rejected had no formal means by which to demand reconsideration. But male citizens did. Their experience as members of guilds, militias, parish councils, or other interest groups not only heightened their political awareness but also taught them the potential value of collective action. A faction of citizens might form a committee or deputation to pursue their objectives. If thwarted by the magistrates, such opposition groups might appeal to the city's ruler, who could respond by revoking the city's old charter and granting a new one that reduced the magistrates' authority. Alternatively, citizens who opposed the actions of the current magistrates might take their complaints to some court of law that claimed jurisdiction over the city's affairs. There were always lawyers willing to argue such cases and judges willing to hear them. The city's magistrates, of course, could also appeal to the ruler or to the courts. But in many cases it was wiser to make concessions to disaffected citizens rather than to run the risks that outside involvement might entail.

Sometimes there were public demonstrations or even outbreaks of violence. The most vigorous expressions of popular protest in cities often took the form of food riots. To insure that the community had an adequate supply of grain or bread was one of the most fundamental obligations of urban leaders, and their failure to do so could trigger violent outbreaks. Groups that normally remained politically passive— notably women—often played a leading role in such episodes. Yet the actual frequency of such riots was small, precisely because magistrates knew how dangerous it was to let granaries become empty or to let bakers charge too much for bread.

But violence could also break out over constitutional issues. Occasionally when groups of disaffected citizens felt they had exhausted all other means of achieving their aims, they resorted to force. Council members might be overpowered, imprisoned, or forced into exile, and a new group of council members representing the opposition group would take power. This was high-risk behavior, for the ousted magistrates would try to convince the ruler or other powerful authorities that such insubordination had to be repressed by force. Yet such episodes recurred sporadically throughout the sixteenth and seventeenth centuries in cities all over Europe. Rare as they were, these events were widely publicized and long remembered.

A particularly dramatic rash of civic uprisings broke out in the second decade of the seventeenth century. In the German city of Frankfurt am Main, a citizens' uprising of 1612–1614 was directed simultaneously against the city's patrician magistrates and the local Jewish community. Not only the ruling magistrates but also the Jews were banished from the city until intervention by the Holy Roman Emperor brought about the restoration of the old regime, the return of the Jewish community, and the execution of the citizen leaders. In La Rochelle, on the west coast of France, an equally dramatic uprising in 1613–1614 led to the overthrow of the existing magistrates, many of whom were confined to dungeons for almost a year. The new government formed by the citizen rebels remained in power for more than a decade. Other urban uprisings, with various outcomes, occurred during the same decade in places like Utrecht in the Netherlands, Wetzlar and Worms in western Germany, Stralsund and Stettin on the Baltic, and elsewhere. In the 1680s a civic uprising in the German city of Cologne lasted for almost six years until the movement was finally suppressed and the ringleaders executed.

Food riots and other spontaneous surges of popular protest continued into the eighteenth century, as did litigation against urban rulers. But sustained uprisings of citizens against their own magistrates did not. The growing power of centralized states had much to do with this. As standing armies grew and towns became the seats of permanent garrisons, it became steadily easier for magistrates to summon the help they needed in suppressing disorder. At the same time, and even more importantly, the administrative reach of the state increasingly penetrated into the city. The traditional distinction between city and state officials declined as members of the urban elite moved into positions of service to the state. The extent to which magistrates and citizens alike focused on the city as the primary source of their political identity steadily diminished.

Many cities grew larger during the eighteenth century, but this did not necessarily transform urban politics. As population growth overwhelmed existing resources, city governments in many regions grappled with growing problems of poverty and the provision of poor relief. But most urban regimes stuck to traditional assumptions and arrangements for dealing with such problems and continued trying to send poor people back to their (often rural) place of origin.

Until the end of the eighteenth century the outward forms of urban politics remained remarkably constant. Magistrates and citizens alike clung stubbornly to the traditional institutions of urban life and rituals of urban governance. And despite growing criticism from Enlightenment thinkers who regarded guilds as obstacles to economic growth, almost everywhere in Europe the guild system remained intact. Major changes in the institutional structure of urban life only came about with the onset of the French Revolution and the wars to which it gave rise. In 1797 Napoléon Bonaparte swept away what had once been the grandest and most self-confident urban regime in Europe: the doge, senate, and Great Council of Venice. His action prefigured the less dramatic but no less thorough changes that lay ahead for the institutional structure of countless other European cities in the early decades of the nineteenth century.

See also **Absolutism** *(in this volume);* **Moral Economy and Luddism; Urban Crowds** *(volume 3);* **Church and Society** *(Volume 5); and other articles in this section.*

BIBLIOGRAPHY

Beik, William. *Urban Protest in Seventeenth-Century France: The Culture of Retribution.* Cambridge, U.K., 1997. An important analysis that illuminates both the patterns of popular protest and the ambivalent response of the authorities in French cities of the early absolutist era.

Brady, Thomas A., Jr. *Ruling Class, Regime and Reformation at Strasbourg, 1520–1555.* Leiden, Netherlands, 1978. A classic attempt to interpret the Reformation in one major city through a collective biography of the community's political leaders.

Finlay, Robert. *Politics in Renaissance Venice.* New Brunswick, N.J., 1980. Shows in dramatic detail how family rivalries and factional conflict underlay the seemingly incorruptible system of politics in sixteenth-century Venice.

Friedrichs, Christopher R. *Urban Politics in Early Modern Europe.* London and New York, 2000. A brief overview that describes the interplay of political forces in early modern cities in the light of modern theories of urban politics.

Halliday, Paul D. *Dismembering the Body Politic: Partisan Politics in England's Towns, 1650–1730.* Cambridge, U.K., and New York, 1998. Describes the interaction between politics on the municipal and the national level in an era when religious conflict was evolving into partisan politics.

Lindemann, Mary. *Patriots and Paupers: Hamburg, 1712–1830.* New York, 1990. Argues that traditionally paternalistic approaches to the problem of urban poverty lasted until the end of the eighteenth century, giving way only after 1800 to new, more punitive attitudes.

Livet, Georges, and Bernard Vogler, eds., *Pouvoir, ville et société en Europe, 1650–1750.* Paris, 1983. A selection of essays on power and society in early modern cities, both in France and elsewhere in Europe.

Mauersberg, Hans. *Wirtschafts- und Sozialgeschichte zentraleuropäischer Städte in neuerer Zeit; dargestellt an den Beispielen von Basel, Frankfurt a.M., Hamburg, Hannover und München.* Göttingen, Germany, 1960. An older but still authoritative description of the political and economic institutions of selected German and Swiss cities.

Nussdorfer, Laurie. *Civic Politics in the Rome of Urban VIII.* Princeton, N.J., 1992. Shows how municipal government functioned in a city whose overlord was the Pope himself.

Robbins, Kevin C. *City on the Ocean Sea: La Rochelle, 1530–1650: Urban Society, Religion, and Politics on the French Atlantic Frontier.* Leiden, Netherlands, 1997. A major study that illuminates the social underpinnings of political conflict in an important French city.

Schilling, Heinz. *Religion, Political Culture, and the Emergence of Early Modern Society: Essays in German and Dutch History.* Leiden, Netherlands, 1992. Translations of key essays by the leading German interpreter of urban political culture in early modern Europe.

Soliday, Gerald Lyman. *A Community in Conflict: Frankfurt Society in the Seventeenth and Early Eighteenth Centuries.* Hanover, N.H., 1974. Shows how a classic urban constitutional dispute was rooted in social conflicts.

Walker, Mack. *German Home Towns: Community, State, and General Estate, 1648–1871.* Ithaca, N.Y., 1971. An influential interpretation that argues that some key elements of modern German politics can be traced to the political culture of small towns in the early modern era.

URBAN INSTITUTIONS AND POLITICS: THE MODERN PERIOD

Theresa M. McBride

The nineteenth century remade cities into new and strange places that challenged conventional political and social categories. Industrialization and intensified urbanization drastically renovated the physical layout of the preindustrial city. What had been the seat of administrative, commercial, and religious power in the traditional topography of royal palaces, town halls, and church spires increasingly gave way to the geography of manufacturing, commerce, and parliamentary politics. In Vienna, like many other older cities, the old city walls were torn down during the nineteenth century, when the enemy ceased to be a foreign invader—like the Turkish armies that had menaced the Habsburg imperial capital for centuries—and came to be an enemy within—the revolutionary people who were demanding constitutional protection and political rights. With a huge tract of open land made available by the demolition of the old defense works, the face of a new city was constructed on the the Ringstrasse, the ring road that replaced the line of the old fortifications. Across a small park, the parliament building (the Reichsrat, site of the legislative assembly) directly faces the Hofburg (residence of the emperor and center of the hereditary and authoritarian monarchy), symbolizing the autocratic emperor's resistance to liberal and nationalist demands for political reform. While the centuries-old Habsburg empire managed to survive until 1918, the traditional elites increased their political power at the regional and local level. Clustered along Vienna's Ringstrasse were the institutions so cherished by nineteenth-century liberals in their struggle against the autocratic empire: constitutional government, embodied in the Reichsrat; the power of the municipal government of Vienna, expressed in the medieval Gothic style of the Rathaus; education, intellectual life, and high culture, represented by the university and the Burgtheater.

The rebuilding of Vienna in the mid- to late nineteenth century parallels the transformation of countless European cities as a result of political events and of demographic and economic pressures. Vienna, Paris, Berlin, and London were all substantially rebuilt in the course of the nineteenth and early twentieth centuries and absorbed millions of new residents. Suburbs were added outside the old city walls; broad boulevards cut through the old city center; new administrative and cultural buildings were constructed. And as the topography of the city changed, so did its politics.

NINETEENTH-CENTURY URBAN POLITICS: IN THE HANDS OF THE ECONOMIC ELITES

The traditional politics of European cities was not democratic, but was based rather on the exercise of collective political power by the urban elites. The core of the elite continued into the modern period to be composed of merchants, those no longer active in business but living off their investments, and many professionals, especially lawyers. Urban political power remained firmly in the hands of this elite of upper-middle-class notables (called *notables* in France and *Honoratioren* in Germany) because of the property requirements for participating in local elections, the qualification of voters according to taxes paid, and the unpaid nature of local administrative positions such as those in city councils. The relative autonomy of urban governance, counterposed to the autocratic power of the monarchy, allowed for the evolution of a sense of citizenship and of a political identity that was focused on the city. When the French Revolution swept away the institutional structures of countless European cities after 1789, this tradition of urban governance helped to shape the development of liberal politics. By abolishing the remnants of feudalism throughout Europe, the French Revolution and Napoleonic Empire accomplished a revolution from above. To take one example, the promulgation of a Prussian constitution in 1808, after the Prussian defeat by the French, gave Prussian cities representative institutions and a degree of self-government. The result was a dramatic shift in the political climate in

Vienna City Hall. The Neues Rathaus, built by Friedrich von Schmidt between 1872 and 1883. CORBIS

these cities. The urban elites became active in demanding constitutional government, economic modernization, national unification, and new forms of citizenship.

City governments often played an active role in the struggle for liberal reforms in the nineteenth century. They did so in order to perpetuate their own power and to promote the economic interests of citizens, who still made up a small percentage of the adult male population even with the beginnings of liberal constitutionalism. Through such institutions as chambers of commerce, employers' associations, and parliamentary lobbies, as well as through social and familial relationships, the economic elites who dominated urban institutions successfully influenced state policy, particularly in areas that affected them. Local politics was the chosen arena of the urban elites because politics was more loosely organized and freer of the control of landed property owners, and because informal contacts and social relationships retained their importance. Their political constituency did not reach downward toward a popular base, but instead stretched outward through the network of family, social, and business relationships that tied together the urban elites. They often resisted democratization and preferred to perpetuate the political tutelage of the urban lower classes. In this way, the nineteenth-century elites survived the transition to parliamentary government and electoral politics remarkably un-

scathed until the early twentieth century, despite the expansion of formal citizenship over the course of the century.

Urbanization promoted a sense of urban identity and local patriotism. People were proud of their cities, and rivalries between cities were frequent. Local elites tried to endow their cities with institutions and services that would serve the inhabitants well, and they implemented improvements that would give their cities distinction. A city's reputation might well be associated with its cultural institutions, such as museums, which could be the linchpins in the reconstruction of the city center. The Rijksmuseum in Amsterdam, the National Gallery in London, and the Alte Pinakothek in Munich, all built between 1800 and 1830, helped enhance the reputation of the cities in which they were constructed and drew tourists to the city as leisure travel increased. Although most were state museums, the attachment of the bourgeois elites to these cultural institutions could be very strong, because they represented a means to fulfill the elite's aspirations for cultural leadership and social legitimacy. Such institutions replaced early modern civic organizations like guilds, which had provided a public identity for earlier cities.

Poor relief was provided at the municipal level throughout most of the nineteenth century. With the rapid growth of cities and industrialization in the first half of the nineteenth century, demands on city agencies increased along with the growing populations of indigents from among those arriving in search of work in urban industry. Most cities sought to cut costs, and they often tried to expel poor migrants. Even as national welfare legislation took shape in the later nineteenth century, city governments retained a substantial role in the provision of poor relief and health services, such as they were. The city's role was particularly important in countries like France that emphasized a decentralized approach to social welfare.

URBANIZATION AND THE EXPANSION OF LOCAL GOVERNMENT'S ROLE

Urbanization could be experienced as a very rapid and disorienting process in the nineteenth and early twentieth centuries, as modern cities swelled by population growth and migration. Intense urban growth had significant implications for urban politics. Class antagonisms were sharper in the nineteenth-century cities than in the countryside and there was a widespread belief that urban crime rates were higher. Middle-class observers (our only sources for this) considered the urban poor and working people "the dangerous classes." Incidents of civil strife were interpreted by the elites as symptoms of social breakdown; under new conditions, formerly innocuous popular festivities could seem threatening, when thousands of people crowded into the narrow streets of the city. Police forces were created or expanded across Europe to replace the traditional use of the state's army to keep order. Suppressing crime and urban disorder supplied the rationale for extending the power of municipal authorities. Crowd control and regulation of popular leisure became prime concerns, along with crime fighting. Some urban elites attempted to outlaw begging.

The demands on city governments extended well beyond the need to control crime and civil strife. Local postal services, fire protection, sewers, water, streets, schools, and the administration of poor relief were all areas in which nineteenth-century cities became increasingly involved, long before national governments saw fit to do so. Berlin's first postal service was set up in 1800 by the tradesmen's guilds; messengers walked through the streets announcing themselves with handbells to collect and deliver mail. Probably because of the mail service, houses in Berlin were numbered for the first time and street names were posted at street corners.

With urbanization came the formation of an identifiable metropolitan culture by the turn of the twentieth century. This urban identity was not as strong in eastern and southern Europe where the links between the town and country remained strong because rural workers migrated seasonally to find work in industry, but maintained a political and social identity as rural people. The new urban culture did not obliterate other identities based on class, ethnicity, or gender, but it did define a common way in which city dwellers related to the city and shared patterns of leisure and consumption. A clear separation developed between urban and rural peoples. City people were considered to be typically "modern" and they viewed rural people as ignorant, narrow-minded, and suspicious. Perhaps no city underwent quite so dramatic a transformation as Berlin. What had been only a provincial capital for the Prussian kingdom reinvented itself as a major metropolis over the course of only a few decades. Between 1848 and 1905, the population of Berlin leaped from 400,000 to 2 million, developing huge suburbs around the city, which added another 1.5 million. Berlin outstripped its rivals to become, by 1920, the world's third-largest city. The dizzying pace of development in the span of a lifetime fixed the city's identity as quintessentially "modern," unfixed, and dynamic, and Berlin became synonymous with the avant-garde in the arts and with a glittering urban culture in the first quarter of the twentieth century.

Britain was the most rapidly industrializing area of Europe in the nineteenth century, and British cities faced the challenge of meeting new urban needs early on. Reform legislation in the 1830s opened cities to control by middle-class elements, and this furthered on expansion of urban government functions, including the police. The London sewer system, established in 1848, was generally regarded as the model of an integrated sewer system, and Glasgow became the first city to harness a natural resource in this way by bringing highland water to its citizens in 1859. But the supply of new services did not transform urban politics in the early Victorian years. Local government in both England and Scotland were characterized by administrative confusion: the number of parochial boards (dominated by local property owners) with responsibilities for sewerage, water supply, public works, transportation, schools, housing, and welfare multiplied, their overlapping jurisdictions creating a chaos of private interests and weak public authority. Order was imposed on this welter of conflicting responsibilities by the creation of popularly elected county councils around the turn of the twentieth century. The largest cities of England, Scotland, and Wales became largely self-administering, with wide powers over police and education. The industrial city of Glasgow earned a reputation for dynamic government with effective action against urban overcrowding, slum clearance, and the early municipalization of water and gas supplies, but such municipal activism came late to London until the long overdue unification of municipal administration in the elected body of the London County Council in 1888.

By the end of the nineteenth century, frustrated by the poor quality of private services available or provoked by public health crises, such as periodic outbreaks of cholera (known to be spread by infected water supplies), urban administrations across Europe were pushed to expand their authority over previously unregulated spheres of urban life. Urban governments had to expand to meet the demands arising from their control over public utilities and the appropriation of public services for their citizens. Believing that municipalization of its water supply would provide higher quality and lower cost than the market, the French city of Lyon finally municipalized its water in 1900. Even though the city paid a yearly compensation to the private water company and increased the size of its workforce, it was turning a profit within two years. By 1904, nearly 2,000 English cities had municipalized their waterworks, 152 their gasworks, and 118 their tram systems. After an Italian law in 1903 that permitted municipalization of public services, most major cities in southern and central Italy started running their own trams and water and electricity boards. Local government expanded further into the lives of its citizens. Until World War I, municipal governments had a far greater impact on the daily lives of city dwellers than did the central government. Cities not only took over the provision of water and gas, but implemented universal schooling, police and fire protection, and welfare services, and built streets, sewers, and housing.

As the functions of municipal government expanded, control of city hall was jealously guarded by the urban elites. For the most part, increasing democratization as a result of the extension of the suffrage by the end of the nineteenth century and in the aftermath of World War I, mass politics, and ideological conflict emerged at the national level. Local politics could be a refuge in which the political ambitions of the urban elite still could be fulfilled. While there was some change of the social composition of French city councils, for example, with the increase in representatives from the middle and lower-middle classes, the urban elites continued to dominate city councils through the 1920s and 1930s. In spite of the reform in 1884, which mandated the free election of French mayors, the majority of city councils continued to be made up of professional men and important merchants. No industrial worker was elected mayor even

of an industrial city until the interwar period. Enormous political power was vested in the mayor, who exercised extensive authority as the registrar of births, marriages, and deaths; as judicial officer entitled to prosecute breaches of the law; and as president of the local council, as well as the agent of the state for implementing national laws. In this "regime of the elected mayor," which extended into the 1950s in France, political parties of all persuasions, including reformist strains of socialism, focused on control of local government in their political tactics. In other countries, like Spain, where national politics were less democratic, local politics could be more dynamic. Thus antidynastic parties began to establish populist urban political machines that took over city governments and disrupted old patterns of patronage after the turn of the century. From the late nineteenth century onward, city governments in many industrial regions were increasingly captured by socialist or (after World War I) communist majorities. In Germany, no local city councils were dominated by the Social Democratic Party until 1918, when universal suffrage led to the sharing of power by liberals and socialists. The resultant control of urban administrations provided key power bases for the parties, even when they were excluded at the national level. Reformist city governments characteristically sought to expand urban social welfare and housing efforts to secure their political power.

THE DECLINE OF
LOCAL GOVERNMENT'S AUTHORITY
AFTER WORLD WAR I

After World War I, the depression and political turmoil produced further changes in urban politics. In theory, fascism in Italy and in Germany espoused a strong, centralized state. This could mean the nationalization of public services and the usurpation of local authority. In Italy in the 1920s, the imposition of fascist governance introduced powerful, appointed local leaders to implement state policies in the regions. Benito Mussolini (1883–1945) dissolved local councils and dismissed elected mayors in 1926; regional authority was assumed by the prefect, who was often a member of the old ruling elite of property owners rather than of the middle classes. In effect, the fascist "reform" simply meant that the provincial nobility regained control of local government. In Germany in the early 1930s, Nazism took local government very seriously, building a political movement out of the economic distress of the middling and lower middle classes by promoting economic revival and vigorous leadership. The Nazi electoral surge between 1930 and 1933 and the Nazi seizure of power were accomplished to a large extent at the local level. However, after 1933 the Nazification of local government brought cities under the direct control of the central authority: Hitler's second-in-command Josef Goebbels (1897–1945) was given the title of Gauleiter (district leader) for Berlin even before the Nazis came to power there. In both Italy and Germany, the fascist era resulted in generally greater centralization of public authority, even though fascists used local politics to come to power.

World War II accelerated the process by which the central government took on previous municipal functions. Under postwar governments, the central government played the major role in rebuilding after the destruction of the war, removing decrepit structures and constructing new housing, building new avenues and squares, installing the infrastructure to provide for public health and transportation, and many other amenities. Housing has remained perhaps the greatest challenge for governments in the twentieth century. In the postwar era, the provision of adequate housing was too great a burden for local governments and was increasingly taken on by national governments. In Britain, subsidized housing provided fully a third of all housing stock by 1939. In France few cities rushed in to provide public housing, in spite of the need, before the national government assumed responsibility for the construction of public housing. Migration and urbanization have been dramatic features of postwar life in capitalist Western Europe, and the older urban centers have been ringed by public housing or new working-class suburbs. Growth of the urban population generated even faster increases in the demand for housing and other services.

Where national governments were unresponsive to the needs, municipal governments had to assume responsibility. Reformist local governments emerged in France in the 1920s, especially in the urban "red belt" of working-class suburbs that ringed Paris and other cities in France, and in Germany in the Weimar period after 1918, when political power passed from the upper middle classes to the newly enfranchised citizenry at large. After World War II, reform became the agenda of both Christian Democrats and the Social Democratic Party in Germany, spurred by the process of de-Nazification and the need to construct safeguards against the weaknesses of the Weimar government. But political and administrative reform took second place to the extraordinary physical reconstruction of German cities after the destruction of the war.

In Italy, with its long history of city-states, political reform was more likely to be achieved on the local level in the postwar era. For example, the central Italian city of Bologna became a showpiece of reformist local government in the 1950s and 1960s, earning a wide reputation for efficiency and honest administration. Building schools and housing, providing better street lighting, public transportation, and new sewers, the communist-dominated city council avoided budget deficits, in the same era when the Italian national government was monopolized by the Christian Democrats, who directed an increasingly corrupt system of political patronage. Thus, political reform and the objectives of the Italian left were realized on the local level while remaining blocked at the national level.

URBAN POLITICAL ISSUES IN THE POSTWAR ERA

The economic miracle experienced by Western Europe since 1950 revived the cities of London, Paris, and Vienna. These cities remained at the center of their country's national lives as the hubs of service and commercial economies and the centers of vast transportation networks. But at the same time, urban politics and urban governments were transformed by the expansion of suburbs, which changed the very nature of city life. The effects of suburbanization seem to defy attempts at a unified administrative structure for city governance. European cities experienced a widening gulf between an "inner" city and an "outer" one, as the challenge of controlling growth and providing basic services to the spreading "conurbations" have foundered on deep social, racial, and economic divisions.

Europe's major cities were marked by increasing social polarization and a tidal wave of political terrorism and civil unrest in the 1960s, 1970s, and 1980s. Migration into Europe from outside the prosperous capitalist western states revived the urban elites' fear of the "dangerous classes" who inhabit the working-class suburbs and inner-city neighborhoods. At the end of the twentieth century, the immigrant and working-class populations continue to live at the outskirts of the city, marginalized by de-industrialization, high unemployment, social and racial differences, and the high rents of the New Europe. These suburbs are seen as tinderboxes, ready to explode and ungovernable, as demoralized, unemployed youths loiter and form gangs. The marginalization of these urban populations jeopardizes political solutions to urban problems. The prosperity of postwar Europe has remade European cities, and the urban nature of life in the New Europe has lent a particular immediacy to the problems of urban society.

See also **The Liberal State; Fascism and Nazism** *(in this volume);* **Police** *(volume 3); and other articles in this section.*

BIBLIOGRAPHY

Allen, William Sheridan. *The Nazi Seizure of Power: The Experience of a Single German Town, 1930–1935.* New York, 1973.

Anderson, Michael. *Family Structure in Nineteenth-Century Lancashire.* Cambridge, U.K., 1971.

Blanning, T. C. W. "The Commercialization and Sacralization of European Culture in the Nineteenth Century." *Oxford Illustrated History of Modern Europe.* Edited by T. C. W. Blanning. Oxford and New York, 1996. Pages 120–147.

Cohen, William B. *Urban Government and the Rise of the French City: Five Municipalities in the Nineteenth Century.* New York, 1998.

Fritzsche, Peter. *Reading Berlin, 1900.* Cambridge, Mass., 1996.

Garside, P. L. "London and the Home Counties." *The Cambridge Social History of Britain, 1750–1950.* Edited by F. M. L. Thompson. Volume 1. Cambridge, U.K., and New York, 1990. Pages 471–539.

Ginsborg, Paul. *A History of Contemporary Italy: Society and Politics, 1943–1988.* London and New York, 1990.

Hohenberg, Paul M., and Lynn Hollen Lees. *The Making of Urban Europe, 1000–1950.* Cambridge, Mass., 1985.

Lees, Andrew. "Historical Perspectives on Cities in Modern Germany: Recent Literature." *Journal of Urban History* 5, no. 4 (August 1979): 411–446.

Magraw, Roger. *France, 1815–1914: The Bourgeois Century.* New York, 1986.

McKibbin, Ross. *Classes and Cultures: England, 1918–1951.* Oxford and New York, 1998.

Porter, Roy. *London: A Social History.* Cambridge, Mass., 1995.

Read, Anthony, and David Fisher. *Berlin Rising: Biography of a City.* New York, 1994.

Schorske, Carl E. *Fin-de-Siècle Vienna: Politics and Culture.* New York, 1980.

Sheehan, James J. "Liberalism and the City in Nineteenth-Century Germany." *Past and Present* 51 (May 1971): 116–137.

Smout, T. C. "Scotland, 1850–1950." *The Cambridge Social History of Britain, 1750–1950.* Edited by F. M. L. Thompson. Volume 1. Cambridge, U.K., and New York, 1990. Pages 209–280.

Thompson, F. M. L. "Town and City." *The Cambridge Social History of Britain, 1750–1950.* Edited by F. M. L. Thompson. Volume 1. Cambridge, U.K., and New York, 1990. Pages 1–86.

Walker, Mack. *German Home Towns: Community, State, and General Estate, 1648–1871.* Ithaca, N.Y., 1971.

Waller, Phillip J. *Town, City, and Nation: England, 1850–1914.* Oxford, U.K., and New York, 1983.

STREET LIFE AND CITY SPACE

W. Scott Haine

The topic of street life and city space is burgeoning at the forefront of social history. Its vast scope embraces the gestures and actions of people—vendors pitching their wares, patrons conversing in taverns or elegant cafés, children playing on back streets, dandies promenading on fashionable boulevards, beggars cowering from the gaze of affluent shoppers. Streets may be host to the explorations of tourists; the daily routines of people walking, driving, or taking mass transit; the carnivals that echo medieval sites of sociability and festivity. The study of city space has recently led historians to ask about the functions and meanings of buildings—from majestic cathedrals, imposing city halls, and banks, to factories, residences, hospitals, and asylums. Streets and other open spaces also reflect the history of transportation (from walking to the use of horses, carriages, subways, cars, and in-line skates) and communication (from the gossip of neighbors to television and other electronic media).

For most of history, streets and their places of commerce, their squares, and their parks have comprised a large part of any city, often one-third of a city's area. Why has it taken social historians so long to focus on these central urban spaces? The anthropologist Gloria Levitas offers one of the best explanations, quoting the French philosopher Auguste Comte (1798–1857): "We reserve till last research into subjects closest to our social selves." Another probable cause is that face-to-face interaction on streets or in cafés and bars, once a given in all societies, has become rare, fascinating, and exotic in the contemporary developed world and endangered in developing countries. Telephones, cars, and televisions—and now various computer technologies—have rendered much face-to-face interaction optional rather than mandatory in daily life. Those coming of age after the year 2000 may not realize that streets are not simply traffic routes, that home and work are not always separated, and that the street can be a center of sociability as well as mobility.

Streets and the spaces intimately dependent on them, such as bars, taverns, and cafés, are in essence the interstitial spaces of a city, at the intersections of public and private life, home and workplaces, and male and female spaces. Not only are such spaces at the center of the recurring patterns of daily life, they have also played a vital role in wars, rebellions, and revolutions. What would the Middle Ages have been without its street vendors, singers, and magicians? Carnivals and processions were central to Renaissance life. Much of the fighting of the French and Russian Revolutions occurred on the streets of Paris and Saint Petersburg, respectively. And how could the social and intellectual life of Paris, Vienna, or London have been as vibrant, from the seventeenth century onward, without cafés?

THE MULTIFUNCTIONAL MEDIEVAL STREET

The origin and foundation of modern European street life and city space emerged during the Middle Ages. In general, medieval cities developed without the elaborate planning characteristic of urban growth during and after the Renaissance. Weak and undeveloped national and local governments did not have the power to design, decree, or enforce specific street layouts, much less to regulate the activities that went on within them. Instead, urban communities built their houses around the principal buildings of the powerful, the holy, and the wealthy: the castles of the warrior nobility, the monasteries and churches of the Catholic clergy, and the markets and fairs of the merchants and traders. Those who built medieval towns had in mind shelter, commercial activity, and military or religious protection rather than a rational street plan. Across Europe, the typical medieval house had a ground floor shop or workshop (production and retail usually shared the same space), with living quarters on the second floor. Houses lacked halls or corridors, so rooms simply opened one upon another, and windows tended to be small and primitive. The best facades, often with porticos and balconies, usually faced the

The Street as Center of Sociability. Street scene in Aquila degli Abruzzi region of Italy, 1952.
©HENRI CARTIER-BRESSON/MAGNUM PHOTOS

street, and the best and biggest rooms opened onto the public realm. As one scholar has noted, the medieval house "forced the members of an extroverted society into the street." (Contemine, p. 443).

Apart from churches, however, few truly "public" buildings existed. During the medieval (A.D. 400–1500) and Renaissance (1300–1600) eras, tav-erns and inns were virtually the only enclosed spaces where the public gathered. Untamed countryside reigned outside the city walls, and often inside as well, for wolves often ravaged cities during the winter. Parks were nonexistent; the only green or open spaces were small gardens or the cemeteries next to the churches.

Streets, an afterthought in medieval construction, became the center of urban expression in the medieval and Renaissance periods. Aside from a few main thoroughfares devoted to horse-and-cart traffic, most medieval streets were more like footpaths, residential and haphazard. With living and working quarters in the same building, people met on the street, and a dense fabric of sociability developed. Bakers, butchers, carpenters, apothecaries, and craftsmen often sold their products at their own doorsteps. In addition, the streets swarmed with a wide variety of vendors hawking products and services: old clothes, food and wine, haircuts and shaves, medical and dental services. Letter writers and knife grinders mingled with magicians, cardsharps, mimes, and minstrels.

Each crier tried to create a distinctive call. As a result, medieval streets reverberated with sounds and songs, and scholars down through the ages have found much musical, artistic, and theatrical merit in these street trades. Indeed, the mid-nineteenth-century French scholar Georges Kastner believed that the polyphonic quality of medieval music was inspired, in part, by these street vendors. Modern research has shown that traveling vendors played a vital role in linking long-distance trade networks and allowing the poor of the countryside or mountainous regions of Europe to make a living.

The romantic image of conviviality and song wafting through narrow medieval streets would be quickly dashed, however, if one looked downward. Cobblestones or bricks were reserved for main streets, and lesser routes were not only unpaved but lacked any efficient means of waste and water disposal. Medieval streets thus had a horrifically pungent smell in summer and became swamps or ice rinks (depending on latitude) in winter. At best, a gutter running down the middle of the street served as a sewage system, and in some cities pigs ran loose as all-purpose garbage eaters.

City space in medieval cities showed little of the segregation by class that became prevalent later. In Italian cities, such as Florence, powerful families often staked out a section of the city and would be surrounded by their own retainers and servants rather than by other wealthy families. Any segregation in these densely packed cities was based upon trade rather than economic status. Artisans, such as jewelers or carpenters, often organized into associations called guilds, which protected the skills and economic status of their members by fixing prices and standards of quality, and setting the terms of apprenticeship. During the medieval period, guildhalls became vital centers of economic and social life for these artisans, and some guilds remained influential into the nineteenth century.

Gender differentiation in the use of space was clearly defined. Paintings and illustrations reveal women at home; in a favored scene, a woman is portrayed at the window. Other female spaces included churches, markets, ovens, water wells, and flour mills, as well as courtyards and alleys around the home. When venturing out into the street, women often traveled in groups. Historians have found that during the course of the Renaissance, upper-class women lost much of the access to street life they had had during the Middle Ages. Women from the lower classes continued to be a a vital part of the street trades and the markets throughout early modern and modern European history.

The distinction between public and private life was blurred in medieval cities, and interactions within the family blended into a broader sociability encompassing the neighborhood. Street and tavern life was subject to a detailed series of customs enforced by designated groups. Social drinking, for example, was often governed by rituals surrounding the passing of a common cup. Groups of young unmarried males in their late teens and early twenties known as youth abbeys often organized festivities and monitored morality in their neighborhoods. Especially strong during the twelfth to the sixteenth centuries, these associations of young men led the celebrations at the end of Lent, for example, and censured husbands who were too submissive to their wives or couples who could not produce children. In addition, guilds and groups of lay Catholics joined together in confraternities and also sponsored street processions and entertainments.

All told, medieval urban society, accustomed to vendors hawking their wares in markets and streets, did not make rigid distinctions between work and leisure, freedom and constraint, or individual and group. The notion of a lone, detached observer walking the streets, reflecting on the crowd and the urban spectacle (the French "flaneur") was inconceivable in this age of customary, constraining, and obligatory sociability. Instead of the artistic individuality that would prevail in the nineteenth and twentieth centuries, the medieval world spawned a convivial communality, especially in the marketplace. Russian literary critic Mikhail Bakhtin (1895–1975), one of the most penetrating and influential interpreters of the role of the marketplace and carnival in medieval and Renaissance life, discerned in the rough, foul, jocular, and boisterous language of the marketplace and carnival, as exemplified in François Rabelais's (c. 1483–1553) *Gargantua and Pantagruel,* a language freed from social norms and hierarchies, a language that created a solidarity among the poor and commonplace people. Not merely verbal, this communication also included the gestures, singing, and hawking of the marketplace. Indeed, this festive "grotesque body" eluded the spatial and moral constraints and decorum embodied in churches, palaces, courts of law, and the homes of the wealthy. Confirmation of Bakthin's thesis can be found in a description of London's fish market as "the college of bad language." (Schmiechen and Carls, p. 16). On the other hand, groups widely developed rituals and rules to govern various social occasions and interactions. Popular spontaneity thus had its limits.

The marketplace was not simply a place of ribald revelry, as Bakhtin has himself acknowledged. In the popular mind, market transactions were supposed to embody what E. P. Thompson called a "moral economy." This concept, found across Europe, held that there was a "just price" for staples. When the price of bread soared, for example, whether from poor harvests, economic dislocation, or war, the populace suspected merchants of hoarding staples in order to make excessive profits. In such an instance, people would stage grain riots, seizing the stock of grain or bread and distributing it to the people at the "just price," then giving the money to the merchants. Public authorities did not usually view such riots as a threat to public order, but rather as a safety valve or what might be called a primitive public opinion poll. The prevailing assumption was that after the poor had had a chance to act out their power—during a carnival, for instance—they would return to their lowly position.

RENAISSANCE URBAN TRANSFORMATION

As far back as the fourteenth century, more orderly sites for commercial transactions began to emerge. First commercial exchanges and then stock markets were a vast improvement over exchanges on streets, courtyards, porticos, churches, or taverns, permitting merchants, traders, wholesalers, and insurance brokers to conduct their transactions with greater efficiency. When the Amsterdam stock market was completed in 1631, it set the standard with its modern, freewheeling form of speculation and its spatial layout, in which each banker, broker, or trader had a numbered spot. Moreover, only those deemed to have sufficient capital were permitted into this temple of enterprise and speculation.

The latter part of the Renaissance was more important for ideas, ideologies, and innovations concerning street life and city space than for a radical change in the texture of urban life itself. The consolidation of monarchical and papal bureaucratic governments (new monarchies), the increasing wealth of the urban merchant and commercial elite, and a rising cult of antiquity combined to produce ambitious plans to redesign cities along Renaissance notions of perspective. Straight and broad streets, on either a grid or a radiating axial, provided dramatic vistas for monumental buildings and easy access for troops and military supplies to the more elaborate fortifications needed to resist increasing cannon power. These broad streets also allowed for easier surveillance and repression of urban disorder.

The most dramatic example of Renaissance urban transformation occurred in Rome under the popes. Following the sack of Rome (1527) and the rise of the Protestant Reformation, the papacy was determined to recreate Rome, building a more secure and imposing capital of Catholicism. The project culminated in the papacy of Sixtus V, who ruled from 1585 to 1590, and employed such Renaissance artists as Michaelangelo (1475–1564) and Bernini (1598–1680). A new network of streets connected the Holy City's myriad monuments, from Roman ruins to Saint Peter's Basilica. A series of fountains and obelisks also brought coherence and unity to the urban plan. Along the new streets, typical of Rome and other Renaissance cities, construction conformed to the street pattern rather than dominating it. In Florence, which pioneered these new trends in urban planning during the thirteenth and fourteenth centuries, merchants and bankers built sumptuous townhouses along the broad new avenues. These neighborhoods were among the first in which segregation by income and status became the norm.

Although this wealthy urban elite also built social welfare institutions such as hospitals and foundling homes, the growing wealth of cities was most prominently expressed in the construction of purpose-built sites for leisure activities. As had happened in the case of markets and exchanges, more of the activities that had once occurred on the street now found their own individual spaces. After 1650 theaters, tennis courts, opera houses, cockpits, bullrings, racecourse tracks, and an assortment of pleasure gardens arose across the European urban landscape. Although these places of amusement and recreation were primarily intended for the upper classes, they were frequented by a wide spectrum of urban society. Class distinctions were nonetheless maintained: in theaters, for example, the upper and middle classes sat in side loges, apart from the lower classes who were relegated to the pit in front of the stage. These centers of diversion initiated the process by which communities tied to specific neighborhoods and streets became more fully integrated into the larger urban environment.

CONTROL AND DECLINE OF STREETLIFE IN THE SEVENTEENTH AND EIGHTEENTH CENTURIES

The seventeenth and eighteenth centuries, the historian Philippe Ariès has argued, produced a wide variety of social institutions based upon friendship and affinity: clubs, intellectual and scientific societies, reading rooms, academies, bookstores, art galleries, and freemasonry. Ariès also noted a proliferation of taverns and the arrival of coffee and chocolate houses, thanks to coffee from the Middle East starting about 1650 and the new chocolate beverages from the Americas. (Ariès, 1989, pp. 2–17). Italy stood in the forefront of the new street patterns, and England was home to many of the associations based on friendship and affinity. The fifteenth-century Court of Bone Compagnie was one of the first clubs, and Masonic lodges emerged a few centuries later. The emergence of these sites of sociability reflected the gradual decline of street life, owing in part to the increased ability of national and local governments to regulate street life and in part to the creation of structures (as noted above) that absorbed some of the street's functions. A small but telling indicator of the decline of the intimate and sometimes promiscuous medieval community is the declining use of communal cups during these decades and the smaller number of youth abbeys willing to counter governmental regulation and repression.

Although streets remained remarkably "cluttered" by modern standards, important changes resulted from the growing power of monarchical and urban governments. For one thing, streets became increasingly and truly "public," that is, unencumbered and open to any pedestrian or vehicle. The French town of Limbus, for example, banned chicken pens and the parking of hay carts in the street, while within the premises of numerous other cities and towns, pigs were forbidden to run free. Civic authorities prohibited the dumping of garbage in the street. By the end of the eighteenth century, Paris and other cities had begun to place numbers on buildings, the better to identify and to regulate them. Police forces became more organized and elaborate. In an attempt to impose order on streets and other urban spaces, Louis XIV (1638–1715) created the position of Lieutenant General of Police in Paris in 1667 and established a network of asylums for the insane, the poor, and the idle. As policing of the street increased, public life began retreating into shops, taverns, and parks. For instance, capital-poor Amsterdam traders transacted their business in cafés near the stock exchange, such as the Café Rochellois, the Café Anglais, and the Café de Leyde. In London, the famous Lloyds of London insurance firm first conducted its business in a coffeehouse.

Growing segregation by neighborhoods led to increasingly differentiated street life. The upper classes, in their luxurious townhouses on broad avenues, used the street to display their elaborate sartorial fashions and their carriages and fine horses. Esplanades were developed on both sides of city walls, which had their original military importance, and became fashionable places for upper-class promenades and also, unfortunately, for depredations by the city's youth. The lower classes, out of necessity rather than pleasure, continued to use city streets as they had in the Middle Ages—as extensions of their cramped living quarters and as work and leisure spaces. The middle class, on the contrary, retreated increasingly into their homes. Bourgeois children were not allowed to play on the street, young women were severely restricted to the home, and even the males felt out of place among both aristocratic display and what they perceived to be lower-class depravity. In England, where middle-class domesticity was most fully developed, Georgian terrace houses were built with the servants' quarters and kitchen on the street side and the bedrooms and living areas in the interior. By the late eighteenth and early nineteenth centuries, English Protestant Evangelicals—among them William Wilberforce (1759–1833), Hannah Moore, and Sarah Stickney Ellis—were advocating a rustic domesticity in newly emerging English suburbs outside of London. In these verdant enclaves, virtuous middle-class families could avoid the immorality and drunkenness of the city streets.

THE RISE OF THE PUBLIC SPHERE

The growing reach of central governments and the decreasing pull of local communities led to the emergence of modern politics in urban space. The expanding literate stratum of urban society, which included the middle classes as well as the nobility, became concerned with governmental actions and demanded that their own views be considered in what is today called public policy. Private individuals gathered in the coffeehouses that were spreading across Europe along with the popularity of this beverage introduced from the Middle East. They discussed public matters, with reason rather than status as the main criterion for the validity of their arguments. The emergence of newspapers in England, Holland, France, and Italy in the later seventeenth century added another morning ritual to these spaces. Still too expensive for most of the literate population, newspapers relied on cafés for subscriptions and circulation among their clientele.

London and Paris developed two of the most important café societies of this era. During the early 1700s, such writers as Joseph Addison (1672–1719), Sir Richard Steele (1672–1729), Henry Carey (1687–1743), Eustace Budgell (1686–1737) met at a coffeehouse in Russell Street known as "Button's," were Addison and Steele published their influential newspapers, the *Tatler* and the *Spectator*. Later in the century, the Paris café La Procope in particular was frequented by the central figures of the French Enlightenment: George-Louis Buffon (1707–1788), Jean Le Rond d'Alembert (1717–1783), Paul-Henri-Dietrich d'Holbach (1723–1789), Denis Diderot (1713–1784), Nicolas-Joseph-Laurent Gilbert (1751–1780), Henri-Louis Lekain (1729–1778), Jean-François Marmontel (1723–1799), Alexis Piron (1689–1773), Jean-Jacques Roussea (1712–1778), and Voltaire (François-Marie Arouet [1694–1778]).

In one of the most influential studies fusing social and intellectual history, Jürgen Habermas has termed such spaces and intellectual critical conversations the "public sphere." Habermas believes that the rationality and equality in evidence in coffeehouses also surfaced in clubs, debating societies, and other academic and scientific associations that emerged in the seventeenth and eighteenth centuries. Montesquieu (1689–1755) captured well the ambiance of these cafés in his *Persian Letters* (1721): "It is a merit of the coffeehouse that you can sit there the whole day and half of the night amongst people of all classes. The coffeehouse is the only place where conversation may be made to come true, where extravagant plans, utopian dreams and political plots are hatched without anyone even leaving their seat." In one of his most memorable images, the nineteenth-century French historian Jules Michelet (1798–1874) imagined café philosophers peering into their coffee cups and seeing the approaching 1789 French Revolution.

POLITICS AND URBAN SPACE FROM THE FRENCH REVOLUTION THROUGH THE NINETEENTH CENTURY

At the end of the eighteenth century, political upheaval in France and the industrial revolution in England inaugurated a century of contestation, dislocation, and transformation in street life and city space. The storming of the Bastille fortress in eastern Paris in July 1789 and other riots across France redefined the market riot and politics in public spaces. No longer could collective popular demonstrations be dismissed as periodic expressions of frustration and excitement bound to dissipate. Now they had the po-

tential to overthrow monarchies and replace them with republics. This new concept of popular street mobilization became enshrined in the French word "journée," literally "day" but also carrying a new revolutionary connotation. The specter of revolution in the streets has haunted Europe ever since.

The French Revolution created new urban spaces and rituals. A series of monuments, holidays—centering on 14 July, the day that the Bastille fell—and parades celebrated and made concrete the new French nation, founded, according to its ideology, upon the will of the people. This "national liturgy" was adopted by the other nations of Europe during the nineteenth century. National holidays became important modern festival days, celebrated with speeches, fireworks, dancing, eating, and drinking.

Two new institutions, at the nexus between taste and leisure, also emerged during the French Revolution: the museum and the modern restaurant. After the fall of the French monarchy in 1792, the revolutionaries turned the former royal palace of the Louvre, in the center of Paris, into the first modern museum. As for restaurants, chefs who had recently catered to royalty and aristocracy now found work in their own commercial establishments, satisfying the appetites of the Paris middle classes. Soon restaurant critics such as Anthelme Brillat-Savarin (1755–1826) emerged to evaluate the new culinary marketplace.

An innovative type of drinking and eating establishment also emerged for the Parisian lower classes. The working class café, introduced newspaper reading, working-class organization, and political agitation into public drinking establishments and other sites of traditional boisterous and bacchic plebeian sociability, fusing the old tradition of popular revolt, dating back to the grain riots of the Middle Ages, with the radical politics (and newspaper reading) of the Enlightenment and the Revolution. Often these places hosted meetings of labor militants, striking workers, and political radicals. In the nineteenth century, formalized labor unions, socialist and labor political parties, and workers' clubs continued to meet in the café, which had become a veritable working-class institution. In 1890 Karl Kautsky (1854–1938), leader of the German Social Democratic Party and disciple of Karl Marx (1818–1883) and Friedrich Engels (1820–1895), well summed up its role as "the proletariat's only bulwark of political freedom" under the politically repressive conditions of that era, concluding that "the tavern is the only place in which the lower classes can meet unmolested and discuss their common affairs. Without the tavern, not only would there be no social life for the German proletariat, but also no political life." This type of working-class drinking establishment spread to England and later to Germany and Russia. In contrast, the labor movement in the Scandinavian north relied more on the temperance movement than on café sociability for its growth and consolidation.

Industrialization intensified the links between politics and urban space. English cities grew at an unprecedented rate between 1780 and 1850, and by 1851 England was the first nation in the world to have a majority of its population living in cities. French, German, Italian, and Russian cities echoed this growth and soon contained an explosive mixture of disoriented rural laborers, overworked and underpaid in workshops and factories, living in squalid slums and subject to periodic economic crises.

Marx and Engels believed that these new industrial cities were producing a new revolutionary class, the proletariat, that might overthrow the capitalist class. In his study of Manchester and other English industrial areas, Engels noted that the class conflict hidden behind factory walls appeared in all its raw, unvarnished intensity on the city streets in the form of poverty, begging, and theft. The street was also the site of organized working-class demonstrations and protests. For this reason workers and their allies fought throughout the nineteenth century to maintain access to the street, often in the face of police and military repression. Though they had cafés and meeting halls, the workers realized that in terms of space they were still at a disadvantage, vis-à-vis the bourgeoisie. The following editorial from a radical Parisian paper, *L'organisation du travail,* during the 1848 Revolution is eloquent on this point: "The street is the first, the most sacred of all the clubs. What do you want, *Messieurs les bourgeois?* The people do not have access to your gilded, ornate salons."

The street during the nineteenth century was the crossroads of hope and despair for the working class. While the French Revolution of 1789 created the modern political demonstration (journée), the subsequent Revolutions of 1830, 1848, and 1871 (the Paris Commune) brought street barricades. After an initial entrance into history during the Fronde rebellion (1648), barricades returned to Parisian streets in 1827 and their use spread to the rest of Europe during the continent-wide 1848 revolution. The space inside the barricade embodied the communal society so many of the revolutionaries wished to create, and often cafés became the headquarters of these incipient revolutionary republics. Although barricades reappeared after World War I and again at the end of World War II, Engels was largely correct when he wrote in the late 1880s that widened streets and improvements in military firepower had rendered barricades obsolete for revolutionaries.

NINETEENTH CENTURY URBAN RENOVATION: ORGANIZING AND DISCIPLINING THE STREETS

Bourgeois response to the threat of revolution and disorder was threefold. One strategy envisaged the physical improvement of the street to make it a safer, cleaner, and more efficient space. Another strategy concentrated on creating new disciplinary and welfare institutions that would moralize deviants or remove them from the street. A third strategy involved a revived emphasis on urban renewal (inspired by the Renaissance example of Rome) or suburbanization (following the example of the late-eighteenth- and early-nineteenth-century middle-class Protestant evangelicals in England).

After 1800 the introduction of the sidewalk—virtually unknown before then—addressed the need to alleviate the increasingly crowded and chaotic streets of rapidly growing cities. The sidewalk (with a convex road for cart, carriage, and other horse traffic) provided gutters, underground drains, sewers, and water and gas mains for sanitation. Lighting, bathroom facilities, kiosks, benches, and newspaper stands reflected an extraordinary rationalization of street functions. (Bedarida and Sutcliff, 1980, p. 386). Street renovation also helped London, Paris, and other cities cope with an unprecedented rise in traffic, seen even before the arrival of the automobile. While the population of inner-city Paris grew by 25 percent between 1850 and 1870, its traffic leaped as much as 400 percent (Berman, 1988, p. 158). After 1850, further improvement was made by paving the street with natural asphalt, a better surface than the earlier British macadam. These new methods were an essential part of the urban renovations that transformed many, especially continental, cities.

The two most dramatic examples of nineteenth-century urban renovation were Paris and Vienna. The transformation of the French capital under the Second Empire of Louis Napoléon Bonaparte (Napoléon III [1808–1873]) and his Prefect of Paris, Baron Georges-Eugéne Haussmann (1809–1891), resulted in an updating of the Renaissance principles of urban beautification. Broad, straight boulevards appeared, along with uniform facades and the latest innovations in sewers, water supply, and lighting. In addition, department stores, terrace cafés, sumptuous music halls, and an ornate opera house made Paris the showpiece of nineteenth-century European cities and insured that its international fairs, especially those of 1889 and 1900, were the most spectacular of the world expositions. A similar transformation occurred in Vienna when, after 1850, the old fortifications were demol-

Arrival of the Automobile. Piccadilly Circus, London, 1910. RADIO TIMES HULTON PICTURE LIBRARY/LIAISON AGENCY

ished and a new circular boulevard, the Ringstrasse, surrounded the capital of the Austro-Hungarian Empire with a range of public buildings, stately residences, and impressive recreation sites. The broad boulevards also provided ample room for armies to repress demonstrations and destroy barricades.

On these new domesticated and shimmering boulevards, the bourgeoisie felt at home. Especially in Paris and Vienna but also in London, the middle class no longer disdained display on public thoroughfares. The protected semipublic arcades, passages, and galleries of Paris and London, popular during the first half of the century, fell into disfavor with the advent of the bright new boulevards (Bedarida and Sutcliff, 1980, p. 386). Those known as ramblers or idlers in London became known in Paris as flaneurs or boulevardiers. These detached observers of the street scene might be wealthy and discriminating bourgeois or journalists, writers, and painters. The French writers Victor Hugo (1802–1885), Charles-Pierre Baudelaire (1821–1867), and Émile Zola (1840–1902) all used "flaneur" to encapsulate the strange mixture of rootlessness, disorientation, exhilaration, and freedom that seemed to be part of the fabric of the "modern" city. Walter Benjamin's (1892–1940) insightful reflections on commodification, alienation, and identity formation under modern capitalism were inspired by the writings of these authors. He dubbed the Paris of that era as "capital of the century."

Anthony Vidler and Thomas Markus (inspired by Michel Foucault [1926–1984]) designated the nineteenth century as essentially the age of confinement and discipline. Hospitals, prisons, schools, reformatories, asylums, dispensaries, orphanages, and workhouses emerged by the hundreds across Europe. "Crippleages" incarcerated disabled people—those who, in past centuries, had lived and begged on the street but who were now judged to be impediments to efficient movement or flow.

Marketplaces and their raucous ambiance remained a vital part of urban life through the early nineteenth century in most European countries. Then growing concerns about public morality, sanitation, and street congestion surfaces, particularly in England. Markets were moved off the streets and into specially built facilities that often resembled churches or Greco-Roman temples, an architecture the Victorians believed would ennoble the act of buying and selling. As in exchanges and stock markets, each vendor had his own booth, stall, or shop. Rationalized commerce led to fixed pricing, which diminished the tradition of bargaining at the market. The "grand age" of these market halls lasted from 1830 to 1890.

The nineteenth century also accentuated the trend of spatial segregation by class. England's system of class separation was the most overt: not only did the bourgeoisie now live in exclusive suburbs, but they also frequented cafés, now transformed into exclusive gentlemen's clubs, admitting members only. The continental bourgeoisie, for the most part, stayed in the city, in the newly renovated districts. Instead of turning their cafés into English-style clubs, the bourgeoisie of Vienna and Paris relied on the high cost and fashionable ambiance of their establishments to keep out the proletariat. They also chose western sections of their cities for these establishments, where prevailing easterly winds blew any bad odors toward proletarian areas.

WORKING-CLASS URBAN CULTURE IN THE LATE NINETEENTH AND EARLY TWENTIETH CENTURIES

More than ever before, working-class districts were pushed to the periphery of cities. On working-class streets, vendors remained central suppliers of commodities, and most shops catered to a population that could seldom buy more than what they needed for each day. Street life still centered on sociability rather than self-display or spatial mobility.

During the second half of the nineteenth century and first quarter of the twentieth, a distinctive working-class subculture evolved. Although still possessing minimal purchasing power compared to their social and economic superiors, workers nevertheless developed a unique pattern of social life. For instance, they were increasingly able to own several sets of clothes, including the famous "Sunday best." After work, they often changed into clothes that diminished the sartorial distance between the classes. Hats, however, continued to signal class difference: the bourgeois wore the formal top hat while the proletarian stayed with the cap. The laboring population also adopted the bourgeois ritual of promenading, usually not on the fashionable central boulevards and parks but rather on the outer boulevards and fortifications of their own parts of town. With the advent of cheap train trips to the seaside or riverside, workers began to develop their own limited notion of the "weekend."

The central institutions of proletarian culture, however, were the café, the dance hall, and the music hall, often combined in one shop. To the chagrin of labor leaders, these institutions remained much more popular than labor halls, workingmen's clubs, or universities. The number of cafés in France and pubs in England provides an indication of the popularity of these establishments. In France the number of cafés jumped from some 365,000 in 1870 to 482,000 in 1913 and to 507,000 in 1938. In England and Wales, the number of pubs and alehouses stood at around 40,000 in 1800 and more than doubled by the 1860s through the 1880s (105,552 in 1860 and in 1880, now including beer houses, 106,751).

TWENTIETH CENTURY URBAN SPACE: THE DECLINE OF STREET LIFE

After the turn of the twentieth century, new technologies and new urban and architectural theories led to radical changes in the urban fabric. London had developed its underground subway system by the 1870s, and mass-transit systems in most other major cities became fully operational after 1900. These forms of rapid transit began to break up the solidarity of working-class neighborhoods. This process of social fragmentation would proceed much more quickly after it finally became feasible for the working classes to own automobiles in the 1960s, some forty years after the middle classes had become car owners. The most important impact of mechanized mass and individual transportation was the definitive separation of work from home; with cars, even the lower classes could now contemplate living outside the city. (This trend, towards a seperation of work an home life, incidentally, began to reverse with the rise of Internet communication.) The English reformer Sir Ebenezer Howard (1850–1928) was an early and influential proponent of the proletarian urban exodus. His vision of "garden cities" purported to moralize the workers through a return to the country, taking much the same course Protestant Evangelicals had advocated for the middle classes a century earlier. Variants of Howard's ideas helped shape suburbanization throughout Europe, especially after World War I.

Although influential, Howard's pastoral vision paled in comparison to a set of radical new theories developed by a generation of architects and urban planners who came of age after 1900. This cohort included the Swiss-born and French-based Charles Édouard Jeanneret (1887–1965), who became famous under the adopted name of Le Corbusier; the Bauhaus school in Germany, including Ludwig Miës van der Rohe (1886–1969) and Walter Gropius (1883–1969); the Italian Antonio Sant'Elia (1888–1916); and the Spaniard Arturo Soria y Mata. These visionaries were inspired by leftist ideologies, such as anarchism, socialism, and communism, and their projects were often imbued with utopian zeal. Although each proponent developed nuanced and complex theories of space, their basic goals were similar: to overcome crowding, congestion, dirt, disease, and lack of ventilation and sunlight, all factors they saw as typical of the nineteenth century. They urged the building of new towns, cities, or districts with broad highways to accommodate the automobile and high-rise housing, thus supplying sufficient space, sunlight, and hygiene for the masses. "Form must follow function," they declared, and denounced architectural ornamentation and embellishment as decadent and bourgeois. This purely functional approach included separating home from work space and creating separate but integrated sites for shopping and leisure.

Traditional street life was doomed to disappear in the face of these heady futuristic visions. According to Le Corbusier, the street was "no more than a trench, a deep cleft, a narrow passage." Few of these architects received commissions to build or redesign cities during the 1920s or 1930s, although they propagated their theories through various organizations and in manifestos and books. Le Corbusier was especially active as an organizer. In 1930 he promulgated the Athens Charter and formed the International Association of Modern Architects (Congrès International d'Architecture Moderne, CIAM). Neither the Russian Revolution (1917) nor the rise of European fascism, first in Italy then in Germany, produced any distinct practical or theoretical breaks in street life or city space. The radical right in Europe adapted to their own purposes such left-wing tactics as street demonstrations and café organizing. Revolutionary workers in Russia created a new type of workers' organization, the soviet, or council, to take over and run the factories. Under the Popular Front government in France during the interwar era, radical social movements achieved a unique development in the use of public space. After the left-wing electoral victory in the spring of 1936, French workers, rather than taking to the streets as they had done traditionally, commandeered and occupied factories and forced employers to grant unprecedented concessions.

The unparalleled destruction of the European urban fabric during World War II provided a golden opportunity for the architectural and urbanist visionaries to implement what became known as the modernist or international style of architecture. Old city centers were rebuilt and "new towns" emerged on the periphery. The spare and functional style of modern architecture ensured a clear visual and social distinction between buildings devoted to home and those designed for work. Zoning ordinances consecrated this rigid distinction in law. Increasingly streets were given over exclusively to cars. As a result, the old-fashioned working-class neighborhood disintegrated or was bulldozed into oblivion. Face-to-face interaction on streets or in cafés, once a given of city life, became ever rarer. This decline in sociability was exacerbated by the arrival of television in the 1950s and 1960s.

New suburban developments or satellite cities tended to be built without any commercial establishments or, indeed, any type of shop within walking distance. English Mark I and Mark II new towns did not even include such intermediate spaces between public and private space as porches or porticos. High-rise apartment complexes were especially stark in their juxtaposition between home space and the newly emerging distant shopping center. Many workers, clerks, supervisors, and managers adapted and enjoyed this novel lifestyle oriented around work, the commute, and the now-affordable panoply of new consumer durable goods (refrigerators, washing machines, stereos). Even in areas where traditional street and café life remained an option, neighborhood sociability became much less dense due to the faster pace and greater variety of options brought about by affluence.

THE REVALORIZATION OF THE STREET IN THE LATER TWENTIETH CENTURY

A profound alienation came to plague a significant number of the inhabitants of these new towns, and by the end of the 1950s some urbanists and architects called for a renewed orientation toward street life, neighborhood values, and sociability. The researchers Michael Young and Peter Willmott in England and Henri Coing in France, finding that even gossip networks could not develop in high-rises, documented an increase in alienation and a decline in mental health. During the 1950s two other researchers, Allison Smithson (1928–) and Peter Smithson (1923–), argued that the more traditional street life of inner-city London's East End exhibited a liveliness and effervescence that could be an antidote to the excesses of technological changes. These observations were confirmed subsequently by a number of American scholars, such as Jane Jacobs and Herbert Gans (1927–). Inspired by these sociological findings, a new generation of architects and planners, some from Le Corbusier's CIAM, started an architectural and urban movement concerned with reviving the social functions of streets and cafés. In 1962 the Danish architect Jan Gehl promoted the prohibition of cars on Copenhagen's Stroget, thus initiating an international movement to create pedestrian walkways in downtown areas.

The revalorization of the street also found advocates among social movements that emerged in Europe, as well as in the United States, during the late 1960s and early 1970s. The most utopian postwar vision of the streets found expression during the events of May 1968. Paralyzing France for several weeks, students and workers in this revolt proclaimed that retaking the street for life and freedom could transform society. Of the thousands of slogans and graffiti this popular explosion produced, one of the most famous was "Under the street, the rage." A new wave of feminism also developed during this time, declaring that women could not be fully liberated unless they had as much right as men did to explore the street. During the last decades of the twentieth century, such English feminists as Elizabeth Wilson and Doreen Massey even explored the possibilities of a woman as flaneur (that is, as a flaneuse?) in the contemporary city.

After 1970 the movement to restore a social dimension to street and urban life became incorporated into the plans of many developments. For instance, English Mark III towns incorporated city centers, and Cergy-Pontoise, a satellite town in the region of Paris, created intermediate zones for sociability between the residences and the freeway. In 1985 the socialist Mitterrand government in France initiated a cultural and architectural program for suburban enrichment ("Suburbs '89 – Banlieues '89") aimed at constructing cafés, libraries, and other public amenities for housing (often high-rise apartments) built after 1945. Gehl's concept of pedestrian malls also became popular across Europe. For example, the southern French city of Toulouse renovated old marketplaces, as London did with Covent Garden. In general, street life revived more successfully than café life. The number of cafés in France and England, respectively seventy-five thousand and fifty-five thousand at the turn of the twenty-first century, continued to decline. Currently, the largest number of drinking establishments in Europe is found in Spain, where urban renovation never reached the level achieved in the rest of western Europe.

By the 1990s a new generation of critics had begun to argue that the attempt to rebuild urban communities was often elitist and artificial. Most of the renovation had led to gentrification that benefited the tourist and upper classes more than the working class. In addition to being drained of all historic association with the popular culture once at the heart of street and café life, many of these new city centers had become subject to a new technological form of surveillance. Great Britain led the way in the installation of closed-circuit television cameras. Indeed, Great Britain had more public closed-circuit television (CCTV) systems than any other advanced capitalist nation: by August 1996 all major British cities except Leeds had them. Such systems can pose severe threats to civil liberties and to the simple enjoyment of urban space. On the other hand, television surveillance does respond to the perception of many government, busi-

Street Games in London's East End. Children playing cricket in a street in Millwall, East London, August 1938. ©HULTON GETTY/LIAISON AGENCY

ness, and public establishments that urban spaces, especially streets and malls, are no longer safe. Nan Ellin, in his *Postmodern Urbanism,* summarized this approach as "form follows fear." How to balance recreation of urban community and the latest techniques of surveillance is one of the dilemmas facing the twenty-first century.

CONCLUSION

This summary of the social history of street life and city space challenges any simple notion of "progress" in social and cultural history. On the one hand, innovations that removed sewage, dirt, and dust from the streets and sidewalks that separated pedestrians and terrace café and restaurant customers from carriage and then car traffic on the street were significant improvements in terms of sanitation, safety, and sociability. On the other hand, especially since World War II, changes that have turned streets over to cars and to an unprecedented degree separated the spaces of work, family, and leisure, have spawned as much alienation as efficiency. The result has been, since the

1980s, an attempt to restore multifunctionality, the hallmark of city life in the medieval and Renaissance eras. An opening and welcoming urban environment will be crucial during the twenty-first century, as European cities will undoubtedly accept millions of new immigrants—now, however, not from the hinterlands of their own nations but from the rest of the world. It is on the streets and in the public places that the process of cultural assimilation, expression, and creation will continue.

The popular French singer Edith Piaf (1915–1963) captured the vitality of the street when, in a reflective moment, she told a friend:

> Life is not given to you as a gift when you come from the street. You learn to live at the maximum at each instant as it passes, before it bids you bye-bye! You also learn how to cry and to laugh and to play. This is a rough but good school, a thousand times more worthwhile than the schools of the rich. You learn to give to the people what they want without too much fuss.

See also **Civil Society** *(in this volume);* **Social Class; The Middle Classes; Working Classes; Moral Economy and Luddism; Urban Crowds** *(volume 3);* **Festivals; Holidays and Public Rituals** *(volume 5); and other articles in this section.*

BIBLIOGRAPHY

Introduction to the History of the Street

Anderson, Stanford, ed. *On Streets.* Cambridge, Mass., 1978.

Çelik, Zeynep, Diane Favro, and Richard Ingersoll. *Streets: Critical Perspectives on Public Space.* Berkeley, Los Angeles, and London, 1994

Fyfe, Nicholas R., ed. *Images of the Street: Planning, Identity, and Control in Public Space.* London and New York, 1998.

Leménorel, Alain. *La rue, lieu de sociabilité? Rencontres de la rue.* Actes du colloque de Rouen, 16–19 novembre 1994 avec la participation d'Alain Corbin. Rouen, France, 1997.

The Street Throughout History

Ariès, Philippe. "Introduction." In *A History of Private Life.* Vol. 3. *Passions of the Renaissance.* Edited by Philippe Ariès and and Georges Duby. Translated by Arthur Goldhammer. Cambridge, Mass., 1989. Pages 1–11.

Brown-May, Andrew. *Melbourne Street Life: The Itinerary of Our Days.* Kew, Victoria, 1998. An excellent study of streets in a European settler society.

Leguay, Jean-Pierre. *La rue au Moyen Age.* Rennes, France, 1984. Covers the medieval street.

Farge, Arlette. *Fragile Lives: Violence, Power, and Solidarity in Eighteenth-Century Paris.* Translated by Carol Shelton. Cambridge, U.K., 1993.

Farge, Arlette. *Subversive Words: Public Opinion in Eighteenth-Century France.* Translated by Rosemary Morris. University Park, Penn., 1995.

Farge, Arlette. *Vivre dans la rue à Paris au XVIIIe siècle.* Paris, 1979.

Garrioch, David. *The Formation of the Parisian Bourgeoisie, 1690–1830.* Cambridge, Mass., 1996.

Garrioch, David. *Neighborhood and Community in Paris, 1740–1790.* Cambridge, Mass., 1986.

Muir, Edward. *Civic Ritual in Renaissance Venice.* Princeton, N.J., 1981.

Trexler, Richard C. *Public Life in Renaissance Florence.* Ithaca, N.Y., and London, 1991.

Weissman, Ronald F. E. *Ritual Brotherhood in Renaissance Florence.* New York, 1982.

Winter, James H. *London's Teeming Streets, 1830–1914.* London and New York, 1993.

Overviews of Literature and Urban Life

Berman, Marshall. *All That Is Solid Melts into Air: The Experience of Modernity.* New York, 1988.

Stallybrass, Peter, and Allon White. *The Politics and Poetics of Transgression.* Ithaca, N.Y., 1986.

Tester, Keith, ed. *The Flaneur.* London and New York, 1994. Covers the literature of the flaneur.

Buildings and Living Spaces

Bedarida, Francois and Anthony Sutcliff. "The Street in the Structure and Life of the City, Reflections on Nineteenth-Century London and Paris." *Journal of Urban History* 6, no. 4 (August 1980): 379–396.

Contemine, Philippe. "Peasant Hearth to Papal Palace: The Fourteenth and Fifteenth Centuries." In *A History of Private Life.* Vol. 2. *Revelations of the Medieval World.* Edited by Georges Duby. Translated by Arthur Goldhammer. Cambridge, Mass., 1988. Pages 425–505.

Fishman, Robert. *Bourgeois Utopias: The Rise and Fall of Suburbia.* New York, 1987. On the rise of English suburbs.

Markus, Thomas A. *Buildings and Power: Freedom and Control in the Origin of Modern Building Types.* London and New York, 1993. An exploration of buildings and their meaning in urban life.

Young, Michael, and Peter Willmott. *Family and Kinship in East London.* Berkeley and Los Angeles, 1992. Discusses the rise of English suburbs.

Gender and Urban Space

Bladh, Christine. "Women and Family Structure in Late 18th Century Stockholm." In *Women in Towns: The Social Position of Urban Women in a Historical Context.* Edited by Marjatta Hietala and Lars Nilsson. Stockholm, 1999. Pages 89–109.

Brown, Judith C., and Robert C. Davis. eds. *Gender and Society in Renaissance Italy: Men and Women in History.* London and New York, 1998.

Cohen, Samuel Kline. *Women in the Streets: Essays on Sex and Power in Renaissance Italy.* Baltimore and London, 1996.

Nord, Deborah Epstein. *Walking the Victorian Streets: Women, Representation, and the City.* Ithaca, N.Y., and London, 1995.

Tebbutt, Melanie. *Women's Talk? A Social History of "Gossip" in Working-Class Neighborhoods, 1880–1960.* Aldershot, U.K., and Brookfield, Vt., 1995.

Von Ankum, Katharina. *Women in the Metropolis, Gender, and Modernity in Weimar Culture.* Berkeley, Los Angeles, and London, 1997.

Walkowitz, Judith R. *City of Dreadful Delight: Narratives of Sexual Danger in Late-Victorian London.* Chicago, 1992.

Street Life: Commerce, Leisure, and Politics

The Concept of the "Public Sphere"

Darnton, Robert. "Presidential Address: An Early Information Society: News and the Media in Eighteenth-Century Paris." *American Historical Review* 105 (2000): 1–35.

Habermas, Jürgen. *The Structural Transformation of the Public Sphere: An Inquiry into a Category of Bourgeois Society.* Translated by Thomas Burger with the assistance of Frederick Lawrence. Cambridge, Mass., 1989.

Street Vendors and Markets

Fontaine, Laurence. *History of Pedlars in Europe.* Translated by Vicki Whittaker. Durham, N.C., 1996.

Milliot, Vincent. *Les "cris de Paris," ou, Le peuple travesti: Les représentations des petits métiers parisiens (XVIe–XVIIIe siècles).* Paris, 1995.

Schmiechen, James, and Kenneth Carls. *The British Market Hall: A Social and Architectural History.* New Haven, Conn., and London, 1999.

Taverns and Cafés

Brennan, Thomas. *Public Drinking and Popular Culture in Eighteenth-Century Paris.* Princeton, N.J., 1988.

Clark, Peter. *The English Alehouse: A Social History, 1200–1830.* London and New York, 1983.

Gutzke, David W. *Protecting the Pub: Brewers and Publicans against Temperance.* Suffolk, U.K., and Wolfeboro, N.H., 1989.

Haine, W. Scott. *The World of the Paris Café: Sociability among the French Working Class, 1789–1914.* Baltimore and London, 1996.

Hurd, Madeleine. *Public Spheres, Public Mores, and Democracy: Hamburg and Stockholm, 1870–1914.* Ann Arbor, Mich., 2000. Covers taverns and cafes.

Phillips, Laura L. *Bolsheviks and the Bottle: Drink and Worker Culture in St. Petersburg, 1900–1929.* DeKalb, Ill., 2000. Covers taverns and cafés.

Roberts, James S. *Drink, Temperance, and the Working Class in Nineteenth-Century Germany.* Boston, 1984.

Segal, Harold B., trans. and ed. *The Vienna Coffeehouse Wits, 1890–1938.* West Lafayette, Ind., 1993.

Tlusty, Ann. *The Culture of Drink in the Early Modern German City.* Charlottesville, Va., 2001.

Leisure

McClellan, Andrew. *Inventing the Louvre: Art, Politics, and the Origins of the Modern Museum in Eighteenth-Century Paris.* New York, 1994.

Ravel, Jeffrey S. *The Contested Parterre: Public Theater and French Political Culture, 1680–1791.* Ithaca, N.Y., 1999.

Sherman, Daniel J. *Worthy Monuments: Art Museums and the Politics of Culture in Nineteenth-Century France.* Cambridge, Mass., 1989.

Spang, Rebecca L. *The Invention of the Restaurant: Paris and Modern Gastronomic Culture.* Cambridge, Mass., 2000.

Thacker, Christopher. *The History of Gardens.* Berkeley and Los Angeles, 1979.

Children and Adolescents

Davin, Anna. *Growing Up Poor: Home, School, and Street in London, 1870–1914.* London, 1996.

Humphries, Stephen. *Hooligans or Rebels?: An Oral History of Working-Class Childhood and Youth, 1889–1939.* Oxford, 1981.

I wish to thank all scholars who helped me online, especially Christine Bladh, Andrew Brown-May, and Edward Stanton.

SUBURBS AND NEW TOWNS

Alexander Cowan

SUBURBS, NEW TOWNS, AND URBAN CORES: SHIFTING BOUNDARIES AND CHANGING MEANINGS

No single definition of the suburb fits all circumstances. Suburbs have existed for as long as humans have lived in urban centers, but their sizes, forms, and demographic and social importance changed almost out of recognition between the sixteenth century and the twenty-first century, outstripping the changes to the urban core around which they are located. Traditionally the medieval suburb was an area of housing beyond the physical boundaries, usually fortifications of some kind, that marked out the limits of an urban center. Its location gave it a number of characteristics. It was unprotected, and it was neither urban nor rural but contained elements of both. Its legal status and that of its inhabitants was ambiguous. Its population consisted of recent arrivals from elsewhere and former residents of the urban center. The latter included some who chose to leave the urban center in search of a better quality of life, who tended to be well off, and some who were forced to leave it because their presence was unacceptable, who were generally poor.

Even at this comparatively early stage of urbanization, the diversity of suburban form and organization underlined the fact that the only feature shared by all suburbs was a negative characteristic. Suburbs were agglomerations of housing not perceived as part of the urban core. Definitions of the urban core changed from the area within a fortified enclosure to an area of dense housing on a street plan inherited from the sixteenth and seventeenth centuries, containing centers of commerce, government, religious practice; public buildings; and a mixture of housing for the rich and the poor and to the twentieth-century central business district. Along with those definitions the nature of the suburbs surrounding the core also changed.

The distinction between urban core and suburb altered over time. The core expanded, and new suburban growth took over many of the functions of older suburbs, which in turn took on new roles. The construction of new fortifications for fiscal and defense purposes enclosed areas that once were suburbs and incorporated them within the urban core. Similarly the outer expansion of suburbs incorporated existing villages and settlements within the suburban area, changing their status but providing new nodes for commerce and sociability. The introduction of mass transport, such as the tram, the railway, and eventually the bus, in the nineteenth and early twentieth centuries facilitated the construction of suburban housing outward along the transport network and further afield as satellites of the towns providing employment.

Until the early twentieth century Europe exhibited a clear distinction between suburbs and new towns. Suburbs were extensions of the urban core, and their development was partly organic and partly the result of planned expansion. New towns, on the other hand, were urban centers developed on entirely new locations to carry out one of a range of specialized functions, commercial, industrial, military, recreational, or administrative. New town construction in the twentieth century also took place as a distinctive exercise. New towns were developed in response to the continuing growth of the urban population, much of which was expected to locate in the suburbs of large cities. To control and direct this demographic and economic growth, national governments and town planners alike proposed to channel it into planned locations away from existing urban areas but connected to them. The alternative was, as one commentator wrote about London in the 1930s, that the extensively decentralized urban area would become a "confluent pox." Ironically, these desired distinctions between suburbs and new towns subsequently eroded to the point that it became scarcely possible in some cases to distinguish the functions of one from the other or even to distinguish a new town from a recent satellite or commuter suburb. For this reason these two forms of urban organization have been combined in a single article that discusses them separately.

The history of suburbs can be studied in terms of urban policies and transportation, while new towns often are examined through the schemes of idealist reformers and urban planners. Social history looks more at the types of people involved in both settings and at the functions the settings served. Not surprisingly nineteenth-century industrialization marks a sharp break in the histories of both types of community and an expansion of their importance.

SUBURBAN GROWTH SINCE THE SIXTEENTH CENTURY: PUSHING BEYOND THE URBAN CORE

The biggest physical change to the suburb after the sixteenth century was the ratio between populations of the suburb and the urban core. The population showed considerable diversity even at the end of the Middle Ages. Only one person in four of the population of Tudor York lived in the suburbs, but over a third of the inhabitants of Carmona, Spain, did so in 1528 and half the population of Winchester in 1600. A majority of the population of Ubeda, Spain, lived beyond the walls in 1595. Suburban growth was particularly marked in Europe's largest cities, setting the pattern for the eighteenth and nineteenth centuries. By 1700 London's suburbs contained three times as many people as the population of the City itself. In many towns population growth may have been accommodated within the walls. Suburban expansion was often a sign that an individual urban economy had continued to expand.

The shape of suburban development was closely related in many towns to the construction, modification, and later demolition of fortifications. Medieval suburbs developed in the shadow of city walls because these fortifications were not expected to fulfil a major defensive role. During the sixteenth and seventeenth centuries many preexisting suburbs were demolished to make way for fortifications of a new design, particularly in areas of endemic warfare, such as the southern Netherlands. New systems of citadels, earthworks, and bastions required much more space than the old curtain walls, and they also depended on the retention of open spaces beyond to allow for an open line of fire against advancing troops. On the one hand, this removed existing suburbs. On the other, the enlarged urban space enclosed by new fortifications enabled construction of new quarters as extensions of the existing urban core. The new fortifications built in Marseilles in 1666 effectively doubled the surface available for urban development and consequently met the demand for houses to accommodate incomers and the wealthy in search of comfortable, well-designed housing. Both of these demands later fueled European suburban expansion.

From the late seventeenth century the decline in siege warfare encouraged towns to remove their fortifications altogether, but this did not in itself facilitate suburban development. In many towns the walls were replaced by promenades, tree-lined areas designed to allow a socially exclusive minority to walk or ride away from the noise, smell, and congestion of the urban core. These in turn became boulevards for wheeled traffic. In Vienna the final removal of the walls permitted the city to construct "The Ring," a broad boulevard flanked by major public buildings imitating the old fortifications, as a way of delimiting the urban core. Similarly the line of fortifications in Milan separated the *circondario esterno* (outer ring) from the *circondario interno* (inner ring), although it was not built on in the same way, and marked an important boundary for tax purposes. Suburban growth was often shaped and encouraged by the construction of boulevards. Both Barcelona and Valencia, for example, in the last third of the nineteenth century constructed new quarters that stretched out beyond the line of the old fortifications.

The major impetus to suburban growth came in the nineteenth century and the early twentieth century as a result of industrialization and widespread population movements. In parts of Europe other than England the construction of multistory tenement blocks within the urban area prevented decentralization on a large scale. By the mid-nineteenth century, more markedly in England than elsewhere in Europe, the pattern of a small proportion of the urban population inhabiting the core while the large majority lived in some form of suburban housing was already visible. This movement was accompanied by an absolute decline in the populations of the central core in capitals such as London, Paris, and Berlin. Over 1.25 million new houses were built in Greater London between 1921 and 1939, and the population of the metropolitan area rose from 7.5 million to 8.7 million. The population of central Paris fell from 3 million to 289,000 between 1921 and 1931, while the suburban area grew from 1.5 million to 2 million. In other French cities the proportion of suburban inhabitants was around 80 to 90 percent. Living outside the central core had become the norm, but the continuous and often unexpectedly rapid growth of the suburbs meant that this norm was constantly redefined.

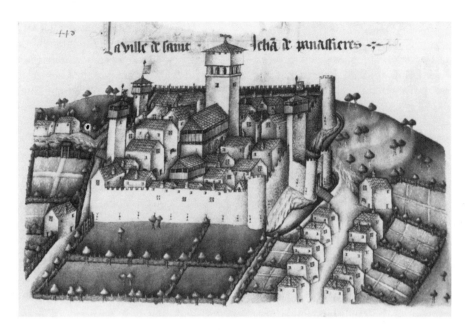

Town and Suburbs. The town of Panissières (Loire department, France) with *faubourgs* extending outside its gates. From *Armorial* by Guillaume Revel, fifteenth century. BIBLIOTHÈQUE NATIONALE, PARIS, FRENCH 22297

TRANSPORT, COMMUTING, AND SATELLITE TOWNS

The key to all suburban expansion after the beginning of the nineteenth century was the combination of migration and increasingly efficient forms of transport. The development of trams, buses, suburban trains, and the motor car transformed the shapes and sizes of urban centers, making it possible to commute to work over increasing distances and bringing satellite towns within the orbit of urban areas. Transportation also facilitated the zoning of urban areas so schools, hospitals, recreational facilities, and commercial centers were located at points accessible by public or private transport. Above all it created a new kind of urban space, in which entire neighborhoods functioned as dormitories, leaving a small population of the elderly, the very young, unpaid mothers, and the unemployed to inhabit the streets during working hours.

Unrestricted private enterprise in transport in the late nineteenth century led to patchy coverage of the suburbs. High rail and tram fares encouraged the wealthy to move further out but were a disincentive to working people. Where new access was granted the results were striking. The tram reached the Parisian suburb of Bobigny in 1902, and within ten years the population had more than doubled. In the late nineteenth century a circular railway was constructed in Berlin some five kilometres from the center, linking all the lines from outside the city. The construction of the metropolitan line in London encouraged suburban development to the northwest. Railways and developers established close links once they shared an interest in moving a new and affluent population into the suburbs.

The new forms of transport increased the development of satellite communities. As a suburban phenomenon, however, they predated the great population expansion of the late nineteenth century. Vienna's complex fortification system in the late seventeenth century displaced its suburban expansion to separate communities such as St. Ulrich. A number of villages north of London, such as Somerstown and Pentonville, were linked to the capital by ribbon development in the eighteenth century and gradually became integrated into the suburbs. To the south of London the development of the railway and a number of local factors encouraged the growth of existing centers, such as Bexley and Bromley, in the mid-nineteenth century. Their expansion eventually met suburban growth moving out of the city, and they were incorporated into the metropolitan area. Similar developments took place around Berlin. After World War II the development of better road networks and an exponential growth in the use of the motor car brought many other towns into the orbit of major metropolitan areas. Some were centers of considerable age, others were entirely new, and some were a hybrid of the two.

SOCIAL COMPOSITION

Suburbs and the poor. A long association has existed between poverty and suburbs. The medieval suburb provided an opportunity for subsistence migrants to find work and cheap accommodations in the town free from regulation by the urban authorities. The suburbs were often their first point of contact and offered the most opportunities for unskilled employment, both industrial and agricultural. For the indigent poor, too, the suburbs provided shelter and partial protection from exclusion policies practiced by the urban authorities. By the late twentieth century the suburbs were home to some of the poorest of the urban population, who had been displaced there by changes to the organization and the housing stock of the urban core. In earlier years the same three factors, inward migration, displacement from the core, and employment opportunities, constantly brought the poor to the suburbs.

As social zoning among the suburbs developed in the nineteenth century, the poor lived in two contrasting parts of the suburbs, those areas closest to the core and those on the extreme periphery of the suburbs. In the first case, the poor moved out of the center of towns into suburban housing originally constructed for the wealthy several generations before. These "walking suburbs" had lost their attraction as more modern and comfortable housing became available further out and their proximity to the countryside was removed. Such houses, often lacking the most desirable facilities, were subdivided into rooms and tenements to accommodate a high-density population in search of work nearby. Developments in transport in the late nineteenth century also ensured a heavy concentration of the poor close to the urban core. Railway lines cut off many of the older suburbs from the business center. Their viaducts and marshaling yards left islands of housing that rapidly degenerated into slums. When cheap transport for unskilled workers was introduced in the early twentieth century, more suburban housing further out came within the economic capacities of workers employed in the center.

For the poor employed on the periphery, on the other hand, housing on the edge of the suburbs was essential. This pattern was established in the late Middle Ages, when early economic zoning ensured that certain economic activities took place outside the walls, such as tanning, fulling, washing and dyeing cloth, glassmaking, slaughtering, and activities with a high fire risk. Many industries required water, and most produced unpleasant by-products. Hence tanning and cloth dyeing took place in the Parisian Faubourg St.-Marcel, across the Seine in an area bordered by little housing. Gunpowder factories operated on the outskirts of many Dutch cities in the seventeenth century, and soap was made in Triana, a Sevillian suburb on the right bank of the Guadalquivir. The textile industry in particular moved out from the centers to the suburbs. During the eighteenth century the growth of the silk industry was a major force in suburban expansion in Nîmes and Lyon. In Lyon the physical appearance of the early nineteenth-century suburb of La Croix-Rouge was shaped by the weavers' need for buildings to provide enough daylight and space to operate a Jacquard loom.

Agricultural workers and gardeners experienced the same need to live on the edge of the housing area. Agriculture continued to occupy large proportions of the urban population well into the eighteenth century. In the seventeenth century 15 to 20 percent of the population of Vienne in the Dauphiné worked on the land, mostly in vineyards. The numbers of market gardeners and fishermen in Strasbourg were high enough to justify guilds of their own. Most rural employees chose to live as close as they could to their work.

Industrialization came comparatively late to many urban centres, but once large-scale urban industrial production was established, access to transport for raw materials and for distribution of the finished product, in addition to the need for large sites to accommodate production, dictated sites on the edge of the town. Housing soon followed. The Italian companies of Breda and Pirelli, which had initially chosen to build factories in Milan behind the main railway station, moved out to the Sesto San Giovanni for more space. Fiat did the same in Turin. The attractions of the periphery also drew out many smaller enterprises, hoping to benefit from conditions that paralleled those in the preindustrial suburb, such as lack of unionization, little external regulation, and a cheap labor force.

In a common pattern throughout Europe, many migrant industrial workers moved to the suburbs in search of cheaper housing at the end of the nineteenth century and the beginning of the twentieth century, a development that brought with it uncontrolled suburban growth of the most chaotic nature. Some suburbs, such as the quarter of Campo Fiesa in Brescia, began with municipal housing but were effectively abandoned as factories developed around them. Others, like the Parisian suburb of Bobigny, were initially collections of shacks without proper foundations, paved streets, water supplies, or sewers. By contrast, interwar and post-1945 planning policies organized outer suburbs for the poor. Municipal estates were built to let to the inner-city poor, whose homes were demolished in slum clearance programs. These estates

Barcelona and Its Suburbs. General view of Barcelona, showing new quarters built in the nineteeth century; smoke rises from industrial sites on the city's outskirts. Museo de Historia de la Ciudad, Barcelona/Institut Amatller d'Art Hispànic

varied among low- and medium-rise blocks, particularly in the United Kingdom and the Netherlands, and high-density, high-rise blocks set in green spaces on the edge of other continental cities. But all improved the material conditions for their first inhabitants. Toulouse constructed ten thousand buildings between 1948 and 1961, providing more than thirty thousand new homes, each with several bedrooms, its own WC (toilet), and bathroom.

Suburbs and the wealthy. In spite of the heavy concentration of the poor population outside the urban core, the words "suburb" and "suburban" became synonymous with homes for families of medium to high incomes. These suburban quarters were in marked contrast to housing for the poor. In the early modern period they were a hybrid between developments within the urban core and areas of housing beyond the walls, but they shared much with the later suburban developments after industrialization. New quarters were built between the sixteenth and eighteenth centuries to accommodate wealthy townspeople, members of the elite, merchants, administrators, and professionals. These people generally desired to escape from the dif-

ficulties of life in old, cramped housing on narrow streets increasingly choked with wheeled traffic, market stalls, pedestrians, and artisans. Specifically they were motivated by a new sense of the urban lower classes as "dangerous" and by a real drive to find a healthier environment free from the contagion and smoke of urban sectors. Thus wealthier suburbs often located to the west of major cities, so the prevailing winds would protect the residents from urban smoke.

The motives for suburban development were articulated in several ways. New quarters such as the Marais in Paris and Covent Garden in London featured large, regular buildings to reflect the high status of their inhabitants and the sense of order the elite wished to impose on the city. They included frequent squares and other open spaces. London developed the area between the old walled City and the royal palace in Whitehall, and in Paris the Marais originally was a swamp. Elsewhere the new buildings either appeared in open areas within the existing walls or in areas created by the extension of fortifications.

While these buildings represented one element of the flight from the old urban core, a second trend also played a part in early suburban development. The use of the area beyond the walls for semiagricultural activities diversified to meet the recreational needs of wealthy townspeople. Some of the space was used for gardens and promenades, where townspeople could take the air on long summer evenings and Sundays or grow fruit and vegetables for their own use, introducing an element of the rural into their lives. The richest of all divided their lives between the urban and the rural by using summer houses further afield. The wealthy of Amsterdam constructed country houses on the Isle of Walcheren and in the Vechte Valley. Venetians built villas along the Brenta River and much further away. The merchants of Lübeck spent time on farms several hours ride from the city. The semirural aspect of preindustrial suburban development was accentuated by the presence of of ecclesiastical institutions, charitable buildings, and hospitals surrounded by gardens and other green spaces.

From the eighteenth century suburban development for the wealthy followed divergent patterns. While much housing in the urban core in Scotland and in continental Europe was remodeled to meet middle-class demand, considerable suburban development extended English towns, a pattern not followed elsewhere until much later. The earliest were the so-called "walking suburbs" built so their inhabitants could easily access activities in the town center. Many, like Jesmond in Newcastle upon Tyne and Camden in North London, reproduced the urban terraces of the eighteenth century on a smaller and less ornate scale. Gardens were kept to a minimum, but an element of the rural was introduced by planting trees along streets. Elsewhere landlords capitalized on a demand for a protected semirural environment, permitting the wealthy to live away from their work, surrounded by greenery, and far from the pollution of the industrial city. During the middle third of the nineteenth century Manchester, Glasglow, Oldham, Nottingham, Liverpool, and Birmingham built estates of detached and semidetached houses with gates and park keepers.

In succeeding generations the exclusivity of such enclaves was threatened by the introduction of comparatively cheap transport, permitting families of lesser means to move into and beyond these suburbs. The wealthy attempted to distance themselves from their more modest neighbors by moving outward. Increasing numbers of semidetached houses with small gardens along roads, tramways, and railways accommodated a rising demand from the middle classes and the labor aristocracy. Other European urban centers also experienced suburban expansion but with the important difference that the middle classes in areas such as Grünewald, Friedenau, and Lichterfelde near Berlin lived in apartment blocks rather than in semidetached houses. After the 1970s an interesting inversion of trends occurred, in which high-rent luxury accommodations became available in the urban core of many English towns, while demand grew on the Continent for small houses on estates surrounded by lawns and greenery.

REGULATION OF SUBURBS

The suburbs began as unregulated urban growth, and the social, political, and economic problems of urbanization in the nineteenth and early twentieth centuries brought attempts to regulate housing, public services, and the urban environment. The largest metropolitan areas created new local administrations, such as the London Country Council established in 1888. The new authority of *Grossberlin* united Berlin with its suburban neighbors in 1920. Together with radical governments in Vienna and elsewhere, these authorities put forward plans to coordinate road and rail transport, develop low-cost housing, and provide water, gas, electricity, and sewers. Many of these plans reached their full potentials in the mid-twentieth century. National legislation increasingly controlled the provision of low to medium cost rented accommodations, such as the French Ribot Law of 1922.

CULTURAL RESPONSES TO THE SUBURB

Suburbs always have received a bad press, much of it arising from their ambiguous status. For many in the early modern period the rural world represented an unknown series of threats. Fortifications, whatever their state of repair, reassured those who lived within them that they were protected from such threats. The presence of housing beyond them and its tendency to attract immigrants who took unregulated employment or engaged in activities that threatened the social and moral order made the suburbs a source of anxiety for the more established members of urban society. Miguel de Cervantes referred to Triana, a suburb of Seville, as a rendezvous for dishonesty. John Graunt described the suburbs of seventeenth-century London as places where "many vicious persons get liberty to live as they please." Neither writer was entirely wrong.

As time went on many fears were transferred to urban areas as a whole. The nineteenth century was full of literary warnings about the iniquity of urban life, but few explicitly mentioned the suburbs. Emile Verhaeren's description of a world characterized by

Fortified New Town. Palmanova, a fortified city in northern Italy established by the Venetian Republic in the late sixteenth century. AEROFILMS, LTD.

the smell of sulfur and naphtha, the rumble of factories, and the sound of the crown owed much to the experience of the industrial suburb. New criticisms of the suburbs largely were written by observers who lived elsewhere. One French senator called the suburbs of nineteenth-century Paris "a great stain of ugliness on the beautiful face of France." A mid-twentieth-century polemic—LeCorbusier's Charte d'Athènes—went even further, saying, "The suburb symbolises the union of urban detritus with urban planning." The suburbs have found few defenders. One was the English poet John Betjeman, whose work celebrated "Metroland," the suburbs on the northwest edge of London along the Metropolitan Line. His images of tennis clubs, fresh-smelling lawns on summer evenings, and amateur dramatics conjure an inimitable picture of middle-class life between the wars.

THE GROWTH OF NEW TOWNS FROM THE SIXTEENTH CENTURY THROUGH THE TWENTIETH CENTURY: CHANGE AND CONTINUITY

The sixteenth century through the eighteenth century: military and princely towns. All new towns shared one characteristic that differentiated them from suburbs: they were planned towns. They were created in response to a perceived need and reflected a well-defined set of ideals about what a town should be and how its inhabitants should live. Such ideals were also influential in shaping urban changes in existing towns but were most well developed where everything was planned from the drawing board. Unlike the previous wave of urbanization in the twelfth century, the new towns of sixteenth- to eighteenth-century Europe were not marked by a search for economic prosperity.

335

Garden City. Bath Road, looking East, Bedford Park (Chiswick, Middlesex, England), 1882. Illustration by B. Francis Berry. THE ART ARCHIVE/EILEEN TWEEDY

Commercial and industrial expansion tended to take place in established centers. Instead, the driving force in new-town creation was political, reflecting new forms of warfare in the developing territorial states and new needs of self-expression by princely rulers.

Military new towns, such as Philippeville in the Spanish Netherlands, Venetian Palmanova close to Habsburg territory, and Neuf-Brisach in the Rhineland, were expansions of the citadels built alongside cities close to sensitive borders. These symmetrical, star-shaped urban fortresses were designed to house soldiers, supplies, and support institutions. They were not planned to expand, and the absence of any voluntary civilian population prevented them from adapting to changing political conditions, nor did they take on new economic functions. They survive as relics of their time. Unlike the inland fortresses, towns established to house naval dockyards, such as Rochefort and Brest in France and Portsea on the south coast of England, flourished well into the eighteenth century, but likewise rarely took on new economic functions.

The princely town expressed contemporary concepts of the ideal city more fully. Towns like Karlsruhe, Versailles, and Mannheim were built when a newly powerful ruler chose to move away from his existing urban residence and start afresh on a new site. These princely towns had two overlapping functions. They were concrete expressions of the ruler's power and, unlike the military new towns, they were conceived of as centers of prosperous economic activities, supplying the needs of the prince and his household and

functioning of their own accord. To ensure their rapid success, immigrant artisans and merchants, often fleeing from religious persecution, were encouraged to settle on condition that they brought useful skills and injections of capital. Some princely centers flourished, but many did not. Often the original plans were subverted by the unwillingness of new residents to conform to what was expected of them. The three streets in Versailles, designed to meet at the royal palace as a focal point, never fully developed along the monumental lines of their original plans. But the planners' failure was Versailles's success, leading to the organic development of an urban center that resembled its older neighbors.

Nineteenth century: industrial new towns. In each phase of urbanization the sponsorship of new towns reflected the distribution of political and economic power. The predominance of the territorial state in early modern Europe encouraged princely residences and military or naval centers, but as industrial activity grew during the nineteenth century, the impetus passed to industrialists and landowners. Much industrial activity took place in extensions of existing towns, but several new towns took advantage of favorable locations to develop factories and housing close to raw materials and transport routes. Their exponential growth and the dominance of their industrial enterprises soon swept away any attempts at planning or regulation. Middlesborough's tenfold growth between 1841 and 1891 swallowed its original grid

336

plan. The coal-mining town of Le Creusot, France, whose population rose from four thousand in 1841 to twenty-five thousand in 1911, was entirely controlled by industrialists until the latter part of the century, when its size became too big to handle. It had no local administration and no forces to keep order.

Twentieth century: new towns as antidotes to the suburbs.

The new towns of the twentieth century were both a new phenomenon and a continuum with their predecessors. They were born out of several influential groups' concerns about the rapid growth of the industrial city. Town planners, municipal authorities, and national governments alike were affected by the prospect that the industrial city would continue to grow at an uncontrolled rate. The experience of the suburbs was particularly instructive. Living conditions in poor suburbs were perceived as even worse than in the remains of the historic urban cores. The pressure of newcomers and the poor quality of housing materials created major sanitation problems. The rapid occupation of all available open spaces by housing, workshops, and factories excluded schools, hospitals, and recreational facilities. The weight of the population also posed potential threats to the political order. The modern new-town movement arose from the belief that urban organization had reached its limits. Further progress was only possible by starting again with planned, controlled constructions that offered space, light, and greenery. In a way, too, the new town offered town dwellers a kind of rural dream.

The early phases of new-town development began in England toward the end of the nineteenth century, under the influence of Ebenezer Howard, whose concept of the "garden city" shaped much suburban development in England and on the Continent, especially in Holland and Scandinavia. The garden city was an attempt to remove housing from a linear, high-density environment. It proposed instead a semirural but still intensely regulated network of curving roads, parks, and gardens, in which houses located on estates were linked to major access routes. Early garden cities provided a new environment for the wealthy, but they were also models for new towns. Welwyn Garden City and Letchworth were built north of London in the interwar years; Le Vésinet, close to Paris, had seventy kilometers of roads; and the *Kolonien* were built outside Berlin. These new towns experienced similar problems of economic attachment to their preindustrial predecessors. They flourished primarily because they were located close to major urban centers that provided them with their populations, but they also filled a new role as commuter towns. Welwyn grew largely because of its proximity to London.

New Towns in the Twentieth Century. Housing near Copenhagen. ©GEORGE GERSTER, PHOTO RESEARCHERS

The postwar period saw a boom in new-town development, particularly in England and France. National legislation encouraged developments that benefited regional and national economies. These new towns were not entirely new in the sense that they incorporated existing urban communities. Although others were located in several regions, including Stevenage and Harlow close to London, Telford in the West Midlands, Corby in the East Midlands, Washington, Peterlee, and Killingworth in the northeast, and Cumbernauld close to Glasgow, Milton Keynes came to characterize the new town in the United Kingdom. The original plan for Milton Keynes incorporated several small towns, but the town generated green spaces, water recreations, and a shopping and business center. For a long time known only for the concrete cows in its fields, an early attempt at public art, Milton Keynes eventually established an art gallery.

The new towns initiated in France in the 1970s are also difficult to distinguish from others linked to existing towns. At the end of World War II the outer suburbs of many French towns were augmented by *grands ensembles,* high-rise groupings of low-rent accommodations, followed by even more ambitious projects. Toulouse–Le Mirail was planned for 100,000 inhabitants with a university campus and a mixture of public and private housing, schools, green spaces, and shops. It failed to live up to its planners' expectations. Private developers took little part. The shopping center was unable to compete with a nearby hypermarket, and the university had an air of living in exile. Other new towns of the same period, such as Évry, Corbeil, L'Isle d'Abeau, and Le Vandreuil, shared the same objective of creating a social mix as did Le Mirail, and to some extent they achieved it at the expense of slower growth. High-density, low-rent developments were delayed in an attempt to attract wealthier residents, some of whom chose to settle in nearby villages and use their cars to benefit from the new town's extensive facilities.

As time passed the expectations that European new towns would become mature communities came to pass. The age mix eventually resembled that of older towns. The young families who were the original inhabitants grew older and put down roots, and other, younger families moved from the cities to the new towns.

CONCLUSION

The modern history of suburbs and new towns reflects the burdens, real and imagined, of the industrial city and the new transportation facilities. Both settings, though particularly the suburbs, raise questions about the human impact of commuting and about the relationships among the different social groups spread along the suburban-urban continuum. Suburbanization, for example, decreased the visibility of poverty with obvious implications in terms of policy responses.

On the whole, suburbs and new towns differ in terms of top-down versus bottom-up development. Suburbs arose mainly from changes in the numbers and motivations of suburban residents, reflecting social issues such as evolving attitudes toward the lower classes and toward disease. Although attitudes and conditions changed, major continuities can be found between preindustrial and industrial suburbs. This is not the case with new towns, which depended more on formal planning and expert initiatives. While the needs of armies and princes shaped the work of early modern town planners, industrialization created new problems arising from the scale of the accompanying demographic and urban expansion. Accordingly, the impetus behind the planning of new towns changed. The social history of new towns and suburbs embraces inherent complexities; however, the study of these two developments has often addressed social issues common to both.

See also **Migration** *(volume 2);* **Social Class** *(volume 3);* **Housing** *(volume 5); and other articles in this section.*

BIBLIOGRAPHY

General

Cowan, Alexander. *Urban Europe, 1500–1700.* New York, 1998.

Friedrichs, Christopher R. *The Early Modern City, 1450–1750.* New York, 1995.

Suburbs

Certeau, Michel de. *The Practice of Everyday Life.* Vol. 2. Minneapolis, Minn., 1998.

Crossick, Geoffrey, ed. *The Artisan and the European Town, 1500–1900.* Aldershot, U.K., 1997.

Fishman, Robert. *Bourgeois Utopias: The Rise and Fall of Suburbia.* New York, 1987.

Morris, Jonathan. *The Political Economy of Shopkeeping in Milan, 1886–1922.* Cambridge, U.K., 1993.

Morris, R. J., and Richard Rodger, eds. *The Victorian City: A Reader in British Urban History, 1820–1914.* London, 1993.

Sutcliffe, Anthony, ed. *Metropolis, 1890–1940.* Chicago, 1984.

Thompson, F. M. L., ed. *The Rise of Suburbia.* Leicester, U.K., 1982.

Wakeman, Rosemary. *Modernizing the Provincial City: Toulouse, 1945–1975.* Cambridge, Mass., 1997.

New Towns

Braunfels, Wolfgang. *Urban Design in Western Europe.* Translated by Kenneth J. Northcott. Chicago, 1988.

Rosenau, Helen. *The Ideal City: Its Architectural Evolution in Europe.* London, 1983.

Rubenstein, James M. *The French New Towns.* Baltimore, 1978.

Section 8

RURAL LIFE

AGRICULTURE

James R. Lehning

Agriculture has until the last two centuries occupied most of the population of Europe, and this has made it a topic of major significance for social historians of virtually every historical period. Its study has required the use of a variety of primary sources, such as leases, registers of feudal obligations, notarial archives, land-holding records, inquiries into rural conditions, and records from markets for agricultural goods. Historians of medieval and early modern societies see agriculture as the principal source of subsistence and wealth, providing the basis for human existence. It also served as a determinant of social and political relations in society, with institutions such as the family and local community organized around exploitation of the land. Political institutions were also organized to extract surpluses produced by agriculture to support other activities, such as warfare and religion. Agricultural production also is viewed as an important constraint on the possibilities of economic, social, and political transformation. While social historians would disagree on the rigidity of the relationship of agriculture to these other aspects of historical processes, few would deny the necessity of considering them as possibilities and of exploring their particular expressions in different times and places.

Agriculture in Europe at the end of the Middle Ages was characterized by great diversity from region to region and by dependence on farming practices that limited its productivity. Beginning in England and western Europe in the sixteenth century, production of grains increased due to expansion of the area of land under cultivation and the introduction of the intensive farming techniques of convertible husbandry, replacing fallow with legumes that restored the soil and provided pasture for livestock. These methods increased the productivity of the soil and diversified agricultural products, creating a model of agricultural revolution that other parts of Europe attempted to adopt, but with only mixed success in some parts of the Continent in the twentieth century.

AGRICULTURE IN THE LATE MIDDLE AGES

From the perspective of the rural village, Europe in the sixteenth century was made up of a combination of arable fields, natural pastures, woodlands, and wastelands. From the English Midlands across northern France, southern Denmark and Sweden, northern Germany, Poland, and into Russia these lands were often combined into an agrarian regime known as open field or champaign, in which the arable was cultivated in open fields in which each household held strips or furrows. South of this great European plain, the open fields were often divided into small irregular plots. In other areas, such as the enclosed fields of western and central France, in Walachia, and in parts of Lower Saxony, Westphalia, Bavaria, Schleswig, the Baltic lands, Brandenburg, and Hungary, isolated individual farmsteads existed with barriers of trees, hedges, or stone walls separating them from their neighbors.

The cultivation of grains, the principal foodstuff of Europe, took place in a system of crop rotation intended to avoid depleting the mineral content of the soil. In much of northern Europe this was a three-field system: in early autumn a winter cereal such as rye or wheat was planted in one field; in the spring, a second field was sown with barley, oats, or another small grain; the third field was left fallow to restore minerals, and especially nitrogen, needed to grow crops. In early or mid-summer the winter grain was harvested, followed by the spring grain in late summer. Then, in the autumn, the fallow field was planted in a winter cereal, beginning the process again. Farther south a two-field system, alternating grain and fallow, was used.

Rotation systems were maintained in areas of open field by customary rules enforced by the village community, which set common dates for planting and harvesting crops and which also allowed customary rights such as gleaning, which permitted the village

The Pattern of Fields. Fields interspersed with vineyards near Lognac-Jarrac, in the Bordeaux wine region of France. AEROFILMS LIMITED

poor to gather grain fallen on the ground after the first cut of the harvest. Gleaning, rights to pasture animals on the village common lands, and rights to fallen wood in communal forests were important supplements to the incomes of those in the village who lacked adequate land for subsistence. But while most families were able to keep barnyard animals such as chickens, and occasionally a goat, ownership of livestock such as cows or pigs was unusual. In most of the plain of northern Europe, the plow used was a heavy wheeled one, with a coulter in front to cut the turf, and a moldboard to turn the furrow to the side. In southern Europe, the plow used was a lighter one, without wheels, coulter, or moldboard, that only scratched the earth. Harvesting was occasionally done with a scythe, but more often the more labor-intensive sickle was used, since it did less damage to the ears of the grain and left a higher stalk, providing more straw for the villagers.

The productivity of this agricultural system was low in modern terms. The restoration of soil fertility by fallowing took one-third or one-half of the arable

Moldboard Plow. The moldboard, an iron plate, turns the soil into ridges along the furrow as the peasant plows. German miniature, c. 1500. BY PERMISSION OF THE BRITISH LIBRARY, LONDON (ADD 17012 FOL. 3)

land out of cultivation each year. The principal fertilizer used was animal manure, produced by grazing animals either on natural meadow and pasture or on fields left fallow, but the small number of livestock limited its availability. In these conditions yields were relatively low: Slicher van Bath's compilation shows medieval returns on seed planted for wheat of about four to one, rising by the late eighteenth century to between six and seven to one on the Continent and to nine or ten to one in England. Rye and oats were also important cereal crops, producing slightly higher returns on seed than wheat (pp. 328–333).

In many parts of rural Europe the community itself was in an uneasy relationship with a lord who possessed ultimate control over the land. In medieval and early modern Europe land tenure was rarely in the form of a fee simple, in which the cultivator possessed complete control over the land. More often, some form of leasehold was the case, in which the tenant was restricted in the cultivation of the land and was required to pay rents, entry fines due when the land was inherited, and other obligations, such as the requirement to use the lord's court, to grind grain in his mill, to provide a number of days of labor service, and to pay the tithe in support of the parish church. These requirements could be very severe, as in eastern Europe where serfdom gave peasants few avenues of recourse against their lords; in other areas, however, customary law or centralizing monarchies protected peasant communities against the excessive demands of their lords, especially after the Black Death in 1348 had removed the late-medieval labor surplus in rural Europe.

These institutional aspects of agrarian society affected the ways in which the soil was cultivated. In an economy whose principle purpose was the production of foodstuffs, one form of agricultural household economy in early modern Europe consisted of a peasant family attempting to produce enough to feed its members, leading to a polyculture with an emphasis on grains. But dues, fines, and services owed by the peasant to his lord, and the tithe owed to the Church, also shaped production. Where these were paid in kind, peasants could be required to produce crops stipulated by the lord, and lords who were oriented toward the markets of towns and cities in their region or even in other parts of Europe could insist on the planting of more salable crops. Peasants could also be forced into the market themselves. Where dues had been commuted into money payments, peasants had to sell a part of their crop to gain the money to pay these dues. Especially in the more commercialized areas of western Europe, these markets could be very significant forces in agriculture, spurring practices such as those in the Upper Rhine, where the multiple governments of the region followed a policy intervening in the markets for meat and grain to ensure an adequate supply for the cities and towns of the region.

THE ORIGINS OF AGRICULTURAL IMPROVEMENT

Beginning in the sixteenth century, especially in England and Holland, the low returns that characterized European agriculture began to increase. While solid data is lacking, and there has been disagreement among historians over its interpretation, this increase apparently occurred in two long phases: slow growth in the second half of the sixteenth century and the first half of the seventeenth, then again in the latter part of the eighteenth century and the nineteenth century. These increases occurred as a result both of more intensive farming and of bringing more land under cultivation. Improved crop and rotation systems increased the productivity of the land, breaking the closed circuit of traditional agriculture by the introduction of new crops, especially clover and turnips. These crops replaced fallow with a useful crop, increasing the supply of fodder, and allowing more livestock and greater manure production. They also helped the fields: clover fixed atmospheric nitrogen into the soil, replacing the nitrogen depleted by the growth of cereals; and turnips smothered weeds in fields, improving later cereal harvests.

To some extent, although how much is subject to debate, these increases in production took place within the existing agrarian system. For example, swamp drainage, as in Holland and eastern England, increased available land, and open-field systems adjusted in some places to changing economic circumstances. M. A. Havinden showed that, in seventeenth- and eighteenth-century Oxfordshire, in the middle of English open-field country, improvement took place through subtle changes in the open-field system. The area of grassland was increased through planting sainfoin and clover as winter feed for livestock. Combined with the increased supply of manure provided by larger herds, these crops increased the fertility of the soil and allowed elimination of some, but not all, fallows. Pulses, planted as a part of more intensive cultivation, increased the feed supply for livestock. Arable land planted in grain decreased, but the higher productivity of the soil not only maintained the previous level of production, but also allowed a shift from rye, barley, and oats to wheat. Thus, without a significant modification of the landscape, an ascending spiral of increased productivity and production occurred.

ENCLOSURE: THE ENGLISH MODEL

Individual ownership of fields allowed for even more rapid improvement. Especially in England and northwestern Europe, increased security of tenure allowed yeomen and peasants to increase the productivity of their fields by adopting some aspects of convertible husbandry. More controversially, improvement also came about through the enclosure of common fields, a practice that especially marked English agricultural history. Enclosure took place by common agreement in many English villages in the late Middle Ages and in the sixteenth and seventeenth centuries, and much of England outside of the Midlands had already been enclosed in this fashion before 1700 or had never been cultivated in open fields. But while about three million acres may have been enclosed by private agreement, another six to seven million acres were enclosed by parliamentary act, a technique that dominated enclosure after 1700 and was especially prevalent after 1750.

Enclosure by agreement could be a time-consuming and expensive process, requiring the consent not only of property owners but also of those with only use rights to the land. Enclosure by parliamentary act was easier, since it required the approval of the lord of the manor (who might be the instigator), the tithe owner, and the owners (but not those holding only use rights) of four-fifths of the land. Following passage of the act, the lands of the village were surveyed and redistributed as private holdings to the property owners. The result by either method could be a dramatic transformation of the lands of the village. Great Linford in Buckinghamshire, for example, was enclosed by agreement in 1658; new hedges were planted, roads and ditches were built, and enclosed pastures, most of them eventually rented to tenants supplying the London market for meat and dairy products, replaced the old open fields.

In classic histories of English agricultural development, such as Chambers and Mingay's *The Agricultural Revolution 1750–1880,* enclosure provided the basis for the implementation of convertible husbandry and for increases in labor and crop productivity, a necessary step toward agricultural revolution. This has been criticized by scholars such as Robert Allen, and it must be recognized that increases in production in some places were more the result of bringing more acreage under cultivation than of higher yields from existing arable lands. In County Durham, for example, studied by R. I. Hodgson, parliamentary enclosure in the late eighteenth century brought commons, moors, and wasteland under grain cultivation, and while some of this was farmed under improved rotations incorporating clover and turnips, much of it was cultivated under the older three-field system. David Grigg's study of south Lincolnshire showed that production was increased in the late eighteenth century by bringing marginal land under cultivation and by improving drainage. While the high grain prices of the Napoleonic era spurred production increases, they worked against the adoption of intensive farming techniques. But when prices fell after 1814, these techniques became necessary for farmers to survive, and,

Enclosure. Green fields near Looe, on the coast of Cornwall, England. ©BUDDY MAYS/CORBIS

in what later came to be called high farming, sheep-rearing, fertilizers, root crops, and claying were used to increase returns on seed.

Enclosure took place because of the prospect of increasing income by bringing unused land under cultivation, gaining higher productivity through more intensive farming, and charging higher rents for more valuable land. But it brought costs, both public and private, associated with the passage of the act itself, and with the physical changes to the land. The costs of enclosure may have been high and charged disproportionately to smaller estates, and enclosure created some farms that were too small to be economically viable. One consequence therefore was the sale of smaller farms and estates at or shortly after enclosure. This might mean consolidation of larger estates, but there is also evidence of an increase in the number of owner-occupiers, especially during the most intense period of enclosure, the Napoleonic Wars.

English agricultural development was therefore a very complex process, with both intensive and extensive aspects. But for most commentators on agriculture it has served as a model against which agricultural systems in other parts of Europe and, in the twentieth century, the world are measured. This English model emphasizes the efficiency and higher productivity of larger farms over peasant smallholders because of their ability to make use of better crop and rotation systems, to increase animal husbandry, and to implement new farming techniques. It therefore points to the necessity of consolidating landholding, as occurred in England through enclosure, as the avenue to agricultural growth.

While it is increasingly doubtful, as we have already seen, that England itself followed only this path to agricultural development, it is certainly true that Continental Europe (except Holland) has had diffi-

culty meeting the expectations of this model of supposedly successful "agricultural revolution." It has instead seemed hindered by peasant cultivators focused on autoconsumption rather than production for a market, the ability of the peasant community to resist innovation, and the absence of improving landlords. While, as in England, the Continent saw a slow recovery of agricultural production in the two centuries after the Black Death in 1348, it also experienced the long seventeenth-century depression marked by low prices and declining rents on land. In Spain and Italy the decline appears to have begun early in the century, perhaps as early as 1600 and accelerated after the 1620s. In France, the reign of Louis XIV (1643–1715) was marked by initial stagnation and then, beginning around 1660 or 1670, a sharp decline in regions as different as the Beauvaisis, Provence, and the west.

THE AGRICULTURAL REVOLUTION

The eighteenth century, in contrast, was a period of rising prices in much of Europe as market demand rose for agricultural products, stimulating attempts to increase production. A slow increase in population began with the recovery after the late fourteenth century, increased into the seventeenth century, and then accelerated in the eighteenth. Rural smallholders in some parts of Europe living through both agriculture and by employments such as spinning and weaving cloth for urban merchants were unable to produce enough to feed themselves and, along with growing urban populations, this created increased demand for agricultural products. The first quarter of the century saw only minor indications of the transition from depression to growth, but Fernand Braudel and Ernest Labrousse's *Histoire économique et sociale de la France* shows that after 1726 prices steadily increased until they leveled off in the 1780s (pp. 329–405). Further east, in the Baltic and North Sea area, the demand for grain and cattle also came from international trade with England and northwestern Europe.

Increased demand was only one of the factors in the late eighteenth century stimulating agricultural improvement in continental Europe. The dissemination of literature advocating scientific farming, and the foundation of schools to teach these methods, began the process of spreading the methods imported from Holland and England. The physiocratic doctrines elaborated in France beginning in the 1750s argued that land and agriculture were the sole sources of wealth, and combined with mercantilistic doctrines in central and eastern Europe these theories encouraged rulers to adopt policies improving agriculture. Anglomania among the educated classes in eastern and central Europe did the same. There were therefore numerous attempts by rulers and their administrators to enclose communal lands and consolidate landholdings in the states of the Holy Roman Empire, in Scandinavia, in the Habsburg Empire, and in Russia and Poland.

The effects of these changes on agricultural production and techniques, however, have been difficult to establish. Cultivation by peasants of crops that fell outside of the rent system was one possible response to increased market demand for agricultural products. Landlords might have difficulty exploiting the opportunity through more intensive farming because of problems in obtaining adequate effort from peasant laborers, competition with peasants for common lands, and a shortage of manure.

In France, the first part of the eighteenth century saw a shift from earlier abandonment of arable to clearing wastelands for cultivation, a trend that became more pronounced after mid-century but that may have added only about 2.5 percent to the arable of the country by 1789. There was also a slow decline in fallowing and a shift from rye to wheat production. But only in the second part of the century is there evidence of any significant increase in agricultural production, the result not only of these modest improvements in agricultural practices but also of more favorable weather in the last few decades of the Old Regime.

When placed against the English model, especially the intensive farming that seemed to contribute so much to the increased agricultural production of that country, continental Europe has therefore seemed marked by agricultural stagnation. But the regional diversity of the early modern economy, pre-eighteenth-century attempts at expansion in the agricultural sector, and the multiple routes, outside of enclosure, toward this expansion are becoming increasingly apparent to historians. This is especially the case in northwestern Europe, where yields around 1800 seem to have been as high as in England. Philip Hoffman has argued that in some parts of France, such as Normandy, the area near Paris, and parts of southeastern France, there were spurts of growth in the sixteenth and seventeenth centuries. These were the result of both intensive and extensive improvements. New crops were planted, meadow and arable increased, and market-oriented vineyards developed. But political crises such as the Wars of Religion and state tax policies disrupted these growth spurts. There is also evidence from Basse-Auvergne and Dauphiné showing the ability of smaller farmers to adopt diversified crop rotations.

Thus, in this revisionist view, increases in agricultural production occurred, and it was not so much small farms, immobile peasants, or weak markets that hindered agricultural growth as it was events outside of agriculture that disrupted this growth when it did occur.

Commercialization also was an important factor in increasing agricultural production in central Europe in the last decades of the eighteenth century. Increased fodder made more livestock possible, increasing as much as 150 percent between 1750 and 1800 in parts of Prussia. This enabled farmers to decrease fallowing and increase grain production, and specialization in commercial crops, especially wheat for export to western Europe, became more common.

But even as production increased, agriculture in much of continental Europe continued to use older rotation and cropping systems; livestock and artificial fertilizers were rare, and returns on seed remained low. Improvement continued to be slow into the nineteenth century. Gabriel Désert and Robert Specklin claim that in France, in spite of the turmoil and disruptions of the Revolution and empire, fallows were reduced by 20 percent, the amount of arable planted in wheat increased by 10 percent, and, following an estimate made by the Société d'économie politique, the gross agricultural product increased by 11 percent in the quarter century between 1789 and 1815 (pp. 107, 138). But in many parts of the country techniques remained unchanged. In 1840 fallowing and wasteland remained common, especially in the south and west, where more than 30 percent of the land area was unused; only in the north and east, and some parts of the southwest, had significant progress been made in bringing more land under cultivation.

Division of common lands in France also occurred slowly, in spite of pressure from agricultural reformers. Increasing production in the first half of the century was made difficult by one long period of price decline until the early 1830s and another at mid-century, and by increases in land rents and labor costs. Nonetheless, by mid-century, cereal production had increased by more than 40 percent over the beginning of the century, and an increased part of this was wheat, replacing rye as the principal grain for market. Other crops, such as potatoes and sugar beets, had also been introduced, and this greatly increased food supply. Livestock increased by a quarter to a third, especially during the 1830s and 1840s.

Land reforms carried out in Prussia and some west German states in the first half of the nineteenth century provided opportunities for division of commons and consolidation of landholding. At the same time, improvements in transport made commercial

Fowler's Steam Plow. J. Folwer demonstrated a steam plow in 1858. By 1864 his factory, in Leeds, employed nine hundred people. Illustration from S. Copland, *Agriculture, Ancient and Modern* (1866). MANSELL COLLECTION/TIME INC.

agriculture more attractive. Agricultural production in central Europe slowly increased in the decades before 1840: cereal production in Prussia rose from 4.6 million tons in 1816 to 6.8 million in 1840, the weight of livestock increased, and other parts of German Europe witnessed similar gains. As in France, these gains were in many places the results not only of the implementation of scientific farming methods but also of the reduction of fallow and cultivation of former wastelands and meadows. But across Europe these increases in production were fragile: the crisis of the late 1840s dropped production back to close to the levels of the turn of the century, reminding Europeans how closely they lived to bare subsistence.

THE GROWTH OF COMMERCIAL AGRICULTURE AFTER 1850

It was during the two decades after 1850 that the countryside in western and central Europe, spurred by transport and market improvements, truly opened toward great increases in production. Secondary roads were improved, making it easier for products to get to markets and for manufactured equipment, such as

scythes and the improved Dombasle plow, to reach peasants. The railroad, especially secondary lines, created national markets for agricultural products: grain and livestock could be sent to major cities, ending the threat of famine there, and fertilizer could be shipped to peasants anxious to increase the productivity of their land. Prices rose after 1850, as did both rural wages and emigration from the countryside to cities, increasing rural incomes and stimulating agricultural production for the market. Gabriel Désert has shown that while in France the expansion of the area planted in cereals ceased in 1862, other crops, such as potatoes, beets, and vines were in full expansion, as was livestock (pp. 247–251), and Maurice Levy-Leboyer estimated that the value of French agricultural production increased by 80 percent between 1852 and 1882 (p. 803).

It is not clear that these increases were due to substantive changes in agricultural practices. In France, rising prices certainly contributed to the increased value, and production increased by only 25 percent. The productivity of the soil increased only slightly, and, for cereals, remained 38 percent behind that of Great Britain. France lagged far behind other European countries in the production of livestock. A similar pattern is found elsewhere. In Prussian Upper Silesia grain production had increased rapidly between 1846 and 1861, growth due to increases in both acreage under cultivation and yields. These slowed after 1861, and from the 1860s to the 1890s growth in production continued but at reduced rates. Only after 1890 did yields again rise, generating growth in production even though acreage under cultivation stagnated.

The weaknesses of continental European agriculture became apparent in the twenty-five years after 1870, when a long decline in agricultural prices occurred. This was the consequence of the development of a global market that created competition, especially in cereals, with producers in other parts of the world. Unless protected by tariffs, many European grain producers, aristocrat and peasant alike, had trouble dealing with cheap imports from the Americas. Although prices improved somewhat in the 1890s and after the turn of the century, the ability of wheat producers in the North American Midwest to undersell European farmers even in European markets pointed out in glaring fashion the limitations imposed by the low productivity of European agriculture at the end of the nineteenth century. The depression forced difficult choices on many of the small peasant farmers in western and central Europe, and for some a retreat from the market and a return to production aimed primarily at autoconsumption was a logical strategy. For others, however, the depression forced rapid adoption of means, such as chemical fertilizers, that increased land productivity. Concentration on commercial dairy farming was a key recourse in Holland and Denmark. While agricultural production stagnated in some countries, such as England, it increased rapidly in Germany, Austria, Hungary, and Scandinavia.

In parts of central Europe and farther east the development of agriculture was complicated by the survival into the nineteenth century of serfdom, a system that left many peasants in servitude to their lords, with little incentive or resources to increase the productivity of the land they worked. The end of serfdom in these lands came in the course of the nineteenth century. But creating free peasants was one thing and increasing agricultural productivity another. Agricultural reformers in the bureaucracies of Russia, Austria-Hungary, and Prussia sought to improve agricultural productivity, but without launching major reforms of landholding and without great success. Eastern European agriculture remained marked by farms composed of scattered plots of land, a low level of investment, poor links to markets, and a low level of productivity.

These problems were especially evident in the Russian Empire, the world's largest exporter of cereals at the end of the nineteenth century. Emancipation of the serfs in Russia in 1861 did little to increase output or change methods of cultivation. After the turn of the century, there was some consolidation of landholding, encouraged by the Stolypin reforms of 1906, which attempted to divide communally held lands into individual farms. These farms, it was hoped, would use improved rotations, plant grass crops, and become more productive, creating the exportable surplus on which the Russian economy depended.

But by the eve of World War I Russian agriculture had made only slight improvements in production. Heavy taxation and unequal terms of trade between towns and countryside limited investment in agriculture. Russian agriculture was still focused on cereal production and often used three-field rotation systems that left much land fallow each year. Even after a decade the reforms of 1906 had only affected a small proportion of the countryside. Russia suffered from increased competition from American wheat in its traditional export markets of northwestern Europe in the second half of the nineteenth century, and like all European wheat producers it faced declining prices from 1873 until the 1890s. Its most important crop remained grain, and the continuation of communal agriculture in most villages into the 1920s, with its periodic redistribution of land, meant that individual peasants had little ability or incentive to improve the land that they farmed.

WESTERN EUROPEAN AGRICULTURE IN THE TWENTIETH CENTURY

The development of a global market for agricultural products in the late nineteenth and twentieth centuries conditioned developments in the agricultural systems of all countries in Europe. The uneven improvement in productivity that characterized the eighteenth and nineteenth centuries resulted in different abilities to compete in the global market, leading to different strategies in the twentieth century to increase production and productivity. The inability of agricultural systems to compete even in their own domestic markets led in the 1890s to protective tariffs in many countries. But while this protection may have limited the social effects of competition and preserved small peasant farms, it also reduced incentives to increase agricultural productivity.

Social experiments, such as collectivization in the Soviet Union and in eastern Europe, were intended to increase production, as were policies of consolidation and of intense cultivation of smaller farms. The record of these policies is inconsistent, but it appears that peasant family farmers were able to raise productivity while large collective farms struggled to meet production goals.

In France, for example, the many small farms of less than 5 hectares that existed in the nineteenth century declined dramatically from more than half of landholdings in 1929 to about one quarter in 1983. Very large farms, of more than 100 hectares, increased only slightly, but medium-sized farms of 5 to 100 hectares came to dominate French agriculture (60 percent in 1983). The poorer regions of the south and the Massif Central followed the north and east in reducing fallowing and the use of artificial fertilizers. Falling farm prices that began in the late 1920s and continued through the 1930s accentuated the rural exodus that began in the late nineteenth century, and after World War II the shortage of labor encouraged the adoption of labor-saving machinery not only on the large cereal farms of the north and east but even on the poorer family farms of the south and west, where after 1945 a "tractor revolution" mechanized production.

These developments were widespread in western Europe. The years of prosperity between the end of World War II and the recession of 1973–1974 transformed western European agriculture through a combination of increased competition and state management. The most important aspect of this was the Common Agricultural Policy of the European Economic Community formed in 1958. This policy was highly controversial, but the EEC took some steps toward accomplishing its goals of creating a single market for agricultural goods with common prices, protecting the farmers of the member countries against foreign competition, and promoting rationalization of agricultural production. Its pricing mechanism tended to set prices higher than market because of political pressures, and the result was not so much rationalization as overproduction, whose costs are borne by the member nations through a system of price subsidies that limited the market impetus for change in the structure of agriculture.

The EEC did open new markets within Europe for farmers in its member countries, although for some products, such as wine, it removed the protection that tariffs had provided since the 1890s. Some governments passed measures, such as French laws of 1960 and 1962, encouraging the retirement of older farmers and the consolidation of property holding. Greater organization and cooperation among farmers improved crops, livestock, and farm management. Productivity increased to the point that surplus, rather than shortage, became the major problem in agricultural policy making.

Many of the changes in western European agriculture over the twentieth century could be seen in Buzetsur-Tarn, a village in southeastern France that in the nineteenth century was dominated by small family farms either owned, sharecropped, or leased by their cultivators. Agricultural improvement during the nineteenth century came about not through dramatic increases in the productivity of wheat fields, but through the development of crops—hay, vegetables, and wine—that could be transported to market on the railroad that came to the town in 1864. But the phylloxera infestation of the 1880s and 1890s hurt the vineyards, and by the period between the World Wars market gardening was also in decline. Peasant polyculture revived, with farms again producing primarily wheat, fodder, and a little wine. There was some mechanization of harvesting between the wars, the result of the rural labor shortage. Fertilizer was used, but only in small quantities.

Significant increases in agricultural productivity came only after 1950. Between 1950 and 1962 most farmers acquired tractors. Dairy products replaced vegetables as a market crop, and by the 1960s a new generation of farmers adopted intensive methods to increase crop yields. Combines and seed drills came into use. Dairy farming increased the amount of manure available, but new seed varieties required intensive artificial fertilizing. In the 1970s the use of herbicides and fungicides became common. To maximize their ability to use these new methods of cultivation, the young farmers of Buzet took advantage of the French government-sponsored process of *remembrement*, the consolidation through exchanges of scattered landholdings into large fields. Irrigation projects were developed to deal with summer drought, and improvements in drainage, made cooperatively with European Economic Community assistance, increased the production of winter crops and made it possible to work in the fields without getting stuck in the muddy clay.

AGRICULTURE IN EASTERN EUROPE IN THE TWENTIETH CENTURY

Such success stories remain tenuous in western Europe because of the threat of declining crop prices to the newly efficient and productive family farmers in villages such as Buzet. But they remain a different experience than that of eastern Europe in the twentieth century. The emancipation of serfs in Russia and elsewhere in eastern Europe in the nineteenth century

An Agricultural Society. Country meeting of the Royal Agricultural Society of England at Bristol, 1842. In the foreground are agricultural implements. Painting by Richard Ansdell. ROYAL AGRICULTURAL SOCIETY OF ENGLAND/SALFORD MUSEUM AND ART GALLERY, MANCHESTER, U.K.

opened the possibility of reforms of the agricultural systems there by developing private landholding and improving rotation systems, but in the twentieth century the hopes of agricultural reformers remained only imperfectly fulfilled.

While most of eastern Europe was agricultural prior to World War I, the great landed estates of the Austro-Hungarian Empire and present-day Poland had not been able to increase their productivity. Throughout the region, land reforms were carried out in the aftermath of World War I. Romania, Czechoslovakia, and Yugoslavia became countries of small peasant proprietors. Ambitious plans for reform in Hungary and Poland were delayed and then moderated for political reasons. Both countries had many large landowners, especially in eastern Poland and central and eastern Hungary, who produced cereals or other products, such as timber, for national and international markets.

The motives for land reforms were political, social, and national, and little thought was given to their economic consequences. Increasing production was difficult for small peasant farmers who lacked capital to invest, technical knowledge and equipment, and efficient transportation. For example, wheat raised in Hungary was unable to compete against American wheat in the Munich market because of high relative production and transportation costs, even though only a few hundred miles separated Hungary from Munich. East European agricultural production therefore stagnated between the World Wars, in some instances actually declining in the 1920s before recovering in the early 1930s. There was some mechanization in the 1920s, but in the 1930s, with declining prices and cheap labor, many tractors stood idle for lack of economic incentives to use them.

Bumper wheat and rice crops around the world created a glut of basic foodstuffs in the world market in the late 1920s, cutting farm incomes across eastern Europe. As the Great Depression spread, prices for manufactured goods remained relatively high, creating a "price scissors" for peasants, in which they contin-

ued paying high prices for manufactured goods while receiving less for the crops they sold. This was especially severe in 1932–1934, striking smallholders particularly hard because, unlike large landholders, they were not protected by government export policies. Peasant purchasing power did not recover significantly in the 1930s, leaving them not only with a declining standard of living but also unable either to make improvements to increase productivity and become more competitive, or to repay loans drawn in the 1920s to improve farms or carry operating expenses from one year to the next. Many of the peasants who had received land in 1919 were forced to sell it back to their former landlords to pay debts, and agriculture throughout eastern Europe became divided into large farms of over fifty hectares and peasant smallholders with less than five hectares.

In Russia, the disruptions caused by the Revolution of 1917, the civil war that followed, the collectivization of agriculture in 1929–1930, the Nazi invasion during World War II, and Soviet pol-

icies aimed at managing agricultural production and organization transformed the country from the largest exporter of grain in the world at the beginning of the century to the world's largest importer of grain and livestock products by the 1980s. Particularly devastating was the policy of forced collectivization, in which individual farms and communally held lands were brought into either collective farms (*kolkhozy*) or the more disciplined state farms (*sovkhozy*).

While one aspect of collectivization was the creation of a rural landscape in which mechanization and other modern farming techniques could be used, it nevertheless proved disastrous. In the short run, collectivization destroyed independent family farmers, the kulaks; led to the slaughter of horses, cattle, and other livestock by peasants to avoid turning them over to the collective farms; and created a famine in the early 1930s. In the long run, the modest gains of the Stolypin era (1906–1916) and the market-oriented New Economic Policy (1923–1928) in the productivity of arable land were reversed. The total grain harvest of the former imperial territory only regained its 1913 level in 1952–1954; the number of livestock returned to its 1928 level only in 1956.

A Virgin Lands program begun in 1954 brought under cultivation previously unused lands throughout the USSR, especially in eastern Kazakhstan. This program began to pay off in 1956, helping produce a record grain crop in that year. But these lands did not initially require fertilizers, and while wheat production increased initially, problems remained in other parts of the agricultural sector, such as vegetables and livestock. The diversion of equipment and expertise to the virgin lands in the east led to decreased returns in older agricultural areas in the western areas of the USSR. A goal set in the 1950s of matching American diets was never met because of low production of meat and dairy products. By 1963 the natural fertility of the virgin lands was exhausted, harvests declined, and a drought made grain shortages again a part of Soviet life. In 1963, for the first time, the Soviet Union became an importer of wheat.

The Soviet experiment in managing agricultural production through collectivization was extended after World War II to the countries of eastern Europe that became Peoples' Democracies. A first collectivization drive occurred immediately after the consolidation of Communist power in the late 1940s, but met with resistance from peasants seeking to maintain control of the farms they had only recently gained through the breakup of landed estates at the end of World War II. But there were significant variations from country to country. Private agriculture remained the rule in Yugoslavia, which after its political break with Moscow in 1948 ceased to emulate the Stalinist economic model, and in Poland, where only about 23 percent of the land was put into collective and state farms during the Stalinist phase from 1948 to 1956. During the October 1956 revolt in Poland 80 percent of collective farms were dissolved by their members, and by 1970, private farms still made up 86 percent of the arable land in that country.

In other parts of Eastern Europe, a second collectivization push, in 1958–1961, was more successful and often brought most of the land into state or collective farms. In Czechoslovakia, for example, only 15 percent of the population worked in agriculture by 1968, but over 95 percent of agriculture was collectivized. In Hungary, where peasant opposition to the regime had been an important part of the unsuccessful 1956 revolution, a drive begun in 1959 nevertheless brought virtually all land into the state sector by 1961. The German Democratic Republic also collectivized most of its agricultural land in this period.

But collectivization was no more successful in Eastern Europe than in the Soviet Union in raising productivity. Only the German Democratic Republic matched western European increases in productivity. In most of the Peoples' Democracies, economic planning focused on industrializing what were, except for Czechoslovakia, primarily agricultural economies. These policies siphoned investment away from agriculture, making improvement in productivity difficult and, in many of the Peoples' Democracies, minimal. In Hungary, the collectivized ownership structure was not questioned, but by the late 1960s more importance was given to market forces for collective farms, and production increased as prices were allowed to rise. Private plots, which were the most productive form of agriculture in all of the Peoples' Democracies, were actively encouraged and, as producers of livestock, dairy products, eggs, vegetables, and fruits, became important parts of the agricultural sector. In Poland, the 1970s saw, perversely, attempts to reduce the importance of private agriculture: state investment went into the inefficient state sector, while private farmers found it difficult to obtain supplies. As a result, the proportion of land privately farmed had fallen to 75 percent in 1980. But agricultural supplies had also decreased. The government was forced to pay increased price subsidies to maintain urban food prices at a reasonable level, and there were a series of political crises triggered by government attempts to reduce the gap between prices at the point of supply and those in urban markets.

After the fall of the Peoples' Democracies of Eastern Europe in 1989 and the breakup of the Soviet Union in 1991, the countries of Eastern Europe moved at varying speeds toward more market-oriented economies and greater integration into the world market. In countries where private landownership was already widespread and where producer and consumer prices for agricultural products quickly were turned over to the market rather than state policy, such as Hungary, this occurred rapidly. The results of these changes were a movement of population from agriculture to other sectors of the economy (in Hungary farm labor dropped from 19 percent in 1992 to 8 percent in 1997 as a share of employment) and increases in labor productivity. Elsewhere, as in the Czech Republic or Russia, reforms were slower, accentuating long-term shortfalls and decreases in agricultural production. The collapse of the Eastern Bloc also disrupted market systems throughout eastern Europe. Even in the most advanced countries, the search for adequate markets and prices for agricultural goods remained a major task, and became even more difficult as the more advanced countries moved into the European Union, leaving their former trading partners behind. Agriculture in Eastern Europe therefore continued to face its long-standing problems of raising production and productivity, while facing new challenges of finding markets for its products.

CONCLUSION

The histories of European agriculture since the Renaissance emphasize both the prominence of a specific model of agricultural change, an agricultural revolution in which large enclosed estates allowed the implementation of intensive farming practices and increased the productivity of the land and overall agricultural production, and the rarity with which that model appears to have actually occurred. In England, the basis for the model, increases in production were the result of extensions of cultivation as well as improvements in productivity, and these improvements were achieved by yeomen farmers as well as on large estates. On the Continent, well into the twentieth century, placing more land under cultivation was often as important as increases in productivity in raising agricultural output, and many parts of Europe remain unable to increase productivity levels to those attained at the end of the English model. The history of European agriculture remains marked by uncertainties paralleling those of soil, weather, and blight that mark the cultivation of the land itself.

See also **Capitalism and Commercialization** *(in this volume);* **Peasants and Rural Laborers** *(volume 3); and other articles in this section.*

BIBLIOGRAPHY

Allen, Robert C. *Enclosure and the Yeoman.* Oxford, 1992.

Amann, Peter. *The Corncribs of Buzet: Modernizing Agriculture in the French Southwest.* Princeton, N.J., 1990.

Aston, T. H., and C. H. E. Philpin, eds. *The Brenner Debate: Agrarian Class Structure and Economic Development in Pre-Industrial Europe.* Cambridge, U.K., 1985.

Bloch, Marc. *French Rural History.* Translated by Janet Sondheimer. Berkeley and Los Angeles, 1966.

Blum, Jerome. *The End of the Old Order in Europe.* Princeton, N.J., 1978.

Braudel, Fernand, and Ernest Labrousse, eds. *Histoire économique et sociale de la France.* 3 vols. Paris, 1970.

Chambers, J. D., and G. E. Mingay. *The Agricultural Revolution 1750–1880.* New York, 1966.

Cleary, M. C. *Peasants, Politicians, and Producers: The Organisation of Agriculture in France since 1918.* New York, 1989.

Conquest, Robert. *The Harvest of Sorrow: Soviet Collectivization and the Terror-Famine.* New York, 1986.

Désert, Gabriel. "Prosperité de l'agriculture." In *Histoire de la France Rurale.* Vol. 3: *Apogée et crise de la civilisation paysanne: 1789–1914.* Edited by Georges Duby and Armand Wallon. Paris, 1976. Pages 221–253.

Désert, Gabriel, and Robert Specklin. "Victoire sur la disette." In *Histoire de la France rurale.* Vol. 3: *Apogée et crise de la civilisation paysanne: 1789–1914.* Edited by Georges Duby and Armand Wallon. Paris, 1976. Pages 107–141.

Grigg, David. *The Agricultural Revolution in South Lincolnshire.* Cambridge, U.K., 1966.

Haines, Michael. "Agriculture and Development in Prussian Upper Silesia, 1846–1913." *Journal of Economic History* 42 (1982): 355–384.

Havinden, M. A. "Agricultural Progress in Open-Field Oxfordshire." *Agricultural History Review* 9 (1961): 73–83.

Hodgson, R. I. "The Progress of Enclosure in County Durham, 1550–1870." In *Change in the Countryside: Essays on Rural England, 1500–1900.* Edited by H. S. A. Fox and R. A. Butlin. London, 1979.

Hoffman, Philip T. *Growth in a Traditional Society: The French Countryside, 1450–1815.* Princeton, N.J., 1996.

Kerridge, Eric. *The Agricultural Revolution.* London, 1967.

Lehning, James R. *Peasant and French: Cultural Contact in Rural France during the Nineteenth Century.* New York, 1995.

Levy-Leboyer, Maurice. "La croissance économique en France au XIXe siècle." *Annales: Economies, Sociétés, Civilisations* 23 (1968): 788–807.

Medvedev, Zhores A. *Soviet Agriculture.* New York, 1987.

Morineau, Michel. *Les faux-semblants d'un démarrage économique: Agriculture et démographie en France au XVIIIe siècle.* Cahiers des Annales 30. Paris, 1971.

Overton, Mark. *Agricultural Revolution in England: The Transformation of the Agrarian Economy.* New York, 1996.

Pavlovskii, Georgii. *Agricultural Russia on the Eve of the Revolution.* New York, 1968 (1930).

Poitrineau, Abel. *La vie rurale en basse Auvergne au XVIIIe siècle.* Paris, 1965.

Reed, Michael. "Enclosure in North Buckinghamshire, 1500–1750." *Agricultural History Review* 32 (1984): 133–144.

Rosenthal, Jean-Laurent. *The Fruits of Revolution: Property Rights, Litigation, and French Agriculture, 1700–1860.* New York, 1992.

Scott, Tom. *Regional Identity and Economic Change: The Upper Rhine, 1450–1600.* Oxford, 1997.

Seton-Watson, Hugh. *Eastern Europe between the Wars, 1918–1941.* New York, 1962.

Slicher van Bath, B. H. *The Agrarian History of Western Europe* A.D. 500–1850. Translated by Olive Ordish. London, 1963.

Sutherland, D. M. G., and T. J. A. Le Goff. "The Revolution and the Rural Economy." In *Reshaping France: Town, Country, and Region during the French Revolution.* Edited by Alan Forrest and Peter Jones. Manchester, U.K., 1991. Pages 52–85.

Thirsk, Joan, ed. *The Agrarian History of England and Wales: Volume 4, 1500–1640.* Cambridge, U.K., 1967.

Turner, Michael. *Enclosures in Britain 1750–1830.* London, 1984.

Van Zanden, J. L. "The First Green Revolution: The Growth of Production and Productivity in European Agriculture, 1870–1914." *Economic History Review* 44 (1991): 215–239.

Wunder, Heide. "Agriculture and Agrarian Society." In *Germany: A New Social and Economic History. Volume 2: 1630–1800.* Edited by Sheilagh Ogilvie. New York, 1996. Pages 63–99.

LAND TENURE

Liana Vardi

Types of property and patterns of landownership might, on the surface, seem to belong less to social history than to economic history, describing the distribution over time and space of small and large farms, or to legal history as a branch of contract law. Land tenure, however, is woven into the very fabric of society, reflecting concepts of property, hierarchy, and individual rights. Describing changes in land tenure thus involves describing changes in the society at large. This makes understanding land tenure both interesting and challenging.

Land tenure in preindustrial Europe has long been the focus of historiographical debate. Painstaking research into landholding has been driven by more than antiquarian curiosity. The resulting information has figured prominently in scholarly debates about distribution of land and about peasants' need for and attachment to the land. Those who equate country life with rural idiocy might not view the peasants' dispossession of their land with as much distress as those who imbue rural life with rustic virtues. If owning land is linked with independence and dignity, then dispossession will seem a cruel blow. The study of land tenure has thus been able to evoke strong feelings: a desire to do justice to the dispossessed; a drive to understand the process of modernization, associated (until recently) with large-scale farming and treating small properties as hindrances to progress; and a wish to go beyond generalizations to recover the full complexities of the past with its variations, exceptions, negotiations, and multiple agencies. Until the 1970s, historians tended to equate country life with land, meaning that gradations in landownership were taken to represent gradations in wealth, disregarding the import of secondary or alternate sources of income. Thus, forms of property and tenure were profoundly intertwined for much of European history. In fact, in its simplest and most reductive form, the history of land tenure in much of Europe might be taken as the emergence and eventual victory of private property over previous forms of tenure.

As the defining feature of rural life, land tenure holds much less sway than it used to. Historians used to fasten on the constraints that antiquated land tenure imposed. They attached importance to both legal and cultural constraints. First, the excessive "surplus extraction" by lord, church, and state left the peasant with the bare minimum. Second, the terms of tenure were so rigid that they allowed peasants and farmers little room to innovate, and should they manage to get around those, they would be trapped by the demands of communal farming and grazing. Third, peasant value systems were geared toward family survival rather than economic profit. To that end, peasants were always struggling to get more land or to hold on to their small properties, rather than concentrating on making these commercially viable.

Late-twentieth-century scholarship focused more on how peasants, be they freeholders, or long-term or short-term tenants, took advantage of economic opportunities, negotiating loopholes or disdaining constraints altogether. The collection, *The Peasantries of Europe* (1998), edited by Tom Scott, is a case in point. Its authors view the organization and accessibility of markets as far more important than legal categories and treat peasants as responding to market forces, by choice or of necessity. Rare is the author who still clings to the notion of a downtrodden peasantry crushed by feudal oppression or to a "romantic" view of the past with its moral economy of mutual aid and communal institutions. In the same way, gone is the notion that peasants were backward and routine-bound, living in self-sufficient worlds (even if they paid state taxes) or "part-societies" (a term favored by rural anthropologists in the wake of Robert Redfield and updated by Eric Wolf).

LAND TENURE IN THE MIDDLE AGES AND THE SEIGNEURIE

Any discussion of land tenure involves by implication a discussion of feudalism and seigneurialism (manorialism for British historians, *Herrschaft* for German ones), for they imparted to land tenure much of its

Working the Land. Peasants plowing fields from a French illuminated manuscript, fifteenth century (Cotton Aug. A V, fol. 161v). By PERMISSION OF THE BRITISH LIBRARY, LONDON

complexity, including a superfluity of attributes that centuries of practice and resistance whittled down and finally abolished. The history of land tenure in Europe must therefore begin in the Middle Ages, when these systems originated.

Land has always been important, of course. Until the mid-nineteenth century, because of its low yields, agriculture was the major occupation of Europeans and 80 percent of the population, and in some cases more, were engaged in the cultivation of the fruits of the soil, edible and nonedible. To own land, therefore, meant the ability to feed, house, and clothe oneself and one's family. It also meant creating the surpluses that allowed other social groups to survive without working the land, be they nobles, churchmen, or city dwellers. Except in extreme circumstances, agriculture was always capable of producing such surpluses so that the possession and marketing of this produce was a profitable proposition. Ownership and control over land therefore provided the most obvious form of wealth and prestige, and this is why it was not left to the people who worked it.

In the Middle Ages all the land in any given country belonged in theory to the Crown, although actual ownership had devolved, via land grants, to the nobility in return for military services, to the church in recognition of its spiritual services, and to commoners by dint of immemorial possession that no one chose to contest and that the Crown, at some point,

agreed to recognize. Such full-fledged peasant owners were always a minority. Noble recipients of land granted domains to other nobles, in turn, so that the countryside became a patchwork of properties of different sizes, whose possessors were arranged hierarchically and linked by a chain of allegiance. Land thus expressed one's place in society. It symbolized, first and foremost, military might as lords were required to support their superiors in battle, and, likewise, to protect the people who worked their land against aggression. This was the primordial contract struck between lord and commoner. Just as the priest was meant to pray for his salvation, so the knight was meant to offer him protection, in return for which the peasant granted both a share of his produce. For some historians, this contractual relationship was real and all benefited from the arrangement. Others argue that the relationship was exploitative and rested not so much on mutuality as on an unequal distribution of power.

In addition to military power, land signified access to economic resources, and ownership brought with it administrative, judicial, and policing powers. When a lord obtained a tract of land (a seigneurie), sometimes in one large chunk, sometimes in several, he also obtained rights of justice over it. The peasants who were settled and working the land, or whom he brought to the land, were under his jurisdiction and subject to his law. Even if the lord could not act totally arbitrarily and was bound, to some extent, by customary or civil law, he had the right to judge, fine, and condemn his peasants as if they were his subjects. Where the state remained sufficiently organized and strong, the peasants could take their cases before this higher authority. But the devolution of power from the Crown to the lords in the Middle Ages reduced that capacity, until that time when the state began to reconsolidate and reclaim these rights. The high point of the seigneurial system in any given country was when most peasants fell under its dominion.

Before the Middle Ages some peasants had owned land outright, but, except for a few pockets where such independent owners survived for centuries (this land being known as alodial), most peasant owners eventually came under the control of a lord, and had to pay him a fee in recognition of his superior ownership of their properties. In one way or another, then, most peasants were tenants and owned tenancies. The full-fledged owner or seigneurial lord was not necessarily a nobleman. The Crown, the church, and wealthy burghers also owned seigneuries.

Besides the judicial and military powers it conferred, a seigneurie was viewed as an income-producing unit, subject at all times to fluctuations in prices, and the vagaries of supply and demand. Although landowners did not subscribe to some medieval version of the *Financial Times,* they were acutely aware of where profits lay and eager to make the most of them. Thus, depending on the region, they might view it as more sensible to lease as much of their land as possible, or on the contrary to hold on to it or "buy" it back from the peasants (whether peasants were coerced into selling or driven to sell by poverty and debt remains open to debate). A landowner might hire laborers or, even better, retain a steady supply of workers by granting them some land and demanding, in return, that they work his land three, four, and even in extreme cases six days a week. Feudalism granted the lord the power to enforce such decisions, which is why feudal economics cannot be separated from power.

Western European lords, as a rule, did not till their domains themselves. Their estates were divided into two distinct parts: the demesne, that part of the land that remained under their direct control, and tenures allocated to peasants. When the lord divvied up his domains or settled peasants on new land he insured himself a ready supply of workers who either worked part-time on his fields, or paid him a rent with which he hired servants. In Germany this system was called *Grundherrschaft* to distinguish it from *Gutsherrschaft* (most common in eastern Europe), where most of the estate remained under the lord's direct control.

Late medieval tenures were either long-term or perpetual leaseholds (emphyteutic), where the peasants received one or several plots, a garden, orchard, perhaps vineyard, or any combination or fraction of these to treat as their own and pass on to their heirs or even sell in return for a number of fixed dues, services, and fees that they owed the lord. The peasants were the de facto owners, having the use value of the land, but the lord remained the final proprietor and peasants continued to owe him dues and/or services in recognition of that fact.

Under the most oppressive conditions of tenure, serfdom, peasants were bound to the estate and forced to work the lord's domain in return for their allotments. Their servile status could be based on personal bondage—known as *Leibeigenschaft* in German, *mainmorte* in French, *Remença* in Spain, and neifty in England—or it could be a condition attached to the land, meaning to the peculiar demands of tenure on a seigneurial estate: the type of relationship that the English called villenage. In western Europe as of the later Middle Ages, personal bondage had been superseded by land based bondage and greater personal freedom. Labor services were commuted to cash, hold on tenures became more secure, and some of the more humiliating seigneurial rights were dispensed with. Peasants recovered their mobility, their ability to bequeath or to marry outside the seigneurie without the consent of their lord. Most important, most tenures became hereditary. Whenever possible, the lord converted previous constraints into payments. Thus, seigneurial relations were transformed into primarily economic transactions. Personal serfdom, on the other hand, was introduced into eastern Europe at the time when it was disappearing in the West, a process known as the second serfdom.

TENANT FARMING AND SHARECROPPING IN THE PREMODERN ERA

Most peasants and serfs, that is free and unfree rustics, possessed tenancies. The terms and nature of tenancy varied. They ranged from quasi ownership to full-fledged economically based rentals. Along with emphyteutic leaseholds, which were either perpetual or lasted up to ninety-nine years, there existed tenures of one to three lives (that of the husband, the wife, and their son, who could upon their death renegotiate for himself three further lives), medium-length tenures of eighteen to twenty-four years, and short-term rentals of one, three, six, or nine years; multiples of three were the most common for they reflected the three-field rotation cycle. Shorter leases were, much like modern rentals, gauged economically on the basis of market prices—in England this was called rack rent—rather than having the fixed fees of hereditary rights of tenure. The tenant-farmer typically paid a high entry fee (or fine) and an annual rent based on the anticipated returns from the land during the length of the lease. From the late Middle Ages onward this became the most common way of leasing the demesne, that part of his domain that the lord did not parcel out as tenures, especially in continental Europe (except east of the Elbe). From the demesne the practice eventually spread to other tenures as lords tried to increase their profits by reducing the number of emphyteutic tenures and making peasants pay returns proportional to their produce. This might happen, for example, when bad economic conditions coupled with high state taxation drove peasants into debt and forced them to relinquish their holdings. The lord might then buy the plots and rent them back under new terms. The progression in the types of tenancies, that is, the changing demands and needs of lords, can be reconstituted through surviving leases, grants, litigation, and sometimes legislation.

Rentals came in two basic forms: the fixed rents described above, which were adjusted with each new contract, and sharecropping agreements, where the landowner and renter supposedly shared the produce equally, hence the terms *métayage* in French and *mezzadria* in Italian from the words meaning "half." Although this terminology was most common, sharecropping agreements might only involve the payment of one-fifth or one-third of the produce, fitting better the Spanish usage of the term *aparcería,* or partnership. But in Spain also sharecropping ranged from one-third to equal shares in the produce. Sharecropping prevailed in some parts of Europe but not in others. It was, for example, unknown in England and much of northern Europe, but common in Italy, France, Spain, and parts of the Rhineland throughout the sixteenth, seventeenth, eighteenth, and nineteenth centuries.

Sharecropping contracts have generally been taken as a sign of poverty: the tenant, being unable to furnish any capital, relied on the owner to provide the seeds, animals, and running capital to work the farm, in return for which he offered his labor and tools and handed over half his produce. Sometimes, the landlord agreed to pay state taxes. In parts of north and central Italy, where sharecropping emerged in the twelfth century as a substitute for serfdom, small landholders with a few parcels took on sharecropping contracts, which augmented what they grew on their own plots (this combination of ownership and rental seems most typical of Piedmont). These farms of about ten to thirty hectares produced a little of everything: cereals, fruits, vegetables, and wine. As S. R. Epstein explains, this arrangement suited landlords, whose main concern was to reduce labor costs. Unlike specialized cash crops, the mixed production kept the workforce busy all year round, but was also less profitable in the long run. In Lombardy and in the south, where farms were much bigger, from 50 to 130 hectares, tenant-farmers *(masseri)* either hired laborers or sublet the less fertile parts of their land. By the eighteenth century tenant-farming had become more common in north and south Italy than sharecropping, which however survived in central Italy until the nineteenth century. Another arrangement that became widespread was the grouping of farms under common management *(fattoria)* worked either by tenant-farmers or day laborers. Sharecropping was slow to disappear from areas where it had existed for centuries. For example in 1862 there were still 400,000 tenant-farmers and 200,000 sharecroppers in France.

In the later Middle Ages, peasants did not lease for brief periods but had hereditary rights to tenancies, which were recognized by customary law (or the custom of the manor, hence in England peasants were known as customary tenants). As territorial states began to consolidate in the fourteenth and fifteenth centuries, rulers upheld this customary law. In the case of England, unfree peasants came to be called copyholders because they were given a copy of the documents attesting their right to their tenure. The revival of Roman law, favored by centralizing rulers, was at first detrimental to peasants because Roman law defined much more bluntly the difference between free and servile status, and serfs were forbidden recourse to public courts and were left at the mercy of their masters.

Yet, because it was not in the long-term interest of most rulers to relinquish control over vast numbers of their subjects, territorial lords sided with peasants against seigneurial lords. Where once a "contract" had bound lord and peasant, with the first protecting the second in adversity in return for labor and rent, now the state inserted itself as the protector of the peasants against the demands of the lords. The Germans had a name for it: *Bauernschutzpolitik,* peasant protection policies. Peasants could once again appeal to public courts, and were liberated from the most onerous of seigneurial exactions. Instead they became liable to the public fisc. In France, as of 1439, the king forbade seigneurs from levying taxes and replaced them with his own. To put it bluntly, in this "trade" one bloodsucker replaced another. Seigneurial payments had not all been extinguished and continued to be a drain on peasant incomes. The demands of the state, however, represented the most onerous fiscal burden from then on.

SEIGNEURIAL DUES

Hereditary tenures owed periodic, usually annual, payments in cash or kind. The amounts were fixed at the time of the agreement. By the twelfth century inflation had reduced cash payments to insignificance, even if they were supplemented by a capon or some eggs. Where an additional rent was paid in kind (in France this was called a *champart* or *terrage*) it could be onerous: as much as 8 percent of the peasant's crop in France (likewise in Spain) levied right after the harvest. In the Middle Ages, lords derived as much as 90 percent of their income from various seigneurial payments. This amount diminished substantially over the next centuries, as lords came to depend primarily on rents and on income from royal and princely courts. By the late eighteenth century, seigneurial payments commonly represented 15 to 30 percent of revenues, although in some Germanic lands they might still amount to 50 percent, as they had in 1500. Payments varied from place to place because tenures were created at different times under different circumstances. No one can do justice to the multiplicity and variety of fees that might be asked of European tenants. Jerome Blum reports that a seigneurie in northwest Germany listed 138 different obligations. Such a variety defies generalization, and few scholars attempt it. Faced with a baffling array of incommensurable data, they are more likely to focus on dynamics within a specific region.

Lords not only charged a quitrent, or fixed fee, they were also entitled to collect a series of incidental fees, called casualties. Some related directly to their "eminent" possession of the land and were levied when a tenant sold his tenure (these went by different names: *lods et ventes* in French, *laudemium* in Latin, *Lehnsgeld* in German) or when he bequeathed it (in English, heriot). This fee might be trivial or rise to one-quarter of the value of the holding. Other payments had once signified the peasants' servile status: their lack of mobility, their inability to marry out of the seigneurie without the lord's consent (the fee known as marchet or formariage), or their obligation to support the lord's expenditures in war, contribute to his ransom, or help pay for his daughter's wedding. Lords could reclaim the land if a peasant died intestate, and had the right to forestall a sale (*retrait seigneurial*). In Catalonia, lords went so far as fining servile peasants whose wives committed adultery (*cugucia*). Paul Freedman has reminded us how deeply peasants resented such degrading payments, how hard they fought for their abolition, and how much they spent on manumissions, that is, the release from bondage. The bundle of offensive payments known as *mals usos* (bad customs) were rescinded in Catalonia in 1486 after a successful peasant rebellion.

By the eleventh century lords throughout Europe charged fees for the use of various services they monopolized: flour mills; bread ovens; wine and olive presses; local markets; passage on roads, bridges, and rivers; weights and measures; and forests or fishponds; and they fined anyone found poaching or bypassing their facilities. Casualties and *banalités* (seigneurial monopolies) were a way for lords to get additional moneys from their tenants, especially those tenants who had secure holdings with fixed rents, which brought lords little revenue. These payments could be changed or increased at will, although they tended to be governed by the custom of the manor/seigneurie. Labor services, which had been the hallmark of serfdom, were generally commuted into rent. Where they survived into the early modern period, they amounted to two or three days' labor a year, although sometimes as many as fourteen. Service days fell at harvest time, and peasants highly resented this interference with their own farming. But for the most part, payments that pertained to servile status were either abolished outright or withered into insignificance as part of the liberties western European peasants gained in the fourteenth and fifteenth centuries. That made payments directly linked to land and various *banal* monopolies all the more important to lords. These survived for centuries in most of continental Europe, to disappear only in the late eighteenth century and nineteenth century.

Despite the clear coercive power of lords, the balance of power between them and their tenants was also governed by economic forces and demographic factors. The support of the state played an important role, and peasant resistance should not be underestimated. Rural communities fought excessive seigneurial exactions with lawsuits and uprisings. Moroever, seigneuries did not always coincide with villages, but could be spread over several, or cover only a part of any given village, depending on how and when they had been constituted. Thus, most peasants lived in villages with multiple owners and lords. As time went on, peasants could also appeal to a reconstituted central state. Everywhere, there were multiple, competing authorities, and peasants learned quickly how to play one against the other.

Although there is no uniformity, scholars estimate that by the eighteenth century peasants paid half of their net profits to the state in taxes, to the church as tithes, and to the seigneurs in rents and dues. In Germany, 60 percent of peasant payments went to the state (representing 25 percent of average output), 30 percent to the lords, and 10 percent to the church. In the mid-eighteenth century the French physiocrat François Quesnay believed a similar distribution to be true of France. Taxes, dues, and tithes might take from one-third to one-half of peasant produce in France and Spain, but only one-third in Switzerland and Austria. These figures sometimes include rent and sometimes not. State taxation increased everywhere, rising to intolerable amounts in wartime, and hitting peasants especially hard since they bore the brunt of the burden. Rents also fluctuated depending on economic circumstances. They rose during the eighteenth century, cutting into tenant-farmer profits. The difficulty in assessing the weight of such exactions is not merely that demands might fluctuate from year to year, but that no one can say for certain how much peasants produced. Payments were either tendered in coin or kind, meaning primarily wheat, the most valuable of cereals. Average yields in Europe before the agricultural revolution have been estimated to lie anywhere between 2:1 and 10:1, although 4:1 seems the most likely. Peasant expenditures have been calculated on that uncertain basis. Given the uncertainty about peasant incomes, estimates reinforce both bleak and sanguine views of the peasant estate.

SERFDOM AND THE STATE

Historians assess the factors that were most significant in altering agrarian relations in the fourteenth century differently. Some (*Annales* school historians in particular) have emphasized demographic factors. Others (particularly marxists) have argued that the crisis was political and signified a long-term transformation of the feudal economy and its mode of surplus extraction into its absolutist version. These arguments were particularly ferocious in the 1970s, culminating in what is known as the Brenner debate, after Robert Brenner's attack on neo-Malthusian interpretations. Research on peasant resistance in the 1980s and 1990s has bolstered the Brenner side of the debate by fastening on local power relations. While few contest the significance of the demographic crises of the fourteenth century, they disagree about the peasants' ability to profit from them, which, not surprisingly, varied from place to place.

The late thirteenth and fourteenth centuries witnessed population explosion, land hunger, and rising prices with concomitant declining wages, followed by a series of catastrophes—crop failures, wars, and epidemics, of which the worst was the Black Death of 1348. These disasters drastically reduced population, lowered demand for food, collapsed agricultural prices, and raised wages. While lords had been eager to take advantage of favorable economic conditions to regain control of the fields, peasants after the plague were able to improve their lot significantly. Lords who had acquired vacated farms were looking to rent them. Depopulation put peasants in a position of strength, and many won freedom from serfdom, reduced rents, and secure tenures from lords eager to attract them. This was not the universal response, however.

Lords, conscious of their power, tried at first to compel peasants to remain on their land by reinstituting a harsh serfdom that severely restricted their mobility. They failed in this because peasants fled to more welcoming terrain or openly rebelled. Lords were successful in England and Catalonia, where serfdom was reintroduced with the support of temporarily weakened states. By the late fifteenth century, however, serfdom had been officially abolished in Catalonia and had disappeared from England. Italy also underwent a form of refeudalization between the fourteenth and sixteenth centuries, which consisted primarily in the landowners' recognition of the overlordship of territorial states rather than in the enserfment of the peasants.

In eastern Europe, which is a case apart, serfdom was successfully introduced in the sixteenth and seventeenth century by lords who controlled large estates and wanted them worked by compulsory labor services. In Germany east of the Elbe, Hungary, Bohemia, Poland, the Danubian Principalities, and Russia, serfdom became the norm at a time when it disappeared almost completely from western Europe. In those regions, lords' control over a servile population was ratified by state legislation and survived until abolished in the nineteenth century.

The reinstitution of serfdom in England and Catalonia in the fourteenth century, and later in eastern Europe, was achieved with the collaboration of recreated territorial states, whose rulers needed the support of their nobilities, and whose royal decrees upheld seigneurial law. State formation had two major consequences: the introduction of civil law that competed with customary law, and taxation that vied with the lord's exactions.

COMMUNAL ASPECTS OF LAND TENURE

One factor that made tenure so complex was that no owner or renter in pre-modern times had the exclusive usufruct of his property. All land had a communal dimension, and most villages also owned land communally. These should not be conflated.

Villages consisted of arable fields and pastures and areas that were considered too sterile to till—wastes, swamps, roadways, and fields that had been abandoned and never reclaimed. Often, the barren lands were turned into communal meadows; in some places they belonged to the seigneur, in others to the village community by dint of immemorial possession or documentary evidence. In northern France where the adage "nulle terre sans seigneur" (no land without a lord) obtained, the land was presumed to belong to the lord unless the community could prove otherwise. In the south the opposite was true, for there it was the seigneur who needed to show proof: "nul seigneur sans titre" (no lord without a title). This distinction became especially important in the eighteenth century, when both seigneurs and villagers claimed to own such communal land or "commons." This land was used primarily for grazing cattle and, while extremely important to all peasants, was crucial for smallholders who had no other way to pasture their animals. A vast literature examines that question for England during the period of enclosures, when the commons vanished. Communal properties were important in Spain, Italy, Alpine regions, and elsewhere where pasturing was a major activity. The privatization of the commons in early modern Europe (usually by state decree), to feed a growing population, went hand in hand with an expansion of the arable at the expense of pasture.

Besides this unclaimed/communal land, all land became at some point communal, notably in regions of open-field farming. The village arable was divided into large sections—two in the case of biennial rotation and three in triennial—that were planted at the same time with the same crop or left fallow. These fields, either when fallow and overgrown with weeds or after the harvest, would be turned into grazing grounds, primarily for sheep. Given the lack of fodder, grazing on the stubble made the possession of animals possible. Also, manure was the principal form of fertilizer before the advent of chemicals, making pasturing a necessary part of farming. All land was declared "open" to pasturing after the harvest, including artificial meadows where the community shared in the second crop. The lord, whose estate might be separate from or mingled within the peasant fields, was also entitled to graze his flocks on the stubble.

It was long presumed that lords were opposed to communal forms of farming and wished them replaced with enclosed private properties; but by the eighteenth century it was they, more often than not, who profited most from communal lands. Villagers

Open Fields. Open fields near Laxton, Nottinghamshire, England, August 1967. [For a photograph of enclosed fields, see the article "Agriculture" in this section of the Encyclopedia.] ©TED SPIEGEL/CORBIS

benefited from the quid pro quos such as the right to scavenge for berries or wood in seigneurial and communal forests. As long as one was a village resident with some land, whether owned or rented, one was entitled to send one's animals on the communal grazing grounds, be they fallow or waste (the number of animals that could be pastured was sometimes prorated), and to share other use rights. For this reason, "closed" villages in Germany and Austria carefully controlled residence and membership in the village community.

Such seasonal devolution of fields into the common domain, such rights of pasture (which, if they spread beyond the village boundaries, were known as intercommoning), and the entire series of use rights came under severe attack in the eighteenth century, and they were replaced—sometimes easily, sometimes after a hard struggle—with enclosed farms and individual property rights. French Revolutionaries who decreed individual property rights and abolished feudal tenures as of the summer of 1789 could not agree about the fate of communal properties, and allowed Old Regime practices to stand. In Spain and Italy, restrictions on property rights eroded in the early modern period as communities sold their commons, usually to settle communal debts. Liberal reformers in the eighteenth and nineteenth centuries made privatization a byword for liberty and progress.

In England, where philosophers had linked independence with individual property since the late seventeenth century, agricultural development was equated with big compact farms liberated from communal servitudes, where each farmer could grow what he wanted, when he wanted, without interference. Land was removed from common cultivation and enclosed as of the sixteenth century, though the pace quickened in the seventeenth and eighteenth centuries. English scholars continue to argue the benefits and drawbacks of enclosures, assessing its effects on productivity and on a small peasantry deprived of communal grazing grounds. Elsewhere in Europe, the survival of communal practices into the modern period was taken, until recently, as a sign of economic backwardness.

FRAGMENTATION OF LANDHOLDINGS

A farm of twenty to twenty-five hectares had since the Middle Ages been taken as the basic unit of taxation, going by the Latin name of *mansus,* or "hide" in English, *Hufe* in German, *mas* in Spanish, and *manse* in French (but also *charrue* as the unit of land that could be cultivated with one plow). Smaller properties were assessed as proportions of the basic unit. Whether owned or leased, this was the amount considered necessary for self-sufficiency, for living off farming alone.

Yet, as of the twelfth century fragmentation became the norm, and the majority of peasants lived on far less, putting their survival at risk in times of dearth. The drop in population in the fourteenth century allowed the reconstitution of larger farmsteads but the process of fragmentation began as soon as population rose once more. That is why some seigneurs and territorial rulers insisted on impartible inheritance, which maintained viable farms and thus more secure bases for taxation and dues. In England, as in Catalonia, nobiliary models of primogeniture, favoring the eldest son, spread early to the peasantry (in Spanish, *hereu*). In the rest of Spain, however, all heirs shared in the inheritance. In the Hohenlohe region of Germany, the counts in 1562 and again in 1655 forbade peasants to divide their holdings. Regimes of impartible inheritance governed four-fifths of Germany, much of Austria, and a few regions of France. There, the child who inherited the farm had to compensate siblings with cash. In areas of partible inheritance, such as Castile, most of France, southern Germany, and Italy, patrimonies were split among all surviving children, although, there too, one heir could opt to buy out his siblings by common agreement. Peasant choices depended on family strategies for survival. The more one delves into what peasants actually did with their properties, the more complicated things look. One should keep in mind that the amount that peasants owned was not necessarily the amount they farmed. Early modern European peasants owned about one-third of the land directly, either as freeholders with full prop-

erty rights or as seigneurial tenants with de facto ownership. But they tilled the remainder by leasing it from noble, ecclesiastical, and absentee urban landlords. The most successful, as we shall see, were the tenant-farmers of vast estates. But below them were plowmen (*laboureurs* in French, *labradores* in Spanish, and what Germans usually mean by *Bauer*) with some land of their own, and the farming implements (plows, horses, or oxen) to take on additional rentals. In most places in Europe, the best land had been granted to the privileged, so that rentals were generally more fertile and thus more profitable than peasant plots. Even peasants with only a few acres might rent a plot or two from other villagers—those too old to till it themselves or those who had moved away while keeping property in the village—or from the parish church. This land was not usually of high quality, but it provided a supplement. A mix of property and leasehold was therefore quite common.

Nonetheless, there was evident growing fragmentation and in the early modern period land tenure became more and more polarized between big holdings on the one hand and small or even tiny tenancies on the other. Demographic upsurge accounts for increased fragmentation at a time when it was no longer possible to extend the arable by cultivating the wastes or by clearing and colonizing new land. Several mitigating factors might explain why peasants would be willing to subdivide tiny plots: access to the commons, the availability of rental property, supplementary work on large estates, the option of planting vines (which necessitated little land for a decent return), and cottage industry. Although the result could be pauperization and eventually "proletarianization" as peasants made do with only a house and selling their labor, it is wrong to think of peasants as lemmings, accepting misery as their lot.

Everywhere, near-landless peasants became a majority. Spain in 1792 reported 16.5 percent peasant owners, 30.5 percent renters, and 53 percent day laborers. In early modern Italy, farms in the central regions covered 10 to 30 hectares, whereas in Lombardy they ranged from 50 to 130 hectares and were surrounded by subdivided smallholdings, as were the *latifundia* in the south and in Sicily. In England, near-landless squatters and cottagers made up 20 to 90 percent of the rural population, depending on the region; overall they amounted to 20 to 30 percent in the sixteenth century, but close to 50 percent in the seventeenth century. The same was true of France where three-quarters of peasants tilled less than 5 acres (2.2 hectares). Fragmentation occurred even in areas of compact farms. In Austria in 1600, big, middling, and small peasantries represented respectively 9, 61,

The Ideal Farm. *The Farm,* painting (c. 1751) by Jean-Baptiste Oudry (1686–1755). Musée du Louvre, Paris/Roger-Viollet, Paris/The Bridgeman Art Library

and 31 percent of the rural population. By 1700 the proportion was 18, 29, and 53 percent. In Saxony full holdings fell from 50 percent of tenures in 1550, to 25 percent in 1750, and 14 percent in 1843.

While tiny peasant holdings multiplied, large farms increased in size. In France, especially around Paris, tenant-farms grew from an average of 50 hectares (or two *charrues*) in the fifteenth and sixteenth centuries, to 80 hectares in the seventeenth century. The disruptions of the Fronde, the demands of the fisc, and the long drop in prices in the late seventeenth century caused havoc among middling peasants. Their abandoned holdings were integrated within existing farms, so that the average farm covered 135 hectares by the second half of the seventeenth century, and 210 hectares in the eighteenth century. Farms were much bigger in England than in France. In the eighteenth century, a large English estate was reckoned at 10,000 acres, or 4,000 hectares—ten times the size of the biggest French equivalent. In France, Jean-Michel Chevet reports, farms of 50 to 100 hectares grew at the detriment of farms in the 10 to 50 hectare range or smaller. The ranks of middling peasants thinned everywhere, although they fared better in Germany than elsewhere. There, rich farmers grew richer and poor ones poorer, but some middling peasants managed to hold onto their family farms, often with the help of landlords who extended them credit in difficult times.

Farms increased in size as lords consolidated their domains in order to profit from price rises (or, as happened in England, Spain, and parts of Germany, to convert their estates from arable to pasture when food prices dropped, and then back again to cereals when market conditions changed). In Italy, France, and England, the richest peasants were not substantial landowners in their own right. Rather they farmed the new, enlarged demesnes for the lords and owned only a few plots of their own. Such tenant-farmers prospered, especially where they managed to stay in place for generations. They intermarried, controlled village councils and vestries when they could, collected dues for the seigneurs and tithes for the church, acted as moneylenders to other peasants, and marketed grain on distant markets or dealt with urban grain merchants. Nicknamed *coqs de village* in France, they were a tight-knit oligarchy and for eighteenth-century agronomists they figured as the acme of rural society and hopes for future developments.

Historical revisionism has not downplayed the importance of rich tenant-farmers. Rather, scholars have examined more closely the "losers" in this trend toward bigger and bigger farms: the middle and small peasantry. In doing so, they have altered our picture of agrarian change. Thus, Robert C. Allen has argued that the agricultural revolution in England owed much to the middling groups of landowners (the yeomen) with 60 to 100 acres (25 to 40 hectares). They prospered in the sixteenth and especially the seventeenth century, introducing new crops, doubling their productivity, and laying the ground, so to speak, for the eighteenth-century large-scale improvements on big estates. Yet, by the eighteenth century large farms had the clear advantage over middling and small peasantry, although many more survived into the mid-nineteenth century than had been supposed.

Not too long ago, farm size was taken as the indicator of economic health: the bigger, the more efficient. The European ideal had once been the small, intensive, and highly productive family farm of medieval and early modern Flanders. By the eighteenth century this model had been superseded by the extensive farming (preferably of a specialized sort) using hired laborers—full-time servants, seasonal migrants, or local small peasants—which prevailed in Britain. This version governed analyses of economic growth from the eighteenth century onward. England was the model, France and other European countries poor replicas. Few people contest that the agricultural revolution began in England (though they disagree as to when) but they balk at the implicit value judgements. Local studies have shown that English progress was slower and more sporadic than once thought. Studies have also demonstrated that open-field farming could be as productive as enclosed properties. Concomitantly, research has revealed far more complicated and often advanced patterns on the Continent. The common understanding is that there was no right or wrong way to "modernity," but rather a multiplicity of paths. Regions once considered backward (Spain, for example), appear to have been as responsive to economic stimuli as "capitalist" England. If historians now uncover blockages in the way of economic growth, it is more in state taxation and the organization of markets than in seigneurial exactions, customary constraints, or forms of land tenure.

CONCLUSION

Land tenure, the historian Jerome Blum argued, can be divided into "good" and "bad." Good tenures made the least financial demands on peasants and their hold on them was most secure; bad tenures were accompanied by high demands for labor or rents and were revocable at will. Michael Bush has challenged that view, claiming that the best tenancies were in fact those that owed labor services, since peasants could spare the extra hands, profit from the security of tenure, be spared the fluctuations in prices, and avoid the dispossession of disinherited siblings that most western Europeans suffered. It is perhaps safest to say that peasants both lost and profited from agrarian regimes. The advent of private property in the eighteenth and nineteenth century, which abolished feudal eminent possession and made peasants the true proprietors of their holdings, freed peasants from irksome and sometimes onerous payments. At the same time, the concentration of land in a few hands—which progressed at different rates in different regions—meant that small and middling peasants were unable to compete in the long run, and had to abandon for good the small-scale part-time farming that had ordered peasant lives for centuries.

The mechanization of agriculture at the end of the nineteenth century, the important capital outlay that it required, and the vast properties that made it worthwhile transformed the European countryside yet again. Peasants, unable to compete, sold out, though in some parts of Europe not until after World War II. In Eastern Europe collectivized farms were imposed by Communist regimes, and briefly attempted by left-wing governments in the West, for example in Spain in the 1930s. Yet, it was the resilience of small-scale mixed farming that saved some Third World countries from total destitution in an era when foreign experts and the World Bank imposed on them the model of large-scale cash cropping. Such realizations are bound to complicate further our approach to and understanding of land tenure in the West.

See also **The Annales Paradigm; Marxism and Radical History** *(volume 1); and other articles in this section.*

BIBLIOGRAPHY

Allen, Robert C. *Enclosure and the Yeoman.* New York, 1992.

Aston, T. H., and C. H. Philpin, eds. *The Brenner Debate: Agrarian Class Structure and Economic Development in Pre-industrial Europe.* New York, 1985.

Audisio, Gabriel. *Les français d'hier.* Vol. 1: *Des paysans XVe–XIXe siècle.* Paris, 1993.

Blum, Jerome. *The End of the Old Order in Rural Europe.* Princeton, N.J., 1978.

Bloch, Marc. *French Rural Society: An Essay on Its Basic Characteristics.* Translated by Janet Sondheimer. Berkeley and Los Angeles, 1978.

Brewer, John, and Susan Staves, eds. *Early Modern Conceptions of Property.* London and New York, 1996.

Bush, M. L., ed. *Serfdom and Slavery: Studies in Legal Bondage.* London and New York, 1996

Chevet, Jean-Michel. *La terre et les paysans en France et en Grande-Bretagne: Du début du XVIIe à la fin du XVIIIe siècle.* Paris, 1998.

Epstein, S. R. "The Peasantries of Italy, 1350–1750." In *The Peasantries of Europe from the Fourteenth to the Eighteenth Centuries.* Edited by Tom Scott. London and New York, 1998. Pages 75–108.

Freedman, Paul. *The Origins of Peasant Servitude in Medieval Catalonia.* Cambridge, U.K., 1991.

Overton, Mark. *Agricultural Revolution in England: The Transformation of the Agrarian Economy 1500–1850.* Cambridge, U.K., 1996.

Poussou, Jean-Pierre. *La terre et les paysans en France et en Grande-Bretagne aux XVIIe et XVIIIe siècles.* Paris, 1999.

Redfeld, Robert. *Peasant Society and Culture: An Anthropological Approach to Civilization.* Chicago, 1956.

Ringrose, David. *Spain, Europe, and the "Spanish Miracle," 1700–1900.* Cambridge, U.K., 1996.

Rösener, Werner. *The Peasantry of Europe.* Translated by Thomas M. Barker. Oxford, 1994.

Scott, Tom, ed. *The Peasantries of Europe from the Fourteenth to the Eighteenth Centuries.* London and New York, 1998.

Vassberg, David. *Land and Society in Golden Age Castile.* Cambridge, U.K., 1984.

Wolf, Eric. *Peasants.* Englewood Cliffs, N.J., 1966.

SERFDOM: WESTERN EUROPE

Liana Vardi

Serfdom is a form of bondage. Unlike slavery in the Roman Empire or in the American South, where the slave was considered chattel for the master to treat as he or she pleased and had no legal recourse, serfdom came in many variants, and the rights and obligations of serfs differed from place to place. Serfdom was primarily a means of attaching peasants to the land, restricting their mobility and choice of how, where, and when to dispose of their own labor, and of extracting payments in return for services over which the landowner had a monopoly. Hence serfdom, like slavery, was predicated on the use of power by one group over another, but unlike slavery it rested on a modicum of consent because, despite the unequal distribution of power, the system was more responsive to peasant pressure and needs.

In the medieval West serfdom was a way of organizing agricultural production and governing people. In its latter function, and marxists would argue in the former as well, serfdom was thus linked to the fragmentation of power associated with the breakup of the Roman Empire and its successor states and the devolution of public powers to local lords. This process, known as feudalism, took centuries to evolve and then centuries to decline, so the history of serfdom becomes a pendant to western European state building. This article examines the social, economic, and political aspects of serfdom and reviews its cultural ramifications.

EMERGENCE OF SERFDOM

In the middle of the nineteenth century Karl Marx posited three stages of economic development: the ancient or slave mode of production, the feudal mode of production, and the capitalist mode of production, which he envisioned as eventually superseded by communism. Feudalism, in this schema, was a political system in which the ruling class extracted agricultural surpluses from peasants through the use of extraeconomic coercion. The survival of the ruling class depended on this oppression of the peasantry, an oppression most clearly displayed in the institution of serfdom. What was serfdom in this marxist model? In an era of extremely low yields, crops had to be grown on vast tracts of land to produce surpluses and required armies of laborers. Slavery was one answer to this problem but, with the disintegration of the Roman Empire and the disappearance of steady supplies of slaves, a homegrown version was devised that took some though not all the elements of slavery by evolving new ways of tying labor to the land. The decay of the state and its replacement with autonomous lordships was the natural consequence of this localized, low-level productivity. This version privileged the inner logic, the imperative dictating the forms both of serfdom and feudalism. The economic limitations of the era imposed the system most suited to surplus extraction.

Historians have not totally abandoned this interpretation but have introduced nuances and chronologies that render the process more diffuse, haphazard, and uneven. Local circumstances and local arrangements have become more important than abstract models in explaining how feudalism and serfdom actually worked. Moreover, the association between Roman slavery and medieval serfdom, once commonplace, has been challenged by interpretations that posit a break between the two in the ninth and tenth centuries and the full emergence of serfdom only in the eleventh.

Roman agriculture relied on slaves both on large estates and on small farms. On the bigger estates, slave gangs housed in dormitories cultivated the crops, while family farms might use one or two slave helpers. In the late Roman Empire, slaves were settled on estates divided into two sections: the reserve of land retained by the landowner and a series of plots given to the slaves to till as their own, hence their name *servi casati* (hutted slaves) or *coloni* (colonists), growing enough food to sustain themselves and their families. To remedy the labor shortage, slaves were permitted to marry. They were given a stake in the estate through plots, which they farmed and could pass on to their heirs. In return for these plots, the slaves owed the landowner rent, dues, services, and most importantly labor on their domains. Some slaves were not given land but were retained on the estate as servants. They were called *mancipia* to differentiate them from the landed serfs. Slaves passed on their servile status to their children. Later those enserfed by dint of their birth, a condition referred to in English as neifty, were known as bondsmen and bondswomen. In other languages they were *nativi per corpora, nativi domini de sanguine; hommes de corps, Leibeigene, and Erbuntertanen*. The historian Michael Bush has considered medieval serfdom an amalgam of this settlement of slaves and another late Roman development, the tying of peasant tenants to an estate by imperial decree. Those who rented land were forbidden from moving away, reducing them to bondage because of the land they occupied. They came to be called tenurial serfs, tenants of lands in villeinage, *serfs à la glèbe, Gutsunternanen,* and *servi terrae*. The origin of enserfment, via blood or via land tenure, continued to differentiate types of servility. Descendants of settled slaves generally owed more services than tenurial serfs who retained a higher status.

In the cases described above, slave and peasant were turned into serfs without their consent. Yet from the seventh to the tenth centuries, one finds repeated instances of peasants giving themselves into bondage, apparently willingly, and most frequently to churches and monasteries, to whom they donated their land, renting it back as bonded laborers. The reasons were manifold: piety, desire for protection in unsettled times, debt, and in some cases crime. These voluntary enserfments demonstrate that serfdom is a complicated process with numerous causes and ramifications that do not readily yield to simple schema.

SERVILE OBLIGATIONS

Whatever the means of their enserfment, over time serfs became liable to a range of payments and were expected to perform labor services for their lords. The most important services were agricultural labor on the demesne or that part of the estate the lord retained as his own, haulage and cartage, military aid or its equivalent, upkeep of the lord's castle, and food and lodging for the lord's men when they visited the area. Serfs remained at the master's mercy, meaning that he could dictate to them the terms and nature of their obligations at will. This arbitrariness, mainly the lot of bondsmen, was one of the most resented aspects of serfdom and the most combated. By the late Middle

Servile Obligations. Peasants receive orders from their lord before going to work in the fields. Facsimile of a miniature from *Propriétaire des choses,* fifteenth century, Library of the Arsenal, Paris. NORTH WIND PICTURE ARCHIVES

Ages serfs demanded and gradually obtained fixed dues and services, a situation that most tenurial serfs already enjoyed, except in those places and times when lords extended their demands and imposed harsher terms on all their dependants, a process examined below.

Although the system was predicated on labor services on the demesne, the trend in Western medieval serfdom was to reduce this forced labor. In region after region labor services fell by the thirteenth century from an initial three to six days a week to a maximum of a couple of weeks a year known as *corvées,* boons, or *noctes*. Since the several days they owed consisted of plowing and harvesting, the most important phases in the agricultural calendar, this continued service to the lord interrupted the serfs' work on their own plots. The reduction of labor services and their commutation into cash arose from the lords' increasing need for revenue. Over time they gave up tilling their properties directly and leased more of the demesne since collecting rent from serfs was more lucrative than feeding them. What is more, the rise in population in the twelfth and thirteenth centuries provided cheap seasonal labor for lords who continued to farm their domains.

Initially serfs paid symbolic annual rents on their tenures, a few coins supplemented by a fowl, eggs, a piece of linen, or another gift in kind, that expressed the lord's continued primary ownership of that land. The commutation of labor services to cash created an additional rent due either in cash or kind depending on the time and place.

Different types of tenures developed. While most serfs enjoyed long-term or perpetual leases known in Roman law as *emphyteutic,* other tenures were leased for shorter periods ranging from three to twenty-four years and rents were adjusted at the termination of each lease. One of the perceived advantages of serfdom for the peasant, historians reckon, was that it ensured long-term tenure, in the best of circumstances at fixed rents.

Since the system was predicated on the control of labor, serfs could not leave the estate, dispose of their land, or marry out of the lord's jurisdiction without his consent and the payment of a fee. They remained bound to the land with the greater independence that came from "owning" their plots and passing them on to their heirs and from the symbiotic relationship that made the landowners dependent on their work and their rent. This arrangement of demesne and peasant tenures with their array of labor services and rents, commonly referred to as the manorial system, spread throughout Europe in Carolingian times.

Attached to the manor or living alongside it was a free peasantry that survived the Roman Empire and the reconfiguration of barbarian tribes into small kingdoms in the fifth, sixth, and seventh centuries. These peasants owned farms large enough for a family to till, roughly the area worked by one plow, called *mansi, manses,* hides, or *Hufen,* that later became units of taxation. Free peasants answered to their territorial ruler, whether a king, duke, or count. They could appeal to his law, and they paid him taxes. To benefit from common pastures and woods, these free peasants might also pay a fee to the local landowner or lord. Their land, however, remained their sole property and was known as allodial. The debates about serfdom and its extent rest on divided opinions about the resilience of this free peasantry or its reduction, gradual or abrupt, to servitude around the eleventh century.

Debates about this process arise in part from the lack of documentation in an age when record keeping was decentralized and haphazard and invading Vikings, Saracens, and Magyars plundered monasteries and dispersed their archives. Debates also hinge on the changing meanings of terms inherited from Rome. Latin terms for slave, such as *servus* for men and *ancilla* for women, came to suggest different levels of dependency and were applied to serfs and freemen alike. At this juncture the new word "slave" (*esclave, esclavo, schiavo,* or *Sklave*) emerged in Europe from the Slav merchants who provided actual slaves in medieval times. The coexistence of personal and tenurial forms of servitude complicated matters because servitude was tied to individuals in some cases and to land in other cases. Over time free peasants might rent land on which they owed servile services, whereas serfs might till free land. Mixed marriages raised further questions about status. Did they enslave the freeman or free the slave? In Germany, for example, children's servility derived from the status of their mother. Roman law did not recognize slaves as it did free peasants, though research suggests that the law in the late empire did. In other words, slaves could not appeal to the royal or comitial courts that supplanted the Roman ones. Membership in village communities was initially denied to personal serfs though it might be extended to tenurial serfs. In time, however, the community came to accept and integrate them all.

Historians who question the continuity between Roman slavery and medieval serfdom point to a decrease in slavery in the ninth and tenth centuries. In Spain, for example, the upheavals caused by the invasions and the weaknesses of the post-Carolingian state allowed many to gain their freedom. When serfdom was imposed in the eleventh century, it fell on a free peasantry whose independence had deteriorated because of poverty. Subdivision of plots among heirs made successful farming difficult. Growing indebtedness forced many to forfeit or sell their land and to rent instead. In this version, only a minority of European peasants owned land by the eleventh century. What differentiated the remainder was the range of obligations attached to their tenures. Free tenants paid rent and owed services specified in leases, contracts, or by local custom. Serfs owed services and rent at the discretion of their lords. Since it was not in the interest of lords to alienate their tenants, conditions for serfs usually followed the custom of the manor, so in England these were sometimes called customary tenants. Changes in the nature of lordship in the eleventh century granted lords increased powers.

NEW FORM OF LORDSHIP

Roman and barbarian law codes defined person and status clearly, differentiating a citizen from a slave. The dilution and gradual erosion of these law codes into local customs as royal and public powers weakened in the aftermath of new invasions and the disintegration of the Carolingian state makes it extremely difficult and controversial to reconstruct a linear progression in rural relations and to generalize its extent. It is as if rural society disappeared into a tunnel to

371

reappear several centuries later with a different configuration. In some cases, slaves and freemen became serfs. Generic terms for "peasant," including *rustici* in Italian, *Bauer* in German, and *vilain* in French, entered the languages, although the equivalent term "villein" in English was confined to the unfree. Historians have associated these phenomena with two trends. As early as the ninth century, society was viewed by jurists and clerics as divided into three groups: those who prayed and those who fought supported by those who worked. All rustics were thus treated as part of the laboring class, one strain in the leveling process. More pertinent was the devolution of power lower down the social hierarchy from monarchs and counts to their knights and supporters, who were granted or who seized territories and legal and pecuniary rights over them. What had once been public authority was converted to and confused with private authority. These new lords, ensconced in castles their estates, acquired banal (pronounced bay-nal) lordship in English, *seigneurie banale* in French, and *Grundherrschaft* in German. The fact that free and unfree peasants lived on territories designated as banal lordships merged their status, for all became subject to the lord's law.

For some historians this process of dissolution began in the ninth century if not earlier. For others the transformation occurred around the year 1000. This latter thesis was put forward by the French medievalists Marc Bloch and Georges Duby, who posited a mutation in the eleventh century that significantly altered social relations in the French countryside. In this version, lords enjoyed uncontested authority for perhaps a century and a half. Then a hierarchy was reestablished and power accrued once again to counts, dukes, and as of the thirteenth and fourteenth centuries to monarchs. The overall thesis has been challenged by historians who question the date and the extent of the transformation. These scholars argue that changes in the eleventh century were neither clear-cut nor drastic, that lords did not obtain absolute authority, and that terminology is too uncertain to support wholesale assertions.

For Bloch, moreover, serfdom was characterized by three payments known in French as the *chevage,* a poll tax levied arbitrarily; the *formariage* (merchet), a fee to the lord for the right to marry a woman from outside the seigneurie by which the bride became a serf; and the *mainmorte* (heriot), which limited the serf's freedom in allocating his inheritance. All those liable to these restrictions and the fees that accompanied them were considered serfs, meaning the majority of peasants. Further research has demonstrated that the distinction between free and unfree loosened

as of the eleventh century, so even freeborn peasants might be liable to some of those fees. Consequently the payments did not necessarily indicate free or unfree status, at least in France. Common subjection to banal lordship became the defining criterion for payments and services. Categories such as "free" and "unfree" disappeared, yielding instead the mixture of independence and dependence that typified all medieval social relations.

ASPECTS OF BANAL LORDSHIP

The confusion of public and private powers allowed lords to prosecute, levy taxes on, and collect dues from their tenants, servile or not, and from the surviving free peasantry. The lord's role in defending the peace at a time when no other public authority existed meant that peasants of all stripe had to rely on the protection of his law court and his castle. This also meant that the lord had the means at hand to police his territory and to secure his peasants' obedience and, as long as neighboring lords cooperated, the power to pursue runaway serfs. In return for protection, peasants helped build and maintain castles and fortifications, and they might be asked to perform guard duty. As weaponry became more sophisticated and costly, they were no longer expected to follow their lord into battle, a drop in status in this warrior society. Yet they were expected to help him defray its costs. The commutation of physical services to monetary payments became more common as seigneurs needed more money to fight their wars and to provide their households with luxuries

The Austrian historian Otto Brunner has suggested that protection lay at the heart of the system. The lord ensured the safety of the inhabitants against marauders and protected their "rights" to their land against intruders. His authority resembled that of a head of household. Although the undisputed master, he was supposed to act for the benefit of his tenants and not arbitrarily. As lord he defended and upheld local custom, which devolved from old tribal law. The relationship between lord and peasant was not merely paternal but mirrored that between lord and vassal. The peasant, serf or free, who held a tenure from a lord owed him aid and fidelity, in some cases sealed by an oath. The lord bestowed on the peasant protection in times of war, food in times of famine, and at all times intercession with outside powers.

German historical tradition is more firmly attached to this feudal model than the English or the French. Werner Rösener, for example, attributes reciprocal obligations to the fact that both serfdom and

Harvesting. *Summer,* engraving by Pieter Brueghel the Elder (c. 1515–1569). PHILLIPS, THE INTERNATIONAL FINE ART AUCTIONEERS, UK/THE BRIDGEMAN ART LIBRARY

feudalism originated in the Roman estate system and in Teutonic tribal customs, which stressed clientage and oath taking. This similarity between serfdom and the feudal ceremonies of vassalage can be clearly perceived in the ritual of seisin, which took place at the death of a serf and the transfer of his holding to his heir. With a symbolic gesture, sometimes in the form of a rod passed to and fro, the lord "recovered" his land and then "granted it anew" to the heir, who thus acknowledged the lord's primary ownership and hence his right to dues and services.

The fee on marriage (merchet) gave rise to a peculiar legend built around the ritual accompanying the lord's agreement to a serf's marriage. In some places he gestured toward or even crossed over the marriage bed. Over time this practice expanded into the myth of the "lord's first night," the right of the lord to deflower the bride. In the eighteenth century, thanks to plays by Voltaire and Pierre-Augustin Beaumarchais and to Wolfgang Amadeus Mozart's opera *The Marriage of Figaro* (1786), this so-called right encapsulated for contemporaries all the horrors and humiliations of serfdom.

Banal lordship gave unscrupulous lords a free hand to increase their demands from their tenants, who lost their capacity to appeal to outside authorities. What is more, the distance from or dissolution of public justice meant that it became increasingly difficult for peasants to prove their original freedom by a court writ, in the case of England, to demonstrate that they held allodial land protected by the king. The lord's main asset was his law court. Although the devolution of public and royal power meant that some lords obtained what is known as high or blood justice allowing them to judge criminal cases, symbolized by a gallows, real profits came from low and middle justice, that is, civil suits and the settlement of local disputes, and in particular from fines for contravening the lord's orders and decrees. Peasants were fined for every breach of the peace, for quarrels and insults, for petty thefts, for indecent behavior, for scavenging, and for planting and harvesting before the official date. Judges in these cases were the lord's appointed stewards, who received a portion of the fines. Interestingly, although slaves had no legal existence and could not be called as witnesses, serfs, whatever their origins, were treated as full members of the community and served on the lord's court.

Banal power gave the lord the further right to monopolize some basic facilities and to force his peasants to use them. These monopolies most commonly consisted of the flour mill, the communal oven, and the winepress. The lord also charged tolls on markets, duties on goods crossing his territory,

373

and fees for the use of his forest and for the right to hunt and fish.

Banal authority therefore could prove extremely remunerative. The weight of these exactions varied from place to place since, by definition, banal authority was local and private. It could even vary from one manor to another, depending on the particular terms granted a tenant, serf, or peasant. At its harshest, banal authority yielded one-third of the lord's revenues above and beyond rent and taxes. Lords were eager to maintain such prerogatives and only desisted when peasants fled en masse or when an outside authority intervened to challenge the legality of lordly demands. Banal lordship was eventually defeated by peasant resistance and by the development of state power, which staked its claims to peasant revenues.

PEASANT RESISTANCE

Banal lordship gave lords power over their peasants, serfs and free alike, that exceeded the presumed compensation for their use of the lord's land in perpetuity or for limited time periods. Excessive or new demands, the subjection to a humiliating string of payments, and arbitrary treatment already were decried by peasants as "bad customs" (*mals usos, mauvaises coutumes, malos usos*) in the tenth and eleventh centuries. Their grievances often went unheeded by lords and rulers, even if they were duly noted by clerics. Some historians have even posited that the worse abuses only existed in the minds of monks.

Peasants resisted in big and small ways. They dragged their feet, performed services perfunctorily, pilfered, were late in their payments, or fled. The village community, once it became better organized, provided some autonomy from the lord and mutual support in case of conflict. When conditions grew intolerable, peasants rebelled. In a society controlled by landowners with full policing powers, intolerable conditions often were imposed by lords seeking to increase their revenues and to reduce all peasants to the status of serfs. Rebellious peasants might succeed in convincing their lord to rescind some of the worst abuses or, most likely, to let them buy them off. Commutation of services to rent was one such result. Peasants neither rebelled constantly nor fled their lords at the slightest provocation because the system provided them with some important benefits. They were given protection in insecure times but more importantly they owned their land, even if in return for rent and services, and could pass it on to their heirs. This made it hard to pick up and leave. Lords for the most part wanted to keep good tenants, even servile ones, and so did not always treat them harshly, even if they had the authority to do so. In fact another cause of peasant rebellion in the late Middle Ages and certainly one of its most common justifications was the perceived decline in mutualism, the sense that the system was breaking down and that lords were no longer fulfilling their obligations. When lords failed to render services and merely demanded them, the peasants felt justified in rebelling.

Peasant rebellions became more common in the late thirteenth century and the fourteenth century with worsening economic conditions. Population growth had fragmented holdings, increasing peasant demand for land and encouraging landowners to raise rents, even on plots where rents were fixed. The drop in population by one-third in western Europe as a result of the Black Death in 1348 caused the retreat of serfdom in some regions as lords facing depopulated villages granted peasants franchises to induce them to stay. In England, on the other hand, the Black Death made lords apply legal constraints more severely, tying peasants to their estates. A peasant rebellion in 1381 demanded the end of the lords' arbitrary powers, asking the king to force lords to follow local customs and to provide fixed terms. Although the rebellion failed in the short-term, as of 1400 serfdom was on the decline, and it soon disappeared altogether from England. In 1525 German peasants rebelled against the reintroduction of serfdom as lords began once more to tie peasants to their estates. Although the revolt was brutally put down, western German peasants managed to regain their freedom, whereas their eastern German counterparts saw their liberties extinguished.

THE END OF SERFDOM

How widespread was banal lordship? What proportion of peasants were enserfed? Historians can provide only vague estimates. When historians relied principally on legal definitions of the free and the unfree, they concluded that most European peasants were serfs in the Middle Ages. In the second half of the twentieth century, however, historians turned to regional studies to undertstand how feudalism and serfdom functioned at the manorial, village, or county level. This has yielded a much more complex picture of the phenomenon, blurring distinctions. Serfs and the freeborn recombined in different configurations depending on the time and place. Few therefore are able or willing to hazard overall conclusions. Still, it appears that servitude did not exist in most of Scandinavia but was widespread in Denmark. It was weak in Spain except for Catalonia. In Italy serfdom was commuted into payments early as townspeople helped peasants gain franchises from lords. Seigneurial dues disappeared altogether in the fourteenth century from central and northern regions of Italy but lasted longer in the south. The Normans introduced serfdom into Sicily and England when they conquered those areas in the eleventh century. Serfdom prevailed in northern France, Flanders, southwestern Germany, and England and gradually vanished from these areas between the twelfth and fifteenth centuries. At its height in England, in the fourteenth century, 40 percent of peasants were serfs. In France, on the other hand, by the end of the twelfth century only 20 percent of peasants remained in servitude. In those areas in France, Germany, or Switzerland where serfdom survived into the fifteenth century, it was not abolished until the French Revolution or its aftermath. Out of 27 million total inhabitants, several hundred thousand serfs still existed in France in 1789, located mainly in Burgundy and Franche-Comté, whose serfdom derived from the type of tenure. Their servile payments varied from severe to light, depending on the locality. Moreover, lords throughout France retained most of their monopolies and their right to levy feudal dues on peasants, serf or free, through the early modern period. All such vestiges of feudalism were swept away during the Revolution.

From the first, individual serfs could buy their freedom, although the price of this manumission varied from place to place. The more general process of liberation, on the other hand, required the connivance of the state with the peasants. This happened when territorial rulers began to rebuild their authority and to reclaim from lords their rights to peasant incomes and taxation. This process went hand in hand with the right of appeal to the king's law courts. In England freemen recovered this privilege as of 1200. Reference to Roman imperial law helped late medieval territorial rulers justify their claims to power. One of the consequences of this reintroduction of Roman law was that it brought back sharp distinctions between the free and the unfree, meaning freeman and serfs, where medieval practice had blurred these distinctions. Some peasants therefore were relegated to the status of the unfree, increasing their lords' arbitrary powers over them. If monarchs wanted to liberate peasants and serfs from the lords and turn them into taxable subjects, they needed to support peasants against their lords, heed their grievances, and reduce the lords' capacity to levy dues and taxes and to have full legal powers over them. Except for Catalonia, such emancipation occurred piecemeal and not by general decree. French peasants, for example, bought their free-

dom in the thirteenth and fourteenth centuries with payments to the crown.

Rulers' collusion with lords, on the other hand, retarded such liberation. Servitude was enforced in England in the eleventh century and again in the fourteenth century because the developing state sided with lords. Lords, moreover, agreed to support each other by not granting asylum to runaway serfs. In Catalonia lords also managed to dictate terms, and the king permitted the introduction of serfdom there in the thirteenth century, much later than elsewhere. Servitude was abolished when a stronger monarch backed the peasants' demand for redemption in 1486, after a series of local rebellions.

Since serfdom disappeared in western Europe gradually, unlike in eastern Europe, where it would be abolished officially in the nineteenth century as in Catalonia, in the sixteenth century, the process has been ascribed to

(a) the blurring of free and unfree under banal lordship;
(b) peasant resistance and the support of the state;
(c) changes in husbandry and development of the village community;
(d) land clearance, new settlement, and the granting of franchises; and
(e) changes in mentality.

Of these causes, the last three still need discussion in this article.

Changes in agricultural practices altered the way the village community functioned and transformed the place of the peasants within it. The most important changes in agricultural practice were the introduction of the heavy plow triennial rotation, improved husbandry, and what is known as open field farming sometime between the eleventh and thirteenth centuries. These contributed to a rise in crop yields from the measly 2.5 to 1 in the sixth and seventh centuries to 4 to 1 on the poorest soils and 10 to 1 on the best by the thirteenth century, allowing a significant rise in population. The western European population tripled between 1000 and 1300, growing from about 15 million to 45 million. In England, where the Domesday Book (1086) provides information for the eleventh century, estimates are that the population quadrupled between 1086 and 1348, the year of the Black Death.

The new plow allowed the tillage of heavy northern soils, best suited to cereals, where the light Roman plow had been next to useless. These improved plows were pulled by oxen and, in the richest areas, by horses, who were more effective but also more expensive. Given the expense of the plow and

Planting. The illustration for March from *Très riches heures du Duc de Berry* showing peasants at work on a feudal estate. VICTORIA & ALBERT MUSEUM, LONDON/THE BRIDGEMAN ART LIBRARY

especially of the team of oxen or horses, only the richest peasants, free and unfree, could afford them. They owed more labor services than the poor as lords demanded that they plow their demesnes. In villages the distinction between rich and poor peasants became more important than that between the freeborn and serfs.

Another innovation was triennial rotation. Given the lack of adequate fertilizer, soils were exhausted quickly. To allow the land to rest and recover some of its fertility, farmland was usually divided into two rotations. Half of the land was planted while the other half remained fallow, and the following year the order was reversed. The introduction sometime in the twelfth century of triennial rotation complicated this arrangement. A third rather than half of the land lay fallow, one-third was sown in the fall with the main cereal crop, usually wheat, and another third was sown in spring with oats to feed horses and cattle. This system increased crop yield, and it also led to a realignment of the fields. Although no one knows when the system emerged exactly or why, by the thirteenth century most villages had switched to open field farming. The entire village arable was divided into three sections rather than each farm, and peasants owned segments in each of the sections. This arrangement required the cooperation of all villagers. Dates for sowing, plowing, and harvesting had to be set so one peasant would not trample another's crop entering the fields. The lord's ban often regulated this communal farming, setting the dates and policing the fields to make sure no one contravened them. This merger of plots was yet another element that diluted the difference between serfs and freeman.

The third factor in transforming the status of serf and peasant was the reclamation of land and the extension of the arable that began in the eleventh century. In some cases peasants just cleared bits of the forest to extend their own plots and to settle their children. This was done with or without the consent of the lord. More important were the colonization schemes undertaken by lords, who sought to increase the number of dues-paying tenants. Opening up land was costly. Trees had to be felled and marshes drained. Lords invested heavily in such enterprises, providing tools and materials, sometimes in association with other lords. Attracting settlers became so important to the future income of lords that they were willing both to pay the initial price and to grant these new settlers, known in French as *hôtes* or guests, advantageous terms, such as personal freedom and fixed rents. Some scholars have argued that extending their banal authority was sufficiently lucrative for lords to offset the loss of servile duties. Lords were coming to rely on monetary rents and on the casualties of the ban for their income. Release from serfdom was granted to new settlers on old manors or to new settlements, and these franchises were gradually extended to older peasant communities lest all the tenants flee.

Given these developments and the importance of the peasant community in regulating economic life and in creating new solidarities, some historians have minimized the importance of legal categories such as free and unfree in defining peasants, focusing instead on their economic status and on the internal functioning of the community. Yet, as other scholars point out, serfs were eager to buy their freedom and found the taint of servitude humiliating, even where it was not onerous in practice.

SERFDOM IN MEDIEVAL CULTURE

Granting that serfdom arose out of the debris of the Roman Empire and disappeared from most of western Europe in the sixteenth century yields about seven hundred years during which serfdom was not only practiced but also theorized. Christian theology made its peace with the physical bondage of slavery and serfdom by stressing the freedom of the soul. Yet, as Paul Freedman's 1999 study shows, the issue was not clear-cut, and debates about serfdom abounded in the Middle Ages. Although medieval thought accepted inequality as a matter of course, ancient justifications of slavery were difficult to transpose because serfs, unlike slaves, were Christian and native-born. Instead, servitude was treated as the consequence of sin. A life of toil was Adam's curse but also his means of redemption. Serfdom was considered the product of another sin. Noah's son Ham laughed at his father's nakedness and was condemned along with his descendants to serve his brothers. This biblical explanation for the origin of serfdom was especially popular in Germany. In France and Spain another legend served the same purpose. Serfs were said to be the descendants of those cowards who had refused to follow Charlemagne into battle against the Saracens in the eighth century, choosing bondage or the payment of a servile tax instead. In England serfdom was attributed to the Norman conquest, before which all Englishmen had supposedly been free. Hence serfs in the fourteenth century believed that records existed that might prove their original liberty.

Everywhere rustics were mocked, reviled, and depicted as no better than beasts. Be they wealthy or poor, medieval characterizations reduced all peasants to the level of serfs. Although nobles and ecclesiastics depended on peasant labor, agricultural work was consistently debased. The struggle against serfdom, from the peasants' perspective, involved fighting its arbitrariness and burdensome payments and asserting their humanity and the dignity of labor. Stories like that of the Swiss peasant-hero William Tell challenged the notion of the cowardly peasant. Parts of the scriptures and classical authors such as Virgil and Horace showed that peasant labor could be associated with rustic virtue. More importantly, peasants argued that Christ had liberated all human beings from sin, including from Ham's curse.

During the Middle Ages, in the words of Freedman, "freedom was understood not as a release from all bonds to others but as immunity from the arbitrary will of others." Peasants denounced lordship, which consisted in this power, as unjust, capricious, and degrading. By the fourteenth century in France, the fifteenth century in England and Spain, and the sixteenth century in western Germany, territorial rulers were ready to heed those complaints and to liberate the peasants from this thrall. The most demeaning aspects of bondage were eliminated seigneurie by seigneurie. Peasants became free to move, to marry as they pleased, and to sell their plots without the lord's intervention. Rents, fixed dues, and obligations took the place of serfdom. The days of the lords and the economic system that bolstered their authority had passed.

See also **The Medieval Heritage** *(volume 1);* **Peasants and Rural Laborers; Slaves; Rural Revolts** *(volume 3); and other articles in this section.*

BIBLIOGRAPHY

Barthélemy, Dominique. *La mutation de l'an mil, a-t-elle eu lieu?* Paris, 1997.

Bloch, Marc. *Feudal Society.* Translated by L. A. Manyon. Chicago, 1961.

Blum, Jerome. *The End of the Old Order in Rural Europe.* Princeton, N.J., 1978.

Bourin, Monique, and Michel Parisse. *L'Europe au siècle de l'an mil.* Paris, 1999.

Boureau, Alain. *The Lord's First Night: The Myth of the Droit de Cuissage.* Translated by Lydia B. Cochrane. Chicago, 1998.

Brunner, Otto. *Land and Lordship: Structures of Governance in Medieval Austria.* Translation and introduction by Howard Kaminsky and James van Horn Melton. Philadelphia, 1992.

Bush, M. L., ed. *Serfdom and Slavery: Studies in Legal Bondage.* London and New York, 1996.

Duby, Georges. *The Early Growth of the European Economy: Warriors and Peasants from the Seventh to the Twelfth Century.* Translated by Howard B. Clarke. Ithaca, N.Y., 1974.

Duby, Georges, and Armand Wallon, eds. *Histoire de la France rurale.* Vol. 1. Paris, 1975.

Freedman, Paul. *Images of the Medieval Peasant.* Stanford, Calif., 1999.

Freedman, Paul. *The Origins of Peasant Servitude in Medieval Catalonia.* Cambridge, U.K., 1991.

Genicot, Léopold. *Rural Communities in the Medieval West.* Baltimore, 1990.

Goetz, Hans-Werner. *Life in the Middle Ages from the Seventh to the Thirteenth Century.* Translated by Albert Wimmer. Notre Dame, Ind., 1993.

Little, Lester K., and Barbara H. Rosenwein, eds. *Debating the Middle Ages.* Malden, Mass., 1998.

Rösener, Werner. *The Peasantry of Europe.* Translated by Thomas M. Barker. Oxford, 1994.

Scott, Tom, ed. *The Peasantries of Europe.* London and New York, 1998.

SERFDOM: EASTERN EUROPE

Boris B. Gorshkov

Serfdom was a system of relations between the owners of land and the peasant tenants who resided on it. These relations involved a variety of social, sociopsychological, cultural, economic, legal, and political aspects that together made serfdom a complex societal institution. During the fourteenth and fifteenth centuries, just when serfdom had begun to decline in many parts of western Europe, a similar institution based on servility emerged in eastern Europe. During the seventeenth and eighteenth centuries, east European serfdom matured and approached its climax; by the mid-nineteenth century it had declined and was abolished. Serfdom in eastern Europe was influenced by a multiplicity of political, economic, cultural, and intellectual developments that occurred in the world and the continent in general, and in each east European state in particular, throughout its existence. Although it reflected many similar economic and legal characteristics, such as its agricultural orientation and the juridical rights lords enjoyed over peasants, east European serfdom was by no means identical to its west European counterpart. Serfdom in eastern Europe was not monolithic; it differed from one state to another. The varied geography, ecology, and climate of eastern Europe lent strong regional variation to this institution. During the period of its existence, east European serfdom also experienced important social changes. Historians of east European serfdom traditionally emphasize its political or economic aspects; they concentrate on the consolidation and centralization of state power or focus on the development of master-serf economic and labor relations. Some of these studies are monochromatic in their portrayal of east European peasants as slavelike, dark, passive, and isolated. Although this essay does not ignore these traditional approaches to serfdom in eastern Europe, namely in Austro-Hungary, East Elbian Germany, Poland, Prussia, the Baltic States, and Russia, its analysis turns on a discussion of relatively dynamic social and economic factors and, where appropriate, on regional variations.

ORIGINS OF SERFDOM

Before the sixteenth century, when serfdom became a legally established institution, east European peasants, unlike the majority of the peasantry of western Europe, enjoyed a considerable degree of freedom. They lived on the land in settlements known as communes. Although sometimes these lands belonged to the peasants themselves, the majority of communes were settled on lands that belonged either to an individual landlord, to the church, or to the state. A peasant village and the landlord's lands on which it was settled constituted the landlord's estate, known as the manor. Peasant-tenants who resided on landlords' lands were free to move and to act, for the most part, subject to their own will. Peasants either worked the landlord's fields or paid annual fees for the land they utilized. Reciprocally, the landlord administered justice and provided his peasants with certain legal and military protections. Thus, traditions of lord-peasant relations originated long before serfdom became a legally established institution.

The process of enserfment in eastern Europe consisted of the gradual economic and legal binding of free peasant-tenants to the land and in some cases to the lord; this process took several centuries. Enserfment was not a result of a single factor but a product of a combination of many complex historical forces. Internal political, economic, and social developments within the east European states (such as centralization and expansion, warfare, epidemics, and so on), as well as the general political and economic situation outside the region, were perhaps the most important key factors in the development of serfdom. Yet, the gradual binding of the majority of the east European population to the land was also a product of the mentality of the early modern aristocracy of eastern Europe. The aristocracy viewed enserfment as the only solution to the political, economic, and social changes it faced.

The deterioration of the status of free peasant tenants, the earliest stage in the enserfment of peasants, began in eastern Europe by the fifteenth century. Landlords, who were gaining political and economic strength, exerted more and more power over the subjects who populated their lands by increasing their economic and juridical subjugation. Political factors played a role, where weak governments encouraged landlord control for lack of other measures; this was compounded in Russia by the steady expansion of territory. But economic factors loomed larger. These included the expansion of markets and the sixteenth-century price revolution, processes that intensified this protoenserfment. The growth of cities, and towns and the development of nonagricultural villages provided new demands for agricultural production. Willing to seize these new economic opportunities, the lords sought to expand the size of their estates. The export of cereals became a basic element of the agricultural economy of the southeastern, central, and Baltic regions of Europe. For example, during the sixteenth century grain exports from Poland increased as much as tenfold. The Netherlands, England, Spain, and Portugal became major consumers of east European grain. Although agricultural productivity in eastern Europe was relatively low, the inexpensive labor of economically dependent peasants kept agricultural production cheap. In order to secure the labor force, landlords shifted their peasants from traditional rent in kind (agricultural commodities) to labor duties. In areas where nonagricultural activities predominated (such as in the northern and central areas of Russia), peasants usually paid rent in kind (various products of cottage industry). Later on, as the money economy expanded, rent in kind was largely succeeded by money rent.

The desire of the landlords to increase estate production put increased economic pressure on the peasants, resulting in indebtedness and economic dependence upon landlords. The indebtedness tended to fix peasants for lengthy periods of time on landlords' estates. Landlords viewed these long time residents as bound to the estates. Others, the more active and energetic peasants, preferred to flee from the estates. The increasing indebtedness, along with the devastation from warfare, famine, epidemics, and pestilence that beset the early modern east European landscape, caused mass peasant migrations from the old settled areas to the peripheries. In order to prevent these migrations, the emerging and consolidating state power sought to eliminate the territorial mobility of peasants.

Political consolidation and centralization of some east European states, as well as the integration of new lands into the existing states, accompanied and, indeed, accelerated the process of enserfment. The ties between the landlord and the peasant, with the latter's waxing economic dependence upon the former, were juridically strengthened. For example, in Poland, a 1496 statute introduced, and later the 1501 law code reinforced, limits on peasant mobility. By 1540 Polish peasants were tied to the land and could not migrate without authorization from landlords. In 1538 the Brandenburg Landtag prohibited unauthorized migration and bound thousands of Brandenburg peasants to the land. During the 1580s and onward a series of decrees heavily restricted peasant movement in Russia (early limited restrictions originated in the late fifteenth century). The 1649 law code finally tied millions of Russian peasants to the soil. Additionally, in order to provide financially for their bureaucratic and military needs, the consolidating states introduced various taxes and duties on the peasantry. During this period, similar processes occurred in most parts of eastern Europe. The legislation not only restricted peasant mobility and increased the economic burdens upon peasants but also gave landlords legal, juridical, executive, and police powers over them. On their estates, landlords became tax collectors, judges, and policemen, on behalf of the state. The state transformed the economic dependence of the peasant upon the landlord into the peasant's legal dependence, indeed subordination, thus almost completely destroying peasant freedom.

Another factor that stimulated the deterioration of the position of the peasantry was slave labor. Although slave labor had declined by the sixteenth century, a small number of slaves still existed in some parts of eastern Europe. On the one hand, as the bondage of economically dependent peasants increased, their status gradually fused with that of the slaves. On the other hand, slaves were included in taxation, which eventually eliminated their slave status. Thus, as a result of all these factors, by the mid-seventeenth century serfdom became a legally established institution in eastern Europe. Legal restrictions on their mobility reduced millions of peasants to the status of serfs tied to the soil and to the lord.

SERFDOM AND THE LAW

Originating from the economic needs of the landowning nobility and then bolstered by the politics of the state, east European serfdom was a social institution that lasted over two hundred years. Perhaps the most important social feature of east European serfdom, like any other serfdom, is that it occurred in a society numerically dominated by the peasantry. At the time serfdom was established, the peasantry accounted for about 80 to 90 percent of the population of the region. Approximately half of the peasants lived on individual landlords' lands and thus were serfs, whereas the balance who lived on church and state lands did not fit into the category of serfdom. Landlords constituted only about 1 percent of the population and owned lands populated with large numbers of peasants who performed agricultural or other labor. An average landlord's estate held several hundred peasants, with individual estates running from a handful to tens of thousands of peasants (several Polish, Hungarian, and Russian magnates owned hundreds of thousands). East European landlords thus lived in an overwhelmingly peasant society. With a few exceptions (the Baltic regions, Polish-Ukrainian lands), most peasants and landlords were of the same ethnicity and shared common cultural and religious roots. Peasants constituted the very essence of their respective nations, being the major social element and the principal source of the national economy and culture.

The complexities and ambiguities of east European serfdom require emphasis. Despite the essential oppressiveness of serfdom, the legislation that enforced it also enabled peasants to sustain their basic economic and social needs. The laws that tied millions of east European peasants to the land at the same time provided the peasantry with the ability for temporary employment outside the ascribed place of residence, as well as for various trading, commercial, and even entrepreneurial pursuits within and away from the village. On the one hand, serfs were sometimes bought and sold at the will of their landlords; on the other, they were protected by laws against personal insult and unreasonable corporal punishment. In Russia, despite bans on serf complaints against their lords, peasants often sued the lords in state courts and sometimes succeeded in bringing to trial those who violated their rights. Serfs also frequently applied to legal institutions seeking emancipation. Having the goal of preserving hierarchy, serfdom simultaneously and somewhat paradoxically opened the door to a certain social mobility for peasants. These legal loopholes constituted a basis for maintaining a certain balance between the interests of the state and the nobility on one side and these of the peasantry on the other.

In fact, neither the state nor the landlord had an interest in totally attaching the peasants to the land. In order to sustain the economic needs of the state and of the landlord, peasants had to have a certain freedom to move (this was particularly crucial in those areas where agriculture was not a primary occupation or where nearby urban centers offered greater earning possibilities). None of the laws in eastern Europe that restricted peasant freedom provided for complete bondage. For example, the notorious Russian 1649 law code indeed heavily restricted the peasant's ability to move. Not commonly realized is that, at the same time, the law granted the peasant the right to migrate temporarily, with proper authorization, in order to seek employment outside the estate. No authorization was required for those peasants who temporarily migrated within thirty-two kilometers of the estate, a legally sanctioned unofficial and uncounted migration. (By the end of the eighteenth century about a quarter of the serfs of Russia's central provinces officially temporarily migrated each year.) Thus, east European serfs were never completely bound to the land; they could be and in fact often were on the move. This provided peasants with opportunities to establish a certain degree of autonomy from their lords.

The social, economic, and cultural importance of the peasants thus allowed them to stretch the boundaries of serfdom. Nevertheless, because legislation in east European states established the authority of the lord over the peasantry, in Russia and Poland the lords came to view and treat peasants as their private property. In estate surveys peasants were listed under the heading of private property. Contemporary legal documents disclose that serfs were sold, mortgaged, and given as gifts. The sale of serfs occurred throughout eastern and central Europe and approached its high point in the eighteenth century. For example, during the American War of Independence (1775–1783) German landlords sold about 29,000 young peasants to the British as soldiers. Russian rulers authorized the sale of serfs to encourage mining and industry. In Russia, the sale of peasants reached its apogee during the reign of Catherine the Great, as attested to by newspaper advertisements of such sales. In most cases, east European peasants were sold with the land they populated and farmed. In other words, these transactions simply signified the transfer of entire villages or large parts of villages to new owners. The sale of serfs without land, which did occur in some cases, provoked contemporary social critics to condemn this practice as the most inhumane and brutal feature of serfdom.

In order to restrict such sales, some states introduced minute regulations into existing laws on the possession of peasants. Eventually, laws banned outright the sale and mortgage of peasants without land, as well as newspaper advertisements of such sales. Some state legislation restricted unreasonable punishment and mistreatment of peasants. Strict sanctions and penalties awaited lords who transgressed the new rules. For example, the Polish law of 1768 provided the death penalty for lords who deliberately caused the death of serfs. In Russia, during the reign of Catherine the Great (1762–1796), about twenty landowners were tried for causing the deaths of their serfs. Two were exiled to Siberia for life and five were sentenced to hard labor for life. Although the number of lords tried and sanctioned was modest, the fact of their harsh punishment arguably served as a lesson to other landowners. New laws increased state regulation of the lord-peasant relationship in such a way as to place sterner limits on the lord's authority. This legislative tendency accelerated toward the end of the eighteenth century and continued until the final abolition of serfdom.

THE SOCIAL INSTITUTIONS OF SERFS: FAMILY AND COMMUNE

More important than legal restrictions of the landlords' power, peasants themselves deployed a wide array of extralegal means to dilute the lords' influence. Peasants developed and maintained cultural values, customs, traditions, and institutions that enabled them to survive by maintaining a balance between external forces and their own communal and individual needs. When conditions became unendurable, peasants protested, withheld their labor, rebelled, and even murdered offending authorities and lords. Hallowed tradition and indigenous institutions, plus a hint of threat, enabled peasants to set limits on the landlords' power and authority, as well as to achieve a certain independence from them.

The family. The family was one such institution. In most cases regarding family affairs and strategies, as well as actual decision making, the family enjoyed a significant degree of autonomy from the landlord. The family was headed by its eldest member, usually the grandfather, known as the patriarch. Patriarchs had a dominant role in making decisions about and supervising the daily activities of other family members and represented the family in communal institutions. Some historians argue that the position and authority of the patriarch in the family was unchallengeable and that this arrangement simultaneously contributed to the development of patriarchal culture among the peasantry. In contrast, some anthropological researchers emphasize the patriarch's responsibility to the family and point out that all major family matters, such as the household economy, property, and the marriage of children, were usually settled in family meetings that consisted of all adult family members, males as well as females. In certain cases the family meeting could displace an inept patriarch and appoint a new family head. For these scholars, the authority of the patriarch was not unlimited; the process of decision making resulted from discussion and compromise among all concerned parties rather than exclusively from the authoritarian will of the patriarch.

Many peasants, particularly in Russia, spent a considerable part of their lives in structurally complex, two- and three-generational households. The family ties of peasants were usually extensive. Structural complexity, however, is not peculiar to households in eastern Europe. Family systems throughout preindustrial Europe were widely diverse depending upon local patterns of political and economic settlement, demography, culture, and ecological factors. Anthropological research illustrates that in preindustrial eastern Europe peasant household structures varied. For example, in southern Estonia extended households were common, whereas nuclear family households prevailed in northern Estonia. In Hungary complex households were more typical for serfs than for other categories of peasants. In Russia, as well as in other parts of eastern Europe, extended families often reflected a certain stage of family development and were quite changeable. For example, young couples lived under the same roof with their parents until they had saved enough money to start their own households. Some historians note that the household size of serf families slightly increased between the seventeenth and nineteenth centuries. Thus, family structures among east European serfs were varied, while usually fitting one or another definition of extended or complex family.

Peasant marriages, performed according to local tradition and custom, received full legal sanction. A marriage contract was usually agreed upon by the couple's parents. Landlords rarely intervened in marriage contracts and usually did not separate serf families. The marriage age of serfs was relatively low in comparison to that of nonserf peasants and to west European peasants of that period. For example, in mid-nineteenth-century Russia, the average marriage age for men was twenty-three and for women nineteen. The pattern of low marriage age for serfs to a certain degree reflected the economic pressures of serfdom because the newly married couple constituted a work unit with its own share of communal land and property. Each couple had the legal and common right to establish its own household.

The commune. Most east European peasant families lived in villages (settlements with households, small stores, mills, communal buildings, a church, and a cemetery); one or more of these villages constituted the peasant commune. The peasant commune was the most important economic and social feature

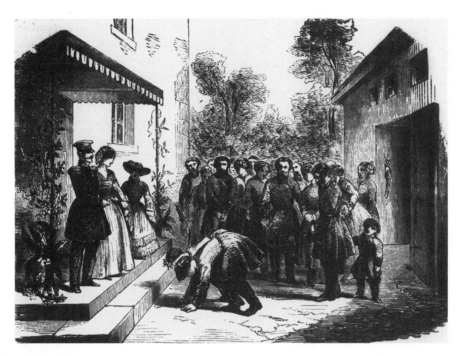

Russian Serfs. A serf couple about to marry present themselves to the estate owners. Nineteenth-century print. ©BETTMANN/CORBIS

of east European serfdom. Through the commune's assembly, represented by the family heads (the patriarchs), the peasants managed village resources, directed economic and fiscal activities, and maintained internal order. The authority of the commune over the village varied, depending upon local custom and the degree to which the landlord restricted its autonomy. The serf commune was a site for interactions between the landlord and the village; the communal elders consulted the lord about appropriate taxes, duties, obligations, and recruitments into the military. The commune controlled land redistribution where it occurred; coordinated agriculture (for example, made decisions about suitable crops and determined the dates of sowing and harvesting); sold, exchanged, or leased lands; and rented or bought additional land as needed. The profit from the sale and lease of communal property was deposited in the communal treasury or divided directly among the households. The commune checked weights and measures, determined the quality of bread and beer, and set the wages of day laborers. The commune often supervised the moral behavior of its members and regulated the religious and social life of the village.

Community assemblies also had important juridical functions, such as resolving intra- and inter-village conflicts and representing the community's interests in all legal institutions. In Austria, Germany, and Lithuania, village community courts settled internal disputes and levied sanctions against guilty parties. In seventeenth century Russia, village commune representatives participated directly in the landlord's court, whereas in eastern Germany they acted as advisers to it. Additionally, in some regions communal assemblies filed suits in courts seeking adjudication when deprived of their interests and rights by their own lords or anyone else. Some even won their cases.

Scholars debate the role of the commune in the agricultural economy, the degree of its autonomy from the landlord, and many other specific aspects that cannot reasonably be addressed here. Some specialists argue that serf communes carved out a certain autonomy primarily because they served as instruments of the landlords. In this interpretation, the communes upheld the landlords' interests, ensuring that every household fulfilled its manorial and state obligations. In contrast, other observers comment that the commune did not always act in the landlords' interests. Communal obligations were usually agreed upon with the lord in advance, with firm commitments from both sides. When lords unilaterally increased already negotiated and fixed duties, communes often protested vociferously and refused to comply.

The commune's practice (in Russia and to some extent in other parts of eastern Europe) of periodic redistribution of arable land among households also remains a subject of scholarly controversy. Some historians claim that redistribution was largely a result of serfdom. In this interpretation, landlords required peasants to redivide their lands in order to coordinate each household's landholdings with its labor capability based upon the number of hands in the family, with the overall goal of maximizing the household's labor effectiveness and productivity. Other historians suggest that land redistribution was not an innovation of the state or of the landlord but rather a traditional peasant practice aimed at maintaining a rough land equality among households based upon their size. Whether land redistributions originated from the commune or were imposed by landlords, it is clear that this practice occurred in parts of Russia up until the turn of the twentieth century and even beyond. Land redistribution was common in areas in which agriculture dominated the peasant economy and especially where soil quality was varied (for example, in the Black Earth regions of southern Russia). In areas where agriculture was not important, land redistribution fell into disuse. The periodicity of land redistributions, where they occurred, varied from one to five, ten, or even more years.

In addition to its important economic, social and juridical functions, the commune, indeed village life as a whole, fostered a collective consciousness among the serfs. Through village life, rich in tradition, custom, religious and national holidays, as well as innumerable communal celebrations, serf peasants maintained a sense of solidarity and cohesiveness. Overemphasis on intravillage conflicts has led some observers to question the sense of communality among the peasants. Private conflicts among peasants, however, did not undermine village solidarity. Indeed, one of the chief functions of the commune was to contain and adjudicate conflict. Furthermore, peasants who migrated into cities for employment sustained themselves in the unfamiliar urban environment by forming fraternal associations (in Russia the famous urban *zemliachestvos*) directly based upon the respective peasants' village and district origins. In essence, at the first opportunity many peasants who had left the village recreated familiar communal mores, hardly a practice consonant with reflexive mutual hostility.

Solidarity among the serfs expressed itself in numerous cases of collective insubordination, refusal to work, disturbances, and rebellions large in size and duration. Popular protest usually broke out when the quality of justice, as it was understood by the peasants, deteriorated. The village commune was a crucial element in initiating popular protest. Serfs first presented their disagreements and complaints collectively to their lords or local officials. If the latter failed to resolve the disputes, the serfs resorted to one or another form of protest, which was often accompanied by customary collective rituals and symbols of misrule. Naturally, serfs showed the greatest concern about increases in duties and demands upon them. From 1800 to 1861, for example, 371 out of 793 (47 percent) disturbances in the central Russian provinces were caused by increases in feudal obligations. In addition to collective forms of protest facilitated by the commune, serfs actively used various forms of individual protest, such as work slowdowns, deception, manipulation of legal norms, and fleeing. These latter forms of protest were primarily associated with the serfs' unfree status. (Although most eastern European cities could not guarantee their freedom, for peasants running away was the primary means to escape serfdom.) Thus, the strong collective consciousness noted above among serfs did not undermine their individual motivations, as also witnessed by their individual economic pursuits (trading, temporal migration, and so forth).

Thus, although often organized by local communal institutions, most peasant revolts had no concrete political or generalized economic goals. Rather, the recurrence of peasant insurrections in eastern Europe throughout the centuries of serfdom reflected the structural changes of east European society, such as the growth of population, state centralization, imposition of new heavy taxes and obligations, the development of a market economy, and the transformation of popular mentality.

THE ECONOMIC ACTIVITIES OF SERFS

The degree of autonomy that east European serfs carved out for themselves within the contexts of familial and communal life also aided the serfs' independent economic activities. In areas where agriculture was the basic element of the economy, serfs worked roughly half of their time for the landlord and the balance for themselves. For example, in the 1740s an average peasant household of Silesia had to work for its lord 177 days a year or approximately three days a week, along with some payment in kind. Three days a week was the usual amount of time most east European serfs had to give their lords, although some were faced with even higher requirements. In non-agricultural areas, where serfs usually payed rent in kind or in money, they could spend the greater part of their time working for themselves. In the 1840s, in order to meet all obligations and pay all feudal dues and state taxes, east European peasants spent from 17 to 86 percent of their income, depending on region and the economic conditions of the household. An average serf household paid out in dues and taxes from 30 to 50 percent of its annual income.

Although the agricultural economy predominated in eastern Europe, serfs, as well as other categories of peasants, were usually multioccupational. The local economy and the serfs' occupations depended largely upon regional characteristics such as soil fertility and climate. In Prussia, the Baltic region, and the southern regions of Russia and non-Russian eastern Europe, the national and local economies were based mainly on agriculture and specifically on grain production. The microeconomy of the northern regions of eastern Europe usually combined various nonagricultural and agricultural activities. With economic expansion during the late eighteenth century, this regional specialization became more notable. In fact, in certain regions agriculture became a seasonal occupation, and the nonagricultural pursuits largely dominated the peasant economy. One study of peasant economic activity in the central nonagricultural Russian provinces shows that from 60 to 93 percent of the regions' peasants engaged at least part-time in one or another nonagricultural activity. For example, in Moscow province the peasants devoted only 3.5 months a year to agriculture and the rest of the year to domestic industries and commerce.

Serf peasants engaged in various nonagricultural activities. About a half of those so employed were hired workers, whereas others were small traders, craftsmen, self-employed in services, and even, though rarely, rich merchants and entrepreneurs. The degree to which east European serfs engaged in various trading, manufacturing, and commercial activities is striking. Large numbers of peasants maintained cottage industries as a seasonal business for the entire family that produced not only for the local market but for the national and international ones as well. Textile making was the dominant type of domestic industry. Millions of peasants spun, wove, and finished various kinds of fabrics in their villages. For example, in 1780 in Tver' province of central Russia, about 280 thousand female peasants wove canvas during the nongrowing season. Peasants sold their products to traveling traders and merchants (themselves often serf peasants), who sold them in various national and regional markets and fairs. Trading peasants, composed of serfs and nonserfs, were often the dominant force in national and local markets throughout eastern Europe.

The peasants' protoindustrial activities during the late eighteenth and the early nineteenth centuries energized many serf villages, providing a basis for the economic and social advancement of those who availed themselves of the opportunity. The peasants' role in the development of east European national economies likewise expanded. After starting out as artisans, craftsmen, and small traders, the more able serfs founded manufacturing concerns and textile mills. Perhaps the single most striking example of serf entrepreneurialism was Ivanovo Voznesensk, a textile city in central Russia's Vladimir province. During the late eighteenth and early nineteenth centuries, several serf traders established textile mills in the small village of Ivanovo on the Sheremet'ev family estate. Eventually the former quiet village transformed itself into the bustling textile city that Friedrich Engels later called "the Russian Manchester." Similar developments occurred in many parts of eastern Europe.

The expansion of the peasantry's economic activities had wide-ranging repercussions. For example, it had an impact on education, on the social mobility of the serfs, and on state laws that regulated the peasantry. New laws eased peasant entry into nonagricultural activities, in part by restricting the lord's authority over serfs. In Russia and elsewhere, statutes enabled serfs to engage in virtually all kinds of economic activities and regulated those activities. The Russian laws of 1827, 1828, 1835, and 1848 progressively limited the power of the lords over peasants engaged in licensed commercial and business enterprises and introduced private property rights for serfs. These laws ultimately applied to many tens of thousands of serfs. Simultaneously, numerous technical and other schools opened their doors to peasants. By learning and engaging in various crafts and trades, peasants became acquainted with the national economies of their respective states. Through economic advancement and education, some serfs even entered the upper social echelons. Although the number of such fortunate individuals was modest when compared to total serf populations, the phenomenon impressed contemporary observers. One mid-nineteenth-century Russian wrote that self-made peasants were forging to the head of merchant communities and emerging as leaders in public affairs.

THE END OF SERFDOM

The abolition of serfdom differed sharply from one east European state to another. In Prussia the royal edict of 1807 ordered the emancipation of that nation's serfs, and that same year Napoleon emancipated the serfs of Poland. Imperial Russian decrees of 1816 and 1819 freed the peasants of the Baltic states. The peasants of the Austrian Empire gained freedom as a direct result of the revolutions of 1848–1849. In Russia, the famous imperial edict of 1861 abolished serf-

Emancipation of the Serfs. Reading the edict of emancipation to the serfs of the Prozorov estate, near Moscow, 1861. SOVFOTO/EASTFOTO

dom there. Romanian peasants, the last European serfs, were freed in 1864, bringing to an end centuries of European peasant bondage.

Although serfdom ended as the immediate result of social revolutions, political developments, or juridical decisions of state authorities, the process of abolition had begun long before these final decisions. As noted, new laws had begun to restrict the authority of the lord over his peasants. Serf involvement in commercial and entrepreneurial activities and the social advancement of some wrought new attitudes in society toward serfs and serfdom itself. Contemporaries increasingly viewed serfs as an active societal and economic force. For most contemporary intellectuals and enlightened statesmen (not to mention various rulers of east European states), serfdom was a malign anachronism. Many tracts and discussions attacked serfdom, sometimes invoking the western European example and Enlightenment ideals. Even the archconservative Nicholas I of Russia (1825–1855) blamed his Romanov ancestors for this "unmitigated evil," which, unfortunately, he could not bring himself to eliminate. Although serfdom did

not completely block significant social and economic changes, informed east European society long viewed it both as a moral evil and an obstacle to rapid societal development. In Russia, defeat in the Crimean War (1853–1856) served as a final impetus to end an outmoded institution that hindered Russia's economic and military development.

State decrees effected the various emancipations but the roots of emancipation lay in long-term east European economic and social changes. By the second half of the eighteenth century, the accelerating tempo of population growth, economic expansion, and the peasants' protoindustrial activities shed an increasingly harsh light on serfdom's petty and major oppressions. Progress, more limited than it could have been, took place not because of serfdom but despite it, in large measure because of the independent activity of millions of serfs who, in the face of their unfree status, exerted an influence on their nations' affairs. In this regard, we might recall that in announcing the emancipation of Russia's serfs, Alexander II stated only that it was better that they should be freed from above than from below, that is, that they should free themselves by force. We would be wiser to view the peasants as actors rather than as ciphers. Serfdom was an indisputable social evil but serfs were not hopeless victims who passively submitted to that evil. Instead, many took a more active stance than we have realized in influencing their own history.

See also **Absolutism; Protoindustrialization** *(in this volume);* **The Aristocracy and Gentry; Peasants and Rural Laborers; Rural Revolts;** *(volume 3); and other articles in this section.*

BIBLIOGRAPHY

Aleksandrov, Vadim A. *Obychnoe pravo krepostnoi derevni Rossii XVIII–nachalo XIX v.* Moscow, 1984.

Aleksandrov, Vadim A. *Sel'skaia obshchina v Rossii (XVII–nachalo XIX v.).* Moscow, 1976.

Blackwell, William. *The Beginnings of Russian Industrialization, 1800–1860.* Princeton, N.J., 1968.

Blum, Jerome. "The Condition of the European Peasantry on the Eve of Emancipation." *Journal of Modern History* 46 (September 1974): 395–424.

Blum, Jerome. "The Internal Structure and Polity of the European Village Community from the Fifteenth to the Nineteenth Century." *Journal of Modern History* 43 (December 1971): 541–576.

Blum, Jerome. *Lord and Peasant in Russia from the Ninth to the Nineteenth Century.* Princeton, N.J., 1961.

Evans, Richard J., and W. R. Lee, eds. *The German Peasantry: Conflict and Community in Rural Society from the Eighteenth to the Twentieth Centuries.* New York, 1986.

Fedorov, Vladimir A. *Krest'ianskoe dvizhenie v Tsentral'noi Rossii, 1800–1860.* Moscow, 1980.

Field, Daniel. *The End of Serfdom: Nobility and Bureaucracy in Russia, 1855–1861.* Cambridge, Mass., 1976.

Gromyko, Marina M. *Mir russkoi derevni.* Moscow, 1991.

Hagen, William W. "How Mighty the Junkers? Peasant Rents and Seignorial Profits in Sixteenth-Century Brandenburg." *Past & Present* 108 (August 1985): 80–116.

Hagen, William W. "Seventeenth-Century Crisis in Brandenburg: The Thirty Years' War, the Destabilization of Serfdom, and the Rise of Absolutism." *American Historical Review* 94 (April 1989): 302–335.

Hagen, William W. "Working for the Junker: The Standard of Living of Manorial Laborers in Brandenburg, 1584–1810." *Journal of Modern History* 58 (March 1986): 143–158.

Hellie, Richard. *Enserfment and Military Change in Muscovy.* Chicago, 1971.

Hoch, Steven L. *Serfdom and Social Control in Russia: Petrovskoe, a Village in Tambov.* Chicago, 1986.

Istoriia krest'ianstva SSSR s drevneishikh vremen do Velikoi Oktiabr'skoi socialisticheskoi revoliutsii. 2 vols. Edited by Viktor I. Buganov and I. D. Koval'chenko. Moscow, 1987–1990.

Istoriia krest'ianstva Rossii s drevneishikh vremen do 1917 g. Vol. 3. Edited by Vadim A. Aleksandrov. Moscow, 1900; 1996.

Istoriia krest'ianstva v Evrope: Epokha feodalizma. 3 vols. Edited by Zinaida V. Udal'tsova. Moscow, 1985–1986.

Kahan, Arcadius. "Notes on Serfdom in Western and Eastern Europe." *Journal of Economic History* 33 (March 1973): 86–99.

Kieniewicz, Stefan. *The Emancipation of the Polish Peasantry.* Chicago, 1969.

Kolchin, Peter. *Unfree Labor: American Slavery and Russian Serfdom.* Cambridge, Mass., 1987.

Melton, Edgar. "Enlightened Segniorialism and Its Dilemmas in Serf Russia, 1750–1830." *Journal of Modern History* 62 (December 1990): 675–708.

Melton, Edgar. "*Gutherrschaft* in East Elbian Germany and Livonia, 1500–1800: A Critique of the Model." *Central European History* 21 (December 1988): 315–349.

Millward, Robert. "An Economic Analysis of the Organization of Serfdom in Eastern Europe." *Journal of Economic History* 42 (September 1982): 513–548.

Moon, David. "Reassessing Russian Serfdom." *European History Quarterly* 26 (1996): 483–526.

Moon, David. *The Russian Peasantry, 1600–1930: The World the Peasants Made.* London and New York, 1999.

Mooser, Joseph. "Property and Wood Theft: Agrarian Capitalism and Social Conflict in Rural Society, 1800–50. A Westphalian Case Study." In *Peasants and Lords in Modern Germany: Recent Studies in Agricultural History.* Edited by Robert G. Moeller. Boston, 1986.

Pallot, Judith, and Denis J. B. Shaw, eds. *Landscape and Settlement in Romanov Russia, 1613–1917.* New York, 1990.

Peters, Jan, ed. *Gutherrschaftsgesellschaften im europäischen Vergleich.* Berlin, 1998.

Rudolph, Richard L. "Agricultural Structure and Proto-industrialization in Russia: Economic Development with Unfree Labor." *Journal of Economic History* 45 (March 1985): 47–69.

Rudolph, Richard L. "Family Structure and Proto-industrialization in Russia." *Journal of Economic History* 40 (March 1980): 111–118.

Schissler, Hanna. "The Junkers: Notes on the Social and Historic Significance of the Agrarian Elite in Prussia." In *Peasants and Lords in Modern Germany: Recent Studies in Agricultural History.* Edited by Robert G. Moeller. Boston, 1986.

Scott, Tom, ed. *The Peasantries of Europe from the Fourteenth to the Eighteenth Centuries.* London and New York, 1998.

Wall, R. et al., ed. *Family Forms in Historic Europe.* Cambridge, U.K., 1983.

Wirtschafter, Elise Kimerling. "Legal Identity and Possession of Serfs in Imperial Russia." *Journal of Modern History* 70 (September 1998): 561–597.

PEASANT AND FARMING VILLAGES

Palle Ove Christiansen

Peasants and villages are among the most studied themes in social history, but researchers have always had difficulty finding general definitions able to cover the forms, in time and space, in which agrarian people have organized and localized themselves under political conditions and those given by nature.

WHAT IS THE EUROPEAN VILLAGE?

The European village normally carries associations of a small consolidated agricultural community, in the ancien régime sometimes consisting of only a few farms. But especially in central and southern Europe villages could appear as built-up areas with five to ten thousand inhabitants. The basic difference between village and town, before the widespread abolition of town and commercial privileges in the 1800s, could seldom be expressed in area or population but was more of a legal and cultural character. The usually modest structures built to shelter shepherds and for cheese production, and so forth, in the various systems of transhumance from European mountain regions, are normally not considered independent villages, as pastures that are exploited in this manner usually belong to village in the lowland. The same applies to so-called satellite villages used for seasonal lodgings or wine production, for example. The concept of the village never refers only to the permanent, dense, rural settlement, but to the entire surrounding area legally available regardless of how much of it is exploited. Large areas with scattered farmsteads can also constitute villages.

The village was the most common form of habitation for the greater part of Europe's population far into the 1800s, and as an organized food producing unit it goes back to around 7000 B.C. for southeast Europe, and around 500 B.C. for northwest Europe. The village has always been characterized by cattle raising and farming in the broadest sense, and since the late Middle Ages, by relations to population groups who did not themselves take part in the primary production of foodstuffs. Investigators like Eric Wolf, Teodor Shanin, and Frank Ellis have spoken of peasants as traditional agriculturists, who run their family-based farms, organized in villages or other cooperative units, to satisfy their own consumption, but who also through production of a surplus are dominated by outsiders and thus are part of larger political and economic systems.

RELATIONS TO MANORIAL ESTATES AND TOWNS

Most European peasant villages from the Middle Ages up to the 1800s and 1900s can be best viewed in relation to the manorial estate and the market town respectively. The relationships between the village and the lord's estate and between village and town have constituted basic conditions shaping villages and village life that cannot be explained solely through scrutiny of the individual village.

The relation to manorial estates. The peasant's praxis in the village in historical Europe should be understood in light of the demand on one hand to perpetuate his own farm and family, and on the other to feed other social estates such as the seigneurs, the church, and the king. Georges Duby (1968) has pointed out that village-estate relations existed both before and after European feudalism, and that the seigneur's close protection of the peasant and the king's outer defense continued in various configurations up into the 1800s.

In the medieval social structure the village lord, through his right to the peasant's or the village's dues, allocated land to the peasants or the village. This was this case regardless of whether the relation between lord and peasant was one of sharecropping, lease, rent, or lifetime *faeste* (a Scandinavian form of semi-feudal dependent tenancy) combined with varying types of personal legal ties to the land, the estate, or the peasant occupation itself. In some places private manorial estates also administered the tax to the supreme prince and the tithe to the church.

To obtain the village resources necessary to sustain himself economically the non-free peasant had to pay dues to the lord, who was responsible for administration over the peasants as a social category. It was especially in the collection of dues in the form of produce, money, or corvée (labor service) to the lord that the estate exerted influence over the village's internal affairs. Where the dues included corvée a large part of the village's labor force was used outside its own area, as a rule in the direct cultivation of estate's demesne lands. From the 1400s and 1500s up to the 1800s, this demand was most pronounced in the great grain-growing regions in central and eastern Europe and the Baltic countries. The manorial dues to the lord assumed very different forms according to the natural conditions and local tradition. In the Mediterranean region dues in olives and fruit were not uncommon. In grazing and mountain regions the dues were often paid in cows, goats, sheep, and wool. Along the Atlantic coast dues were often paid in fish. And special products of almost every kind, such as poultry, honey, hides, and textiles, have also been used. Most familiar, however, are grain dues in the form of rye, barley, and wheat (for bread, porridge, and beer). Dues were normally assessed on the individual farm, but especially early on and in eastern central Europe collective dues have existed, for example in the form of a head of cattle paid by the peasants of a midsized village.

Just as the married male peasant at the head of his household was a nucleus of village's organization, in the ancien régime he was accorded a place together with his fellow villagers in the society's hierarchical structure as producer of food and taxpayer. It was this position of villages and peasants within a hierarchical society of fixed social estates, a relation absent in so-called primitive societies and ones without seigneurialism, which made peasant and village societies specific historical categories in Europe.

The relation to market towns. If the seigneur was able to demand dues in the form of money, or if the king, the duke, or the feudal overlord demanded taxes paid in cash, the peasant was forced to convert some of his products to money at the market. In regions with great distances between the market towns rural markets were periodically held for small producers to exchange products. Where the towns were close together, as in northwestern Europe, the peasants often had to retail their most important commodities in the market towns or else sell them to the town's merchants. With Poland as the best known exception, the market towns were often outside the seigneurs' juris-

diction and were instead protected by the country's prince. In areas where the peasant had no natural access to salt and iron, these basic needs also forced him into contact with the commodity market, in other words the town. This stable market commerce did not mean, however, that production activities in the old village were governed by market principles of supply and demand.

Even though market dependency increased quantitatively from around 1500, the village-town relationship is of long standing. This relationship is significant for understanding the regional variations in domestic utensils, clothing, dyes, and small metal goods, which in differing quantity and composition have been a fixed element in the mode of life of European peasant villages, and which probably attained their greatest diversity in the 1800s. Börje Hanssen's studies of the Österlen region in southern Sweden (1952) describe villages in the 1600s and 1700s as part of a complex network with both market towns and rural fairs. Hanssen also shows that frequent town contact does not necessarily lead to changes in the peasant or folk culture. This was implied in Robert Redfield's (1941) criticized but nonetheless widely used continuum model of social change, based on his early studies of Central America. Although the isolated peasant and the self-sufficient village have by and large never existed in Europe, spatial contact has not automatically led to cultural adaptation.

Ferdinand Tönnies's classical dichotomy between *Gemeinschaft* (community) and *Gesellschaft* (society) has greatly influenced the modern public's stereotyped conception of city versus country (village). All concrete investigations show, however, that the small village is not exclusively homogeneous and the great city differentiated. Studies have also demonstrated that there have always existed rather large contingents of village people in cities, such as servants, small tradespeople, carters, fishermen, and laborers, some of whom moved back to their villages after a few years. At the same time many villages have been home to culturally urban people such as clergymen, estate functionaries, and regional technicians like surveyors and officers.

DIVERSITY AND COMPLEXITY OF VILLAGES ACROSS EUROPE

Within Europe's boundaries innumerable forms can be found under which village peasants have lived and still live, which because of their variety are nearly impossible to discuss in general terms. This diversity stems from factors ranging from geopolitical circumstances, state administration, and landlord policies, to market access and local ecological conditions. Attempts have been made to speak of differences on the basis of varied forms of European estate systems, the topographical adaptation of peasant village structure, and variations in the cultivation systems in the old village, that is, the village prior to land consolidation reforms.

Many features of present-day European village structure have roots in an earlier dependency on nearby manorial estates, and even in estate structures and settlement patterns that were developed in the 1500s, a period of population and price increase. In European estate organization the distinction is often made between indirect cultivation, in which the lord lives off dues in the form of foodstuffs or money from the peasants on the tributary tenant land, and direct cultivation, in which the lord himself engages in large-scale production on his demesne land. Under indirect cultivation the distance between the peasants' own places of habitation and the estate is not especially important. Before the 1500s and 1600s this type of estate organization was found especially in thinly populated areas in the east, and in the west on scattered tracts such as crown land, in areas with dispersed peasant settlements and interior soil, and in regions where the early feudal estates were, after the 1500s, unsuccessful in reestablishing an effective direct cultivation based on serfs or hard corvée.

With direct cultivation the distance from the demesne to the agricultural laborers or the peasants who through their labor dues cultivated this land had to be as short as possible, which as a rule necessitated that the farms be more closely grouped. This also made easier the lord's supervision of the labor force. Because of recruitment of the village population for corvée, this estate cultivation in northeastern Europe could result in a considerable density of villages in regions that earlier had more scattered settlement. In these otherwise agrarian areas, the estates also produced goods for export to western Europe, largely by compulsory labor dues. In some places all the way up to the 1900s the manorial exploitation resulted in pauperized village societies. Research has shown that even though the pressure from lords on peasants intensified in Mecklenburg, Swedish Pomerania, East Prussia, Poland, the Baltic countries, and the Russian regions, as compared to most places in western Europe, there were far greater differences in both east and west than hitherto assumed.

Scholars have long been tempted to discern a pattern in the innumerable typologies of European village forms. Historians, geographers, and linguists have examined the geographic distribution of settlement patterns, systems of succession, village names,

Fortified Church. The Catholic church at Cisnadie, Romania. Photograph by Staffan Widstrand, 1990. ©STAFFAN WIDSTRAND/CORBIS

and number of farms per village. Some have distinguished between street villages, terrain villages, round villages, and dispersed settlements. A particularly important aim has been to set up frameworks describing the establishment and physical structure of villages, but it has been difficult to find patterns. Nonetheless, research has demonstrated some regularities; for instance, people settled to form villages where there is fertile soil, sufficient water and forest, facility of clearing land, and lines of communication.

Hamlets, that is, small clusters of houses with no actual historical village organization, are found everywhere in Europe. There are also the agro-towns and villages surrounding *Kirchenburgen,* or fortified churches. Agro-towns have evolved from the Middle Ages well into the 1800s in Southern Italy, Sicily, Andalusia, and in southeastern Hungary. There are examples of very large villages of this kind, sometimes with over thirty thousand inhabitants, which besides their peasant and agricultural laborer population include urban social categories and have urban institutions. In the Mediterranean area the inhabitants of agro-towns prefer to be associated culturally with an urban ethos, whereas agro-towns on the Great Hungarian Plain have always had a more rural character. The fortified church is primarily a phenomenon of eastern central Europe. Best known are the Saxon villages in Transylvania (Romania), where from the 1400s many churches were fortified and encompassed by ramparts and ring walls as protection against the Turks and roaming Vandals, giving the villages a striking physical appearance.

Particularly before the post–World War II mechanization, climate and soil differences have also produced great disparities in conditions between Mediterranean and transalpine agriculture, and consequently

391

Agro-Town. Village of Ecija, Andalusia, Spain. Engraving from *Civitates orbis terrarum* (1567). By permission of the British Library, London

in village configuration and organization in these two regions, relative to available resources. Some investigators speak of the transalpine ecotype as compared to the Mediterranean, and Lynn White (1962), extending Marc Bloch's theories as presented in his *French Rural History* (originally published in 1931), has endeavored to summarize some of the main characteristics of villages and village production and their evolution in southern and northern Europe respectively. Since the Middle Ages Mediterranean peasant agricultural practices adapted to a dry climate and light soil, as distinct from the northern European practices adapted to heavy soil in a humid climate. According to White and other investigators, the respective conditions determined whether people settled in small or larger villages, used light or heavy plows, and tilled equilateral versus long fields; they also accounted for differences in village organization and location.

Despite the fact that even at the end of the twentieth century great differences existed between the two parts of Europe, the variations present in either period cannot be explained solely on the basis of ecological adaptation or technological diffusion. Before mechanization, and particularly in the early open-field village, it is the village and not the individual farm that is the relevant unit for analysis of the overall exploitation of nature and the relationship of peasants and their livestock to historically determined scarce resources. In modern farming, however, both in the south and the north, it is the farm which is the pivotal unit.

VILLAGE ORGANIZATION IN THE ANCIEN RÉGIME

According to Jerome Blum, the European village community arose in the Middle Ages as a corporate body managing communal resources, directing certain common activities, and supervising certain aspects of the communal life, and it persisted for as long as the open-field village was in existence, and as far as certain communal interests such as the exploitation of peat bogs were concerned, all the way up to the modern era. Formally the village community was run by the village assembly headed by the village headman. In some places this post was rotated among the farms in the village, and in certain regions the seigneur had to approve the choice of new headman. The village assembly decided important internal matters in the village and often acted as a go-between for the individual farm or inhabitant and the seigneur, the church, and the state, especially in areas of central and eastern Europe where the dues were assessed collectively on the village as a whole.

Generally the village had a large degree of independent authority which could, especially in areas of Switzerland, Austria and Southern Germany, include its own local court. The village assembly in some freehold areas could also sell, buy, rent, and rent out communal land. Even in those parts of Europe where the seigneur could sell or reallocate both peasants and village land, and thus intervene in all internal village relations, he often let the village take care of itself so long, as he got his dues punctually.

The village assembly gave guidelines for how communal areas with grazing land, forest, bog, meadow, or lakes should be exploited, and how fences and roads ought to be maintained. It decided when sowing and harvest should begin or be concluded, which of the two cultivated territories under the widespread three-field rotation system should be laid out the next year and with which crops, and which zone was to be opened for grazing. The village assembly moreover could hire village herdsmen, decide which of the peasants was to feed the communal bull each year, assist in firefighting, and issue petty fines for disturbing the peace.

The formal farm-village relationship functioned on the basis of the so-called village law, which dates from the Middle Ages but which worked on the basis of oral tradition until the 1800s or even longer. Perhaps all households, or at any rate all households with land, originally had a vote in the village assembly, but in the 1600s and 1700s in many places less than one third of the households in the village were represented, and the most prosperous village inhabitants enacted statutes that stripped the landless or those with limited land of influence. This phenomenon is often interpreted in connection with the general population increase since the 1500s and especially the 1700s, when there was greater competition for the village's resources. As a rule only male farm representatives could sit in the village assembly but in some areas in Russia widows also had a vote, and in certain places in France both women and men took part in the meetings of the village assembly. In these areas the local priest and even the seigneur could be members, but otherwise the village assembly was reserved exclusively for the peasant estate. In the 1800s, representative democracy in some countries resulted in the creation, as the lowest administrative unit, of parish councils in which persons from all social estates could have a seat.

In many places the village assembly's earlier rather sovereign position had already been undermined before the abolition of the open-field system eliminated its most pivotal functions. Particularly in northeastern central Europe—when from the 1500s to the beginning of the 1800s much peasant land was incorporated in the demesne lands and the inhabitants made into cottagers or day laborers (a process termed *Bauernlegen* in German)—the village assemblies were depleted of their traditional functions and authority. Under intensive large-scale production in both east and west, the seigneurs were in many places successful in eliminating some of the village headman's functions. They were able to replace the headmen with so-called peasant bailiffs or with headmen who were also estate functionaries of a sort, since besides administering the village's own affairs they were supposed to summon their fellow villagers to corvée on the demesne farm. However, in western and central Europe with the Enlightenment of the 1700s the state endeavored to safeguard some of the peasants' rights vis-à-vis the seigneurs, perhaps not for the peasants' sake alone, but to secure for the nation a more solvent tax basis, a greater number of inhabitants, and more—and more loyal—soldiers. This state intervention in village affairs could not help but standardize the functions of the village assemblies.

The best known example of the village assembly or commune's regulating function, in which the commune acted as the de facto owner of the peasant land, is found in Russia in the 1700s and 1800s. Under this system the peasants had permanent right only to their house and outbuildings, to communal areas such as commons and forests, and to only a little cultivated land. In return, at regular intervals the village assembly (*mir*) apportioned shares of the village land to the individual peasant household, usually in relation to how many mouths it had to feed or how many adult workers it contained. Where in most peasant communities the household had to adapt its domestic size and consumption to the amount of land, in Russia it was the village assembly which redistributed the village land to the households according to their size and need. This system is known in different variants in a number of areas in both eastern and western Europe.

Corporative organization of various forms existed in European villages into the twentieth century. Best known are the southern Slavic brotherhoods, where the dangers of isolation rendered collaboration among rural inhabitants necessary, and the non-family-based guild in Germany, the Nordic countries, and England, which had a role in organizing large work projects in the village.

OCCUPATIONAL GROUPINGS, STRATIFICATION, AND LIFESTYLE

The old village has often—in national ethnography from the late 1800s and in discussions of equality and national character—been held out as a democratic unit to be emulated. Recent research has shown, however, that the preindustrial village was often strongly socially differentiated, often strayed from the communal ethos, with its norms of mutual cooperation, suggested by its formal organization.

The village has nearly always been compounded of more occupational groupings than peasants, even though the peasants were originally predominant. From the 1600s great inequality of resources and affluence prevailed within the old peasant category, alongside which there often lived smallholders, cottars, artisans and small tradesmen, landless laborers, servants, and hired hands. The latter population elements increased markedly in the 1800s. Often they did not have independent representatives in the village assembly even though in numbers they might constitute the majority of the village population. The occupational designations were not necessarily attached

Village Government in Russia. *The Village Meeting,* painting (1895) by Nikolai Petrovich Bogdanov-Belsky (1868–1945). STATE RUSSIAN MUSEUM, ST. PETERSBURG, RUSSIA/THE BRIDGEMAN ART LIBRARY

permanently to the individual person or family; a young couple might start out as day laborers, later become peasants for twenty to twenty-five years, and end as cottars or lodgers. Nor was being a servant a permanent occupation in continental Europe, but rather a phase in the life cycle of young people, before they got married and perhaps took over an independent cottage or a farm. For smallholders and cottars the combination of farming and wage labor is very old, but in the 1900s it became widespread among the ranks of small farmers as the lower limit for viable farming was pushed upward.

In the case of southwestern Germany, the historical-anthropological studies of Hans Medick (1996) and David Sabean (1990) have shown what a variety of social and cultural forms existed in the villages of the 1600s, 1700s, and 1800s, and how women and men acted in their preoccupation with material interests, social position, and religious norms. In areas with partible inheritance where both sons and daughters were heirs, as Sabean in his book on Neckarhausen in Württemberg revealed, clashes between parents and adult children, between fathers and sons-in-law and between brothers-in-law over inheritance

of plots of land could be an immediate part of daily life in the village. Under these conditions family and blood relations were apparently of far greater significance in the village than often assumed.

In a study of east Danish villages Palle O. Christiansen has shown how in the 1700s the villagers' different interests and the estate's economic policy toward the villages as dues payers led to almost constant conflict in estate villages even where peasants otherwise had large adjoining lands. The everyday life of the villagers was remote from the commonplace notions of a corporate community. Village life was rather to be perceived as a conflictual coexistence between two essentially different peasant lifestyles, one lived in an often rather jolly day-to-day perspective and the other more ambitious and provident. The village can thus be understood as a kind of unity of opposites, in which the two lifestyles with a basis in the estate's praxis contributed mutually to reproducing each other. The balance between the two lifestyles might vary according to the estate's administrative praxis and the village's resources, particularly forest, but this duality was found in all villages belonging to the estate.

Differences in behavior among villagers may be perceived even into the twenty-first century. These differences result from the modern division of labor and the new presence of culturally urban people in the village, and also from the multiethnic composition of many villages, which often has roots both in late-medieval colonization in eastern central Europe and state-directed population movements of the 1700s and 1900s. In Hungary and Romania, especially until 1945, there were many German (Swabian or Saxon) minorities who lived in the same villages as Magyars, Romanians, and Roma (Gypsies), each speaking its own language. In the Balkan countries the diversity of nationality, language, and religion could be even greater, and has persisted into the twenty-first century.

AGRARIAN REFORMS: VILLAGE CONSOLIDATION AND FARM DECENTRALIZATION

An extensive complex of state-directed agrarian reforms, implemented especially in the 1700s and 1800s, aimed to modernize the old open-field village and

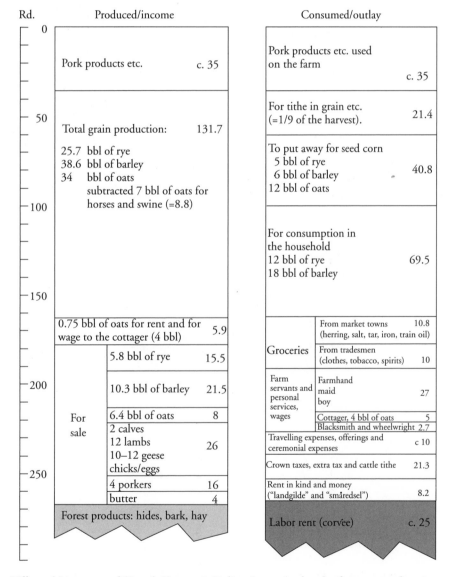

Villagers' Interests and Estate's Economic Policy. Income and outlay for a peasant farm in Giesegaard, Denmark, c. 1780. Adapted from Palle Ove Christiansen, *A Manorial World: Lord, Peasants, and Cultural Distinctions on a Danish Estate, 1750–1980* (Oslo: Scandinavian University Press, 1996), p. 157.

GØRSLEV

The two maps show the east Danish village of Gørslev, on the Giesegaard manorial estate, before and after the 1798 consolidation. On the map from 1781 Gørslev is an open-field village. The farms' often over fifty strips lie in the village's three fields, spread out among scrub, bogs, and irregular patches of forest. To the south is the old common, whose western segment peasants had begun cultivating in the 1700s. The village's entire area was 1,010 hectares, of which 470 hectares were culti- vated and around two-thirds was sown and harvested each year.

Consolidation and decentralization took place in 1798 and 1799, and the map from 1805 shows how the peasants' new large and contiguous areas covered the vil- lage's entire surface. The lord's forest, however, was kept outside and fenced in with straight stone walls. Straight lines predominate, as compared with the map from 1781. The new plan encouraged the laying out of kilometers of

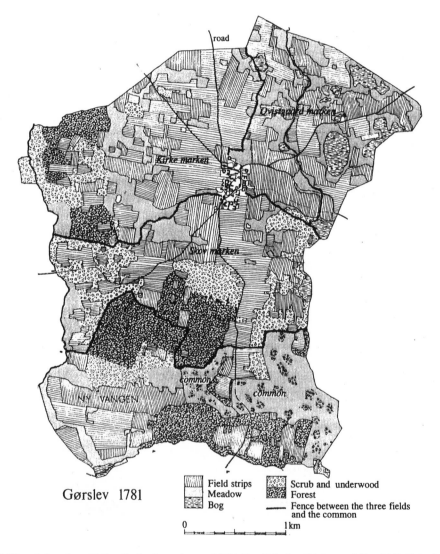

Gørslev 1781

Field strips
Meadow
Bog

Scrub and underwood
Forest
Fence between the three fields and the common

0   1 km

Peasant Village before Consolidation. Gørslev, Denmark, around 1781. From Palle Ove Christiansen, *A Manorial World: Lord, Peasants, and Cultural Distinctions on a Danish Estate, 1750–1980* (Oslo: Scandinavian University Press, 1996), p. 134.

roads, fences, and ditches, along with the rebuilding of around 700 linear meters of houses, stables, and barns.

The consolidation is a mixture of star and block consolidation. Eight farms remained in the village center and received triangular plots, while ten peasants moved to the village's outskirts and got more quadrangular parcels. Only a part of the peasants' parcels were cultivated, and it took generations before all arable land was under the plow.

Before the consolidation the village consisted of twenty farms (run by extended families) with large adjoining lands, six so-called field or forest cottages (inhabited by nuclear families) with moderate adjoining lands, twenty-eight cottages with grazing rights on the common, and ten families or persons who were lodgers. After the consolidation there were eighteen large farms, four cottages with moderate adjoining lands, seventeen cottages with a little land, and twelve to fourteen landless cottages. Grazing rights disappeared together with the common.

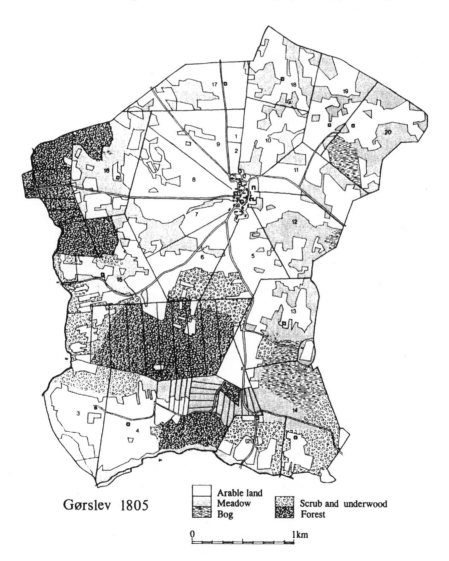

Gørslev 1805

Arable land
Meadow
Bog
Scrub and underwood
Forest

0   1km

Peasant Village after Consolidation. Gørslev, Denmark, around 1805. From Palle Ove Christiansen, *A Manorial World: Lord, Peasants, and Cultural Distinctions on a Danish Estate, 1750–1980* (Oslo: Scandinavian University Press, 1996), p. 318.

emancipate the peasant families as individual and independent citizens by means of the abolition of serfdom, conversion of corvée, and transition to peasant freehold. The earliest examples come from small countries like Savoy, Switzerland, and Denmark. The most important physical changes in the village have to do with the so-called technical reforms, that is, the conversion of open fields, divided into scattered strips, into consolidated, enclosed holdings, and the decentralization of individual farms. These reforms disturbed irrevocably the classical farm-village relation, though in most cases without resolving the inequalities that had arisen between big and small peasants.

In some areas in France and Southern Germany since the 1500s, villages have carried out consolidations of scattered strips themselves, and similar consolidations occurred in eastern Schleswig-Holstein. The first and most systematic centrally authorized consolidation, the English enclosures of the shared pastures and common fields, were organized in the 1500s and 1600s. The most extensive governmental enclosures of villages, however, took place in the following century, mainly in the Midlands. The most significant visual changes were the fences between the plot owners' main parcels, which also made it possible to put together the smaller tilled strips, particularly from the late 1700s. On many estates consolidated land that was not leased out was traditionally left for sheep farming and hunting.

On the Continent consolidations took place generally much later than in England. Except for a few precursors in the 1600s and early 1700s overall most consolidations in Schleswig-Holstein, Northern Germany, and Denmark began in the mid-1700s, and through the following century in other parts of Europe. In large parts of Russia, Poland, and what later became Czechoslovakia, as well as in areas of Switzerland and southern Germany, consolidation did not gather momentum until the 1900s.

Consolidation as a rule apportioned the village's communal areas such as commons and forests among the individual farms, and gathered each farm's often innumerable small fields into a single large parcel or a few bigger parcels which the peasant himself could decide when and how to cultivate. This led to a greater emphasis on the individual peasant within the village. He no longer had to wait for his neighbor in communal projects, and he saved time driving and walking to his fields and back. The peasant could obtain much cleaner and better manured soil, and by effective personal fencing keep neighbors and their livestock out of his fields and avoid the danger of contagion that came with earlier communal grazing. The great expense of consolidation notwithstanding, the governments and proprietors tended to reckon that the individual peasant, through his hopefully greater initiative, would become more solvent and that he would exploit resources like forest and grazing land less ruthlessly. They also hoped that the village could better support an augmented and more affluent population.

In many places consolidation was followed by the removal of farmsteads from the old village nucleus to the new field which the peasant had been allotted. A single large quadrangular parcel with the farmstead in the middle was considered the most effective setup but was not always possible, because of both the natural contours of the land and the expense involved in moving many farmsteads out onto the fields.

There is hardly any doubt that consolidation combined with the gradual introduction of more effective crop rotation raised productivity, though the old village was not nearly as inefficient as some of its modern critics have asserted. The improved yield from the consolidated lands—in hay production especially—did not occur until after old boundaries and ditches were slowly adjusted to the new field contours and otherwise untitled land was brought under cultivation, which took several years. Thereafter the productivity and commodity production per farm could be increased, which was reflected in augmented dues, more cows, and larger sales. Most important, perhaps, was that the new individual and farm-centered production held a very great potential in that the clearly defined, assembled parcels, often quite large and making more efficient use of the land than scattered strips, for many years henceforth allowed hitherto uncultivated areas to be brought under the plow. This was the case in Denmark and southern Sweden, for example, as well as in northwestern Germany and France.

The pattern of village transformation described above was not universal, however. In some areas peasants have always dwelled on their field plots rather than in village centers, although the cultivation of these fields over time has not always resulted in field contours which are suitable for modern motorized production. This is true in southwestern England, Ireland, all of southwestern France, Holland, Belgium, and the district west of Bremen in Germany, plus in Latvia and Serbia. Conversely there exist places, particularly in southern Europe, where peasants have no wish to move out of the village center, either so as not to reduce their already diminutive plots or because it is considered more urban and therefore finer to live in the village center than on the open land.

THE MODERN
PEASANT-FARMER AND
THE VILLAGE

In the consolidated village the village assembly's primary activities were eliminated, but in many places the organization remained in existence but with fewer and other tasks under its province. The removal of many farms from the village center could also change the physical configuration of the village. The old village changed its character rather than merely disintegrating. Even though the big, communal projects vanished and many families, particularly in transalpine Europe, moved out onto the fields, family, neighbor, and cooperative relations continued to exist. Moreover, many villages in the 1800s and especially the 1900s became small service centers, with artisans and shops for daily necessities.

The modern peasant-farmer, on his separate parcel of a size able to feed his family at the minimum, is inconceivable without a local service network and access to the larger market for both purchases and sales. Actually it is only in its modern form that it is possible to speak of the farmstead as both an economic unit and a home (see Eric Wolf, 1996, p.13). Although some European peasant farms have very low productivity, family farms have simultaneously turned out to have a far greater potential than was believed by reformers. The extinction of European family farms has often been prophesied, without their disappearing. Even though family farms face problems, and even though many have been combined, the structure itself continues to be reproduced.

The larger family farm's strength appears to be connected with the fact that in continental Europe it never became a small capitalistic enterprise. That is to say that the agriculturist often did not behave like the English tenant farmer or perform farm labor, even though modern agriculture involves large commodity production and is also dependent upon operational investments and loans. The independent peasant freehold of the 1800s and 1900s made it possible for the family-based farm at the end of the twentieth century to invest and become involved in the market, while at the same time the farm did not always have to pay interest on its own equity or include the family's labor in calculating the production price relative to the market wage. Just as in the case of smallholdings earlier, family members often supplemented their income with domestic industry or wage labor with the aim of keeping the farm and the home intact. This nucleus of agricultural activity contributed to the continued functioning of many villages. Simultaneously, some governments and the European Union also subsidized family production and services in villages, so as to maintain a degree of activity in marginal areas.

LAND REFORM MOVEMENTS
AND NEW VILLAGES
AFTER 1918 AND 1945

The parcelling out of land to peasants with the aims of stemming social unrest among agricultural laborers, limiting overseas emigration, and securing the necessary labor force for farmers and estates, began at the end of the 1800s. The land reforms after World War I in Czechoslovakia, Prussia, Finland, and part of Denmark, and after World War II in Yugoslavia and Italy, had the direct aim of reducing the extent and power of the still existing great estates, while at the same time obliging a rural but landless population's demand for land. The governments also sought to prevent a large-scale influx to the cities, which were rarely able to supply jobs to both a growing population and men returning from war. State land reform and the laying out of smallholdings in new so-called rationally planned villages has often paralleled the appearance of social movements of a populist character, which in opposition to both estate production and urban proletarianization have argued for healthy rural work and the small independent family farm. It was often pointed out that productivity per area unit in these small farms was greater than on estates, whereas the productivity per time unit was disregarded, inasmuch as surplus time in the village was seldom able to be used productively in other ways.

Many of the smallholdings which through centralized land reforms were portioned out in the 1900s have been so localized that the often extensive rural settlements can be spoken of as villages. These new villages came to function as intended in many places, but in others problems of various kinds arose. In southern and central Europe plots were never inhabited or farmed because they were too small or inexpedient from the outset, roads or water mains were never laid, people did not venture to move out of the old villages, or cattle thefts proliferated. These settlements, alongside the deserted villages, stand today as ghost towns. Other smallholdings were combined and new families moved into the houses, but particularly up until around 1960 these new smallholder villages had a symbolic progressive and antifeudal aura about them in those sections of Europe historically characterized by extensive seigneurial estates.

Hungarian Collective Farm. The village of Karzag, Hungary, 1956. ERICH LESSING/ART
RESOURCE, NY

COLLECTIVIZATION AND
DECOLLECTIVIZATION IN THE 1900s

A very different kind of land reform took place in
parts of eastern Europe in the twentieth century. The
collectivization of village peasants which took place
from 1929 to 1938 in the Soviet Union and in all
socialist countries after 1948 with the exception of
Poland and Yugoslavia fundamentally changed conditions in rural areas in that part of Europe. In socialist
agriculture the distinction must be made between
conditions on the collectives proper and state farms,
which are more reminiscent of large estate production
with a paid labor force. The collectivization of large
amounts of village land meant combined production
on a large scale on former peasant farms, which thus
were not modernized as individual family enterprises.
At the same time the peasants got the right to personally farm so-called private plots. Despite the fact
that these personal plots often were only one-third
and one-half hectares, through their occupiers' intensive cultivation they had a very large yield. Mechanization took place primarily on the often very extensive
state farms and on the collective fields, whereas production on the small personal plots was intensified
mostly through comprehensive allocation of family labor and low-technological equipment. Thus, in much
of eastern Central Europe the socialist experiment often not only preserved but also developed a classical
peasantlike cultivation which characterized village life
in the otherwise strongly industrialized societies.

Socialist agricultural and industrial planning
also had other conspicuous consequences. In Romania in the 1970s and 1980s, many villages in the
plains districts were completely depopulated and the
peasants relocated in large central towns engaged in
either large-scale farming or the State's high-priority
industries.

Following the anticommunist upheavals in 1989–
1991 in eastern central Europe decollectivization has
taken place. Peasants have divided the former collective fields, often according to the land division that
applied before the forced collectivization. Many small
family farms were reestablished in the villages in this
way. The result has been a large difference in the exploitation and possession forms in the countries in
question. In some places financial magnates have tried
to buy up land to combine into large private farms,
while simultaneously small peasants have collectively
sold the large machines from the former collectives,
which are useless on their own small holdings, and
instead have bought a horse and a couple of cows. In
such villages it is possible to see peasants build small
timber stables for their newly acquired livestock in the
same style as at the beginning of the twentieth century. The family's reestablished agricultural enterprise
supplements other sources of income such as wage
labor and other small production.

DEPOPULATION
AND URBAN NEWCOMERS

Much of Europe, particularly in the 1900s, saw a migration from the country to the city, gradually draining many villages of young people. Frequently the lands have been so small and inaccessible, and the prestige in living in a rural area so low, that families have not been able to sell their property in the villages, which are therefore gradually depopulated. After 1991 this has also been the case in villages in the former socialist countries, where the ethnic German inhabitants moved to Germany. Remaining are only old people and empty houses, possession of which is in some cases eventually taken by Roma.

Partial depopulation is not a new phenomenon, though the background for deserted villages always has to be perceived in a specific historical context. Rural depopulation was known in the Middle Ages (due to epidemics), in the Thirty Years' War in the 1600s, in the 1800s due to the great waves of emigration, and after the two world wars and in the Soviet Union and Romania due to deportations and forced migrations. The problems in many villages at the beginning of the twenty-first century are not only connected with young people leaving for urban centers to get education and jobs. The dwindling of the population bases is exacerbated by the fact that many small tradespeople have to close shop and that schools are amalgamated; in addition, state policies that are poorly suited to rural conditions can contribute to depopulation.

At the same time, since the 1960s, especially in northwestern Europe, a change has occurred in the pattern of migration in that numbers of people are moving away from the large cities in order to settle in villages and small rural towns. This is not only a result of the late modern anti-industrial attitude among well-educated population groups, but also has to do with better transportation possibilities (roads and private automobiles), cheaper homes in the country, and new forms of electronic communication. The increased demand for rural houses (including vacation homes) in such areas, often close to large well-functioning centers, has also resulted in planned expansions of many older farm villages. These villages exhibit a wholly new form of discourse characterized by both traditional agrarian viewpoints and strong culturally urban interests.

See also other articles in this section.

BIBLIOGRAPHY

Bloch, Marc. *French Rural History: An Essay on Its Basic Characteristics.* London, 1966.

Blum, Jerome. *The End of the Old Order in Rural Europe.* Princeton, N.J., 1978.

Blum, Jerome. "The European Village as Community: Origins and Functions." *Agricultural History* 45 (1971): 157–178.

Blum, Jerome. "The Internal Structure and Policy of the European Village Community from the Fifteenth to the Nineteenth Century." *Journal of Modern History* 43 (1971): 541–576.

Brunt, Lodewijk. "Social Change in a Dutch Village." In *Beyond the Community: Social Process in Europe.* Edited by Jeremy Boissevain and John Friedl. The Hague, Netherlands, 1975.

Christiansen, Palle O. "Culture and Contrasts in a Northern European Village: Lifestyles among Manorial Peasants." *Journal of Social History* 29 (1995): 275–294.

Christiansen, Palle O. "The Household in the Local Setting: A Study of Peasant Stratification." In *Chance and Change: Social and Economic Studies in Historical Demography in the Baltic Area.* Edited by Sune Åkerman et al. Odense, Denmark, 1978.

Christiansen, Palle O. *A Manorial World: Lord, Peasants, and Cultural Distinctions on a Danish Estate, 1750–1980.* Oslo, 1996.

Duby, Georges. "Manorial Economy." In *International Encyclopedia of the Social Sciences.* New York, 1968.

Ellis, Frank. *Peasant Economics: Farm Households and Agrarian Development.* Cambridge, U.K., 1988.

Franklin, S. H. *The European Peasantry: The Final Phase.* London, 1969.

Galeski, Boguslaw. *Basic Concepts of Rural Sociology.* Manchester, U.K., 1972.

Hanssen, Börje. "Fields of Social Activity and Their Dynamics." In *Transactions of the Westermarck Society.* Vol. 2. Copenhagen and Åbo, 1948. Pages 99–133.

Hanssen, Börje. *Österlen: En studie över social-antropologiska sammanhang under 1600– och 1700–talen i sydöstra Skåne.* Stockholm, 1952. Basic study in Swedish of the relationships between villages, fairs, and towns.

Hofer, Tamás. "Agro-Town Regions of Peripheral Europe." *Ethnologia Europaea* 17 (1987): 69–95.

Koefoed, C. A. "Udskiftningens gang gennem de europæiske lande . . ." *Tidsskrift for landøkonomi* (1933): 566–595; 629–665; 705–722. Important presentation in Danish of village consolidation (with maps) in all European countries.

Koefoed, C. A. *My Share in the Stolypin Agrarian Reforms.* Odense, Denmark, 1985.

Medick, Hans. *Weben und Überleben in Laichingen 1650–1900: Lokalgeschichte als Allgemeine Geschichte.* Göttingen, Germany, 1996.

Redfield, Robert. *The Folk Culture of Yucatán.* Chicaco, 1941.

Sabean, David. *Property, Production, and Family in Neckarhausen, 1700–1870.* Cambridge, U.K., 1990.

Sampson, Steven L. *National Integration through Socialist Planning: An Anthropological Study of a Romanian New Town.* Boulder, Colo., 1984.

Shanin, Teodor, ed. *Peasant and Peasant Societies: Selected Readings.* 2d ed. London, 1988.

Tai, H. C. "The Political Process of Land Reform: A Comparative Study." *Civilisations* 18 (1968).

Turner, Michael. *Enclosures in Britain 1750–1830.* London, 1984.

Tönnies, Ferdinand. *Community and Society.* Edited and translated by Charles Price Loomis. New York, 1957 (1887).

Verdery, Katherine. *Transylvanian Villagers: Three Centuries of Political, Economic, and Ethnic Change.* Berkeley, Calif., 1983.

White, Lynn, Jr. *Medieval Technology and Social Change.* Oxford, 1962.

Wolf, Eric R. *Peasants.* Englewood Cliffs, N.J., 1966.

COLLECTIVIZATION

Lynne Viola

The collectivization of agriculture was a central feature of twentieth-century (mainly) marxist regimes in countries ranging from Eastern Europe to Africa, Asia, and Latin America. Although Marx never fully or explicitly envisioned collectivization, marxist regimes deemed collectivized agriculture an essential condition of socialism following the example set by the Soviet Union in its collectivization drive of the First Five-Year Plan (1928–1932). Collectivization proved to be a transformative experience for many regimes and their people, resulting in violence, repression, population dislocation, and food shortages, while simultaneously increasing the political rigidity of administrative controls in the countryside.

The aim of collectivization was to create a large-scale socialized agricultural economy, based on modern techniques of agronomy and animal husbandry and organized into state and collective farms. While state farms were to replicate the conditions of nationalized industry with state ownership and a salaried rural workforce, collective farms were to be profit-sharing organizations, in which farmers tilled the land collectively and governed and managed the farm through a collective farm assembly and elected officers. Collectivization was meant to transform the rural sector, replacing communal forms of peasant land tenure and small, private farms, as well as ridding the countryside of a rural bourgeoisie, capitalism, and the market.

The idea of collectivization was founded upon ideological, economic, and political factors. The tenets of Marxism-Leninism judged collectivization to be not only a more just and rational economic system than capitalist modes of farming based on market forces, but also presumed collectivization to be the logical outcome of the progressive dynamics of class forces in the countryside. Marxist-Leninists grafted urban concepts of class and class struggle onto the peasantry in what was, at best, an awkward fit. They divided the peasantry into poor peasants and rural proletarians (the natural allies of the working class), middle peasants (a large and politically wavering in-termediate stratum sharing features common to both proletariat and bourgeoisie), and kulaks (a rural bourgeoisie with social and economic power disproportionate to its relatively small numbers). They assumed that poor peasants and agricultural laborers would rally to the side of the collective farm on the basis of their class interests, swaying the middle peasant to their side and defeating the kulak in the process. In practice, peasants rarely performed according to class principles, instead uniting together in defense of com-

Encouraging Collectivization. A Soviet poster of the 1930s urges "Peasant woman, go to the collective farm" despite the interference of opponents. ©The Fotomas Index (U.K.)

403

mon interests—subsistence, ways of life, and belief—threatened by the theory and practice of collectivization. The poor peasant in most cases failed to come to the aid of the working class (in the concrete form of mobilized urban Communists and factory workers who implemented collectivization), and the regime's inability to provide a clear and consistent definition of the kulak most often meant that politics rather than social or economic status determined who was classified as a kulak.

Collectivization was viewed as an essential ingredient in the "construction" of socialism. In the Soviet Union and elsewhere, socialist construction meant not only the eradication of rural capitalism, but also the industrialization and modernization of the country. The collectivization of agriculture would facilitate the control and transfer of economic resources from the rural to the heavy industrial sector in a process the Soviet Communist theorist E. A. Preobrazhensky labeled in the 1920s "primitive socialist accumulation." By increasing grain production and mechanizing agriculture, collectivization was expected to free up capital and labor for industry, and food resources for a growing urban industrial workforce. And although most historians agree that collectivization did not pay for industrialization, at least in the short-term, it is clear that this expectation was an important motivation behind collectivization, particularly in conditions of economic isolation.

Finally, collectivization was a central aspect of state building, as regimes sought to expand political and administrative controls to the countryside, where in the Soviet Union and most of Eastern Europe (with the exception of Czechoslovakia) the majority of the population lived. The peasant commune and scattered, small private farms represented semiautonomous loci of power. Through the mobilization of urban forces, an expansion in rural party membership, and the creation of new, Soviet organs of power (the state farm, collective farm, machine-tractor stations, and so forth), the Communist Party endeavored to offset its relatively weak base of power in the countryside. Auxiliary policies aimed against religion and the kulak sought to eliminate the alternative power centers of the church and local authority figures.

In reality, the Soviet Union in the 1930s and the countries of Eastern Europe after World War II faced a largely resistant peasantry and smallholding farming population, uninterested in collectivized agriculture and generally impervious to marxist class principles. Collectivization consequently was a top-down, state-initiated transformation based on coercion and the mobilization of outside forces and animated by a fiercely urban bias and antipeasant prejudice.

While collectivization in Eastern Europe generally occurred with less violence, and in some cases more in the breach, collectivization in the Soviet Union represented an upheaval of cataclysmic proportions.

THE RUSSIAN REVOLUTION, COLLECTIVIZATION, AND THE PEASANTRY

The peasantry presented the Communist Party of the Soviet Union with the most formidable challenge of the revolution. Communist definitions generally sought to explain away the peasantry, to see it as a transitional class that would disappear with the advent of socialism. Communists expected the peasantry to dissolve into the working class—as indeed had been the case elsewhere in Europe—as the industrialization of the country expanded and siphoned off labor from the countryside. Until that time, however, the peasantry represented a glaring social, economic, and political contradiction to the premise and reality of the revolution.

Soviet power was based upon a "dictatorship of the proletariat and poor peasantry." In 1917, when the Bolsheviks championed peasant revolutionary goals as their own, V. I. Lenin claimed that "there is *no* radical divergence of interests between the wage-workers and the working and exploited peasantry. Socialism is *fully* able to meet the interests of both" (Lenin, vol. 35, p. 102). In fact, the dictatorship, and the "alliance" it derived from, combined mutually irreconcilable aims and quickly broke apart in conflict. It could not have been otherwise given the contradictory nature of the October Revolution, a "working-class revolution" in an agrarian nation in which the industrial proletariat accounted for little more than 3 percent of the population, while the peasantry constituted no less than 85 percent. In fact, there were actually two revolutions in 1917—an urban, socialist revolution, and a rural, bourgeois or antimanorial revolution. The two revolutions represented different and ultimately antithetical goals. Following its forced expropriation and partition of the nobility's lands in 1917, the peasantry desired no more than the right to be left alone: to prosper as farmers and to dispose of their produce as they saw fit. Although some peasants may have shared the socialist aims of the towns, most were averse to principles of socialist collectivism.

The 1917 Revolution had the unintended consequence of reinforcing many aspects of peasant culture and, specifically, a number of important features underlying and strengthening community cohesion. Although human and material losses from years of war and the famine that followed in the wake of the Russian Civil War (1918–1920) took a tremendous toll on the peasantry, the revolution, in combination with this time of troubles, had the effect of revitalizing the peasant community. Peasants engaged in massive social leveling during the revolution and civil war. The percentages of poor peasants fell from a prerevolutionary level of some 65 percent to around 25 percent by the mid-1920s, while the proportion of wealthy peasants declined from roughly 15 percent (depending on calculation) to about 3 percent in the same time span. The middle peasant became the dominant figure in Soviet agriculture as a result of wartime losses; social revolution and redivision of wealth; and the return, often forced, of large numbers of peasants who had quit the commune to establish individual farmsteads in the prewar Stolypin agrarian reforms, Prime Minister Petr Stolypin's post-1905 "wager on the strong," whereby the tsarist government endeavored to weaken communal land tenure by encouraging individual, hereditary forms of land ownership and the emergence of a stratum of strong, individual farmers in order to create a conservative base of support for the regime in the countryside.

Socioeconomic differentiation remained fairly stable through the 1920s, showing only very slight increases at the extremes. Leveling reinforced village homogeneity and cohesion while strengthening the position of the middle peasant. The kulak never regained his prerevolutionary economic status or social standing in the village and was by no means the dangerous counterrevolutionary described in the Stalinist rhetoric of the collectivization era. The commune itself was bolstered as most of the individual proprietors among the peasants (many of whom had benefited from the Stolypin reforms after 1905) returned to communal land tenure, which constituted approximately 95 percent of all forms of land tenure in the mid-1920s, thereby standardizing the peasant economy. And although peasant households splintered as the liberating effects of the revolution encouraged and enabled peasants' sons to free themselves from the authority of the patriarchal household, most peasants, especially women and the weaker members of the community, clung all the more tenaciously to customary and conservative notions of household, family, marriage, and belief in order to survive the crisis of the times. While the revolution no doubt dislodged and altered significant aspects of peasant lives, historians increasingly believe that the basic structures and institutions of the village demonstrated considerable continuity over the revolutionary divide, in many cases becoming stronger as a defensive bulwark against economic hardship and the destructive incursions of warring governments and armies.

The strengthening of homogeneity and the endurance of peasant culture in the 1920s should not imply that the peasantry was a static, unchanging rustic fixture. Profound processes of change had long been at work in the countryside, accelerating in particular in the late nineteenth and early twentieth centuries. Alternative patterns of socialization appeared at this time as peasant-workers and soldiers returned permanently or on visits to their home villages. Urban patterns of taste and, to a lesser extent, consumption also began to make an appearance in rural Russia as personal contacts between town and countryside became more common. A market economy made inroads into the prerevolutionary countryside, altering the economy of the peasant household as well as the internal social dynamics of the commune. Family size declined as extended families slowly began to give way to nuclear families, and marriages began to be based less exclusively on parents' choice. Peasant culture did not stagnate, but evolved over time, absorbing change and pragmatically adapting what was of use. Fundamental structures and institutions of peasant community persisted, demonstrating the durability and adaptability of the peasantry as a culture.

Similar patterns of change persisted into the Soviet period, coexisting, sometimes peacefully, sometimes not, with the prevailing patterns of peasant and community relations and dynamics. Although many interactions between village and town were disrupted during the revolution and civil war, the town and state continued to have an enormous impact on the countryside. Tens of thousands of peasant-workers returned to the village during the civil war, bringing with them new ways and practices not always in line with those of the community. A vast number of peasants served in the army during the world war and civil war, and they, too, returned with new ideas, sometimes at odds with their neighbors. From some of these groups emerged the village's first Communists and members of the Young Communist League (Komsomol). The Communist Party, in the meantime, although in practice generally neglectful of the countryside through most of the 1920s and preoccupied with industrial and internal party politics, was, in theory, committed to remaking the peasantry, to eliminating it as an antiquated socioeconomic category in an accelerated depeasantization that would transform peasant into proletarian. The party, the Komsomol, peasant-workers home on leave, groups of poor peasants, and Red Army veterans all became dimly lit beacons of Communist sensibility in the village. Efforts at socialization and indoctrination occurred in periodic antireligious campaigns, literacy campaigns, election campaigns, campaigns to recruit party and Komsomol members, campaigns to organize poor peasants or women, and so on, as the state attempted to build bridges into the countryside in the 1920s. The state succeeded in establishing pockets of support in the village, which would serve not only as agents of change but also as new sources of cleavage and village disjunction as new political identities emerged and interacted within the peasant community.

Collectivization was to destroy most of these "cultural bridges," leaving what remained of the state's small contingent of supporters entrenched against a hostile community. Most of the natural cleavages and fault lines that crisscrossed the village in ordinary times receded into latency during collectivization as the community found itself united against a common and, by this time, deadly foe. During collectivization, the peasantry acted as a class in much the way Teodor Shanin has defined class for peasantry in *Peasants and Peasant Societies:* "That is, as a social entity with a community of economic interests, its identity shaped by conflict with other classes and expressed in typical patterns of cognition and political consciousness, however rudimentary, which made it capable of collective action reflecting its interests" (p. 329). The era of the New Economic Policy (NEP), a relative golden age for the peasantry, came to an abrupt end with the collectivization of Soviet agriculture.

Collectivization encapsulated the original fault lines of the revolution, between a minority class in whose name the Communists professed to rule and the majority peasantry whose very reality appeared to block the revolution. Stalin's collectivization was an attempt to eliminate the fault line, to solve the accursed peasant problem by force, to create a socialist society and economy from above. It was a campaign of domination that aimed at nothing less than the internal colonization of the peasantry. Collectivization was intended to ensure a steady flow of grain to the state to feed the nation and to pay for industrialization. It was also intended to enable Soviet power to subjugate the peasantry through the imposition of administrative and political controls and forced acculturation into the dominant culture.

COLLECTIVIZATION IN THE SOVIET UNION

In November 1929, Stalin proclaimed that the middle peasant had begun to flock to the collective farms. In fact, collectivization had increased dramatically by this time, surpassing the relatively modest rates projected for the socialized sector of agriculture after the Fifteenth Party Congress of December 1927 placed col-

lectivization on the immediate agenda. At the Sixteenth Party Conference in April 1929, in its First Five-Year Plan on agriculture, the central committee of the Communist Party had projected the collectivization of 9.6 percent of the peasant population in the 1932–1933 economic year, and 13.6 percent (or approximately 3.7 million households) in 1933–1934. These projections were revised upward in the late summer and fall of 1929, when first *Gosplan* (the state planning commission) called for the collectivization of 2.5 million peasant households in the course of 1929–1930, and then *Kolkhoztsentr* (the central agency at the head of collective-farm administration) resolved that 3.1 million peasant households would be incorporated into collective farms by the end of 1929–1930 (Davies, *The Socialist Offensive,* pp. 112, 147).

In actuality, by 1 June 1928, 1.7 percent of peasant households were in collective farms; and between 1 June and 1 October 1929, alone, percentages rose from 3.9 to 7.5. The increase was especially marked in major grain-producing regions. The Lower Volga and North Caucasus surpassed all other regions with percentages of collectivized peasant households reaching 18.1 and 19.1, respectively, in October (Davies, *The Socialist Offensive,* p. 442). The high rates achieved in the regional collectivization campaigns lay behind Stalin's statement that the middle peasantry was entering collective farms. By arguing that the middle peasant was turning voluntarily to socialized agriculture, Stalin was claiming that the majority of the peasantry was ready for collectivization. In reality, it was mainly poor peasants who were joining collectives. And, although there was apparently some genuine enthusiasm "from below," the regional campaigns had already begun to resort to coercion to achieve their high percentages.

Even at this stage, collectivization was largely imposed "from above." Orchestrated and led by the regional party organizations, with implicit or explicit sanction from Moscow, district-level officials and urban Communists and workers brought collectivization to the countryside. A volatile antipeasant mood in the cities—especially among rank-and-file Communists and industrial workers and based on bread shortages, continuing news of "kulak sabotage," and long-simmering urban-rural antipathies—infected these cadres and other, newer recruits from urban centers. This combination of official endorsement, regional initiative and direction, and unrestrained action on the part of lower-level cadres intertwined to create a radical momentum of ever-accelerating collectivization tempos. The "success" of the regional campaigns then provided the necessary impetus for Moscow to push up collectivization rates even higher in what became a deadly and continual tug-of-war between center and periphery as reality exceeded plan, and plans were continually revised to register, keep pace with, and push forward collectivization tempos.

The Politburo commission, December 1929.

The November 1929 Communist Party plenum formally ratified the policy of wholesale collectivization, leaving the specifics of policy implementation to a Politburo commission that would meet the next month. The commission called for the completion of collectivization in major grain-producing regions in one to two years; in other grain regions, two to three years; and in the most important grain deficit regions, three to four years. The commission also resolved that an intermediate form of collective farm, the artel—a cooperative that featured the socialization of land, labor, draft animals, and basic inventory—would be the standard, and that private ownership of domestic livestock needed for consumption would be maintained. Any movement to extend socialization of peasant properties beyond the artel would depend on the peasantry's experience and "the growth of its confidence in the stability, benefits, and advantages" of collective farming. The kulak faced expropriation of his means of production (which would then be transferred to the collective farms) and resettlement or exile. The subcommittee on the kulak recommended a differentiated approach to the elimination of the kulak as a class. Finally, the commission warned against any attempt either to restrain collectivization or to collectivize "by decree."

The Politburo commission published its legislation on 5 January 1930. The legislation stipulated that the Lower Volga, Central Volga, and North Caucasus were to complete collectivization by fall 1930, spring 1931 at the latest; all remaining grain regions were to complete collectivization by fall 1931, spring 1932 at the latest, thus accelerating yet again the pace of the campaign. No mention was made of remaining areas. The legislation also specified that the artel would be the main form of collective farm, leaving out any particulars from the commission's work. Stalin had personally intervened on this issue, ordering the editing out of "details" on the artel, which should, he argued, more appropriately be left to the jurisdiction of the Commissariat of Agriculture. The kulak would be "eliminated as a class," as Stalin had already noted in his 27 December 1929 speech at the Conference of Marxist Agronomists, and excluded from entry into the collective farms. Stalin and other maximalists in the leadership were responsible for radicalizing further an already radical set of guidelines by revising the work of the December commission, keeping the legislation vague, and including only very weak warnings against violence.

By the time this legislation was published, collectivization percentages in the Soviet Union had leaped from 7.5 in October to 18.1 on 1 January 1930, with even higher rates in major grain regions (Lower Volga, 56–70 percent; Central Volga, 41.7 percent; North Caucasus, 48.1 percent). Through the month of January, reality continued to outpace planning. By 1 February 1930, 31.7 percent of all households were in collective farms, with rates still higher in individual regions (Moscow, 37.1 percent; Central Black Earth Region, 51 percent; Ural, 52.1 percent; Central Volga, 51.8 percent; Lower Volga, 61.1 percent; North Caucasus, 62.7 percent; see Davies, *The Socialist Offensive*, pp. 442–443).

Dekulakization.

Dekulakization—the elimination of the kulak as a class—had also spread far and wide through the country as regional party organizations enacted their own legislation and issued their own directives in advance and in anticipation of Moscow. A Politburo commission led by V. M. Molotov, Politburo member and Stalin's right-hand man, met from 15 to 26 January in an effort to draw up central legislation on dekulakization. Like collectivization, dekulakization had gone far beyond the initial plans of the December Politburo commission by now, in what had become a melee of violence and plunder. The term "kulak" was defined broadly to include not only kulaks (an ambiguous term to start with) but (using the parlance of the day) active white guards, former bandits, former white officers, repatriated peasants, active members of church councils and sects, priests, and anyone "currently manifesting c[ounter]-r[evolutionary] activities." Following the policy recommendations of December, the commission divided kulaks into three categories: counterrevolutionaries, those refusing to submit to collectivization, and the remainder. The first, most dangerous category was limited to some 60,000 heads of households who faced execution or internment in concentration camps, while their families were expropriated of their properties and all but the most essential items and were sent into exile in remote parts of the country. The second category—primarily the richest kulaks, large-scale kulaks, and former semilandowners—was limited to 150,000 families; deemed somewhat less dangerous but still a threat, they also faced expropriation and exile to remote regions. The main points of exile for these two categories were the Northern Region (scheduled to receive 70,000 families), Siberia (50,000 families), the Urals (20–25,000 families), and Kazakhstan (20–25,000 families). The third category, well over one-half million families, was to be subjected to partial expropriation of properties and resettlement within their native districts. Overall numbers of dekulakized peasants were not to exceed 3 to 5 percent of the population. The OGPU (the political police) was charged with the implementation of arrests and deportations. The operation was to be completed in four months. District soviets, in combination with village soviets, poor peasants, and collective farmers, were responsible for drawing up lists of kulaks and carrying out expropriations.

Collectivization and dekulakization had long since jumped the rails of central control. Brigades of collectivizers with plenipotentiary powers toured the countryside, stopping briefly in villages where, often with guns in hands, they forced peasants, under threat of dekulakization, to sign up to join the collective farm. Intimidation, harassment, and even torture were used to exact signatures. Collectivization rates continued to rise through February, reaching 57.2 percent by 1 March, and the hideously unreal regional percentages of 74.2 in Moscow Region, 83.3 in the Central Black Earth Region, 75.6 in the Urals, 60.3 in Central Volga, 70.1 in Lower Volga, and 79.4 in North Caucasus (Davies, *The Socialist Offensive*, pp. 442–443). The high percentages belied the fact that most collective farms at this time were "paper collectives," attained in the "race for percentages" held among regional and district party organizations. Collectivization often amounted to little more than a collective farm charter and chairman, the socialization of livestock (which might remain in former owners' possession until appropriate collective space was provided), and the terror of dekulakization.

Dekulakization was no fiction. Although deportations often did not begin until later, peasants labeled as kulaks found themselves evicted from their homes or forced to exchange homes with poor peasants; fleeced of their belongings, often including household items, trinkets, and clothes; and shamed, insulted, and injured before the community. Dekulakization was sometimes carried out "conspiratorially," in the dead of night, as cadres banged on doors and windows, terrorizing families who were forced out onto the street, half-dressed. Often, everything was taken from these families, including children's underwear and earrings from women's ears. In the Central Black Earth Region, a county-level official told cadres to "dekulakize in such a way that only the ceiling beams and walls are left."

The countryside was engulfed in what peasants called a Bartholomew's night massacre. As state repression increased, peasant violence increased, and as peasant violence increased, state violence increased, leading to a seemingly never-ending crescendo of arrests, pillage, beatings, and rage. The crescendo came to an abrupt halt, however, when, on 2 March 1930, Stalin published his article "Dizziness from Success," which blamed the outrages on the lower-level cadres—who were indeed dizzy from success—but failed to admit any central responsibility. Soon collectivization percentages began to tumble as peasants appropriated Stalin's name in their struggle against the cadres of collectivization. Peasants quit the collective farms in droves, driving down percentages of collectivized households from 57.2 in March to 38.6 in April, 28 in May, and further downward until hitting a low of 21.5 in September. The decline in regional rates was equally drastic. Between 1 March and 1 May, percentages of collectivized households fell in Moscow Region from 74.2 to 7.5; in the Central Black Earth Region, from 83.3 to 18.2; in the Urals, from 75.6 to 31.9; in the Lower Volga, from 70.1 to 41.4; in the Central Volga, from 60.3 to 30.1; and in the North Caucasus, from 79.4 to 63.2 (Davies, *The Socialist Offensive*, pp. 442–443).

Collectivization resumed in the fall of 1930 at a slightly less breakneck speed. The major grain-producing regions attained complete collectivization by the end of the First Five-Year Plan in 1932; other regions climbed more gradually to that goal, generally reaching it by the end of the 1930s. In the meantime, over one million peasant families (five to six million people) were subjected to some form of dekulakization during the years of wholesale collectivization. Of these, some 381,026 families (totaling 1,803,392 people) were exiled in 1930 and 1931, the two key years of deportation. The deportations were perhaps one of the most horrendous episodes in a decade marked by horror and, through the vast expansion of the use of internal exile, the concentration camp system, and the political police, helped to establish the foundations for the Stalinist police state.

CONSEQUENCES AND AFTERMATH OF SOVIET COLLECTIVIZATION

Collectivization posed a profound threat to the peasant way of life. Peasants of every social strata responded to this threat by uniting in defense of their families, beliefs, communities, and livelihood, and overcoming their ordinary and multiple differences. In 1930, more than two million peasants took part in 13,794 mass disturbances against Communist Party policies. In 1929 and 1930, the OGPU recorded 22,887 "terrorist acts" aimed at local officials and peasant activists, more than 1,100 of them murders

Collectivization in the Soviet Union. Peasants enroll for collective farm, Russia, early 1930s. DAVID KING COLLECTION

(Viola, 1996, pp. 103, 105, 110, 112, 140). Peasant resistance was rooted in peasant culture rather than in any specific social stratum and was shaped by an agency and political consciousness that derived from reasoned concerns centered largely on issues of justice and subsistence, and supplemented by retribution, anger, and desperation. The peasant rebellion against collectivization was the most serious episode of popular resistance experienced by the Communist Party after the Russian Civil War.

In the end, peasant rebels were no match for the vast police powers of the state, and, like most other peasant rebellions, this one was destined to fail. The main element in the peasantry's defeat was state repression. Millions of peasants were arrested, imprisoned, deported, or executed in the years of collectivization. The state dismantled existing authority structures in the village, removing and replacing traditional elites. The devastating famine of 1932–1933, caused by collectivization and the state's inhumanly high grain requisitions, complemented state repression, first robbing peasants of their grain and then depriving perhaps as many as five million people of their lives as starvation and disease took their toll. Repression and a one-sided war of attrition effectively silenced peasant rebels.

Yet repression alone could not and did not end peasant resistance; nor could it have served as the only mechanism of control in the long term. For reasons of sheer necessity, the state largely gave up its revolutionary aspirations in the countryside after collectivization, choosing, pragmatically and cynically, to exert its domination over the peasantry through the control of vital resources, most especially grain. The peasant household continued to be the mainstay of the peasant—if not collective farm—economy, and homes, domestic livestock, barns, sheds, and household necessities were deemed peasants' private property. The private plot and a limited collective farm market remained alongside socialized agriculture to guarantee a minimum subsistence for collective farmers and to supplement the nation's consumer needs. Peasants were co-opted into positions of authority, and in the decades following the death of Stalin, the state gradually extended more of its admittedly paltry benefits from the urban to the rural sector. The Soviet agricultural system became a hybrid system, based on peasant private plots and collective farms, all in the service of the state, but offering the peasantry something in the exchange.

In the long term, the social by-products of industrialization and urbanization proved as efficacious in securing peasant acquiescence as the brute force of the state. Continued outmigration and permanent resettlement in cities of males and young people spread extended families between town and village, bringing peasant culture to the town and fixing in place urban bridges to the village more firmly than ever before. Education, military service, and improved transportation and communications facilitated a certain degree of sovietization in the countryside, or, at the very least, some homogenization across the urban divide.

The Stalinist state and the collective farm system triumphed in the end, but their triumph did not spell the end of peasant culture. The peasantry re-emerged, not unchanged to be sure, from within socialized agriculture. Passive resistance and other "weapons of the weak" became endemic mechanisms of coping and survival for the peasantry within the collective farm. Agriculture stagnated, becoming the Achilles' heel of the Soviet economy, a ceaseless reminder of the ironies of the "proletarian revolution" in peasant Russia. Like the peasant commune before it, the collective farm became a bulwark against change and as much a subsistence shelter for peasants as a control mechanism for the state. Over time, the collective farm became the quintessential risk-aversion guarantor that peasants had always sought. Socioeconomic leveling, a basic and insured subsistence, and some degree of cultural independence, demographic isolation, and feminization of the village maintained and even strengthened aspects of village culture.

To the extent that it was possible, peasants made the collective farm their own. State attempts at decollectivization after 1991 provide ample evidence for this. Decollectivization was blocked by a peasantry grown accustomed to the collective farm. This seeming intransigence was less the result of backwardness, or a "serf mentality," as some interpreters see it, than a simple continuity of peasant needs, values, and ways of living. Decollectivization, moreover, demonstrated continuity with earlier state efforts to remold the peasantry. Its implementation was top down, based on some measure of force (although nothing like that of collectivization), and relied counterproductively on a tradition-bound equalization of small land parcels in cases of privatization, revealing all the usual elements of the cultural manipulation and imperialism of state modernization. Peasants in post-Communist Russia and other former Soviet republics have responded to decollectivization with skepticism and hostility, having molded the collective farm at least partially to their own needs.

COLLECTIVIZATION IN EASTERN EUROPE

Collectivization in the Communist countries of Eastern Europe (defined here as the former German Democratic Republic, Czechoslovakia, Hungary, Poland, Bulgaria, Romania, Yugoslavia, and Albania) followed similar patterns to Soviet collectivization. Following occupation by Soviet military forces at the end of World War II, these countries were subject to a pro-

cess of sovietization, which, in the years before the death of Stalin in 1953, was tantamount to Stalinization. Political repression, the nationalization of industry, and the beginnings of agricultural collectivization were carried out in the years between 1948 and 1953. As in the Soviet Union, collectivization was a state-directed policy and met with little or no support from the peasantry. Collectivization in Eastern Europe also entailed the elimination of a rural bourgeoisie, leading to national policies of dekulakization. By 1953, collectivization in most of Eastern Europe had only been partially implemented. The brief "thaw" in policy following the death of Stalin meant in most cases a respite for the peasantry and a temporary halt in collectivization. The second stage of collectivization came in the late 1950s, with the result that collectivization was completed throughout Eastern Europe by 1962, with the notable exceptions of Poland and Yugoslavia, which did not experience a second collectivization drive and had largely abandoned collectivization after the initial drive of the late Stalin period.

The motivations behind collectivization were fairly uniform through Eastern Europe. Following Soviet patterns of ideology and economic and political development, Eastern European collectivization was based on theories of rural class struggle, the idea of "primitive socialist accumulation," and the extension of political and administrative controls to the countryside. Most important, Eastern European collectivization came with Soviet hegemony, as an imported by-product of military occupation and sovietization.

Eastern European collectivization exhibited patterns of national variation. While the initial collectivization drive in Poland was relatively moderate, collectivization in Bulgaria, for example, was brutal and much closer in style to the Soviet drive of 1930. And in spite of initial collectivization campaigns, private agriculture continued to dominate the rural economies of Poland and Yugoslavia. In Hungary the policies of the New Economic Mechanism after 1968 gradually introduced market forces into the socialized agricultural economy, diminishing the intensity of collectivization. And, as in the case of the Soviet Union, a private sector based on the household economies of collective farmers played an important role in both collective farmers' income and the nation's consumer needs throughout Eastern Europe.

Peasants often resisted collectivization in Eastern Europe. Although peasants and farmers sometimes offered active forms of resistance to collectivization, the more widespread and long-term reaction of the rural population to socialized agriculture was passive resistance in the form of foot-dragging, pilfer-

Soviet Collective Farm. *A Collective Farm Festival,* painting (1937) by Sergei V. Gerasimov (1885–1964). TRETYAKOV GALLERY, MOSCOW/NOVOSTI/THE BRIDGEMAN ART LIBRARY

ing, and the like. Eastern Europe also experienced patterns of demographic change similar to the Soviet Union, with population movement between rural and urban sectors.

After 1989, with perestroika and the end of Soviet domination in Eastern Europe, policies of decollectivization and property restitution were initiated in much of Eastern Europe. These policies were not entirely successful. In most cases, reform policies were hastily constructed and implemented in the more general context of a complex economic restructuring of the system entailing myriad economic problems and disruptions. In general, where collectivization was most entrenched (Bulgaria, Romania, Albania), decollectivization was most problematic. As of the late 1990s, decollectivization was a continuing process, necessitating new policies, new legislation, and the rewriting of legal codes.

See also **Peasants and Rural Laborers** *(volume 3); and other articles in this section.*

BIBLIOGRAPHY

Conquest, Robert. *The Harvest of Sorrow: Soviet Collectivization and the Terror-Famine.* Oxford and New York, 1986.

Davies, R. W. *The Socialist Offensive: The Collectivisation of Soviet Agriculture, 1929–1930.* Cambridge, Mass., 1980.

Davies, R. W. *The Soviet Collective Farm, 1929–1930.* Cambridge, Mass., 1980.

Fainsod, Merle. *Smolensk under Soviet Rule.* Cambridge, Mass., 1958.

Fitzpatrick, Sheila. *Stalin's Peasants: Resistance and Survival in the Russian Village after Collectivization.* New York, 1994.

Hughes, James. *Stalin, Siberia, and the Crisis of the New Economic Policy.* Cambridge, U.K., 1991.

Hughes, James. *Stalinism in a Russian Province: Collectivization and Dekulakization in Siberia.* London, 1996.

Kingston-Mann, Esther. *Lenin and the Problem of Marxist Peasant Revolution.* Oxford and New York, 1983.

Korbonski, Andrzej. *Politics of Socialist Agriculture in Poland: 1945–1960.* New York, 1965.

Lenin, V. I. *Polnoe sobranie sochinenii.* 5th ed. 55 vols. Moscow, 1958–1966.

Lewin, Moshe. *Russian Peasants and Soviet Power: A Study of Collectivization.* Translated by Irene Nove. New York, 1975.

Medvedev, Zhores A. *Soviet Agriculture.* New York, 1987.

Millar, James R., and Alec Nove. "A Debate on Collectivization: Was Stalin Really Necessary?" *Problems of Communism* 25 (1976): 49–62.

Pryor, Frederic L. *The Red and the Green: The Rise and Fall of Collectivized Agriculture in Marxist Regimes.* Princeton, N.J., 1992.

Rakowska-Harmstone, Teresa, and Andrew Gyorgy, eds. *Communism in Eastern Europe.* Bloomington, Ind., 1979.

Shanin, Teodor, ed. *Peasants and Peasant Societies.* 2d ed. Oxford, 1987.

Sokolovsky, Joan. *Peasants and Power: State Autonomy and the Collectivization of Agriculture in Eastern Europe.* Boulder, Colo., 1990.

Swain, Nigel. *Collective Farms Which Work?* Cambridge, U.K., 1985.

Turnock, David, ed. *Privatization in Rural Eastern Europe: The Process of Restitution and Restructuring.* Cheltenham, U.K., 1998.

Viola, Lynne. *The Best Sons of the Fatherland: Workers in the Vanguard of Soviet Collectivization.* Oxford and New York, 1987.

Viola, Lynne. *Peasant Rebels under Stalin: Collectivization and the Culture of Peasant Resistance.* Oxford and New York, 1996.

ESTATES AND COUNTRY HOUSES

Priscilla R. Roosevelt

nce, Europe's country residences
ategories. Foremost were the vast
ing estates that the aristocracy of
controlled and administered.
val fiefdoms persisted well into
Powerful landowning families
creating dynastic alliances to in-
nd landholdings. The second
ing arose in Renaissance Italy:
ountry house, a rural pleasure
d to urban life, as the city was
r source of income. But own-
tates exported urban comforts
ce all country residences were
in a rural setting, and country
damentally different from their
hbors.

ouse reached its apogee in
ngland through a successful fu-
pes of country life. In England
nonymous both with wealth and
here else was there a similarly self-
nt elite. The architecture, furnish-
country seats throughout the Brit-
the political authority, social status,
of the landed gentleman, who shot
nds, and roamed his tenant farms in
day but dressed in tails each evening.
gnificance, these country houses have
ous social histories.

untry life gave rise to a widespread
lomania on the Continent. But in
the conditions for a similar culture of
re absent, and hence social (as opposed
or economic) histories of continental
re rare. Whereas the English lord ignored
solutism focused attention on it. The
or example, were thoroughly tied to Ver-
nobleman Jean de La Bruyère explained
an . . . at home in his province lives free
substance; . . . at court he is taken care
ved" (Ford, 1953, p. vii).

Only in the reign of Louis XVI (1774–1792) did French court life lose its significance. Other continental elites also reached their zenith of power and independence in the same period, the era of enlightened absolutism, under Frederick the Great of Prussia, Joseph II of Austria, and Catherine II of Russia. The model of country splendor at Frederick's Sans Souci in Potsdam found echoes in suburban villas near Berlin and Vienna, though the traditional strongholds of Prussia's nobility remained, in essence, medieval, as did those of great Austrian landowners. Russia lacked comparable medieval manors; the vast majority of its country houses were built in a single century, between 1762, when Catherine the Great ascended the throne, and 1861, when the serfs were emancipated. Although the Russian elite spoke French, as estate owners they too were Anglophiles. Some Russian country estates were major sources of income; though the country house had little political impact, it played an enormous role in Russia's cultural development.

THE IDEOLOGY AND ARCHITECTURE OF THE COUNTRY HOUSE

As James S. Ackerman points out in *The Villa,* the country house of Renaissance Italy embodied a radical ideological innovation. Heretofore, country grandees had been surrounded by armed retainers. Their sparsely furnished and intermittently occupied castles and châteaus were grand symbols of territorial hegemony. Well into the English Renaissance, many great houses, among them Longleat (1568–1569) and Wothorpe Lodge (1610), retained the great chambers, turrets, and towers signifying authority in medieval times.

Renaissance Italy contained politically ambitious and economically prosperous city-states whose leading citizens identified easily with their Roman forbears. The rediscovery of the works of classical Roman authors such as Virgil, Pliny the Younger, Horace, Cato, and Vitruvius, whose poetry and prose idealized

413

Italian Renaissance Villa. Villa of Cafaggiolo, built for the Medici rulers of Florence by Giusto van Utens around 1599.

the long-vanished arcadian retreats of Roman states-men and intellectuals, gave rise to a cult of country life centered on the bucolic leisure activities available at a country house. Classical writers had used the word *otium* to describe their country pursuits. The antith-esis of *negotium,* a preoccupation with business, *otium* could mean either the informality and arcadian relax-ation Virgil described in his *Eclogues* or the pursuit of salubrious mental and physical activity he praised in his *Georgics* (which also contained practical farming advice). In the fourteenth century the seminal work *Vita solitaria* by the great classical scholar Petrarch, along with his letters extolling the many pleasures of country life, gave new life to the ancient pursuit of *otium.* But for the owner of a country house, labor was not the backbreaking, monotonous routine of the rural poor; rather, it was seen as the reinvigoration of soul and spirit. Voltaire designing his garden at Ferney, and Marie Antoinette in her Versailles dairy serving guests fresh milk from prize cows, were both pursuing this ideal.

Villa architecture and landscaping, paintings of country houses and paintings within their walls, and a rich literature about country house life soon en-shrined the new cult. Renaissance villas sprang full-blown from readings of the ancient texts, since no Roman country houses had yet been excavated to provide concrete models. The earliest Medici co[untry] residences, at Trebbio (1427–1433) and Cafag[giolo] (1443–1452), demonstrated the lingering infl[uence] of medieval towers and battlements. The Medic[i villa] at Fiesole, by contrast, situated on a comma[nding] height with sweeping views of the Arno valle[y and] Florence, reflected the new aesthetic of Leon B[attista] Alberti's *De re aedificatoria* (On the art of bui[lding], completed 1452, published 1485), which attack[ed the] fortress as incommensurate with the values [of the] peaceful citizens of a republic. As Ackerman no[tes, the] Fiesole villa was the first modern country hou[se de]-signed solely on the basis of aesthetic and hum[anist] values. Slightly later, Lorenzo de' Medici c[ommis]-sioned Giuliano de Sangallo to design a grand [country] house at Poggio (1485). With its templelike [pediment] resting atop a colonnade spanning the enti[re] facade, and its imposing split staircase, the [Poggio] house expressed the sense of dynastic grand[eur that] informed later structures such as the new H[ardwick] Hall, built in England at the end of the sixtee[nth cen]-tury. This imposing, symmetrical house ha[d a] facade pierced by countless windows and [was] adorned with the initials of Elizabeth H[ardwick,] countess of Shrewsbury. Her contempora[ries, the] Maignarts of Normandy, far more modest Fr[ench] pro-vincials, likewise highlighted family status

Latin inscriptions glorifying their ancestors along the Italianate galleries of the facade of one estate house, and they built a new, more magnificent house on another estate in the early seventeenth century. During the next two centuries countless country houses were built or remodeled throughout Europe, as the stylish country residence, complete with coat of arms and family tree, portraits of ancestors and mementos of their achievements, became a necessity for families wishing to assert their high social standing.

No architect had a more profound impact on the form of Europe's country houses than Andrea Palladio (1508–1580). Palladianism provided an international architectural vocabulary for Europe's elite, making neoclassical grandeur synonymous with authority and good taste. The eighteen country houses Palladio designed for wealthy patrons from Venice, Padua, and Vicenza innovatively adapted the elegant forms of classical Roman architecture to the practical functions of a country house. The stables, storerooms, and other service areas of a working farm were all incorporated into a single balanced architectural plan, often as elegant pavilions attached to the main house by covered colonnades. The enormous variety of Palladio's houses made them a particularly rich resource for later designers. The long, low Villa Barbaro at Maser (1557–1558), its salon walls enlivened by Paolo Veronese's frescoes of romantic landscapes and evocative Roman ruins, was one model. The Villa Rotunda (1560–1591) has an entirely different aesthetic. Designed as a pleasure palace, its cubic form, crowned with a dome and with Roman porticoes on each facade, dominates the landscape. Palladio described his creations in his *I quattro libri dell'architettura* (Four books on architecture; 1570), an illustrated compendium of advice and plans for country house builders that found scores of devotees throughout Europe.

In Holland, Palladian villas appeared alongside their baroque precursors in the republic's golden age, the seventeenth century. Enclaves of elegant mansions arose around the major cities of Leiden and Haarlem, and along the banks of the river Vecht between Utrecht and Amsterdam. Their names, such as Hofwijk, "away from court," or Zorghvliet, "fly from care," were expressive of the country house ideology. The Dutch spent immense sums on the building and furnishing of these houses. Visitors found them sumptuous, with large, well-tended parks and all the leisure activities—hunting, gardening, or playing the squire among tenant farmers—that jaded courtiers might find physically and morally restorative.

In England, Palladianism found its first convert in the architect Inigo Jones (1573–1652), but others appeared after 1715, when two source books appeared

simultaneously: the first volume of Colen Campbell's *Vitruvius Britannicus,* and a two-volume edition of Palladio. Richard Boyle, third earl of Burlington, a passionate adherent, borrowed freely from the Villa Rotunda for the design of his suburban Chiswick House (1727–1729). The rotunda, however, never gained the popularity of Palladio's columned porticoes and symmetrical room arrangements. In Russia and in Ireland, the Palladian combination of a central block linked to two wings by curved colonnades was particularly fashionable. The refined simplicity and balance of Palladianism suited Enlightenment ideals far better than the excessively decorative baroque. But it was more widespread in countries without older indigenous secular architectural traditions, such as Russia or the United States, than in England, where it competed from the mid-eighteenth century onward with a revival of the Gothic and, later, with a diffused historicism embracing numerous earlier styles.

In the heyday of estate building (in England, from 1660 to 1730 and from 1790 until well into the nineteenth century), architects also designed interior decor and furnishings, and decorators doubled as landscapers. Charles Cameron (1730s–1812), a Scottish architect whose treatise on Roman baths won him commissions from Catherine the Great, not only designed the central complex (a Palladian bridge, gallery of worthies, and Roman baths) of Tsarskoe Selo, the summer palace of the Russian imperial family, but also sketched designs for its interior decor and furnishings. Eighteenth-century designers worked in many styles as well as forms, including rococo and chinoiserie, which added grace, variety, and fantasy to their vocabulary. Robert Adam (1728–1792), famed for his neoclassical interiors, was also renowned for his Gothic villas and castles.

In eighteenth-century Russia, European styles came in rapid succession. The earliest country houses, along the road to Peterhof, the royal residence outside St. Petersburg, were predominantly Italian baroque, like St. Petersburg itself. Like the Dutch villas that perhaps inspired them, these courtiers' houses had playful names such as Neskuchnoe, "not boring," and Mon Plaisir, "my pleasure." In 1762 Catherine the Great commissioned Antonio Rinaldi to design a small palace with rococo and chinoiserie interiors at Oranienbaum. But in 1764 she embraced neoclassicism, Russian courtiers followed suit, and the great age of Russian estate building (1762–1825) saw grandiose neoclassical houses proliferate throughout central Russia. Both foreign and Russian architects, such as the self-taught Nikolai Lvov (1751–1803), who translated and published Palladio's *I quattri libri,* designed country houses, some of which, such as Lvov's

Country Life. *Merry Company in the Open Air,* painting (c. 1615) by Willem Pietersz Buytewech (c. 1591–1624). WALLRAF-RICHARTZ MUSEUM, COLOGNE, GERMANY/THE BRIDGEMAN ART LIBRARY

own Nikolskoe-Cherenchitsy and Gavrila Derzhavin's Zvanka, were clearly modeled on the Villa Rotunda. Russian Gothic was rare, reserved for outbuildings as a decorative contrast to the main house, until the reign of Nicholas I (1825–1855), a period when, throughout Europe, romanticism encouraged historicism in architecture. Nicholas's Gothic "Cottage" initiated the search for a Russian national style and opened the doors to stylistic experimentation, culminating in the fanciful, symbolic, and eclectic architecture of late-nineteenth-century Russian country houses, some Gothic, others neoclassical, still others Swiss chalets or grandiose variations on traditional Russian village architecture.

LANDSCAPE DESIGN

In Renaissance Italy the landscaped surroundings of the villa had been rigidly geometrical. Clipped hedges and topiary, geometrically arranged paths, a profusion of statuary, and fountains remained in vogue through the seventeenth century, culminating in the magnificent designs of André Le Nôtre for the formal gardens of Versailles, widely imitated by country house landscapers. But during the eighteenth century, talented English landscapers imbued with a new sensibility to nature devised changes that altered the entire concept of the landscape. Batty Langley, in his *New Principles of Gardening* (1728), suggested the straight garden path be replaced by sinuous designs he termed "artinatural." Charles Bridgeman left plantings untrimmed and created vast expanses of lawn at Stowe, his most renowned commission. By mid-century, in the work of the most noted practitioners such as William Kent, who designed the Elysian Fields at Stowe, the garden became indistinguishable from the idealized, untrammeled landscapes of fashionable painters such as Claude Lorrain and Nicolas Poussin. Walls were replaced by the ha-ha, a deep invisible ditch with a sunken wall that kept farm animals out of the garden. In the second half of the century Lancelot "Capability" Brown (who worked on 188 gardens) emphasized water in the landscape, and Humphrey Repton in his 220 commissions enthroned the picturesque.

The English, or informal, garden was as demanding as its predecessor on owners' resources and designers' ingenuity. Tenant farms were sacrificed in a competition for vast landscaped parks that by the early nineteenth century sometimes encompassed thousands of acres. Throughout Europe, legions of workers were set to resculpting garden terrain, creating natural-looking ponds and lakes, brooks and waterfalls, and sloping hillsides, or moving full-grown trees to function as accents in the landscape. Areas of light and shade, hills and plains, open spaces and verdant glades alternated to inspire particular moods or emotions. The best designers emulated the four levels of association—the philosophical, the allegorical, the historical, and the picturesque—found at showplaces such as Stowe.

Evocative garden structures—Palladian or rustic bridges, Grecian temples, obelisks, mosques, pagodas, shell-encrusted grottoes, and ruins—enhanced the sense of communication with other times and places. The much emulated landscape of Stowe boasted a neoclassical Temple of British Worthies and a Gothic Temple; Alexander Pope's Twickenham had a *paradiso* (an artificial hill) taken from Italian models. Ruins, whether Roman bridge or Gothic abbey, had historical allusions but were also frankly picturesque, as were other inventive or extravagant follies such as one pavilion shaped like a pineapple. (A folly is a small fanciful building designed exclusively for picturesque effect.) Toward the end of the eighteenth century, Polish magnates engaged in competitive folly building. Princess Izabela Czartoryska's garden at Powazki outside Warsaw had the usual ruins, grottoes, temples, and waterfalls. In addition, various small thatched huts were built for family members, humble on the outside but inside sporting luxuries such as the Sèvres porcelain tiles used on the princess's bathroom walls. A rival, Princess Elzbieta Lubomirska, favored exotic structures at her Mon Coteau, "my hillside," including a pagoda, a Turkish pavilion, and a North American Indian tepee. In Russia the landscaper Andrei T. Bolotov designed numerous amusing surprises for the grounds of Count Alexei Bobrinskoi's estate, Bogoroditsk. Visitors were temporarily trapped on the *paradiso* when a hidden sluice opened and water filled a moat. The grotto, sunk into a hill and decorated with many different types of stone, had a mirrored interior. Bolotov also constructed ingenious shams, among them a ruined monastery on a nearby hillside. In western Europe by this time, the taste for exotic structures in the garden had waned, spurred by Jacques Delille's influential poem of 1782, titled "Les jardins, ou l'art d'embellir le paysage" (Gardens, or the art of embellishing the landscape), which warned against their excessive use. The picturesque garden, emulative of a wilder, more unadorned nature, now came into vogue in England and France.

The eighteenth-century revolution in landscaping enlarged the private space around the European estate, increasing its distinction from its surroundings. Yet at the same time, the notions of grandeur and taste embodied in these private paradises escaped their boundaries to reach a wider audience. Owners of famous English houses and gardens began opening them to touring continental aristocrats, who picked up ideas for their own houses and pleasure grounds at Stowe, Blenheim, Chatsworth, and a host of lesser properties. In addition, by mid-century not only country house architectural guides but illustrated works on park design and decoration circulated widely. These "how-to" manuals aided the many estate owners who wanted fashionable garden paradises but lacked the financial means to hire expert landscapers.

ESTATE INTERIORS AND OCCUPANCY

As Mark Girouard demonstrates in his *Life in the English Country House* (1978), the alterations in country house interiors over time provide a guide to changes in customary practices and in the role of the house. The Elizabethan and Jacobean house was the setting for elaborate rituals attending the lord's daily activities. The ceremonial center of the house moved from the medieval, ground-floor great hall to the great chamber on an upper floor, used for welcoming visitors, dining in state, masques, dancing, and other public activities. Long, elegant galleries provided space for indoor exercise and for increasing numbers of family portraits. Bedchambers (private spaces) were entered through withdrawing chambers (semiprivate), which were also used for small dinners, as were informal sitting rooms or parlors. In the "formal house" (1630–1720), the ceremonial space grew. The great chamber, now called a salon or saloon, remained central. Surrounding it were suites of apartments: withdrawing chambers and bedrooms, now much more public. The ejection of servants from the great hall and the revolutionary invention of a backstairs with servants' rooms off it made the staff less visible. Libraries, studies, and pictures other than portraits made their debut.

In the early eighteenth century, a great increase in travel and country entertaining brought the "social house" into being. The great hall shrank, and the main floor of the house now consisted of a series of high-ceilinged drawing rooms, their walls hung with landscapes as well as portraits. The largest saloon was used for balls; other rooms, diversified by function, might include a library, billiard room, music room, dining room, and often a separate breakfast room near a winter garden or conservatory. A state bedroom, long obligatory for a grand house, was retained as part of the entertaining space, though in most instances it was never occupied by royalty. The furnishings of these public rooms reflected the collecting habits of generations of scions on the grand tour: antique furniture and sculptures, rare books, collections of coins,

Country Palace. Entrance gate to Eszterháza, the palace of the Eszterhazy princes, 1761–1781. The palace contained 120 rooms during the time of Prince Miklós József the Magnificent (1714–1790). ESZTERHÁZA PALACE, FERTÖD, HUNGARY/ERICH LESSING/ART RESOURCE, NY.

minerals, and weapons. Suites of private apartments for family members were now relegated to the floor above the reception rooms, or in the aboveground rusticated floor below.

In most country houses until the nineteenth century, the public rooms opened into each other, creating linear axes of enfilades along the facades of the house. Furniture was often placed stiffly along the walls, and guests promenaded along the enfilade. As the nineteenth century progressed, formality waned and the sphere of intimacy and privacy grew. A circular arrangement of rooms became more normal for new houses, as did circular seating for gatherings. In Russia the enfilade was deliberately interrupted by closing doors and placing barriers such as bookcases against them. Rigidly symmetrical architecture also went out of fashion; in England the Gothic style saw a second revival in the Victorian age.

The eighteenth and early nineteenth centuries marked the heyday of the great country house in part because of gradual improvements in travel: first, asphalt paving and carriages fitted with springs, then railway lines. Whereas in Elizabethan England owners had traveled from town to country not only with most of their servants but most of the furniture, by the late eighteenth century it was possible to migrate from a well-staffed and furnished city house to an equally welcoming country estate for the summer. As with so many aspects of country house life, occupancy patterns varied enormously. Throughout this period, some houses were occupied year-round, others rarely visited. A few eighteenth-century Russian grandees, for example, built lavish country mansions on lands granted by the Crown, entertained the empress once, and then returned permanently to St. Petersburg.

MASTERS AND SERVANTS

The proper functioning of a great house depended on a large and well-trained staff. As early as the sixteenth century, important English houses had books of regulations to guide staff in matters of dress and deportment. The size of these staffs varied considerably. In a large house such as the earl of Dorset's Knole in the seventeenth century, 111 servants regularly dined in the servants' hall. In parts of eastern Europe, staffs for considerably smaller houses regularly exceeded this number. The Wilmot sisters, who visited Princess Dashkova's estate, Troitskoe, in Russia in the early nineteenth century, reported that Russian nobles considered staffs of two or three hundred quite normal. This huge number of retainers usually had its own village, close to the great house, with separate quarters for male and female servants, a bathhouse, kitchen and dining hall, and laundry. Russian serfdom (a de facto form of slavery abolished only in 1861) partially explains the huge numbers of servants. House serfs appeared to cost little, as their cash wages were small; moreover, positions tended to multiply as the supply swelled due to natural increase. The typical Russian staff also included resident serf artists, artisans, and entertainers, who in western Europe would have been temporary employees.

In medieval England, upper servants (who were frequently poor relations) often fraternized with the masters, and others bedded down haphazardly in the great hall or outside their masters' apartments. By the mid-eighteenth century, this informality had vanished, and a rigid upstairs-downstairs division of life in the house was standard in much of western Europe. The steward and housekeeper were at the top of the servant hierarchy; beneath these major chatelains were a host of underservants, ranging from ladies' maids and footmen to chars and scullery maids. The elaborate ranking system ruling the servants' hall extended to personal servants of visiting guests: the higher one's master's position, the higher one's own place at the servants' table.

In eastern Europe, by contrast, particularly in countries such as Russia and Austria until the abolition of serfdom, the household remained more medieval. The hierarchy was less formalized, and well into the nineteenth century maids and valets slept on pallets in the hall. In every household there were residents of indeterminate status: not family members, not really part of the staff. Certain staff members were privileged, particularly nannies and fools (anachronistic west of the Rhine). But maids and footmen, foreign visitors noted, sometimes danced alongside their masters during a ball. As in western Europe, the upper staff was sharply distinct in dress and deportment from the lower staff and groundsmen, stable hands, and agricultural laborers. Russian memoirists speak of the existence of "two kingdoms" on the estate, one centered on the life of the estate house, the other the domain of the bailiff, embracing all the working portions of the estate.

OCCUPATIONS AND DIVERSIONS

Historians like Girouard warn against the widespread myth of the benevolent squire, devoted to his servants and tenant farmers, possessed of a strong sense of public service and duty, and leading a halcyon existence in a finely appointed country house with a first-class library. Many owners fell well short of this mark. Some were boorish, or bad managers, or perpetually drunk; others were willful eccentrics. In mid-nineteenth-century Russia, N. E. Struisky, a former governor of Penza province, amused himself by interrogating and torturing his serfs. In contemporaneous England, the main occupation of the equally demented duke of Portland was the construction of elaborate tunnels beneath his Welbeck Abbey.

Custom and economic necessity induced more quotidian landowners to spend a portion of each morning consulting with bailiff or accountant, ordering purchases or repairs, visiting the stables and inspecting livestock, supervising the sowing or harvest, or in other activities promoting their domain's economic well-being. English landowners began to take a serious interest in model farming in the early nineteenth century and to supervise agricultural practices on the estate more closely. Meanwhile their wives attended to the smooth functioning of household and family, giving instructions to cooks, housekeepers, nursemaids, and governesses, and checking the pantry and storerooms. In nineteenth-century England wives and daughters often visited the village sick and needy; in Russia landowners built, and wives and daughters frequently ran, the peasant hospital. In economic respects, Russian landowners' practices were comparatively backward. Although many Russian nobles imported prize livestock and took pride in their stud farms, agricultural affairs were usually left to the bailiff, and model farming was considered eccentric. Only the early twentieth century saw major attempts at improved agricultural equipment and methods.

The manor house was the center of the rural community, and throughout Europe owners sponsored traditional entertainments to strengthen and reaffirm the sense of social cohesiveness. The early nineteenth century saw an increase of landowner paternalism toward tenant farmers or peasant villages and the local lesser gentry, and an upswing in entertainments on their behalf. In Russia landowners (who habitually justified serfdom by referring to their paternal care of the "souls" in their keeping) regularly celebrated major religious and agricultural landmarks such as Christmas, Lent, Easter, and the harvest with ceremonies or festivities involving their peasants. Long tables were set up in the courtyard, and the master's family broke bread with their peasants. The earl of Egremont was famed for his annual feasts at Petworth, to which hundreds of locals were invited; at other country estates, festivities including games and dancing as well as food and drink lasted into the night or even for several days. Celebrations of landmarks in the landowning family's history—weddings, births of heirs, christenings, and funerals—also involved the whole community.

Entertaining one's peers was another important aspect of country house life, for through it patronage connections, advantageous marriages, and enhanced community standing could be achieved. On the most basic level, entertaining consisted of receiving one's neighbors according to well-established protocols. In England new country house owners received visits from the community; in Russia they were expected to make calls on their neighbors. Other types of country house entertaining changed enormously over time and varied from country to country. The lavish balls and spectacular illuminations of a royal progress in Elizabethan England might be compared to the similarly spectacular balls, fireworks, and theater staged for Catherine the Great's journeys across Russia some two centuries later. Throughout Europe by the eighteenth century, rather than all do the same thing at an evening party guests instead chose between dancing, cards, or conversation. In the 1770s a visit to the magnificent château of the duc d'Harcourt, four miles south of Caen, offered a wide variety of diversions: walks in his delightful English garden, hunting in his game-filled forests, elevated conversations with philosophers and seductive women, dancing, and music.

From the eighteenth century on, amateur theatricals or musical entertainments were a staple of country evenings. A few English aficionados built private theaters on their estates, and theater in billiard rooms or libraries was widespread. But estate theater and extravagant entertaining reached their apogee in eighteenth-century Russia, where noble amateurs trod the boards but where talent could also be bought and sold. Renowned actors such as Mikhail Shchepkin began their careers as serf entertainers. Most talent was homegrown, but one magnate sent a serf boy to Europe to study the violin, and many prided themselves on troupes of expensively trained entertainers. By the 1820s such ostentation was frowned upon, and with the emancipation of 1861 it vanished entirely. Yet to the end of the old regime, amateur country theater of the type described in Anton Chekhov's *The Seagull* flourished in estate living rooms.

Across Europe outdoor activities also became progressively less formal. In England foxhunting was the exception to this rule: the nineteenth-century cult of vigorous outdoor exercise transformed it into an organized sport of considerable social importance. But in general houseguests were increasingly left to devise their own patterns of daily amusement. Shooting game, from deer and partridge in Scotland to wild boar and bears in Russia, was a perennial favorite for men. On many estates, boating, bathing, lawn bowling or croquet, and, at the end of the nineteenth century, tennis were available. A bracing stroll or ride, sketching in the park, or reading in the garden became more popular. In Russia picnics in the woods and mushroom hunting were favorite diversions.

The reach of country hospitality altered over the centuries as well. In England it progressed from a feudal casualness and inclusiveness embracing anyone who dropped by to the select guest lists for nineteenth-century house parties, the most celebrated of which were published in the newspapers. Farther east on the Continent, the feudal model obtained well into the nineteenth century, partially due to the infinitely greater distances between town and country and to the inferior transportation system. Even in the early twentieth century, although the railway network had vastly expanded, many east European estates remained too remote to visit without spending the night. In Russia the presence of thirty or more for daily dinner was considered quite normal, and estate owners were accustomed to entertaining and lodging all well-born passersby, there being virtually no inns. For Russian nobles, estate hospitality was not merely a tradition but an important part of their identity, and the most wealthy pursued it on a grand scale. In the 1770s Count Peter Sheremetev invited anyone "in decent dress" to enjoy the grounds of his suburban estate twice a week throughout the summer. They could boat on his artificial lake, stroll the grounds, play games, or enjoy outdoor theater and fireworks. At Prince Alexei Kurakin's estate near Orel in the 1820s, every guest who arrived, bidden or unbidden, was automatically assigned quarters and a carriage. Many stayed for weeks on end, some for months or even years. Only economic necessity put an end to these practices.

The Hunt. View near Offley, Hertfordshire, England, by D. Wolstenholme, c. 1840. BRITISH MUSEUM/THE ART ARCHIVE

COUNTRY HOUSES AND ESTATES IN THE TWENTIETH CENTURY

The extent to which European landowners' fortunes declined in the late nineteenth century has been much debated. In England and Russia agricultural recession and mounting maintenance expenses led the aristocracy to sell a large percentage of its lands, but some historians argue that the proceeds were profitably reinvested. There can be no doubt, however, that in England the elite's monopoly of landownership and the link between land and political power were broken as the peerage accommodated itself to the new commercial class. In 1868 Benjamin Disraeli's lack of a country estate almost disqualified him for the portfolio of prime minister. But between 1886 and 1914, of two hundred new peers in the House of Lords, only 25 percent were from the traditional landed elite, and only 30 percent of the remainder bothered to acquire country estates.

Marriage to American heiresses solved the economic woes of some English and French aristocrats. In Russia clusters of dachas—country villas for week-

end or summer use—sprang up as some landowners became developers. At Serednikovo outside Moscow, for example, the Firsanovs built not only a profitable dacha settlement, Firsanovka, three miles from the manor house, but a railway station to provide access. Just prior to the Great War, peasants owned 40 percent of Russia's arable land, yet vast estates in central and southern Russia were still owned by landowners whose agricultural innovations were bringing profits, and who were immersed in local political, economic, and social activities. Elsewhere in eastern Europe, aristocrats also held onto their estates. In the Austro-Hungarian Empire, where twenty-four families owned more than 250,000 acres each, there existed small kingdoms such as the Esterhazys' 735,000 acres in Hungary or the Schwarzenbergs' 360,000 acres in Bohemia.

At the turn of the century, the European aristocracy was one large family, its country houses united through generations of advantageous marriages. A single family might have estates in Bohemia, Poland, and Russia, administered through a central accounting office in Vienna, and move between these residences

421

Garden Party. Garden party organized by the National Trust, Ightam Mote, Kent, England, c. 1985–1995. ©Patrick Ward/Corbis

tates. In Russia revolution supplied the coup de grâce. Owners were dispossessed and many houses looted or destroyed. The 10 percent that survived were put to new public use as orphanages, insane asylums, sanitoriums, or agricultural institutes.

The interwar years did little to halt the decline in England and France, though Girouard argues that the English country house enjoyed an Indian summer between 1900 and 1940 similar to that in Russia between 1861 and 1917. However, just prior to World War II the English country house was so visibly at risk that in 1939 the government approved a plan to offer owners tax and other relief in exchange for public access to their houses. Known as the "Country House Scheme," the plan was administered by the National Trust (founded 1895) and saved numerous endangered houses. Elsewhere, little changed until the post–World War II period, when the pattern of Soviet Russian takeovers of houses was repeated in communist Eastern Europe.

At the beginning of the twenty-first century, although very little remains of the original substance of country life, both the great houses themselves and the symbols of grandeur associated with them have shown remarkable tenacity. In England the highly successful National Trust has collaborated with owners in promoting tourism as a survival mechanism. Throughout Europe many historic houses are now schools, foundations, corporate retreats, country clubs or spas, or, in Spain and Portugal, government-run tourist destinations. They have been joined by countless weekend villas. Some of these are "manors" fashioned from humble older structures such as Cotswold cottages or Burgundy farmhouses. Others are new, with design elements—porticoes and columns, gazebos and "great halls"—appropriated from earlier symbols of country magnificence. Those elements, and the frequency with which such suburban dwellings, regardless of the size of house or lot, are called "manors" or "estates," seem calculated, nostalgic appeals to the earlier forms and ideals of country life.

with little sense of national boundaries. But the nostalgic tone of some articles in new illustrated publications such as *Country Life* in England or *The Capital and the Estate* in Russia shows that Europe's aristocratic arcadias were already on the defensive. World War I permanently altered this way of life. In England, Ireland, France, Germany, and Italy, many owners perished or lost their means of support for their es-

See also **The Aristocracy and Gentry; Servants** *(volume 3); and other articles in this section.*

BIBLIOGRAPHY

Ackerman, James S. *The Villa: Form and Ideology of Country Houses.* Princeton, N.J., 1990.

Beik, William. *Absolutism and Society in Seventeenth-Century France.* New York, 1985.

Beard, Geoffrey. *The Work of Robert Adam.* London, 1978.

Beckett, J. V. *The Aristocracy in England, 1660–1914.* New York and Oxford, 1986.

Bence-Jones, Mark. *Life in an Irish Country House.* London, 1996.

Bentmann, Reinhard, and Michael Muller. *Die Villa als Herrschaftsarchitektur: Versuch einer kunst- und sozialgeschichtlichen Analyse.* Frankfurt, 1970.

Bluche, François. *La vie quotidienne de la noblesse francaise au XVIIIe siècle.* Paris, 1973.

Bovill, E. W. *English Country Life, 1780–1830.* London: Oxford University Press, 1962.

Bush, M. L. *The European Nobility.* 2 vols. Manchester, U.K., 1983–1988.

Cannadine, David. *The Decline and Fall of the British Aristocracy.* New Haven, Conn., 1990.

Dewald, Jonathan. *The European Nobility, 1400–1800.* Cambridge, U.K., and New York, 1996.

Dewald, Jonathan. *The Formation of a Provincial Nobility: The Magistrates of the Parlement of Rouen, 1499–1610.* Princeton, N.J., 1979

Ford, Franklin L. *Robe and Sword: The Regrouping of the French Aristocracy after Louis XIV.* Cambridge, Mass., 1965.

Girouard, Mark. *A Country House Companion.* Wigston, U.K., and New Haven, Conn., 1987.

Girouard, Mark. *Life in the English Country House: A Social and Architectural History.* New Haven, Conn., and London, 1978.

Hunt, John Dixon, and Peter Willis, eds. *The Genius of the Place: The English Landscape Garden, 1620–1820.* Cambridge, Mass., 1988.

Jenkins, Philip. *The Making of a Ruling Class: The Glamorgan Gentry, 1640–1790.* Cambridge, U.K., and New York, 1983.

Kazhdan, T. P. *Khudozhestvennyi mir russkoi usad'by.* Moscow, 1997.

Roosevelt, Priscilla. *Life on the Russian Country Estate: A Social and Cultural History.* New Haven, Conn., 1995.

Scott, H. M., ed. *The European Nobilities in the Seventeenth and Eighteenth Centuries.* 2 vols. London and New York, 1995.

Sinclair, Andres. *The Last of the Best: The Aristocracy of Europe in the Twentieth Century.* London, 1969.

Somerville-Large, Peter. *The Irish Country House: A Social History.* London, 1995.

Spring, David, ed. *European Landed Elites in the Nineteenth Century.* Baltimore, 1977.

Stone, Lawrence. *The Crisis of the Aristocracy, 1558–1641.* Oxford, 1965.

Wilmot, Martha. *The Russian Journals of Martha and Catherine Wilmot.* London, 1934.

FAIRS AND MARKETS

Montserrat M. Miller

Although their origins are much older, fairs and markets of one form or another have been important components of Europe's commercial economy since the eleventh-century recovery of urban life. Emerging wherever surplus was great enough to stimulate exchange, markets nearly always involved the retail sale to urbanites of staple goods, especially food, produced in the countryside. Fairs, on the other hand, which could be much larger than markets, more frequently featured the sale of costlier items such as cloth, livestock, and agricultural implements, as well as wholesale trade in a range of goods. And while markets were usually weekly or daily, fairs tended to be held less often. Both fairs and markets proliferated through medieval Europe, expanding and contracting in response to economic cycles linking regions together in relationships that involved the production, consumption, and exchange of goods, money, ideas, and cultural practices. While the importance of fairs declined after the 1300s, a highly complex, specialized, and hierarchical network of markets continued to develop and by the eighteenth century was operating at the foundation of Europe's dynamic economy.

During industrialization, fairs and markets were neither entirely eclipsed by shops and more formalized arrangements for high-level wholesale exchange nor rendered insignificant within the economy. Indeed markets in the nineteenth century were reorganized by governing authorities to better serve the conditions of crowded cities and were often covered with impressive iron and glass roofs that signaled new levels of municipal efficiency and pride. Likewise, mammoth fairs became symbols of industrial might or, on a smaller scale, deliberate expressions of the regional folk culture that was so important to emerging nationalist identities. Although interest in building new markets dwindled in the early twentieth century, in some areas there was resistance to the larger, and ultimately preponderant, trend toward shops and stores and then super and hypermarkets. While specific social and cultural practices appear to have been transformed by these structural shifts in the commercial system of distribution, parallels remain between the consumer megacomplexes of the late twentieth century, and even internet shopping, and the older forms of exchange in Europe's fairs and markets of the past.

In its treatment of fairs and markets, the social history literature emphasizes a number of themes. When focusing on the earlier period, empirical research on fairs and markets frequently tests the limits of economic models postulating the inexorable workings of supply and demand. Another theme involves the emergence and operation of the central place and network systems of exchange upon which the industrial economy was built. Scholars have also frequently used markets to explore the social relations that linked peasant societies to the more elite and formalized expressions of the dominant culture. The nineteenth and twentieth century work is more focused on the relationship of fairs and markets to the state and questions of gender and social class within an urban, industrial context. So fairs and markets are of significance to historians working on a number of specific questions related to Europe's economic, political, cultural, and social past.

MARKETS IN THE MIDDLE AGES

In the early Middle Ages, markets existed in some form everywhere that economic life teetered above complete self-sufficiency. Wherever towns survived there were markets to supply the population with the relatively small surplus of agricultural goods available. Though villages tended not to have markets, all towns certainly did. In this period before Europe's economic recovery, markets were frequently small, and their offerings quite limited. Typically, peasants brought their extra foodstuffs to sell to passersby, and in some places they were joined by artisans selling locally manufactured goods such as pottery and baskets. Seignorial or ecclesiastic authorities set the market days and often regulated such elements as pricing. Lining up along a

The Village Fair. Painting (1908) by Boris Kustodiev (1878–1927). Tretyakov Gallery, Moscow/Scala/Art Resource, NY

church wall, or in some other specified place within or just outside the town, vendors traded goods for money, and markets thus operated as one of the only venues for local exchange in an economy otherwise marked by subsistence.

All of the late-ninth- and tenth-century changes in the European countryside that stimulated agricultural productivity also acted to expand market operations. More surplus translated into more goods for sale, more hawkers and vendors on town streets, more market days, and longer market hours. Expanding markets thus stimulated urban growth. Where new markets emerged, villages often grew into towns; where towns expanded, the process of growth usually involved the construction of new defensive walls encompassing peripheral areas where successful new markets had become established. So the simpler, smaller markets of the early Middle Ages were transformed by the tenth-century rise in agricultural productivity, and then population, into clamoring centers of economic and social exchange.

By the late Middle Ages, markets had become much more crowded and lively, characteristically featuring a cacophony of sights, sounds, and smells. Vendors, usually women, competed for the attention of customers as crowds of people milled through the market's array of open-air stalls, each specializing in particular goods such as meat, fish, eggs, poultry, bread, vegetables, cheese, and sausage. Although artisans and merchants operated market stalls as well, they were more often drawn toward sedentary points of sale from within shops attached to or near production or storage. Retail food vendors, on the other hand, were slower to move to the more permanent quarters of the shop, although bakeries, and in some places butchers, were exceptions to the rule.

While some trade was certainly spontaneous and unregulated, markets were in general tightly controlled. Initially operating under ecclesiastic or seignorial auspices, emerging royal authorities were quick to claim their right to charter markets. In fact, more royal market charters were issued in some areas than the number of actual markets that operated; it was one thing to receive a market charter and quite another to invest in stall construction and management of a successful operation (Matte, 1996). Whether seignorial, ecclesiastic, or corporate, market authorities determined the hours of operation; charged vendors stallage; set prices and tolls; and monitored weights, measures, and the terms of exchange. Authorities usually operated public scales so that weights could be independently verified. There are innumerable instances of vendors receiving severe punishment for violations that were interpreted as transgressions against the common good. Indeed most historians who study markets maintain that vendors and customers shared a set of "moral economy" precepts about the way in which markets should operate and that these community standards of fairness were reinforced by market authorities as part of their claim for popular legitimacy.

Although the growth of marketplaces was deeply intertwined with the process of urbanization, markets also served as one of the several complex and dynamic links that bound villages, towns, and cities to the countryside that surrounded them. In the eleventh and twelfth centuries, town life, and in many ways town culture, became increasingly differentiated from that of the countryside. The towns, where free men could engage in commerce, featured greater opportunities for mobility than the countryside, where the social order was more static. And characteristic elements of town life such as guild corporatism, which came to permeate town culture, were largely foreign in the rural world. Yet markets constituted the most quotidian and direct link between urban and rural life through this period. Urban marketplaces distributed goods produced in the countryside, and urban demand shaped rural agricultural production. Markets drew a segment of the rural labor force, mainly composed of women, into towns to work in their stalls, and market sales injected money into the rural economy. Along with coins earned on trade and the odd goods that peasant vendors may have purchased in town, news, information, and wide-ranging cultural practices traveled back into rural areas at the end of the market day. An ongoing flow of humanity from countryside to town and back was part and parcel of successful markets everywhere.

Attention to the nature and dimensions of the catchment zones that extended outward from urban nodes into the rural countryside has led historians to conceptualize Europe in terms of the development and growth of a series of central places: villages, towns, and cities ringed by the overlapping areas within which money was directly exchanged for goods and labor. Indeed the central-place functions of towns were to a great extent reflected in the number, size, frequency, type, and scope of markets that were held within the corporate boundaries. Increases and decreases in the size and number of urban markets were directly linked to the expansion and contraction of central-place catchment zones. Markets are therefore one of the key places where historians look to observe the nature and extent of rural/urban interplay during the preindustrial period. So while markets were physically located in urban settings their connections to the rural world were extensive and complex.

FAIRS IN THE MIDDLE AGES

Like markets, some of Europe's fairs had origins that dated back even to Roman times, but much more than town markets, fairs, especially the larger ones, often linked far-distant regions together in a network. In their twelfth and thirteenth century heyday, especially, performers and entertainers, peddlers, specialized merchants, and financiers spent much of their year traveling the circuit of fairs that extended across Europe. Frequently sponsored by municipal corporations and trading houses, fairs stimulated economic growth by periodically bringing a concentration of buyers, sellers, performers, and onlookers together in one specific physical place. Fairs were festive occasions that combined entertainment, wholesale exchange, banking, and the retail sale of agricultural implements, farm animals, and manufactured goods.

From the late middle ages until the first quarter of the seventeenth century, the network of fairs that reached from the Low Countries through France to northern Italy, with branches extending outward in various directions, served as the main western European institutions for high-level finance and credit. This stimulated economic growth and urban specialization in both north and south. The old Champagne fairs, which reached their zenith in the thirteenth century, drew in practically the whole commercial and financial capitalist elite. Such fairs were the venues for international trade between merchant houses, and they were the points at which currencies and bills of exchange were settled. Beginning in the fourteenth century, however, the royal authorities more frequently extended exemptions from duties and tolls to high ranking merchants and merchant houses, causing fairs to decline. Such exemptions made fairs less attractive. By the seventeenth century, fairs had lost many of their highest-level economic functions in western Europe and had been largely replaced by banks and the establishment of more sedentary structures for wholesale trade. Perhaps the foremost historian of European fairs and markets in the early modern period, Fernand Braudel, called fairs archaic forms of exchange (Braudel, p. 93). In eastern Europe, for example, where the economic trajectory was less dynamic, fairs flourished much longer, reflecting the later emergence of modern financial capitalist structures.

In western Europe the likes of the Champagne fairs were replaced in the economic system by an essentially new form of higher-level market. Frequently called exchanges or *bourses,* these institutions had become established in the Mediterranean cities of Genoa, Florence, Pisa, Venice, Barcelona, and Valencia by the fourteenth century (Braudel, p. 99). Usually housed in special buildings, *bourses* of various types emerged not long afterward in the commercial cities of northern Europe as they increasingly dominated long-distance trade. The exchanges of Bruges, Antwerp, Amsterdam, and London had taken their place within the highest ranks of the economic order by the early 1500s. As was the case with many markets and fairs, the exchanges of Europe became more specialized as the economy expanded. Major cities opened exchanges that concentrated on the sale of grain, cloth, insurance, merchant company stocks, and government shares. These *bourses* incorporated many of the wholesale and banking functions that had earlier been the province of fairs.

EARLY MODERN PERIOD

Both fairs and markets persisted through the early modern period, with some noteworthy modifications. Fairs, shorn of many of their highest-level financial functions in western Europe, remained much-anticipated cultural and economic events on a regional level. In other words, although fairs lost some of their network functions, they retained much central-place importance. Many small-scale manufacturers organized production around the temporal rhythm of the fairs, still usually seasonal and periodic, and depended on them for much of their annual sales. Alongside the crowded calendar of religious holidays, fairs continued to represent one of the main secular institutions for regional sociability and cultural diffusion. Urban markets remained important through the early modern period as well. They grew in number and size, especially from 1450 and 1650, while population growth and urbanization were linked. During these centuries towns and cities had to devote more attention to market regulation and policing and to find new places within the walled environs where markets could be held. While market management came to represent an ever more urgent problem for municipal authorities, the expansion of markets heightened their cultural impact on the urban quarters where they were held.

Because scholars have generally come to view culture as a body of shared ideas and practices that is always in the process of being created and recreated when individuals interact, the complex exchanges taking place within fairs and markets have assumed great social historical significance. The discursive exchanges and behaviors associated with fairs and markets can be interpreted as forces acting to create, re-create, reinforce, or undermine the various rural and urban cultures that existed in Europe at any given time. In just

one morning, a single vendor might have spoken directly to and/or exchanged looks with hundreds of other participants in the fair or market. Female consumers would most likely have only rarely come into close contact with as many people at one time as they did when they went about the process of shopping for food at town markets. Because fairs and markets were nuclei of commerce and thus places where face-to-face contact was concentrated, they were among the most intensive points for the generation and recreation of popular culture. Indeed, the atmospheres of fairs and markets, easily read by the regular participants, reflected collective attitudes of optimism or fear. News traveled fast from one stall to another, and a failure to comprehend the cultural rules governing exchange in fairs or markets could carry with it grave economic consequences.

In song and folk tales regional fairs appear over and over as much-anticipated occasions for status display and entertainment, as well as places to buy colored ribbons and other minor luxuries of a festive nature. Through performances, ceremonies, and economic exchange, rural groups came into contact with one another at fairs, observing local differences and absorbing cultural elements that ranged from new variations on old stories and songs to changes in styles of dress. Moreover, because fairs brought rural and urban groups into contact with one another, they represented points at which popular traditions intersected with more formal and dominant cultural expressions. The differences in dress, speech, and behavior between urban and rural groups could easily be observed at fairs, and, as a consequence, broader diffusion of dominant cultural forms was effected.

Regional fairs also remained occasions for the display and reinforcement of social hierarchies. Because among other things they were the sites of servant hiring and the livestock trade, fairs drew in the most successful farmers. There the lowest-ranking members of the agricultural order could see crisp representations of the rural hierarchy and their place within it. Fairs also always featured women and children, explicitly engaged in displays of social rank, wearing their finest clothes and seeking to spend a bit of money on something that would be perceived as fun. Fairs offered the opportunity for children and women to see how their economic means placed them in relationship to others, and thus refined their sense of place within the social hierarchy. So in a number of ways fairs offer abundant historical insight about the social and cultural context of rural life in early modern Europe.

Regular urban markets operated as important social institutions through the early modern period as

Nineteenth-Century Fair. St. James's Fair at Bristol, painting by Samuel Colman (1804–1840). CITY OF BRISTOL MUSEUM AND ART GALLERY, BRISTOL, U.K./THE BRIDGEMAN ART LIBRARY

well. Markets were hierarchically arranged and both reflected and reinforced the urban social order. The most prosperous vendors, frequently butchers, had the largest or best-positioned stalls. Butchers defined themselves as skilled laborers, required apprenticeships, and operated their stalls from within a well-established tradition of guild membership. Poulterers, sausage and cheese vendors, and fishmongers sometimes created similar guild associations as well. Vendor groups with guild membership and using artisanal language to define themselves wielded greater influence with market and corporate authorities than those traders who sold bulk produce such as cabbage, or, later on, potatoes. Making no claims to skilled labor, vegetable vendors of all varieties were much less likely to belong to guilds. The relatively low level of prestige associated with their trade was reflected in the size/or location of their stalls within the market. At the bottom of the market and social hierarchy were ambulatory or itinerant vendors, operating legally or illegally, in a range of goods. Ambulatory trade was often carried out by the most marginalized members of society and frequently raised the ire of both established vendors who paid stallage and the law enforcement authorities. So

while market vendors represented a category of urban retail merchants, they were also a group within which sharp hierarchical relationships existed.

As at fairs, the cultural dimensions of urban markets were rich, complex, and shaped by rank and hierarchy. Through the butchers and other types of vendors holding guild membership, markets were drawn into the festivals and ceremonies of the artisanal community. Because markets sold food, they were starting points for the celebration of all Saints days and other holidays that involved the preparation of special family meals. In extending credit, individual vendors often determined whether the poorest of households would mark holidays with any type of special foods at all. By the early eighteenth century, even modest European cities held a half dozen food markets daily. With dense urban settlement clusters around them, markets had become one of the most crucial types of public spaces in the city, especially for women. Neighborhood reputations could be made or broken through behavior in the markets, and markets were places within which female consumers often sought to defend the honor of their homes. In fact, markets had come to rival churches, government build-

Renaissance Market. Market of fabric and furniture merchants, Bologna, fifteenth-century miniature. Museo Civico, Bologna, Italy/Alinari/Art Resource, NY

ings, and public squares as the most-frequented sites of social and cultural exchange.

INDUSTRIALIZATION

The long process of industrialization brought tremendous change in the scale and functions of urban places in Europe. After a lull of approximately a hundred years, the mid-eighteenth century ushered in a period of major urban growth and demographic expansion. The technological and organizational shifts necessitated by the factory system of production urbanized new areas, often with chaotic results that strained inadequate infrastructures. England's midland cities in the late eighteenth and early nineteenth centuries exemplify this. Industrial growth accelerated the urbanization of older cities as well, presenting civil authorities with real problems of provisioning an expanding population. Municipal governments all across the continent understood the connection between revolutionary fervor and the availability of food at what were popularly held to be just prices. Bread riots, after all, were not uncommon, and such spontaneous outbursts had been known to set off much larger uprisings. Issues of provisioning thus were often urgent.

Although the towns and cities of Europe in the late eighteenth and early nineteenth centuries certainly featured many shops, most foods other than bread and sometimes meat, were sold in the daily markets, the vast majority of which were still held in squares with no protection from the elements. Industrialization forced authorities to face the task of making the old urban market system work under conditions of greater density and changing social composition. Most cities first pursued a strategy that involved expanding the number of stall permits and extending the length and number of vendor rows in already-existing markets. As a consequence, food markets simply became larger and more crowded. In many places, such expansion reached the limits of the possible during the first half of the nineteenth century: where city walls remained in place and population density high, streets became impassable during market hours and neighbors complained about piles of garbage and raucous noise. Problems of sanitation led to outbreaks of disease and caused considerable additional concern on the part of municipal authorities. Another solution had to be found. Nearly everywhere in this period city governments sought to expand the provisioning system by establishing new markets. But space within old urban cores was scarce. In Barcelona, new markets were built on the lots made available as a result of the popular anticlerical attacks

that led to the destruction of several convents in the 1840s. Elsewhere space for markets was made either where port facilities were being expanded to meet the needs of the industrial system of maritime transport or in the areas beyond the defensive walls that were being developed as new bourgeois residential districts.

One of the principal characteristics of nineteenth-century cities was an increase in scale, especially with the emergence and extension of the rail network that facilitated the transport of raw materials to the burgeoning factories located in close proximity to the source of labor. Cities spread over what had been fields and peasant cottages, and new districts with streets laid out in grid patterns often became fashionable areas. In these areas, cities were built from the ground up in relatively short time, and room was nearly always reserved for new markets. In fact, the general physical appearance of most nineteenth-century cities underwent considerable transformation. In addition to the new peripheral bourgeois neighborhoods, broad boulevards, monuments to national figures, and larger public squares and parks became characteristic parts of the industrial city. These new elements in the physical appearance of cities were promoted by the political authorities, who sponsored them as tangible evidence of progress, efficiency, and both municipal and national pride. The Hausmannization of Paris is just the best-known example of a much larger trend in nineteenth century urban makeovers. All across Europe, from Vienna to Madrid, the results of the nineteenth-century urban transformations remain visible to even the most casual of observers.

Alongside triumphant arches and grand boulevards the older organizational arrangement of urban public markets often represented discordance and incongruency. No matter how large markets grew or how many were authorized by municipal authorities, as long as they were held in the open air they remained sloppy and noisy affairs that were increasingly less acceptable to emerging middle-class aesthetic sensibilities. The solution that many municipal authorities chose was to build market halls and move market sales indoors, where consumers and vendors alike could escape the elements and engage in exchange under more permanent, hygienic, and rationalized conditions. Market-hall design ranged from sturdy one-story poured-concrete structures with arched porticoes along exposed walls to grand iron-truss halls with glass roofs and elaborate decorative elements. By the 1860s, both London and Paris had constructed a series of new covered market halls linked to the rail network. Berlin did not begin its market-building project until twenty years later, and there, the results were less successful (Lohmeier, p. 111).

Shopping Arcade. Galeries St. Hubert, Brussels, 1990. OWEN FRANKEN/©CORBIS

More generally, the new combination of municipally operated covered markets located near train stations worked well, allowing for a more efficient and larger-scale wholesaling system that linked the city directly to both its immediate catchment zone and to distant sources of provisions. European municipal authorities built such structures as part of a larger strategy to expand the provisioning system and to rationalize the use of urban space. The inauguration of market halls, such as the one which took place in Barcelona in 1876 to mark the opening of the *Born* structure, were often accompanied by much fanfare and ceremony glorifying both the modern state and the progress that governing authorities could bring through their stewardship of the industrialization of the economy.

The second half of the nineteenth century also marked a new era in the history of fairs. London's 1851 *Great Exhibition of the Works of Industry of All Nations* set the standard. In the following decades mammoth fairs became more common. Designed as international exhibits of modernity, nineteenth-century fairs involved large-scale construction projects that often looked like fairylands of light, water, and space. London's Crystal Palace from the 1851 Exhibition is one such example. The Ciutadella Park in Barcelona, built for the 1888 *Exposición Mundial,* is another. Inaugurated by the highest-ranking political authorities, nineteenth-century fairs drew in tens of millions of visitors and put the host region's highest cultural expressions on display while serving to lift bourgeois confidence in progress to new heights. Like the old Champagne fairs, they brought together potential buyers, sellers, and onlookers and established the tone for trading relations that operated at the uppermost levels of economic exchange. Most historical interpretations of the nineteenth-century European world's fairs also emphasize the important role they played in diffusing popular criticism of the established political and social order.

In eastern Europe, where urbanization and industrialization proceeded more slowly, large state-sponsored international exhibitions were organized less frequently; nonetheless, the region certainly had its vibrant nineteenth-century fairs. Those held at Leipzig and Novgorod were especially well known for bringing European and Asian merchants together to exchange a wide variety of goods. Moscow also held a series of larger fairs, international in scope, but not industrial exhibitions in the same sense as the western European and American varieties.

A second era of world's fairs in western Europe began with the 1925 *Paris Exposition Internationale des Arts Décoratifs et Industriels Modernes* and was followed by a number of others during the years of the Great Depression. Here, too, the European industrial world's fairs of the twentieth century promoted consumer confidence in a future that promised to be much brighter than the difficult present in which they were set.

THE TWENTIETH CENTURY

In most areas of Europe, but especially in the northwest, municipal authorities stopped building covered markets in the early twentieth century, when the number and variety of food shops and stores increased while many of the covered markets began a process of long and slow decline. The growing capitalization of the distribution system and technological advances in the food-processing industry drove much of this shift. Increases in the scale of agricultural production, mechanical refrigeration, and the food-processing industry had stimulated the expansion of wholesale distribution networks for several decades. Food retailers able to buy in larger quantities could reduce costs and increase profit margins. Individual market vendors with small retail establishments found themselves at a disadvantage.

While grand covered markets moved toward extinction in most places, some municipal authorities undertook great efforts to facilitate the adaptation of public food markets to twentieth-century economic conditions. The best example of this is Barcelona, where the city government issued a new municipal market code in 1898 that prevailed with only minor modifications over the course of the next half century. Modern refrigeration chambers were added to all of the city's markets, and individual vendors were allowed to double and triple the size of their stalls and eventually to bequeath their vendor licenses as real property from one generation to the next. Such measures facilitated the social and economic consolidation of urban-dwelling retail vendors who purchased wholesale from middlemen, privileging them over rural producers who had long traveled into the city on a daily basis to sell the surplus from their small family plots. Under such conditions, market stalls came to resemble small shops, and indeed the shopkeeper and vendor population became difficult to distinguish. Barcelona's urban retail market vendors took their place in the ranks of the new lower middle class alongside telephone operators, department store clerks, and minor office workers. Where public policy explicitly protected vendors, daily food markets stood a better chance of enduring through the middle of the twentieth century and beyond.

More generally through western Europe in the postwar period, supermarkets and self-service stores, and then suburban hypermarkets, gradually laid claim to the bulk of retail sales in food. Outside the communist block, Europeans increasingly chose to make fewer, albeit bigger, provisioning excursions, and as in the United States, the weekly grocery-shopping trip became a domestic ritual. Daily shopping in public markets in most places became the province of older women who maintained the traditions followed by their mothers. Most historians of markets, in fact, assert that their ultimate demise was set in motion by the combined effects of higher levels of female employment outside the home, mass marketing of electrical refrigeration, and the spread of the automobile. All undermined the need for daily shopping trips as part of a household routine. Nonetheless, the vast majority of European cities had at least one or two public markets still in operation in the late twentieth century, although many of these featured a significant number of small shops aimed at tourists alongside stalls that catered to neighborhood consumption. Again, the city of Barcelona is noteworthy in that forty-one food markets remained in operation there at the close of the twentieth century, with significant modernization undertaken by a public-private governing body.

The decline of public markets in twentieth-century European cities brought changes in urban sociability patterns. As long as every household in the city was provisioned daily through a trip to a public market and to specific shops neighborhood women were linked together in a network of commercial and social relationships. With vendors often living in the immediate environs, markets were hubs of neighborhood news and information and places where face-to-face contact was maintained in an otherwise densely populated and largely anonymous setting. Going to market daily had been one of the main ways that women in the burgeoning industrial cities got to know

Twentieth-Century Market. Street market in Krasnodar, Russia, 1992. SOVFOTO/EASTFOTO

who their neighbors were, heard about their neighbors' affairs, and found out about some of the goings on in other apartment houses of the district. The decline of public markets reduced levels of neighborhood social exchange among women and dried up a crucial pool of local gossip and information. The structures through which urban cultures and subcultures were created and re-created among women were changed as a result.

While self-service stores, supermarkets, and hypermarkets proved to be profitable enterprises that created new employment, their expanding share of the retail sale of food reduced women's independent entrepreneurial opportunities in many areas. Women, held in Western culture to inherently possess verbal skills useful in petty trade, had dominated the ranks of market vendors since time immemorial in most regions. Through the nineteenth and early twentieth centuries, operating a market stall was a reasonably accessible option for women from the lower ranks of the social order. Market-stall operations required little capital and could usually be undertaken alone and combined with the responsibilities of household and children. With the eclipse of markets by shops, stores, and supermarkets, women's independent opportunities in the retail commercial sector were narrowed.

CONCLUSION

Although by the end of the twentieth century the fairs and markets that operated all across the European landscape from the eleventh-century revival of urban life through the nineteenth century remained in most places only as relics of the past, a degree of persistence and continuity was still identifiable. Small regional fairs remain common, and some cities' provisioning systems, such as Barcelona's, feature a combination of municipal markets, shops, and super/hypermarkets. In many ways the European variant of the late-twentieth-century shopping mall, and even internet dotcoms, can be viewed as larger scale versions of traditional markets. Their distinction from the older institutions for retail commerce lies more in scale, capitalization, and technological foundation than in fundamental arrangement. Likewise, trade fairs and exhibitions, common in virtually every area of the economy, are distinctly reminiscent of the old European fairs whose role in high finance and wholesale trade had been crucial in the process of economic expansion. Fairs and markets have been integral parts of Europe's history, and their study promises to reveal much about the way the economy works today.

See also other articles in this section.

BIBLIOGRAPHY

Alexander, Sally. *St. Giles's Fair, 1830–1914: Popular Culture and the Industrial Revolution in 19th Century Oxford.* Oxford, 1970.

Braudel, Fernand. *Civilization and Capitalism, 15th–18th Century.* Vol. 2: *The Wheels of Commerce.* Translated by Sian Reynolds. London, 1982.

Burgess, Malcolm. "Fairs and Entertainers in Eighteenth Century Russia." *Slavonic Review* 38 (1959): 95–113.

Burton, Benedict. *The Anthropology of World's Fairs: San Francisco's Panama Pacific International Exposition of 1915.* Berkeley, Calif., 1982.

Drew, R. F. "The Siberian Fair, 1600–1750." *The Slavonic and East European Review* 39 (1961): 423–439.

Farmer, D. L. "Marketing the Produce of the Countryside, 1200–1500." In *The Agrarian History of England and Wales.* Vol. 3. Edited by E. Miller. Cambridge, U.K., 1991. Page 345.

Fontaine, Laurence. *History of Pedlars in Europe.* Durham, N.C., 1996.

Forman, S. and J. F. Riegelhaupt. "Market Place and Market System: Toward a Theory of Peasant Economic Integration." *Comparative Studies in Society and History* 12 (1970): 188–212.

Greenhalgh, Paul. *Ephemeral Vistas: The Expositions Universelles, Great Exhibitions, and World's Fairs, 1851–1939.* Manchester, U.K., 1988.

Kowalski, Maryanne. *Local Markets and Regional Trade in Medieval Exeter.* New York, 1995.

Lindenfeld, Jacqueline. *Speech and Sociability at French Urban Marketplaces.* Amsterdam and Philadelphia, 1990.

Lohmeier, Andrew. "*Bürgerliche Gesellschaft* and Consumer Interests: The Berlin Public Market Hall Reform, 1867–1891." *Business History Review* 73 (spring 1999): 91–113.

Masschaele, James. "The Multiplicity of Medieval Markets Reconsidered." *Journal of Historical Geography* 20 (1994): 255–271.

Mate, Mavis. "The Rise and Fall of Markets in Southeast England." *Canadian Journal of History* 31 (April 1996): 59–87.

Mikesell, Marvin W. "Market Centers of Northeastern Spain: A Review." *Geographical Review* 50 (1960): 247–251.

Miller, Montserrat. "Market Vendors of Barcelona: Community, Class, and Family in a Twentieth Century Southern European City." Ph.D. diss., Carnegie Mellon University, 1994.

Mintz, Sidney W. "Men, Women and Trade." *Comparative Studies in Society and History* 13 (1971):247–269.

Rydell, Robert W. *The Books of the Fairs: Materials about World's Fairs, 1834–1916, in the Smithsonian Institution Libraries.* Chicago, 1992.

Rydell, Robert W. *World of Fairs: The Century-of-Progress Expositions.* Chicago: University of Chicago Press, 1993.

Tilly, Charles. "Food Supply and Public Order in Modern Europe." In *The Formation of National States in Western Europe.* Edited by Charles Tilly. Princeton, N.J., 1975. Pages 380–455.

Walton, Whitney. *France at the Crystal Palace: Bourgeois Taste and Artisan Manufacture in the Nineteenth Century.* Berkeley, Calif., 1992.

Section 9

STATE AND SOCIETY

ABSOLUTISM

David Parker

First used at the end of the eighteenth century, the term "absolutism" is loosely employed by many historians as a synonym for absolute monarchy. It is most commonly associated with the personal rule of Louis XIV of France (1661–1715) and his contemporaneous rulers: Peter the Great (1682–1725) of Russia; Frederick William, the Great Elector of Brandenburg (1640–1688), and his son Frederick (1688–1713), who became the first king of Prussia in 1701; Charles XI of Sweden (1660–1697) and his son Charles XII (1697–1718). To these names may be added the so-called enlightened despots or absolutists of the eighteenth century, notably Catherine the Great of Russia (1762–1796), Frederick the Great of Prussia (1740–1786), and Joseph II of Austria (1765–1790).

Despite this unavoidable reference to particular monarchs, it is generally understood that absolutism cannot be equated with complete or total control by the ruler. Such a form of rule was beyond the reach of early modern states, where a ruler's effectiveness was limited by poor communications, constant difficulty in mobilizing adequate resources, and, above all, the need to satisfy the interests and aspirations of the nobility. Continued use of the term "absolutism" can, however, be justified to describe monarchical systems of government that were largely unrestrained by national or local representative institutions. The disappearance or weakening of these institutions, marked by the demise of the French Estates General in 1614–1615, the Castile Cortes after 1665, and the Brandenburg Estates after 1685, was the practical counterpoint to the increasingly powerful idea—clearly articulated and debated at the time—that monarchs were accountable to no one but God.

THE STRUCTURE OF THE ABSOLUTIST STATE

In absolutist as opposed to constitutional systems, representative institutions played no part in the lawmaking process; lawmaking was the prerogative of the king, who could override custom and the laws of his predecessors. Nor did absolute monarchs require consent for taxation. The growth of royal authority was frequently accompanied by a decline in municipal autonomy and in the independence of the church, while there was a tendency for seigneurial jurisdictions to be subsumed within a national legal framework. Paradoxically, the elevation of the personal authority of kings went hand in hand with the bureaucratization of their regimes as ever greater numbers of fiscal, judicial, and administrative officers were required to sustain them. Absolute monarchs also had at their disposition armies of ever greater size and firepower—to finance them was the essential reason for the expansion of the machinery of state.

These generalizations should, however, be applied with care. In Castile the disappearance of the Cortes was accompanied by a strengthening of seigneurial jurisdictions together with noble tax-raising powers as the Crown alienated many of its regalian rights. In Sweden, where the members of the Riksdag explicitly recognized in 1680 the Crown's legislative sovereignty and its powers of taxation, the curiously consensual nature of the process allowed the Riksdag to survive and to reassert its constitutional role within fifty years. Even in Louis XIV's France the survival of important provincial estates meant that representation and consent to taxation were not entirely emasculated; and in the half century after his death the parlements, although far from representative of anybody except their venal officeholders, were able to resurrect their right to remonstrate against objectionable royal edicts. In doing so, they severely dented the monarchy's absolute pretensions. Thus while absolute monarchies may be clearly differentiated from those that formally limited the power of the Crown—notably in England, Poland, and Hungary—absolutism was a tendency with considerable variations rather than a defined structure.

Only in France, for instance, had there developed by 1700 a practice of direct ministerial responsibility for the great departments of state (finance, war,

In the Shadow of Louis XIV. *Louis XV as a Child,* portrait by Hyacinthe Rigaud (1659–1743). Louis XV (1710–1774) succeeded his great-grandfather, Louis XIV, in 1715. METROPOLITAN MUSEUM OF ART, NEW YORK, PURCHASE, MARY WETMORE SHIVELY BEQUEST, IN MEMORY OF HER HUSBAND, HENRY L. SHIVELY, M.D., 1960 (60.6)

and foreign affairs). Elsewhere a collegial style of administration, largely inspired by Axel Oxenstierna's reforms in Sweden in 1634, found favor. Between 1717 and 1720 Peter the Great established no fewer than eleven collegial departments falling into three groups: war and foreign affairs, financial affairs, and trade and industry. Each college was theoretically controlled by eleven high officials headed by a president; the presidents came together in the senate, which had earlier replaced the old privy council as the supreme administrative body under the king. There were clear parallels with the emerging structures of the Prussian state, where, at almost the same time, the General Directory was established as an umbrella body for four departments but with a limited degree of functional specialization. Even in France the emergence of functionally defined royal councils did not ensure a clear demarcation between the business brought before them.

Reorganizing the central government, however, was a relatively easy task compared with that of effec-

tively directing local agencies. In Spain the monarchy was dependent on eighty or so *corregidores* (royal appointees), who presided over town councils and acted as chief magistrates. But because they were not career bureaucrats and were often drawn from the municipal oligarchies they were supposed to control, their commitment to royal interests was uncertain. They did not exist in at least half the country, where primary jurisdiction belonged to the local seigneurs. Not until the following century, with the disappearance of the provincial Cortes and the development of a system of royal intendants on French lines, did the Spanish monarchy begin to remedy this situation. However, as French experience itself showed that intendants were unable to fulfill their responsibilities without *subdélégués* (subdelegates) drawn from the local officeholders, the significance of their replication in Spain should not be exaggerated. In Prussia coordination of local government was improved by integrating the administration of the royal domains with the military-fiscal administration that had evolved during the wars of the seventeenth century; the resulting provincial chambers were then subordinated to the General Directory. Nonetheless, the regime's effectiveness continued to depend on the rural commissioners, or *Landräte,* nominated by the county squirearchy. Under Frederick II they acquired extensive administrative, judicial, fiscal, and military responsibilities.

Not surprisingly, in the vast and growing spaces of the Russian Empire the coordination of local and central administrations posed particular problems. Between 1708 and 1718 Peter the Great introduced a degree of decentralization, by transforming the old military provinces into eight sometimes vast *guberniyas* headed by governors with a full range of fiscal and judicial powers. Subordinate officials seem to have been displaced by military commandants. The resulting slippage of power in turn led within a decade to a renewed strengthening of upward lines of authority; in theory, all local agencies were subordinated to the new central colleges. However, the governors, appointed by the tsar, retained significant powers, and the military commandants soon gave way to civilian *voevodas* appointed by the senate. After 1728 Russia was governed by nine governors, twenty-eight provincial *voevodas,* and about seventy local *voevodas.* The resulting uncertainty about the chain of command contributed to tensions between local and regional authorities, and from 1764 there was a return to decentralized modes. The number of *guberniyas* increased while the police and fiscal powers of the colleges were redistributed to provincial chambers. Only in small and homogeneous Sweden was the integration of central and local control effected without noticeable uncertainty; but even there, royal governors and judges increased their presence by an accommodation with older, more egalitarian institutions, notably the jury system.

VENALITY OF OFFICE

In contrast to those in central and eastern Europe (with the exception of the Prussian judiciary), institutional structures in France and Spain were dependent on sale of office. By the end of Louis XIV's reign the total number of venal offices, if those in the tax farms, municipalities, and army are included, may have been as high as seventy thousand or more, compared with around five thousand at the beginning of the sixteenth century. Information from Spain is less complete, but by the 1630s the sale of senior administrative offices together with those in the municipalities, which were vital to the financial and social stability of the body politic, was commonplace. It has been suggested that in Castile there were twice the number of offices per head of population as in France. In both countries the resulting patrimonial nature of the system was further reinforced by the practice of using private financiers to sell offices, tax concessions, and alienated regalian rights.

Venality was both a means of getting the bureaucracy to pay for itself and a source of additional revenue. In its absence other means had to be found to sustain expanding civilian and military establishments. The Swedish Crown partly solved the problem through the *reduktion,* by which, in diametric opposition to French and Spanish practices, it exercised the regalian right of calling in lands alienated to the nobility. This was accomplished in an increasingly comprehensive and aggressive manner in 1655, 1680, and 1682. The most influential of Sweden's reforms, however, was the cantonal, or allotment, system of maintaining an army. The government negotiated contracts with each province for the supply and maintenance of infantry soldiers, who were given either a cottage or accommodation on a farm. The advantages of this practice were considerable, enabling an army to be kept in permanent readiness at minimal cost while reducing more brutal methods of conscription, heavy war taxation, and the billeting of unruly troops on resentful communities; in the short term, at least, it helped a small country compete with, and even inflict military defeats on, their wealthier or more populous rivals.

In 1727 the cantonal system was introduced in Prussia with remarkable results. Although Prussian revenues increased by only 44 percent between 1713 and 1740, the size of the army more than doubled to 83,000. The annexation of Silesia in 1745 and West Prussia in 1772 took the population from 2.2 to 4.76 million. By 1786 it was 5.4 million, and the size of the army had correspondingly grown to 200,000. With about 4 percent of the population in arms Prussia exceeded all its rivals in the militarization of the populace. However, neither Prussia nor Austria, where a similar system was adopted in the 1770s, was able to emulate Sweden's success in controlling costs, for military reform in Sweden had been accompanied by the introduction of an audit department with the aim of adhering to a balanced budget, which placed it decades ahead of its rivals.

The variation in the incidence of venality has encouraged Thomas Ertman to postulate a typological difference between the "patrimonial" absolutisms of Latin Europe and the "bureaucratic" ones of the east. Yet bureaucratic absolutisms also displayed powerful patrimonial characteristics. In Russia the payment of salaries for local government officers was withdrawn in 1727, leaving them to "pay themselves" from the proceeds of their business. Not until 1763 were all officials salaried. The Prussian *Landräte* were paid a modest salary, but it came from the provincial chamber, not from the king; moreover, these were key positions much sought after by the more powerful nobles, who used them to establish patronage networks, which they deployed in the interests of family and allies. As far as military posts were concerned, no country emulated French practice, which by the 1770s had generated 900 colonels to 163 regiments. Even so, the Prussian officer corps grew dramatically during the reign of Frederick the Great, and many hundreds of captains supplemented their salaries by taking a cut of the company expenses and soldiers' pay made over to them by the state. The patrimonial character of the absolutist regimes was not, therefore, a simple consequence of venality. It might be more accurate to suggest the opposite—that venality was but one expression of the patrimonial dynamics that shaped absolutist regimes.

ABSOLUTISM AND WAR

If it is indisputable that the emergence of absolutist regimes was a response to the bellicose turmoil of the seventeenth century, it is equally apparent that this was not the only possible outcome. In Sweden the military difficulties of the 1670s produced a lurch toward absolutism, but those of the Great Northern War (1700–1721), notably the military debacle at Poltava in 1709, led directly to a reassertion of constitutional rule; indeed in 1719 the Riksdag ended the hereditary monarchy established in 1544. During the same period, pressures of the War of the Spanish Succession on England accentuated rather than diminished parliamentary control of the burgeoning bureaucracy, the army, and the navy. The modern state may, in the most generic sense, be a product of warfare, but this is an insufficient explanation for the divergent forms of its development and cannot convey the full array of conditions required to produce a specifically absolutist variant.

Attempts by modern historians to address this problem have largely concentrated on the conditions under which states set about maximizing revenues. According to Charles Tilly early modern states were shaped by the interaction between their coercive capacities and their capital accumulation and concentration. Venice (capital intensive) and Russia (coercive) are positioned at opposite ends of the spectrum, with England, France, and Spain somewhere in the middle. Ertman, noting that Tilly's model can accommodate neither Hungary nor Poland, which despite being "militarily exposed" produced constitutional rather than absolutist regimes, has offered an explanation based on the prior character of representative and local government. Assemblies encompassing the three estates (nobility, clergy, and commoners), which could easily be divided, were less well equipped to survive than territorial-based assemblies, which tended to be more strongly rooted in local government. Brian Downing, on the other hand, relates the survival of constitutional practices to a plurality of factors: the capacity to exploit foreign territories; the protection offered by difficult terrain; diplomatic skill; or simple good fortune.

THE SOCIAL FOUNDATIONS OF ABSOLUTISM

While these modern interpretations reject oversimplified connections between war and absolutism, they confine themselves largely to the dynamics of state finance, giving little weight to socioeconomic matters. This perhaps reflects the fading power of older class-based analyses of absolutism, which, in either Whiggish or marxist terms, fastened on the rise of the middle classes or the bourgeoisie. By the end of the twentieth century most historians, marxists included, had abandoned Friedrich Engels's notion that an equilibrium between nobles and bourgeois allowed the monarchy to rise above both. Indeed the longevity of such ideas is surprising since absolutism was most securely rooted in Prussia and Russia, where the bourgeoisie was insignificant, and positively rejected in the United Provinces and England, where it was most powerful.

If the association of absolutism with the bourgeoisie is to have any credence, one would expect it to be established in western Europe, where the urban populations were larger and commercial activity more vigorous. Yet even there the connection is doubtful. The Spanish monarchy's dependence on the compliance and resources of privileged urban centers is deceptive, for these towns had effectively become the patrimony of the *caballeros* (noblemen). State investors also made up the middle and upper cadres of the judiciary, the army, the church, the royal governors of the cities, and the king's secretaries and councillors. These noble urban oligarchs had little resemblance to a bourgeoisie. The entrenchment of their position was echoed in the countryside, particularly in the south, by the consolidation of seigneurial authority. During Philip IV's reign (1621–1665) some fifty-five thousand families—no less than 5 percent of the population—were sold into seigneurial jurisdiction, and at least 169 new *señores* (lords) were created with the right to appoint village magistrates and officials. One telling consequence of this process was a dramatic reduction in appeals to the royal courts at Valladolid and Granada.

Similar observations may be made about the social foundations of absolutism in France, where, despite the intendants, who held office by virtue of revocable commissions and not by purchase, the realm continued to be administered, taxed, and judged by rentier officeholders who at the higher levels formed the ranks of the *noblesse de robe* (judicial nobility). While much of the capital for the purchase of office came from trade, this diversion of merchant wealth into rentier and usurious investments inhibited the progress of capitalism. It is thus not possible, as some historians have suggested, to attribute urban patriciates' royalism to the support of a bourgeois class for the economic protection offered by the Crown. Such royalism is better explained by the deep social conservatism of urban elites, who aspired to advance their families through the purchase of office, land, and title. In any event, the bourgeoisie played no significant part in formulating the mercantilist policies that Richelieu (Armand-Jean du Plessis) presented to a handpicked assembly of notables (nobles, magistrates, clergy) in 1627. Not until 1700, with the establishment of the Council of Commerce, did the trading bourgeoisie achieve a modest level of influence at the highest levels. Even then, the Council's proceedings reveal a persistent attachment to local interests, traditional social values, and a corporate mentality.

Traders and manufacturers were frequently hostile or indifferent to government economic initiatives yet without a principled basis for their opposition that might have suggested a developing sense of class interest.

Only about Sweden is it possible to argue that absolutism rested on some equilibrium between classes. But here it was the peasantry, not the diminutive bourgeoisie, that acted as the counterpoise to the nobility. Not only was the Swedish peasantry largely composed of freeholders but, uniquely in Europe, it was recognized as a separate estate of the realm with an autonomous political role. Although diminished as Charles XI gathered power to himself and an inner circle of councillors, the peasants' influence ensured the nobility would bear the brunt of fiscal retrenchment by relinquishing many of its lands. True, this was not accomplished without consolidating royal support among the lesser nobility, who, reinforced by an influx of newcomers, dominated the *reduktion* commission. But what is remarkable about the recovery of alienated lands was the extent to which it was carried through; even the president of the council was not spared significant losses, despite his personal appeals to the king. However the unusual balance of social forces in Sweden did not, as events were to show, provide the most propitious basis for an enduring absolutism.

ABSOLUTISM AND THE NOBILITY

Elsewhere in Europe the absolute state consolidated its position at the expense of the peasants, partly by increasing their tax burden and partly by reinforcing their subordination to landlords. Perhaps the most famous landmark in this process was the Russian law code of 1649, which bound the Russian peasant to the soil, a plight aggravated in 1722 by the imposition of the poll tax, from which the nobility was exempt. By comparison the Prussian peasantry was well-off. Nevertheless, in addition to providing or finding the labor to cultivate the lords' demesnes—up to sixty days per year in a fifth of cases and twenty-six days in another two-fifths—it also met the largest part of the tax burden. Even in western Europe, where estate ownership and jurisdiction were no longer coterminous, the landed classes retained a remarkable ability to extract taxes, seigneurial dues, and tithes from a legally dependent peasant population. In both Castile and France half the peasants' product was consumed in payments that sustained non-peasant classes. Inevitably, there was a certain tension between the demands of the central state and landlords for the peasants' surplus. Indeed during the massive endemic unrest in the 1630s and 1640s it was not unknown for French tax officials to encourage their tenants to resist the demands of the fisc, or royal treasury. Yet this curious situation also indicates that the absolute state was not, as is sometimes suggested, an *independent* competitor against the seigneurs but a state managed by them.

All this suggests that the dynamics of absolutism were generated by noble society itself. From at least the mid-sixteenth century the European nobility had been badly shaken and divided. In part this was due to the soaring costs of war, but warfare was itself the outcome of internecine conflicts within the nobility. The centuries-long struggle between the Valois and the Bourbon against the Habsburgs was the ultimate expression of noble rivalry. Such rivalry was also manifest in the civil wars that, compounded by religious passions, tore France and Germany apart. In Russia the governing boyar elite was terrorized, depleted, and left reeling by the onslaught of Tsar Ivan IV between 1565 and 1572, and when the ruling dynasty died out in 1598, Muscovy slid into chaos. Claimants to the throne set up rival governments within a few miles of each other, while Sigismund III Vasa of Poland, who had previously been deposed as king of Sweden by his uncle (Charles IX of Sweden), invaded the country in 1610 and had his son elected tsar by a group of boyars. Only the opposition of other nobles finally secured the throne, in 1612, for Michael Romanov, a member of a distinguished but non-titled family related to the previous dynasty. The Russian throne was to remain prey to adventurers, among whom one might count Catherine the Great, who had no claim to it whatsoever. Sweden, too, in the last years of the sixteenth century was destabilized by deep factional rivalries, accentuated by religious division. Having seized the throne, Sigismund's uncle subsequently ordered the execution of his leading aristocratic opponents.

The assertion of regal authority was accompanied by a growing differentiation within the ranks of the nobility and the emergence of a handful of very powerful and influential families. In Brandenburg, for instance, on the eve of the Thirty Years' War thirteen families had already achieved an extraordinary concentration of both office and wealth, holding between them one-third to one-half of seigneurial land. As historians have long suggested, this may in part have been due to a decline in noble revenues, a decline compounded for some by the catastrophic effects of decades of war on rural economies. Many lesser nobles found themselves little better off than their tenants, while others consolidated large fortunes. But the polarization was also an outcome of the jostling for place and favor, to which monarchs contributed with measures that simultaneously recognized noble aspirations and strengthened their own powers of patronage. As early as 1520 Charles V of Spain created four distinct noble ranks, with a tiny handful of grandees at the top and large numbers of often very poor *hidalgos* (yeomen) at the bottom. All expanded significantly in the 150 years that followed, with the number of titled nobility rising from 69 in 1530 to 212 a century later. In Russia new ranks within the boyar elite were created in the sixteenth century to accommodate pressure from social upstarts, although Ivan IV tripled the number of service gentry, much to the chagrin of some of the magnates. In Sweden the monarchy began to recover from the turmoil of the early seventeenth century by incorporating the nobility as a formal estate of the realm and introducing grants of hereditary status. The order was further divided into three: the titled nobility (twelve families), members of the council of state (twenty-two families), all other untitled nobles. This process, however, excluded four hundred families.

Having consolidated their position, European monarchs were able to exploit divisions between and within noble ranks and deploy their own powers of patronage further to restructure the relationship with the nobility. This process was particularly evident in the last decades of the seventeenth century, when the Brandenburg Junkers, the Swedish inner circle, the Russian boyars, and the overmighty French subjects all had their grips on the levers of power reduced. Between 1640 and the 1670s aristocratic domination of the Russian Duma fell from 70 to 25 percent. Most dramatically, in Denmark the almost overnight establishment of absolutism in 1661 was rapidly followed by the effective dissolution of the old nobility as a distinct social group; not only did it lose its monopoly of important offices, but its numbers and its wealth collapsed. In 1660, 95 percent of privately owned manors were in the hands of the old nobility; by 1710 that had been reduced to 38.5 percent.

However, in every case, these developments were only a phase in the integration of noble and monarchical interests. In Denmark the absolute monarchy almost immediately set about creating a new nobility by introducing in the 1670s the titles of baron and count, expressly designed to enable Crown officials of common origins to acquire noble privileges and status. Their land was also protected from market forces, making it subject to primogeniture and entail. Entailed estates made up one-fifth of agricultural land in 1800. A similar renewal of the nobility took place

in Sweden, where the number of noble families rose from 150 in 1627 to 556 in 1700; half of these families owed promotion to Charles XI. In Russia a hereditary nobility did not exist, save for the princes, until the reign of Peter the Great. His extraordinarily elaborate Table of Ranks—with its fourteen grades; 262 functions, from general admiral to court butler; and tripartite classification into military, court, and civil nobility—was intended to create a Western-style noble estate. The process was not complete until 1785, when Catherine the Great's Charter of Nobility confirmed its legally privileged status. Matters followed a slightly different course in Prussia, where the Great Elector turned to the German imperial nobility to replace the Junkers. However, despite having to contend with an influx of newcomers, the Junker's never lost their virtual monopoly of the key posts in the provincial administration.

The refashioning of the nobility increased rather than diminished the preoccupation with rank and the concentration of power and wealth in the hands of a few families. Everywhere access to the highest councils was facilitated by family connections, which were constantly reinforced by the head of the clan, who secured advantageous marriages, offices and pensions, and other favors for kin and clients. Where patronage was bolstered by hereditary officeholding, as in France, the upper echelons of the state became the preserve of dynasties of ennobled officeholders. In Russia the 180 or so nobles who occupied the first four ranks were a self-perpetuating elite collectively described as the *generalitet*. Moreover, two-thirds came from old aristocratic families, who showed a remarkable staying power, particularly if connected to the royal family. While power and wealth were not perhaps as closely linked as in France, the political hierarchy was certainly underpinned by economic differentials. In 1797 four-fifths of landowners owned fewer than 100 serfs each, and a mere 1.5 percent of them had over 1,000 each, accounting in aggregate for 35 percent of the serf population. Moreover, as in western Europe, the monarchy was on hand to reward favored and influential families; Catherine the Great gave away 400,000 serfs, three-quarters of whom were acquired by the partition of Poland.

To a greater or lesser extent, nobles, which it is worth stressing rarely exceeded 1 percent of the population except in parts of Castile, were the managers and beneficiaries of the absolute state. But playing the power game could be dangerous. No fewer than 128 Russian nobles had their estates confiscated between 1700 and 1755, and a number of ministers were either executed or exiled. French absolutism was less brutal, but dissent could lead to prison or exile, and financiers were always vulnerable to the government's periodic investigations into their wealth. In the years before Louis XIV's accession the resentment felt by those who lost out in the intense competition for power and wealth threatened to plunge France back into civil war. The success of Richelieu and Jules Mazarin, both from relatively modest noble backgrounds, in achieving supreme public office, ducal status, and unrivaled fortunes in the process offended old grandees and the new officeholding elite alike. Resistance to ministerial tyranny and corruption erupted in the War of the Fronde (1648–1653). Fortunately for Mazarin, the Fronde largely served to expose the divisions between grandees, lesser nobles, parlements, tax officials, municipalities, and others, all of whom claimed to be the most loyal and suitable servants of the king. The chief minister's clientele also proved, as had that of Richelieu, more resilient and effective than those arrayed against him. However, Louis XIV's decision to dispense with a first minister was perfectly in tune with the public mood. Ironically, in doing so, he inherited not only a governmental machine but also a vast patronage system, which he manipulated with consummate success.

At the same time the French upper classes began to realize that they could ill afford to engage in perpetual conflict and that they might benefit from a king strong and prestigious enough to bring some order. This conviction was reinforced by three decades of tax revolts—themselves facilitated by upper-class rivalries, which both set a bad example and created opportunities for revolt. There is an evident parallel with the situation in Russia, where repeated waves of peasant resistance provoked demands from the service nobility for the suppression of the peasants' right of movement.

Versailles, to which the court moved in 1682, was the ultimate expression of all these pressures. Both the seat of government and the residence of an ever growing royal family, the very building embodied the inseparability of the public and the private. It served also, in the words of Françoise Bertaut de Motteville, as "a great market," made seemly by elaborate rules of etiquette, where courtiers jostled for position, pensions, and marriages. Through its preoccupation with rank and privilege the court gave renewed vigor to the social hierarchy, legitimating the privileged position of those who attended on the king. Not least Versailles created a dazzling stage for the king's deification as a great sun god whose rays brought light and order where there was darkness and confusion, a ruler systematically and consciously portrayed in prose, verse, painting, and music as the bringer of war, peace, abundance, and justice.

Absolute Monarch. Louis XIV (1638–1715) with plans for the château of Versailles. Anonymous French artist. Musée et Domaine Nationale de Versailles et de Trianon, Versailles, France/©Archivo Iconografico, S.A./ Corbis

THE LEGITIMATION OF ABSOLUTISM

As these observations suggest, the absolute state even in the west was hardly a progressive or modernizing force. Despite the growth of centralizing bureaucracies and a degree of functional specialization, the elevation of royal authority reflected its success in recovering control of patrimonial systems that had sometimes appeared to be on the verge of succumbing to their inherent instability. Ideologically, too, the elevation of royal authority was a largely conservative response to the disorders afflicting the body politic. Although some historians have seen in French absolutism a manifestation of the modern idea of legislative sovereignty enunciated by Jean Bodin in 1576, it was largely legitimated by essentially traditional ideas. Bodin himself harnessed the concept of sovereignty to Thomist and neo-Platonic teleologies, which had by no means been vanquished as overarching ideologies by the end of the seventeenth century. Absolute power replicated that of God and was in harmony with the divinely ordained cosmos.

The overriding need, according to Bodin, was to restore the integrity of the monarchical order and the social hierarchy on which it depended. In fact his conception of the social hierarchy was not merely idealized but also very French. In most of the countries discussed here, hereditary monarchs and nobilities, titles, and estates of the realm were recent creations, but this did not prevent monarchs and nobles from asserting an ancient and imprescriptible role as the mainstays of a universal order. Heightened religious feelings also bolstered monarchical ideology by encouraging kings to assert their divine authority. If the Protestant kings of Prussia and Sweden did not radiate the sacral aura of Louis XIV, an "austere concept of divine providence" served Charles XI and the Great Elector just as well in imparting a sense of duty to those around them (Melton, p. 87). Protestant and Catholic authorities alike did not doubt that the rebellion and disorder of the age were results of man's inherent sinfulness, even signs of divine displeasure. Historians have also emphasized the way in which an increasingly neostoical and classical culture put a premium on both general good order and personal self-discipline. This went along with the progressive abandonment of the constitutional ideas and rights of resistance that had been espoused by many nobles in the sixteenth century.

THE LAST STAGE OF ABSOLUTISM: ENLIGHTENED DESPOTISM

After 1760 the equilibrium of the absolutist regimes was once more disturbed. The Seven Years' War (1756–1763), sparked in part by Prussia's annexation of Silesia from Austria, ushered in several decades of intense great-power rivalry. Poland was wiped off the face of the map. The French monarchy, debilitated by fighting in Europe and overseas, never recovered. By dint of a massive debasement of the coinage and its plunder of Silesia and Poland, the Prussian regime managed somewhat better. Even so, the war chest bequeathed by Frederick II to his successor was rapidly exhausted in the turbulent years between 1787 and 1794. In 1795 Prussia was forced to sue for peace with France, ceding all territory on the west bank of the Rhine. Russia, while jostling to assert its position as a major European power, was also pushing up against the Turkish Empire in the east with three bouts of open conflict (1768–1774, 1783–1784, 1787–1792). The pressure exerted on rudimentary financial systems, inelastic economies, and a resentful population had a predictable effect. New peaks of unrest were reached in the revolt of the Cossacks under Yemelyan Ivanovich Pugachov in 1773 and in Bohemia two years later, when a forty-thousand-strong army was

required to restore order. In France a run of poor harvests brought an end to years of relative calm in the countryside and prepared the way for the peasant uprising in the summer of 1789.

It is difficult to characterize the highly ambivalent and often contradictory responses of the absolute states to the worsening situation as simply enlightened. The administrative centralization of Joseph II, the rigidly mercantilist regime of Frederick II, and Catherine's Legislative Commission, which for the first time gave the nobility a role as an estate of the realm, are among the many policies of conservative hue. Nor was this surprising, given that the impetus for reform was precipitated by pressures similar to those that had ushered in the absolutist regimes a century earlier. Even Joseph II's determined attempts to abolish labor services and reduce the burdens of seigneurialism may be construed as efforts to generate more state revenue.

On the other hand, absolutism had brought into being a class of now experienced and educated nobles, state servants who began to see that reform was necessary if their regimes were to survive as great powers. This realization was heightened by an awareness of the immense technical superiority of English agriculture, industry, and commerce, to which these regimes repeatedly turned for expertise and practical assistance. Even in Prussia, where the University of Halle was a bulwark of opposition to physiocratic ideas, Frederick the Great understood that the rural world ought to be freed from its burdens, although he achieved almost nothing outside the royal domains. In this changing intellectual climate, many nobles had by the 1770s absorbed utilitarian assumptions about the origins, purpose, and nature of government that had little in common with the religious teleology of their predecessors. Ideas of natural equality and meritocracy gained ground.

However, there was a self-evident contradictoriness in absolutist regimes attacking the hierarchical society of which they were so much part. When Joseph II died, his reforming program was in tatters. In France resistance to reform precipitated a chain of events that led to the destruction of absolute monarchy and the entire privileged order. Even then, although revolution and industrialization accelerated the pace of change and hastened the transformation of the nobility and the emancipation of the peasantry, the political superstructures of central and eastern Europe displayed an extraordinary resilience. Not until the 1870s was Prussia absorbed into a quite different type of state, and not until the twentieth century did the Russian regime finally disintegrate under the impact of a classic combination of war and social unrest.

446

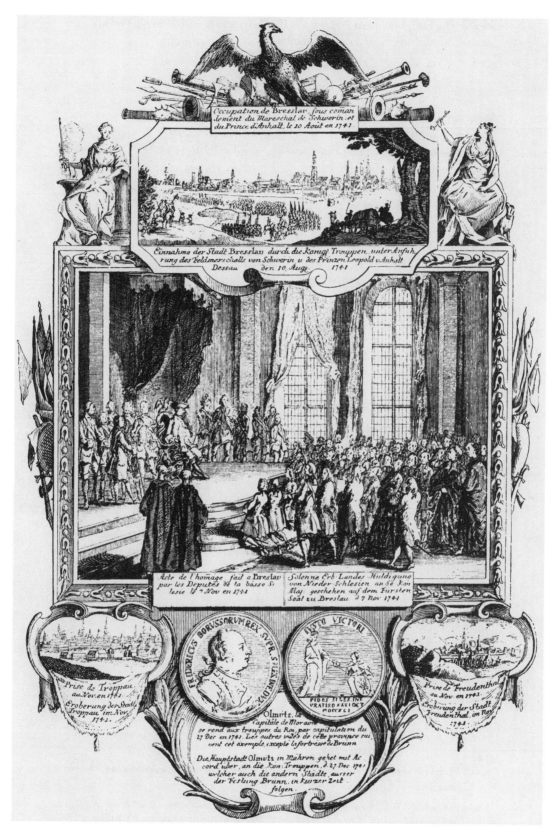

Monarch and Estates. The deputies of Lower Silesia swear loyalty to their new master, Frederick the Great of Prussia, at Breslau, 7 November 1741. Austria ceded Silesia to Prussia the following year. Engraving by J. D. Schleuen. ULLSTEIN BILDERDIENST, BERLIN

See also **The Enlightenment** *(volume 1);* **The Aristocracy and Gentry; The Military** *(volume 3); and other articles in this section.*

BIBLIOGRAPHY

Anderson, Perry. *Lineages of the Absolutist State.* London, 1974.

Beik, William. *Absolutism and Society in Seventeenth-Century France: State Power and Provincial Aristocracy in Languedoc.* Cambridge, U.K., 1985.

Bonney Richard, ed. *Economic Systems and State Finance.* Oxford, 1995.

Crummey, Robert O. *Aristocrats and Servitors: The Boyar Elite in Russia, 1613–1689.* Princeton, N.J., 1983.

Downing, Brian M. *The Military Revolution and Political Change: Origins of Democracy and Autocracy in Early Modern Europe.* Princeton, N.J., 1992.

Dukes, Paul. *Catherine the Great and the Russian Nobility.* Cambridge, U.K., 1967.

Ertman, Thomas. *Birth of the Leviathan: Building States and Regimes in Medieval and Early Modern Europe.* Cambridge, U.K., 1997.

Hoffman, Philip T., and Kathryn Norberg, eds. *Fiscal Crises, Liberty, and Representative Government, 1450–1789.* Stanford, Calif., 1994.

Köpeczi, Béla, Albert Souboul, Éva H. Balázs, and Domokas Kosáry, eds. *L'absolutisme éclairé.* Budapest, Hungary, and Paris, 1985.

LeDonne, John P. *Absolutism and Ruling Class: The Formation of the Russian Political Order, 1700–1825.* New York, 1991.

LeDonne, John P. *Ruling Russia: Politics and Administration in the Age of Absolutism, 1762–1796.* Princeton, N.J., 1984.

Liublinskaia, Alexandra Dmitrievna. *French Absolutism: The Crucial Phase, 1620–1629.* Cambridge, U.K., 1968.

Meehan-Waters, Brenda. *Autocracy and Aristocracy: The Russian Service Elite of 1730.* New Brunswick, N.J., 1982.

Melton, Edgar. "The Prussian Junkers, 1600–1786." In *The European Nobilities in the Seventeenth and Eighteenth Centuries.* Vol. 2. Edited by H. M. Scott. London, 1995.

Miller, John, ed. *Absolutism in Seventeenth-Century Europe.* Basingstoke, U.K., 1990.

Munck, Thomas. *The Peasantry and the Early Absolute Monarchy in Denmark, 1660–1708.* Copenhagen, Denmark, 1979.

Parker, David. *Class and State in Ancien Régime France: The Road to Modernity?* London, 1996.

Parker, David. *The Making of French Absolutism.* London, 1983.

Rosenberg, Hans. *Bureaucracy, Aristocracy, and Autocracy: The Prussian Experience, 1660–1815.* Cambridge, Mass., 1958.

Scott, H. M. ed. *Enlightened Absolutism: Reform and Reformers in Later Eighteenth-Century Europe.* Basingstoke, U.K., 1990.

Scott, H. M., ed. *The European Nobilities in the Seventeenth and Eighteenth Centuries.* London, 1995.

Thompson, I. A. A. *Crown and Cortes: Government, Institutions, and Representation in Early Modern Castile.* Aldershot, U.K., and Brookfield, Vt., 1993.

Tilly, Charles. *Coercion, Capital, and European States.* Rev. ed. Oxford, 1992.

Upton, Anthony F. *Charles XI and Swedish Absolutism.* Cambridge, U.K., 1998.

THE LIBERAL STATE

Adrian Shubert

Liberalism as a political philosophy has a long history and incorporates complex influences from a number of countries. The word was first applied to a political movement in Spain in 1812, referring to the advocates of constitutional government. This use then extended to other countries. The political systems intended by their founders to be liberal incorporated this intellectual tradition but not it alone. They were also informed by traditions of eighteenth-century enlightened absolutism and the experience of popular revolution that began in France in 1789 and touched virtually all the Continent by 1848.

The European liberal state was a product of the coming together of these influences. Local circumstances guaranteed differences in emphasis and detail among countries, but the fundamental features of the liberal state were strikingly consistent. The hallmark of all liberal states was the creation of written constitutions that established representative governments based on highly restricted suffrage determined by wealth, literacy, or both. The right to vote was characteristically limited to between 1 and 10 percent of the population. The liberal state was also far removed from any conception of a "minimum" or "night watchman" state. Indeed once liberals came to power, state building was among their primary objectives. The liberal state was much more extensive in its reach across Europe and directly touched more of its citizens than had its ancien régime predecessor.

The watchwords of the builders of Europe's liberal states were centralization and homogenization. In large part these concerns derived from the experience of eighteenth-century enlightened reformers, whose goals were to enhance national military and economic power and to strengthen the Crown and bring it into closer contact with its subjects. Such a program meant that reformers and the liberals who succeeded them were simultaneously engaged in eliminating state intervention in a number of areas, primarily economic; in building the power of the state by weakening the multiplicity of privileges, intermediate institutions, and private jurisdictions that stood between govern-

ment and subjects (or citizens); and in increasing the number of the state's own agents. This perspective was forcefully expressed by Pablo de Olavide, a reforming official in Spain under Charles III (1759–1788), when he described the ancien régime as:

> A body composed of other and smaller bodies, separated and in opposition to one another, which oppress and despise each other and are in a continuous state of war. Each province, each religious house, each profession is separated from the rest of the nation and concentrated in itself . . . a monstrous Republic of little republics which contradict each other because the particular interest of each is in contradiction with the general interest.

Before liberals could build they had to destroy many of the institutions that characterized the ancien régime. These institutions did not always surrender quietly, especially religious institutions, which were often the most significant targets of such changes. Olavide ended up in the clutches of one of those intermediate bodies, the Inquisition. Across much of Europe and especially Catholic Europe the churches were the liberals' most persistent and most dangerous opponents.

The great era for the construction of liberal states was between the Restoration and the revolutions of 1848. Even Britain, which already had a parliamentary form of government with highly restrictive suffrage, saw an attack on a range of customary economic practices that had constituted breaks on the free play of market forces and had offered some form of protection to ordinary men and women. The regimes established under the Restoration were subject to a series of conspiracies and military coups that sought to restore or install parliamentary government. These were most frequent in southern Europe, where liberals wanted rulers to proclaim the Spanish Constitution of 1812. Few of these uprisings were successful, although the Spanish revolution of 1820 was defeated only by French intervention in 1823. Dynastic conflicts provided the opportunity for liberals to achieve definitive victories in Portugal and Spain in the 1830s, while in Belgium independence from the Netherlands, achieved with the aid of foreign intervention, was accompanied by the creation of a constitutional system. Greece became a constitutional monarchy in 1843, and Denmark and the Netherlands did so in 1849. In Italy, Piedmont became a permanently liberal state in 1848, and it imposed that liberalism on the rest of the peninsula between 1860 and 1870.

While most of western Europe had liberal political systems by 1848 or 1849, this was not the case in other parts of the Continent. Austria did not establish a constitutional government until 1860, Sweden until 1864, northern Germany until 1867, and Germany as a whole until 1871.

The circumstances that produced liberal states in Europe have been the subject of long-standing and ongoing debates. The central issue undoubtedly has been the extent to which the revolutions that did away with the ancien régimes of Europe can be identified with a specific social class, the bourgeoisie. The marxist interpretation, which holds that liberal states were the product of bourgeois revolutions, has been particularly influential. In this view industrial development produced a bourgeois class that eventually seized power from the feudal aristocracy. The classic examples of bourgeois revolutions were England and France, and the influence of these interpretations was such that they became normative. Scholars assessed the histories of other countries in terms of how closely they matched these models. Those countries with significantly different patterns were frequently deemed "peculiar" or to have "failed." Moreover in countries such as Germany, Italy, and Spain the "failure" of the bourgeoisie to make its revolution was frequently asserted as the reason they succumbed to dictatorship in the interwar period. This was, for example, the central thrust of Antonio Gramsci's analysis of Italian unification, his concept of "passive revolution," and the thinking behind Germany's *Sonderweg* (special path).

After the 1960s and especially after the 1980s the concept of bourgeois revolution and the identification of liberalism with a specific class were increasingly questioned. In country after country historians were unable to locate an industrial bourgeoisie that seized power and recast state and society to its specifications. These changes were most striking in the French Revolution. The classic marxist view of Georges Lefebvre was challenged by historians such as Alfred Cobban, G. V. Taylor, and above all François Furet. Research uncovered not a new class tied to industry but a composite elite of nobles and commercial and professional bourgeois who were similar intellectually and culturally. Historians began to locate the causes

of the revolution not in the economy but in the realms of politics, ideology, or culture. Similar trends have been present in the historiographies of England, Germany, and Spain. Perhaps the extreme example of this trend was Arno Mayer's controversial claim that, far from a bourgeois revolution, the aristocracy remained the dominant class across Europe on the eve of World War I.

BUILDING THE LIBERAL STATE

The architects of Europe's liberal states had an expansive vision of the proper areas of state activity. The first continental liberal state was created in France during the Revolution (1789–1815). The revolutionaries quickly abolished the institutions of the ancien régime and replaced them with new ones that brought the state into a direct relationship with its citizens. War was the single greatest impetus to the construction of this new centralized state. The French pioneered many institutions and structures that were widely copied across Europe, and not just by liberals.

TERRITORY AND ADMINISTRATION

Under the ancien régime national territory was characteristically divided into units of significantly different sizes that, more important, enjoyed different relationships with the Crown. In France the *pays d'état* and in Spain the Basque Provinces and Navarre had special privileges regarding taxation and military service that were not shared by other parts of the realm. Such a situation offended liberals, for whom legal privilege of any sort was anathema and who sought to bring all parts of their country and all its citizens into equal relationships with the central state. Thus one of the first measures liberals undertook was the division of the national territory into new units of roughly equal size that did not enjoy any privileges.

A new division of the national territory into units of roughly equal size was considered a pressing need by early governments of the French Revolution. In January 1790 the country was divided into eighty departments, an arrangement retained by all the regimes that followed. France became the model for other countries. Portugal and Spain were divided into provinces in 1833, Piedmont divided in the 1850s, and Italy divided following unification in 1861. Where they existed, internal customs barriers were also eliminated.

In addition to the unequal division of national territory under the ancien régime, the individuals who lived there held unequal status. The liberal vision of equal citizens required elimination of all such privi-

The Danish Parliament. First session of the Danish Parliament, established in 1849 in response to the Revolutions of 1848. Painting (1860–1864) by Constantin Hansen. OLE HAUPT/NATIONALHISTORISKE MUSEUM, FREDERIKSBORG, DENMARK

leges. Much was subsumed under the "abolition of feudalism," the elimination of seigneurial rights and legal jurisdiction and of special legal status for designated groups, such as the nobility and the clergy. Thus Spanish liberals abolished the Inquisition, and Piedmont's Siccardi Laws, passed in 1850, did away with church courts and legal immunities for the clergy, demanded government approval for donations of property to religious institutions, and eliminated penalties for nonobservance of religious holidays. This freedom also applied to the economy, including the destruction of the guilds. More significantly in societies that were still primarily agricultural, it removed privileged constraints on the use and sale of land, the most important of which was the expropriation of the lands of religious institutions.

The legal complexes of the ancien régime were replaced by rationalized legal codes that applied to all citizens. Again the model for much of the Continent was the French Napoleonic Code, established in 1804. Even before it established a constitution, Piedmont adopted a civil code (1837) and a penal code (1839) on the Napoleonic model. The 1837 code became the

basis for the Italian Civil Law Code of 1865. Piedmont's 1859 criminal code was extended to all of Italy except Tuscany and remained in place until the approval of the Zanardelli Code in 1889. Portugal passed a penal code in 1852 and a civil code in 1867. Spain's first penal code, passed in 1848, was revised in 1870, but Spain had no civil code until 1889. Even then it did not supersede local civil laws in several parts of the country.

This division of the national territory was a prerequisite for the creation of a centralized, hierarchical administrative structure through which the policies of the central state could be transmitted to the provinces, towns, and villages of the nation. As Javier de Burgos, the architect of Spain's version of this structure, put it, the goal was to construct "a chain that starts at the head of the administration and ends with the last local policeman." The inspiration for this highly centralized administrative structure came from France and the figure of the prefect, the appointed agent of the state in each of the departments. In Spain, Burgos's creation of the provinces was accompanied by the creation of a new figure, the civil governor, who was

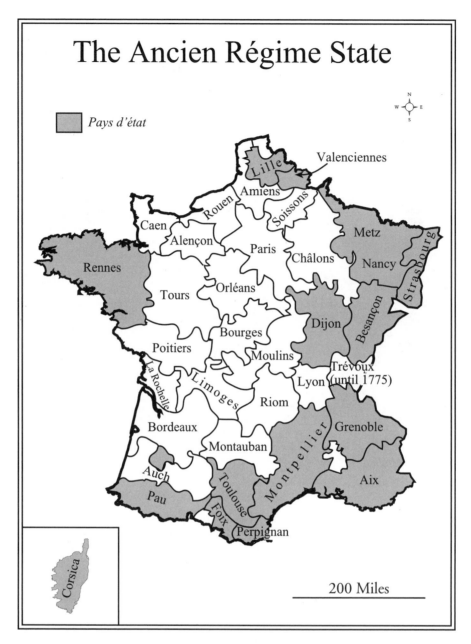

The Ancien Régime State

▢ *Pays d'état*

The Ancien Régime State. The provinces of France under the ancien régime. *Pays d'état* were provinces that had provincial estates (legislative assemblies).

the agent of the central government. These officials were invested with a wide range of responsibilities, including public order, education, welfare, statistics, and economic development. Similar developments took place in Portugal during the 1830s and in Piedmont during the 1850s as Camillo Cavour sought to build a state capable of expansion in northern Italy. He created powerful provincial officials, known as prefects, and immediately imposed them on the whole of Italy after unification in 1861.

Typically provinces were further divided into counties and municipalities, each with its own local official subordinate to the civil governor or prefect. In some cases, such as in Portugal and Spain, appointed mayors formed the lowest rung on the ladder of centralized administration. The issue of appointed versus elected mayors was often a point of division between moderate and more radical liberals.

Belgium and Britain took different paths. Belgium experienced centralized administrative systems

The Liberal State

The Liberal State. The departments established during the French Revolution.

under Napoleon and as part of the Dutch monarchy, but when the country achieved independence in 1830 it left cities and towns a wide degree of autonomy, including the power to impose local taxes, subsidize schools and churches, and control the police and the militia. Brussels, Liège, Ghent, and Antwerp had the power to call out the militia independent of central government approval. At the provincial level the key institution was the elected council, not the provincial governor. Appointed for life, governors chaired the councils but did not act as the local agents of the state administrations, as did prefects in the French model.

As citizens made new demands on government, the Belgian government delegated tasks to local and provincial institutions or created new semipublic ones.

Britain developed a strong central state that left a number of functions to local governments or voluntary associations. As a result the direct presence of the central state in the lives of its citizens was much less apparent than elsewhere in Europe. This approach represented a continuity from the ancien régime, which relied on a range of indirect agents, such as chartered municipalities, justices of the peace, overseers of the poor, householder constables, and local associations.

The last decade of the eighteenth century and the period after 1815 saw efforts to make the central government more efficient while expanding the scope for the actions of individuals and free institutions. Included in this approach was an attack on customary rights and other long-standing constraints on economic freedom, such as the Assize of Bread, which permitted judicial control of bread and ale prices.

The 1830s and 1840s brought a significant expansion of the central state. The Anatomy Act (1832) created a central inspectorate to regulate the use of the dead for research, and the Factory Act (1833) created a specialized inspectorate staffed by professional civil servants responsible to the home office. These inspectors constituted a new species of central government agent. Over the next two decades analogous services were established to oversee poor law institutions, public health, mines, prisons, and schools. In 1836 a centralized system for registering births, deaths, and marriages was added. The government also began to regulate new areas, such as railways in 1842 and working hours in the Ten Hours Act of 1847.

Despite all these changes, local governments remained important and through most of the century affected more people directly than did the central state. A large number of new laws affecting areas such as baths, washhouses, lodging houses, public libraries, laborers' dwellings, and industrial schools left implementation to local authorities. The central government sought to achieve greater uniformity by creating the Local Government Board (1871) and by mandating local health authorities and medical officers of health (1872), but even in these functions it did not assume direct control.

POLICE

Burgos was far from unique in seeing policing as an important feature of the new state apparatus. France obtained a national police force in 1798. The Gendarmerie Nationale patrolled rural areas and highways and reported to the war minister. It was complemented by the Sûreté Nationale, an urban police force reporting to the interior minister and responsible, among other things, for political intelligence. The Sûreté gradually took over the municipal police of the major cities. By the end of the century France had more than twenty thousand gendarmes. Spain's Civil Guard was created in 1844 on the model of the Gendarmerie, and by 1880 it boasted almost two thousand posts and more than sixteen thousand men throughout the country, often in small rural towns. United Italy immediately was endowed with two highly

centralized police forces, the Carabinieri, numbering 24,626 in 1889, for the countryside and the Guardia de Sicurezza Publica for the cities. Unsurprisingly both were extensions of Piedmontese institutions.

Policing and justice was another area in which the British government extended its reach, albeit gradually at first. Municipal governments lost to the lord chancellor the power to appoint magistrates, although they gained the right to establish watch committees to oversee the police. The County and Borough Police Act (1856) made the creation of police forces mandatory and, more significantly, made them subject to central inspection. The pace picked up after around 1870. A centralized criminal records system was established in 1869, and ten years later the newly created director of public prosecutions put criminal prosecution squarely in the hands of central authority. Special Branch, with a mandate to watch political dissidents, was created in 1884. The Prison Act of 1877 gave the state increased control of the prison system. Overall, expenditures on police rose from 1.5 million pounds in 1861 to 7 million in 1914.

MILITARY SERVICE

The French Republic pioneered the mass mobilization of the citizenry as an emergency measure in 1793, but the principle of involving all the nation's young men in military service remained one of the hallmarks of liberal states, at least on the Continent. France introduced conscription in 1798 and retained it in various forms throughout the nineteenth century. The St. Cyr Law of 1818, the cornerstone, established a period of service of six years, but the term varied between five and eight years until 1889, when it was set at three years. People with enough money could purchase a substitute for their sons, but that practice was eliminated in 1873.

Spain introduced national service in 1837 but permitted the purchase of exemption with provision of a substitute until 1912. Immediately after unification Italy imposed conscription, one of the causes of widespread disturbances in the South in the early 1860s.

EDUCATION

Education proved the most contentious area for state expansion. It almost always brought the state into direct conflict with powerful religious institutions, for whom control over the minds of the young was considered essential. For many continental countries France once again provided the model. The Guizot

Law of 1833 required that every commune provide an elementary school, and two years later a corps of school inspectors was created. A child labor law in 1841 required education for all children under the age of twelve. The major expansion of the school system came with the Ferry Laws of the 1880s, which made public elementary schools totally free, instituted compulsory education, provided subsidies for school buildings and teacher salaries, and established an elaborate system of inspections. Between 1878 and 1885 the state budget for education increased by 250 percent.

Spain legislated a national school system in 1857, but the Moyano Law left municipalities holding the financial responsibility. In 1900 the central state created an Education Ministry and assumed the obligation of paying teachers. The Piedmontese school system was established by the 1859 Casati Law, and it extended to all of Italy after unification. The law created a powerful Ministry of Public Instruction that controlled public education and had oversight of private schools. The minister had direct control over all instruction and exercised it through an inspectorate. Local and provincial elective boards operated under the control of the prefects.

The British government had to tread lightly in the education field. Both the established Anglican Church and the Nonconformists opposed state intervention, and bills to create a national school system were repeatedly defeated in Parliament. The government could make only annual grants, beginning with a modest 20,000 pounds in 1833, rising to 189,000 by 1850 to 724,000 by 1860. After 1839 this grant was supervised by the Privy Council's education committee. The British experience was thus significantly different from those of many continental states, which early on created nationwide school systems, at least on paper. The British passed no equivalent of the Guizot, Moyano, or Casati Laws. Even the Education Act of 1870, which set out a commitment to a national system, did not overcome the religious issue. It created a situation in which, by the end of the century, the Education Department had to deal with over two thousand school boards and the management of more than fourteen thousand individual schools.

An integral part of education was the question of language, specifically the extension of the national language to all citizens. In 1863 about a fifth of the French population did not speak French, and under the Third Republic patois remained deeply entrenched in more than twenty departments. The pressure of an extended school system and universal military service steadily extended French. Italy faced a similar situation, but its dialects were more persistent. At the end of the century the Poles in eastern Prussia were forcibly educated in German.

In Spain, where the existence of Catalan, Basque, and Gallego made the issue particularly complex, the state attempted to legislate the use of Spanish. Catalan was prohibited from use in notarial documents in 1862, and five years later plays written in "dialects" were censored. Catalan was banned from the Civil Register in 1870 and from the justice system in 1881. In 1896 the government forbade speaking Catalan on the telephone, and in 1902 the state tried to require that priests teach the catechism in Spanish only. Austria, a multinational and multilingual empire, faced the most difficult situation. Its 1867 constitution permitted elementary schooling in the "language of the country," but this raised the question of minorities within each "country."

CENSORSHIP

Liberal constitutions promised freedom of expression and freedom of the press, yet those freedoms were almost always immediately circumscribed by restrictive legislation. The Piedmontese *Statuto,* which became the constitution of Italy after 1860, contained a typical formula, promising a "free press subject to the constraints of the law." Liberal states exercised censorship throughout the nineteenth century, passing laws, establishing agencies, and appointing officials for the purpose. Commonalities existed throughout Europe. Theater and caricature were more rigidly controlled than printed material; printed material directed at the lower classes was more stringently censored than that aimed higher up the social scale; and the press of the organized working class was frequently a special target. Governments also regularly evaded their own laws with administrative measures. As new technologies generated new forms of communication, such as photographs and moving pictures, they, too, were subjected to state censorship.

PUBLIC HEALTH

Liberal states often actively legislated in the area of public health, although not always in the same way. Peter Baldwin has argued that two forms of state intervention controlled contagious diseases such as smallpox, cholera, and venereal disease. Germany and France responded with obviously interventionist measures, such as quarantines, compulsory vaccinations, and regulation of prostitutes. For example, Germany's Contagious Disease Law (1900) required that the sick be sequestered. In contrast, Britain and the Nordic countries opted for an emphasis on voluntary vaccinations and on controlling the environmental conditions that caused disease. Apparently less interventionist, this was a different form of intervention. As Baldwin wrote, the voluntary and environmentalist strategy "cost more resources and administrative muscle than many [states] could muster" (Baldwin).

In Portugal, health laws in 1835 and 1844 created a national network of health authorities to issue death certificates and enforce new rules on burials, for instance, requiring location of cemeteries at a minimum distance from populated areas. These measures were not always well received, especially by peasants who saw in them a new form of taxation and an attack on long-held customs.

RESISTANCE

In many parts of Europe the construction of the liberal state provoked resistance and on occasion even full-scale counterrevolutions. Opposition came primarily from the Catholic Church, whose temporal power, material assets, and internal management were targets of the liberal state's ambitions. But ecclesiastical opposition represented a danger to the liberal state only when it tied into significant popular discontent. Such discontent was most common in rural areas, particularly those characterized by the existence of a relatively egalitarian smallholding peasantry and numerous secular clergy who were well integrated into local life. If these peasants spoke a language other than the official one of the state, the possibilities increased further. Resistance was provoked by certain aspects of liberal state building, including the sale of local common lands, taxation, the imposition of military service, the assertion of greater control over natural resources, or the application of laws that, as with public health, threatened deeply held local customs. Local clergy frequently were influential in or even led resistance movements. The presence and extent of counterrevolution corresponded to the vigor and rapidity with which liberals built their new state. It was most significant in France, Portugal, Italy, and above all Spain.

The French Revolution was marked by numerous outbreaks of counterrevolution in a number of rural regions. There is no simple, overarching explanation for these movements, which were triggered by varying combinations of local landholding patterns and social conflicts, the effects of the intrusion of the new state apparatus into the countryside, the revolutionary abolition of feudalism, the imposition of conscription, and the attack on the church. Fourteen departments revolted in western France alone in March 1793, and further upheaval occurred in the north and the south. In the Vendée, where counterrevolution was most deeply rooted, a guerrilla war continued until 1796, followed by further outbreaks in 1799–1801, 1815, and 1832.

Counterrevolution outlived the revolution in other parts of France. The Forest Code of 1827 gave unprecedented power to a new, centralized forest administration. Some saw the activities of its local agents in controlling the use of forest resources as an attack on long-established use rights, especially in royal and communal forests, provoking resistance known as the War of the Desmoiselles in the department of the Ariège.

The clergy had a prominent role in generating popular support for the absolutist side in Portugal's War of the Brothers (1829–1834) and in the decade-long antiliberal violence that followed. New regulations requiring death certificates and the location of cemeteries at a minimum distance from villages were taken by many people, especially in the rural north, as a new tax and an attack on traditional practices regarding the dead, who, it was believed, should be kept close to the living. The 1845 Health Law was a primary cause of the Maria da Fonte revolt that spread across the north of the country in 1846 and 1847 and provoked British and Spanish intervention.

In Italy the imposition of the Piedmontese administrative system, taxes, conscription, and the sale of common lands provoked a massive wave of banditry across the south in the years immediately following unification. The imposition in 1869 of a new tax on grinding grain generated widespread peasant disturbances in the north and center of the country.

Counterrevolution was strongest and most persistent in Spain. Beginning with the "liberal triennium" of 1820 to 1823, peasants in various parts of the country, but especially in Catalonia, Valencia, the Basque Provinces, and Navarre, participated in antiliberal movements. In the 1820s they were motivated by conscription, a prohibition on burials inside churches, tax increases, and what was seen as anticlerical legislation. These issues and a defense of regional privilege (*fueros*) were the mass base for the Carlist movement, which fought a seven-year civil war against the liberal state between 1833 and 1840 and a second, shorter one from 1874 to 1876. The anticentralist legacy of Carlism carried on into the Basque nationalist movement that emerged in the 1890s.

Belgium had a very different experience. From the country's independence in 1830 the Catholic Church supported a liberal state that subsidized its activities and permitted religious schools and even

Dans les écoles des couvents, on enseigne aux enfants
la haine de tout ce qui n'est pas clérical

Liberal View of Catholic Education. "In convent schools, children are taught to hate everything that isn't clerical." A Belgian print (1912) satirizes a Catholic schoolroom in which a nun equates the political opposition with the devil, liberals with rascals, and socialists with hooligans. LIBERAAL ARCHIEF, FONDS WILLEMFODS, GHENT, BELGIUM

lived with religious toleration. When liberals attempted to secularize the schools in the 1880s, the Catholic Church and its supporters reacted but not by challenging the existence of the liberal state itself. Instead, Catholics mobilized politically and successfully fought for power through electoral means.

NEW DEPARTURES

During the last quarter of the century the liberal state responded to new circumstances by moving in new directions. On the one hand, the new intellectual trends were a reaction to the consequences of industrialization. On the other, the emergence of mass political movements, especially socialism, were encouraged by the granting of universal or near-universal male suffrage in Germany (1871), France (1875), Spain (1890), Belgium (1894), Norway (1898), Finland (1905), Sweden (1907), and Italy (1912). Liberal politicians in some countries, such as Germany, had trouble adjusting to the tumult of mass politics and were often outpaced by socialists or conservatives.

As a result new reform measures were almost as likely to be the work of conservative governments as of liberal ones. The first move came from the newly unified German Reich. Chancellor Otto von Bismarck's motivation was to preempt the rapidly grow-

ing Social Democratic Party, which he banned in 1879. Through the 1880s the German government introduced a series of social insurance measures unprecedented in their nature and scope that included sickness insurance in 1883, accident insurance in 1884, and disability and old-age insurance in 1889. Within the working class at least, Bismarck's laws mandated obligatory participation and income-related contributions, provided universal coverage, did not involve means testing, and were administered centrally. By 1913, 15 million Germans had sickness insurance, 28 million had accident insurance, and 1 million received pensions. These measures were accompanied by government regulation of a range of work-related areas, such as compulsory factory regulations, the creation of labor exchanges and industrial courts, the beginnings of arbitration, and legislation limiting the number of hours women could work each day.

These German initiatives were a model that was copied or at least appealed to elsewhere. Bismarck in turn claimed to have learned valuable lessons from Napoleon III's experiments with a national pension fund and an accident insurance fund. The German model became increasingly influential in Britain after 1905. It had a major impact on David Lloyd George and was specifically referred to as an inspiration for

MAJOR SOCIAL LEGISLATION, 1883–1914

Accidents	*Sickness*	*Pensions*	*Unemployment*
Germany, 1884	Germany, 1883	Germany, 1889	Norway, 1906
Austria, 1887	Italy, 1886	Denmark, 1891	Belgium, 1907
Norway, 1894	Austria, 1888	Italy, 1898	Denmark, 1907
Finland, 1895	Sweden, 1891	Belgium, 1900	United Kingdom, 1911
France, 1898	Denmark, 1892	United Kingdom, 1908	France, 1914
Denmark, 1898	Belgium, 1894	France, 1910	
Italy, 1898	Norway, 1909	Netherlands, 1913	
Netherlands, 1901	United Kingdom, 1911	Sweden, 1913	
Sweden, 1901	Switzerland, 1911		
Belgium, 1903	Netherlands, 1913		
United Kingdom, 1906			
Switzerland, 1911			

the landmark 1911 National Insurance Act. In France the German model was in the forefront of parliamentary debates of welfare bills both as something to be copied and something to be avoided.

In the twenty-five years before World War I governments across Europe moved into new areas of activity. The 1890s saw the creation in Britain of the Labor Department of the Board of Trade; the Conciliation Act (1896), through which the state became the arbiter of labor disputes; and the Workman's Compensation Act (1897). The real thrust of this new, social liberalism came after 1908, with the Liberal governments of Herbert Henry Asquith and Lloyd George. Old-age pensions were available on a means-tested basis to the elderly and very poor in 1908, and three years later the National Insurance Act introduced compulsory health insurance for all wage workers and some unemployment insurance.

Between 1892 and 1910 France introduced a series of social welfare measures. Early workplace legislation was either toughened or extended. In 1892 France placed limits on working hours of children, adolescents, and adult women and in 1900 set the working day for adult males in so-called mixed workshops at a maximum of ten hours. This was extended to all adult workers two years later. Insurance for workplace accidents was introduced in 1898, but it was not compulsory and excluded all agricultural workers and some industrial ones. Old-age pensions came in 1910. These carried some state financing and

in theory participation was obligatory, although in 1912 only 7 million of 12 million eligible workers were involved.

In Italy this development began with the creation of a Labor Council composed of representatives of business, parliament, and organized labor to study labor issues and a commission to supervise emigration in 1902. The bulk of these new initiatives were associated with the governments of Giovanni Giolitti, including restrictions on the employment of children and the first protection of female labor in 1907 and the nationalization of the life insurance industry in 1912. Spain's Social Reform Institute, six of whose twelve members were Socialists, was created in 1883 to advise the government on labor issues, but the first significant legislation was slow in coming. Workers' compensation was established in 1900 and the eight-hour day in 1918.

The Scandinavian approach was the furthest removed from that of Bismarck. There political parties more associated with the right than the left promoted social welfare legislation, but the result was social programs that provided universal coverage and were financed entirely by taxes rather than by premiums. Denmark introduced such pensions in 1911 and Sweden did so in 1913.

Much of this social legislation fit within liberal conceptions of individual effort and responsibility, but that was considerably more difficult when the state began to intervene directly in family life. France was a pioneer. In 1889 the state claimed the authority to make abused and neglected children its wards. Over the next two decades the French state also intervened between husbands and wives, passing laws that limited husbands' authority over their wives and their earnings. The state also funded mandatory maternity leave for all wage-earning women after 1913 and instituted means-tested family allowances for dependent children once a family had its fourth child. The British government curtailed parental authority with the Children's Act (1908), which required medical examinations for all children and established a system of probationary and juvenile courts. As was true with other areas of social provision, the political support for intervention in the family varied. In Britain socialists and feminists were the strongest advocates for such legislation; in France conservatives, nationalists, and Catholics were the advocates.

At the same time that intervention in the lives of citizens increased, the liberal state faced the problem of reinforcing its legitimacy and generating identity and loyalty in the face of mass political movements on both the right and the left that rejected its basic tenets. A common response was, as Eric Hobsbawm has argued, to invent new traditions. The range of such practices was great, and the actual mix varied from country to country. For example, France's Third Republic eschewed the use of the historical past, while the German Reich embraced it.

At their literal flimsiest, such traditions included issuing historical postage stamps. The first appeared in Portugal in 1894 to commemorate the five-hundredth anniversary of the birth of Prince Henry the Navigator (1394–1460). Greece (1896), Germany (1899), Spain (1905), the Netherlands (1906), Switzerland (1907), Austria-Hungary (1908), Italy (1910), and Belgium (1914) soon followed. Nations created new holidays, such as France's Bastille Day, established in 1880, and Spain's Día de la Raza, commemorating the voyage of Columbus, in 1912, and new ceremonial occasions. The first, Queen Victoria's jubilee of 1887, was copied elsewhere and repeated in Britain and its empire. The Great Exhibition of 1851, which featured the Crystal Palace, quickly evolved into frequent international expositions and world's fairs that promoted both the host and the participating nations. Liberal states also built large numbers of public buildings, statues, and other monuments.

AFTER THE LIBERAL STATE

Universal male suffrage, mass parties, and state involvement in social welfare suggest that before World War I the liberal state was already turning into something else. The murderous effects of the war and the emergence of new forms of behavior, especially among women, exacerbated prewar concerns about the condition of the family and the level and health of national populations. Across Europe the relation between the state and the citizen changed significantly as the state became deeply involved in numerous areas that had previously been considered private life. In much of western and central Europe the liberal state was giving way to the welfare state.

The welfare state reached its full flowering in the first three decades after the end of World War II. But in contrast to the interwar years, the emphasis on collective health gave way to what Mark Mazower

State as Guarantor of Pensions. "The state guarantees all payments" of the V.O.V. (voluntary old-age insurance program), proclaims a Dutch poster of the 1950s. INTERNATIONAL INSTITUTE FOR SOCIAL HISTORY, AMSTERDAM

(1999) described as a concern to "expand opportunities and choices for the individual citizen." Fuelled by full employment and rapid economic growth, public spending, especially on social services, increased significantly, as did the taxation that funded it. Rather than a single model of the welfare state, considerable differences developed among nations. Probably the most famous internationally was the Swedish Social Democratic version, where the goal was to reduce inequality. The British approach used taxation to provide a basic minimum for all citizens, while Belgium, France, and Germany established voluntary insurance plans in which contributions were linked to earnings.

By the 1970s the welfare state was challenged by neoconservatives, who advocated monetarist policies, pruning the state, and a less-intrusive relationship between the state and its citizens. This movement was strongest in Britain, embodied by Margaret Thatcher, prime minister from 1979 to 1990. But even in Britain the state's share of economic activity, measured in public spending as a percentage of GDP, was not significantly reduced. Thatcherism weakened local government to the benefit of the central state. The ideological attack on the welfare state contributed to the changing position of some social democratic parties, which began to advocate approaches such as the "Third Way" of British prime minister Tony Blair or the "New Middle" of the German counterpart Gerhard Schroeder. In general, however, people on the Continent remained attached to the welfare state and resisted the lure of a return to something that was much closer to the liberal state of the nineteenth century.

See also other articles in this section.

BIBLIOGRAPHY

Books

Baldwin, Peter. *Contagion and the State in Europe, 1830–1930.* Cambridge, U.K., 1999.

Baldwin, Peter. *The Politics of Social Solidarity.* Cambridge, U.K., 1990.

Blackbourn, David. *The Long Nineteenth Century: A History of Germany, 1780–1918.* New York, 1998.

Blackbourn, David, and Geoff Eley. *The Peculiarities of German History: Bourgeois Society and Politics in Nineteenth-Century Germany.* Oxford, 1984.

Clark, Martin. *Modern Italy, 1871–1995.* London, 1996.

Cobban, Alfred. *The Social Interpretation of the French Revolution.* New York, 1999.

Cruz, Jesus. *Gentlemen, Bourgeois, and Revolutionaries: Political Change and Cultural Persistence among the Spanish Dominant Groups, 1750–1850.* Cambridge, U.K., 1996.

Davis, John A. *Conflict and Control: Law and Order in Nineteenth-Century Italy.* Atlantic Highlands, N.J., 1988.

Doyle, William. *Origins of the French Revolution.* New York, 1999.

Furet, François. *Interpreting the French Revolution.* New York, 1981.

Gould, Andrew C. *Origins of Liberal Dominance: State, Church, and Party in Nineteenth-Century Europe.* Ann Arbor, Mich., 1999.

Gramsci, Antonio. *Prison Notebooks.* New York, 1992.

Gray, John. *Liberalism.* Minneapolis, Minn., 1995.

Hennock, E. P. *British Social Reform and German Precedents: The Case of Social Insurance, 1880–1914.* Oxford, 1987.

Hobsbawm, Eric. *Age of Extremes: The Short Twentieth Century, 1914–1991.* London, 1994.

Lefebvre, Georges. *The Coming of the French Revolution, 1789.* New York, 1957.

Mayer, Arno. *The Persistence of the Old Regime.* New York, 1981.

Mazower, Mark. *Dark Continent: Europe's Twentieth Century.* New York, 1999.

Pedersen, Susan. *Family Dependence and the Origins of the Welfare State: Britain and France, 1914–1945.* Cambridge, U.K., 1993.

Riall, Lucy. *The Italian Risorgimento: State, Society, and National Unification.* London, 1994.

Sahlins, Peter. *Forest Rites.* Cambridge, Mass., 1994.

Sheehan, James J. *German Liberalism in the Nineteenth Century.* Chicago, 1978.

Shubert, Adrian. *A Social History of Modern Spain.* London, 1990.

Stone, Judith F. *The Search for Social Peace.* Albany, N.Y., 1985.

Weber, Eugen. *Peasants into Frenchmen: The Modernization of Rural France, 1870–1914.* London, 1977.

Edited Collections

Bellamy, Richard, ed. *Victorian Liberalism: Nineteenth Century Political Thought and Practice.* New York, 1990.

Flora, Peter, and Arnold J. Heidenheimer, eds. *The Development of Welfare States in Europe and America.* New Brunswick, N.J., 1981.

Goldstein, Robert Justin, ed. *The War for the Public Mind: Political Censorship in Nineteenth-Century Europe.* Westport, Conn., 2000.

Hobsbawm, Eric, and Terence Ranger, eds. *The Invention of Tradition.* Cambridge, U.K., 1983.

Mommsen, Wolfgang, ed. *The Emergence of the Welfare State in Britain and Germany, 1850–1950.* London, 1981.

Chapters in Books

Gatrell, V. A. C. "Crime, Authority, and the Policeman-State." In *The Cambridge Social History of Britain, 1750–1950.* Edited by F. M. L. Thompson. Vol. 3. Cambridge, U.K., 1990. Pages 243–310.

LeGoff, T. J. A., and Donald M. G. Sutherland. "Religion and Rural Revolt: An Overview." In *Religion and Rural Revolt.* Edited by János M. Bak and Gerhard Benecke. Dover, N.H., 1984. Pages 123–145.

Thane, Pat. "Government and Society in England and Wales, 1750–1914." In *The Cambridge Social History of Britain, 1750–1950.* Edited by F. M. L. Thompson. Vol. 3. Cambridge, U.K., 1990. Pages 1–81.

DEMOCRACY

Charles Tilly

Even today, visibly viable democracies remain a minority among European forms of rule. Like tyranny and oligarchy, democracy is a kind of regime: a set of relations between a government and persons subject to that government's jurisdiction. (A government is any organization, at least partly independent of kinship, that controls the principal concentrated means of coercion within a delimited territory or set of territories.) The relations in question consist of mutual rights and obligations, government to subject and subject to government. A regime is democratic to the extent that:

1. regular and categorical, rather than intermittent and individualized, relations exist between the government and its subjects (for example, legal residence within the government's territories in itself establishes routine connections with governmental agents, regardless of relations to particular patrons);
2. those relations include most or all subjects (for example, no substantial sovereign enclaves exist within governmental perimeters);
3. those relations are equal across subjects and categories of subjects (for example, no legal exclusions from voting or officeholding based on property ownership prevail);
4. governmental personnel, resources, and performances change in response to binding collective consultation of subjects (for example, popular referenda make law);
5. subjects, especially members of minorities, receive protection from arbitrary action by governmental agents (for example, uniformly administered due process precedes incarceration of any individual regardless of social category).

Thus democratization means formation of a regime featuring relatively broad, equal, categorical, binding consultation and protection. Summing up variation in all these regards, we can block out a range from low to high protected consultation. Any move toward protected consultation constitutes democratization; any move away from protected consultation, de-democratization. These are obviously matters of degree: no polity anywhere has ever conformed fully to the five criteria. Hence to call any particular polity democratic means merely that it embodies more protected consultation than most other historical polities have.

PROBLEMS OF DEFINITION

Why stress such abstract standards when we might simply check for familiar constitutional arrangements, such as legislative assemblies, contested elections, broad franchise, and the like? Certainly any social historian of European democracy must pay close attention to the extensive constitutional innovations that occurred in these regards after 1750. Yet three facts speak against the adoption of straightforward constitutional tests for democracy: the origins of most democratic practices in undemocratic regimes; the frequency with which ostensibly democratic constitutions remain dead letters; and the contingent, erratic emergence of democratic regimes from struggle.

First, almost all major democratic institutions initially formed in oligarchic regimes, as means by which narrow circles of power holders exercised constraint on each other and on their rulers. To take the obvious example, Britain's Parliament combined a House of Lords assembling the realm's peers with a House of Commons in which the country's small landholding class held sway. That bicameral legislature eventually became a worldwide model for representative governments. In standard adaptations of that model, an upper house speaks for territories, self-reproducing elites, and/or powerful institutions, while a lower house more nearly speaks for the population at large. In Britain itself, however, the House of Lords never became a means of democratic consultation, and the House of Commons hardly qualified before the reform bills of 1832 and 1867 expanded the national electorate to include most male working-class householders.

Second, many constitutions that look quite democratic on paper remain dead letters. Rulers cook elections, jail opponents, restrict the press, disqualify voters, bypass legislatures, suborn judges, award contracts to cronies, and terrorize popular movements despite constitutional provisions forbidding all of these activities. For instance, when Louis Napoleon Bonaparte reacted to opposition following his popular election as French president in 1848 by executing a coup d'état in 1851, he did not dare to repeal the 1848 constitution's provision for general manhood suffrage, but his henchmen immediately set to work intimidating Louis Napoleon's opposition, cutting back voters' lists, restricting the press, and weakening the national assembly. With little change in its nominal constitution, France took giant steps away from protected consultation. Not the sheer existence of standard democratic forms of organization, but their integration into effective protected consultation, signals the presence of democracy. We must trace the history of democratic processes, not merely of their simulacra.

That injunction leads to the third reason for avoiding concentration on the enactment of constitutions: the erratic, contingent emergence of democracy from struggle. As we shall see abundantly, European democratization did not result mainly from cool contemplation of political alternatives. It always involved intense political struggle. It often resulted from international war, revolution, or violent domestic conflict. Rarely, furthermore, did the struggle simply align one well-defined bloc of democrats against another well-defined bloc of antidemocrats. People changed sides, third parties intervened, and democratic institutions often formed haphazardly as compromise settlements of otherwise intractable conflicts. To explain democratization, we must examine a wide range of political struggles and detect democracy-producing processes within them—even where participants themselves did not know they were advancing democracy.

CONDITIONS FOR DEMOCRACY

In principle, we could search for democratic processes within households, associations, firms, churches, and communities, just so long as each one contained something like a government—a distinctive position or organization controlling its principal concentrated means of coercion. Some analysts of democracy argue, indeed, that democracy originates in such smaller-scale settings before spreading to a national or international scale, while still others claim that robust democracy can only operate on a small scale, among people who know and care about each other personally. Here, however, we will concentrate on the larger scale, asking how, when, and why national regimes moved toward protected consultation in Europe since the Renaissance.

Governmental capacity. Part of the answer concerns changes in governmental capacity. Governments vary significantly in control by their agents over people, resources, information, and spaces within their jurisdiction. Capacity matters to democracy because below some threshold governmental agents lack the means of implementing protected consultation. Beneath the minimum, democracy gives way to anarchy. Anarchists and utopians, to be sure, have often taken the relative democracy of some crafts, shops, and local communities as warrants for the feasibility of stateless democracy on a large scale.

The historical record, however, suggests another conclusion: where governments collapse, other predators spring up. In the absence of effective governmental power, people who control substantial concentrations of capital, coercion, or commitment generally use them to forward their own ends, thus creating new forms of oppression and inequality. As the Soviet Union collapsed after 1989, for example, the dismantling of central authority did not release a liberating wave of democratization but gave a new set of tycoons, tyrants, and violent entrepreneurs (many of them, to be sure, former members of the Soviet state apparatus) room to ply their trades. If high governmental capacity does not define democracy, it looks like a nearly necessary condition for democracy on a large scale. In European experience on a national scale, extensive increases of governmental capacity always preceded and underlay the formation of democratic regimes.

We cannot, however, conclude that expansion of governmental capacity reliably fosters democracy. In fact, expanding governmental capacity promotes tyranny more often than it causes democracy to flower. In the abstract calculation that quantifies governmental experiences, the relationship between governmental capacity and democracy is no doubt curvilinear: more frequent democracy results from medium to medium-high governmental capacity, but beyond that threshold substantial cramping of democratic possibilities prevails as governmental agents come to control a very wide range of activities and resources.

Citizenship. Citizenship only forms on the higher slopes of protected consultation. Only where governmental capacity is relatively extensive, where established rights and obligations vis-à-vis governmental agents involve some significant share of a government's subject population, where some equality of access to government exists among subjects, where consultation of those persons makes a difference to governmental performance, and subjects enjoy some protection from arbitrary action can we reasonably begin to speak of citizenship. Although citizenship of a sort bound elite members of Greek city-states to their governments and elite members of many medieval European cities to their municipalities, on the whole citizenship on a national scale only became a strong, continuous presence during the nineteenth century. Understanding its emergence requires attention to political changes, including revolutions, but also to the social forces unleashed by industrialization, such as the rise of working-class movements.

Democracy builds on citizenship but does not exhaust it. Indeed, most Western states created some forms of citizenship after 1800, but over most of the nineteenth century the citizenship in question was too narrow, too unequal, too nonconsultative, and/or too unprotective to qualify their regimes as democratic. The regimes we loosely call "totalitarian," for example, typically combined high governmental capacity with relatively broad and equal citizenship, but afforded neither binding consultation nor extensive protection from arbitrary action by governmental agents. Some monarchies maintained narrow, unequal citizenship while consulting the happy few who enjoyed citizenship and protecting them from arbitrary action by governmental agents; those regimes thereby qualified as oligarchies.

In searching for democratic regimes, we can take relatively high governmental capacity for granted because it is a necessary condition for strong consultation and protection. We will recognize a high-capacity regime as democratic when it installs not only citizenship in general but broad citizenship, relatively equal citizenship, strong consultation of citizens, and significant protection of citizens from arbitrary action by governmental agents. By these criteria, Europe produced no national democratic regimes before the late eighteenth century. Then, by comparison with their predecessors, the (slave-holding but at least partly democratic) United States of the 1780s, the abortive Dutch Patriot regime later in the same decade, and the French revolutionary regimes of 1789 to 1793 all added significant increments to protected consultation.

Consultation and protection.

Both consultation and protection require further stipulations. Although many rulers have claimed to embody their people's will, only governments that have created concrete preference-communicating institutions have also installed binding, effective consultation. In Europe, representative assemblies, contested elections, referenda, petitions, courts, and public meetings of the empowered figure most prominently among such institutions. Whether polls, discussions in mass media, or special-interest networks qualify in fact or in principle as valid and effective preference-communicating institutions remains highly controversial.

On the side of protection, democracies typically guarantee zones of toleration for speech, belief, assembly, association, and public identity, despite generally imposing some cultural standards for participation in the polity. A regime that prescribes certain forms of speech, belief, assembly, association, and public identity while banning all other forms may maintain broad, equal citizenship and a degree of consultation, but it slides away from democracy toward populist authoritarianism as it qualifies protection. Thus the five elements of democratization—categorical relations, breadth, equality, binding consultation, and protection—form and vary in partial independence of each other.

DEMOCRATIZATION

Yet in any particular era, available precedents make a difference. Previous historical experience has laid down a set of models, understandings, and practices concerning such matters as how to conduct a contested election. During the early nineteenth century, France's revolutionary innovations offered guidelines for democratic theory and practice. After World War II, similarly, existing regimes of Western Europe and North America provided models for dozens of new regimes, including those of former European colonies. This political culture of democracy limits options for newcomers both because it offers templates for the construction of new regimes and because it affects the likelihood that existing power holders—democratic or not—will recognize a new regime as democratic.

Historical development.

Over the long run of human history, the vast majority of regimes have been undemocratic. Democratic regimes are rare, contingent, recent creations. Partial democracies have, it is true, formed intermittently at a local scale, for example in villages ruled by councils incorporating most heads of household. At the scale of a city-state, a warlord's domain, or a regional federation, forms of government have usually run from dynastic hegemony to oligarchy, with narrow, unequal citizenship or none at all, little or no binding consultation, and uncertain protection from arbitrary governmental action.

Before the nineteenth century, furthermore, large states and empires generally managed by means of indirect rule: systems in which the central power received tribute, cooperation, and guarantees of compliance on the part of subject populations from regional power holders who enjoyed great autonomy within their own domains. Seen from the bottom, such systems often imposed tyranny on ordinary people. Seen from the top, however, they lacked capacity: the intermediaries supplied resources, but they also set stringent limits to rulers' ability to govern or transform the world within their presumed jurisdictions.

Only the nineteenth century brought widespread adoption of direct rule, the creation of structures extending governmental communication and control continuously from central institutions to individual localities or even to households, and back again. Even then, direct rule ranged from the unitary hierarchies of centralized monarchy to the segmentation of federalism. On a large scale, direct rule made substantial citizenship, and therefore democracy, possible. Possible, but not likely, much less inevitable: instruments of direct rule have sustained many oligarchies, some autocracies, a number of party- and army-controlled states, and a few fascist tyrannies. Even in the era of direct rule most polities have remained far from democratic.

Varieties of democratization and paths to democracy.

Figure 1 schematizes variation and change in regimes. Where low governmental capacity and little protected consultation prevail, political life goes on in fragmented tyranny: multiple coercive forces, small-scale despots, and competitors for larger-scale power are possible, but no effective central government. The diagram's opposite corner contains the zone of citizenship: mutual rights and obligations binding governmental agents to whole categories of people who are subject to the government's authority, those categories being defined chiefly or exclusively by relations to the government rather than by reference to particular ties with rulers or membership in categories based on imputed durable traits such as race, ethnicity, gender, or religion.

At point A of the diagram's triangular citizenship zone, a combination of little protected consultation and extremely high governmental capacity describes a regimented state. We might call such a state totalitarian; Nazi Germany illustrates political processes at that point. At point B, protected consultation has reached its maximum, but governmental capacity is so low the regime runs the risk of internal and external attack. Nineteenth-century Belgium never reached that point, but veered repeatedly toward it. Point C—

maximum governmental capacity plus maximum protected consultation—is probably empty because of incompatibilities between extremely high capacity and consultation. This line of reasoning leads to sketching a zone of authoritarianism in the diagram's upper left, overlapping the zone of citizenship but by no means exhausting it. It also suggests an idealized path for effective democratization, giving roughly equal weight to increases in governmental capacity and protected consultation up to the point of entry into citizenship, but then turning to deceleration, and ultimately mild reduction, of capacity where protected consultation has settled in.

Figure 2 sets limits on real histories of democratization by sketching two extreme paths:

1. a strong-state path featuring early expansion of governmental capacity, entry into the zone of authoritarianism, expansion of protected consultation through a phase of authoritarian citizenship, and finally the emergence of a less authoritarian, more democratic, but still high-capacity regime. In European historical experience, Prussia from 1650 through 1925 came closer to such a trajectory than most other states

2. a weak-state path featuring early expansion of protected consultation followed only much later by increase in governmental capacity on a large scale, hence entry into the zone of effective citizenship from below. Although few European states followed this trajectory very far because most of them that started succumbed to conquest or disintegration, Switzerland—shielded from conquest by mountainous terrain, rivalries among adjacent powers, and a militarily skilled population—came closer to this extreme than most other European regimes.

All real European histories fell within the extremes. Most described much more erratic courses, with reversals and sudden shifts in both dimensions, and the vast majority entered or approached the zone of authoritarianism at one time or another. The schematic map simply makes it easier to describe the concrete paths of change we are trying to explain.

Elements of democratization.

Democratization emerges from interacting changes in three analytically separable but interdependent sets of social relations: inequality, networks of trust, and public politics.

> *Categorical Inequality:* Categorical inequality— collective differences in advantage across boundaries such as gender, race, religion, and class—declines in those areas of social life

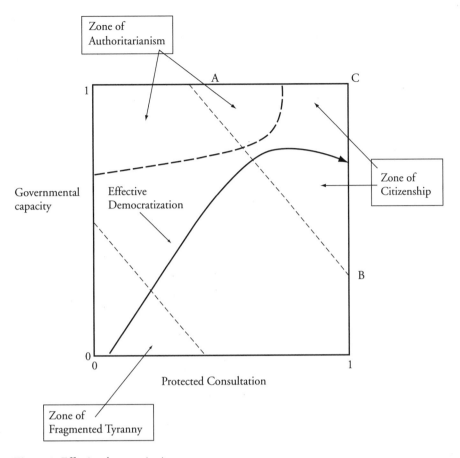

Figure 1. Effective democratization.

that either constitute or immediately support participation in public politics. Buffers arise that reduce the representation and enactment of those inequalities in collective political life. For example, rich and poor alike perform military service, pay taxes, serve on juries, and gain access to courts.

Trust Networks: A significant shift occurs in the locus of interpersonal networks on which people rely when undertaking risky long-term enterprises such as marriage, long-distance trade, membership in crafts, and investment of savings: such networks move from evasion of governmental detection and control to involvement of government agents and presumption that such agents will meet their long-term commitments. Subjects do not necessarily come to trust individual leaders, but they do make commitments on the presumption that the government will meet its own commitments. For example, people increasingly invest family funds in government securities, rely on governments for pensions,

allow their children to serve in the military, and seek governmental protection for their religious organizations.

Public Politics: Partly in response to changes in categorical inequality and trust networks, and partly as a consequence of alterations within the political arena itself, the bulk of a government's subject population acquires binding, protected, relatively equal claims on a government's agents, activities, and resources. For example, governmental agents quell rebellions against wartime conscription, taxation, and expropriation not only with threats and punishments but also with displays of fairness, acts of mercy, enactments of bargains, and articulations of rules for future conscription, taxation, and expropriation.

Only where the three sets of changes intersect does effective, durable democracy emerge.

Conquest, confrontation, colonization, and revolution. Most of the time, alterations in categorical

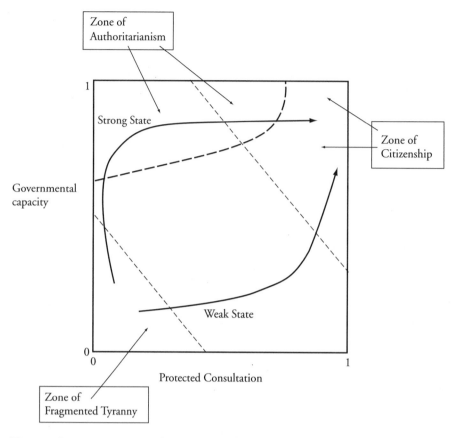

Figure 2. Strong-state versus weak-state paths to democracy.

inequality, trust networks, and public politics occur slowly and incrementally. Nevertheless, certain shocks sometimes accelerate these processes, producing surges of democratization. In European experience since 1500, the chief shocks have been conquest, confrontation, colonization, and revolution.

Conquest is the forcible reorganization of existing systems of government, inequality, and trust by an external power. In the history of European democratization, the most famous example is no doubt conquest by French revolutionary and Napoleonic armies outside of France, which left governments on a semidemocratic French model in place through much of western Europe after Napoleon's defeat. Reestablishment of France, Germany, Italy, and Japan on more or less democratic bases after World War II rivals French revolutionary exploits in this regard. Conquest sometimes promotes democratization because it destroys old trust networks, creates new ones, and provides external guarantees that the new government will meet its commitments.

Confrontation has provided the textbook cases of democratization, as existing oligarchies have responded to challenges by excluded political actors

with broadening of citizenship, equalization of citizenship, increase of binding consultation, and/or expansion of protection for citizens. Nineteenth-century British rulers' responses to large mobilizations by Protestant Dissenters, Catholics, merchants, and skilled workers fit the pattern approximately in Great Britain, but by no means always—and certainly not in Ireland. Confrontation promotes democratization, when it does, not only because it expands and equalizes access to government but also because it generates new trust-bearing coalitions and weakens coercive controls supporting current inequalities.

Colonization, with wholesale transplantation of population from mother country to colony, has often promoted democratization, although frequently at the cost of destroying, expelling, or subordinating indigenous populations within the colonial territory. Thus Canada, the United States, Australia, and New Zealand began European settlement with coercive, oligarchic regimes, but rapidly moved some distance toward broad citizenship, equal citizenship, binding consultation, and protection. (Let us never forget how far short of theoretically possible maximum values in these four regards all existing democracies have always fallen; by these demanding criteria, no near-democracy has ever existed on a large scale.) Colonization of this sort makes a difference not merely because it exports political institutions containing some rudiments of democracy but also because it promotes relative equality of material conditions and weakens patron-client networks tied closely to the government of the colonizing power.

As England's Glorious Revolution of 1688–1689 illustrates, revolutions do not universally promote moves toward broad, equal citizenship, binding consultation, and protection. Let us take revolutions to be large splits in control over means of government followed by substantial transfers of power over government. As compared with previous regimes, the net effect of most revolutions over the last few centuries has been at least a modicum of democratization, as here defined. Why so? Because they typically activate an even wider range of democracy-promoting processes than do conquest, colonization, and confrontation. Revolutions rarely or never occur, for example, without coalition formation between segments of ruling classes and constituted political actors that are currently excluded from power. But they also commonly dissolve or incorporate nongovernmental patron-client networks, contain previously autonomous military forces, equalize assets and/or well-being across the population at large, and attack existing trust networks. Revolutions sometimes sweep away old networks that block democratization, and they promote the formation of governing coalitions far more general than those that preceded them.

DEMOCRATIZATION IN SWITZERLAND

To watch the impact of revolution, conquest, and confrontation (if not of colonization) on categorical inequality, trust networks, and public politics from closer up, consider the remarkable experience of Switzerland from the late eighteenth century to 1848. Up to the eighteenth century's end, Switzerland operated as a loose, uneven confederation of largely independent cantons and their dependent territories. Although the Confederation had a Diet of its own, it operated essentially as a meeting place for strictly instructed ambassadors from sovereign cantons. Within each canton, furthermore, sharp inequalities typically separated comfortable burghers of the principal town, workers within the same town, members of constituted hinterland communities, and inhabitants of dependent territories who lacked any political representation. In Bern, for example, 3,600 qualified citizens ruled 400,000 people who lacked rights of citizenship, while in Zurich 5,700 official burghers governed 150,000 country dwellers. Within the ranks of citizens, furthermore, a small—and narrowing—number of families typically dominated public office from one generation to the next.

Both the countryside's great eighteenth-century expansion of cottage industry and the mechanized urban industrial concentration that took off after 1800 increased discrepancies among the distributions of population, wealth, and political privilege. Cantonal power holders controlled the press tightly and felt free to exile, imprison, or even execute their critics. From the outside, the confederation as a whole therefore resembled less a zone of freedom than a conglomerate of petty tyrannies. The majority of the population who lacked full citizenship, or any at all, smarted under the rule of proud oligarchs. Meanwhile, politically excluded intellectuals and bourgeois formed numerous associations—notably the Helvetic Society—to criticize existing regimes, promote Swiss national patriotism, revitalize rural economies, and prepare major reforms.

The French Revolution and democratic reforms. The French Revolution shook Switzerland's economic and political ties to its great neighbor while exposing Swiss people to new French models and doctrines. From 1789 onward, revolutionary movements formed in several parts of Switzerland. In 1793 Geneva (not a confederation member, but closely tied to Switzerland) underwent a revolution on the French model. As the threat of French invasion mounted in early 1798, Basel, Vaud, Lucerne, Zurich, and other cantons followed the revolutionary path. Basel, for example, turned from a constitution in which only citizens of the town were represented in the Senate to another giving equal representation to urban and rural populations.

Conquered by France in collaboration with Swiss revolutionaries in 1798, then receiving a new constitution that year, the Swiss confederation as a whole adopted a much more centralized form of government with significantly expanded citizenship. The central government remained fragile, however; four coups occurred between 1800 and 1802 alone. At the withdrawal of French troops in 1802, multiple rebellions broke out. Switzerland then rushed to the brink of civil war. Only Napoleon's intervention and imposition of a new constitution in 1803 kept the country together.

The 1803 regime, known in Swiss history as the Mediation, restored considerable powers to cantons, but by no means reestablished the old regime. Switzerland's recast confederation operated with a national assembly, official multilingualism, relative equality among cantons, and freedom for citizens to move from canton to canton. Despite some territorial adjustments, a weak central legislature, judiciary, and executive survived Napoleon's defeat after another close brush with civil war, this time averted by the intervention of the great powers in 1813–1815. In the war settlement of 1815, Austria, France, Great Britain, Portugal, Prussia, Russia, Spain, and Sweden accepted a treaty among twenty-two cantons called the Federal Pact as they guaranteed Switzerland's perpetual neutrality and the inviolability of its frontiers.

Switzerland of the Federal Pact operated without a permanent bureaucracy, a standing army, common coinage, standard measures, or a national flag, but with multiple internal customs barriers, a rotating capital, and incessant bickering among cantonal representatives who had no right to deviate from their home constituents' instructions. The Swiss lived with a national system better disposed to vetoes than to concerted change.

With France's July 1830 revolution, anticlericalism became more salient in Swiss radicalism. After 1830, Switzerland became a temporary home for many exiled revolutionaries (such as Giuseppe Mazzini, Wilhelm Weitling, and, more surprisingly, Louis Napoleon), who collaborated with Swiss radicals in calling for reform. Historians of Switzerland in the 1830s speak of a Regeneration Movement pursued by means of publicity, clubs, and mass marches. A great spurt of new periodicals accompanied the political turmoil of 1830–1831. Empowered liberals began enacting standard nineteenth-century reforms such as limitation of child labor and expansion of public schools. Nevertheless, the new cantonal constitutions enacted in that mobilization stressed liberty and fraternity much more than they did equality.

Protestant-Catholic divisions and civil war.

With a Protestant majority concentrated in the richer, more industrial and urban cantons, an approximate political split between Protestant-liberal-radical and Catholic-conservative interests became salient in Swiss politics. In regions dominated by conservative cities such as Basel, the countryside (widely industrialized during the eighteenth century, but suffering a contraction in cottage industry during the early nineteenth) often supported liberal or radical programs. In centers of growing capital-intensive production such as Zurich, conflict pitted a bourgeoisie much attached to oligarchic political privilege against an expanding working class that bid increasingly for a voice in public politics and allied increasingly with dissident radicals among the bourgeoisie. In these regards, political

divisions within Switzerland resembled those prevailing elsewhere in western Europe.

The political problem became acute because national alignments of the mid-1840s pitted twelve richer and predominantly liberal-Protestant cantons against ten poorer, predominantly conservative-Catholic cantons in a Diet where each canton had a single vote. (Strictly speaking, some units on each side, products themselves of earlier splits, qualified as half-cantons casting half a vote each, but the 12/10 balance of votes held.) Thus liberals deployed the rhetoric of national patriotism and majority rule while conservatives countered with cantonal rights and defense of religious traditions. Three levels of citizenship—municipal, cantonal, and national—competed with each other.

Contention occurred incessantly, and often with vitriolic violence, from 1830 to 1848. Although reform movements were already under way in Vaud and Ticino as 1830 began—indeed, Ticino preceded France by adopting a new constitution on 4 July 1830—France's July Revolution of 1830 and its Belgian echo later in the year encouraged Swiss reformers and revolutionaries. As the French and Belgian revolutions rolled on, smaller-scale revolutions took place in the Swiss towns and cantons of Aargau, Lucerne, St. Gallen, Schaffhausen, Solothurn, Thurgau, Vaud, and Zurich. Thereafter, republicans and radicals repeatedly formed military bands (often called free corps, or *Freischärler*) and attempted to take over particular cantonal capitals by force of arms. Such bands failed in Lucerne (1841), but succeeded in bringing new administrations to power in Lausanne (1847), Geneva (1847), and Neuchâtel (1848).

The largest military engagement took place in 1847. Switzerland's federal Diet ordered dissolution of the mutual defense league (Sonderbund) formed by Catholic cantons two years earlier. When the Catholic cantons refused, the Diet sent an army to Fribourg and Zug, whose forces capitulated without serious fighting, then Lucerne, where a short battle occurred. The Sonderbund had about 79,000 men under arms, the confederation some 99,000. The war ended with thirty-three dead among Catholic forces and sixty dead among the attackers. The defeat of the Sonderbund consolidated the dominance of liberals in Switzerland as a whole and led to the adoption of a cautiously liberal constitution, on something like an American model, in 1848.

A last ricochet of the 1847–1848 military struggles occurred in 1856. Forces loyal to the king of Prussia (effectively, but not formally, displaced from shared sovereignty in Neuchâtel by the republican coup of 1848) seized military control over part of Neuchâtel's cantonal capital, only to be defeated almost immediately by the cantonal militia. Prussia's threats to invade Switzerland incited other European powers to hold Prussia in check. From that point on, the liberal constitution applied to all of the Swiss Federation. Between 1849 and 1870, furthermore, all Swiss cantons terminated their profitable, centuries-old export of mercenary units for military service outside of Switzerland. Thereafter, only papal guards and a few ceremonial military units elsewhere represented Swiss soldiery outside of Switzerland itself.

Swiss democracy. Between 1830 and 1847, Swiss democracy receded into civil war. Only military victory of one side wrenched the confederation back toward a democratic settlement. As of 1848, we might call Switzerland as a whole either a weak democracy or a democratic oligarchy. Property owners prevailed and only males could vote, but the confederation transacted its business through elections, referenda, and parliamentary deliberations, as well as making citizenship transferable among cantons. Democratic institutions comparable to those that now prevail in western Europe still took a long time to form. Women could not vote in Swiss federal elections, for example, until 1971. By the middle of the nineteenth century, nevertheless, Switzerland had formed one of Europe's more durably representative regimes.

The Swiss experience is remarkable for its transition to representative government in the presence of consistent linguistic differences. Important distinctions have long existed between Switzerland's Germanic-speaking northern and eastern cantons, its French-speaking western border cantons, its Italian-speaking southern rim, and its Romansh-speaking enclaves in the southeast. Switzerland also features sharp town-to-town differences in the Alemannic dialects known generically as *Schwyzerdütsch,* which actually serve as languages of choice for spoken communication in nominally Germanophone Switzerland. With dominant cleavages based on religion and inherited from the Reformation, the Swiss have rarely fought over linguistic distinctions.

Switzerland is even more remarkable for the vitality of representative institutions in company with fairly weak state structures. Similar regimes elsewhere in Europe generally succumbed to conquest by higher-capacity (and much less democratic) neighbors. Switzerland's topography, its ability to summon up military defense when pressed, and rivalries among its powerful neighbors gave it breathing room similar to that enjoyed by Liechtenstein and Andorra. Switzerland's tough independence likewise inspired Europe's regional politicians, so much so that Basque nationalists of the nineteenth century proposed that

their own land become the "Switzerland of the Pyrenees."

Whatever else we say about the Swiss itinerary toward democracy, it certainly passed through intense popular struggle, including extensive military action. The same process that produced a higher-capacity central government, furthermore, also created Switzerland's restricted but genuine democracy: as compared with what came before, relatively broad—if unequal—citizenship, binding consultation of citizens, and substantial protection of citizens from arbitrary action by governmental agents were established. As compared with late-nineteenth-century French or British models of democracy, however, the Swiss federal system looks extraordinarily heterogeneous: a distinctive constitution, dominant language, and citizenship for each canton; multiple authorities and compacts; and a remarkable combination of exclusiveness with the capacity to create particular niches for newly accepted political actors. Through all subsequent constitutional changes, those residues of Swiss political history have persisted. In all democratic polities, similar residues of past struggles and compromises remain.

DEMOCRATIZATION IN EUROPE

The Swiss experiences of 1798, 1830, and 1847–1848 should remind us of a very general principle. Rather than occurring randomly and separately country by country, shocks such as conquest, confrontation, colonization, and revolution bunch in time and space. They bunch partly because similar processes—for example, wars, depressions, and mass migrations—affect adjacent countries. They also bunch because a shock to one regime reverberates among its neighbors. As a consequence, democratization occurs in waves.

Europe's first important wave of democratization arrived with the French Revolution. Although the French themselves retreated rapidly from the radical democratic reforms of 1789 to 1793, French regimes from 1793 to 1815 all embodied broader and more equal citizenship (if not always binding consultation or effective protection) than their prerevolutionary predecessors. As French armies conquered other European territories, furthermore, they installed regimes on the French model, which means that in general they increased protected consultation by comparison with the regimes they displaced. Even after Napoleon's defeats between 1812 and 1815, both the French model and French-style constitutions left residues of democratic practice through much of western Europe.

Europe's next wave of democratization arose with the revolutions of 1847–1848 in Sicily, Naples, Piedmont, Lombardy, France, Austria, Hungary, Wallachia, and Prussia. By 1851, to be sure, counterrevolutionary movements and external invasions had reversed most democratic gains in all these regions. Still, from that point on at least the forms of protected consultation prevailed as benchmarks for European regimes. In different ways, furthermore, the revolutions of 1847–1848 promoted or enabled democratic reforms in the Netherlands, Belgium, and Switzerland as well. On balance, the struggles of 1847–1851 moved western and central European regimes significantly in the direction of broad, equal, categorical, binding consultation and protection—that is, toward democracy.

After 1848, revolution receded as a democratizing shock in Europe. Portugal, Spain, and the Balkan countries experienced repeated forcible seizures of power between 1848 and World War I, but protected consultation advanced little or not at all in those regions. In 1870 and 1871, France's revolutionary changes opened the path to a turbulent but broadly democratic Third Republic that survived to World War II. Precipitated by Russia's loss in the Russo-Japanese War, Russia's revolution of 1905–1906 temporarily introduced a radically democratic regime, but succumbed to tsarist counterforce soon thereafter. In the aftermath, the tsar instituted a series of political and economic reforms that, compared to pre-1905 regimes, moved Russia modestly in the direction of protected consultation.

Over Europe as a whole, nevertheless, confrontation took over from revolution as the chief promoter of democratization between 1849 and World War I. In western and central Europe, mass labor movements formed, making impressive gains in representation through strikes, demonstrations, electoral campaigns, and a wide array of organizational activities. In Austria, Belgium, Denmark, France, Germany, Italy, the Netherlands, Norway, Sweden, Switzerland, and the United Kingdom, for example, eligible voters reached 50 percent of adult males through hard-fought reforms at various dates from 1848 to 1912.

In those same countries, most workers acquired the right to strike—previously an illegal activity—through parallel struggles between 1848 and 1921. Legalization of labor unions, formation of labor parties, proliferation and reduced repression of popular media, regularization of nonmilitary policing, and expanded freedom to associate and assemble all constituted increases in protected consultation. They all rested, furthermore, on rising governmental capacity, the capacity both to deliver services and to enforce popular rights over the frequent opposition of landlords and capitalists.

With World War I, the pendulum swung back to conquest and revolution. Conquest, in fact, then promoted revolution; such wartime losers as Germany and Russia experienced deep democratizing revolutions. In Germany, a social democratic regime came to power, and after extensive struggle (contained by the victorious Allies) the country emerged from its war settlement with a broadly democratic regime. In 1917, Russia's March and October Revolutions brought in first a liberal and then a radical regime. Although many analysts of 1917 claim to detect in the Bolshevik seizure of power an irresistible impulse to totalitarianism, as compared with preceding regimes, the initial transformation installed breadth, equality, consultation, and protection to an almost unimaginable degree. What remains hotly debated is how much and how soon a vast civil war, the formation of the Red Army, creation of a centralized Communist Party, and management of economic disaster reversed those early democratic gains.

That was not all. Hungary (also on the losing side as part of the Austro-Hungarian empire) passed through a brief radical revolution only to see it terminated by separate attacks of monarchist and Romanian forces. Elsewhere in Europe, struggles that had begun with strike waves during the war's later years swelled to massive postwar mobilizations in nominal winners Italy, France, and Great Britain. In Ireland, resistance to British rule greatly accelerated with the Easter Rebellion of 1916 and culminated in the formation of an Irish Free State (1922), now a British dominion similar in status to Canada and Australia, with a similarly democratic constitution. (With severe costs for democratic practice in both parts of Ireland, Ulster remained attached to the United Kingdom.)

One outcome of these diverse struggles was widespread adoption of proportional representation, an electoral system that increased the chances of small parties—hence minority interests—to place spokespersons in national legislatures. Another was considerable expansion of the suffrage, including female suffrage. As of 1910, Finland alone granted full voting rights in national elections to women. By 1925, the roster had expanded to Iceland, the Irish Free State, Norway, Sweden, Denmark, Estonia, Latvia, Lithuania, the Soviet Union, Poland, Germany, the Netherlands, Luxembourg, Czechoslovakia, and Austria. (By that time, most other regimes had made lesser concessions to female suffrage: while British men voted at twenty-one, for example, British women thirty and older had the vote.)

472

De-democratization occurred during the 1920s and 1930s. Fascist regimes seized power in Italy and Germany, the Salazar dictatorship displaced Portugal's weak parliamentary regime in 1932, and Spain slid from a half-dozen years of republican government (1931–1936) into civil war and an authoritarian regime that lasted until Generalissimo Francisco Franco's death in 1975. Dictatorial leaders came to power in Greece, Lithuania, and Latvia, while Stalin's rule grew increasingly despotic in the Soviet Union. Despite minor advancements of protected consultation in western Europe, by 1940 Europe as a whole had slid back considerably from the democratic heights it had reached in the aftermath of World War I. German conquests of Poland, Austria, Czechoslovakia, France, Belgium, the Netherlands, Luxembourg, and Yugoslavia, the formation of a German puppet regime in Norway, and the alignment of Romania, Hungary, and Bulgaria with the German-Italian-Japanese axis reduced European democracy even further.

Evaluation of the postwar settlement raises thorny issues. On NATO's side of the Cold War divide, the United States, Great Britain, and their allies used force and persuasion to establish extensively democratic regimes in most European areas outside Iberia and the Balkans. Impelled by popular mobilization and encouraged by Western Europeans and North Americans, Greece, Spain, and Portugal replaced authoritarian regimes with parliamentary democracies during the 1970s. That much looks like a great wave of deliberately promoted democratization.

On the Warsaw Pact side, however, newly installed socialist regimes of the 1940s generally promoted relatively broad, equal, and categorical citizenship while placing severe limits on both consultation and protection. Simultaneously, socialist states used their rising capacities both to equalize entitlements at the base and to increase repression of dissidents. Depending on the relative weight given to breadth, equality, consultation, and protection, then, we might rate Eastern European shifts in democracy between 1940 and 1950 as anything from minor losses to substantial gains.

In any case, the breakup of the Soviet Union and the Warsaw Pact, beginning in 1989, introduced a new bifurcation into Eastern Europe. In Russia, Belarus, and Ukraine after 1989, mighty political transformations but little or no increase in protected consultation occurred despite the introduction of parties, oppositions, and contested elections. In those territories declines in state capacity undermined protection, equality, and even the breadth of political rights. In the former Yugoslavia and Albania, shattered by civil war, democracy declined from its already modest earlier levels except for the emergence of an independent and relatively democratic Slovenia. Elsewhere in the former Soviet bloc, the record varies but on balance shows increases in protected consultation. One more wave of democratization—this one just as vexed and incomplete as those of 1789–1815, 1847–1850, and 1914–1922—is rolling slowly across Europe.

See also other articles in this section.

BIBLIOGRAPHY

Aminzade, Ronald. *Ballots and Barricades: Class Formation and Republican Politics in France, 1830–1871.* Princeton, N.J., 1993. The emergence of an industrial working class promoted popular republicanism that differed in important ways from its bourgeois cousin.

Andrews, George Reid, and Herrick Chapman, eds. *The Social Construction of Democracy, 1870–1990.* New York, 1995. The authors, mostly social and political historians, take up the social origins of democracy in the comparative spirit of Barrington Moore.

Burawoy, Michael, and Katherine Verdery, eds. *Uncertain Transition: Ethnographies of Change in the Postsocialist World.* Lanham, Md., 1999. Not only the editors but also other perceptive observers offer close-up studies of a world in turmoil.

Collier, Ruth Berins. *Paths toward Democracy: The Working Class and Elites in Western Europe and South America.* New York, 1999. Bold, yet careful, comparison of multiple political transitions.

Dahl, Robert A. *On Democracy.* New Haven, Conn., 1998. Admirably compact, concrete, and accessible exposition of Dahl's conception and defense of democratic institutions.

Downing, Brian M. *The Military Revolution and Political Change: Origins of Democracy and Autocracy in Early Modern Europe.* Princeton, N.J., 1992. As the subtitle hints, extended and well-documented argument for the revision of Barrington Moore's classic theses by considering the financing of military organization and the survival of medieval representative institutions.

Downs, Charles. *Revolution at the Grassroots: Community Organizations in the Portuguese Revolution.* Albany, N.Y., 1989. How direct democracy and demands for its institutionalization actually worked in 1974–1975.

Fish, M. Steven. *Democracy from Scratch: Opposition and Regime in the New Russian Revolution.* Princeton, N.J., 1995. Russian politics under Gorbachev as a series of social movements under the influence of a rapidly changing state-shaped political opportunity structure.

Giugni, Marco G., Doug McAdam, and Charles Tilly, eds. *From Contention to Democracy.* Lanham, Md., 1998. Essays on relations between social change and social movements.

Hanagan, Michael, and Charles Tilly, eds. *Extending Citizenship, Reconfiguring States.* Lanham, Md., 1999. Why citizenship matters, historically and politically.

Held, David. *Models of Democracy.* 2d ed. Stanford, Calif., 1996. Varieties of democracy in history and the choices they offer today.

Herzog, Don. *Poisoning the Minds of the Lower Orders.* Princeton, N.J., 1998. Rich, riotous reflections on discourses of inequality, copiously illustrated from British literature and public life between 1750 and 1830, almost entirely uncontaminated by social scientific work on its subject.

Koopmans, Ruud. *Democracy from Below: New Social Movements and the Political System in West Germany.* Boulder, Colo., 1995. Political process in comparative perspective.

Laba, Roman. *The Roots of Solidarity: A Political Sociology of Poland's Working-Class Democratization.* Princeton, N.J., 1991. Laba counters the idea of an intellectual-led revolution with a grassroots account of worker initiatives.

Linz, Juan J., and Alfred Stepan. *Problems of Democratic Transition and Consolidation: Southern Europe, South America, and Post-Communist Europe.* Baltimore, 1996. Reflective, tentative comparisons of democratization and its failures in three critical world areas.

Markoff, John. *Waves of Democracy: Social Movements and Political Change.* Thousand Oaks, Calif., 1996. How and why democratization comes in bunches with extensive popular mobilization.

Moore, Barrington, Jr. *Social Origins of Dictatorship and Democracy.* Boston, 1993. Reprint of 1966 book with new preface by James C. Scott and Edward Friedman. A grand comparison—and theoretical analysis—of modern politics' alternative forms and their origins.

Morgan, Edmund S. *Inventing the People: The Rise of Popular Sovereignty in England and America.* New York, 1988. Whence and wherefore the idea of government by the consent, and in the interest, of the governed.

O'Donnell, Guillermo, Philippe C. Schmitter, and Laurence Whitehead. *Transitions from Authoritarian Rule: Prospects for Democracy.* Baltimore, 1986. Vast inquiry into democratization and related transitions.

Prak, Maarten. "Citizen Radicalism and Democracy in the Dutch Republic: The Patriot Movement of the 1780s." *Theory and Society* 20 (1991): 73–102.

Putnam, Robert D., with Robert Leonardi and Raffaella Y. Nanetti. *Making Democracy Work: Civic Traditions in Modern Italy.* Princeton, N.J., 1993. An exploration of how embedding democratic institutions in civic reciprocity and sociability makes them work.

Rueschemeyer, Dietrich, Evelyne Huber Stephens, and John D. Stephens. *Capitalist Development and Democracy.* Chicago, 1992. How industrialization generated uncontainable popular demands, thereby opening the way to democracy.

Schwartzman, Kathleen C. "Globalization and Democracy." *Annual Review of Sociology* 24 (1998): 159–181.

Schwartzman, Kathleen C. *The Social Origins of Democratic Collapse: The First Portuguese Republic in the Global Economy.* Lawrence, Kans., 1989. How the fragmentation of a semiperipheral state's bourgeoisie made a democratic regime vulnerable.

Somers, Margaret R. "Citizenship and the Place of the Public Sphere: Law, Community, and Political Culture in the Transition to Democracy." *American Sociological Review* 58 (1993): 587–620.

Tilly, Charles. *European Revolutions, 1492–1992.* Oxford, 1993. The interplay of state transformations and revolutionary situations.

Tilly Charles, ed. *Citizenship, Identity, and Social History.* Cambridge, U.K., 1995. Historically informed analyses of citizenship and its politics.

THE WELFARE STATE

Steven M. Beaudoin

Gone are the days when social history could be described as history with the politics left out. Social historians today are just as concerned with politics and state structures as they are with the material conditions of daily life. Indeed, those who would attempt an analysis of such pillars of social history as working-class protest or childhood would soon discover that such issues are inexorably tied to the state. This is particularly true of any study of poverty in modern society. The welfare state has thus become a central concern of social historians, who study its social, economic, and ideological roots; its role in shaping class relations and gender ideals; its economic consequences; and the strategies it fosters among the recipients of assistance. In fact, given the institutional nature of the welfare state, state, local, and private relief agency archives offer rich sources of information for social historians. In this way, the welfare state has become a staple of European social history.

If the welfare state's place in the study of history is easy to determine, the same cannot be said of its definition. For many scholars, the welfare state is the combination of government programs designed to assist the needy. By providing such services as housing, monetary assistance, and health care, these programs assure a level of subsistence below which no citizen should fall. Other scholars, however, adopt actuarial concepts and define the welfare state as the set of policies devised to redistribute risk. In a capitalist society, they argue, welfare comprises the insurance programs that protect citizens against the hardships that might result from periods of economic inactivity like those caused by illness, unemployment, and old age. Some even argue that education is part of the welfare state, for it prepares recipients for a productive work life. For all that they differ, these divergent views share at least one element: they all revolve around the issue of security. For the purposes of this essay, the welfare state includes those programs and policies forged with the goal of easing life's insecurities, from elite fears of beggars to working-class anxieties over industrial accidents. This definition underlies a history of the welfare state that begins with sixteenth-century attempts to rationalize relief and prohibit begging, and ends with early-twenty-first-century programs of national health insurance and family allocations.

EARLY-MODERN ANTECEDENTS OF THE WELFARE STATE

Beginning roughly with the sixteenth century, secular authorities throughout Europe began to take a more active interest in poor relief, resulting in efforts to rationalize, professionalize, and bureaucratize systems of assistance. While historians previously argued that such concerns were the result of Protestant theology's rejection of good works as a means to salvation, current work indicates that some secularization also occurred in Catholic states, although an upsurge in piety and charitable giving following the Council of Trent (1545–1563) limited the rate of centralization and rationalization. The breakdown of older religious institutions, the decline of traditional private sources of security, such as the local community, the growth of state bureaucracies in general, and the social and economic consequences of an emerging commercial economy during the sixteenth and seventeenth centuries all appear now to be more likely causes of this transformation in welfare provision. Marxist historians, in particular, have seized upon the last development, linking poor relief reform to a rising mercantile economy. By allowing urban elites to regulate the supply of labor, new systems of assistance formed an important bridge in the European transition to capitalism. Another group of scholars, who base their work primarily on the rise of new institutions, such as the *hôpital-général* established in Paris in 1656, emphasize the reformers' desires to promote certain ideals and social order by enclosing social marginals.

Like the causes, the results of new concerns with poor relief varied enormously. In the Flemish city of Ypres, for example, a 1525 poor law charged a new committee of four civil supervisors with the regulation

Guardians of Orphans. *Ufficiali dei pupilli* (officials in charge of underage orphans), Florence, from a 1503 copy of statutes that date from 1384. ARCHIVIO DI STATO, FLORENCE

of individual parish committees, which in turn visited recipients' homes, collected alms, and managed the poor box established in every church. In an accommodation with existing charitable institutions, the new board of supervisors also centralized the collection of gifts in a "common chest" and redistributed them to various establishments throughout the city. At the same time, legal begging was strictly curtailed. While such reforms won the praise of the Holy Roman Emperor Charles V (1500–1558), his support did not result in similar measures throughout his domains. In Spain, political, economic, and social structures conspired to slow the pace of, if not prohibit, centralization and rationalization. The more firmly entrenched religious institutions, which had traditionally overseen charity, and the fiscal weakness of the state throughout the seventeenth and eighteenth centuries, made the establishment of more expensive, secular charity boards almost impossible. Only a handful of cities, such as Zamora, followed the lead of Ypres and other early modern Catholic urban centers.

England lies on the other side of the spectrum as the only European state to implement successfully a national system of relief founded on a set of acts, passed in 1598 and 1601, known as the Elizabethan Poor Law. This legislation prohibited begging, made parish poor rates mandatory, and rationalized the delivery of aid by empowering overseers of the poor and justices of the peace to determine eligibility and regulate distribution. The implementation of the Speenhamland system in 1795 extended relief to those whose wages fell below a certain level, on the basis of the price of bread and family size. Commercial wealth,

historians argue, rested at the heart of such a comprehensive system of relief.

The impact of these reforms on the poor themselves seems to have been limited, except, of course, in England, where the Speenhamland system not only expanded the rolls of recipients, but also increased the number of men among those who sought assistance—a category heretofore almost completely composed of women. Throughout the rest of Europe, however, the poor were left to devise strategies that included kin networks and informal and unofficial alms, as well as new institutions created by elite reformers. In short, the new establishments and systems that emerged from efforts to centralize and rationalize poor relief did not replace older measures; they only expanded the options.

THE TRIUMPH OF LIBERALISM

In many respects, the French Revolution represents the apex of this movement to secularize and rationalize poor relief. The Revolution nearly destroyed the old system of aid by nationalizing the Church's property, by taking away the financial basis of religious poor relief, and by firmly establishing the right of all French citizens to government assistance if unable to work. Unfortunately, the various programs that revolutionaries constructed were impossible to implement in the midst of war and civil unrest. In matters of social welfare, then, the Revolution's legacy was little more than a contentious debate over the roles of the state and of private charity. From this time forward, social welfare became linked to questions of state obligation and citizens' rights. State-mandated and organized assistance was equated with the radical politics that had burdened Europe with more than two decades of war.

In the Revolution's wake, laissez-faire capitalism and other tenets of classical liberalism began to hold greater sway than early modern arguments for greater state involvement. According to most classical liberals, the state had no right to violate private property in order to effect a redistribution of wealth. Individuals alone were responsible for their livelihoods and, through thrift and foresight, for preparation for the vagaries of illness and old age. A legislated system of social welfare would only serve to instill a sense of entitlement among the working class that would destroy the moral fabric of the nation. This principle did not preclude all state assistance, but rather restricted it to assistance for the truly needy, those whose plight moved the collective heart of the nation. Increasingly, however, the line drawn between the truly needy and the "undeserving" poor included fewer and fewer people as worthy of help. Poverty, many classical liberals maintained, was not the product of economic insecurity, but of moral failings. During much of the nineteenth century, then, public assistance became stingier and more punitive in nature.

The result was a retrenchment of state aid throughout much of Europe. In early-nineteenth-century Hamburg, for example, the burghers responded to economic instability, a growing population of laboring poor, and the upheavals of Napoleonic warfare by cutting back on the more generous assistance available as late as the 1790s. The 1817 regulations for the Allgemeine Armenanstalt, or General Poor Relief Agency, restricted state aid only to the registered poor, and even these services, like medical care and weekly alms, were reduced. Relief officers rephrased their mission to include the alleviation of poverty, not its prevention, as the city had once defined it. Accompanying this shift was an emphasis on volunteerism. The state pared down its responsibilities and left private charity to fill the gap. As the historian Mary Lindemann noted in *Patriots and Paupers* (1990), Hamburg's governors ceased to allow any sense of social conscience to shape state policies.

The same thing might be said of England's ruling elite. The Poor Law Amendment Act of 1834 abolished outdoor relief for the able-bodied and their families by instituting the concepts of "less eligibility" and "the workhouse test." Those who could work were placed in workhouses and segregated from the "worthy" poor, such as orphans, the aged, and the insane. At the same time, elected guardians under the supervision of a central Poor Law Commission replaced informal parish vestries as poor-relief administrators. With these measures, reformers hoped to bring uniformity to English public assistance while ensuring that relief did not damage the economy by artificially raising free-market wages.

Perhaps nowhere is the shift from increasing state involvement to its near absence more evident than in Russia. In 1775, Catherine the Great reformed provincial government to create provincial social welfare boards charged with establishing new institutions of public assistance, such as almshouses and orphanages. Though these boards failed to stimulate a civic spirit among her subjects, as Catherine had hoped, they did become significant contributors to the social welfare of Russian peasants before emancipation. With emancipation in 1861, however, Russian public assistance virtually disappeared, a casualty of limited powers of taxation, political fears of excessive

The Dauphine's Bounty. Marie-Antoinette, wife of the Dauphin (who became Louis XVI of France in 1774), distributes alms to the poor. Engraving (1773) after a drawing of J.-M. Moreau the Younger. BIBLIOTHÈQUE NATIONAL DE FRANCE, PARIS

local autonomy, and a resurgent belief that charity must be private and morally based.

By the middle decades of the nineteenth century, most European states had retreated from the realm of social welfare, causing some scholars to argue that it is not the rise of the welfare state that demands explanation, but this more puzzling gap in the long history of state assistance. Be that as it may, the end result was the same: poverty had become the domain of local governments and private institutions like charities and mutual aid societies. While charitable activity increased, becoming a symbol of middle-class gentility, especially among women, the poor themselves suffered both from want and the moralizing control of their social superiors. Many charities, for example, restricted assistance only to mothers and couples who could prove Christian marriage. Moreover, sufficient assistance became an accident of birth, for localized relief meant a highly unequal system of aid based upon residency. Paupers who could not prove long-term residency in a given city faced deportation to their native cities. As the century drew to a close, however, calls for enhanced state services increased. By the 1870s, Europe was poised to undergo yet another shift in state support for social welfare.

THE RISE OF THE WELFARE STATE

The final decades of the nineteenth century witnessed a growing concern with social welfare and state functions. Grouped under the more general problem known to contemporaries as "the social question," poverty seemed at the base of Europe's many difficulties, from working-class protest to degeneration. The rise of such attention was evident not only in the reams of paper used to disseminate a wide array of opinions on the subject, but also in the public and private actions devised to address these concerns. Much of this activity sprang from bourgeois anxiety over socialist politics and working-class radicalism, which began to express itself in a growing number of strikes as well as at the polls. To many observers, municipal and private charity was no longer sufficient to deal with the vagaries of a maturing industrial economy, all too evident in the depression that began in 1873 and lasted well into the 1890s. Only the central state, many argued, could support a more comprehensive system of assistance. Moreover, in the context of social Darwinism, the state was said to have a duty to protect the nation from racial decadence and deterioration, a decline that was said to be clearly evident in a number of social studies conducted in working-class slums throughout Europe.

Although most of Europe's elite shared this sense of fear and dread, their answers to those anxieties were far from uniform. New programs and policies were shaped as much by state structures, political considerations, and previous social welfare measures as they were by concern with riot and national decline. In the history of German social welfare, for example, historians have typically emphasized a long tradition of Prussian etatism to explain the innovative social insurance programs that the German chancellor Otto von Bismarck (1815–1898) ushered through the new Reichstag between 1883 and 1889. These measures differed significantly from previous forms of poor relief because they were founded upon contributory systems of social insurance. The 1883 compulsory program against workers' illness pooled workers' and employers' contributions to fund up to thirteen weeks of relief, which in 1903 was extended to twenty-six weeks. An 1884 law insuring workers against workplace accidents operated in a similar fashion. Finally, the pension law of 1889, financed by employers, workers, and state subsidies, provided workers a small pension if they reached seventy years of age.

While this legislation was indeed innovative, particularly in its obligatory nature, these programs did not completely eschew earlier traditions of social welfare. The bourgeois principle of self-help remained the central tenet of social welfare, and German workers contributed the lion's share for their own insurance. Moreover, whenever possible, older institutions, such as mutual aid societies, retained a place within the newer state structure. In fact, social insurance did not supplant municipal and private charity, which remained the primary sources of assistance for the indigent, especially women and children. Finally, the laws benefited only industrial workers. By 1913, only 14.5 million workers received insurance out of a population of approximately 65 million.

These limitations, according to many historians, serve only to highlight the conservative political intent behind them. Bismarck designed these first steps toward the modern welfare state with the goal of wooing the working class away from the powerful German Social Democratic Party. His social welfare policies, according to this view, were an exercise in authoritarian state-building, nothing more. However, George Steinmetz (1993) has offered a new interpretation of German social welfare, including in his study similar reforms in poor-relief legislation that also date from the last decades of the nineteenth century. In an interpretation reminiscent of studies of early modern welfare, Steinmetz argues that the programs instituted under Bismarck promoted a bourgeois strategy of capitalist development, which included the creation and maintenance of a free labor market. Moreover, middle-class reformers constructed this system over the objections of conservative Junkers. According to Steinmetz, the development of German social welfare owes more to bourgeois economic needs and political clout than to an authoritarian state with traditional agrarian support.

Regardless of the motives that spawned them, the three measures that formed the core of German social welfare also served as a model for reformers throughout Europe. States as diverse as Norway, Spain, and Holland all established insurance against accidents in the 1890s, while Austria and Italy reinforced similar programs with sickness insurance and old-age pensions, respectively. Frequently, however, similar programs took very different organizational forms, particularly in Scandinavia. In Denmark, for example, a set of measures created between 1891 and 1907 established the outlines of what one scholar has labeled the "solidaristic" welfare state. The 1898 Accident Insurance Act covered only wage earners, and under the Sickness Insurance Reform of 1892, sickness insurance remained voluntary and rested on a base of sickness funds and mutual aid societies, funded by participant contributions but also subsidized by the state. There was significant innovation in the realms of old-age pensions and unemployment insurance, a new type of safeguard. The Old Age Relief Act of 1891 established a right to pensions drawn from a fund financed by taxes, not worker contributions. These pensions were offered to all indigents over sixty years of age. Unemployment insurance followed the same principles as sickness insurance. It was voluntary and, although subsidized by the state, relied on participant contributions.

These innovations highlight the different sources of social welfare reform in Europe; Denmark's social insurance programs were the result of social and political compromise among the most important political parties, the Social Democrats on one side and the Agrarian Liberals and Conservatives on the other. The Radical Liberals, who represented both rural smallholders and urban intellectuals, officially organized in 1905 around a program of greater state involvement and acted as important mediators among opposing groups before and after their formation as an independent party. Danish social insurance thus rested on a foundation of peasant-liberalism and consensus, essential ingredients to later reforms.

In Britain, reforms fell somewhere between the German and Nordic models. An 1897 Workmen's Compensation Law provided employer-paid insurance for workplace accidents, while a 1908 Old Age Pension Act established pensions for the indigent over seventy years of age. As in Denmark, old-age pensions were supported by a general tax fund, not worker contributions. The inclusion of this measure precipitated a constitutional crisis that culminated in the substantial weakening of the House of Lords. Liberal and Labour politicians followed up this new policy the following year with the establishment of Trade Boards, which were empowered to end "sweated labor" by setting minimum wages in various trades, a list that grew with time. Finally, the 1911 National Insurance Act capped this period of vigorous reform with programs for both sickness and unemployment insurance. This last bill was the product of significant compromise, however. Sickness and unemployment insurance was contributory and compulsory, but only for certain classes of workers. Health insurance affected only manual workers and those earning less than 160 pounds annually. Moreover, only the insured worker received medical assistance, not his family. Mutual aid societies and private insurers also received special attention; approved societies retained a central role in dispensing medical assistance. As for unemployment insurance (Part II of the National Insurance Act), legislators limited this experimental program to only a small group of relatively well-paid trades that suffered from periodic unemployment, such as ironfounding, shipbuilding, and construction.

As in Germany, then, new social programs added significantly to older relief institutions, but did not supersede them. Private charitable associations like the Charity Organisation Society retained a significant role in social welfare, a role they sought to enhance through cooperation with new state institutions. In fact, a growing number of historians now argue that European politicians designed their programs to complement voluntary organizations. The rise of the welfare state was not a complete break with the past, it was a gradual transformation. Nowhere was this more evident than in France.

The history of French social welfare has long suffered from the belief that little occurred to rival German and Scandinavian innovation. In the realm of maternal and pronatalist welfare, however, France took the lead among industrialized nations. By 1914 the French government had spent millions of francs establishing regional centers for prenatal care, a family allowance program awarding assistance to needy families with four or more children, and legislation granting women compensation for prenatal and postpartum leaves from employment. Yet in other forms of social welfare, French assistance remained traditional, eschewing social insurance for poor relief. Despite extremely limited programs, such as insurance for work-related accidents, legislated in 1899, and old-age pensions for workers, instituted in 1910, the vast majority of French citizens continued to rely only on poor relief, which remained municipal and heavily dependent on private charity.

While the 1893 legislation granting free medical assistance to the indigent and the 1905 system of pensions for the elderly indigent decreed rights to assistance based upon citizenship, they relied almost completely on municipal and departmental funding and organization. In response, most cities increased their reliance on private charities. Between 1870 and 1914, for example, municipal subsidies to private charities in Bordeaux increased by 230 percent. In essence, then, France trod a middle path between earlier clasically liberal dependence on municipal assistance and private charity on the one hand, and the social insurance schemes of its northern neighbors on the other. This curious development arose from French concepts of the state and citizenship. Against the historical backdrop of the French Revolution, politicians were reluctant to establish new rights to assistance that would entail the creation of a vast bureaucracy. They therefore, limited a citizen's right to relief and made such rights municipal obligations. However, overriding concerns over falling birth rates and degeneracy convinced these same leaders to be inventive with maternal and pronatalist welfare. Moreover, they could fit such innovations into their political ideologies by reminding themselves that women and children were not true citizens. In short, the delicate relationship between citizens and their state was not altered by assistance for women and children. Consensus on these measures was thus much easier to attain in the cantankerous arena of French politics. The end result was a system of social welfare less out of place among the other European states than previously believed.

The decades before World War I thus witnessed some startling innovations in social welfare. Having relinquished a role in such matters during the early years of the nineteenth century, most European states now played a prominent role not only in providing assistance, but also in the reconceptualization of social welfare. Few social insurance schemes relied exclusively on workers' contributions. State subsidies now supplemented traditional reliance on self-help. At the same time, proponents of social welfare spoke in terms of citizens' rights and state obligation, not voluntary relief. Even more important, programs that depended on general tax funds and not members' contributions, like the British and Danish pension plans, introduced limited measures of income redistribution, not just the redistribution of risk enforced in compulsory social insurance programs. The outlines of the modern welfare state were clearly visible in these developments. But those who benefited remained relatively few in number.

New programs affected mainly factory workers, leaving artisans, shopkeepers, and rural workers to rely on charity. Moreover, those who were not consistently part of the labor pool, particularly women, benefited little if any. In fact, women's relationship to the budding welfare state was dominated by the rhetoric of maternalism. Women deserved assistance only because their continued reproduction was central to the nation's future. As a result, women did not figure into social insurance as workers; more often than not they entered onto welfare rolls as dependents, ineligible for equal benefits. Ironically, while many welfare programs thus recognized the importance of women's reproductive labor, male politicians simultaneously refused to equate it with the productive labor of men, which received higher remunerative value both on and off the job. These shortcomings would become evident in the decades after the World War I, though real change would come only after World War II, if at all.

THE HEYDAY OF THE WELFARE STATE

The devastation of World War I demonstrated to all concerned just how inadequate welfare reform before 1914 had been. Yet few major breakthroughs were forthcoming. Instead, the reforms implemented during the interwar years merely extended insurance programs to additional categories of workers without altering basic assumptions and structures. Despite new social insurance legislation in France in 1928 and 1930, most workers remained uninsured. By the mid 1930s approximately 10 million workers—those whose wages fell below an established minimum—were eligible for a host of private and public insurance funds paid for by worker and employer contributions. In Denmark, the Great Social Reform of 1933 was more a rationalization and reorganization of earlier measures than a bold new step in a different direction. Danes could choose between active and passive membership in funds, and, despite the government's renewed commitment to universal compulsory social insurance, the latter provided very little protection. The interwar welfare state also remained a gendered entity. The new fascist states of Italy and Germany implemented maternalist welfare measures to rebuild their populations, while forcing many women to leave better-paying jobs to be replaced by unemployed men. French politicians also extended family allowances, which would later become a mainstay of the French welfare state.

There were exceptions to the general lack of innovation in social welfare policy. Sweden, for example, began to secure a reputation for social welfare, which it would consolidate after 1945. Between 1933 and 1938, the Swedes implemented such programs as state-subsidized loans to newlyweds; maternity benefits for approximately 90 percent of all mothers, including free childbirth services; state subsidies to voluntary unemployment benefit societies; and low-interest housing loans for large families. In the new Soviet Union, too, social welfare underwent significant change. Soviet citizens were now entitled to full employment, daycare centers, and free medical care. But such new rights, and the freedoms they were meant to produce, existed more on paper than in reality. Unemployment gave way principally to small make-work programs, while free day care and communal responsibility quickly deteriorated, leaving only doubled workloads for women who entered factories while remaining responsible for the bulk of their family's daily upkeep.

When the hardships of the Great Depression struck in 1929, most European states responded by cutting back on welfare benefits. For most of Europe, it was only after World War II that the modern welfare state became reality. Although no consensus exists, many historians credit the war's varied impacts to explain this postwar expansion of social programs. Fascism's demise tarnished the traditional right and promoted the rise of new political forces, most prominently, the Christian Democrats, that did not oppose state-supported social welfare. Parties on the left also gained increased stature from their participation in resistance movements and wartime coalition governments. One argument holds that, especially in Britain, the privations of war also returned a sense of community to war-torn populations that made the redistribution of risk and income more acceptable after 1945. Perhaps most important, the postwar years witnessed the rise of a new consumer economy in which large retailers overwhelmed the small shop owners, who had long been foes of social insurance. More middle-class families, now tied to the fortunes of large corporations, acknowledged the benefits of an extended system of social welfare that would include them. Throughout Europe, then, the basic outlines of what we now call the welfare state gradually emerged from the rubble of World War II.

In Eastern Europe, Soviet domination brought social programs modeled after Russia's, including state-supported housing, health care, and education. In Western Europe, Great Britain and the Scandinavian states led the way by creating social-insurance schemes that were compulsory and universal. In addition, contributory funding was replaced with a combination of flat-rate benefits, which guaranteed basic services to all citizens regardless of need, and supplementary programs designed to assist the needy. All of this required substantial state subsidies derived from increased tax revenues. Although many continental states like France and Germany did not immediately adopt similar measures, the basic outlines of the British and Scandinavian systems were implemented there later in the 1950s and 1960s, albeit with significant modifications rooted in earlier patterns of welfare development in each country.

Based largely on plans known as the Beveridge Report (1942), drawn up during the war by William Beveridge (1879–1963), the British welfare state made participation compulsory and benefits universal. British citizens paid flat-rate contributions and received flat-rate benefits. Since contributions had to be set low enough for the majority of British citizens, the state used tax revenue to supplement funding for such programs as National Health Insurance, implemented by 1948. The state also used tax monies to assist the needy with both housing and education costs, greatly altering the shape of British society.

It was in Sweden, however, that the true epitome of the welfare state arose after World War II. During these years a strong economy, the consolidation of the Social Democratic government, and administrative reforms dictated by wartime needs paved the way for a host of social programs. Between 1946 and 1959, Swedes created a social welfare system that combined universal flat-rate benefit programs for old-age pensions and child allowances with income-contingent programs for housing, health care, and supplementary pensions. The former guaranteed benefits to all citizens, while the latter replaced contributory schemes with means testing.

In 1963, the National Insurance Act coordinated most of these programs into three types of insurance: the health and parental insurance system, the basic pension system, and the national supplementary pension system. The first system provided benefits for medical and dental costs, as well as compensation for loss of income due to illness or childbirth and child care, including up to six months' leave to care for children under eight years of age (payable to either the father or mother since 1974). The basic pension system paid benefits to all retired or disabled Swedes, as well as family pensions for dependents that had lost a family provider. Finally, supplementary pensions were based on pensionable income earned before retirement, an income that had to be above a base amount but less than 7.5 times that same amount. In addition to this National Insurance, Sweden also maintained work injury and unemployment insurance programs. All of this was supplemented with public

Free Health Care. Norwegian poster.
UNIVERSITETSBIBLIOTEKAT I OSLO BILLEDSAMLINGEN

assistance for those whose needs were not adequately met by insurance. This entire system rested squarely on state funding through taxation, employer contributions, and interest income from special insurance funds. Swedes reinforced this commitment to social insurance in 1981 with the Social Services Act, designed to reduce the place of individually oriented means-tested programs for a greater reliance on general, structurally oriented programs that would protect individual privacy.

In both France and Germany, on the other hand, the immediate postwar years saw mainly the extension of social welfare along lines already established before 1945, particularly through the extension of contributory social insurance funds linked to separate classes and occupations. In France, the self-employed and white-collar middle managers opposed participation in a national social security system established in 1948, prompting the maintenance of numerous private funds. Ironically, when the petty bourgeoisie sought admission to the national pension system in the 1960s, it was the unions who now opposed the expansion of social welfare to include their poorer fellow citizens. In the end, the self-employed and white-collar middle managers won admission. A similar situation occurred in Germany, as wealthy artisans fought during the 1950s to retain a separate fund within the white-collar worker insurance system. In 1959, however, less-affluent artisans succeeded in joining their fund to the workers' pension insurance system over the objection of the Social Democrats. Soon after, various reforms in the 1960s gave France and Germany many of the trappings of the Scandinavian welfare states, including unemployment and health insurance for the entire population and a host of state agencies devoted to public health and social work. At the same time, early characteristics have not completely disappeared. Germany's welfare system remains quite corporatist in nature, while France's retains a significant role for a host of public and private insurance funds. Similarly, the system of family allowances that emerged before World War I and was later extended during the interwar years remains a central pillar of French social welfare. Payments are based on the number of children and are allotted to all French families. Such measures are designed to support population growth, not redistribute income.

The impact of the expansion of European social welfare cannot be overstated. The welfare state has fundamentally altered class relations as well as the relations between the citizenry and the state. While class distinctions clearly remain, the divisions have become less stark. Workers are now active participants in a consumer culture that they share with the middle class. Governments also claim a much greater role in what was previously defined as private life, particularly family life. Young families now raise their children with state assistance and remain free of the direct responsibility of caring for elderly relatives. Just how important the welfare state has become in the lives of most Europeans is evident in the response to growing demands from conservatives to curtail welfare spending. The welfare state entered a period of crisis in the late 1970s, as rising oil prices created stagflation. Near the turn of the century, concern over rising government debt was aggravated by an aging population and discontent with immigrant demands for the right to participate in social insurance and assistance programs. Yet the welfare state has not been abandoned. Indeed, government plans for austerity have been met with street demonstrations. While some governments, like Margaret Thatcher's (1925–) in Great Britain (1979–1990), have successfully withdrawn the state from various arenas of economic life through privatization, the basic outlines and institutions of the welfare state remain intact. Perhaps the greatest impact of the welfare state has thus been the recognition that the state does indeed have a vital interest in actively supporting the welfare of its citizens.

THE WELFARE STATE AND SOCIAL HISTORY

Social history has played an integral role in our understanding of the welfare state, particularly of its origins. Initially, two schools of thought emerged. The first, espoused primarily by marxist historians, depicted the welfare state as a set of measures designed to dull the sharp edges of capitalism and thus lure workers away from social revolution. Other historians, however, joined social scientists in presenting the growth of state-supported social welfare as a product of modernization. As western societies developed industrial economies, insecurity among the proletariat grew. So did their political voice. The end result was a state that responded to working-class interests with social insurance. These interpretations have not fared well under increased scrutiny. Later analysts discovered that the development of the welfare state owed as much to the demands of the petty bourgeoisie as to working-class radicalism. At the same time, other scholars began to emphasize the importance of state structures and political ideologies in shaping the contours of the welfare state. The end result has been a new social interpretation that highlights the fundamental roles of middle-class voters and their political ideologies. The welfare state grew earliest and strongest not only in those nations where the middle-class became convinced that it, too, could benefit from tax-funded programs to redistribute risk and income, but also in those countries where middle-class ideology did not prohibit a strong, interventionist state. The timing of welfare reforms depended on how soon each nation's bourgeoisie could be won over to these two arguments.

The particular shape and impacts of the welfare state have also proven fertile soil for social historians.

This is especially true for those interested in gender and the family. Social insurance first grew out of contributory schemes that posited men as workers and women as dependents. And unions in many nations expressed little desire to see this pattern altered. In Britain, for example, unions linked social insurance to the concept of the family wage. Therefore, even after 1945, whether they worked or not, married women received lower benefits than men and unmarried female workers. British social welfare was thus built on a family model that envisioned married women as secondary sources of income, perpetuating a reliance on married women for part-time work. In other countries too, social welfare posited women as recipients of need-based relief and mothers' pensions, but not as full-fledged citizens. In France, on the other hand, politicians faced with depopulation recognized that married women would always remain integral members of the labor pool. The result was a social security system based on individual participation regardless of sex or marital status and a system of family allowances that rewarded all families for having children, including single mothers. This, many historians argue, played a significant role in the different paths English and French feminists chose later in the twentieth century, with British feminists taking a much more aggressive stance against the state.

Finally, social historians have begun to spend more time analyzing the transformation from reliance on private charity to the welfare state. While much work remains to be undertaken in this direction, current research already indicates that an easy distinction between public and private in the rise of the welfare state is untenable. Private charities often figured prominently in the plans of welfare reformers and remain integral parts of the welfare states that function today. In these and other ways, then, social history continues to add significantly to our understanding of the welfare state in Europe.

See also **Charity and Poor Relief: The Early Modern Period; Charity and Poor Relief: The Modern Period** *(volume 3);* **The Family and the State; The Elderly** *(volume 4);* **Standards of Living** *(volume 5); and other articles in this section.*

BIBLIOGRAPHY

Accampo, Elinor Ann, Rachel G. Fuchs, and Mary Lynn Stewart, et al. *Gender and the Politics of Social Reform in France, 1870–1914.* Baltimore, 1995.

Ashford, Douglas E. *The Emergence of the Welfare States.* Oxford and New York, 1987.

Baldwin, Peter. *The Politics of Social Solidarity: Class Bases of the European Welfare State, 1875–1975.* Cambridge, U.K., 1990.

Canning, Kathleen. "Social Policy, Body Politics: Recasting the Social Question in Germany." In *Gender and Class in Modern Europe.* Edited by Laura L. Frader and Sonya O. Rose. Ithaca, N.Y., 1996.

Cawson, Alan. *Corporatism and Welfare: Social Policy and State Intervention in Britain.* London, 1982.

Crew, David. "The Ambiguities of Modernity: Welfare and the German State from Wilhelm to Hitler." In *Society, Culture, and the State in Germany, 1870–1930.* Edited by Goeff Eley. Ann Arbor, Mich., 1996.

Donzelot, Jacques. *The Policing of Families.* Translated by Robert Hurley. New York, 1979.

Esping-Andersen, Gøsta. *The Three Worlds of Welfare Capitalism.* Princeton, N.J., 1990.

Flora, Peter, ed. *Growth to Limits: The Western European Welfare States since World War II.* 2 vols. Berlin and New York, 1986.

Flora, Peter, and Arnold J. Heidenheimer, eds. *The Development of Welfare States in Europe and America.* New Brunswick, N.J., 1981.

Forsberg, Mats. *The Evolution of Social Welfare Policy in Sweden.* Translated by Victor Kayfetz. Stockholm, 1984.

Fuchs, Rachel Ginnis. *Poor and Pregnant in Paris: Strategies for Survival in the Nineteenth Century.* New Brunswick, N.J., 1992.

Grossmann, Atina. *Reforming Sex: The German Movement for Birth Control and Abortion Reform, 1920–1950.* New York, 1995.

Hatzfeld, Henri. *Du paupérisme à la sécurité sociale; essai sur les origines de la sécurité sociale en France, 1850–1940.* Paris, 1971. Reprint, Nancy, France, 1989.

Himmelfarb, Gertrude. *Poverty and Compassion: The Moral Imagination of the Late Victorians.* New York, 1991.

Hong, Young-Sun. *Welfare, Modernity, and the Weimar State, 1919–1933.* Princeton, N.J., 1998.

Jenson, Jane. "Both Friend and Foe: Women and State Welfare." In *Becoming Visible: Women in European History.* 2d ed., Edited by Renate Bridenthal, Claudia Koonz, and Susan Stuard. Boston, 1987. Pages 535–556.

Jutte, Robert. *Poverty and Deviance in Early Modern Europe.* Cambridge, U.K., and New York, 1994.

Koven, Seth, and Sonya Michel, eds. *Mothers of a New World: Maternalist Politics and the Origins of Welfare States.* New York, 1993.

Lindemann, Mary. *Patriots and Paupers: Hamburg, 1712–1830.* New York, 1990.

Lindenmeyr, Adele. *Poverty Is Not a Vice: Charity, Society, and the State in Imperial Russia.* Princeton, N.J., 1996.

Lynch, Katherine A. *Family, Class, and Ideology in Early Industrial France: Social Policy and the Working-Class Family, 1825–1848.* Madison, Wis., 1988.

Mandler, Peter, ed. *The Uses of Charity: The Poor on Relief in the Nineteenth-Century Metropolis.* Philadelphia, 1990.

Pedersen, Susan. *Family, Dependence, and the Origins of the Welfare State: Britain and France, 1914–1945.* Cambridge, U.K., and New York, 1993.

Rose, Sonya O. "Protective Labor Legislation in Nineteenth-Century Britain." In *Gender and Class in Modern Europe.* Edited by Laura L. Frader and Sonya O. Rose. Ithaca, N.Y., 1996.

Steinmetz, George. *Regulating the Social: The Welfare State and Local Politics in Imperial Germany.* Princeton, N.J., 1993.

Sullivan, Michael. *The Development of the British Welfare State.* New York and London, 1996.

Swaan, Abram de. *In Care of the State: Health Care, Education, and Welfare in Europe and the USA in the Modern Era.* Oxford and Cambridge, U.K., 1988.

Thane, Pat. *Foundations of the Welfare State.* London, 1982.

Thane, Pat, and Gisela Bock, eds. *Maternity and Gender Policies: Women and the Rise of the European Welfare States, 1880s–1950s.* New York, 1991.

CIVIL SOCIETY

Guido Hausmann and Manfred Hettling

The end of the cold war has signaled—for the time being—the end of one of the grand utopias of the nineteenth century. Although communist ideology in its many variations eroded before the end of the cold war, its demise accompanied as well as resulted from the end of utopianism. Beginning in the 1970s intellectuals from Poland, the Czech Republic, Hungary, and other states in the former East bloc proclaimed "civil society" as a new "political program," not as a utopia. Herein lies a cause for the post-cold-war attraction all over Europe of the "civil society" model of social organization. This social organization, rooted in European antiquity and the Catholic Middle Ages but also distinctly influenced by the Reformation, contains many local, regional, and national shadings. Variations of civil society emerged in eighteenth-century Europe and North America and spread to other communities.

THE TERM "CIVIL SOCIETY"

The various terms for civil society indicate the various traditions out of which it grew. Examples include the German *bürgerliche Gesellschaft,* the French *société civile,* the Anglo-American "civil society," the Italian *civile condizione,* and the Russian *burzhuaznoe/grazhdankoe obshchestvo.* Enlightenment thinkers of the eighteenth century like Denis Diderot (1713–1784), Voltaire (1694–1778), and Jean-Jacques Rousseau (1712–1778), in France; David Hume (1711–1776) and John Locke (1632–1704) in England; and Immanuel Kant (1724–1804) in Germany defined the essential attributes of civil society. Among these were the idea of contractual relationships, the reduction of religion to a private conviction, individual human rights, and political freedoms.

In the ancient tradition descending from Aristotle, the term *societas civilis,* or civil society, always designated a political society—that is, a community of citizens bound together in a governing political bond as free and equal participants. A later tradition

of the term originated in the early nineteenth century and was related to the emancipation of the newly risen middle classes from the feudal social order. The term "civil society" designated a society of private individuals distinguished by their ownership of property: in this more modern understanding of "civil society," the term does not include the notion of political participation. As Georg Wilhelm Friedrich Hegel (1770–1831) declared, civil society and the state stand in opposition to each other. In the Anglo-American tradition, the ancient understanding of the term prevailed. Here civil society remained connected to political participation—ever a predominant theme—whereas the two were separate on the European continent for a long time. Use of the term since the late twentieth century calls for the ancient bond linking the self-organization of citizens for their economic benefit with political participation and seeks to overcome the separation of apolitical civil society from the politics of the state.

The various traditions of the concept share the designation of a self-organizing society; they differ in how much this community participates in the political rule of the state. The claim to a political voice did not necessarily call into question the legitimacy of traditional monarchies. Such a claim could lead to the antimonarchical, revolutionary pathos of post-1789 France, but the outcome could also be a long-lasting, highly stable monarchy—if such a monarchy accepted its transformation into a political institution that represented only the common political goals of civil society. In the German-speaking world the tradition stemming from Hegel and Karl Marx (1818–1883), which defined civil society as a philosophical and ideological category, continued to exercise significant influence; this tradition held an apolitical understanding of the concept and called for a relatively strict division of state and society. A stronger reception of Anglo-American contract theory first arrived in (West) Germany after 1945.

The cornerstone of civil society was the self-organizing individual who had the right to bond with others in free associations. The individual citizen was defined as free from religious rule and as entitled to participate in political institutions by virtue of being an individual. In the Anglo-American states the right and natural freedom of the individual was of primary importance. This idea grew out of the Protestant tradition that made religious freedom an individual's indivisible right. This tradition interpreted religious freedom not as the result of tolerance—an instance of grace by the state—but as an inalienable human right, one that preceded the actions of any social institution. In the French tradition a concept of human rights prevailed that protected the individual from the state: freedom is understood as the restriction of potential state interference. No effective Russian tradition of individual rights ever developed. Unlike in Poland, no trace of the Renaissance, of humanism, or of the Reformation left its mark in Muscovite Russia. Only in the eighteenth century, Scottish, English, French, and—transmitted through East Prussia and the Baltic—German sources spread the European concept of freedom. However, alongside the ideas that asserted the primacy of individual rights were the equally lasting European concepts that projected individual freedoms onto the collective—the nation, state, or monarchy. These fit into a wholly different tradition.

The German Enlightenment tradition mixed different interpretations of the individual. Kant's model of civil society described the individual in various functions and social conditions. In Kant's view the legal foundation for civil society lay in the following principles: the freedom of every member of society based on his or her being "human"; the equality of members as "subjects"; and members' independence as "citizens." As a human being, anyone has the right to pursue happiness in his or her own way. As a subject everyone has to follow the law. As a citizen, anyone is a "lawmaker"; that is, he or she participates in the formation of the political will of society (or, in the parlance of American pragmatism, he or she will make the decisions that directly influence others). Freedom is conferred on all people, and at the same time every person—whether man or woman, rich or poor, aristocratic or bourgeois—is bound to obey the law. For Kant, restrictions on these universal proclamations and decrees came only with a final distinction, the "quality" of citizens. With this addendum, Kant articulated what was and is contained in all concepts of civil society, that not all people, but only those who meet certain prerequisites, gain a political say. Since Kant, the criteria for the exclusion of individual groups have fundamentally changed. Estate privileges (aristocracy), legal categories (patriciate, citizen status), economic requirements (property), and sex (the exclusion of women) no longer set limits to participation. As before, however, there still exist restrictions based on age, capacity for rational choice, criminal record, and national citizenship.

Equality only prevails within these social restrictions; only those people selected by these filters can form through their associations the core social element of any civil society. Association is the complementary concept to civil society. Whereas Thomas Hobbes (1588–1679) in *Leviathan* (1651) placed the individual under the absolute sovereignty of the state in order to prevent civil war between individuals, all theorists of civil society—Locke in England, Alexis de Tocqueville (1805–1859) in France, Kant in Germany—have identified its uniqueness as the ability of persons to freely form associations among themselves in order to support one another and to regulate social life. The American pragmatism of John Dewey (1859–1952) also stands in this tradition.

Associations in civil society differ in principle from earlier forms of association in that the individual's identity is only partially defined by his or her participation in such groups. Associations and face-to-face communication exist in all societies; even totalitarianism could not do away with them. The aspect of association specific to civil society is based on functional differentiation: people participate only with a part of themselves; thus many different kinds of social circles can join together resulting in infinitely variable possibilities for interaction. The paradox is this: by limiting the common bond within associations, civil society makes an infinite variety of associations possible. Herein lies the tense relationship between particularity and universality that defines the dynamic of civil society.

Two decisive transformations have taken place in civil society since the eighteenth century: women gained the right to political participation in the twentieth century, and economic status is no longer a criterion for such participation. With these changes a central component of any conception of civil society as it had existed from the eighteenth to the beginning of the twentieth century also changed: political decision making was no longer the exclusive domain of men with property. Every society contained different expressions of this same phenomenon. In England political exclusion based on ownership, which has been called the politics of "possessive individualism" (C. B. Macpherson), prevailed. In France the political privileges of the propertied bourgeois dominated for a long time, despite the universalist political pathos connected to the term *citoyen*. In Germany, too, and even more in eastern European societies, economic hurdles to political participation were raised.

These restrictive models of civil society defined "independence" as the decisive category for participation. They attached an economic and moral value to the term so that it signified one's permitted conduct as well as one's membership in society. Bourgeois optimism for progress in the nineteenth century mediated the growing tension between real social inequalities and the utopian nature of commonly held middle-class ideals. The attainment of utopia would liberate the excluded, who as individuals would one day fulfill certain criteria and enter civil society, so that they, too, could become fellow "lawmakers." Many reached this goal, many did not. The workers' movement and the women's movement grew out of the attempt to change civil society's rules of exclusion. Apart from economic barriers to political participation, in western European societies there were restrictions based on religion and national origin (if often on an informal level), while in eastern Europe—that is, the Russian Empire—there were formal restrictions against non-Christians (Jews, Muslims), which provoked protest movements.

The development toward conferring the principles of civil society on those excluded from participation seemed to signal the implementation and redemption of the civic ideal of individual self-fulfillment and civic equality. This optimism broke down, however, in many European societies at the end of the nineteenth century. Optimism for civic progress turned into fin-de-siècle criticism of civilized culture, and in practice optimism deteriorated into the authoritarian regimes of the interwar period. Ultimately, in Germany and the Soviet Union, it contributed to Hitlerism and Stalinism. The utopian potential first reappeared at the end of the twentieth century in the societies of Eastern Europe but was restricted to a political program for the transformation of the then socialist societies. Both the *social* utopia of civil society, based on the independence of the individual through his or her participation in ownership and education, and the *political* utopia of civil society, based on equal participation of all members, had lost little of their attraction. Nevertheless, in no way did a mere "revolution to catch up" (Jürgen Habermas) occur in Eastern Europe, as some observers in the West judged it. From its beginnings in early modern times, the concept of civil society has been flexible enough to produce very diverse forms of social organization.

HISTORIOGRAPHY

In the 1980s and 1990s the interpretations of Jürgen Habermas and Reinhart Koselleck fueled the discussion of civil society. It is perhaps no accident that these two thinkers emerged in Germany in the years after 1945. Both of them attempted to explain the collapse of civil society in Germany in the years before 1945. Reflection on this failure to build a lasting civil society provoked analysis of its structure in the postwar era. Another track in historiography follows the thought of Michel Foucault on the disciplinary and regulatory character of civil society. This mode of analysis uses the opposition between the promise of a universal society and the redemption of the particular individual to formulate a rigid critique of bourgeois ideology. It sharpens critical skepticism toward the paradoxes and unfulfilled potential of civil society, but in the process often forgets that this kind of self-criticism is a founding principle of civil society.

Historical research beginning in the 1970s and 1980s concentrated on analyzing various organized associations in the eighteenth century, the media, and individual social support networks. Investigations of the social substrata of civil society, including the bourgeoisie or middle classes, led to wide sociohistorical analyses of bourgeois professional groups and numerous microhistorical studies of cities as the space of middle-class activity. The economic and social heterogeneity of these professional groups, brought to light by empirical research, led scholars since the mid-1980s to analyze more closely the cultural practices, symbols, and images that dominated this world, in order to show the homogenizing forces presumed to operate within a differentiated society. Some researchers pose the question whether one could even speak of a middle class ("bourgeoisie") or whether the plural form, "middle classes," ("bourgeois societies") was more suitable. Much work concentrated on analyzing patterns of behavior and the cultural molding of individuals; an international comparative history of terminology also slowly developed.

ELEMENTS OF A BOURGEOIS SOCIETY: THE PUBLIC SPHERE AND SOCIABILITY

Four characteristics define an ideal type of civil society, and the political theorizing of the eighteenth century already described them all: criticism, functional differentiation, sociability, and the media.

Nothing is more necessary for the process of enlightenment—for the gradual formation of a bourgeois society—than the freedom to criticize. In Kant's formulation, criticism is the potential "for reason in all matters to be put to public use." Free criticism, the results of which are open and to which all people are entitled, is the *conditio sine qua non* for the proper dynamic of a civil society.

Criticism is free, but a restriction exists. The freedom to criticize is conferred on an individual only in a socially compartmentalized function performed by the individual: for example, on a scholar within the literary and journalistic marketplace but not within an official public office. The attribute of a critic is conferred, potentially, on any person, regardless of sex, social position, or religious worldview. Historically, this means that within the existing estate-based social system of the eighteenth century, a sphere was constituted to which all persons had access, while at the same time they remained bound by the restrictions and regulations of their social environment.

Civil society occurs within designated, bounded social spheres and provides "spaces of interaction" (Koselleck) in which sociability can take place. In these spaces of interaction a specific form of face-to-face communication arises. Here society determines—ideally for all, but in fact for the few—that the restrictive social conditions of daily life are suspended. In their absence individuals interact with no prescribed or imposed purpose. Bourgeois sociability is based on this tension between the equality gained within these spheres of interaction and the continued inequality in the outside world. This tension gives rise to the impetus and promise of bourgeois self-improvement. The arenas of sociability complement the division and regulation of individual roles required for society to function.

Civil society is based not only on the sociability within spheres of interaction. It also links these spheres and enables them to communicate. The linking of disparate spheres of interaction takes place both in direct exchanges between people and also through institutions that make interaction possible. Both aspects, sociability as face-to-face communication and as mediated forms of networking, are required for the functioning of the public sphere in civil society.

One should not underestimate the role of the media in the exercise of sociability in the eighteenth century. Letters, printed writings, newspapers were indispensable for sociability. They created an intellectual horizon that stretched far beyond the daily world and made possible the first public world of readers in which the freedom to criticize could flourish. Similarly, one should not underestimate the fundamental significance of interpersonal communication in the personal sphere within the mass-media world of the twentieth century. Both are crucial for civil society.

The public sphere thrives in social arenas that are structured to promote sociability and connected by forms of media. Within these distinct spaces, individuals conduct themselves according to a functional division of roles. In the arena of sociability, the object criticized and the mode of rational criticism must be free of constraints. No restrictions can exist other than that the actors satisfy the requirements of their roles.

One can distinguish in this way the public sphere in civil society from similar forms of public conduct in premodern times. There were premodern forms of the "representative public sphere" where individuals decided the rules of civic conduct. There were also spheres dedicated solely to the enjoyment of public life; indeed, public life in the Middle Ages encompassed more areas of daily life than it does today. During the Middle Ages, individuals met at public gatherings and communicated as equals; for an example one need only refer to village communes. In these diverse forms of community the form of the public sphere did more than merely recreate the representational courtly model. Three elements distinguish the modern public sphere and bring it into an effective relationship with the rise of bourgeois society. First, the principle that criticism could be voiced on all issues; second, the functional division of roles; third, the growing significance of mediating institutions. (For example, the itinerant preacher no longer communicated the news; information was transmitted in writing.)

Sociability, the public sphere, and civil society do not stand one after the other in a tight causal relationship throughout European history, however. Eighteenth-century thought considered the opposite of rational conduct, "asocial sociability" (Kant), an important, complementary expression of the human craving for individualization. Forms of sociability also pervaded premodern societies, existing throughout the lower social strata to the same degree as in the middle and higher social strata. Pubs in market squares, restaurants, folk festivals, folk theaters, and religious festivals and celebrations offered a variety of options as diverse as the sociability at the courts. The spectrum of social forms has changed, but sociability as face-to-face communication has lost none of its importance. The public sphere in its more narrow sense as a political public space, however, holds a unique position in the development of modern civil society. In this sphere, the "lawmakers," that is, people making decisions for those who cannot directly participate, can address one another (Dewey).

The outward forms of the bases of civil society have been historically variable. Crucial moments in the history of such interaction would include the spread of the movable-type printing press in the fifteenth and sixteenth centuries; the explosion of a reading public, the emergence of salons, academies, lodges, public gathering places, and so on in the seventeenth and eighteenth centuries; the transformation of media in the nineteenth century with the spread of daily newspapers that gradually pushed the censors aside. The rise of the commercialized press and sensational journalism hindered direct political interference in the media. In the United States and France such mass journalism spread in two waves, in the 1830s and again from the 1860s to the 1880s; in Russia and Germany it made its appearance in the final third of the nineteenth century. Print mass media focused on the novelty value of a news item rather than on an ideology. This tendency permitted the rise of an economically independent media market; at the same time, this initiated a dangerous process in which the individual reader was no longer an active, rational participant but a passive consumer of information conveyed through the marketplace. Many describe this as a decline, but civil society has always developed mechanisms to foster the independent political decision making of individual citizens, even under conditions dominated by the marketplace. In the twentieth century came the rapid spread of new media forms such as film, radio, television, and the Internet—all accompanied by intense public discussion about the dangers and consequences these would have for the political functioning of civil society.

Two examples, coffeehouses and reading societies, can be sketched briefly to illustrate how sociability and the journalistic public sphere were linked. The English coffeehouse emerged in Europe as the first institution that promoted the public exercise of reason. Late-twentieth-century research has supported and also modified Habermas's thesis on this phenomenon. From the mid-1660s coffeehouses spread not only in London (where there were already more than eighty in 1663) but also in many English, Scottish, and Irish towns; their triumphant march could barely be halted by a temporary prohibition against them in 1675. Not only men but also women, and not only members of the urban upper classes were among the rising number of visitors. Patrons discussed national and international events (what became known as coffeehouse politics) as well as local issues. Behind this phenomenon were rising beer prices, which made the coffeehouse a money-saving alternative to the pub and a popular place for the circulation of news. It competed with traditional social venues such as cockfights, lawn-bowling lanes, and "church-a les." As a drink, coffee not only was less expensive than beer but also symbolized the advance of rationality and the sober calculation of self-supporting people, where alcoholic drinks would be pushed aside.

The reading societies that arose in France and Germany in the second half of the eighteenth century contributed to public sociability and promoted the public sphere of journalism. Here members of the middle classes met to read (newspapers, reference works, and books were too expensive for everyone to buy for themselves), and this created spaces in which people could converse about issues of general interest outside their narrow professional interests or family ties. Reading societies became classic arenas for enlightened reasoning. They also allowed the possibility for entertainment, such as smoking, billiards, and card games, which increased their attractiveness.

Other forms of association were the academies and learned societies, while Masonic lodges served as middle-class forms of association par excellence. The principle of free association quickly proved very attractive to many different social groups, greatly contributing to the success of civil society. It was even attractive and useful to those who sought to oppose it. For instance, freedom of association benefited emerging free-market societies, and opponents of the free market in a short time banded together in associations designed to curtail its effects. All modern organizations and political parties since the nineteenth century grew from these roots.

The extent to which such associations defined public life can distinguish individual societies. They dominated public life in countries where state institutions were weak, such as England, Switzerland, the United States, and also the Netherlands and Scandinavia. In countries with a strong statist tradition such as France, Prussia, and especially Russia, they competed with the hierarchical structures of state authority. In Russia up to 1917 middle-class associational life could operate only in large cities. This was also one reason why in Russia no "bourgeois" social order could succeed. For a long time in southern Europe patriarchal clientele relationships and kinship networks were more significant than anything else.

Critics of Habermas argue that a single (middle class) public sphere never existed, only various sectional public spheres that competed with one another. In a historical perspective, there is no question that numerous communications networks developed in Europe. However, these various sectional public spheres were politically successful within the evolving national civil society only if they adopted its structural organization as their model. Just as political opponents of free association quickly adopted it as their organizational principle, public associations that resisted the free market served as the political decision makers that helped integrate into society the very free-market relations they sought to oppose. This in no way excluded differentiations between competing publics, but the many communication networks were always linked to one another. In this respect, the Internet is only the latest example of this type of interaction that provides all individuals with a potential connection as individuals to one another.

SOCIAL STRUCTURES OF THE BOURGEOIS MIDDLE STRATA

One cannot understand civil society without understanding the extensive social and economic transformation that seized European societies from the end of the eighteenth century. With literacy, secularization, industrialization, and urbanization, among other processes, came new professional groups and social strata based on education and property that increasingly eroded the traditional order based on birthright. Included in the new order were the entrepreneur and the salaried employee, the manager and the rentier, the lawyer and the engineer, the doctor and the teacher. This does not mean that in the European Middle Ages and in the early modern era there was no social and geographic mobility. Yet the bases for the new bourgeois social order were different: they were rooted far more firmly in individual attainment of property and educational credentials rather than in an estate-prescribed social position. It depended less on estate-based rank and lifestyle than on class condition. Place in the market economy determined social stratification in middle-class society. Late-twentieth-century studies have hotly debated the extent to which different social groups—the bourgeoisie (the economic middle class), the old urban citizenry, and the professions or the university educated (the "free professions")—formed this class. Are government officials, pastors, and priests included as well as lower-wage employees and handworkers? It is disputable whether one can designate heterogeneous occupational groups with a collective singular noun, such as "bourgeoisie" or "middle class." For this definition it is of central importance to establish its outer limits vis-à-vis the lower strata (peasants and manual laborers) as well as against the aristocracy, although it includes the notion of mobility for all and embraces the integration process (of becoming part of the bourgeoisie). Moreover, as a rule the demarcation from the lower classes was much stricter than from the upper classes. In Germany, though, the threshold into aristocracy was always higher than in England or France. In Russia from the early eighteenth century the Table of Ranks of Peter I (1672–1725) allowed the possibility of rising into the personal or hereditary nobility, and the non-Russian elites (the Cossacks elders of the Ukraine, the Polish aristocracy, the Baltic German barons, and so

on) were also incorporated into the imperial aristocracy in the eighteenth and nineteenth centuries. As it did in other European countries, the aristocracy in Russia up to the twentieth century shielded itself from the lower classes.

However, even when by demarcating the boundary with the aristocracy and the lower classes a distinctive social profile of a middle social stratum is produced, it still displays an important degree of inner heterogeneity. While in Germany the traditional corporate urban citizenry still had great significance in the late eighteenth and nineteenth centuries, in England, where highly skilled master craftsmen had never played a comparable role, the importance of this old urban citizenry had long vanished.

From various social subgroups a special petite bourgeoisie emerged at the end of the nineteenth century in many European societies. Out of the old middle stratum, self-employed master craftsmen, small businessmen, and shopkeepers, a quickly growing throng of salaried employees and officials completed the new middle stratum. Those with university educations (the free professions) are another subgroup that developed its own diverse traditions and social positions in all the European countries. At the end of the nineteenth century in France one segment began to establish a separate social identity as "intellectuals" critical of the existing social order. But in Germany at least to the end of the nineteenth century the majority of the educated middle class understood themselves to be members of the bourgeoisie and sought employment in civil service. In Italy the university educated, especially lawyers, referred to themselves from 1875 as *borghese* and *ceto medio* (middle class), terms which had formerly served to describe the medieval and early modern middle class. In the twentieth century the university-educated in Italy first differentiated themselves as *borghesia umanistica,* and the term *borghese* increasingly referred to an economically defined social class composed of industrialists, businessmen, and bankers. In Italy and Germany the middle class long had a strong connection to the state and only gradually emerged more self-conscious and independent. In Russia a segment of those with a higher education considered themselves the *intelligentsia* and obtained their own social identity through their criticism of the aristocracy, the merchantry, and especially the autocratic political order. But in the Russian Empire well into the nineteenth century only civil service offered a means of subsistence. The rapid growth of the free professions, the limited possibilities of making a living by offering one's services on the free market, and the barriers to mobility in civil service led in Germany and Russia to increasing fragmentation and social isolation from the end of the nineteenth century. These also encouraged the political radicalization of a segment of university-educated intellectuals who could no longer be integrated into society.

The question of the economic, social, and cultural homogeneity of the "middle classes" remains one of the more difficult subjects for historical analysis. Some scholars study the specific forms of association and community in order to discover the networking and overlapping of social milieus that were once separate. Over time it has become clear that the analysis of these middle strata has for a long time been done too much from the perspective of a marxist-influenced view of class conflict. Studies have shown the crucial importance of the merchant strata in all Western societies well into the nineteenth century. The property owners, the overwhelming numbers of economically independent actors, clearly dominated the nineteenth century and were collectively the characteristic social type for the structure of the middle classes. The fundamental social roots of all civil societies—with the exception of Russia up to the beginning of the twentieth century—go back to the traditional figure of the property owner.

The common moral and social value system of the middle strata lay in the notion of ownership. Yet this included no common *political* value system for a class that had been described as taking political action in earlier times in pursuit of "possessive individualism." By the end of the nineteenth century the link between this social type and any distinct political value system disappeared. With this the far-reaching transformation of civil society took place. The increasing heterogeneity within the middle classes, which were the core of civil society, dissolved any close, direct link between political participation and economic status. Though many contemporaries at the time perceived this as a crisis, the societal form of civil society proved flexible enough to carry out this new social openness in a creative way.

In the twentieth century on the one hand the social-welfare state guaranteed a minimum economic status for its citizens (though there were and are huge differences between individual countries). On the other hand the spectrum of institutions and bureaucratic organizations was differentiated to such an extent that both participation and protest produced numerous possible reactions. It almost seems that the principal problem facing modern civil society after the twentieth century is no longer the social question but how to mobilize individual citizens into living politically engaged lives. Traditionally, engagement was not a problem because engagement—the role of the "lawmaker"—was for the propertied class inextricably

wedded to the pursuit of their self-interest. The survival of civil society was based on dissolving this traditional bond between economic and political interest. Yet contemporary civil societies must reclaim individual citizens, whom no direct economic interest mobilizes into political action, for involvement in the public sphere. Optimists like Albert O. Hirschman trust that this phenomenon merely reflects the inevitable swing between the pursuit of private interests and the active shaping of public life. Insofar as civil society has lost its direct link to social support groups since the end of the nineteenth century, greater room has been created to find different political answers to social problems. This is the basis for the continuing stability and attractiveness of civil society as a societal model.

CULTURAL VALUES, BOURGEOIS IDENTITY, AND CIVIC CONSCIOUSNESS

One of the founders of modern sociology, Max Weber (1864–1920), claimed that self-interest guides the actions of people, but ideas function as the switchmen that determine the rails on which the dynamic of self-interested action moves. Civil society always was and is based on a system of values, practices, and relational models. According to the anthropologist Clifford Geertz, its citizens are said to be "tangled in self-spun webs of meaning." Civil society requires such a system of rules, or "ideal types" of values and behavior models, that cultivate a specific "quality" in the character of the citizen and shape a "civil" way of life. This "bourgeois identity" always formulated a kind of ideal or utopian design for its conduct in the world. An image of utopia determined the direction in which the individual first develops into a citizen and defined the vision according to which any society will change into a civil society.

Every civil society requires an ethic of civic consciousness, a system of ideal types, of values and practices that mediate between the various ways of living in the world. After religion had lost its comprehensive role of explaining the world and structuring life, competing spheres of values and ways of living existed side by side in a tense relation. Such cultural symbol systems served as "switchmen"; their institutionalization into actual ways of conducting one's life (religion, relationships, economy, politics, law, art, love/sex, science, nature) has the force to structure in advance the direction in which motivations lead human conduct. Individuals carry out the "civic" direction of their lives along the idealized path of a given symbol system guided by the self-interested dynamic of their specific way of life. Thus there is only an apparent conflict between society and the individual. The urgent struggle between liberalism and communitarianism could therefore probably be only settled violently, because it has reduced the age-old interlocking of ideas and interests into an imaginary contradiction. From the outlook of eighteenth- and nineteenth-century liberal theorists of civil society, this opposition still appeared as an impermissible curtailment of individual freedom.

Since its beginnings, the cultural system that regulates civil society has undergone many transformations. Following industrialization and urbanization, the web of signification, in which and with which people interpreted their experiences and directed their actions, became dysfunctional. The decades around 1800 and around 1900 can both be understood as times of such radical change. Around 1800 "bourgeois identity" emerged as a cultural system that was adequate for a specific kind of social structure and social interaction and that interpreted societal experiences in an intelligible and tension-reducing way. From the 1890s the critique of cultured civilization, articulated by citizens and often indebted to their civic ideas, gave expression to the widening gap and growing tension between the mechanisms of social interaction and the systems that endowed them with meaning. The third fundamental period of radical change within civil society began in the 1960s, with the sweeping transformation of the values of western societies. Criticized by the orthodox of the left and right as destroying values and promoting social erosion, this transformation can also be understood as a process in which civil society's cultural system of rules provided new "switchmen" for human conduct.

This radical change caused many to diagnose a critical juncture in the history of civil society. Habermas, for example, perceived a "structural transformation of the public sphere" but later changed his diagnosis. He originally assumed a collapse of the public sphere and the disappearance of critical journalism. The more the public sphere extends outward, and with it the values of civil society, the more it loses its primary political function: to place all public events under the control of a critical public. In mass democracy and under the influence of mass media, critical public opinion turns into conformity and the cultivated, rational public turns into a cultural consumer. Habermas revised this thesis in 1990 after the transformation of values since the 1960s and the beginning of the collapse of communism in the Eastern European states. Yet others have continued with dire predictions. The idea that the independent individual—

the critical citizen—would not survive in the public sphere of the mass media, as well as the argument that the public sphere as a genuine space of civil society would succumb to a tyranny of the private sphere, has found proponents (Sennett). De Tocqueville's insight, developed in his book on America, again proves valid: civil society delivers itself from danger with the same principles that threaten its continuation. However, the German example in the twentieth century indicates that civil society's capacity for self-preservation is imperiled under certain conditions. The structural transformation of the public sphere has not yet proven to be such a threat.

Looking back on the twentieth century, one can understand the astonishing vitality of civil society today in the following way. Late-nineteenth-century critics perceived a crisis in the no longer reconcilable tension between the value system (with its standards of conduct always oriented to the property owner) and the prevailing logic of business. One cannot understand the political crises and the movements opposing civil society of the twentieth century without understanding these insecurities. The ongoing transformation of values at the beginning of the twenty-first century will establish a new system of values that will prescribe new "switchmen" for different forms of behavior.

OPEN QUESTIONS

Those who emphasize the multifaceted and non-utopian character of civil society recognize the variety of cultural traditions and influences that have contributed to its character. At the same time elements such as the social contract, individual human rights, and political freedoms are core concepts of the European tradition. How civil societies in the twentieth century in the middle of Europe could break apart despite participating in this tradition will be the focus of future research. These studies will also seek to determine the prerequisites for a lasting civil society. A question of particular urgency will be how societies on Europe's periphery or outside Europe can build a civil society. These societies have already to some extent been in continuous contact with Europe. Often, however, neither the elites nor the tradition-bound majorities of these countries permit an open discussion of this question. This resistance hinders consensus building on subjects such as how to retain and change particular traditions and how to integrate "new" elements of civic, political culture so that the formation of a civil society is not perceived as a hegemonic takeover. The questions of modern nation building and middle-class society, of individuals and associations, and of the civic public sphere and civic consciousness indicate in any case that a complex image of humanity and a system of values form the basis of civil society. It does not merely concern a liberal economic system and the making of a middle social stratum. In the end, civil society's potential rests in its ever-changing character over the course of the nineteenth and twentieth centuries, especially its capacity to reform itself through open discussion about its own principles and procedural techniques, including the transformation of its own mechanisms of exclusion with regard to women, the lower classes, other nationalities, religions, and races. From here there are many possibilities for further research. In the center of it all are the elements of middle-class society and their relationships to one another throughout historical change: the public and freely accessible use of reason, spheres of direct social interaction, and mediated interaction. Prospective research will focus less on classic social history than on its connection with cultural, political, and economic history. There is less potential for research within a narrow national-historical perspective than in a comparative perspective that encompasses both European and non-European societies.

Translated from German by Mark Georgiev

See also **Middle Classes; New Social Movements; Professionals and Professionalization** *(volume 3);* **Reading** *(volume 5); and other articles in this section.*

BIBLIOGRAPHY

General

Calhoun, Craig, ed. *Habermas and the Public Sphere.* Cambridge, Mass., 1992.

Cohen, Jean L., and Andrew Arato. *Civil Society and Political Theory.* Cambridge, Mass., 1992.

Geertz, Clifford. *Interpretations of Culture: Selected Essays.* New York, 1973.

Gellner, Ernest. *Conditions of Liberty: Civil Society and Its Rivals.* London, 1994.

Goodman, Dena. "Public Sphere and Private Life: Toward a Synthesis of Current Historiographical Approaches to the Old Regime" *History & Theory* 31 (1992):1–20.

Habermas, Jürgen. *The Structural Transformation of the Public Sphere: An Inquiry into a Category of Bourgeois Society.* Translated by Thomas Burger with the assistance of Frederick Lawrence. Cambridge, Mass., 1989.

Hirschman, Albert O. *Shifting Involvements: Private Interest and Public Action.* Princeton, N.J., 1982.

Inglehart, Ronald. *The Silent Revolution: Changing Values and Political Styles among Western Publics.* Princeton, N.J., 1977.

Keane, John, ed. *Civil Society and the State: New European Perspectives.* London, 1988.

Koselleck, Reinhart. *Critique and Crisis: Enlightenment and the Pathogenesis of Modern Society.* Oxford and New York, 1988.

Macpherson, C. B. *The Political Theory of Possessive Individualism: From Hobbes to Locke.* Oxford, 1962.

Michalski, Krzysztof, ed. *Europa und die Civil Society: Castelgandolfo-Gespräche.* Stuttgart, Germany, 1991.

Sennett, Richard. *The Fall of Public Man.* New York, 1977.

Weintraub, Jeff, and Krishnan Kumar, eds. *Public and Private in Thought and Practice: Perspectives on a Grand Dichotomy.* Chicago, 1997.

On Individual European Societies

Bácskai, Vera, ed. *Bürgertum und bürgerliche Entwicklung in Mittel- und Osteuropa.* 2 vols. Budapest, Hungary, 1986.

Banti, Alberto M. *Terra e denaro: Una borghesia padana dell'Ottocento*. Venice, 1989.

Clowes, Edith W., Samuel D. Kassow, and James L. West, eds. *Between Tsar and People: Educated Society and the Quest for Public Identity in Late Imperial Russia*. Princeton, N.J., 1991.

Daumard, Adeline. *Les bourgeois et la bourgeoisie en France depuis 1815*. Paris, 1987.

Davidoff, Leonore, and Catherine Hall. *Family Fortunes: Men and Women of the English Middle Class, 1780–1850*. Chicago, 1987.

François, Etienne, ed. *Sociabilité et société bourgeoise en France, en Allemagne et en Suisse, 1750–1850: Geselligkeit, Vereinswesen und bürgerliche Gesellschaft in Frankreich, Deutschland und der Schweiz, 1750–1850*. Paris, 1986.

Frykman, Jonas, and Orvar Löfgren. *Culture Builders: A Historical Anthropology of Middle-Class Life*. Translated by Alan Crozier. New Brunswick, N.J., 1987.

Goodman, Dena. *The Republic of Letters: A Cultural History of the French Enlightenment*. Ithaca, N.Y., 1994.

Hall, Catherine. *White, Male, and Middle-Class: Explorations in Feminism and History*. Cambridge, U.K., 1992.

Hausmann, Guido. *Universität und städtische Gesellschaft in Odessa, 1865–1917: Soziale und nationale Selbstorganisation an der Peripherie des Zarenreiches*. Stuttgart, Germany, 1998.

Hettling, Manfred. *Politische Bürgerlichkeit. Der Bürger zwischen Individualität und Vergesellschaftung in Deutschland und der Schweiz von 1860 bis 1918*. Göttingen, Germany, 1999.

Hull, Isabel V. *Sexuality, State, and Civil Society in Germany, 1700–1815*. Ithaca, N.Y., 1996.

Im Hof, Ulrich. *Das gesellige Jahrhundert: Gesellschaft und Gesellschaften im Zeitalter der Aufklärung*. Munich, 1982.

Kaplan, Marion. *The Making of the Jewish Middle Class: Women, Family, and Identity in Imperial Germany*. Oxford, 1991.

Kocka, Jürgen, and Allen Mitchell, eds. *Bourgeois Society in Nineteenth-Century Europe*. Oxford, 1993.

Landes, Joan B. *Women and the Public Sphere in the Age of the French Revolution*. Ithaca, N.Y., 1988.

Lindenmeyr, Adele. *Poverty Is Not a Vice: Charity, Society, and the State in Imperial Russia*. Princeton, N.J., 1996.

Pilbeam, P. M. *The Middle Classes in Europe, 1789–1914: France, Germany, Italy, and Russia*. Chicago, 1990.

Price, Roger. *A Social History of Nineteenth-Century France*. London, 1987.

Rieber, Alfred J. *Merchants and Entrepreneurs in Imperial Russia*. Chapel Hill, N.C., 1982.

Ringer, Fritz K. *Education and Society in Modern Europe, 1815–1960*. Bloomington, Ind., 1979.

Schorske, Carl E. *Fin-de-siècle Vienna: Politics and Culture*. New York, 1981.

Siegrist, Hannes, ed. *Bürgerliche Berufe. Zur Sozialgeschichte der freien und akademischen Berufe im internationalen Vergleich*. Göttingen, Germany, 1988.

Wehler, Hans-Ulrich. *Deutsche Gesellschaftsgeschichte*. Vols. 1–3. Munich. 1987, 1995.

The authors wish to express their thanks to the Fritz Thyssen Foundation for its support of a conference comparing civil society in east and west Europe.

NATIONALISM

Caroline Ford

Nationalism has been one of the most powerful forces shaping modern political life in Europe since at least the eighteenth century. It is therefore somewhat ironical that, unlike liberalism or socialism—the two other great "isms" of modern times—there has been a surprising lack of consensus regarding its definition, origins, and consequences. Insisting on nationalism's modernity, most historians from the nineteenth century onward have argued that nationalism is an ideology consisting of a rather inchoate body of ideas and that these ideas inform nationalism as a political and social movement affirming the sovereignty and integrity of discrete nation-states. That ideology was predicated, first, on the notion that the world is divided into nations, each with its own characteristics and destiny. Second, it assumes that the nation is the source of all political and social power. With the "cultural turn" in historical studies, nationalism has also come to be defined as a form of identification, as a collective consciousness, and as a discourse drawing on complex symbolic systems. Social historians have begun to emphasize the relationship between the development of national identities and other forms of collective identification, including class and gender.

The sheer diversity and variety of nationalist movements and ideologies in Europe during the past few centuries make it extremely difficult to classify nationalism politically—as a right- or left-wing phenomenon—over time or to establish its constituent elements in religion, culture, consent, or language. Nationalism assumed a variety of different territorial, ethnic, and cultural forms, and these forms frequently overlapped. Indeed, nationalism as a form of consciousness, as a body of ideas, and as a political movement is nebulous and protean, and it is perhaps in these very qualities that its power resides. How did nationalism come into being in Europe and how has it changed as a political movement between the eighteenth century and the present? Why has it so tenaciously endured, even as the 1992 Treaty of Maastricht and the promise of a new Europe without national frontiers seemed to herald its demise? An-

swers to these questions have been many and varied. How these questions have been answered (and the study of nationalism more generally) are in large part a reflection of the history of European nationalism itself.

THE EMERGENCE OF NATIONALISM: THE CONTEXT

Nationalism and the modern nation-state, as they emerged in Europe, were only thinkable and possible toward the end of the eighteenth century, as hierarchical societies predicated on vertical ties between the ruler and the ruled gave way to more egalitarian societies that were based on horizontal ties between "citizens." Until the end of the eighteenth century, most states in Europe were dynastic and predicated on a corporate social order based on privilege. European society was divided into three orders, consisting of those who fought, those who prayed, and those who worked, and each of these orders was accorded, or not accorded, as the case may have been, elaborate privileges (as members of a corporate body, rather than as individuals) by the monarch. This was a political society of subjects rather than citizens who had common legal rights and duties.

The abolition during the French Revolution (1789) of titles of nobility and of all special privileges attached to corporate bodies laid the groundwork for a society of citizens. This society resulted in a new relationship between the constituent members of a new political order, and indeed in the creation of the modern notion of citizenship, which instantly established a political world based on horizontal rather than vertical ties. While the process by which this society came into being in the monarchical states of Europe was uneven, it was more or less complete by the end of the nineteenth century and provided the structural underpinnings for the development of nationalism in Europe in the nineteenth and twentieth centuries.

Napoleonic Republic. Italian delegates meeting at Lyon, France, in 1802 to proclaim an Italian republic under French tutelage. The delegates elected Napoleon Bonaparte president of the republic. Painting by Nicholas André Monsiau (1754–1837). CHÂTEAU DE VERSAILLES, FRANCE/THE BRIDGEMAN ART LIBRARY

The emergence of nationalism at the end of the eighteenth century was also a by-product of the gradual secularization of European society and political institutions. The decline of the power of universal religious institutions—most notably the Roman Catholic Church—and of the loyalties they inspired both undermined the legitimacy of rule by divine right on the part of Catholic monarchs and opened avenues for other forms of spiritual and political allegiance. From the end of the seventeenth century, new conceptions of time and space, propagated during the scientific revolution, further challenged the certainties of religion and spawned new questions regarding relationships between different geographic areas and peoples.

Finally, the emergence and development of nationalism in the eighteenth century coincided with the spread of literacy and print capitalism, which served to integrate disparate populations through the medium of a common language and culture. The rise in levels of literacy, the spread of national educational initiatives, and the growing focus, particularly among literary elites, on language as a source of national cohesion served as integrative forces.

The development of nationalism in Europe occurred in a series of stages, beginning in the decades preceding the French Revolution, the wars of "liberation," and Napoleonic expansion, which served as a political catalyst for nationalist movements in areas of Europe that had largely been immune from nation-

alism's appeals. This first phase of European nationalism spanned a period from the 1760s to 1848. The second stage of European nationalism, which followed the defeat of the revolutions of 1848, coincided with German and Italian unification, the advent of mass politics, and the new imperialism of the late nineteenth century. World War I inaugurated a third stage in the development of nationalism in the twentieth century, as anticolonial movements in Europe's colonial empires increasingly began to assume a nationalist form, and as the nation-state became the dominant form of political organization in the world.

THE DEVELOPMENT OF NATIONALISM AND ITS HISTORY: STAGE 1, 1789–1848

Although some scholars (especially Benedict Anderson in *Imagined Communities*) have argued that nationalism as a political phenomenon appeared first in the New World among Anglo settlers transplanted from their original homeland or among creoles, both of whom increasingly came to resent the culture of the metropole, it was firmly implanted in the Old World by the end of the eighteenth century. During its first phase, nationalism as a political and social movement was embraced by the middle classes and by literate elites and was largely an affair of the liberal left in Europe as a whole. Literate elites in western and central Europe set out to define the nation and to promote the national cause through the celebration of language and sometimes of religion or a shared historical past. In a fragmented central Europe, writers such as Johann Gottfried von Herder (1744–1803) focused on the importance of the German language in defining nationality, and indeed, language became the key element in defining national community. Jean-Jacques Rousseau's (1712–1778) writings on Corsica and Poland stressed the ways in which language and culture defined a nation's individual character, suggesting that it was only through their preservation and recovery that the nation could be maintained over time.

Governments early on also recognized the importance of linguistic uniformity for the modern nation-state. For a brief time, both at the end of the eighteenth century and then again at the end of the nineteenth, the French state, for example, made war on regional languages and dialects and attempted to impose a standardized French on its citizens through varying administrative mechanisms and public education. This was part of a larger universal "civilizing mission" unleashed by the French state, but it served, above all, the national cause. Indeed, language increasingly came to occupy a place in international territorial conflicts between states. This was manifested in disputes between Danes and Germans in Schleswig-Holstein in the 1860s.

During the course of the nineteenth century, language became increasingly important to definitions of nationality and played an important role in fostering national cohesion for several reasons. First, even in territorial states possessing a multiplicity of languages and dialects, the state's official sponsorship of a national language gave it a permanence and a sense of the eternal that it would not otherwise have acquired. This official language had the advantage, moreover, of being propagated through public education initiatives undertaken by most European states toward the end of the nineteenth century.

Jules Michelet (1798–1874) and Joseph-Ernest Renan (1823–1892) argued against the notion that language, religion, race, ethnicity, or geography were essential defining features of nationality, even as they stressed the importance of the nation as a "spiritual principle." They emphasized the binding power and importance of history or historical forgetting. More than any writer in the first half of the nineteenth century, Michelet, the historian, was instrumental in emphasizing the unconscious historical processes shaping nation formation. Indeed, Michelet indicated ways in which the French, who may not have conceived of themselves as such until the French Revolution, worked

for many centuries to construct a cultural and physical fabric that came to define France in tangible terms. He suggested that the French and the French nation surely existed for centuries, even if the nation as a political unit did not come into being until the French Revolution. A shared history, however, contributed to an acceptance of a common territory or homeland by the time of the French Revolution. And that territory was comprised of citizens sharing a common historical memory. The early-nineteenth-century valorization of the *Volk* and of popular culture in western Europe was part of a larger attempt among intellectual elites to recover (or "invent") a common cultural and national past, and they sought to bring that past to a growing reading public. Some of this literary and historical work, which was pressed into the service of defining the nation, led to it being defined in terms of a kind of historical essentialism. This historicism, dedicated to uncovering a prenationalist past, allowed literary elites and political leaders to invoke an "eternal" France or Germany, whose "natural" national traits were endowed by history, language, and geography. As a certain kind of historical essentialism came to define national identities and to inform nationalist movements in the first half of the nineteenth century, the construction of ethnic identities along similar lines was not far away.

Popular protonationalism. As governments and literary elites debated the constituent elements of nationhood in the old states of Europe, including Britain and France, and in central Europe and the Italian Peninsula, where unified nation-states did not exist before the latter half of the nineteenth century, popular forms of protonationalism emerged. Much of this popular protonationalist sentiment was born, however, from armed conflict or war, rather than from a romantic attachment to language or a common historic past. Indeed war has been pivotal to the development of nationalism since the eighteenth century. The role of war in forging national sentiment became evident in the Battle of Valmy of 1792, when a poorly equipped French army faced a formidably trained Prussian force and resisted it behind the battle cry, "Vive la Nation!" This prompted Johann Wolfgang von Goethe (1749–1832) to proclaim that the battle marked a new epoch in human history. During the French Revolution, the *levée en masse* (mass levy of troops) of 1792, proclaimed in the name of the *patrie en danger* (the fatherland endangered), created Europe's first citizen army and justified itself in the name of a nation of citizens sharing common interests and concerns. The *levée en masse* drew on the experience of the Seven Years' War (1756–1763) and the dynastic rivalries be-

Bulgaria Personified. *Bulgarian Freedom,* anonymous print, c. 1877–1878. St. Cyril and St. Methodius National Library, Sofia, Bulgaria

tween European states in the eighteenth century, particularly those between Britain and France. Thus, long before the nation-state in its modern form came into being, wars were beginning to be fought in its name, in the name of a patriotism that would soon find its expression in nationalism. Linda Colley's important work on the impact of the French revolutionary wars on the development of British nationalism suggests as much, as she explores the decisive role played by a series of eighteenth-century wars in fostering British patriotism: the War of the Spanish Succession (1701–1714), the War of the Austrian Succession (1740–1748), and the French revolutionary and Napoleonic wars (1792–1802 and 1803–1815). Prussia's defeat in the Battle of Jena in 1806 was a testament to the tenacious power of the national idea in a French army of citizens, rather than subjects.

War and revolution mobilized large numbers of people at home, who rallied to a domestic cause. Even though many of those who fought in the great wars of the eighteenth century were not yet citizens, countless numbers justified their participation in patriotic terms. This popular protonationalist sentiment was soon translated into more or less successful wars of

liberation across the continent and led to the transformation of the map of Europe at the Congress of Vienna (1815). Moreover, this settlement was soon followed by a war of liberation against Ottoman rule, which led to the creation of a new kingdom of Greece in 1829. Belgium became an independent nation-state after its 1830 revolt, while Poland, an unsuccessful aspirant to national sovereignty, revolted in the same year, suffering defeat in the name of national self-determination.

From the French Revolution to 1848 nationalism tended to be linked to liberal, even democratic, left-wing movements, and culminated in the "national" revolutions of 1848 in central Europe and in the Italian Peninsula. In both regions nationalism was primarily a movement of liberal and republican intellectuals, who defined themselves against and opposed political organizations predicated on dynastic ties. Those who supported national unity in the Frankfurt parliament and in the Italian Peninsula failed to press their demands because of their lack of popular support, internal divisions, and, in the case of Italy, foreign intervention. German and Italian unification had to wait more than a decade after their initial failure.

THE DEVELOPMENT OF NATIONALISM AND ITS HISTORY: STAGE 2, 1848–1914

Nationalism as a movement and as an ideology changed decisively in Europe as a result of the revolution of 1848. The debacle of the revolutions of 1848 in central Europe and the Italian Peninsula indicated that if these two areas of Europe were to be unified, that process would (and did) come about largely through "blood and iron." The failure of that revolution and the realization among political elites, even those who supported monarchism, that nationalism could be harnessed for particular political purposes had a profound impact on its future trajectory. It was war and the stratagems of Prussia's chief minister, Otto von Bismarck (1815–1898), that led to the unification of Germany in 1871, and it was the political aspirations of Camillo Benso, conte di Cavour (1810–1861) and Piedmont's rivalry with the Habsburgs that led to the unification of Italy by 1861. Increasingly, nationalism was linked to the designs of conservative elites during the course of the nineteenth century. Nationalism gradually became a mass phenomenon and, paradoxically, one that was linked to right-wing and sometimes antinationalist causes. The war in Schleswig-Holstein and the Franco-Prussian War of 1871, both of which laid the groundwork for German unification, have often been seen as an expression of Prussian patriotism rather than of German nationalism, waged by Bismarck to ensure Prussian hegemony in central Europe.

Mass nationalism: "blood and soil." By the late 1880s nationalism assumed new forms in Europe. As a movement, it increasingly became a mass phenomenon and was less grounded in the French liberal tradition of consent and contract, or even of a common culture. Race, ethnicity, and language became more important in defining nationality. Of course, this new nationalist discourse was fueled by colonialism and the new imperialism and the literature it spawned regarding the world's races. Much of the national competition among European nation-states was played out in theaters of war on the fringes or beyond the borders of western Europe, particularly in north Africa and the Balkans.

As nationalism and its social constituency changed, so did its political associations. Having been associated with the revolutionary left wing since the French Revolution, by 1900 a new nationalism of blood and soil came to be associated with a bellicose and in some instances racist and anti-Semitic right wing all over Europe. The Dreyfus affair of 1898 in France and the formation of right-wing leagues in Germany contributed to a nationalistic rhetoric that was increasingly strident and xenophobic in nature. Changes in the character of European nationalism were both a reflection of changes in state strategies designed to mobilize their citizenries and a consequence of the democratization of the political process in many European states, with the advent of universal manhood suffrage. In short, a formerly elitist and monarchical right wing saw in nationalism a new source of cohesion and a means to attract a mass constituency.

The early historical work on European nationalism coincided with and reflected its late-nineteenth-century transformation. It resembled the racist, xenophobic, and imperialist rhetoric embodied in fin de siècle nationalism in evoking national traits and stereotypes. This literature was, however, counterbalanced by a serious assessment and critique of the national question by marxists of the Second International. To name a few of them, Karl Kautsky, Rosa Luxembourg, Otto Bauer, and V. I. Lenin devoted themselves to the problem.

World War I demonstrated the power of national identifications, as expressed, for example, in the initial massive working-class support for the war effort—in apparent contradiction with a self-proclaimed socialist ideology—in much of central and western Europe. The war revealed that the development of a national self-consciousness among different social groups did not necessarily occur at the cost of other forms of social consciousness, even if it could supersede them at particular historical moments. Indeed, popular adhesion to causes such as those of World War I or the Boer War attests to the spread of racial ideas and a new jingoist xenophobic nationalism in a number of European nation-states.

THE DEVELOPMENT OF NATIONALISM AND ITS HISTORY: STAGE 3, 1914–1980

It is no accident that World War I gave rise to the first serious and sustained comparative and historical inquiry into the origins and development of nationalism. This early work is primarily associated with Carlton Hayes and Hans Kohn. Hayes's *The Historical Evolution of Modern Nationalism* (New York, 1931) and Kohn's *The Idea of Nationalism: A Study in Its Origin and Background* (New York, 1944) were written in the aftermath of the creation of the League of Nations in 1919 and the breakup of the huge multicultural, multiethnic, and multilingual empires of central and eastern Europe—the Habsburg, Romanov, and Ottoman—and with the creation of wholly new nation-states in those regions. Indeed, many of the

Germany Personified. *Deutschland—August 1914,* painting by Friedrich August von Kaulbach (1850–1920). MUSEUM FÜR DEUTSCHE GESCHICHTE, BERLIN/AKG LONDON

movements dedicated to national liberation in the twenty-five years before World War I were directed against supranational and multinational empires. After World War I, nationalist movements tended to be directed against established national states in Europe. These separatist nationalist movements, which are still very much a part of the European landscape, drew on prewar definitions of nationality based on ethnicity and, in some cases, religion. The League of Nations eventually legitimized the modern nation-state as the only internationally recognized form of political organization in the world. Hayes and Kohn sought to explain how this came to be so, arguing that nationalism was indeed an eighteenth-century invention, despite the claims to a distant historical past among some nations.

Much of this critical interest in nationalism was short-lived, however, as nationalism became suspect as a result of its alliance with fascism, national socialism, and anti-Semitism in the 1930s and 1940s. Moreover, the emergence of a new cold war order following World War II, which led to the disappearance of the autonomy and independence of most of the new states created in eastern Europe in the aftermath of World War I; the rise of supranational organizations, such as the European Economic Community; and the ubiquity of international communism deflected attention away from the study of nationalism as a historical phenomenon. Indeed, it led to the conviction that nationalism represented merely a "stage" in the historical development of Europe, if not the world—a backward and uncivilized one at that—and that the nation-state would ultimately be replaced by other forms of political organization. This was a view taken by both liberals and marxists. Cosmopolitan liberals believed that nationalism was (simply) a stepping-stone to the creation of constitutional sovereign states comprised of citizens sharing common political and civil rights. Marxists regarded the phenomenon as an illusion, an atavism that was manipulated by elites for economic and political purposes. Neither could account for the persistence and pervasive power of nationalism defined in ethnic terms.

The post–World War II era also witnessed the emergence of new nationalist movements in Europe's colonies (or former colonies). During the war itself European and non-European resistance movements emerged in response to German and Japanese attempts to create empires. Nationalism also inspired anti-colonial liberation movements in Africa and Asia in the 1940s, 1950s, and 1960s.

Modernization theorists, writing in the 1950s in the aftermath of World War II, began to argue that nationalism and the formation of nation-states implied ineluctable processes of assimilation. Karl Deutsch's *Nationalism and Social Communication: An Inquiry into the Foundations of Nationality* (Cambridge, Mass., 1953) is a case in point. According to Deutsch, modern nation-states were built by political centers through a homogenizing process of cultural and institutional assimilation and acculturation. This process, achieved through the instruments of mass communication, railways, roads, public education, and conscription, allegedly resulted in the abandonment of traditional allegiances and identities and their replacement with those defined by the metropole. Consciously using the the concept of colonization, Eugen Weber in *Peasants into Frenchmen: The Modernization of Rural France, 1870–1914* (Stanford, Calif., 1976) has suggested that peasants became Frenchmen as they adopted the ideas, values, and culture of the metropole—Paris—and as these values came to replace those of the region and the village. Why would the far-flung populations wish it to be otherwise, John Stuart Mill (1806–1873) asked as early as the nineteenth century. He wrote that no one could imagine that it would be more beneficial to retain one's regional identity in France, for example, when one could acquire all the benefits of French citizenship.

For much of the 1950s and 1960s, nationalism did not receive sustained or concentrated attention from social historians of Europe. They embraced the study of class formation, social mobility, and social revolution with alacrity, writing the history of peoples who formerly "had no history." Much of this "history from the bottom up" either ignored, somewhat strangely, the development of nationalism or focused on the formation of the nation-state and its relationship to movements of social protest. Thus, the first generation of social history did not have much influence on the historical approaches to European nationalism.

Interest in European nationalisms revived slowly and then grew steadily in the late 1970s. The historical literature that emerged in this period challenged the evolutionary views of marxists and liberals, as well as the assumptions that underpinned interpretations of nationalism that were based on the concept of "modernization," for a variety of reasons. The sudden emergence of a number of "ethnic minority nationalist" movements in the very heart of Western Europe—in Scotland, Wales, Ireland, Brittany, Catalonia, the Basque region, and Corsica—made historians question the degree to which one could count on the eventual disappearance of nationalism, and they called into question the process of national integration described by Karl Deutsch and others. How could one account for the appearance of these new nationalisms in some of Europe's oldest nation states? Miroslav

Hroch's pathbreaking and early *Social Preconditions of National Revival in Europe* (Prague, 1968; Cambridge, U.K., 1985), an analysis of the rise of nationalisms in central and Eastern Europe, suggested new ways of thinking about nationalism. He emphasized the role of regional elites and the uneven economic development "within" states, arguing that local elites whose interests were threatened by larger markets and global forces often encouraged the spread of nationalist sentiment to protect those interests. On the basis of this hypothesis, Hroch argued that nationalist movements generally developed in three separate stages. First, nationalist movements assume an apolitical, folkloric character; second, they are taken up by literate elites wishing to inculcate the "national idea" and organize the masses; and third, nationalist movements then truly gain mass-based support. This stage analysis of nationalist movements has deeply shaped the historical literature on nationalism, building on the modernization theorists' "top down" approach that has reinforced much of the historical literature on nationalism since its inception.

DEVELOPMENTS IN NATIONALISM AND ITS HISTORY SINCE 1980

In the 1980s and 1990s historians began to ask new questions about the development of European nationalism and to abandon many of the assumptions that have informed its study since the early twentieth century. As was the case with previous developments, these challenges and questions have in part been shaped by the history of nationalism in Europe. This history includes the breakup of the former Soviet Union; the emergence of nationalist xenophobia in the former Soviet Union; the disintegration of Yugoslavia in the 1990s; the rise of nationalist movements in the Balkans; and the promise of European unity and integration. These developments have refocused scholarly attention on nationalism as a central subject of historical enquiry since the early 1980s, and they have influenced the kinds of questions historians have begun to ask.

Following World War I, President Woodrow Wilson of the United States declared in his famous "Fourteen Points" that the peoples of the former Austro-Hungarian Empire should be given the the freest opportunity for autonomous development. The appearance, disappearance, and reappearance of new nations in eastern Europe have become a fulcrum for the reconsideration of nationalism as a question in Europe as a whole. "Old" nationalisms, which appeared to have withered away, have ostensibly reemerged with

a vengeance. The post-Communist organization of political space in these regions has resulted in the proliferation of new "nations" defined largely in ethnic terms. The "identity politics" rampant in the former Yugoslavia, in Kosovo, Uzbekistan, Slovenia, Macedonia, and Azerbaijan unleashed new and horrible tragedies. To what extent are these nationalisms late-twentieth-century creations or old wine in new bottles? Is this the right historical question to ask? What can the answer to these questions tell us about nation formation more generally and how can these nations be integrated into the international community of nations? Campaigns of "ethnic cleansing" have been launched in a national cause, and language tests have been established, for example, to determine who is a real Ukrainian or Slovene. Religion, ethnicity, and language continue to be divisive and defining features of group claims to sovereignty, territory, and self-determination. Such pernicious and deadly developments have forced historians to reexamine the nature of national identifications and their ultimate consequences. Rogers Brubaker has deftly explored the existence of these nationalisms in this regard, and he has suggested that one must think about nationalism in these regions not in terms of resurgence or recession, using the prevailing literature on nationalism that has focused on the state and nation building, but rather on how nationalism was "reframed" in these areas.

The Flemish, Catalans, Lombards, and Scots have continued to reaffirm their local identities and seek a greater degree of autonomy in Belgium, Spain, Italy, and Britain, respectively, as well as a role in a new Europe. Indeed, as these new "ethnic minority" nationalisms have appeared, Western European politics have also been dominated by debates concerning immigration and the permeability of national borders in a new European Union. Large immigrant populations from former European colonies have flowed into Europe since the late 1960s, and many of these immigrants share little in terms of language, culture, or religion with the dominant cultures of Europe. As a result, Europeans have been forced to ask themselves difficult questions about the relationship between nationality and citizenship. On the one hand, "ethnic minority" nationalisms call for a closer relationship between ethnicity and nation; on the other, massive immigration challenges that relationship.

Citizenship, common people, and symbols. All these developments have resulted in a gradual shift away from historical approaches to nationalism that focus primarily on state formation and social-political elites to ones that resonate more with social historians, such as the exploration of "national consciousness,"

French Nationalism. In a patriotic image made after the Prussian victory over France in 1870, women in Alsatian costume repel a German soldier from French soil. France was forced to cede the provinces of Alsace and Lorraine to the German Empire in 1871; they were restored to France in 1919. ©COLLECTION VIOLLET

the "culture" of nationalism, the process of identity formation (and its limits), and the role of gender in shaping nationalist movements and nationalist discourse. Historians have begun to focus on a new set of questions: Why were individuals willing to fight and die for a community and for people whom they would never meet in their lifetimes? What is nationalism's emotional appeal? How and why are national passions aroused and in what contexts? Out of what symbolic discourses and repertoires are national identities constructed? How—through what imagery—do societies represent their nations, and what is the significance of these representations? If national identities, viewed in historical perspective, are fluid, how and why do they change through time? How and why does nationalism remain such a potent and powerful force in Europe?

In asking these questions, historians of European nationalism have explored three broad themes. First, they have investigated the nature, evolution, and

limits of citizenship and immigration policy in various national contexts. Brubaker, for example, has explored the nature and history of French and German citizenship law to highlight differing conceptions of national identity and belonging. This approach follows older "top down" models by focusing on policy making at the center.

Second, historians have begun to pay far greater attention to the formation of national identities and the creation of a national consciousness among ordinary people. This second approach has further opened the history of nationalism to social historians. Benedict Anderson's *Imagined Communities* (1991), a broad synthetic essay on the emergence and spread of nationalism, has played a pivotal role in this regard. Individual historical studies have provided nuanced historical accounts of the creation of national consciousness through time. Peter Sahlins, for example, has argued that the boundary between France and Spain was as much constructed by Catalans who live on both sides of the border in the Cerdagne between the sixteenth and the eighteenth centuries as it was by the French government in Paris. He therefore challenges the top-down, center-outward approach to understanding the formation of national identities and suggests ways in which local rivalries and issues inform national debates. Similarly, Celia Applegate argues that the formation of a national consciousness in certain areas of Germany was as much a product of a cherished identification with *Heimat* (one's local homeland) as it was a product of German unification. I have argued that attempts by the French state to replace time-honored cultural practices and allegiances and to integrate Catholic Brittany into the secular republican culture of metropolitan France toward the end of the nineteenth century were incomplete at best. This did not mean that a national consciousness failed to materialize in the far reaches of the French hexagon, but rather that a national consciousness was forged through a process of negotiation and selective appropriation on the part of individuals and social groups at the periphery. All these historians have sought to understand how ordinary people, rather than elites and governments, have established a relationship with an imagined national community.

Finally, historians using techniques and insights from the "new cultural history" have focused on the importance of representation and symbolism in understanding nationalism and the propagation of national myths. Maurice Agulhon's work on the role of Marianne as a female symbol of France since the French Revolution, and Lynn Hunt's study of the competing symbols of Hercules and Marianne in revolutionary culture suggest that more attention should

506

be given to how nations and their elites define themselves and export their own images abroad.

How does one explain the survival of national antagonisms and the spread of nationalist movements in the face of transnationalism and larger processes of globalization? In many respects the world has become unified by transnational capitalist organizations. In view of its intellectual poverty as ideology, how and why does nationalism now ultimately seem to be a more powerful mobilizing force than socialism or communism? Is the "resurgence" of nationalism an atavism, an aberration? Historians are only beginning to answer these questions. What seems clear is that nationalism as an ideology and as a political movement is and has been ubiquitous since the eighteenth century and continues to be pervasive in Europe. In the prescient words of Isaiah Berlin, written in 1991, nationalism is not "resurgent" because it never really died.

See also **Emigration and Colonies; Imperialism and Domestic Society; Racism** *(volume 1); and other articles in this section.*

BIBLIOGRAPHY

Agulhon, Maurice. *Marianne into Battle: Republican Imagery and Symbolism in France, 1789–1880.* Translated by Janet Lloyd. Cambridge, U.K., 1981.

Anderson, Benedict. *Imagined Communities: Reflections on the Origins and Spread of Nationalism.* London, l991.

Applegate, Celia. *A Nation of Provincials: The German Idea of Heimat.* Berkeley, Calif., 1990.

Armstrong, John. *Nations before Nationalism.* Chapel Hill, N.C., 1982.

Banac, Ivo. *The National Question in Yugoslavia: Origins, History, Politics.* Ithaca, N.Y., 1984.

Bhabha, Homi, ed. *Nation and Narration.* London and New York, 1990.

Breuilly, John. *Nationalism and the State.* Manchester, U.K., 1982.

Brubaker, Rogers. *Citizenship and Nationhood in France and Germany.* Cambridge, Mass., 1992.

Brubaker, Rogers. *Nationalism Reframed: Nationhood and the National Question in the New Europe.* Cambridge, U.K., 1996.

Colley, Linda. *Britons: Forging the Nation, 1707–1837.* New Haven, Conn., 1992.

Ford, Caroline. *Creating the Nation in Provincial France: Religion and Political Identity in Brittany.* Princeton, N.J., 1993.

Gellner, Ernest. *Nations and Nationalism.* Ithaca, N.Y., 1983.

Hobsbawm, Eric. *Nations and Nationalism since 1780: Programme, Myth, Reality.* Cambridge, U.K., 1990.

Hroch, Miroslav. *Social Preconditions of National Revival in Europe: A Comparative Analysis of the Social Composition of Patriotic Groups among the Smaller European Nations.* Translated by Ben Fowkes. Cambridge, U.K., 1985.

Hunt, Lynn. *Politics, Culture, and Class in the French Revolution.* Berkeley, Calif., 1984.

Hutchinson, John, and Anthony D. Smith, eds. *Nationalism.* Oxford, 1994.

Ignatieff, Michael. *Blood and Belonging: Journeys into the New Nationalism.* New York, 1994.

Nora, Pierre, ed. *Realms of Memory: Rethinking the French Past.* New York, 1996.

Sahlins, Peter. *Boundaries: The Making of France and Spain in the Pyrenees.* Berkeley, Calif., 1989.

Samuel, Raphael. *Patriotism: The Making and Unmaking of British National Identity.* 3 vols. London, 1989.

Smith, Anthony. *National Identity.* Reno, Nev., 1991.

Teich, Mikuláš, and Roy Porter, eds. *The National Question in Europe in Historical Context.* New York, 1993.

Tilly, Charles, ed. *The Formation of National States in Western Europe.* Princeton, N.J., 1975.

Weber, Eugen. *Peasants into Frenchmen: The Modernization of Rural France, 1870–1914.* Stanford, Calif., 1976.

FASCISM AND NAZISM

Alexander De Grand

THE HISTORICAL CONTEXT

Fascism and Nazism developed out of a general crisis of the European political system connected with the rise of the mass participation state from the late nineteenth century to the end of World War I. The mass participation state was marked by five features: an unprecedented expansion of the number of voters brought on by universal manhood suffrage and in some cases by the extension of the vote to women; the development of mass communications; a high degree of mass mobilization, initially by revolutionary socialist parties; new economic and social demands put forward by democratic and revolutionary organizations; and fragmented, poorly organized middle-class political party structures, largely legacies of the nineteenth-century restricted franchise. Fascism was motivated by deep-seated fears of social and political disintegration and of political revolution on the part of both ruling elites and large sectors of the middle and lower-middle classes. These classes had little to gain from a socialist revolution. Fascist and Nazi movements appeared throughout Europe during the period between World Wars I and II, but only in Italy and Germany did they come to power and develop into regimes.

By 1919 liberalism and liberal democracy, focused on individual rights, offered a pallid response to social and economic upheaval brought on by World War I. Political life had been thoroughly radicalized by war and by the Bolshevik Revolution of 1917. Large segments of newly enfranchised masses were moving outside of established social and economic institutions and were falling under the control of revolutionary organizations. Liberal democracy, which relies on competition of individuals and groups in the political and economic marketplaces, offered little assurance of social cohesion in a time of crisis. In contrast, socialism and communism formulated powerful quasi-religious visions of human redemption and solidarity based on the triumph of the peasantry and the working class.

FASCISM AND NAZISM DEFINED

Fascism exploded on the political scene after 1919 as a countermyth, as the first mass movement of the middle class in Italy and Germany, and as a political party through which important sectors of the economic and political establishments sought to preserve the status quo in revolutionary times. Faced with a shattered political order, a highly politicized and fragmented body politic, a revolutionary threat, and a profound loss of faith in the market mechanisms, Fascism put forward a vision of social and political solidarity based on the primacy of membership in the organic nation (Fascism) or race (Nazism). It brought a new word, "totalitarian," into the political lexicon. Because social and economic disintegration after World War I seemed to threaten the very basis of Western civilization, the remedy for it had to be equally drastic or total. Using techniques of mass mobilization pioneered by the left, tactics of combat forged in the trenches of World War I, and modern means of mass communications, Fascism and Nazism promised a new and unified national or racial community.

The Fascist-Nazi political revolutions stemmed from profound anxieties about the disintegration of the social order and of the national or racial unit. Thus, not surprisingly, they shared many characteristics: the cult of the single leader who represented the essence of the nation or race; the single party through which all political life was directed; state control of mass communications and propaganda; the absorption of all independent social, leisure time, and professional activity within the state; the destruction of independent labor organizations; state direction of the economy within the context of private ownership; and the mobilization of society for war against domestic and foreign enemies.

Nonetheless, the Fascist and Nazi regimes were mired in contradictions. They were movements of the middle class, aiming at the restoration of traditional gender and social hierarchies, yet they claimed to be revolutionary regimes that would create new national

509

Fascists Salute. Cyclists saluting the Italian Fascist leader Benito Mussolini, November 1923. Mussolini became prime minister in 1922. ©HULTON GETTY/LIAISON AGENCY

and racial communities. Both regimes at once reflected and mocked bourgeois values. They promised, especially in the case of Italian Fascism, to respect private property and ownership of the means of production. Yet they were built on a vision of mercantilist crisis that implied state direction of a shrinking world economy in which nations and races struggled continuously to survive. Mobilization for warfare undermined aspirations for political and social stabilization and the restoration of traditional values. The regimes put forward a spartan ethic of self-denial, austerity, and subordination of the individual to the group that neither was shared by most Germans or Italians nor reflected the private behavior of the leadership.

Contradictions were overcome by massive mobilization and propaganda efforts. Fascism and Nazism borrowed from their socialist and communist opponents and from traditional religion to create elaborate public rituals, vast public spaces for rallies, and an almost godlike cult of the leader. The central myth was the salvation of the nation or race through rebirth and regeneration. Rebirth could only come through struggle. new values of sacrifice, and constant vigilance against external and internal enemies. Italian Fascism consisted of constantly shifting "battles" for self-sufficiency in grain, population expansion, the value of the lire, and Italian domination of the Mediterranean Sea and against the League of Nations, France,

and England. Germany, in contrast, concentrated its full attention on the perceived Jewish biological, cultural, and economic threat and the drive for outward expansion, especially in eastern Europe.

In so far as Fascism and to a lesser extent Nazism operated according to economic theories, they opted for a corporative model of economic organization as a "third way" between capitalism and communism. Italy attempted to organize economic and social life around functional units that brought together workers and management in the various branches of the economy within a single framework. Strikes and lockouts were outlawed and replaced by mandatory arbitration. However, the destruction of independent trade unions, the close ties between industry and the Fascist and Nazi regimes, and war mobilization resulted in a state-directed autarky with major branches of the economy organized into government-sponsored cartels geared to war production and to the exploitation of conquered territories.

TYPOLOGIES OF FASCISM

During the 1920s and 1930s movements modeled on Fascism or Nazism cropped up throughout Europe. Historians and political scientists have failed to find a common thread that would link the widely divergent

510

experiences of France, Italy, Germany, Austria, Hungary, Spain, Romania, Belgium, England, and Latin American countries. Generally they have used three approaches to analyze fascism and nazism. One approach defines the two movements as modern totalitarianism and links them with the Soviet experience under Joseph Stalin. However, totalitarian theory concentrates on organization of the state and leaves out Italy, which was not truly totalitarian. A second approach finds a fascist minimum that links Italy and Germany and leaves out Soviet communism. The common core is sought in economic structures, either in the form of a crisis of capitalism or of stages of economic development, in a general European cultural crisis, in a revolt of the lower middle classes, or in the psychological trauma of a generation that experienced World War I and subsequent dislocations. Finally, a number of theories deny any connection between fascism and nazism. Fascism has its roots in the crisis of the marxist left, whereas nazism derives from ideas of racial biology common in nineteenth-century Europe.

The diversity of organizations connected with fascism poses problems for any general theory. Some movements were authoritarian-traditionalist, seeking the restoration of traditional values, often by violence, through reliance on religion and ties to conservative forces. Others were overtly fascist or nazi, seeking an autonomous base by mobilizing the lower middle class and peasantry on programs that were always antimarxist but often included anticapitalist populism, extreme nationalism, racial mysticism, and anti-Semitism.

In Austria the nationalist authoritarian paramilitary Heimwehr was allied to right-wing nationalists, its ideology was Catholic corporative, and it drew support from the small-town middle class and the peasantry. In Spain the most notable movement inspired by fascism was the Falange, founded in 1933 by José Antonio Primo de Rivera. The Falange called for an almost mystical national revival through the reassertion of traditional, Catholic values and the struggle against marxism. Eventually the Falange was subsumed into General Francisco Franco's military revolt of 1936. The oldest of the conservative, nationalist movements was the Action Française, founded in France in 1899 by Charles Maurras. The Action Française was monarchist, authoritarian, anti-Semitic, theoretically Catholic, and virulently antidemocratic. Another French movement of the authoritarian right was the Croix de Feu, founded in 1927. After 1936 the Croix de Feu transformed into the French Social Party, which drew from the middle class and peasant farmers. The Belgian Rexist movement, headed by Leon Degrelle, followed the authoritarian, Catholic

model closer to Benito Mussolini's Fascism than to Nazi paganism.

On the radical fascist right, the French ex-Communist Jacques Doriot formed the Parti Populaire Français that initially won a substantial working-class following but gradually lost it as the party was tied to conservative financial backers and gravitated toward the Nazi model during World War II. Sir Oswald Mosley's British Union of Fascists, formed in 1932, adopted the cult of the leader and the violent tactics that marked both fascism and nazism. Mosley's anti-Semitism drew him closer to Adolf Hitler than to Mussolini. Among the most interesting radical movements were the Hungarian Arrow Cross, led by Ferenc Szálasi, which combined extreme nationalism, radical economic and social restructuring, and violent anti-Semitism; and the Romanian Legion of the Archangel Michael, founded by Corneliu Zelea Codreanu in 1927. The Legion called for a peasant society based on extreme nationalism with a dose of Romanian Orthodox Christian mysticism. The movement was violent, confrontational, and extremely anti-Semitic with support from students and poor peasants and few ties to the economic and social establishment. The Arrow Cross and the Legion of the Archangel Michael were suppressed by the conservative Hungarian and Romanian governments in power during the 1930s.

THE ITALIAN FASCIST AND GERMAN NAZI MOVEMENTS

Origins and early development. The Fascist and Nazi movements developed in roughly three parallel stages. The first phase was the radical, quasi-revolutionary movement, which lasted in Italy only from March 1919 to mid-1920 and in Germany continued from January 1919 to the abortive Beer Hall Putsch of November 1923. The second period was marked by the transformation of both movements into broader middle-class alliances. In Italy this took place between mid-1920 and November 1921, when the Fascist movement became the landowners' primary weapon to smash the socialist peasant movement in the rich agricultural Po Valley. In Germany the transformative phase lasted from the reconstitution of the party in 1925 to the first electoral success in 1929. The final step in the party development, preparatory to the seizure of power, was when both movements became truly mass organizations, entered Parliament, and began to negotiate with the economic and social establishments. In Italy this process lasted from the end of 1921 until the March on Rome in October 1922, and in Germany it lasted from 1929 to January 1933.

The radical phase. Anton Drexler formed the German Workers' Party in Munich on 5 January 1919. A few months later, on 23 March, Mussolini launched the first *fascio di combattimento* (combat group) in Milan. The term *fascio* originally meant "group" and was used by both left and right. Members of the *fascio* were *fascisti.* Both movements combined extreme nationalism with radical economic and social programs. For instance, the first Fascist program, inspired by Mussolini's early socialism, called for the eight-hour day, worker participation in management, the vote for women, and a new republican constitution. Backing for the *fascio* came from students, veterans, and young professionals along with former socialists, syndicalists, and anarchists who had joined Mussolini in 1914 and 1915 in breaking with the official Socialist Party over Italian entry into World War I. They shared a complete rejection of the existing political system, a contempt for the Italian political class, and an intense hatred of proletarian-based socialism. The early Fascist movement was solidly northern, with particular strength in Milan, Italy's most modern urban center.

In contrast to the Fascist movement, the German Workers' Party had no ties to the left and was based in Munich, outside Germany's industrial heartland. Hitler joined the movement in late September 1919, and the next year it became the National Socialist German Workers' Party (NSDAP). The new party was extremely small, with 189 members in January 1920 and only 2,000 at the end of the year. The Nazi movement appealed to war veterans, artisans, and the disaffected lower middle class, who were hostile both to socialism and to large-scale commercial and industrial capitalism. In 1921 and 1922 it spread to the small Protestant towns of Franconia and Bavaria and to the major cities Munich and Nürnberg. Spurred by French occupation of the Ruhr Valley, inflation, and economic collapse, by November 1923 the party claimed over fifty thousand members spread throughout a large part of Germany. It had become a broad coalition of the middle class with some working-class support in the industrial Ruhr and Rhineland.

Three things characterize the social history of the early Fascist and Nazi movements. First, the leadership was young, drawn from the generation born in the 1880s and 1890s. Mussolini was born in 1883, Hitler in 1889. Second, the defining experience for both Fascists and Nazis was World War I. Coming of age as the war began, they were stamped by the conflict's violence and the solidarity of the trenches, and they re-created this cohesion in the military formations important to both parties. The Nazis created the Sturmabteilung (SA) in 1921; the Fascists organized *fasci di combattimento*, or squads, modeled after wartime special combat units. These paramilitary formations made both movements something new on the political scene—parties organized not for traditional electoral politics but for violent, ongoing confrontations with political opponents. The third characteristic of both movements was an intense anger and impatience that found outlets in nationalism, hatred of democracy and socialism, and calls for the restoration of social- and gender-based hierarchies. One additional element, extreme racism and anti-Semitism, was present in the Nazi movement from the beginning. For instance, the Nazi program of February 1920 excluded Jews from membership in the future German national community.

The transformative-coalition phase. The transformative phase revealed a high degree of organizational flexibility. Powerful local leaders (*ras* in Italy, *Gauleiter* in Germany) acted with significant independence. The movements' ideological opportunism allowed them to adapt to new circumstances, and the cult of the supreme leader emerged.

The radical-populist Fascist movement reached an impasse with the Italian elections of November 1919. Mussolini's movement was solidly defeated, and the Italian Socialist Party and the Catholic Popular Party represented over half of the new parliament. By early 1920 total membership in the *fasci* dropped to nine hundred. The movement revived from this low point after November, when it spearheaded the agrarian reaction to Socialist peasant organizations and strikes. One of the best social histories of the origins of Fascism in Italy, *Fascism in Ferrara, 1915–1925* (1975) by Paul Corner, analyzes the Fascists' use of long-standing social and economic tensions to gain a popular base. By the end of 1920 the 88 *fasci* had over 20,000 members, and a year later 834 *fasci* had over 250,000 members.

The balance shifted from northern cities to the countryside and small towns of northern and central Italy. New recruits were young professionals, shopkeepers, students, and small and large landowners. They launched well-armed punitive expeditions from provincial centers against unprepared and poorly coordinated peasant unions. Beginning with the areas around Bologna and Ferrara, much of northern Italy turned into a battle zone with the passive acquiescence or active connivance of police and military authorities. This second phase ended at the Fascist congress in November 1921, when the movement officially became the National Fascist Party (PNF). The party fully accepted Mussolini's supreme position and abandoned its republican, anti-Catholic, and radical program in favor of a monarchist and economically conservative agenda.

The Nazi movement reached a similar impasse in late 1923. The movement was outlawed, and Hitler was arrested and imprisoned after the failed attempt to overthrow the Weimar Republic (Beer Hall Putsch) of 3–9 November. The party was reorganized in 1925 on the *Führerprinzip,* or leadership principle, with Hitler as undisputed leader. The Nazi movement attracted middle- and lower-middle-class supporters, but the urban working-class strategy it pursued in 1927 and 1928 made limited gains. In the elections of May 1928 the Nazis won only 2.8 percent of the vote but made a significant breakthrough among the desperate small farmers in the northern state of Schleswig-Holstein, marking the end of the party's urban strategy. The onset of the Great Depression opened the way for major Nazi victories in 1929 and 1930.

The consolidation of the mass movement and the seizure of power.

Fascists and Nazis took power in similar ways. Their paramilitary wings created a climate of violence directed at their Socialist and Communist enemies and the existing political class, which dared not crack down lest the revolutionary left revive. In both countries Parliament was paralyzed. After the 1930 elections successive German governments survived using presidential emergency decree powers. The Italian and German conservative political and economic establishments united to bring the Fascist and Nazi movements into the government, and in both countries the conservatives felt confident they could control any power-sharing arrangement. Thus Mussolini and Hitler came to power legally. The Fascist and Nazi revolutions came after the movements controlled the government.

In 1921 and 1922 the Italian Fascist squads continued their revenge against the Socialist worker and peasant unions in well-organized attacks against whole provinces. The Nazi SA, a massive organization devoted to street fighting and fund-raising, had a social base decidedly more working-class and lower-middle-class than the NSDAP. Once in Parliament both parties courted key constituencies within the established order. The Fascist Party entered the government-sponsored electoral coalition in June 1921, when it won thirty-five seats in parliament, and adopted a new conservative program in November. Weak and divided governments in 1921 and 1922 led all established political leaders to seek an alliance with Mussolini by October 1922. To precipitate events the Fascists decreed a mass mobilization of their squads and the March on Rome that began on 27 October. Faced with violence and potential civil war, King Victor Emman-

uel III first offered the post of prime minister to a conservative. When Mussolini demanded the position for himself, the monarch yielded on 29 October and appointed the Fascist leader to head the government.

During the late 1920s and early 1930s the Nazis formed organizations that incorporated students, teachers, farmers, civil servants, doctors, lawyers, and architects into the movement. Hitler ignored the party's radical economic program and reached out to industrialists. The NSDAP won 108 seats in the September 1930 national elections and controlled several state governments, sweeping aside all the other middle-class political groups. Nazi domination of the political space previously occupied by several fragmented middle-class parties was confirmed in the July 1932 elections, when the party won 230 seats and 37 percent of the votes. By January 1933 party membership had reached 1.4 million people. Social histories have revealed that, of those who voted for the Nazis, 70 percent were middle class, but roughly one-third could be described as working class or unemployed. The rank and file members were small peasant farmers, shopkeepers, artisans, civil servants, teachers, professionals, and small businesspeople. In contrast, the party leadership after 1928 increasingly was drawn from the middle and upper-middle classes. Clearly the NSDAP was a successful mass movement of the middle classes before Hitler's appointment as chancellor on 30 January 1933.

FROM MOVEMENT TO REGIME: THE FASCIST AND NAZI STATES

Until 1934 the Fascist and Nazi movements seemed to run on parallel courses. Both leaders were young when they took power. Mussolini was thirty-nine in 1922; Hitler was forty-four in 1933. Neither man offered a clear indication of his future programs, and they headed movements more suited to seizing power than to governing. The Fascist and Nazi movements proclaimed themselves revolutionary but were in coalitions with conservatives who had decidedly different aims. The two movements had changed their social bases in similar ways during the march to power. As the movements grew, more middle- and upper-middle-class people joined, but remnants of the old lower-middle-class populism remained in the Fascist squads and in the SA. Expectations that the movements would share the spoils with the bases had to be balanced against the realities of governing. The conservative industrialists and landowners' desires for merely the restoring of order had to be reconciled with the drive to total power inherent in Fascism and Nazism.

Nazi Leader. Adolf Hitler arrives at a National Labor Day youth rally in Berlin, 1 May 1934. Seated in the back of the car is Vice Chancellor Franz von Papen. AKG LONDON

How much the Fascist and Nazi regimes were the result of choices made by Mussolini and Hitler has been the subject of much debate between intentionalists and structuralists. The intentionalists stress the role of Hitler in the Nazi regime and, in fact, both regimes must be seen, at least in part, as determined by the wills of their powerful leaders, especially in foreign and racial policies. But the structuralists are correct to see these regimes as also the products of powerful social and economic institutional forces interacting within the contexts of the new dictatorships. The organization of the regimes was largely determined by the social alliances that brought them to power. Moreover policies often were shaped by competition for power among important interest groups within the dictatorships. The implication for social historians is that a simple top-down model of power relationships is inadequate, even in highly authoritarian regimes.

The histories of the Fascist and Nazi regimes can be divided into four periods: consolidation of power and the suppression of the opposition (Italy from 1922 to 1926, Germany from 30 January to July 1933), stabilization of power (Italy from 1926 to 1935, Germany from 1933 to 1936), the drive to totalitarian control (Italy from 1935 to 1939, Germany after 1936), and war and expansion (Italy from 1935 to 1943, Germany from 1936 to 1945).

The repression of the opposition. At the top of the hierarchy was the supreme leader. After 1934 Hitler combined the offices of chancellor and chief of state, while Mussolini formally served as prime minister under the Italian monarch. Both regimes abolished the old constitutions and never replaced them. Instead, they introduced a series of ad hoc constitutional arrangements. Mussolini and Hitler immediately diminished the importance of Parliament. They quickly dissolved the old legislatures and called new elections, Mussolini in spring 1924 and Hitler in March 1933. New electoral laws gave their parties a significant advantage. Mussolini won approval of the 1923 Acerbo law, which gave two-thirds of the seats in Parliament to the party that won over 25 percent of the vote. The Nazis declared a state of emergency on 31 January 1933 and on 4 February issued an emergency decree limiting press freedom and public meetings. The Nazis used the burning of the Reichstag building by a Dutch communist in late February as an excuse to ban that party under a decree for "the Protection of the People and the State" on 28 February 1933. Mussolini ended parliamentary control over the cabinet in December 1925 with a law making the head of government responsible only to the monarch. Hitler accomplished the same end with the Enabling Act of 23 March 1933, which gave the government power to issue laws without the consent of the

Reichstag. Over time even cabinet meetings in both regimes became rarer and less important. Each constituency negotiated directly with the supreme leader or with other power centers on a bilateral basis.

The consolidation of power: economic, social, and religious policies.

Upon taking power, the Fascists and Nazis faced conflicting pressures. The lower-middle-class base of the party and the paramilitary formations sought immediate rewards, such as restrictions on department stores in Germany, larger roles for the Fascist and Nazi militias, and appointment to government offices. Each of these demands conflicted with the desires of industrialists, bankers, the military, and the civil service. Both regimes coped by curbing the power of the party militias and buying off key constituencies.

In Italy this process of concessions worked only partially, and Mussolini never freed himself from the alliance with conservatives. To the landowners the Fascist government offered the suppression of the peasant unions and a substantial degree of local government control. Industrialists received the destruction of Socialist and Communist unions and reaffirmation of the supremacy of the employer within the firm. Over the long term, heavy industry was integrated into a lucrative system of state-sponsored cartels that carved up market shares to the advantage of larger competitors and guaranteed government contracts for military armaments and import substitution. The Italian Catholic Church benefited most notably from the Lateran Treaty and Concordat of 1929, which guaranteed the official status of the church and its autonomous sphere within the Fascist regime. The military won curbs on the power of the Fascist militia. The lower middle class gained increased access to party and state positions and a gradual relaxation of limits on educational opportunities. Of course, the losers in the process were industrial workers and peasants, both male and female, who faced lost political and economic rights and wage reductions with the onset of the depression.

Nazi Germany similarly bought special constituencies. Heavy industry won significant advantages. Unions of all sorts were banned, and not even the Nazi Labor Front had the right to bargain collectively. Arbitration of wages was shifted to the Ministry of Labor, and the rights of management were reaffirmed. In 1934 Hjalmar Schacht, a banker with close business ties, became economics minister, and he dominated policy until 1936. He introduced foreign currency controls, import restrictions, and cartelization in favor of large industrial corporations. Radical demands from the Nazi base, such as the anti–department store campaign, were shelved; handicrafts were brought under the German Craft Trades organization; and small businesses were arranged under a specialized association. In September 1933 the Nazis created an agricultural marketing organization, the Reichsnährstand, which introduced price supports for basic commodities. The so-called blood purge of the SA leadership in June 1934 eliminated a rival to the military establishment, and the army was further satisfied by the decision to rearm.

On the religious front the Nazis attempted to create a party-dominated Evangelical Church but pulled back in the face of resistance from Protestant leaders in 1933 and 1934. In mid-1933 the Nazi government signed a concordat with the Catholic Church modeled on the Lateran accords of Fascist Italy. On paper the Catholic Church was assured of its own sphere of religious influence in exchange for abandoning its political activity and its youth groups. But both the Protestant and Catholic Churches in Nazi Germany were on the defensive before the power of the state.

Fascism and Nazism brought large areas of social and economic life under state control. Both regimes created youth groups (Balilla in Italy, Hitler Youth in Germany); women's organizations (*fasci femminili* and National Socialist Womanhood, and the *Deutsche Frauenwerke*); leisure-time organizations that provided both indoctrination and entertainment for workers (*Dopolavoro*, and the German Strength through Joy); myriad official professional associations for lawyers, doctors, artists, and architects; and social welfare agencies that aimed to increase the birthrate of the "racially healthy" population (the Fascist Woman and Infants Organization, and the Nazi Welfare Organization). To encourage a higher birthrate, the two dictatorships offered housing allowances and family subsidies, forced married women out of the employment market, and imposed special taxes on the unmarried. The number of women workers declined in the Fascist era due as much to the reduced importance of agriculture and textiles as to actual Fascist policy. During the early 1930s the Fascist government closed some state employment to women, and in 1938 it imposed a 10 percent quota on female employment in the state sector and in large firms. The excess of females over males, pressure from middle-class families, and mobilization for war moderated the impact of these measures, but professional advancement was closed in many areas. Politically active women were directed into party and state women's and social welfare agencies. Neither regime closed the universities to women, although the Nazis imposed a 10 percent cap on female enrollment. Nonetheless, on the eve of the war women comprised 30 percent of German university students.

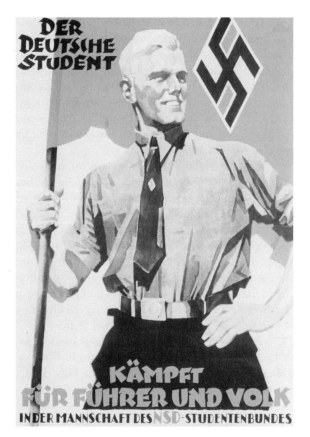

Nazi Student Organization. Poster by Ludwig Hohlwein, 1930s. ©CORBIS

Neither Italy nor Germany encouraged significant upward social mobility. The educational system remained a middle-class bastion. Workers in Italy suffered a significant decline in wages as a result of state-enforced salary reductions during the late 1920s and early 1930s. Prices fell more slowly, resulting in an overall decline in the standard of living. Nazi Germany reached full employment by 1936, and labor shortages kept wages from falling. Both regimes provided sufficient basic foodstuffs but neglected the consumer goods sector. Nonmonetary incentives, such as housing and family benefits, replaced wage incentives.

Both Fascist rule in Italy and Nazi rule in Germany profoundly influenced their respective societies, but it is dangerous to exaggerate their impact. Certainly large areas of working class life remained on the margins of the Fascist or Nazi consensus, and the middle and upper classes could retreat into the sphere of private life. German historians of "everyday life," such as Detlev J. K. Peukert in *Inside Nazi Germany: Conformity, Opposition, and Racism in Everyday Life* (1987), are aware that the Nazi regime failed to resolve any of the historic social and economic cleavages in

Germany. To this extent the "racial community" failed to create a new German, just as Mussolini's "revolution" failed to create the new Fascist Italian. But the two regimes did touch almost all Italians and Germans, even those who retreated into private life, by forcing them into constant daily compromises and involving them in the many official social and economic organizations. In the end the social impact of fascism and nazism cannot be separated from the effects of the war, defeat, and occupation. Certainly in the case of Italy and Germany, the "economic miracle" of the 1950s and early 1960s changed their societies more fundamentally than anything the Fascists and Nazis did.

Differences between Fascist and Nazi regimes.
If the two regimes resembled each other in important ways, they differed in equally important regards both during and after the consolidation of power. First, the Nazis made revolutionary use of the concept of race to undermine existing legal standards and bureaucratic order, to make sweeping changes in cultural life by labeling most modern art and literature Judeo-Bolshevik, and to extend state control into the sphere of private life. The Nazis used racial laws to purge the civil service in 1933; Joseph Goebbels's new Ministry of Propaganda (1933) began to dismantle libraries and museums with a massive, symbolic book burning in the spring of 1933; and the Nürnberg Laws of 1935 took citizenship from Jews and forbade marriage between Jews and non-Jews. Applying racial theory, the Nazis sterilized those deemed physically or mentally defective or born of mixed-race marriages. They encouraged Aryans to have children; indeed divorce was granted on grounds of infertility. In Italy the opposition of the Catholic Church made sterilization or divorce practically impossible but failed to prevent the adoption of anti-Semitic legislation in 1938 that began the physical separation of Italian Jews from Christians.

The two regimes also differed in how the state bureaucracy related to the party and its paramilitary and police organizations. In Italy the Fascist Party was subordinated to the established bureaucracy that imposed the dictatorship, therefore the party never developed its own police and security apparatus. Hitler understood that the German bureaucracy was ill suited to create his racial utopia, and to a much greater extent than in Italy, the party relied on Nazi-dominated organizations to carry out its will. Most important, the SS, the party security agency, paralleled the state security police, the Gestapo. In 1936 Heinrich Himmler merged the state and party police under his control and forged a weapon of totalitarian terror that had no Italian counterpart. The Italian regime rested on a highly effective police apparatus (the OVRA), widespread use of informants, censorship of the media, and even concentration camps in the late 1930s, but it did not use systematic terror.

A final distinction between the two regimes is in the culture. Most of Italian culture survived under Fascism, which applied no official doctrine to purge literature, the arts, or the universities except against overt opponents. Thus Italy's greatest artists and writers remained in the country. In contrast, the Nazis forced German writers and artists into silence or exile. The Nazis gathered much of the best European painting and sculpture in 1937 for the Exhibition of Decadent Art, which subsequently was sold, was destroyed, or disappeared into Nazi private collections.

Fascism, Nazism, and war. Fascism and Nazism were geared for war and expansion. Both regimes started from a vision of a world of narrowing opportunities in which nations and races had to struggle, expand, or die. Hitler's goal of expansion of the German state was rivaled in importance only by anti-Semitic policies. In 1933 and 1934 he assured the military that he would begin rapid rearmament. In 1936, after achieving full employment and economic recovery, the Nazis rejected economic orthodoxy for continued expansion of a war economy. From the re-militarization of the Rhineland in March 1936 to the final disaster of World War II in 1945, Nazism embarked on a series of conquests that had no limits and involved ever-widening aims.

Fascist Italy, a much weaker state, moved more slowly. Mussolini had few options during the 1920s, when Britain and France were dominant, but the revival of Germany after 1933 gave Il Duce (the leader) his opportunity. Mussolini had the more limited ambition of replacing Britain as the dominant power in the Mediterranean. By putting his country on a war footing, he might also break the conservatives' hold over his regime and resume the push for a totalitarian society. Unfortunately for Mussolini, Italy lacked the industrial and military base to compete with Germany and Britain. Mussolini embarked on wars in Ethiopia (1935–1936), Spain (1936–1938), Albania (1939), and France, Greece, and North Africa (1940–1941). Defeat in Greece and North Africa by early 1941 meant the beginning of the end of Italian Fascism, and the regime collapsed after the Allied invasion of Sicily in early 1943. On 24–25 July 1943 Mussolini was outvoted by his fellow Fascist leaders, removed by the king, and arrested. In September, Hitler's army rescued Il Duce and restored him to power as head of a puppet Italian Social Republic that lasted until April 1945. It preceded its German ally in defeat and collapse by only a matter of weeks.

See also **The World Wars and the Depression; The Jews and Anti-Semitism; Racism** *(volume 1);* **War and Conquest** *(volume 2);* **Revolutions** *(volume 3); and other articles in this section.*

BIBLIOGRAPHY

Bosworth, J. B. R. *The Italian Dictatorship: Problems and Perspectives in the Interpretation of Mussolini and Fascism.* London, 1998.

Broszat, Martin. *The Hitler State.* Translated by John W. Hiden. London, 1981.

Corner, Paul. *Fascism in Ferrara, 1915–1925.* London and New York, 1975.

Kershaw, Ian. *Hitler, 1889–1936: Hubris.* New York, 1999.

Kershaw, Ian. *The Nazi Dictatorship: Problems and Perspectives of Interpretation.* 3d ed. London, 1993.

Lyttelton, Adrian. *The Seizure of Power: Fascism in Italy 1919–1929.* Princeton, N.J., 1987.

Mack Smith, Denis. *Mussolini.* New York, 1983.

Payne, Stanley G. *A History of Fascism, 1914–1945.* Madison, Wis., 1995.

Peukert, Detlev J. K. *Inside Nazi Germany: Conformity, Opposition, and Racism in Everyday Life.* Translated by Richard Deveson. New Haven, Conn., 1987.

COMMUNISM

Eric D. Weitz

Communism and social democracy constituted the two major branches of the socialist movement in the twentieth century. Both were direct descendants of nineteenth-century socialism; their differing political and historical relationship to the Russian Revolution marked the essential division between them. Social Democrats were committed to liberal democratic forms of government, from which they imagined a peaceful transition from capitalism to socialism would occur. Universally, they supported the February Revolution of 1917 that overthrew the tsarist regime in Russia. Almost universally, they condemned the October Revolution of 1917, by which the Bolsheviks came to power.

Led by Vladimir Ilich Lenin, the Bolsheviks were initially one faction of the Russian Social Democratic and Labor Party. In the first of a number of name changes, they became the Russian Communist Party (b) in March 1918 and the All-Union Communist Party (b) in 1925, the "b" in both cases standing for "Bolshevik," or "Majority," the name Lenin had dubbed his faction. In reality, the Bolsheviks had only briefly counted a majority within the Russian Social Democratic and Labor Party in the years before 1917. Their opponents, the Mensheviks, or "Minority," were, for the most part, typically social democratic in orientation. In contrast, the Bolsheviks came to believe that they could force-pace developments in Russia, bypassing the phase of liberal capitalism to institute socialism more or less immediately. Far less worried about liberal democratic norms, they were determined to maintain party control of the state as the decisive means of creating socialism. The party itself, accorded almost mystical authority by Lenin and other Bolshevik leaders, was to be a disciplined body that would guide the revolution and mobilize the entire proletarian and peasant population for the cause of building socialism. The Bolsheviks' open advocacy of terror against perceived opponents of the revolution inspired the greatest hostility from Social Democrats, who viewed the inherently undemocratic and brutal measures of terror as a violation of the most cherished principles of socialism.

By according the state enormous power, communism created a new, twentieth-century model of state-society relations, one that would spread from Russia and the Soviet Union to other countries in Europe and beyond in the wake of World War II. To be sure, European states going back to the early modern era promoted economic development, regulated the family and gender relations, and repressed independent expression. Especially in central and eastern Europe, states had a decisive impact upon social history. But no state prior to the twentieth century had such all-encompassing determination to mold society in accord with its ideological commitments, nor did any have the technical means to regulate society on such a vast scale. In the nations under communist party rule, the "workers' and peasants' state" practiced a kind of internal colonialism. The communist state had a developmental and civilizing mission to fulfill, force-pacing industrialization and the collectivization of agriculture, forging nations out of disparate ethnic groups, and, not least, creating the new communist man and woman. To accomplish these dramatic tasks, the state became a gigantic apparatus, one that also violated the most basic democratic standards.

At the same time, the state, like the party, could never simply impose its programs and goals upon society. Especially in the Soviet Union, the effort to create a specifically communist modernity ran smack against the realities of an overwhelmingly peasant society marked also by enormous ethnic diversity. In the countries of central and eastern Europe, the communist states established after 1945 also faced large peasant populations and ethnic diversity, as well as more developed middle and working classes that were often quite hostile to communism. The entreaties and commands of the states were sometimes met with resistance or, more often, sullen apathy or noncompliance. In response, the state grew still larger, while all sorts of inefficiencies and compromises were carried into its institutions. Ultimately, the immobility and apathy of significant segments of their societies sapped the communist states of legitimacy, leaving them in

Lenin Speaks. Lenin addressing a crowd in Moscow, 5 May 1920. Leon Trotsky *(in uniform, right)* leans against the rostrum.
DAVID KING COLLECTION

wreckage all over Europe. Nonetheless, the workers' and peasants' states were able also to attract a good deal of popular support, precisely because they seemed to embody development and progress.

While the history of communism focuses heavily on state-society relations in the Soviet Union and later in its satellite states, there is also a powerful social history of communism in places like Germany, France, and Italy, where the party developed as a potent protest force. Social historians have worked to determine what types of workers and peasants were most likely to become communist. In some cases, as in the area of Bologna, Italy, communist strength owed much to regional traditions of dissent and not just to class issues. Communist movements went through various phases in wooing their constituency. Thus in France in the 1930s new attempts were made to attract young people and women by combining the communist message with social programs and even cosmetic and fashion advice. While communist trade unions were typically more intransigent than their socialist counterparts, many workers sought conventional incremental goals from the unions without much reference

to revolutionary implications. Communist participation in coalition governments right after World War II was vital to the creation of welfare states in France and Italy. Communist-controlled city governments were often very effective in providing social programs. In sum, many communist voters were able to gain not only an outlet for profound social and political grievances but also a variety of practical services as well.

SOCIALIST VARIETIES

In the nineteenth century certain strands of socialism had promoted a vision of the autonomy of workers and their communities. The ideal here was of mostly small-scale communities that were self-governed and that organized production in a common, mutual fashion. This kind of socialism, sometimes called mutualism, had strong resonance in France, Italy, Spain, and Russia. This vision echoed aspects of other efforts to establish autonomous, communal societies in Europe in earlier periods, such as those of Anabaptists in the Reformation or the more radical groups active in

520

the English revolutions of the seventeenth century. In the age of industrialization, these ideas found practical expression in the "houses of labor" that proliferated especially in France and Italy, which served as a kind of combined working-class hiring hall, recreational center, and site of political activism. The various forms of workers' mutual-aid societies, from burial funds to sports associations to early trade unions, were also focal points of autonomous organization, and their supporters were often opposed to any form of state intervention.

The major theorists of socialism and communism, Karl Marx and Friedrich Engels, were notably vague in their prescriptions for the political organization of the future communist society. Yet for all their support of the large-scale features of industrialism, they too captured some of that vision of a world of self-organization in which the state, in their classic phrase, "withered away." Many socialists seemed to agree with that formulation. But Marx and Engels also coined another phrase, the "dictatorship of the proletariat," which would become even more renowned. Marx seems to have meant something quite democratic, almost a Rousseauean notion of the general will. Given his view that society would divide inevitably into two classes, a great majority of proletarians versus a tiny number of powerful capitalists, it is certainly fair to assume that he understood the dictatorship of the proletariat as a situation in which the vast majority of the population would deprive the tiny number of exploiters of their political rights in order to ensure the victory of the revolution. By maintaining power over and against these exploiters, a true democracy, one that ran through all the institutions of society, the economy, family, and polity, would at last emerge.

Other socialists in the nineteenth century had an even more favorable understanding of the state. In 1848 the French socialist Louis Blanc entered the revolutionary government and convinced it to establish national workshops, a kind of state-funded employment program. Some of the utopian socialists, like Claude Henri de Saint-Simon, advocated a prominent role for the state, even the capitalist state, in improving workers' lives and charting the path from capitalism to socialism. The German socialist Ferdinand Lassalle thought similarly. Through democratic participation, the state, over time, would evolve from its capitalist to a socialist nature.

The Social Democratic Party of Germany (SPD) became the major voice of the statist tendency in the Second International, the association of socialist parties founded in 1889. As the largest socialist party before World War I, but also because it was, after all,

German, the filial descendant of Marx and Engels, the SPD wielded great authority. Alongside its explicitly Marxist orientation, the SPD in its early years was greatly influenced by Lassalle's followers and their pro-state position. The SPD grew significantly even in the 1880s, when many party activities were legally banned. It faced its first great ideological crisis in that same decade, when it found itself confronted with a state-run social welfare program pioneered by the German chancellor Otto von Bismarck. Germany was the first state to adopt the key elements of modern social welfare—accident insurance, health insurance, and old-age pensions. Bismarck viewed these measures as a way to ameliorate the difficult conditions of workers in the industrial age and to undermine the appeal of socialism by binding workers to the German state. Socialists could adopt a stance of ideological purity and spurn the social-welfare measures promoted by a semiauthoritarian, capitalist state, or they could work within the state in support of the programs. However minimal the benefits in the early years, however much they expanded the realm of state intervention in workers' lives, the social-welfare programs were immensely popular with workers. Despite their initial opposition, most socialists quickly became advocates and only fought with the state on the size and range of the programs. By the onset of World War I, many Ger-

Karl Marx. ©CAMERA PRESS LTD., LONDON

Friedrich Engels. ©Hulton Getty/Liaison Agency

man socialists worked within the local administration of the social-welfare programs and had also come to demand state mediation of labor disputes. Practically, the SPD was increasingly entwined with the state, despite the ideological hostility expressed by certain wings of the party, especially its leading ideological lights, Karl Kautsky and Rosa Luxemburg. In general, an orientation in favor of the state had come to prevail in the Second International over more anarchist-leaning, small-scale, mutualist visions that rejected the state in toto.

In one of the great ironies of history, V. I. Lenin, on the eve of the Russian Revolution, returned to the antistate position in his famous tract "State and Revolution" (1917). Lenin authored a democratic, even anarchist-sounding treatise that emphasized the withering away of the state after the proletarian revolution. Lenin gave no strict time frame for this process, but it is safe to say that it would not take eons, perhaps a generation or two. Yet at about the same time, Lenin expressed great admiration for the German state in World War I, which he imagined to be a strong, stunning exemplar of rational efficiency. Lenin envisaged revolution as a combination of proletarian (or party) power and the organizational capacities of the Ger-

man state. Lenin, in short, embodied the diverse strands of socialist thinking about the state.

REVOLUTION AND THE STATE

Lenin returned in April 1917 to a Russia in the midst of revolution. He immediately raised the slogan, "All Power to the Soviets," a call that also embodied the contradictory legacies of nineteenth-century socialism. The soviets (councils) were organized more or less spontaneously in factory meetings in which workers elected their own representatives. City soviets were then formed from the representatives of the various workplaces. The movement soon spread to the countryside and the military. "All Power to the Soviets" was seen as an arch-democratic demand, a kind of mutualism writ large, since the soviets were popularly elected, democratic organs. In Lenin's Marxian logic, soviets would necessarily adopt the "correct" position, even if it took some convincing from the Bolshevik Party. In the heady revolutionary days of 1917, Lenin saw no contradiction between democracy and revolution, a position that seemed to be confirmed when the tide of revolution brought Bolshevik majorities in key soviets in the major cities of Petrograd and Moscow and in a few key naval regiments.

When Lenin decided the time was ripe for moving the revolution beyond its initial liberal phase, he and his supporters made certain that their revolution would be seen as the work of the soviets, not the Bolshevik Party. Formally, the revolution was organized by the Military Revolutionary Committee of the Petrograd Soviet, both headed by Leon Trotsky, who had moved his small group of Mensheviks into the Bolshevik Party just a few months before. For all intents and appearances, the revolution carried out on 7 November 1917 was a democratic affair of urban Russia. The program proclaimed by the new revolutionary government was highly democratic. It granted land to the village soviets, self-determination to the national minorities, and workers' control of industry. The government also called for an immediate end to World War I without any indemnities or territorial annexations and promised to convene a constitutional convention. As the new foreign minister, Trotsky opened the safe, read aloud the secret treaties the tsarist government had signed, and theatrically announced that the ministry would issue a few proclamations and then close shop. A minimalist state backed by self-organized workers' and peasants' communities seemed to be in place in Russia in the autumn of 1917.

But the Bolsheviks were immediately confronted with a set of intertwining dilemmas that dramatically posed the problem of the relationship between state and society under a revolutionary regime. With all the hubris of revolutionaries, the Bolsheviks presumed that they knew the correct course (even when there were shifts in specific policies) for Russia and expected workers and peasants to follow suit. But what would happen if workers did not choose to follow the course laid out by the party? Moreover, the revolution had basically been staged in Petrograd and Moscow. The Bolsheviks had taken power through an urban revolution combined with a peasant revolt. Politically, peasants were fickle, willing to support the Bolsheviks when they promised land but by no means committed to the overall political vision of a socialist revolution. How were the Bolsheviks to engineer a revolution in such a minimally developed society? To complicate matters further, the Bolsheviks had seized power in an empire with a dizzying array of ethnic and national groups. How could support be found for a socialist revolution amid this diversity, when ethnicity was often a more critical identity marker than class? In responding to these dilemmas, the Bolsheviks would find that they could not simply impose their ideology and institutions upon society.

The first breach in the putative democratic nature of the young Bolshevik state came very quickly. In January 1918, just a few months after the Bolshevik seizure of power, a constitutional convention convened in Petrograd. The Bolsheviks had won substantial representation in the elections but were still in a minority, while the populist, peasant-based Social Revolutionary Party had garnered the largest proportion of votes. The convention was summarily dismissed by the Bolshevik-controlled Red Guards.

The key event that would define the future development of the state was the civil war that erupted in the spring of 1918. The war was fought on many fronts and included intervention by armies of other European nations and the United States, which allied with the counterrevolutionary forces. The conflict drove home to the Bolsheviks just how tenuous their position was and how much they needed an effective state to remain in power. Building on Lenin's imagination of the German state as a highly efficient, well-oiled machine (never mind the fact that Germany lost World War I), the Bolsheviks proclaimed the policy of War Communism, in which the state seized control of the whole economy and sought to mobilize the entire society to the Bolshevik cause. For some Bolsheviks, notably Nikolai Bukharin, War Communism was not just an emergency policy but the very expression of the new socialist society, which had now abolished private ownership of the means of production. Yet War Communism was a ludicrous policy that failed miserably. The Russian state lacked the depth of its German counterpart, lacked its tradition of efficiency and competence. The Russian empire was sprawling, and it was far more difficult to direct hundreds of thousands of independent peasant landholdings than it was, in Germany, to issue orders to, say, four major firms of the steel industry or the six companies that dominated the chemical industry. Under War Communism, industrial production ground nearly to a halt, and peasants, faced with continual crop seizures, simply stopped sowing. For the first time, the Bolsheviks faced the tenacity of society, which was far greater, its malleability much less, than they had imagined.

War requires an army, and in the modern world armies are put into the field by states. The Bolsheviks had the nucleus of an army in the militias, the Red Guards, formed in the summer of 1917, who played a critical role in the execution of the revolution. But the Red Guards were somewhat unruly and hardly capable of fighting on the many fronts of the civil war. Lenin appointed Trotsky military commissar in March 1918, and it was he who displayed both organizational brilliance and ruthlessness in bringing to life the Red Army. Trotsky imposed a disciplinary regimen worthy of the Prussian kings or the Russian tsars but now combined with the ideological fervor of revolution. In creating an effective army, Trotsky contributed mightily to the emergence of a powerful state.

Still more chillingly, Trotsky created an army that practiced terror. The Bolsheviks were very open in their advocacy of terror, by which they understood the state's systematic application of extraordinary means of repression against opponents of the revolution. They published articles in newspapers extolling terror and openly debated Russian and Western socialists who were appalled at the level of violence in the Russian Revolution. Lenin issued a blistering attack on the German Social Democrat Karl Kautsky, while Trotsky displayed rhetorical brilliance and theoretical vacuity. He argued that the violence of the revolution served the higher goals of socialism and human freedom, while the violence of capitalism, no less endemic, only prolonged injustice.

The Red Army was not the only agency of terror. In December 1917 the Bolshevik state established the first of the many secret police agencies that would play such a profound role in Soviet life, the All-Russian Extraordinary Commission to Fight Counterrevolution, known by its Russian acronym, Cheka. As the institutions of force within the state, the Red Army and the Cheka conducted arbitrary arrests and executions and seized as hostages the families of counterrevolutionaries. Perhaps most drastically, the

Bolsheviks deported entire villages in the Don and Kuban Cossack regions. The villagers were accused en masse of counterrevolutionary activities. This dramatic display of state power was sometimes accompanied by a biological rhetoric that made Cossack peasants into pariahs, incapable ever of incorporation into the new society. These people could not be "civilized" into good socialists; instead, society had to be protected from them by their utter exclusion.

The Bolsheviks ultimately triumphed in the civil war, but it was a costly victory. The cities, so central to the Bolshevik revolution in 1917, had become denuded of their populations. Many of the Bolsheviks' most fervent supporters had been killed in the civil war. Peasants had stopped sowing; industry stopped producing. Famine was widespread. Fatefully, a strong element of militarism came to define Bolshevik culture. Many of the Bolshevik leaders adopted military dress. Iron discipline, already an ideal of Lenin, became ever more prized with the sense that the revolution was made by military might. The heroic male proletarian, who leaves the factory, rifle in hand, to defend the revolution, became an ideal that far surpassed the young woman who also fought for the revolution or labored in the factories. Revolutionary militarism meant a renewed and more fervent centering of masculine power within the institutions of party and state.

The disastrous situation at the end of the civil war forced the state to relax its grip on society. Right at the end of the civil war the Bolsheviks convened for their Tenth Congress. Surveying the devastation before him, Lenin made a strategically brilliant retreat: the state would retain control only of the "commanding heights" of the economy, banks and large-scale industry. Trade and small-scale industry would be afforded, if not exactly free rein, at least a wide range of liberties. Most importantly, the peasants would pay a fixed tax in kind and could then dispose freely of any surplus. To many Bolsheviks, this New Economic Policy (NEP) marked a restoration of capitalism and betrayal of the revolution. For others, it was a strategic retreat born of necessity. Still others, like Bukharin, who radically revised his previous support for War Communism, would come to see in NEP the possibilities for a peaceful transition from capitalism to socialism.

The new policy came to pass along with one last great convulsion of the civil war, the revolt of sailors at Kronstadt in March 1921. The Kronstadt naval garrison had been a major supporter of the Bolshevik revolution in 1917. Now its sailors revolted against the suppression of democratic liberties and the desolate conditions in the countryside, from which many

of the sailors hailed. "Soviets without Bolsheviks," their slogan went, invoking the democratic promise of 1917. It was an eery, sad comment on the entire course of events since October 1917. The Bolsheviks suppressed the revolt, with many of the delegates to the Tenth Congress joining the charge across the frozen Neva River, revolver in hand, to storm the garrison. The contradictions of the revolution—the state's claim to represent the will of the people, its suppression of their will when the people found the Bolshevik state woefully wanting—were laid bare.

BUILDING THE STATE, CREATING THE NEW MAN AND WOMAN

If there was ever a golden period in the Soviet Union, it was the 1920s. The state still exercised repression, but in comparison with what came before and would come afterward, its hand was relatively light. The range of free expression was fairly broad. The economy revived and artistic experimentation flourished. Yet two fundamental structural features emerged in the 1920s. First, the Soviet Union, a federated republic of socialist states, formally came into being at the end of 1922. (From this point it is convenient to speak of Soviets and Communists rather than Russians and Bolsheviks.) Issues of ethnic, national, and religious diversity were now built into the union as a central feature of its existence. Furthermore, the institutions of party and state became formalized. Names would change, reforms would occur, but the essential features of all communist parties and states for the entire twentieth century were firmly established in the 1920s. For the party, the leading organs were the Central Committee, Central Control Commission, and Politburo. For the state, the parallel institutions were the All-Union Congress of Soviets, the Central Executive Committee of the Congress, and the Presidium. The "leading role" of the party was firmly stated in many of the constitutions of Soviet-style states and, practically, by the fact that leading personnel occupied both party and state positions. While the party and state had, technically, discrete functions, the twentieth-century neologism of "party-state" accurately captures the effective intertwining of the two.

In the relative calm of the 1920s, the communist state also articulated more clearly programs designed to forge the new Soviet man and woman. "Forge," a term widely used at the time, conjures up the communist emphasis on the economy and state. Like the metal that emerges out of the blast furnace, the new man and woman would be "produced" through the application of human intelligence and skill. People could not be left to develop on their own but would be crafted by labor, in this case the labor of the workers' and peasants' state.

Propaganda and mobilization, but also repression, constituted the key techniques of this labor. The ideals of socialism were propagated everywhere in the Soviet Union in the 1920s—in schools, institutes, workplaces, academies, the army. A veritable explosion of print culture emerged in the 1920s, as leaflets, pamphlets, and books espousing the ideals of socialism and the campaigns of the Soviet state were disseminated throughout society. New media also expanded dramatically in this period, as the Soviets quickly adopted radio and film for its propaganda drives. Much of the artistic expressiveness of the 1920s, the creation of a variety of modernist genres, served also to disseminate socialist ideas.

But it was also through "practical work," through the mobilization of people in all sorts of campaigns, that the new Soviet man and woman were to be created. Mobilizing university students to teach literacy, urban workers to aid in the harvest, peasants to become involved in the organization of atheists, men to join the Red Army, women to volunteer in orphanages, committed Bolsheviks to work in the Cheka—these were all forms of activism through which men and women would learn the tenets of socialism and become solid citizens of the socialist state. They would reform themselves and those under their tutelage, a civilizing mission not totally unlike other reform efforts in the Western world in the modern period. The result would be ideologically schooled, self-disciplined people who worked selflessly for socialist development. For men, the ideal had profound militaristic connotations, conveyed by the Soviet posters of the period that invariably portrayed muscled men either producing or defending the revolution, hammer or rifle in hand. For women, the ideal was more disparate. Sometimes heroines of the revolution were depicted in fighting formation; other times they were shown as producers or as communist versions of the modern "new woman" of the 1920s—thin, athletic, active in society, and boundlessly happy. But in the 1920s, and still more in the 1930s, maternalist imagery was also prevalent, as if the socialist new woman could somehow combine all of these roles. For both men and women, socialist morality signified serious self-disciplining, a regularized, not promiscuous, sexuality, an aversion to drink and cigarettes and any other superfluous consumption beyond the strict necessities of life, and a devotion to work and politics. In 1936 the Soviet state adopted the pronatalist rhetoric and politics common to many Western countries, including a ban on abortions.

The image of the new socialist man and woman was not propagated only domestically. For all of its particularly Russian characteristics, the revolution and the Soviet Union were very much international phenomena. The Communist Party sought to influence workers and socialists all over Europe and beyond. The major agency for that task was the Communist International (or Comintern), founded in 1919 in Moscow. In the language of the day, the Comintern was to be the "general staff" of the worldwide revolution. Ultimately, the Comintern became the vehicle of Russian control over other national communist parties in Europe and beyond. But for many activists, the Comintern embodied the ideals of international proletarian solidarity against the exploitations and injustices of capitalism. Usually under the auspices of the Comintern, thousands and thousands of communists from around the world came to the Soviet Union and received political and military training in various academies and institutes.

It is impossible to gauge how successful was this vision of the socialist new man and woman that the state promoted in the Soviet Union. Certainly, repression was ever present, even in the 1920s, and ran in tandem with the more positive-sounding aspects of the socialist culture program. Only a minority of the population sought to emulate the ideal in toto. But the partisans of socialism comprised a critical minority. They were the activists in the socialist state, and without their services, the more drastic campaigns of the Stalin era could not have prevailed, nor could the Soviet Union have triumphed over the German invaders in the 1940s. After World War II, many of the foreign communists who had also been inspired by the ideals and had received training in the Soviet Union would play key roles in the communist movements in their home countries.

THE WAR AGAINST SOCIETY

On the economic terrain, grain supply remained a critical problem in the 1920s even though the peasants returned to sowing and harvesting. Moreover, the growing social differentiation in the countryside worried the communists. The real differences between a kulak, a wealthy peasant, and other agricultural toilers were usually quite minimal, but that did not stop the communists from expending great effort to classify and categorize the rural population. The kulak might have had a draft animal or two and hired labor to help out on his land. (Technically, the land was owned by the village soviet, then distributed to individual households.) While kulaks constituted perhaps 5 percent

Celebrating the Socialist Ideal. Participants carry portraits of Marx, Engels, and Lenin in the annual parade commemorating the Bolshevik revolution. Gorky Street, Moscow, 7 November 1955. SOVFOTO/EASTFOTO

of the rural population, they accounted for around 40 percent of the marketed grain. They held therefore a critical position in the economy. Three times the kulaks went on a grain strike—that is, they refused to bring their grain to market, counting on the government to increase the price. In the meantime, Joseph Stalin had accumulated enormous powers through his control of the party organization and its political bodies. (Formally, his powers were based on his position as general secretary of the Central Committee of the Communist Party of the Soviet Union from 1922 to 1953, to which he added many other titles over the years, especially in World War II.) By the late 1920s, Stalin had prevailed in the intraparty factional conflicts. To Stalin and some other leading communists, peasant grain strikes threatened the authority of the state, the very existence of the revolution. He and his supporters had few scruples against deploying state power to rectify the situation.

The outcome was the massive deployment of force against the peasantry, first through grain requisitions that began at the very end of 1928, and then through the forced collectivization of peasant landholdings. These events, which extended into the mid-1930s, constituted the single greatest clash between state and society in the Soviet Union. It was a conflict between a state bent on economic development and human transformation and a vast, largely immobile rural population, wedded to private peasant landholdings and traditional ways of life, who resisted the state's drive to transform radically and unalterably conditions in agriculture. The state sent Red Army detachments into the countryside, along with elite groups of party workers, often idealistic youth. The definition of a kulak came to mean anyone who resisted the program of collectivization. Hundreds of thousands, perhaps millions, of peasants—the exact numbers remain disputed—were imprisoned or sent to labor camps in Siberia (known by their Russian acronym, the Gulag). Many died in transit or from the extremely harsh conditions of the Gulag. In the early 1930s the ineptness of state policies led to horrendous famine in the Ukraine and northern Caucasus. As many as 6 million people may have died from the ravages of hunger. While some scholars argue that the state deliberately promoted the famine in order to break peasant resistance and to suppress Ukrainian nationalism, it seems more likely that it resulted from indifference and ineptness, though the root cause certainly was the deployment of massive force against rural society.

Concomitant with forced collectivization, Stalin initiated the rapid, state-directed industrialization drive, embodied in the series of five-year plans, the first of which was launched in 1928. Economically, the program constituted a huge superexploitation of the still largely peasant society. Whatever resources the state extracted, it channeled into the heavy industrial sector, and the Soviet Union became an industrial powerhouse. Economic development, then, went hand in hand with the massive buildup of the state. Typical of the Stalin era and its emphasis on grand scale were such massive projects as the White Sea Canal, built with convict labor in appalling conditions, and Magnitogorsk, the gigantic steel complex that arose out of almost nothing. Designed to be a model Soviet city, Magnitogorsk eventually produced great amounts of steel, but the community surrounding it endured unpaved roads, crowded apartments that rapidly deteriorated, and inadequate plumbing.

The massive, state-directed efforts of collectivization and industrialization irrevocably transformed Soviet society. The population became immensely mobile—a "quicksand society," in the words of the historian Moshe Lewin—and more urbanized. The palpable presence of the state extended into virtually every geographic area however remote, into every family. Out of a population of around 170 million, 16 to 19 million peasants left their villages in the 1930s to enter the urban, industrial workforce. The number of cities with over 100,000 inhabitants rose in the 1930s from thirty-one to eighty-nine. The migrants were preponderantly young and male and often skilled; they left the village populations disproportionately older and female, trends that the ravages of World War II would only accentuate. Out of some 25 million individual peasant households, the state created 240,000 collective farms.

The state, then, won the battles for collectivization and industrialization, but at great cost. Despite very substantial economic growth in the 1930s and then again in the 1950s and 1960s, state-directed development built all sorts of inefficiencies into the economy. Clearly, the absence of adequate pricing mechanisms and the inattentiveness to markets caused structural inefficiencies. But so did the laggard, slothful work discipline typical of Soviet labor. Assured of employment and at least a minimal existence by the state, presented with few material incentives for hard labor, people worked slowly and inefficiently, if perhaps more humanely, as least by Western capitalist standards. Political repression ensured that peasants could not strike or rebel, but like their counterparts in so many parts of the world, they responded to the demands placed upon them with a baleful indifference. In contrast, they lavished great attention on their private plots, when these were made available to them alongside the collective farms, notably in the 1950s under Nikita Khrushchev. The slow, lumbering character of collective-farm and industrial labor somehow became replicated in the state, which for all its powers displayed many of these same attributes. Society was not infinitely malleable, and the very processes that made the state huge also made it hugely inefficient.

Along with collectivization and industrialization, the systematic exercise of political terror in the 1930s constituted the third element in the massive buildup of the state. To the extent that the terror had any rationality, its goal seems to have been the elimination of all possible political opposition, the full consolidation of Stalin's personal power in the party-state. If collectivization was a war against the peasantry, the Great Terror of 1936–1938 was a war against the party, but one that spilled over into the society at large. Terror, by its very nature, has an accelerating dynamic. In the infamous show trials, many of the leading figures of the revolution were deemed "enemies of the people" and subsequently executed. By 1938, only a handful of old Bolsheviks still sat in the Central Committee; fully 70 percent of the Central Committee members elected in 1934 were sent to the labor camps or executed. The officer corps of the Red Army was similarly affected, as were leading officials in the economic sector and in the Foreign Ministry. But all sorts of individuals, some with no political position whatsoever, found themselves denounced and subject to the arbitrary powers of the state. The system of labor camps expanded dramatically in this period and assumed an important role in the economy, particularly in extraction industries like mining and lumbering. More recent research in Soviet archives has shown that a significant movement in and out of the camps emerged—sentencing was not a one-way ticket. Still, thousands upon thousands of people languished in the Gulag, to be freed only in the 1950s, while many others died from the extremely harsh conditions.

Yet another form of oppression appeared in the 1930s, that of particular ethnic groups. In the 1920s, the Soviets state had first implemented the policy of *korenizatsiia,* or indigenization. In the Soviet view, articulated by Stalin in "Marxism and the National Question" (1913), the nation represented a particular stage of historical development but also had a certain timeless quality to it based on the cultural distinctions among peoples. Progress toward socialism could only come through the national form. Hence in the 1920s, through "indigenization," the Soviets promoted national languages and national elites. National soviets were established, and in a number of cases ethnic Russians were forcibly removed to give indigenous groups greater access to resources. Soviet scholars gave oral languages and dialects written form, and the state consolidated some tribes and ethnic groups and handed them a common language.

But a vital change came with the proclamation of the new constitution in 1936, which, in Stalinist eyes, gave legal form to the triumph of socialism. The nobility and the tsarist state, then the bourgeoisie, had been defeated. Class enemies as social groups no longer existed within the Soviet Union, just wayward individuals. And nations still existed. The very concept of essential nations that had underpinned the development of nationalities in the 1920s and early 1930s now also underpinned the attack on "suspect" nations. Over the course of the 1930s the objects of persecution shifted from class enemies to "enemies of the people," which slid easily into "enemy nations." As a result, beginning in the 1930s and accelerating during the war years, a variety of ethnic groups were deported in the most horrendous conditions from their historic areas of settlement, including Koreans, Chechens, Ingush, Greeks, Germans, and others. By categorizing and searching out all the members of the targeted groups, the Soviet state essentially racialized ethnicity and nationality even though the Soviets explicitly rejected the ideology of race. The state acted as if the qualities that made the members of a particular group dangerous were immutable and transgenerational, carried by every single individual necessarily and inevitably.

All told, around 3.5 million people were removed in these ethnic deportations. According to recent investigations, death rates from the exigencies of the deportations ranged from 9 percent for the Chechens to 46 percent for the Crimean Tatars. And in 1952–1953, it seems that plans were underway for the deportation of the Jewish community. Only Stalin's death in 1953 staved off this possibility.

The vast growth in the exercise of state terror and state repression from the late 1920s into the early 1950s meant that a profound element of fear and guilt crept into social relations, a characteristic best depicted in Russian literature, such as Anna Akhmatova's searing poem, "The Requiem," Aleksandr Solzhenitsyn's *Gulag Archipelago* (1973–1975), Varlam Shalamov's *Kolyma Tales* (1978), or Vasily Grossman's *Forever Flowing* (1970). The screeching sound of the "Black Marias," the secret police autos; the knock on the door at night; the denunciation by one's neighbors; the fearful and secretly joyous silence when a colleague suddenly disappeared, making an office or a promotion available to those who remained—these constituted part of the realities of social relations.

At the same time, the massive uprooting of society created not only a world of fear but also one of opportunities and of confidence in the developmental possibilities of the socialist future. The industrial and agrarian economies had insatiable needs for skilled workers and technicians, and those who could find themselves a spot in technical institutes or universities had unparalleled opportunities for upward mobility. The state deliberately favored children of peasant and working-class backgrounds, granting them unprecedented opportunities for education and advancement. At the same time, the downward mobility of the former privileged classes eased slightly. The 1936 constitution that proclaimed the victory of socialism formally abolished the *lishentsy* (disenfranchised) class. Now all Soviet citizens were considered equal, though social prejudices against those from formerly privileged classes remained quite strong.

The programs that began in the late 1920s, from collectivization to terror, conjured up waves of commitment, especially among youthful Soviet citizens. Stalinism represented for many of them the path out of backwardness, a mixture of nationalism and socialism that inspired pride in the country's development and in the prospects of "building socialism." Fear and terror there were, but they were not the only aspects of the Soviet reality of the 1930s.

WAR AND THE EXPANSION OF THE SOVIET-STYLE STATE

The German invasion of the Soviet Union in June 1941 wrought great devastation, human and material, on Soviet soil. Close to 20 million Soviet citizens died in the course of World War II. The defense and then the rollback of German forces required immense sacrifices. Through all this, the basic institutions of state and society held their ground. Indeed, the repressive, even murderous, side of state policies in some ways accelerated—as the escalation of ethnic and national purges and the maintenance of the Gulag system indicate—even while the population rallied to the defense of the Soviet system against the foreign invaders. At the same time, building on the gender policies of the 1930s, a far more conservative tenor entered into Soviet life. A crass, essentialized Russian nationalism became more and more pronounced. The state did not even shy away from invoking its adversaries of the past, the church and the tsars, as a way of solidifying Russian nationalist sentiment in the struggle against the Germans.

At the end of the war the Red Army, having borne the brunt of the fighting for so many years, was successfully situated all across central and eastern Europe. Communist parties in France, Italy, Yugoslavia, Greece, and elsewhere had played leading roles in the resistance against Nazi occupation. As a result, they emerged in 1945 as vibrant movements with a great deal of popular support. Indeed, communism reached its high point in Europe between 1943, the beginning of full-scale resistance, and 1956, the year of Khrushchev's speech condemning the crimes of Stalin and of the deployment of Soviet troops against the Hungarian uprising.

Communist parties participated in most Western European governments in the immediate postwar years. In Yugoslavia, a unique case, the party had come to power by playing the decisive role in the resistance. It fought successful military campaigns against both the German occupiers and Yugoslav conservatives and fascists and was able to retain power despite the hostility of the Soviets, who resented the independence of the Yugoslav communists. In the West, communists were quickly driven out of governments with the onset of the Cold War in 1947 and 1948. In France and Italy communists were still able to retain enormous influence in the trade unions and other associations of the labor movement as well as in local government, all of which enabled them to pressure successfully for higher wages and improved social benefits for their working-class constituencies. By the 1980s that influence was waning. Communist voting rates in France began to decline in that decade, causing the party to resort to tactics such as hostility to immigration. The Italian party, long more flexible than the French in its willingness to collaborate with other elements, also began to fade.

In Eastern Europe, in Bulgaria, Romania, Hungary, Czechoslovakia, Poland, and the German Democratic Republic, the Soviets were able, in a few short years, to bring to power communist parties loyal to the Soviet Union. Scholars argue fiercely about whether this was the intent of the Soviets from the moment World War II began or whether they had more varied and flexible (or confused) policies that only became fixed and uniform in the context of the emergence of the Cold War between 1945 and 1949. Certainly, the great transformation of power relations within Europe, the utter devastation of Germany, and the surge between 1943 and 1948 of anti-Nazi resistance, mass worker protests, and Communist Party activism in so many countries created a fluid and unprecedented situation. The Baltic states (incorporated directly into the Soviet Union since 1939), Poland, and Bulgaria were probably slated for complete Communist Party control early on, while it is possible that more diverse political solutions would have been acceptable in some of the other countries, especially if a unified, neutral Germany had been established. "Third-way" social and political orders, somewhere between liberal capitalism and Soviet-style socialism, might have become a reality.

But the onset of the Cold War and Stalin's own deep paranoia drastically narrowed the political options by the end of the 1940s. In the Soviet bloc, a uniform pattern was created among the "people's democracies," as they came to be called. (The pattern included the GDR even though it never was called a "people's democracy." As the remains of a divided power and situated on the front lines of the Cold War, the GDR always had a peculiar status.) In all the countries, Communist Party power was secured through the usual mechanisms—an extensive security apparatus, state control over industry and agriculture, and party control over the state. This pattern persisted for the fifty years from the late 1940s onward. Moreover, the state, as in the Soviet Union, had a developmental function. It collectivized agriculture and promoted the development of industry, heavy industry in particular. Both processes occurred on a significant scale throughout the region in the late 1940s and 1950s. The social structure became transformed as people left farming and the villages for industry and the cities. Warsaw, Lodz, Bucharest, Pilsen, and many other cities grew significantly; social mobility intensified as the regimes favored the children of working-class and peasant backgrounds. The huge bureaucracies of communist states also offered avenues of mobility and a means of binding large segments of the population to the system. The state also exercised the heavy hand of repression, most drastically in the early 1950s.

The communist-ruled countries of Eastern Europe were, from the outset, more developed and complex than Soviet society of the 1930s. They had more significant industrial bases and more varied social structures. Over twenty years of experience with eco-

Hungary, 1956. Removing the portrait of Lenin from the Gyor City Hall, Budapest. Calls for democratic reform in Hungary erupted into revolution in October 1956. Premier Imre Nagy (1896–1958) withdrew Hungary from the Warsaw Pact and appealed in vain to the United Nations for help against Soviet intervention. In November Soviet troops invaded Hungary. Nagy's former ally János Kádár formed a new government, while Nagy himself was executed. ERICH LESSING/MAGNUM PHOTOS

nomic planning in the Soviet Union had laid bare many of the inefficiencies of strict central control. To varying degrees and in response to internal social pressures, the communist states experimented with slightly different models from the strict command model that persisted in the Soviet Union. The Poles gave up on collectivized agriculture; the Hungarians introduced market mechanisms in the 1960s. Only East Germany, loyal to the Soviet model to the end, carried out further nationalizations of remaining small businesses in the 1970s.

Economic development also helped create the demise of the very system that promoted it. By the late 1950s, communist states had made material improvements the mark of success of their own system. They promised their populations the consumer life on a scale comparable with the West, yet with the social protections afforded by communism. But the inefficiencies of centrally planned economies, no matter if they had some more flexibilities than the Soviets, could not compete with Western capitalist economies, especially in the more aggressive and competitive global markets in the last decades of the twentieth century. The dead weight of state repression prevented any serious reform efforts and continually antagonized substantial segments of the population. Key professional groups desired autonomy and consideration of their interests within the state. Gradually, new public spheres emerged. In the Soviet Union, the public sphere was largely composed of intellectuals who ran great risks of imprisonment in horrendous circumstances. In Poland, workers rebelled in 1956, 1968, and 1979–1980. Slowly and with difficulty, a common opposition was formed between workers and intellectuals, with significant support from the Catholic Church. In Czechoslovakia a significant reform movement developed within the ranks of the party, only to be crushed by Soviet intervention in 1968. Afterward, an opposition of intellectuals created an underground community that periodically surfaced with public pronouncements in favor of democratic liberties and curbs on state power.

Ultimately, the communist states faced the tenacity of their societies, the sullen resentments against the all-encompassing claims of the party-states and their attempts to infiltrate all dimensions of social relations. Society's self-distancing from the state deprived communism of all legitimacy, even among its own leaders, who by the 1980s seemed more like ossified powerholders than champions of the socialist cause. Within a few short years, by the early 1990s, the systems would all be gone, swept away by the party's inability to manage internal reform in the Soviet Union and by waves of popular protests. Societies took their revenge upon the states that sought to mold, regulate, and repress them. At the same time, these societies were very different from those that had first spawned the socialist and communist movements in the epoch of industrialization; they were more complex, more educated, more white-collar. With the exception of Poland and Romania, the key roles in the revolutions of 1989–1991 were played not by workers, the quintessential activists and protesters of the industrial age, but by students, intellectuals, and the technical intelligentsia. The demise of communism was symptomatic of the end of the classic epoch of industrialization and of the labor movement, socialist and communist, that emerged alongside it.

See also **Marxism and Radical History** *(volume 1);* **Socialism** *(volume 3); and other articles in this section.*

BIBLIOGRAPHY

Cohen, Stephen F. *Bukharin and the Bolshevik Revolution: A Political Biography, 1888–1938.* New York, 1973.

Fitzpatrick, Sheila. *Everyday Stalinism: Ordinary Life in Extraordinary Times. Soviet Russia in the 1930s.* New York, 1999.

Fitzpatrick, Sheila. *The Russian Revolution.* 2d ed. Oxford and New York, 1994.

Getty, J. Arch, and Roberta T. Manning, eds. *Stalinist Terror: New Perspectives.* Cambridge, U.K., 1993.

Goldman, Wendy Z. *Women, the State, and Revolution: Soviet Family Policy and Social Life, 1917–1936.* Cambridge, U.K. 1993.

Hagen, Mark von. *Soldiers in the Proletarian Dictatorship: The Red Army and the Soviet Socialist State, 1917–1930*. Ithaca, N.Y., 1990.

Holquist, Peter. "'Information Is the Alpha and Omega of Our Work': Bolshevik Surveillance in Its Pan-European Context." *Journal of Modern History* 69 (1997): 415–450.

Koenker, Diane P., William G. Rosenberg, and Ronald Grigor Suny, eds. *Party, State, and Society in the Russian Civil War: Explorations in Social History.* Bloomington, Ind., 1989.

Konrad, George, and Ivan Szelenyi. *The Intellectuals on the Road to Class Power.* Translated by Andrew Arato and Richard E. Allen. New York, 1979.

Kornai, Janos. *The Socialist System: The Political Economy of Communism.* Princeton, N.J., 1992.

Lewin, Moshe. *The Making of the Soviet System: Essays in the Social History of Interwar Russia.* New York, 1985.

Lewin, Moshe. *Russian Peasants and Soviet Power: A Study of Collectivization.* Translated by Irene Nove with John Biggart. London, 1968.

Martin, Terry. "The Origins of Soviet Ethnic Cleansing." *Journal of Modern History* 70(1998):813–861.

Naimark, Norman M. *The Russians in Germany: A History of the Soviet Zone of Occupation, 1945–1949.* Cambridge, Mass., 1995.

Siegelbaum, Lewis H. *Soviet State and Society between Revolutions, 1918–1929.* Cambridge, U.K., 1992.

Skilling, H. Gordon. *Czechoslovakia's Interrupted Revolution.* Princeton, N.J., 1976.

Suny, Ronald Grigor. *The Revenge of the Past: Nationalism, Revolution, and the Collapse of the Soviet Union.* Stanford, Calif., 1993.

Tucker, Robert C., ed. *Stalinism: Essays in Historical Interpretation.* New York, 1977.

Verdery, Katherine. *What Was Socialism, and What Comes Next?* Princeton, N.J., 1996.

Weitz, Eric D. *Creating German Communism, 1890–1990: From Popular Protests to Socialist State.* Princeton, N.J., 1997.

Werth, Nicolas. "Un État contre son peuple: Violences, répressions, terreurs en Union sovietique." In *Le livre noir du communisme: Crimes, terreur et répression.* Edited by Stéphane Courtois. Paris, 1997. Pages 43–295.

BUREAUCRACY

Don K. Rowney

"Bureaucracy" is a name given to hierarchical authority structures in modern, complex organizations. Historically, the term has applied to state organizations and to the structure of the behavior of officials until well into the twentieth century. Increasingly, after World War I, bureaucracy has been a concept and term that scholars have applied to firms and large civic organizations, often with the implications of cumbersome inefficiency and impersonal insensitivity in dealings with the public or clients.

BUREAUCRACY AS A CONCEPT AND ORGANIZATIONAL TYPE

Scholars' use of the terms "bureaucracy" and "bureaucratization" is largely owing to the influence of the German sociologist Max Weber (1864–1920), who applied it mainly to agencies of the state. But to think of a bureaucracy merely as an office for the transaction of public business is similar to thinking of supersonic aircraft as a means of conveyance from point A to point B. Historically, the term has embodied an array of political, cultural, and philosophical viewpoints that, in turn, reflect the increasingly pervasive and intrusive presence of state and other large organizations into the modern history of European society. The continuing interest in Weber's work on this process, and the important contributions to this body of scholarship by students and critics of Weber, oblige any extended consideration of bureaucracy to be as much a history of ideas as one of institutions.

Students of modern European history often associate the extension of state administration with the "inevitable" secularization, rationalization, and extension of royal household functions. These developments are characterized as responding to the increasing complexity of military and political functions, commercial and industrial enterprise, as well as to urbanization and the European compulsion to create impersonal legal authorities in public life. This view is especially associated with Weber's work. Weber's near monopoly over thinking about bureaucracy and bureaucratization in modern Europe, however, did not take hold until the 1960s. Between the time of his death in 1920 and the mid-twentieth century—an era that witnessed an explosion in the number and scope of bureaucratic organizations—Weber's influence in Europe generally, and in Germany specifically, was comparatively limited. With the appearance in the 1950s and 1960s of several important studies of his work and influence by scholars such as Wolfgang J. Mommsen, and the convening of the Fifteenth Congress of the German Sociological Association in 1964, commemorating the centenary of his birth, the dominance of Weberian views of bureaucracy and bureaucratic development—the process of bureaucratization—was assured.

In the English-speaking world, Talcott Parsons's *Structure of Social Action* (1937) stimulated interest in German sociology and Weber's ideas about the origins of capitalism and bureaucracy in modern Europe. Later in his career, Parsons would adopt a more nuanced and critical view of Weberian organizational behavior. Nevertheless, Parsons's early understanding of Weber and bureaucratic structural development reinforced the growing importance of structural functionalism in the 1940s and 1950s and the work of the most influential American student of Weber, Reinhard Bendix.

Interpretations of Weber's understanding of bureaucracy are, in fact, based on syntheses of a vast and diverse array of his writings, in particular *Economy and Society, The Religion of China, The Religion of India, The Protestant Ethic and the Spirit of Capitalism,* and *General Economic History.* Owing, moreover, to a proliferation of special editions and translations (especially into English) of Weber's original works, it can be difficult to trace the provenance of Weber's most famous and influential theories, including his views on bureaucracy and bureaucratization. This accounts, at least in part, for the continuing controversy over what Weber actually understood the phenomenon to be.

Max Weber. ARCHIVE PHOTOS

Max Weber was born in Germany and grew up during the Second Empire, an era of remarkable efflorescence in the arts, science, and politics. The son of a successful lawyer, he was educated in the classics and received collegiate and postgraduate training at the Universities of Heidelberg, Göttingen, and Berlin, primarily in law. Eventually he received an appointment as a professor of economics at the University of Freiburg and, later, the University of Heidelberg. Weber's analyses of social structures, religion, and social behavior pervaded North American sociological writing from the late 1930s until the 1980s. His influence in Europe was more restricted than in the United States until the post–World War II period. He continues to dominate scholarship in the field of bureaucracy, although this influence is more limited today owing to increased use by firms and governmental bodies of research from fields such as organizational psychology.

Weber thought that authority structures were the core of social organization but that such structures required validation, or legitimation, by underlying social values. Across an extraordinary range of historical and sociological studies, Weber developed a typology of authority that, depending upon historical circumstances, was reducible to one of three forms: traditional, charismatic, or legal. He thought, moreover, that legal authority was most (although not exclusively) typical of modern societies and expected this authority to broaden its scope and intensify over time. A continuing point of controversy among students of Weber is whether this view of authority and its role in society was prescriptive (or normative) or merely descriptive. In any case, the extension of written legal norms, together with an increasing dependence upon rational (as opposed, for example, to religious) standards of conduct in public life demanded the creation of the organizational structures and behavior that he called bureaucratic. While Weber recognized the importance of bureaucracies in premodern societies, he thought that the fusion of legal norms and rationality with such characteristics of modern life as complex technology, large concentrations of population, and widespread education created a circle of social, political, and economic energies that continually stimulated bureaucratic development in the contemporary world.

Although Weber's view of bureaucracy was explicitly and expertly rooted in historical research, his work, for the most part, does not seem intended to serve as detailed narrative descriptions of the emergence of modern state administrations. Thus, while histories of state and large nonstate bureaucracies written by other scholars are "Weberian" in the sense that they quite frequently draw upon Weber's ideas and use his terminology, the narratives themselves—their factual foundations and developmental sequences—often differ markedly from Weber's. Moreover, as is shown below, there are intellectual perspectives upon which one can draw for constructing and interpreting historical narratives of administrative development that are quite distinct from those that adopt the viewpoint that the history of administration is, in fact, the history of "bureaucratization."

One way of distinguishing schools of different historical narratives that use Weber's concepts and terminology is to ask how they understand the preconditions or generative circumstances for European bureaucratic development. These schools fall into two broad categories. The first is a school of political culture that lays great emphasis on a specific combination of historical circumstances—the need of central governments (usually monarchies) for the management of increasingly complex organizations of growing size and an increasing reliance, over time, upon formal legislation that serves as rules of public conduct. The second is a school of explanation based in economics that owes much to the rise, in the nineteenth century, of large-scale manufacturing and commercial enterprises. Although this work is often set within a Weberian frame of terminology, it also often integrates the analytic and interpretive work of Adam Smith and Karl Marx. Literally, of course, the two schools do not form exclusive categories; in fact, Weber himself frequently combined economics and political culture as independent variables in models or typologies of bureaucratic development.

NARRATIVES OF BUREAUCRATIC DEVELOPMENT: BUREAUCRATIZATION

It is not difficult to find examples of hierarchical and functionally specialized bodies of officials in medieval Europe (for example, in both the court offices of the Holy Roman Empire and the curia of the Roman Catholic Church). Nevertheless, the transformation of secular territorial administrations into specialized administrations for war, finance, the operations of royal courts, and diplomatic and tax administration is generally a phenomenon of the fourteenth to the eighteenth centuries throughout Europe, and not just in western and northern Europe, as some narratives would have it. Certain central government roles (such as taxation and warfare), however, were often coopted by regional territorial authorities or even transformed into commercial activities, with the erstwhile official—a tax farmer or a mercenary soldier, for example—assuming an entrepreneurial role between the state and the taxpayer. Thus it is difficult to find examples of the bureaucratization of state functions that develop in a linear process, moving straight from a traditional, patriarchal system rooted in the society of the royal court to a full-blown system of specializations and hierarchy legitimated by law and rationality.

Part of the reason why bureaucratization (or administrative development of any kind) was tentative and subject to reversal is owing to the limited functions of European states in society before 1800. Generally speaking, even in the eighteenth century state roles were overwhelmingly monopolized by waging war, preparing for war, and paying for recently concluded wars. Other state or court functions were comparatively modest, confined to intermittent diplomacy, the formal organization of the court itself, and, of course, the comparatively complicated functions of

administering tax collections. As Fernand Braudel notes in *The Wheels of Commerce,* these fiscal operations were more smoothly accomplished in some states than in others. But, over time, the political control of military organizations and technology and especially management of the expense of warfare, obliged states to create offices that were staffed by full-time trained officials. As Weber notes, such individuals were often drawn, early on, from the clergy. These constituted one of the few small reservoirs of men in western Europe who were both educated and independent of the landed nobility with whom the monarch often competed.

Gradually, European states began to reach into unattended spheres of social life or, at any rate, to assume responsibility for activities previously in the charge of religious organizations, local communities, and families. For example, some states began, in the eighteenth century, to take an interest in primary education, the redistribution of land, the technical education of farmers, and relief of the circumstances of the poor. The resulting modest extensions of state roles became an occasion for bureaucratization. Eighteenth-century extensions of state roles into uncharted social waters were also often the occasion of virulent political debates over the quality and substance of state administrative roles, their efficiency, honesty, and what today would be called their cost-effectiveness.

Most famously, the effect of the English cleric Thomas Malthus's *Essay on the Principle of Population* (1798) was to convince some policymakers that the only effect of poor relief could be to enlarge the numbers of the poor through encouraging reproduction by a proportion similar to the degree of aid. Applied without limit, such unwise but well-intended aids would extend the problem of want indefinitely until all economic resources were exhausted. By the early nineteenth century, political confrontations over such issues introduced additional elements into what Weber would see as a self-reinforcing circle of bureaucratic enhancement. Demands for increased efficiency, reduced corruption, and the introduction of university-educated officials who, in contrast with officials of earlier generations, were not necessarily members of noble social elites or the clergy would intensify the process of bureaucratization itself.

This new era in the development of state administration often involved the expansion of bureaucracy into previously undergoverned segments of society and began the very slow inclusion of social groups—castes or classes—that previously were excluded from state roles. These developments, in turn, were accompanied by a growing need for formally

Housing the Bureaucracy. The château of Versailles. In the foreground, on either side of the entry court, are buildings that housed the agencies of government of ancien régime France. CHÂTEAU DE VERSAILLES ET DE TRIANON, FRANCE/©PHOTO RMN

specified organizational roles, a clearly defined authority structure, and rules that protected and legally defined the authority of officials who were not necessarily born into the ruling classes. By the nineteenth century the demand for administrators who were educated in the increasingly secular settings of universities or in institutions specially designed for the training of state officials, as in France, was strong and growing.

As John Armstrong notes in *The European Administrative Elite* (1973), however, various artificial roadblocks to the inclusion of lower classes in state administration were virtually universal. As a consequence, at least up to World War I, attempts at civil service reforms (such as those proposed in Britain by Sir Stafford Northcote and Sir Charles Trevelyan in 1853) were very slow to take effect. Many seemingly practical structures and controls had the effect of slowing both social and operational change within services. These included the explicit division of state service into "higher" and "lower" echelons, and practical divisions into a favored and relatively influential central

service and a disfavored, relatively obscure provincial service. Such service divisions combined with examination and educational criteria such as the "classics barrier," an educational bar that essentially excluded individuals who had not learned Greek and Latin by attending elite primary and secondary educational institutions. These constructions meant that, in civil administration and the military, "open elites" were rare until well after World War II. Indeed, a study published by the *Economist* magazine on 19 March 1994 showed that, again in Britain, the most senior positions in the civil service (the twenty offices of the permanent secretaries) were staffed exclusively by males who were overwhelmingly the products both of elite, private grammar schools and the Oxbridge universities. But the increasing pressure on both military and civil administrations to master and apply complex technologies as part of their operations often provided the wedge for lower class entrance into state service, at least at low and middle levels.

With urbanization, industrialization, and growth in population size, state roles—from mass education to welfare and public health—had expanded by the end of the nineteenth century. State offices increased in number and authority, as did the numbers of officials and the size of agency budgets. This increased bureaucratization also broadened opportunities for social mobility via official roles, gradually exceeding the capacity of upper classes to staff even elite offices in some European states.

VARIATIONS IN THE NARRATIVES OF BUREAUCRATIZATION

As noted above, many students of the history of bureaucracy explain bureaucratization in terms of the emergence of political and cultural factors—for example, rational and legal systems of valuing public behavior and political needs of rulers. Others understand the process of European bureaucratization within a framework of economic—rather than cultural and political—stimulus. In other words, they understand the experience as a product of other factors in addition to, or besides, growing rationality and legalism, and they see it as more varied across different European states, owing to the different tempos of the state's economic development. The weight of this second view results from the fact that much of the growth of large, complex organizations has historically occurred outside the boundaries of state institutions. Manufacturing and commercial firms, even early in the nineteenth century, illustrated many of the characteristics of bureaucracy that Weber found in state organizations. Moreover, as Adam Smith showed in the eighteenth century, specialized functions and expert roles were as important in efficient manufacturing as they were in the management of state budgets or artillery brigades. Economies of scale and control of markets that made trusts and combines common in many European countries, and conditions of secure employment that were gradually forced upon employers by professional and trade associations, made it increasingly difficult to distinguish between state and industrial bureaucracies. Moreover, the densely argued view of Karl Marx that large-scale capitalism would continue to expand until it was consumed in revolution meant that, as early as the second half of the nineteenth century, Europeans started to think of themselves as living in a world comprehensively dominated by bureaucracy. This was a vision that haunted such thinkers as Friedrich Nietzsche and became a touchstone for much of leftist politics before World War I.

In fact, the relative importance of both economic and political structures and behavior in accounting for the tempo of European bureaucratization sharply differentiates the experience of European societies in general. In eastern Europe and Russia as well as in Italy, Spain, Portugal, and Ireland, different conditions applied, and narratives of bureaucratization have to be written that are different from those of the earliest industrializers. These differences are owing to significant variations both in political structures and in commercial and industrial behavior.

For example, studies of formal administrative systems in Italy have shown that the endurance of patrimonial forms of local government depended more on the survival or disappearance of forms of social organization than on the presence or absence of legal systems of a specific type. Robert Putnam, in *Making Democracy Work* (1993), in particular, sees long-enduring patterns in public and civic life as critical to differences in social adaptation to administrative systems, whatever the underlying system of law. These differences in forms of civic associations and of the public behavior of private citizens were central to Putnam's explanation of the variations in political development between northern and southern Italy in the late twentieth century.

Similarly, in his study of the history of bureaucratization in Sweden, Norway, Germany, France, and England, Rolf Torstendahl found substantial differences in the levels of both political centralization and bureaucratization over long periods of time. While they were fairly similar with respect to economic measures such as per capita income, urbanization, and levels of employment in manufacturing and commerce, these societies nevertheless demonstrated important differences in social and political traditions, "formed," as he put it, through their different histories.

Eastern Europe and especially Russia present unique problems for anyone interested in creating a narrative history of European bureaucratization. This is owing both to relatively delayed political and economic development and to the introduction of communist political systems in the twentieth century, with their highly centralized state civil administrations and centrally planned economies. Each of these historical circumstances presented special opportunities for the extension of state administrative roles. As Alexander Gerschenkron, among others, showed, the delayed introduction of industrialization and capitalism seems to have required enhanced state roles throughout eastern Europe and especially in Russia. There the need for rapid industrialization was underscored by the catastrophic failure of state foreign and military policy in both the Crimean War (1853–1856) and the Russo-Turkish War (1877–1878). In both instances the weak performance of Russian arms in the face of strategic and tactical challenges that, fifty years earlier,

Russia had successfully mastered, drove home the significance, in practice, of Russia's economic and technical backwardness. It was the state, rather than private enterprise, that took the lead in making the investment decisions essential to the development of heavy industry and the economic and social infrastructures essential to early industrialization.

Russian decisions to industrialize were thus not free of political and administrative freight. By the end of the nineteenth century, state roles in the national economy had burgeoned, with hundreds of new oversight agencies and scores of new programs designed to manage the social behavior of emerging working and middle classes and of the new civic entities—such as urban administrations, schools, and medical facilities—that accompanied industrialization. In detail, these new organizations were not equal in quality to those of France or Germany. Officials were less well trained. Corruption was more common. Bureaucratic self-interest intruded more frequently between an agency and the public it was meant to serve. Much is made in scholarly studies of these organizations of the potential arbitrary intervention of the monarchy and other members of elite society into their activities. In fact, this was a relatively rare occurrence. With advancing industrialization and the integration of the Russian state and economy into European orbits of power, the balance of authority between the monarch and the state bureaucracy was shifting in favor of the latter. In terms of their broad characteristics, the agencies of Russian state administration at the end of the nineteenth century were true bureaucracies in the Weberian sense of the word: hierarchical, legally bound, subdivided according to specialization, and defensive of officials' authority.

Following the Communist revolution of 1917, state intrusion into society became even more pervasive in Russia and, after 1945, in Soviet-occupied Eastern Europe. The vehicles for fresh state intervention were increased political centralization; the rapid development of state-controlled infrastructures such as mass education, medical, electrical, and transport systems; and especially centralized economic planning, pricing, and resource allocation. It seems unlikely, however, that the state organizations which governments created to manage these activities were Weberian bureaucracies. Owing to the arbitrary roles of political police, increasing corruption, gray and black market activities, and especially to the continuing intervention of Communist parties or their surrogates, Weberian prerequisites of legal norms of operation and professional independence of officials were often absent. It may be more reasonable to think of these organizations as systems of "dual supervi-

sion," as Reinhard Bendix would have it in *Work and Authority in Industry* (1956), since that term implies a system that cannot tolerate any degree of worker independence and attempts to avoid this by simultaneous managerial and ideological, or political, supervision. It is important to recognize, however, that arbitrary police and party roles were not universal in the Soviet and Communist bloc states and that there were administrative offices in higher education and scientific research, for example, that operated relatively independently and effectively.

The Weberian view that a circle of mutually reinforcing energies would continually expand bureaucracy in modern European society has been an important touchstone for policy debates and narratives of post-World War II bureaucratization. In the 1950s and 1960s economists such as John Kenneth Galbraith, Wassily Leontief, and Gunnar Myrdal seem confidently to have expected that state roles in planning and development were essential and certain to grow in all three major types of social system—advanced capitalist, communist, and developing. As early as the 1940s, however, proponents of "privatization," deinstitutionalization, and devolution of state functions such as transport, power generation, criminal incarceration, education, and even of poor relief called aspects of the bureaucratization narrative into question. Economists such as Friedrich von Hayek challenged the expectation that increases in the scale of enterprises (whether state or private) would offer proportionate increases in efficiency (economies of scale), lowering the cost of output. Moreover, changes in the cost and structure of many technologies—most notably, computers beginning in the 1970s—also made the decentralized operation of social and economic infrastructures and even policymaking feasible. In *Industrial Constructions* (1996), Gary Herrigel, for example, noted a symmetry in Germany between the "centralization and integration in the economy" on the one hand and state centralization on the other in the 1960s, as contrasted with the economic decentralization in the 1980s that stimulated a "similar reversal in state structure." It could certainly be argued, however, that the opposite has been true at the administrative level of the European Union in Brussels and Strasbourg. There, the last few decades of the twentieth century witnessed a nearly unprecedented expansion of oversight and regulatory administrations in economic, fiscal, educational, and cultural affairs, as well as in some areas of international relations.

Policy and technological change in the 1970s and 1980s also placed the bureaucracies of huge multinational and conglomerate corporations in the private sector under pressure. In the short run (during

538

the 1980s and early 1990s, in particular) this resulted in some corporate "downsizing" and restructuring as well as in the divestiture of enterprises from state ownership. In the longer run, however, there appears to have been a renewed emphasis on bureaucratization in the private sector, taking the form not only of expanding firm size and scope but also of internationalization (or "globalization"). This trend has also increased the importance of organizations made up of other organizations, such as trade and professional associations that engage in political lobbying and negotiate or coordinate wage bargaining nationally or across industries, leading to what Torstendahl calls "corporative capitalism."

ADMINISTRATION WITHOUT BUREAUCRACY

While Weber tended to be preoccupied with state roles and their embeddedness into bureaucratic organizations, large nonstate organizations increasingly captured the attention of other writers. At the same time, these scholars also offered interpretations of organizational and official behavior that were at variance with Weber's views, emphasizing, for example, the unpredictability of participants' behavior in bureaucratic settings.

Roberto Michels, in *Political Parties: A Sociological Study of the Oligarchical Tendencies of Modern Democracy* (1915), studied large political associations representing lower-class interests in Germany. These organizations were created, in the teeth of much opposition, to represent the interests of laborers against large manufacturing organizations, such as the Krupp metal industries trust, and the political interest groups that supported them. Michels (with considerable critical assistance from Weber) concluded that in order to achieve their goals, these labor organizations adopted many of the bureaucratic characteristics of the huge firms with which they competed, obeying an "iron law of oligarchy." They became, that is, bureaucracies with authoritarian leaders in their own right in spite of organized labor's avowed antibureaucratic values. With the passage of time, internal requirements for the survival of working-class organizations conflicted with the workplace objectives of union members. This phenomenon, eventually known as goal displacement, is now recognized as common in formal organizations of all kinds.

Similarly, Frederick W. Taylor's detailed studies of the behavior of workers in large industrial and commercial settings indicated that, whatever the content of formal bureaucratic rules of behavior, workers often

DEVOLUTION AND DECENTRALIZATION: REVERSAL OF BUREAUCRATIZATION?

In his analysis of bureaucratization in the modern world, Max Weber thought that components of bureaucratic systems would interact so as to assure the continued expansion of bureaucratic systems. Beginning in the 1970s, research in political science, economics, and history has suggested that growth in the power and scope of authority of nation-states and firms in the contemporary world may not be inevitable. For example, Charles Sable and Jonathan Zeitlin published a pathbreaking article in 1985 that called attention to "exceptions" to the rule that successful enterprises always became mass producers and thus bigger, more dominant in their industries, and more bureaucratic. In 1987 the historian Paul Kennedy published a highly successful comparative history of several major European states in which he called attention to the factors accounting not only for their historic rise to power, wealth, and global influence but to their "fall" in the later twentieth century.

Decentralization and even breakup of a firm, an industry, or a state, however, do not necessarily lead to a reduction in bureaucracy. The sources of bureaucratization, as Weber noted, arise from the need, in modern society, for managerial and service organizations that are staffed by personnel in whom the public (or the organization's clients) have confidence or whom they regard as "legitimate." The foundations of such legitimacy seem to rest, in most cases, on demonstrations of expertise, detachment, and, above all, professional authority on the part of the organization's staff—the very components that Weber thought would stimulate bureaucratization.

performed below levels of job output that might easily achieve in different circumstances. Universal, formal rules governing the behavior of employees or officials, that is, could be impediments to optimum performance. Taylor set about attempting to reconstruct job site conditions in ways that would enhance worker output and summarized his findings in *The Principles of Scientific Management* (1911). He focused attention on the microstructures of workplace behavior, in contrast to the attention that Weberian analysis paid to the macrostructures. Taylor's time-and-motion studies became famous as examples of strategies that were designed to affect performance in ways that went beyond the global rules and definitions to which Weber attached importance.

After 1910, Taylorism became one of the twentieth century's first management fads. Taylorism's influence became pervasive in some firms in North America and western Europe where management sought to improve workplace productivity without significant additional capital investment. In his attempt to reconstruct a state managerial system without all of the formalities and inefficiencies of the tsarist bureaucracy that leftist revolutionaries despised, the Bolshevik leader Vladimir Lenin seized upon Taylorism as an administrative and organizational strategy that promised both efficiency and humane rationality in the workplace during the early years following the Russian Revolution of 1917. The politics of Russia's revolutionary transformation of administration ultimately overwhelmed Bolshevik ideals in this context.

In both of the preceding cases one sees examples of the abstract analyses and practical workplace strategies that the combination of rapidly developing organizations and critiques of Weberian theories would produce in the mid-twentieth century. These examples could be extended by illustrations, for instance, from the "human relations" school of industrial management. Taken together, these alternative, non-Weberian views of administration may be divided into several disciplinary or educational categories, three of which are administration theory, organization theory, and institutional theory.

Administration theory. State administration, as a special career, research, and educational track, long antedates Weberianism and bureaucratic studies and may be subsumed under the field of administration theory. There is still some controversy over whether the classic, centralized state administration in France was a product of the Napoleonic era or, as Alexis de Tocqueville asserted in *The Old Regime and the French Revolution* (1856), of the ancien régime. In any case, the notion that certain individuals could be prepared for a life of impartial and disinterested administration of organizations was common in many eighteenth-century European states, was central to Napoleonic reforms of state administration, and survived through the turn of the twenty-first century. For example, in France the *grandes écôles* (such as the prerevolutionary École des Ponts et Chausées or the Napoleonic École Polytechnique) and, in Russia, the Tsarskoe Selo Lycée were meant to serve as training institutes for future elite state administrators. These institutions tended to focus on substantive administrative issues, as, indeed,

do their heirs—schools of business and public administration—at the end of the twentieth century.

During the years following World War II, a period of rapid growth of large-scale administrations, research in public administration increased enormously. Work by Dwight Waldo (*The Administrative State,* 1984) and others, spanning two generations, produced theories of administration that attempted to distance themselves from Weber and from the history of bureaucracy. Increasingly, at the end of the twentieth century, public and business administration programs in both the European Union and North America—such as the École Nationale d'Administration—relied on such disciplines as law, economics, organizational psychology, and accounting and derived much of their substantive focus not from theories of bureaucracy but from empirical case studies.

Organization theory. Organization theory and the detailed empirical study of individual and group behavior in complex organizations tend to be found within the disciplines of psychology, economics, and sociology. These offer, in many ways, a much more detailed understanding of administrative and organizational behavior than does bureaucratic research. Herbert A. Simon's *Administrative Behavior: A Study of Decision-Making* (1947), for example, stimulated a broad and rich body of empirical research into specific components of organizational behavior. Within this body of work, the Weberian perspective and the idea of organization as bureaucracy play only a limited role. For example, Chester Barnard (*The Function of the Executive,* 1938) and Fritz J. Roethlisberger and William J. Dickson (in *Management and the Worker* [1961], a celebrated study of social organization in one of the plants of the Western Electric Company) argued in the late 1930s that informal organizations, not meaningfully accounted for by Weberian typologies, always tended to arise within formal organizations. These were unplanned and undocumented structural relations among organization participants that were, in spite of their informality, essential for the operation of the formal organization. Such informal associations not only controlled the personal relations among participants but even effectively controlled what acceptable standards for job output would be. Analysis of the equilibrium between acceptable participant effort and organizational demands was extended by Simon, whose work won the Nobel Prize in Economics, and others. Of course, manipulation of such equilibria to achieve harmonious and cost-effective output is key to contemporary management and administrative science and has become a focal subject in schools of administration.

Institutional theory. A late twentieth-century addition to the corpus of work on large organizations, institutional theory attempts to identify social structures and behavior that render economic exchange less than optimal. As developed by the economist Douglass C. North (*Institutions, Institutional Change, and Economic Performance,* 1990), for example, this work is less interested in the institutions (or organizations) themselves than in their effect on economic performance. Nevertheless, institutional theory addresses the roles of both formal and informal organizations in society, comparatively and historically. Bureaucracy is of interest in institutional theoretical studies to the degree that it helps to explain institutional behavior. But an important underlying assumption seems to be that it is feasible to reconstruct social institutions—or to allow institutions to reconstruct themselves—in ways that limit, or even reverse, the organizational sclerosis that bureaucracy often implies.

SOCIAL AND OCCUPATIONAL MOBILITY ISSUES

The history of social mobility as it relates to bureaucracy in Europe is complex, owing not only to variations in the mobility opportunities for bureaucrats and candidates for bureaucratic appointments over time but also to important differences in the experience of individual countries. Moreover, as noted above, in the case of state bureaucracies one must keep in mind that, at certain points in time, while they may offer the means of upward mobility to individuals who gain official employment, their organizational responsibilities may well include constructing or controlling mobility opportunities for individuals throughout society. As educational administrators or fiscal agents, bureaucrats may well be responsible for shaping the career chances of virtually all future social elites, including their own future colleagues. While this may not mean that they control educational policy or even influence it consistently and significantly, there is ample evidence that bureaucratic elites act as "gatekeepers" who may control access to a vast array of career appointments in many societies. Work by authors such as John Armstrong and Ezra Suleiman, moreover, has shown that, at least until the 1950s and 1960s, this has meant that even very talented children of the lower classes in the democratic states of western Europe could be excluded systematically from elite administrative careers and even from the educational programs that might prepare them to compete for such careers.

This said, it remains a fact that large bureaucratic organizations, whether state or private, have long served as channels for upward social mobility in Europe. Among other factors, the increasing reliance of these organizations on impersonal rules of behavior and their growing need for expertise have enhanced the opportunities of individuals, such as the clerics in early modern western Europe, who may have possessed professional qualifications for elite administrative roles without having the upper-class social credentials that were traditionally associated with administrative power. As a result, beginning as early as the Renaissance, state civil service and certain branches of military service offered opportunities to the bright and ambitious sons of literate, impecunious commoners who had access to formal education, or at least technical training, throughout Europe. These opportunities, however, almost universally excluded the daughters of all social categories (except royal families, and occasionally the children of successful members of professions and of a few industrial magnates). They also denied access to all social categories beneath the relatively privileged, educated minority who should be regarded as a sort of social subelite. The exclusions applied, for example, not only to women but usually to Jews, and often (but not always) to other ethnic and religious minorities.

In western, central and most of eastern Europe, this structure of inclusions and exclusions would not change significantly until much later. That is, career opportunities in bureaucracies broadly, and in senior political or elite administration especially, would not be democratized, reflecting somewhat the social structure of entire societies, until the late twentieth century. In Scandinavia and western Europe women made inroads into institutions of higher and, more slowly, technical education. But usually these individuals were the children of social elites or, at least, of upper-middle-class professionals and the bourgeoisie. Moreover, these educational credentials reliably translated into administrative careers in only a few, relatively undervalued, fields such as lower education and general health care.

The history of career mobility in Russia and the other republics of the Soviet Union after the Russian Revolution of 1917 was quite different from that of the rest of Europe. In Russia, to be sure, literacy, numeracy, and other results of education were so rare in the early twentieth century that even the most open bureaucratic employment policies could never have been democratic in the sense of reflecting the structure of the whole society. Nevertheless, as I note in *Transition to Technocracy* (1989), aggressive state and Communist Party programs aimed at restaffing and reconstructing the entire bureaucratic apparatus with candidates from the lower classes produced a massive turnover and relative democratization of Soviet officialdom in a period of time so brief that its effect has probably never been matched in European history. It is important to recognize, however, that this transformation within a decade, or perhaps fifteen years, was costly in terms of squandering administrative experience and denying both to civil administration and the bureaucracy of the new planned economy educational resources that were essential to their functioning. Forced by restaffing requirements, the rapid expansion of agencies, erratic police and Communist Party oversight, and politically inspired purges to reach ever deeper into the population reservoirs of the working class and peasantry, state administration in Russia suffered a degradation in intellectual resources beginning in the 1920s from which it did not recover until at least after World War II. Indeed, one can argue that the disarray and structural weakness that one finds in the state administrations of Russia and other former Soviet republics at the turn of the twenty-first century is partly owing to the continuing effects of this early destabilization.

Bureaucracy certainly shows no sign of significant retreat in Europe in the twenty-first century. If states are devolving and decentralizing in certain ways, they give no indication of being able to do without the rationality and structured authority that Weber found within modern bureaucracies. Moreover, as sophisticated technologies become ever more crucial to administrative operations in both the public and private spheres, the demand for independent, disinterested, legally protected experts organized into smoothly functioning career hierarchies seems certain to survive. In this critical sense, Weber's view that bureaucracy is a self-reinforcing social construct in modern society, together with his ability to identify the energies that give it life, was historically correct and analytically indispensable.

See also **Secularization** *(volume 2);* **Social Mobility** *(volume 3).*

BIBLIOGRAPHY

Works by Weber and about Weberian Bureaucracy

Armstrong, John A. *The European Administrative Elite.* Princeton, N.J., 1973.

Bendix, Reinhard. *Work and Authority in Industry: Ideologies of Management in the Course of Industrialization.* New York, 1956.

Braudel, Fernand. *The Wheels of Commerce.* Translated by Siân Reynolds. Vol. 2 of *Civilization and Capitalism, 15th–18th Century.* New York, 1981–1984.

Mommsen, Wolfgang J. *The Age of Bureaucracy: Perspectives on the Political Sociology of Max Weber.* Oxford, 1974.

Pintner, Walter M., and Don K. Rowney, eds. *Russian Officialdom: The Bureaucratization of Russian Society from the Seventeenth to the Twentieth Century.* Chapel Hill, N.C., 1979.

Rosenburg, Hans. *Bureaucracy, Aristocracy, and Autocracy: The Prussian Experience, 1660–1815.* Cambridge, Mass., 1958.

Rowney, Don K. *Transition to Technocracy: The Structural Foundations of the Soviet Administrative State.* Ithaca, N.Y., 1989.

Suleiman, Ezra N., ed. *Bureaucrats and Policy Making.* New York, 1984.

Suleiman, Ezra N. *Politics, Power, and Bureaucracy in France: The Administrative Elite.* Princeton, N. J., 1974.

Torstendahl, Rolf. *Bureaucratisation in Northwestern Europe, 1880–1985: Domination and Governance.* London, 1990.

Weber, Max. *Economy and Society.* 2 vols. Edited by Guenter Roth and Claus Wittrich. Translated by Ephraim Fischoff et al. New York, 1968.

Weber, Max. *The Protestant Ethic and the Spirit of Capitalism.* Translated by Talcott Parsons. London, 1930.

Weber, Max. *General Economic History*. Translated by Frank H. Knight. Glencoe, Ill., 1950.

Critical Interpretations of Bureaucracy and Alternative Theories of Administration

Barnard, Chester I. *The Functions of the Executive*. Cambridge, Mass., 1938.

Herrigel, Gary. *Industrial Constructions: The Sources of German Industrial Power*. Cambridge, U.K., and New York, 1996.

Kennedy, Paul. *The Rise and Fall of the Great Powers: Economic Change and Military Conflict from 1500 to 2000*. New York, 1987.

Michels, Roberto. *Political Parties: A Sociological Study of the Oligarchical Tendencies of Modern Democracy*. Translated by Eden and Cedar Paul. New York, 1959.

North, Douglass C. *Institutions, Institutional Change, and Economic Performance*. Cambridge, U.K., and New York, 1990.

Parsons, Talcott. *The Structure of Social Action: A Study in Social Theory with Special Reference to a Group of Recent European Writers*. New York, 1937.

Putnam, Robert D. *Making Democracy Work: Civic Traditions in Modern Italy*. With Robert Leonardi and Raffaella Y. Nanetti. Princeton, N.J., 1993.

Roethlisberger, Fritz J., and William J. Dickson. *Management and the Worker*. Cambridge, Mass., 1961.

Sabel, Charles, and Jonathan Zeitlin. "Historical Alternatives to Mass Production: Politics, Markets and Technology in Nineteenth-Century Industrialization." *Past and Present* 108 (1985): 133–176.

Simon, Herbert A. *Administrative Behavior: A Study of Decision-Making*. 3d ed. New York, 1976.

Taylor, Frederick W. *The Principles of Scientific Management*. Vol. 2 of *Scientific Management*. 3 vols. New York, 1947.

Waldo, Dwight. *The Administrative State: A Study of the Political Theory of American Public Administration*. 2d ed. New York, 1984.

MILITARY SERVICE

Michael S. Neiberg

Taking their cue from the classical Greeks and Romans, some Europeans have traditionally viewed military service as the ultimate positive manifestation of the relationship between the state and the individual. To such people, the military possessed the ability to make loyal citizens out of scoundrels, educated men out of the ignorant masses, and, above all, soldiers out of peasants and workers. To others, military service instead represented the ultimate expression of the nefarious influence of the state on their lives. From this point of view the state removed men from the fields, where their labor might do some good, and placed them in the military, where their efforts were wasted in forced marches, formal parades, and martial training, all to defend an alien state that many saw as the true enemy. A peasant from provincial France, Russia, or Hungary might take orders from an officer who did not even speak his language.

Whether seen as patriotic or coercive, military service became a common feature in male lives from early modern European society forward; by the middle of the nineteenth century it was required of hundreds of thousands of young men in almost all of the states of continental Europe. This essay thematically tracks elements of military service in Europe from the sixteenth century to the present day. It begins by introducing the main types of military service, then proceeds to discuss four specifics: men's motivations for joining the military; the role of military service as an instrument of nationalization; the relationship of officers and enlisted men; and ways men have avoided military service. Finally it presents some concluding thoughts on military service in Europe since 1945.

TYPES OF MILITARY SERVICE

Since the Renaissance, four common types of military service stand out: militia, conscript, volunteer, and mercenary. Societies with few internal conflicts or external enemies have the luxury of relying on a militia: part-time soldiers who assemble only for rudimentary

training and in times of crisis. Among European states, the Swiss are the most famous for their citizen militia. Early modern German states, however, also sustained militias based on noncitizen peasants. One of the militia's greatest strengths is its cost-effectiveness. Because militiamen are civilians for most of the year, the state does not have to pay them except in times of training and war. Since they have ordinarily trained with men from their same locality, they develop important bonds and connections to their towns or counties.

The militia's greatest strengths are, however, also its most important weaknesses. Because its men are not full-time soldiers, they rarely possess up-to-date military knowledge or have much familiarity with modern military technology. These units also lack the military cohesion of regulars. Furthermore, they cannot be called to military service without risking attendant disruptions to a nation's economy. Their local attachments make them much more effective in defense of their homeland (sometimes defined as their county or town rather than the entire state) than they are on the offensive.

Conscript systems are also relatively cheap. Because the state compels military service via threats of punishment and appeals to patriotism, it does not need to compensate its soldiers generously. Conscript systems therefore can often yield large armies, as they did in the Napoleonic period and during the two world wars. The famous *levée en masse* of 1793 was not a draft per se, but it was an important antecedent as it set the precedent that all citizens of France owed military service in some fashion. Such a demand was only possible in the dramatic spirit of the French Revolution. Frenchmen responded to the *levée en masse,* producing fourteen new French armies in just a few weeks.

France's Jourdan Law of 1798 built upon the spirit of the *levée en masse* but went even further. The Jourdan Law, Europe's first large-scale systematic draft, required all young men in France to register; the government then set regional quotas to be met off of

THE *LEVÉE EN MASSE*, 1793

From this moment until that in which our enemies shall have been driven from the territory of the Republic, all Frenchmen are permanently requisitioned for service in the armies. Young men will go into battle. Married men will forge arms and transport supplies. Women will make tents and uniforms, and serve in hospitals. Children will pick up rags. Old men will have themselves carried into public squares, to inspire the courage of warriors, and to preach hatred of kings and the unity of the Republic.

those registers. By 1815 the French system had provided two million men to the revolutionary and Napoleonic armies. Soon other states in Europe were trying to imitate both the national spirit of the *levée en masse* and the quantitative success of the Jourdan system.

Conscription, however, has important drawbacks. Men forced or coerced into military service may not necessarily feel the strong attachment to the army that militiamen feel. (Usually armies rely most heavily on conscription. Navies and air forces ordinarily depend on the threat of conscription into the army to compel men to "volunteer" for their service instead.) In effect, the army that forcibly removed a man from home sometimes became a bigger enemy than the foreign one he was ostensibly being trained to fight. When conscripts saw little connection between their goals and those of the army, friction could easily result. Friction could also result when the social and cultural backgrounds of conscripts differed from those of professionals. Along these lines, Douglas Porch in *March to the Marne* described the heavily royalist and Jesuit-educated French professional officer corps in the early Third Republic period as "an unwelcomed guest at a republican feast" (p. 1).

Conscription can also generate bitter resentment if the system provides loopholes or exemptions for certain classes while obligating others to serve disproportionately. Few military systems can afford to make 100 percent of their young men liable to conscription. They must therefore make decisions about which men they wish to conscript and which men they wish to exempt. In Imperial Germany men drew lots to determine who would serve. Other systems

provided outlets for certain people, a method that often produced intense opposition. For example, allowing the wealthy to buy a substitute commonly rankled those who could not afford such a privilege. On the other hand, becoming a professional substitute could be a promising opportunity for a young man with few attractive alternatives. Government-sanctioned mutual associations emerged in France in the 1830s to locate a substitute for a considerable fee. France finally ended substitution in 1873, but retained controversial exemptions for theology students and priests.

Some military systems rely exclusively on full-time professional volunteers. Britain, due to its traditions opposed to a standing army and the protections provided by the Royal Navy, has most often chosen this system. Even during the crises of World War I, Britain avoided introducing a draft until 1916. Volunteer systems are among the most expensive systems because men must be attracted to military service and kept there. Money is the usually preferred motivation. Ideally, a significant number of volunteers (even in militia and conscript systems) will stay on to become professionals who dedicate themselves to learning the ways of the military. Of course, not all men are true volunteers. Vagrants, orphans, local troublemakers, criminals, and debtors often found themselves "induced" to volunteer.

Finally, a state may pay mercenaries to perform its military service. Mercenaries are among the most expensive ways to man an army. Historically, they had skills that few national armies could match, but their high skill level and advanced weaponry did not come cheaply. Because mercenaries were not national troops, it mattered little if their own personal goals did not overlap with those of the society paying them. Their loyalty to anything but their next payments was almost always in doubt. If their employers failed to make timely payments, mercenaries might pillage or turn on those who defaulted on promised compensations. The rise of national armies in the seventeenth century came about largely as a response to the unreliability of mercenaries. Furthermore, as nationalism came to dominate European politics and warfare, mercenaries made increasingly less sense; an army defined by national goals could scarcely have its fighting done by foreigners. By the time of Napoleon they were already out of favor with many monarchs. By the middle of the nineteenth century they had virtually disappeared.

Many factors control the type (or types, for a state could blend two or more systems) of military service system a society employs. Economics plays a crucial role. So does the nature of a society's civil-military relationship. States like Britain with strong anticonscription traditions can only implement a draft with great difficulty and in times of great crisis. Similarly, mercenaries can only be effectively employed by a state with the resources to afford them. Since their loyalty is uncertain, states prefer to keep them at a distance. Sweden's use of mercenaries in Germany during the Thirty Years' War fits this model as does Britain's hiring of Hessians to fight the American rebels at the end of the eighteenth century.

Because military service systems vary, they matter for understanding the nature of military service itself. The level of voluntary recruitment, the amount of active and passive resistance to the military, and the military's ability to win battles all depend to a large extent on the type of system or blend of systems chosen. When the system and the society it serves are in harmony, the chances of wartime success are enhanced. When they are not, as in the case of Russia in 1905 (see below), the results can be disastrous.

WHY MEN SERVED

The type of military service system in existence in a given society at a given time also affected men's choices in relationship to military service. Even in a system that seeks to conscript a large majority of its young men, those men always have the choice to resist or evade military service. Other important factors in determining how men responded to military service included ideology; economic conditions; a desire for adventure; and the quality of civil-military relations.

Patriotism, or at least regionalism, might be enough to entice men to serve. The perceived immediacy of a threat could unite a nation and compel its men into martial action in the name of defense. Eugen Weber and Douglas Porch have both argued, in two very different books, that most Frenchmen after the Franco-Prussian War of 1870–1871 came (if inconsistently) to understand that their service was important for protecting *La Patrie* (the homeland) from a threatening Germany. French desires for *revanche* (revenge) and the return of Alsace-Lorraine also drew men who wanted to do their part in the great national struggle. They therefore either enlisted voluntarily or at least did not try to avoid the draft in large numbers as they had before 1870.

The enthusiastic crowds of July 1914 were another manifestation of patriotism impelling men to answer their country's call to arms. Thousands of men enthusiastically joined the army in large measure to avenge perceived slights to their nation's honor or to settle old scores with hated neighbors. Exclusively ascribing the wild enthusiasm that some men displayed for war in 1914 to patriotism is to greatly simplify a complex picture. Still, to dismiss national feeling and patriotism as a root cause is also to miss an important point. The men of 1914 were products of an era flush with national feeling. Patriotic sentiments followed them to war and, eventually, to the grave as well.

Other ideological factors could also lead men to join the military. Richard Cobb traced the creation of "Peoples' Armies" in France in 1793 to revolutionary

Mercenaries. Irish soldiers in the service of Gustavus II Adolph, king of Sweden (reigned 1611–1632), 1631. By permission of the British Library, London

zeal and dedication to "internal security." These armies were mobilized to rid France of traitors to the revolution and to remove lasting remnants of the ancien régime. They became, in Cobb's words, instruments of terror in the *départements* of France. Most of these men were artisans and craftsmen who felt that they had a great stake in protecting the success of the revolution. The Peoples' Armies were, in effect, local militia and shared all of the militia's shortcomings. The regular army viewed them as amateurs and they tended to perform more poorly the further they traveled from home. The quality of their performance is less important to our present discussion than the power of ideology to motivate them to volunteer.

Ideology proved to be more important in the twentieth century than it had been earlier. International ideologies such as fascism and communism led men to fight in places quite far from home. The Spanish Civil War is a case in point. Men came from all over Europe, and as far away as North America, either to fight for or against fascism, communism, republicanism, anarchism, and a dozen more ideologies in a brutal three-year conflict.

The ideological fervor of Spain overlapped into World War II as well. Omer Bartov's impressive studies of the Third Reich cite ideology (morally bankrupt though that ideology was) as an important element that brought men into the Wehrmacht and kept them loyal to it. Because of that ideological commitment, he argues, most members of the Wehrmacht were horrified by the bomb plot against Hitler in the summer of 1944. They saw the failure of the plotters to kill Hitler as evidence of the Führer's divine aura. Soldiers, he notes, were more likely than civilians to support the Nazi regime. Stephen Fritz largely agrees, arguing that ideology served to sustain the German soldier throughout the low points of the war on the Russian front.

Alongside ideology, poverty stands out as the most important motivation for military service. The Thirty Years' War produced a near-constant struggle on the part of recruiters to fill the ranks. One study of that war, Geoffrey Parker's *Thirty Years' War,* noted that the recruiters' job was easiest in times of high food prices, economic recession, and budgetary surpluses that allowed them to offer high bounties. When bounties were not possible, the promise of plunder on the enemy's land might serve as a substitute.

Geoffrey Moorhouse's study of the town of Bury in Lancashire during World War I noted that the military served a significant role as employer of last resort. Bury, a coal and textile town, occasionally experienced extended periods of economic downturn, some of them quite severe. The army served as a way to survive

these hard times. Moorhouse notes that the success of British army recruiters in Bury, not unlike their occupational ancestors during the Thirty Years' War, was inversely proportional to the economic health of the city and its region.

The military could serve as a kind of "bridging" institution that might, if he survived, compensate for disadvantages in a man's civilian background. Peter Karsten notes that in contrast to Irish patriots who fought against England, Irish volunteers to the British army were almost always poorer and less literate (especially in English) than the general Irish population. Money served as a crucial incentive in attracting Irish soldiers to British service at twice their proportion in the population as a whole. Of course, ideology played a role as well. Irish troops were willing to serve England, but only as long as that army did not oppress Ireland.

For some men, the military represented a significant rise in their standard of living. Soldiers often ate better than they had as peasants, received more regular medical care, and in many cases (outside Russia at least) military life involved much less work than did full-time agriculture. Many men chose not to return to their birth villages after their term of service ended, reenlisting for as long as they could. In some cases, military service allowed a man to escape problems in his home community such as a defaulted loan, a scandalous love affair, or some other social stigma.

Military service could continue to pay dividends even after retirement. Many states introduced pensions and even rudimentary health-care systems for military veterans. The beautiful, gold-domed Parisian military hospital Les Invalides is one of the most famous and most ornate examples of post-service care for veterans, but it is far from the only one. Military service might also be the key to better jobs in civilian life or a springboard to a business or political career otherwise unattainable.

Some men actively sought to join armies, especially ones with traditions of success or special mystiques. Military systems, especially in western Europe, developed distinct military cultures to attract such men into service. In the sixteenth century Charles V's Spain led the way in creating *tercios,* permanent regiments with their own uniforms, traditions, and patterns of group loyalty. These changes led to regimental traditions in other armies as well. Men might therefore join the military out of a desire to be a member of a particular regiment or tercio. Over time, these regiments produced their own uniforms to further distinguish them from other units. Tercios and regiments attracted men who genuinely sought the camaraderie and martial spirit that military service provided. Militaries motivated by regimental loyalty often translated that élan into greater spirit and efficiency on the battlefield.

Adventure motivated many young men who sought to break away from dreary peasant life or unpleasant factory work. Service overseas in a colonial army promised travel to exotic locales and participation in the "white man's burden" or noblesse oblige. White soldiers also benefited more directly from the colonial system. Imperialism provided the means by which someone from the working classes could achieve bourgeois standards of living. Even enlisted men serving in Asia or Africa might be able to afford a servant. Just by the color of his skin, a European soldier was no longer at the bottom of society. He was instead a soldier with important responsibilities and comforts undreamed of at home.

MILITARY SERVICE AS A NATIONALIZING FORCE

The expansion and contraction of European state borders did not always conform to national or ethnic boundaries. Multireligious and multilingual empires posed challenges for conservatives and others who endeavored to create homogenous nation-states. The military, many hoped, could serve as a "school for the nation," by teaching national customs, religion, language, and history to members of ethnic minorities. The more diverse the empire, the greater the challenge. As Karsten demonstrated, the British army took on the role of teaching English to Gaelic-speaking Irish Catholics, though it was likely much less successful in converting men to Anglicanism.

In France, the army became one institution that, in Weber's phrase, turned peasants into Frenchmen. In the 1850s and 1860s, he contends, peasants showed a determined lack of enthusiasm toward the military and even toward the French state itself. But the Franco-Prussian War and the increased number of Frenchmen experiencing military training changed that approach by the 1890s. The basic education that French peasants learned in school was replicated in the army where literacy and understanding of French citizenship were among the criteria for promotion. Although regional differences still existed (NCOs commonly had to translate an officer's French orders into regional dialects), Eugen Weber argues in *Peasants into Frenchmen* that by 1890 the army "was no longer 'theirs' but 'ours' " (pp. 298–299).

Some states could not meet the challenge. In the Austro-Hungarian Empire, linguistic, religious, and ethnic tensions prevailed over any attempt by the army to impose uniformity. At the outbreak of World War I, Austro-Hungarian army regulations recognized nine main languages; one observer counted twenty-three languages spoken among the troops. Similarly, regional tensions persisted in Italy, where men from the north dominated the officer corps, and in Germany, where Prussians did so. "Nationalization" could thus be interpreted by many enlisted men as an attempt to persuade them to reject their own customs in favor of those fashionable in the big cities, or lose their ethnic or regional identity. In Russia, the army made a concerted effort to inculcate new attitudes, but the heavily peasant force continued to reflect traditional social and regional attachments. Thus nationalization did not always succeed, but where and when a society decided to attempt it, military service almost always played a central role.

OFFICERS AND "OTHER RANKS"

European states in the early modern and modern periods created bifurcated military systems that sharply divided officers and enlisted men. These divisions emerged from medieval distinctions between aristocrats and peasants. As late as World War II, aristocrats dominated the officer corps of many European militaries, increasingly so at their higher ends. These patterns were most pronounced in Russia (before 1917), Britain, and Germany. To be sure, many sons of the middle class moved into the officer corps over time, notably in more technologically dependent services and branches like the navy and artillery. Even in societies that destroyed or marginalized their aristocracies, social elites still came to dominate the officer corps. As a result, officer corps tended to be politically conservative and often suspicious of enlisted men.

Such divisions often created civil-military tensions. In the eighteenth century Prussia was among the states that insisted on nobles in their officer corps, even if they were non-Prussian. The Prussian state was especially suspicious of admitting too many members of the middle class into its officer corps. The attendant dislocations, many Prussians later believed, created important civil-military tensions that contributed to battlefield humiliations at the hands of Napoleon in 1806. The abolition of serfdom in Prussia the following year was partially designed to instill in the peasantry more loyalty to the state and to the army. The partial success of that reform and others improved military morale, though important tensions remained.

Similarly, as we have seen, the French military of the early Third Republic period, especially its more senior officers, were often royalists or Bonapartists.

Prussian Royal Bodyguard. The Prussian royal bodyguard swears allegiance to the newly crowned King Frederick William I in 1713. Engraving by Pieter Schenk I (1660–1718/9). ©THE BRITISH MUSEUM, LONDON

1905. One might reasonably extend his argument to 1917 as well.

In effect, before World War I three discrete groups entered military service, each in different ways. The nobility, in states where it existed, entered at the top, often through purchased commissions. To cite a famous example, Arthur Wellesley, duke of Wellington, purchased a lieutenant colonelcy at the age of twenty-four. His opponent at the Battle of Waterloo in 1815, Napoleon Bonaparte, was able to use his father's minor noble status to gain admission to the French military school at Brienne-le-Château. He went on to further glory as the French Revolution opened up many new opportunities for officers of bourgeois and lower noble backgrounds.

Napoleon also went on to become a great champion of the second group, the bourgeoisie and artisan class. In opening the military "to the talents" he paved the way for many more non-nobles to enter military service. One of Napoleon's most valued subordinate commanders, Michel Ney, "the bravest of bravest," (and, some added, "the dumbest of the dumb") was the son of a master barrel cooper. He entered military service as an enlisted man in 1787, received a commission in 1792, and rose to the rank of marshal in 1804. Thus in just seventeen years he went from artisan's son to one of the most important men in France. Jean-Baptiste Jourdan, the man for whom the Jourdan conscription law of 1798 was named, was the son of a surgeon. He rose from private to marshal in twenty years.

Noble holds on the officer corps weakened as armies grew larger in the nineteenth century. In some nations, such as Germany, conservative officers argued against expanding armies too much on the grounds that doing so would require too many non-nobles to become officers. Nevertheless, aristocratic control of the military diminished significantly in the years prior to World War I, though it did not disappear entirely. Furthermore, as the military increasingly came to need skills that mirrored the skills of civilians, nobles (who ordinarily lacked such skills) became less useful. The financial, administrative, and logistical corps of armies therefore came to be dominated by the middle class.

The third group, peasants and unskilled workers, were expected to fill the ranks. Few rose to the officer corps until huge officer casualties during World War I began to leave armies few alternatives, but many did achieve high enlisted ranks. In many armies, they dominated the noncommissioned officers corps (composed of varying grades of sergeants in the army and petty officers in the navy). Because men from the peasantry and the working classes often identified with people of similar background more than they did

Many of them mistrusted the Republic and had a tumultuous relationship with it. Radicals tried, with little success, to increase the number of non-nobles in the French officer corps. They even proposed that all graduates of the military academy at St. Cyr perform one year of service as a private. Propositions such as these only served to heighten the mutual suspicion between the army and the state on the one hand and between officers and enlisted men on the other. Divisions, both real and perceived, could explode in moments of crisis such as the Dreyfus affair or, to cite an earlier example, the continent-wide revolutions of 1848 (see below).

John Bushnell has argued that the Russian army before 1905 suffered from Europe's most severe divisions between officers and enlisted men. The officers were mostly nobles and products of the Europeanized Russia created under Peter the Great and Catherine the Great in the late seventeenth and eighteenth centuries. The enlisted men, however, were products of peasant Russia and not as greatly affected by the Europeanization movement. The officers, therefore, saw peasant and worker uprisings as threats to Russia, but the men were more likely to identify with such uprisings than to oppose them. To Bushnell, the large chasm between officers and enlisted men helps to explain the series of mutinies in the Russian army in

with their own officers, they might refuse to obey orders that they saw as unjust.

The possibility that soldiers might not obey their officers emerged repeatedly during times of civil strife. Many soldiers were uncomfortable with the role of domestic policeman, especially when they were being asked to police people of similar social backgrounds to their own. During the revolutions of 1848 the Paris National Guard did at times refuse to fire on demonstrators. In Milan, Hungarian, Croat, and Slovene soldiers belonging to the Austrian army sympathized with Italian republicans. Many deserted to the demonstrators, while others allowed themselves to be driven away by an "army" of protestors wielding medieval pikes. Prussia hired Russian soldiers to quell disturbances in the hopes that they would have fewer qualms about shooting demonstrators (they did). While most professional soldiers did obey orders to

disperse crowds, the Paris and Milan examples, on top of the general tensions of 1848, led to later reforms that increased the term of service in many nations and reduced the roles of reserves and national guards.

The mass armies required by the world wars were, out of necessity, products of conscription. The totality of twentieth century warfare encompassed every facet of belligerent societies. Most social exemptions from conscription disappeared; only men with occupations deemed critical to the war effort (these commonly included not middle-class professions, but farmers, miners, and metal workers) were exempted. But the conscriptions of the first half of the twentieth century did not produce the active opposition that earlier versions had. The only clear exceptions to this pattern were in the crumbling Russian and Austro-Hungarian empires as World War I began to turn against them. The relative acceptance of the draft dur-

Russian Reservists. Russian reservists called up for service marching through St. Petersburg, 1914. ©BETTMANN/CORBIS

ing the world wars is a product of its (perforce) more egalitarian nature and the national emergencies that the world wars represented.

Furthermore, by World War II many enlisted men and junior officers had skills of great value to the military. Operating a mid-twentieth-century army was vastly more complicated than operating one a century earlier. Armies needed large numbers of skilled men in jobs such as mechanic, radioman, and logistician. Enlisted men had ceased to be the lowest orders of society. They had become invaluable members of specialized combat teams.

AVOIDING MILITARY SERVICE

Of course, the military comes with the very important drawback of demanding potentially life-threatening service. Europe's chronic warfare and internal turmoil meant that men joined the military with the knowledge that seeing combat at some point in their careers was a distinct possibility. Contemporary military sociologists talk about military service as a trade-off of benefits and burdens. The inherent danger of military service was clearly one such burden. Furthermore, the popular association of soldiering with bad morals and habits lowered the prestige of the soldier considerably at least as late as World War I. In many sectors of European society soldiers were received with more contempt than respect.

The military also involved being subjected to harsh and sometimes arbitrary discipline. Beginning with the period just prior to the Thirty Years' War, firearms technology came to be integrated into all European armies. In order to use such weapons effectively, men had to be drilled to act in unison. The first drill manuals appeared in 1607. Discipline and drill were the means officers used in order to make lines of men act in concert. Discipline became so intense that the men often had more reason to fear their officers and NCOs than the enemy. Intense discipline became a regular feature of military life with harsh punishments (including flogging, denial of food, imprisonment, and even, in extreme cases, death) as the penalties for disobedience.

Even in times of peace, military service could be extremely unpleasant. Russian officers prior to 1905 commonly hired their men out as agriculture laborers and pocketed the profits, and Soviets soldiers did the same work in the post–World War II era. This practice existed in Germany and Austria as well. In many parts of Europe, soldiers had to spend almost all of their money on food and uniforms. Especially in eastern Europe military service itself was seen as a form of slavery. The distinction sometimes seemed slight indeed. Until 1861 Russian peasants could be conscripted for twenty-five years or more and, in many cases, sons of soldiers were automatically conscripted as well.

Given these conditions, many men did what they could to avoid such service, often with the active support of their communities. For the community, encouraging draft evasion made good economic sense: every man lost to the army was one less man available to work at harvest time. Where substitution existed families might make considerable financial sacrifices in order to pay for someone other than an eldest son (and therefore heir to the land and guardian of the family name) to be conscripted. Eugen Weber notes that as late as 1870 some French villages simply registered all new births as girls. In others, birth certificates might not even be filed. Other men beat conscription through self-inflicting or inventing a physical disability.

CONCLUSIONS

Since 1945, military service has come to depend upon the acquisition of men (and, increasingly, women) with the necessary skills to operate highly technical weapons systems. This process, ongoing for more than a century, requires long-term professionals, who are willing to commit enough time to the military to make the investments in training pay off. Conscripts continued to fill the unskilled and semiskilled jobs, but many militaries became disenchanted with the educational backgrounds and motivations of draftees. With the end of the cold war, most European states have reduced or eliminated conscription, with Russia an important exception.

The emphasis on skill has also greatly reduced the importance of ascriptive criteria such as ethnicity and gender. Women had served in militaries in both world wars, but most commonly in traditional "women's roles." Only in the Soviet Union in World War II did significant numbers of women see combat, though as many as 25 percent of British antiaircraft gunners were women. Soviet women served as snipers, tank drivers, and pilots. The most famous of these pilots, the "Night Witches," received the high Soviet distinction of being named a Guards Regiment.

These female services were, however, understood to be either an extreme response to exigent circumstances or a military extension of women's traditional civilian spheres. Since the 1960s, however, women have moved into military roles previously understood to be male. Female generals, fighter and bomber pilots, and ship captains have emerged in almost all European (and, for that matter, many non-European) militaries. Similar patterns have emerged among ethnic minorities and openly homosexual soldiers, groups that in the past have at times been officially marginalized or forbidden from serving. What matters most at the dawn of the twenty-first century is skill.

The military continues to be an option for young men and women who seek a bridge to improve their lives. It is, however, becoming less and less an employer of last resort. Most militaries have minimum education requirements that eliminate the most disadvantaged members of society from serving. Although still seen by many as an alien institution, the military does not inspire the kinds of fear and hatred that it has in the past.

Military service will undoubtedly continue to evoke controversy across Europe. Recent reductions in draft calls in western and northern Europe should attenuate those controversies as men will be forced to enter the military much less often. New controversies are most likely to revolve around women's desires to move into more and more military jobs (special operations and submarines, for example) still understood by many to be the preserves of men. The role of national soldiers in international operations and transnational coalitions (such as joint European defense and the expansion of NATO) are also likely to be contentious. For historians, the most fruitful areas of future research promise to be in comparisons of European experiences of military service. Such studies can illuminate both national and continental patterns, yielding a better understanding of both.

See also **The French Revolution and Empire; The World Wars and Depression** *(volume 1);* **War and Conquest** *(in this volume);* **Social Mobility; The Aristocracy and Gentry; The Military** *(volume 3); and other articles in this section.*

BIBLIOGRAPHY

Bartov, Omer. *Hitler's Army: Soldiers, Nazis, and War in the Third Reich.* New York, 1992. Should be a starting point for any study of the Wehrmacht and its soldiers during World War II.

Bushnell, John. *Mutiny amid Repression: Russian Soldiers in the Revolution of 1905–1906.* Bloomington, Indiana: 1985.

Cobb, Richard. *The Peoples' Armies: the Armées Révolutionnaires, Instrument of the Terror in the Departments, April 1793 to Floreal Year II.* Translated by Marianne Elliott. New Haven, Conn., 1987. Analysis of what the military as an institution meant to revolutionary France.

Fritz, Stephen. *Frontsoldaten: The German Soldier in World War II.* Lexington, Ky., 1995.

Herwig, Holger H. *The German Naval Officer Corps: A Social and Political History, 1890–1918.* Oxford, 1973.

Karsten, Peter. "Irish Soldiers in the British Army, 1792–1922." *Journal of Social History* 17 (1983): 31–65.

Moorhouse, Geoffrey. *Hell's Foundations: A Social History of the Town of Bury in the Aftermath of the Gallipoli Campaign.* New York, 1992.

Parker, Geoffrey, ed. *The Thirty Years' War.* 2d rev. ed. London, 1997. See chapter 6, "The Universal Soldier."

Porch, Douglas. *March to the Marne: The French Army 1871–1914.* Cambridge, U.K.: 1981. Though not totally devoted to the subject of military service per se, it should be consulted before beginning any serious study of French military service in the Third Republic.

Weber, Eugen. *Peasants into Frenchmen: The Modernization of Rural France, 1870–1914.* Stanford, Calif.: 1976. See chapter 17 for his discussion of the army.

Wildman, Allan K. *The End of the Russian Imperial Army.* 2 vols. Princeton, N.J., 1980–1987.